ASPECTS OF RELIGION IN THE SOVIET UNION
1917-1967

ASPECTS OF RELIGION IN THE SOVIET UNION

1917-1967

EDITED BY RICHARD H. MARSHALL, JR.

Associate Editors, Thomas E. Bird and Andrew Q. Blane

THE UNIVERSITY OF CHICAGO PRESS, CHICAGO AND LONDON

International Standard Book Number: 0–226–50700–9
Library of Congress Catalog Card Number: 70–115874

THE UNIVERSITY OF CHICAGO PRESS, CHICAGO 60637
THE UNIVERSITY OF CHICAGO PRESS, LTD., LONDON

DEDICATION

The editors and contributors
who have cooperated in this collection
dedicate their work to

PAUL B. ANDERSON

His interest in religion in the Soviet Union
spans half a century and more.
During most of this time, very few people
concerned themselves with this
important field of study.
The present work is evidence of the fact
that he has successfully communicated
his interest to others and convinced
them of the pressing need for serious and
extensive research in this area.

CONTENTS

viii

FOREWORD

In the twenty years and more which have passed since the end of World War II it has gradually become apparent that Soviet area-specialists have not devoted sufficient time and energy to the study of religion in the USSR. There have been isolated individuals who have made such research their primary occupation and who have tried to influence others to do likewise, but the work and the appeals of these few have elicited only a minimal response.

There are several reasons for this state of affairs. Prior to 1950 the discipline of Soviet studies in the West, particularly in the English-speaking countries, was the concern of only a small number of scholars and statesmen, many of whom had hurried into the field in the forties, often with only rudimentary training. Because of their small number and the assortment of pressing tasks which faced them, these men attended principally to political and economic matters. It is perhaps understandable that in such circumstances a thoroughgoing study of religion in the Soviet Union was ignored or assigned a relatively low priority.

Another contributing factor was the widespread, albeit anachronistic, habit of regarding the study of religion per se as the prerogative of the divinity schools. To the extent that religion was investigated at all in the secular university, the focus of attention was usually narrowed to the area of church–state relations. In the case of the Soviet Union this meant, for all practical purposes, study of the patterns of conflict and accommodation between the government and the principal religious body, the Russian Orthodox church. In sum, there was lamentably little awareness of the richness of religion and its "promise" for scholarly investigation.

Either of the above reasons would doubtless suffice to explain the paucity of research in this area, but there is still one more important factor which must be noted. The few studies on religion in the USSR which were published in the forties and fifties, by such men as N. S. Timasheff, J. S. Curtiss, and M. Spinka,[1] based on the evidence available at the time, tended to agree that a reasonably acceptable modus vivendi had been worked out between church and state during the early years of the war, and that there was little likelihood of any dramatic change in the near future. The effect of this assessment could only have served to reinforce the conviction that the study of religion in the USSR (study, that is, of church–state relations) did not demand greater attention in the foreseeable future.

It is said that where hard facts end, imagination begins. It is, therefore, hardly surprising that in this field—religion in the Soviet Union—a number of gross misconceptions, not to mention deliberate distortions, have gained currency. There have been, on the one hand, groups and individuals whose attitudes in this, as in other matters, were determined by an abiding antagonism towards the Soviet regime. These have characterized official policy as conducting a consistent, single-minded, and coordinated drive to eliminate all vestiges of religion, both institutional and personal. It has been claimed that this aim was largely realized and that the remnants of previous denominational structures are part of "showcase Russia" or are used in the area of foreign policy, and, in either case, are completely staffed by government agents.

At the opposite end of the spectrum are those who tend to view the events of the past half-century as the simple separation of church and state, a universal and desirable concomitant of modern statehood. Those holding such a view are given to quoting from the Soviet Constitution and to citing the public statements of Soviet religious leaders to support their contention that genuine religious freedom obtains in the USSR. To the extent that they consider the problem, they explain the closing of hundreds of churches as justified by the massive indifference towards religion among men and women of working age. (This indifference is, for the most part, substantiated by church attendance figures, although these can be quite mislead-

---

1. The titles of these and other works are to be found in the Bibliography. That the amount of useful and semiuseful material available in English can be contained in such a brief space is ample evidence of the need for research, especially for monographs on special topics.

ing.) In the final analysis the entire matter is dismissed by labelling it simply a Soviet manifestation of the spirit of secularism spawned by the combined processes of urbanization and the technological revolution. (It must be noted that although this last generalization misleads through oversimplification, it does indirectly call attention to one of the many questions which must be carefully evaluated, namely, a determination of which phenomena in this realm are unique to the Soviet scene and which are common to the modern age.)

This is not the place to present a detailed catalogue of the myriad types of misinformation about religion in the Soviet Union which abound in opinion and in print. Nor is it the place to introduce a full refutation of the extreme and very general views described above. Briefly it can be said that the first view overlooks the many shifts of policy which can be historically documented, the variations in the local implementation of such policy, the differences in the treatment of the various denominations, and the subtle but real changes in the ideological posture towards religion which can be gleaned from the writings and remarks of Soviet leaders in the past fifty years. Exponents of the second or "soft" view would appear to be unaware of the harsh repressive measures taken against various religious groups and individuals throughout the last half-century (and as recently as the early sixties) for no other reason than the fact of their religious beliefs. They also do not face up to the contradiction between the guarantees of freedom of confession on the one hand and, on the other, the strictures placed upon religious instruction by a continuing and extensive campaign of antireligious propaganda (not to mention more serious forms of discrimination). Furthermore, they do not seem to be aware of either the tenacity of traditional religion or of the increased interest in religion in the USSR, especially among the intelligentsia, which has been manifested in a variety of ways since Stalin's death.

Mention of the changes of recent years leads to another aspect of the problem which has only recently begun to make itself felt. It is increasingly clear that our information about events prior to 1950 is inadequate and that this has served to mislead us in a variety of ways. How much worse, then, is our knowledge of the situation in the past decade, given the comparatively rapid pace at which changes have taken place in the Soviet Union?

A pertinent example of this process of change or ferment is to be found in what has often been referred to as the "ideological crisis" of the sixties. The monolithic ideology which was the official matrix of life during Stalin's lifetime has gradually come to be viewed by Soviet citizens as philosophically irrelevant and morally bankrupt. Especially among the creative intelligentsia there is at present a greater openness to theism as an ingredient of a new, more appropriate ideology, on both a personal and community level. In addition, the growing vocal agitation for a greater degree of legality in Soviet life has touched the area of religion on numerous occasions. Churchmen and jurists alike have called for the rejection of arbitrary administrative measures, for which there is no judicial review, and for fidelity to existing laws.

During this same period important changes in the study and understanding of Soviet Russia have also taken place in the West. First of all, there has been a great maturation and hence broadening of the general field of Soviet area-studies. Secondly, there has been an enormous increase in the amount of religious material, both official and unofficial, which has come out of the Soviet Union in recent years. (The lack of information is, of course, a continuing problem, but the situation is far better than it was.) Finally, considerable progress has been made towards the acceptance of religion as a legitimate subject for academic investigation. The resulting growth of interest in the place of religion qua religion in Soviet society, as well as in the bearing of religion on other aspects of that society, has brought to the field men of many interests and disciplines, including political scientists, economists, sociologists, historians, and literary scholars.

It is ironic, not to say discouraging, that those who are now interested in issues which touch upon religion and which arise from contemporary developments in the USSR find themselves hampered because of the lack of reliable past research. In other words, far from being able to begin their work on a solid foundation, they find that they must first address themselves to questions which they might rightfully expect to have long since been thoroughly examined.

The state of the study of religion in the USSR is such that it is not now possible to compile an exhaustive inventory of topics which demand immediate attention. But mention of a few of the more obvious ones may serve to emphasize the immensity of the task which lies ahead. One general category would encompass work on the vicissitudes of particular denominations. Even the best of past studies *pro domu suo* have all too often betrayed little or no understanding of the overall patterns of events within other groups or other areas of life. Analysis of present and prerevolutionary modes of existence and self-expression would provide valuable studies in the patterns of adaptability within particular groups. The need for comparative studies, contrasting the situation, attitudes, and behavior of the various denominations, is particularly acute. Still another rich area of possible research is that of the relation of different religious institutions and/or ideologies to other basic institutions and values of Soviet society. Here scholars with experience in fields such as law, philosophy, and literature are needed.

These remarks apply equally to subjects within the field of religion which have not previously been studied and to a large number of those that have. The intense and prolonged antireligious campaign of the last four or five years of Khrushchev's rule is an example of a topic which has yet to be analyzed. Specialists cannot hope to give a full and proper assessment of his time in power while so many important questions in this area remain unanswered. What interpretation is to be put on Khrushchev's part in calling a halt in 1954 to the so-called "Hundred-Days" campaign? Was the subsequent, longer campaign of 1959–64 begun principally on the initiative of Khrushchev or was it more of a collective decision? Was it in any way intended to allay the suspicions of restive neo-Stalinist elements in the party who were alarmed at the denunciation of Stalin and the apparent disposition of the new leadership to consider a program of reform? Could it have been undertaken to demonstrate continued ideological purity to the Chinese Communists at a time when mutual suspicion and discord were beginning to spread to the fraternal parties around the world? Was it intended as a sign to those who greeted de-Stalinization with enthusiasm that their hopes should not be too unbounded? Or, as is more likely, was it a combination of these and other considerations? If so, what are the other considerations and how are priorities to be distributed to these various motivating factors?

To take another insufficiently explored topic, in 1948 the Uniate church was totally suppressed at a time when the Russian Orthodox church was still enjoying a period of relative freedom as a result of the wartime detente. Numerous books and monographs have been written on this subject, yet little light has been shed on a number of basic questions. Was the suppression a result of the regime's fear of the Uniate connections with Rome, hence of a potential source of foreign influence and divided loyalties? Was it in retaliation for the Roman pontiff's expressed hostility towards communism? What part did the wartime collaboration of many inhabitants of the western Ukraine with the Germans play? Was the absorption of the Uniates by the Orthodox church suggested by the latter to the civil authorities? Was this the beginning of a new period of restrictive measures, measures that seemingly touched all the churches except the Orthodox, which was at that point proving to be a useful instrument of foreign policy in the East European countries with large Orthodox populations?

The realization that the study of religion in the Soviet Union and Eastern Europe had been seriously neglected led, although along an often indirect and uncertain path, to the preparation of the present book. Early in the 1960s, through the initiative of Paul B. Anderson and Donald A. Lowrie, a small group of men and women in the New York area began to meet regularly to discuss their work on problems of religion in the Soviet Union and Eastern Europe. One of the first tangible results of their cooperation was the bi-monthly translation service, *Religion in Communist-Dominated Areas*, published under the auspices of the National Council of Churches.

In 1964 William C. Fletcher, who was director of the Centre de Recherches et d'Études in Geneva, joined the group. For several years this organization, now defunct, was helpful in undertaking many valuable studies in this field. In December, 1964, Dr. Fletcher organized a three-day conference at the University of Southern California to examine the state of research in the field. A second, more ambitious gathering was held in the spring of 1966 at Greyston House, one of the conference facilities of Columbia University. Those in attendance at the two conferences were quick to acknowledge the urgent need for research in the field. They also came to see the need for coordination of their efforts. Several participants admitted that they had previously been almost completely unaware of related events in the general field of religion in the Soviet Union outside their own special area of concern, and several were obliged to alter their interpretation of their findings on the basis of the presentations of others.

The book offered here, *Aspects of Religion in the Soviet Union, 1917–1967*, is not simply a random gathering of articles by men of divergent backgrounds. It is, rather, the embodiment of a new and broader academic interest in the field of religion in the Soviet Union, and, in its parts, attempts to illustrate how a variety of disciplines, each with its own approach, can find a place in that field. The book also attempts to fill a few of the gaps noted earlier and to present new information that raises questions about the conclusions of previous research. In the light of what remains to be done, the book makes no pretense at being comprehensive nor does it undertake to offer any broad estimates of, or new consensus on, the meaning of the experience of the past fifty years. To do so would be quite premature. As the title indicates, this book concerns itself only with certain "aspects" of religion in the Soviet Union, an effort which is less a case of modesty than of appropriateness, given the present state of the science. To the extent that this effort sparks interest and raises questions, specialists may look forward to a substantial increase in the attention given to this potentially illuminating but long-overlooked field.

The editors express their appreciation to Sharon Arndt (Stein) and Martha Mock for their assistance in the preparation of the manuscript.

Thanks are due to the publishers mentioned in various footnotes for permission to quote from copyrighted materials.

RICHARD H. MARSHALL, JR.

I

PAUL B. ANDERSON: STUDENT OF RELIGION IN RUSSIA

PAUL B. ANDERSON

1

IN APPRECIATION
OF
PAUL B. ANDERSON

It is particularly fitting that a volume on religion in the Soviet Union should be dedicated to Paul B. Anderson. He has devoted his life to the issues to which this book is addressed.

In fifty years of close association with Russians, Dr. Anderson has become a preeminent Western authority on the Russian Orthodox church. His special field of study has been Orthodoxy in its relation to the cultures and political systems which have constituted its environment, and which in varying degrees the church has helped to form. While specializing on the church in the Soviet Union and its relation to communism, he has amassed, through intimate experience and firsthand research, a unique body of knowledge on church and state not only in Russia but in all of Eastern Europe and the Middle East where Orthodoxy is strong.

There are few people in the West whose personal contact with Russia antedates the Bolshevik Revolution, and fewer still of this company whose field of special concern has been religion. Paul Anderson was introduced to Russia in 1917. He had already spent four years as a YMCA secretary in China, where he was sent by the International Committee of the YMCAs of the United States and Canada. He shared the characteristics of broad perspective, studious curiosity, and Christian dedication which so signally marked the Christian ambassadors of the international YMCA of that period. He

R. H. Edwin Epsy

was selected by Dr. John R. Mott early in 1917 as his private secretary on a special diplomatic mission to Russia which Dr. Mott had undertaken for the United States government.

At the conclusion of this brief assignment Anderson was asked to serve further in Russia. Though only twenty-three years of age, he was assigned to coordinate the work of a half-dozen YMCA secretaries from neutral countries in a ministry to German and Austro-Hungarian captives in Russian prisoner of war camps which were scattered from the Urals to Vladivostok. Under the conditions of the Revolution and with World War I at its height, he gained firsthand experience in handling delicate international problems with people of many nationalities and philosophies of life. Working in Siberia and the heartland of Russia, he also acquired an understanding and appreciation of the Russian people.

Before the end of the war, Paul Anderson changed his location but not his concern. Obliged by the Revolution to leave Russia, he turned to the service of interned Russians in Germany and Russian prisoners of war in Poland. At the end of the war, he became YMCA secretary for Russian people outside of Russia, with headquarters for four years in Berlin and then, until 1941, in Paris.

It was thus that Paul Anderson was launched on a lifetime career with Russians in exile. His specific tasks assumed many forms. In his first assignment he was director of the Russian Correspondence School (initially for war prisoners and refugees who had not yet been relocated) and editor of the YMCA Press, which was to become the major Russian-language publisher outside of Russia.

Dr. Anderson in these early years not only gained a working knowledge of German and French, with a concomitant understanding of the problems of Europe, but began his lifelong study of the Russian language and culture. He identified himself with the life and liturgy of the Russian Orthodox church and gained wide acquaintance with Russian emigrés of many backgrounds, particularly intellectuals and lay and clerical leaders of the church. He developed the Press into a dynamic Christian enterprise which became a prime vehicle for the expression of Orthodox theology and philosophy to the Russians in diaspora and to the wider Western community.

It was during this period that an event which seemed a tragedy at the time took place. The Bolsheviks exiled about one hundred

Russian Christian scholars and a number of clergy to the West. In the years that followed, these men produced some of their best writings and developed their institutions in a new environment unhindered by political control. In 1922, Nicholas Berdyaev joined the YMCA staff as editor and lecturer, attracting many other philosophers and theologians. They produced nearly four hundred scholarly works, published by the YMCA Press in Berlin and Prague and, after 1925, in Paris.

In all of this, Paul Anderson had a guiding hand. When the depression struck in the late 1920s the International Committee of the YMCA confided to him the full responsibility for Russian work in Europe. By this time the YMCA and the Russian Orthodox enterprises were so fully integrated, thanks in large part to the talents of Dr. Anderson, that such notable names as Berdyaev, Bulgakov, Florovsky, Zenkovsky, Zander, Zernov, Pianov, and Nikitin came to symbolize the enterprise. The minds and spirits of these men and women were made available to the world through the efforts of Anderson and others associated with him. He arranged the financing and administrative machinery for institutions as diverse as the Orthodox Theological Institute of St. Sergius in Paris, the Russian Student Christian Movement, and a number of Orthodox summer camps.

Paul Anderson also developed intimate connections with the patriarchs and primates of other Orthodox churches in Europe and the Middle East. Some of them had been his colleagues in earlier years in the YMCA and the World Student Christian Federation. Recently a Roman Catholic woman in Paris recounted to Dr. Anderson that when she had mentioned his name on a visit to the ecumenical patriarch at the Phanar in Istanbul, the patriarch had said, "But Paul Anderson is one of us!" In the November, 1967, issue of *World Communiqué*, the publication of the worldwide YMCA, there appeared a letter from the patriarch to Paul B. Anderson, who still is ecumenical consultant to the World Alliance of YMCAs. The patriarch saluted both Dr. Anderson and other early leaders of the YMCA and the ecumenical movement such as John R. Mott, Archbishop Nathan Soderblom, and Willem A. Visser 't Hooft.

But Anderson's primary identification was with the Russians. As the years went by he won for himself a place of increasing confidence in their counsels. Beginning in the 1920s, he served as their financier, guide, interpreter, and counselor at the great ecumenical conferences.

He was a crucial figure in the development of understanding between the churches of East and West. Some of the experiences of critical importance were the Stockholm Conference on Life and Work in 1925, the first Anglo-Orthodox Student Conference in 1927, the resultant organization of the Fellowship of St. Alban and St. Sergius, the founding of the Russian Clergy and Church Aid Fund in Britain in 1932, the world conferences of the churches at Oxford and Edinburgh in 1937, and the Utrecht Conference in 1938 at which the constitution was drafted for the World Council of Churches.

In the years of burgeoning ecumenical activity since World War II, Dr. Anderson has continued as a key link in Orthodox–Anglican–Protestant dialogue at the great world conferences of these churches and in countless consultations and visitations. He helped organize and lead the first interchange of delegations between the National Council of Churches of the United States and the churches of the Soviet Union in 1956, followed by another exchange in 1962–63. He was consultant and interpreter to an official delegation of theologians from the Church of England to the Russian Orthodox church in 1956. In the fall of 1967 he performed a similar role for a delegation from the Church of the Brethren of the United States. He has been in the Soviet Union five times since World War II, has been a voracious reader of Russian publications, and has been sought out by representatives of the Russian Orthodox church when they have been in Western Europe or the United States. At the same time, he has continued as a trusted counselor to the various branches of the Russian church in exile. He has also traveled widely during these years among the other Orthodox churches of Europe and the Middle East.

In the midst of all of these Orthodox associations, Dr. Anderson has remained a member of the Protestant Episcopal church. This has won him wide respect, and he in turn pays high tribute to outstanding leaders of his own communion, both in the United States and in Britain. Because of his standing among Anglicans, he has been a close consultant to successive archbishops of Canterbury and other bishops and scholars on Orthodox relationships. In the United States, he has been an official delegate of the Protestant Episcopal church in crucial conversations, and continues as an active consultant to his church in this field. He serves in the same capacity in the National Council of Churches, for which five years ago he established and today continues to edit the bi-monthly *Religion in Communist-Dominated Areas*.

Dr. Anderson's contribution has had a special vitality because he has been more than an organizer, diplomat, and man of good will. He has had an instinctive understanding of the basic issues, and has pursued them with the discipline of a scholar. Amidst all his practical activity, he has been able to write two basic books: *Russia's Religious Future* (1935) and *People, Church, and State in Modern Russia* (1944). He has written numerous monographs and articles for scholarly journals, with increasing attention in recent years to issues of international affairs in the crossfire between communist and democratic apprehensions of life. He brings to all his analyses a prudent judgment rooted in a lifetime of experience, and a note of hope and aspiration rooted in his Christian faith.

Rounding out fifty years of intimate association with Russians and the Russian Orthodox church, and having lived a fuller life than most of us, Paul Anderson still looks to the future. He has provided inspiration and encouragement to numerous younger scholars. He is constantly on the lookout for promising men and women who can carry forward his task of interpretation and reconciliation. For those who elect to respond to this need it is certain that his life and work will continue to be their model and guide.

2

REFLECTIONS ON RELIGION IN RUSSIA 1917-1967

I would like to begin by saying that this paper is not a scientific study of religion in the Soviet period. Rather, it is the story of my personal experience with the Russian church in the USSR and in the emigration. Also, I have always been extremely fortunate in being able to augment my own, firsthand information with what I have learned from a host of friends in Russia, in Europe, in the Middle East, in the Americas, and in Australia.

My early training had very little to do with Russia. When I arrived at the Finland Station in Petrograd on a soft "white night" in mid-June, 1917, the entire inventory of my knowledge of things Russian was a brief acquaintance with a Russian political exile at a university, an evening in Shanghai listening to the St. Petersburg Cathedral Choir, and a few Russian lessons from a fellow passenger aboard ship en route to Russia during the First World War. I little suspected, at the time, that my life was to take a totally different direction by dint of my new Russian assignment.

On June 13, 1917, the special diplomatic mission appointed by President Woodrow Wilson to bring greetings to the Russian provisional government arrived in Petrograd. I participated in the work of the mission as private secretary to Dr. John R. Mott, general secretary of the International Committee, YMCA. His task was to establish friendly relations with prominent religious leaders, espe-

Paul B. Anderson

cially with the hierarchy of the Russian Orthodox church. Each morning at eight o'clock I joined Dr. Mott at the Winter Palace, where the mission was housed, and we would transcribe notes of his conversations of the previous day. In this way I learned a great deal about the Russian church and especially about preparations for the forthcoming all-Russian *sobor* ("council") scheduled to convene on August 15. I went with Dr. Mott to Moscow in July when he met with the pre-*sobor* conference. He was personally acquainted with Archbishop Tikhon (who was subsequently elected patriarch) and other church leaders, and I greatly benefited from these associations.

Dr. Mott was a true friend of Russia. I remember one of his favorite quotations, from Tiutchev: "No one can know Russia; one can only believe in Russia." Yet it would have been well if he, not to mention our other diplomatic representatives, had familiarized themselves more systematically with the history and cultural development of the country. Probably most of us in Petrograd in 1917 had drawn the bulk of our "information" from the novels of Dostoevsky, Turgenev, and Tolstoy.

I had the good fortune to be introduced to Russian religious culture of the early twentieth century by some of the men and women who were then contributing mightily to it: Ariadne Tyrkova Williams, Dean Sergius Bulgakov, Archbishop Evlogy of Volynia and Paris, Archbishop Antony Khrapovitsky (a member of the faculty of all four theological academies, one after the other), not to speak of Nicholas Berdyaev, who was our senior editor in the YMCA Press from 1923 until his death in 1947. I should also mention my very earliest tutors in things Russian, men who brought me into direct touch with the political scene: Professor Samuel F. Harper, Major Allen Wardwell of the American Red Cross Mission, Albert Rhys Williams, and John Reed. It was these last two who took me with them to the Smolny Institute on the night of the Bolshevik Revolution for Lenin's dramatic declaration of the advent of Soviet power.

In his conversations with bishops and other church leaders in the pre-October months of 1917, Dr. Mott discerned a mood of revival in the church and a spirit of optimism for the future. My numerous visits to parish churches did not lead me to the same conclusion. I frequently stopped in at the church on Panteleimonskaia Ulitsa, as it was near our YMCA office for prisoner of war service at 8 Mokhovaia Ulitsa. Here, as in the other churches which I visited in Petrograd, I never found many at worship. Later, after the October Revolution, the people were to turn to the church for consolation in the midst of great confusion and uncertainty. I know this personally because, during the time we maintained an office in Moscow, I often visited the parish church on the Arbat and was truly impressed by both the spirit of the service and the devotion of the people.

After Dr. Mott's mission left, I was put in charge of work with prisoners of war. As a result, in the early months of 1918 I traveled the length of the Siberian railway and back, visiting our YMCA field staff. Returning from Vladivostok, I arrived in Krasnoiarsk in time for Easter. This was a marvelous experience. The great cathedral square was filled with peasant carts and the church itself was packed. During this profoundly beautiful service I could not fail to notice a mood of considerable anxiety, caused, no doubt, by the sporadic rifle fire which could be heard in the streets. That year Easter fell on May 1, the great workers' holiday, which the Bolsheviks in Krasnoiarsk celebrated with a large parade. The photographs which I took show banners with the slogans "All Power to the Soviets" and "Workers of the World, Unite!" Although large numbers of men in uniform took part in the parade, there were few onlookers. The public was still undecided about the revolution which had taken place. This was still before the Fifth Congress of Soviets in the summer of 1918 which threw the Social Revolutionaries out of the government and claimed full authority for the Bolsheviks.

My return from the Far East came only days before the Czechoslovak legions began to clash with the Bolsheviks all along the Trans-Siberian railway. I must have been on almost the last train to come through from Vladivostok without incident. I spent several days in Perm visiting prisoner of war camps with our secretary there, and then had a memorable three-day trip by steamer down the river Kama, through the vast virgin forests, to Kazan, and then down the Volga to Samara. Temporary headquarters for YMCA civilian service had been established there, partly because the American YMCA was operating a rural reconstruction service from a leased steamer which stopped at towns along the way, from Nizhny Novgorod to Samara, in order to give demonstrations of modern farm methods.

From Samara I returned to Moscow. During the summer I made several trips to Petrograd, since part of the prisoner of war office staff was still stationed there. Although the nature of my work with enemy prisoners in Russia did not call for systematic contacts with the Russian church, I did manage to acquaint myself with many local churches in Petrograd and Moscow. However, it was not until the YMCA began expanding its services to both civilian and military personnel in Russia in 1918 that I had occasion to deal directly with the Holy Synod. Actually, my errand was a simple one and had nothing to do with the great problems then facing the church as a result of the new legislation which threatened to ruin it. I simply went to buy as many New Testaments as the Synod could supply for use in our local YMCA centers. We obtained several thousand at that time, and I am afraid we sadly depleted their stock. Except for a small edition published in the twenties by the Protestants, no further editions of the Scriptures were produced in Russia until 1956.

Apart from the haunting experience of attending services in Moscow's awe-inspiring Church of Our Savior (which was later torn down by the Soviets and replaced by a large outdoor winterized swimming pool), I remember with special satisfaction going to *Vsenoshchnaia* (Great Vespers) at the New Jerusalem Monastery, famous in the seventeenth century as the place of Patriarch Nikon's exile after his enforced retirement, but destroyed during World War II. While we were spending the weekend at a dacha near the monastery, a new threat to the regime came. Count Mirbach, the German ambassador to Moscow, was shot by an assassin. Everyone wondered if the Germans would void the recent Peace of Brest Litovsk and march into Moscow. International communications at that time were so poor that people in Russia, probably even those in the government, did not know how hard pressed the Germans were. No attack came, but the few Americans still in Russia soon left, including all the consular staff. Of the YMCA people, only Louis Penningroth (in Petrograd) and I (in Moscow) remained.

I did not outlast my colleagues by many weeks. In October it became necessary for both Penningroth and me to leave. We left the country just days before the armistice was signed in France, and we were back home early in December.

I was not to get back to Moscow until 1956, but throughout the intervening time I was deeply engrossed in Russian affairs because of my assignment to what was called Russian work by the International Committee of the YMCA. In May, 1920, I was back in Europe in charge of a party of three—Donald A. Lowrie, James Somerville, Jr., and myself—assigned to do whatever we could for the Russian people, inside or outside the country. Some of my colleagues did spend time in Russia in the ensuing few years. They served there during the famine of 1921–23, representing the American section of the European Student Relief, which was accredited to the American Relief Administration. In connection with this relief work, Ethan T. Colton and Donald A. Lowrie had personal contact with Patriarch Tikhon and other church leaders. Others, Edgar MacNaughten in particular, were in constant touch with leading churchmen and theologians in Kiev.

In 1922 Colton came to Berlin from Moscow and asked me to interpret for him in conveying a message from Patriarch Tikhon to Archbishop Evlogy. This was the historic verbal communication authorizing Metropolitan Platon to assume the duties of head of the Russian church in North America. On this same visit to Berlin, Colton asked me to subscribe to *Pravda* and *Izvestiia*, as well as to other Soviet papers and periodicals of my choice, for the purpose of translating into English articles pertaining to religion. Copies of these translations were sent to America, and a set is now in the Hoover Library at Stanford University, just as we typed them in Berlin.

In 1922 famine was widespread in Russia and the Soviet government was expropriating church property and valuables to help meet the emergency. In general, the first phase of what proved to be a protracted struggle was well underway at the time. Monsignor Constantine Budkiewicz, pastor of a Roman Catholic church in Petrograd who resisted the confiscation of church valuables, was executed in March; Patriarch Tikhon was arrested in May. The government-sponsored "Living Church" was organized in June, and Metropolitan Benjamin of Petrograd was executed in July. It was apparent that matters of great moment were taking place and that we in the West should try to keep abreast of developments. From this time on one of my principal duties was to render whatever service I could in this field. We still had sufficient communication with Russia, primarily through new refugees and visiting foreigners, to enable us to acquire much information beyond that found in the press. Also, I began to collect books and pamphlets and, when they appeared, the new antireligious magazines such as *Bezbozhnik*, *Bezbozhnik u stanka*, and *Antireligioznik*, which figured in the establishment and promotion of the movement called the League of the Militant Godless.

Berlin in the 1920s, with its tens of thousands of refugees, became a Russian cultural center. Music, drama, art, and diverse intellectual activities flourished. It was also an important center of Russian book publishing, with such firms as Ladyzhnikov, Slovo, Heinrich Sachs, and the YMCA each contributing numerous titles every year. Most of the manuscripts published were obtained from Russian emigrés and, until the general embargo of 1923, the greatest sale of these books was in Russia, to which the books were exported either directly or by way of Riga or Warsaw. In addition, Russian books were purchased in large numbers in the Baltic countries, Eastern Poland, Moldavia, and Bulgaria. As our production increased, I found it necessary to visit bookstores in all these countries to promote sales and ascertain interest.

The YMCA soon found itself involved in all aspects of the spiritual and intellectual movements of the Russian emigration. Historically we had had ties with Russia going back to 1900, when the local YMCA in St. Petersburg (*Maiak*, "The Lighthouse") was established, not to mention our work in the Russian Student Christian Movement, which was inaugurated some few years later. Personal ties with Russian church leaders had thereby been maintained over a considerable period. After the Revolution, with the moral and financial backing of Dr. John R. Mott and the International Committee of the YMCA, we helped to establish the Russian Student Christian Movement Abroad. Between 1920 and 1924 the YMCA also operated a correspondence school and two technical schools, one at Wünsdorf near Berlin and the other at Sofia, Bulgaria. Finally, it was also at this time that the YMCA Press was founded; this Russian-language publishing program was legally incorporated in Prague in 1921. It has been my good fortune to have been associated with it ever since.

The YMCA has always published books for its members in every country, but our Russian undertaking was somewhat different. It had the unique task of trying to fill the vacuum created by the Bolshevik suspension of the production of religious books in the Soviet Union. We began with the publication of textbooks on scientific, engineering, and agricultural subjects, but within a few months we were also working in the religious field. One of the first books of a religious nature which we published was a biography of Saint Sergius of Radonezh, written by the novelist Boris Zaitsev. At the same time we planned and published a symposium entitled *Problemy russkago religioznago soznaniia* (Problems of the Russian religious mind). The leading religious philosophers in Berlin at the time contributed to it, including B. Vysheslavtsev, N. Berdyaev, L. Karsavin, V. Zenkovsky, N. Lossky, N. Arseniev, and others. These two books demonstrated that the Press was not an American Protestant propaganda outlet, and established us as producers of the best works in Russian Orthodox thought. In the course of nearly fifty years the Press has published approximately four hundred titles.

During my four years in Berlin, beginning in June, 1920, I also followed the battle that had been joined between the Soviet regime and religion. (My interest was especially keen because I had been in Petrograd on January 23, 1918, when the first decree on religion appeared.) The excesses of the government seemed to most of us to speak for themselves. Because of the incompleteness of our information, however, and the need to speculate as to the meaning of what was available, divergent views occasionally appeared. For example, the establishment of the Living Church was interpreted by some, both in Russia and abroad, as proof of the fact that the authorities were not opposed to religion as such but merely to reactionaries and counterrevolutionaries in the churches. Neither Dr. Mott nor the members of the YMCA group could accept this interpretation. We had men like Colton and Lowrie who were in constant personal touch with the patriarch and the real leaders of the Orthodox church in Moscow and Kiev, and these men knew this was not so.

Julius Hecker, whom I knew very well, was an ardent admirer of the Living Church. He had worked for the YMCA among war prisoners in Austria–Hungary and had initiated Russian-language publications there under YMCA auspices. His writings on religion in Russia were persuasive, and some American Protestants became convinced that Soviet policy on religion consisted of disestablishment and freedom of religion, with a synthesis of the best aspects of socialism and Christianity. His failure to penetrate the real meaning of events subsequently resulted in much hardship for the Orthodox church in America. This was because he had considerable influence in certain Protestant circles in America which ultimately came to support the Living Church. This development in turn affected the struggle between, on the one hand, Metropolitan Platon and his successors in the Russian Orthodox Metropolia in America and, on the other, John Kedrov, who represented the Living Church in the United States, and his successors.

The Orthodox church in Russia was hard pressed during the 1920s. In the first decade of the new regime Iaroslavsky, Skvortsov-Stepanov, and other promoters of atheism wrote numerous pamphlets against religion.[1] The closing of church schools and the prohibition of religious education were a serious blow, as were the arrest and execution of great numbers of bishops and priests, and the seizing of church properties and even churches themselves. Many bishops and priests were exiled to Solovki in the White Sea. We obtained the famous 1926 Solovki letter[2] soon after its composition and thus were able to follow the struggle of the Orthodox church with the Living Church and the efforts of the former to regain legal status and to establish a legitimate locum tenens in the patriarchate.

In Europe there were numerous sources of information regarding religion in Russia, with which we kept in touch. The temporary synod of Russian bishops (organized in Constantinople and later located at Sremski Karlovtsi, near Belgrade) had at its disposal much valuable information, although much of the material it published was biased and tendentious. I visited its head, Metropolitan Antony (Khrapovitsky), in Yugoslavia several times during those years. Another source was Professor George Fedotov, who arrived in Paris in 1926. At the headquarters of the YMCA and the Russian Student Christian Movement, which in the previous year had been transferred to Paris from Berlin, he told of the arrest and exile on a single day of the last forty members of the Russian Student Christian Movement in Leningrad.

A group of us now took up serious study of Soviet antireligious publications. The Soviet press—dailies, periodicals, and books—was our basic resource. Despite their nature and tone, these materials

1. See Joan Delaney, "The Origins of Soviet Antireligious Organizations," chapter 6 below.

2. In 1926 the bishops of the Orthodox church who had been exiled to the Solovki Islands wrote a note to the Soviet government protesting the measures taken against the church and calling for a modus vivendi between them. Included with the complaints of the bishops was a denunciation of the Living, or Renovated, Church. The English text of this document may be found in Nikita Struve, *Christians in Contemporary Russia* (New York: Scribner's, 1967), pp. 351–61.

provided much information on church life and reported incidents of resistance by the church, giving names, dates, and places.

At this time the Russians in Paris, in the French provincial centers, in Czechoslovakia, Yugoslavia, and Bulgaria still felt close ties with their homeland and tried to preserve the religious culture and institutions abroad which they believed had been condemned to extinction in the Soviet Union. In addition to the labors of the Russian Student Christian Movement, expressions of this effort came from the Orthodox Theological Institute of St. Sergius in Paris and were manifest in a great variety of other projects devised by the Russian intellectuals with whom we were working. Berdyaev, Bulgakov, Fedotov, Fondaminsky-Bunakov, Kartashov, Vysheslavtsev, Florovsky, Zenkovsky, Skobtsova (who later became the nun, Mother Maria), the Zernovs, and others were all members of this creative group. Many of them, including Berdyaev and several other philosophers and theologians (nearly one hundred in all), had been exiled in 1922 and 1923, and first made their way to Berlin, where I was living.

Since there was historical precedent for YMCA involvement in Russian cultural and religious activity, I invited Berdyaev, Vysheslavtsev, and Frank to my apartment and asked them what they would like to do abroad. Berdyaev said that they would like to organize an institute similar to the Free Philosophical Academy which he and others had established in Moscow after they had been discharged from the university because of their religious convictions. Our committee agreed to this and thus was launched a cooperative effort starting with the establishment of the Religious Philosophical Academy, with Berdyaev at its head. The Academy began its work in Berlin in 1923, but moved to Paris in 1924, when the locus of cultural and intellectual activity within the emigration shifted to France.

This stimulating and diversified movement could well have been called "Russia in the West." One dimension of our work, however, was an attempt to influence cultural and spiritual (*not* political) development in the Soviet Union itself. This goal was seriously hampered during the interwar years because it was practically impossible to make contact with religious leaders or institutions in the USSR. Very few books or magazines on religious subjects were passed by Soviet censors, while the bishops and clergy there were in personal danger if known to possess Western literature. In general, what contact was maintained came almost exclusively through individual visitors. My own most fruitful relationship was with Metropolitan Elevthery of Kovno, Lithuania, whom I saw frequently. Since he retained his canonical ties with the patriarchate, he was therefore able to visit Moscow.

The new attacks on the churches which accompanied the collectivization of the First Five-Year Plan, especially from 1930 to 1933, aroused the sympathy of non-Orthodox Christian churches in the West and gave rise to committees of protest in England, Holland, Switzerland, and elsewhere. (Perhaps they were spurred by the success of earlier protests which in 1922–23 had helped obtain the release of Patriarch Tikhon and Bishop Cieplak, although it must be admitted that many other hierarchs arrested at about the same time were kept in prison or executed.) In 1930–31 there were numerous articles in the Western press and several mass meetings, all calling upon the Soviets to drop, or at least to modify, their hostile policy toward religion. The new archbishop of Canterbury, Cosmo Lang, invited Metropolitan Evlogy of Paris to join him in a protest meeting in London. The latter accepted the invitation, which immediately caused the Soviets to denounce him and led to his being cut off from the Moscow patriarchate.[3] Despite these protests, the terrors connected with collectivization continued unabated, perhaps because of the government's increased self-confidence. Scores of bishops, and thousands of priests and lay workers were executed or exiled to labor camps, so that by the outbreak of the war in 1939 the episcopate had been reduced to about six in active diocesan service.

We increased our efforts to keep abreast of the situation during the 1930s and to share our information with Western churches. There was a gradual but significant increase in the demand for such information in English (the Synod Abroad, or the Karlovtsi Synod, located in Belgrade and the emigré press in Paris were already providing considerable coverage in Russian) on both the general background and the current conditions of the church's situation under the Soviets. Expanding our translation service, we now began publica-

---

3. The canonical dilemma in which Evlogy then found himself was quickly resolved when Patriarch Photius II of Constantinople "temporarily" received him and established an exarchate for the Russian Orthodox parishes of western Europe. This exarchate was only abolished in 1965 (November 22) by Patriarch Athenagoras I, with the admonition that Evlogy's successor, Archbishop Georges, and his clergy return to canonical communion with the patriarchate of Moscow. This they have refused to do.

tion of a series of brochures entitled "Life in Soviet Russia," which dealt not only with religion but with other aspects of Soviet culture as well. It was at this time that Sir Bernard Pares commissioned me to write the "Chronicle on the Soviet Union" for the *Slavonic Review*, a quarterly publication of the School of Slavonic Studies at the University of London.

The British were much more interested in matters Russian and Orthodox than either the Americans or the French. This was particularly true of the Church of England, whose Anglican and Eastern Churches Association continued to maintain and develop its relationships of some eighty years' standing. The honorary secretary of the association, the Reverend R. M. French, had been a consular chaplain in Russia and was the translator of most of Berdyaev's books into English. Canon J. A. Douglas, honorary secretary of the Church of England's Council of Foreign Relations, Sir Bernard Pares, and Lord Charnwood were all dedicated sponsors of efforts to aid the Russian church. I was regularly in touch with all of these men.

One of the results of the growing isolation of the Russian Orthodox church in the Soviet Union was that it fell behind in the interchurch activities which were finding expression in the rapidly advancing ecumenical movement, as well as in the rapprochement between the Anglican and Orthodox churches. Canon Douglas prepared a lengthy communication on these matters and addressed it to Metropolitan Sergy, the locum tenens of the patriarchal throne in Moscow. This letter was translated into Russian, and I took it to Metropolitan Elevthery in Kovno, who was to forward it to Moscow. The letter was not acknowledged directly by Metropolitan Sergy, but it was subsequently referred to in a message which he sent to the patriarch of Constantinople concerning the patriarch's invitation to the Russians to attend a pro-council of the Orthodox churches scheduled to meet on Mount Athos in 1930.

Sergy's message, by the way, attests to the influence wielded by the Moscow patriarchate in worldwide Orthodox affairs. Since the Orthodox churches require a consensus of the heads of all the autocephalous churches, not just the fiat of the patriarch of Constantinople who is *primus inter pares*, the presence of the Russian church at the proposed meeting on Mount Athos was indispensable. However, between 1925 and 1927, during the interregnum in Russia between

the death of Patriarch Tikhon and the legalization of the patriarchal office and the Holy Synod under Metropolitan Sergy, Constantinople ventured to accredit an emissary to the Living Church. In
preparing for the Mount Athos meeting, the ecumenical patriarch
sent invitations to both the Living Church and to Metropolitan
Sergy. The latter replied that he would not send a representative
unless the invitation to the Living Church was withdrawn. Whether
this demand was met is not yet clear, but at any rate neither group
was represented at the Mount Athos meeting, and the absence of
the Russian church for all practical purposes nullified the effect of the
attempted pro-council.

Although all the churches suffered in the persecution of the thirties,
the Orthodox church was attacked especially vigorously. It did
manage to publish a few issues of the *Journal of the Moscow Patriarchate* with routine information on synodal meetings and a few
excellent articles. But life in the parishes was stifled, priests hounded
and exiled, and the Militant Godless movement constantly announced fresh successes. There seemed to be a slight improvement in the
situation when Stalin declared, at a meeting on the 1936 constitution,
"Why should the clergy be disenfranchised? Not all of them are
disloyal." When the census of the following year revealed, however,
that a large proportion of the public was still religious, severe pressure was applied once again. The Baptists were forced to announce
the closing of their central organization and the Orthodox very nearly
had to do the same.

It may be that one of the factors which contributed to the plight of
the Russian church at this period was the attitude of many in the
emigration toward the patriarchate. When in 1927 Metropolitan
Sergy achieved the legalization of his administration through an
accommodation with the regime, many emigrés accused him of
having "sold out." Many others, however, felt that he had made the
best of a difficult situation and had at least kept the patriarchal office
alive. It is true that the existence of this office did benefit the regime.
For example, the government could use it to prove that it allowed the
church to function, asserting that freedom of religion existed in the
country because it was guaranteed by the constitution. Through the
patriarchate the government also hoped to influence international
groups with which it was involved. In any case, during the thirties the
church was largely defenseless; religious instruction was prohibited

almost completely, publications were all but nonexistent, and there was no possibility of conducting open and fair debate.

Our subscriptions to Soviet periodicals and the supply of anti-religious books and pamphlets stopped abruptly on September 1, 1939, when the Nazi armies began their invasion of Poland. Similarly, the Soviet acquisition of Estonia, Latvia, Lithuania, and the Polish territories east of the Bug River interrupted corollary sources of information. As a result, we in Paris had little news from any source.

At the end of September my wife and two children returned to America. My YMCA responsibilities took me to the Balkans for about six weeks during the early months of 1940. On my return to Paris I found great nervousness in spite of the stalemate at the Maginot line. The evacuation of children was taking place—but not of the children of non-French parents. Consequently the Russian Student Christian Movement Abroad, which by formal agreement was conducting the activities a Russian YMCA would have had, began looking for a large chateau in the country in which to house at least some of the children left behind. Other Russian emigré committees did the same. By June, 1940, after the Nazi armies had bypassed the Maginot line and in a blitzkrieg overcome the French armies in the north, plans for evacuation were ready to be carried out. I was in Pau, just north of the Pyrenees, setting up our "reserve post" when the Italian attack triggered the general fascist advance. It took more than two days to drive back to Paris, where I arrived at five o'clock in the morning. The city was empty. Everything with wheels had joined the exodus. I cleared up things at the office, visited the embassy, and at six o'clock that evening set out again for Pau, getting caught an hour later in the mass of vehicles two miles south of Versailles. The next morning at daybreak German tanks began rolling down the Champs Elysées.

In July I returned to Paris, and remained thirteen months under the German occupation. Our Russian publishing program was stopped, as was the work of all social organizations. Profiting by the historical position of the YMCA as an international organization, and by my own experience as director of YMCA services to German and Austrian prisoners of war in Russia during the First World War, I made contact with the German high command and in December received official permits for visits to internment and prisoner of war camps in France.

On June 23, 1941, we received news of the German invasion of
Russia the previous day. Many Russian emigrés were now interned,
especially intellectuals and priests. Since the president of the Russian
Student Christian Movement was one of those interned, he transferred his responsibilities to me. There is nothing to report on any
"study of Russia" during this period. This study stopped for the
duration at the end of July, 1941, when I was fortunate enough to get
permission to leave, via Portugal, for repatriation to the United
States with embassy personnel.

Back home new tasks appeared in the YMCA Russian work.
Through the Geneva world YMCA office, our staff of neutrals in
Germany asked for books for the hundreds of thousands of Russian
prisoners of war. Our stock of suitable literature was soon exhausted.
Then we bought from the Four Continent Book Corporation as much
as they could furnish, and finally the YMCA financed the reprinting
of Russian classics in large quantity and shipped them on International Red Cross vessels for distribution through Geneva, in
Germany.

There is one interesting conversation to record in this connection.
Dr. Tracy Strong, general secretary of the World Alliance YMCA
and head of its War Prisoners' Aid, wanted permits to service prisoners held in the Soviet Union. An approach was made to the Soviet
ambassador in Stockholm, but without success. Dr. Strong and I
then decided to visit the Soviet ambassador in Washington, Andrei
Gromyko. He received us rather formally and soon asked, "Is it true
that you distribute Bibles to Russian prisoners in Germany?" Dr.
Strong replied that the YMCA gives religious literature only to
persons requesting it, and I told of buying up all available copies of
the Koran in France for North African prisoners held by Germany in
France. No permit was ever given for the YMCA or any other international organization to serve prisoners in Soviet camps. Soviet
Russia was the only belligerent country refusing such service,
despite the fact that Nazi Germany had granted permits for service
to captured Russians.

During my stay in America I was able to get, through the Four
Continent Book Corporation, a number of Soviet papers, journals,
and books. We also received copies of *The Truth about Religion in
Russia*, published by the patriarchate, followed by other books and
pamphlets of the same general content, namely, descriptions of the

contribution of the Russian church to the war effort. At the same time, the Russian church sent Archbishop Alexander to resume contact with the few parishes in the United States which still adhered to the patriarchate. I called on him, and he returned the call at my office in the YMCA headquarters, but did not stay long. He supplied little information on church life in Russia except to say that he had a fine house and a car, whereas he observed that Benjamin, the Russian bishop in New York, lived in poor quarters on Long Island.

It is commonly held that the situation of the church improved markedly when Germany and the USSR concluded their partition of Poland. This is not completely accurate. Despite the addition of several bishops to the episcopate as a result of the acquisition of the the former Polish territories, and the loyal appeal in 1941 of Metropolitan Sergy to all the faithful to come to the defense of the fatherland, it was not until 1943 that Stalin became fully convinced that the church could play a positive role in winning the war. In other words, while there was little further deterioration in the church's situation between 1939 and 1943, the real improvement did not come until the end of this transitional period.

At the close of the war all of the registered churches found their position relatively strengthened. (I will not deal here with the nature of these improvements since they are adequately discussed elsewhere in the present volume.)[4] Patriarch Aleksy has told me personally of conversations which he (then Metropolitan of Leningrad), Metropolitan Sergy, and Metropolitan Nikolai of Krutitsk had with Stalin in 1944. Stalin assured them of his readiness to allow the church to reopen its theological schools, to fill vacant dioceses, and even to hold a synod for the election of a patriarch. These promises were kept, and needless to say the church took advantage of them. In this sense the book, *The Truth about Religion in Russia*, while misleading in some of its remarks about the prewar period, can be accepted as more or less accurate in its description of the late wartime and immediate postwar periods. The Militant Godless movement was closed down, churches were reopened in many areas, priests came out of hiding, theological schools were reopened, and liturgical books were published by the Orthodox church publishing house.

I returned to Paris in November, 1944, attached to the prisoner-

4. See Alexander Bogolepov, "The Legal Position of the Russian Orthodox Church in the Soviet Union," chapter 9 below.

of-war-exchange section of SHAEF. The next summer Canon
Douglas invited me to London for the visit of Metropolitan Nikolai
of Krutitsk. Apart from my casual acquaintance with Archbishop
Alexander in New York, this was my first direct contact with the
modern hierarchy. Thereafter I met frequently with Metropolitan
Nikolai, and the acquaintance rapidly extended to other prelates
who came to Europe or America.

After the war the YMCA Russian work did not get under way
again until 1947. To meet the shortage of paper, we used our international connections to import stocks from Finland. This enabled us
to publish some of the manuscripts written during the war. In 1947
we lost our chief editor, Nicholas Berdyaev. For twenty-four years
we had worked together, building up the YMCA Press publishing
program of creative Russian thought. I count it as one of my
greatest joys to have been associated with Berdyaev in this effort to
maintain and develop Russian Christian culture.

There were other Russian casualties resulting either from the war
or the postwar tensions, especially in France. Mother Maria (Skobtsova), the head of Action Orthodoxe, died in a Nazi camp, as did
its chaplain, Father Dimitry Klepinin, and many more. Father
Sergei Bulgakov died before the war ended. Professor Anton
Kartashov survived only a few years more. But perhaps our greatest
loss was that of Metropolitan Evlogy, also in 1947. In prerevolutionary Russia, Evlogy had been bishop of Kholm, and twice a member
of the national Duma. In the emigration he attracted large numbers
of laymen and clergy by his forward-looking policies. He sponsored
the establishment of the Orthodox Theological Institute in Paris,
which because of its dedication to Sergius of Radonezh was often
referred to as the St. Sergius Institute. He heartily supported our
YMCA work and seldom missed a student-movement conference;
and he gave his blessing to the founding of the Fellowship of St.
Alban and St. Sergius, which began with Russian Orthodox and
Anglican clergy and theological students.

In 1947, when I settled permanently in America, Dr. Donald A.
Lowrie took over the active direction of the Russian work in Europe.
He was to make a splendid contribution by handling the publication
of several theological works, as well as supervising the work of a
committee of persons competent in religious education in preparing
and publishing a five-volume illustrated graded series for church

school use. In 1955 Dr. Lowrie also returned to America, and the
YMCA publishing enterprise was turned over to the Russian Student
Christian Movement Abroad, to be managed by an administrative-
editorial board of five persons, of whom I am still one, which meets
two to four times a year.

In 1948 the Moscow patriarchate was permitted to invite to
Zagorsk representatives of all the autocephalous and autonomous
Orthodox churches, to celebrate five hundred years of autocephaly
of the Russian Orthodox church as well as to hold a conference on
current questions facing these churches. The conference took place,
and the proceedings were published in two volumes, made available
in Russian and French. Recognizing the historical significance of this
conference I took responsibility for translating and publishing it in
English.[5] In many ways the meeting had all the marks of a pan-
Orthodox pro-council, but the delegates of the ecumenical patriarchate made it clear that they had come for the celebration and not
for a conference, so that the conclusions arrived at had only the value
of an unofficial historical record.

Two topics discussed and recorded at this meeting were especially
revealing as to the extent to which the Russian church had fallen
behind the times. One concerned relations with the Roman Catholic
church. Here the reports were merely a rehash of the old quarrels and
prejudices on both sides, and completely neglected the trends which
were already in the making and which later were brought into the
open by Pope John XXIII and Vatican Council II.

The second topic was similar in nature, namely, the question of
the World Council of Churches. This body was to be formally
established later the same year, but the Moscow patriarchate
declined the invitation to join. It is interesting to note that the reason
given for this refusal was that the council was too much engaged in
political matters. This is rather ironic in view of the carefully planned
activities of many representatives of the patriarchate in various
countries at that time and ever since, and of its own avid attention to
political matters within the Christian Peace Conference, which began
in 1958, as well as in the World Council of Churches once the patriarchate did join (for example, at the council's Conference on Church
and Society held in Geneva in 1966).

5. *Proceedings of the Conference of the Heads of the Autocephalous Orthodox Churches,
Held in Moscow, July, 1948* (Paris: YMCA Press, 1952). Also published by the Moscow
patriarchate, as indicated, in Russian and French.

It would seem that in the postwar period the Soviet regime became aware of the possible assistance it might gain from church activities in certain areas of foreign policy. Metropolitan Aleksy had scarcely been elected to succeed Patriarch Sergy in 1945, when he set out on an extensive trip to reestablish the historic ties of the Russian church with the ancient patriarchates of Antioch, Jerusalem, and Alexandria. Certain church practices of the nineteenth century, such as inviting foreign students to come to Moscow to pursue theological studies, or the exchange of visits between dignitaries of the Middle Eastern patriarchates and Moscow, were revived. In the course of time the practice of establishing in Russia a *metokhion* (an ecclesiastical diplomatic mission for contact between autocephalous churches) with a chapel that would be maintained by these sees was also renewed and reciprocated by the establishment of Russian church centers in Alexandria and Damascus.

Historically these practices arose in the eighteenth century, when Imperial Russia and the Russian church assumed a sort of spiritual protectorate over their fellow Orthodox in the territory under the rule of the Turkish empire. These venerable patriarchates were at that time granted vast landholdings, particularly in southern Russia, the income from which helped to support them. When the opportunity of restoring this custom was offered, it was quickly accepted. The Soviet government naturally saw the value of this system and authorized the church to purchase foreign exchange in Moscow and pay sums of money approximately equivalent to the old grants in cash or other benefits. One of the most recent of such grants by the Russian church was for the equipping of a large new hospital in Beirut, built by Metropolitan Salibi in 1966.

Much has been written about the decision of the Russian church in the early 1960s to join the World Council of Churches, contrary to the conclusions of the 1948 conference in Zagorsk. Some have felt that this was essentially a political maneuver, which would enable the Soviet government to increase its influence in the West. Others feel that it is precisely this sort of contact abroad which strengthens the church's position at home. From the beginning I supported the entrance of the Russian Orthodox church, declaring often that the World Council's constituent members and especially its senior staff should make a special effort to understand the peculiar nature and motivations of the church in Soviet Russia. Formal entry of the

Russian church into the council was voted at the New Delhi assembly in 1961. My support of this move was well received by WCC leaders, and its importance becomes evident when one observes how fully the Russian church has entered into all the activities of the council.

When I retired from the YMCA in 1961, after forty-eight years of service, mostly with Russians and other Orthodox peoples, the general secretary of the National Council of Churches in the United States invited me to spend two years helping the council develop an understanding of things Russian and Orthodox. This led to my participation in the 1962 exchange delegation, and to my involvement in the handling of the reciprocal Russian delegation.

It was also at this time that the bulletin *Religion in Communist-Dominated Areas* was born. This came about quite simply. At NCC senior staff-meetings I was asked more than once how I came to know about religious life in Russia. My reply was that I was able to keep up with Russian-language periodicals. To make up for this deficiency, I then agreed to provide the staff and interested committee members with translations which I made from current Soviet papers and journals. As the demand expanded, the Council engaged Blahoslav S. Hruby as managing editor, who is competent not only in Russian but in several other East European languages. His work became even more indispensable after I concluded my two-year term with the NCC. However, I have continued on in the role of editor, hoping to assure balance and truth in dealing with a paradoxical situation—the life of Christian churches in a governmental system whose official goal is "to uproot all religion from the minds and habits of the people."

Western churchmen and politicians generally have much difficulty in trying to grasp the realities of the life of religious organizations in the USSR. This effort is difficult even for those who know the Russian language and who have long maintained close and friendly connections with Russian churchmen in the Soviet Union and abroad. I have myself made six visits to Moscow and several other cities in the USSR in the last eleven years, and I regularly read a great variety of Soviet newspapers, journals, and books—religious, anti-religious, cultural, and philosophical—yet I would not claim to be more than a student and observer.

It is particularly regrettable that the Western churches understand so little about developments in recent years, most notably since the resolution of the Central Committee of the Communist party in November, 1954. The Soviet explanation of what must unquestionably be seen as the beginning of redoubled efforts against religion is that the laws and the constitution have not changed, but that the authorities have simply become more conscientious in the application of this legislation. The party resolution of 1954 was, more than a question of law, a revival of ideological insistence that atheism is not only an essential prerequisite for party membership, but an indispensable tenet of the entire philosophy of the Communist system.[6] Following out this decree the ideologists held a national conference in 1957, established policies, and suggested practices to implement the new program.

By 1960 the party was ready to put the program into action. Metropolitan Nikolai was removed from office and died in December, 1961. (I was in Moscow at the time and attended the first *panikhida*—a prayer service for the dead—at Zagorsk, on the eve of his funeral.) He was replaced by Metropolitan Nikodim. G. Karpov, head of the Council for the Affairs of the Orthodox Church, was also removed and replaced by V. Kuroedov, an inflexible party man. Probably at the behest of the government, the patriarchate in 1961 called a plenary council of the Russian hierarchy to change the constitution of the church. It was decreed that priests would no longer sit on parish councils and would, in effect, become mere employees of these councils. The public explanation of this change by both church and state was that it relieved the clergy of secular, especially financial, concerns, and enabled them to devote themselves wholly to the spiritual responsibilities placed upon them by their ordination.[7]

Thousands of local parish churches were closed between 1959 and 1964. (Some estimates run as high as ten thousand.) A more complete catalogue of the measures taken by the government in this period can be found in the article herein which deals with the subject in detail.[8]

One noteworthy change which took place in this period was in the nature of the antireligious propaganda employed. During the thirties much of the content of this propaganda was taken from nineteenth-century anticlerical literature and from Lenin's diatribes. From the

6. See Joshua Rothenberg, "The Legal Status of Religion in the Soviet Union," chapter 5 below.

7. For a full discussion of this constitutional change see Bogolepov, chapter 9 below.

8. See Donald A. Lowrie and William C. Fletcher, "Khrushchev's Religious Policy, 1959–1964," chapter 7 below.

mid-fifties, however, antireligious workers have been equipped with a more modern and sophisticated approach to matters of religion. Soviet ideologists have now delved into the works of the Russian philosophers who had been assailed by Lenin before the Revolution, but whose thinking and writing were attractive to Russian intellectuals of the 50s and 60s. The pages of *Voprosy filosofii* (Problems of philosophy) and its predecessor, *Pod znamenem marksizma* (Under the banner of Marxism), are also full of articles on Berdyaev, Lossky, Ilyin, and others of those men exiled in 1922, whose works were published abroad and did not reach the USSR until after the war. Similarly, special attention is given to contemporary Western studies in the psychology of religion, the sociology of religion, and ecumenism.

It is still difficult to say whether Khrushchev's removal from power has resulted in any significant changes in the party or the government's attitude concerning religion. One thing, however, seems clear. Despite all the restrictions which have been placed on the churches, the number of believers in the Soviet Union is still considerable. Neither the church nor the state have published formal statistics on church membership. Fortunately, the Soviet Academy of Sciences has enabled us to gain a more accurate appraisal in this area than was previously possible. The academy, as well as other governmental institutions, has made a number of sociological surveys to determine the prevalence of religious sentiments among the population.[9] As yet, the data for a truly comprehensive picture are lacking, but the studies which have been published so far are very interesting.

While it is clear that religious observance has decreased significantly and church attendance has diminished, one must bear in mind that the number of believers cannot be reckoned by counting heads at regular worship services, since the number of believers who do not go to church is still substantial. One has only to attend a church festival in Zagorsk or the patronal feast in any parish to appreciate the volume of the "fringe" church affiliation. Perhaps in the near future our information will be improved, because Soviet sociologists are now trying to be more scientific in assessing such phenomena.

Another factor, which is doubtless a source of chagrin to the party ideologues, is the presence of religious feeling and convictions in the

9. See Bohdan R. Bociurkiw, "Religion and Atheism in Soviet Society," chapter 4 below.

new intelligentsia, men and women born and raised in the Soviet period.[10] Some of these people have no doubt read works of emigré philosophers and theologians, since many of these works are now circulating clandestinely in mimeographed form in the USSR. The interest of these young intellectuals in religious matters may also stem in part from the influence of classical Russian writers, such as Dostoevsky. Finally, personal experience, especially in times of anxiety or distress, must surely have contributed to this new awareness of God.

It may be said, too, that one of the fruits of cultural exchange has been the sharing of ideas on a variety of subjects, religion among them. Especially to be noted are the exchanges organized by European and American churches with the Russian Orthodox and with the Lutherans and Baptists in the USSR, and the student exchanges set up by the YMCA and YWCA over the past decade on a reciprocal basis with Soviet youth organizations. I have twice gone to the Soviet Union as a member of the exchange delegation of the National Council of Churches of the USA, and once as American Episcopal Church observer with the theological delegation of the Church of England. Each such journey has been followed by a return visit of churchmen from the USSR. Both the Russian church and the Soviet state have been very cooperative in facilitating visits to churches and to cultural institutions in the USSR, while the American and European churches and governments have reciprocated splendidly. After the long dry-spell in church relations, and even in tourism, these exchanges have served as opportunities for close examination of the views of both sides.

The church exchanges in which I have participated have been far more than *visites de politesse*. Our first NCC delegation, in February, 1956, came about as a result of a conviction in the staff that the Russian church leadership was not accurately informed on the American position in Korea. When we got to Moscow, the discussion proved to be very frank indeed! So was the conversation on matters of doctrinal and practical differences between the Orthodox and the Anglicans, when first-class theologians of both churches met in Moscow, also in 1956, for a full week of discussions. Careful notes were taken and checked in English and Russian by a two-man team on each side—I served on the Anglican team. Since the record of

10. See George L. Kline, "Religious Themes in Soviet Literature," chapter 8 below.

these discussions runs to 560 typewritten pages, apart from the text of the papers prepared in advance, the seriousness of this undertaking becomes clear. On each successive visit to the USSR, or, when meeting Russian churchmen who have come to the West, I have been left with the conviction of the lasting impression of these encounters, and of their reciprocal significance in the church life of both East and West.

What can be said about the next half-century of religious life in the Soviet Union? I think it is fair to expect that some measure and variety of religion will be preserved, and that among the Christian bodies the Orthodox church and the Union of Evangelical Christians-Baptists will probably continue to be the chief modes of its expression. The net influence of all religious bodies on Soviet life may wane, at least to the extent that Soviet ideology and structure inhibit authentic development of any religious life. To offset this, though, it seems highly likely that Soviet intellectuals who are becoming aware of the religious dimension of human nature will seek to combine their response to the promptings of conscience with the demands of Soviet technological modernity.[11] This effort will increasingly find support from corresponding movements elsewhere in the world. In sum, the dynamic quality of what used to be called the Russian soul will undoubtedly continue to find expression, although perhaps in ways that cannot presently be predicted.

11. See for example, Andrei D. Sakharov, *Progress, Coexistence, and Intellectual Freedom* (New York: W. W. Norton, 1968).

3

A SELECTED BIBLIOGRAPHY
OF THE PUBLISHED WORKS
OF PAUL B. ANDERSON

Author

"Russia Creates New Law on Religion." *The Christian Century*, 9 October 1929, pp. 1246–48.

"The New Law on Religion in Russia." *The Christian East* 10 (1929): 142–48.

"The Fellowship of St. Alban and St. Sergius." *The Christian East* 13 (1932): 2–7.

"Religion and Communism." *Journal of the Fellowship of St. Alban and St. Sergius* 1 (1934): 35–37.

"Father Sergius Bulgakov in America." *Sobornost* 1 (1935): 38–44.

Russia's Religious Future. London: Lutterworth Press, 1935.

"The Soviet Union." In *The Church and the State*, edited by Kenneth G. Grubb, pp. 223–46. Madras Series, vol. 6. New York: International Missionary Council, 1939.

"New Soviet Antireligious Legislation." *Sobornost* 1 (1937): 33–37.

"Soviet Life, 1939." *Sobornost* n.s. 17 (1939): 27–31.

"Religion and Antireligion in the Soviet Union." *Sobornost* n.s. 18 (1939): 28–31.

"In Regard to Statistics." *Sobornost* n.s. 19 (1939): 33–35.

"Russia and the Ecumenical Movement." *Christendom* 9 (1944): 505–15.

People, Church, and State in Modern Russia. London: Student Christian Movement Press, 1942. New York: Macmillan, 1944.

(French edition: *L'Eglise et la nation en Russie sovietique.* Paris, 1946.)

"Toward Mutual Understanding: Two-Way Visit of American and Russian Churchmen." *National Council Outlook,* 26 February 1956, pp. 9–10.

"Churchmen Visit Russia." *The Christian Century,* 18 April 1956, pp. 480–82.

"Russian-American Visitations: A Prelude to Understanding." *Christianity and Crisis,* 9 July 1956, p. 12.

"The Orthodox Church in Soviet Russia." *Foreign Affairs* 39 (1961): 299–311.

Recent Developments in the Soviet Bloc. Testimony of Paul B. Anderson to the US Congress, Subcommittee on Europe of House Committee on Foreign Affairs. 88th Cong., 2nd Sess., Part I: *Recent Trends in Soviet and East European Literature, Arts, Human Rights (Law and Religion), and the Younger Generation.* Wash., D.C., 1964, pp. 94–102, 115–24.

"Religious Liberty under Communism." *Journal of Church and State* 6 (1964): 169–77.

"Ecumenical Aspects of Eastern Orthodox Migration with Special Reference to Australia." *Migration Today,* no. 8 (1967), pp. 1–17. Reprinted in *Eastern Churches Review* 2 (1969): 296–302.

"The Problem of Alienation: Life Without Spiritual or Religious Ideals." In *Religion and the Search for New Ideals in the USSR,* edited by W. C. Fletcher and A. Strover, pp. 13–23. New York: Frederick A. Praeger, 1967.

Foreword to *Communist Russia and the Russian Orthodox Church 1943–1962* by William B. Stroyen. Washington, D.C.: Catholic University of America Press, 1967.

"In response to Yuri Alexandrov." *Ave Maria,* 9 December 1967, pp. 11–12.

"A Decade of Significance for Religion: 1956–1966." In *The New Russia: Communism in Evolution,* edited by Denis Dirscherl, pp. 134–56. Dayton, Ohio: Pflaum Press, 1968.

Editor

Life in Soviet Russia. A series, nos. 1–10. Paris YMCA Press, 1930–43. Three of these are of special interest: (1) *Fifteen Years of*

Religion and Antireligion in Soviet Russia, nos. 2/3 (1933); (2) *Training for Godless Ministry*, no. 6 (1934); (3) *Russia's Religious Future*, no. 10 (1935).

Major Portions of the Proceedings of the Conference of Heads and Representatives of Autocephalous Orthodox Churches in Connection with the Celebration of 500 Years of Autocephalicity of the Russian Orthodox Church: 8–18 July 1948. Paris: YMCA Press, 1952.

Religion in Communist-Dominated Areas. A translation service published semimonthly by the National Council of Churches. From 1962 to present.

Associate Editor, *The Living Church*, weekly magazine of the Protestant Episcopal Church in the United States. From 1944 to present.

II

RELIGION AND SOVIET SOCIETY

INTRODUCTION

Two major themes emerge from the articles found in this section. (1) There has been a continued commitment on the part of the Soviet regime to eradicate all vestiges of religion within that society. (2) Religion, with marked tenacity and through a variety of forms, traditional and new, continues to play a significant, if diminished, role in Soviet society.

The first of these themes—the more dominant one—is reflected in all of the articles with the exception of that by George Kline. In his introductory essay, Bohdan Bociurkiw asserts that the Soviet leadership has been hampered in dealing with religious phenomena by its dogmatic assumptions concerning the nature of religion. He adduces examples in support of his thesis from all periods of Soviet history, but gives particular attention to the last decade. He concludes that at the close of the Khrushchev period the regime could find some satisfaction in the results of its latter-day administrative attack on religious life, but could still not boast of the final elimination of religious belief. A dogmatic reappraisal followed which, though reaching new depths of analysis, still suffered from serious theoretical inadequacies. These concern not only the nature of religion, but the nature of contemporary Soviet society which, according to Bociurkiw, is increasingly secular in character. The paradoxical result for the regime is that, along with a slow erosion of religious belief, this secularization undermines the commitment to ideology in general and creates a growing number of citizens indifferent to or tolerant of religion.

Moving from the question of the dogmatic underpinnings of Soviet religious policy, Joshua Rothenberg's paper focuses on Soviet law as it concerns religion. His basic motif is the law's complexity. Although, viewed historically, Soviet religious legislation has undergone a general increase in severity, law in written statute and law in actual life have often differed, even sharply, for the simple reason that Soviet policy has not always followed its legal codes. Moreover, even when implementation is sought according to existing law the actual result can be highly variegated because directives must be filtered down through a complex bureaucracy which at the local level is usually characterized by differing traditions and personalities.

In their essays, Joan Delaney and Donald Lowrie and William Fletcher concern themselves less with dogma or law than with Soviet antireligious propaganda and practice, in its earliest and latest expressions. Delaney notes that although the antireligious movement began within party circles, it was neither created by party fiat nor directed by careful party control in the first years of its existence. In the movement's first phase several *ad hoc* groups arose which soon clashed over the best means of conducting antireligious work. This conflict was further complicated by personal rivalries and the larger political debates and decisions of the time, in particular the introduction and continuation of the New Economic Policy and the gradual bureaucratization and centralization of the party. By the mid-twenties the party leadership was forced to settle the sharp conflicts within the antireligious movement by establishing party control over all antireligious activity. The centrist guidelines adopted then, although soon abandoned, have recently come under study to determine what applicability they may have to current conditions. This is certainly part of the reassessment to which Bociurkiw refers.

Lowrie and Fletcher put forth that about 1959 the detente established during the war between church and state began to dissolve. It was rapidly replaced by an intense antireligious attack aimed at rooting out all "religious survivals." Coordinated and sophisticated antireligious propaganda pervaded the educational system, the mass media, and the world of literature and the arts. Relatively new features included the introduction of secular rites and concentrated work with individual believers. The campaign was not limited to propaganda alone; legal and administrative pressures were also brought to bear. Some religious bodies (the Orthodox and the Baptists) were forced to alter their bylaws in a more restrictive direction. Scores of houses of worship were closed, and the number of seminaries and monasteries was sharply reduced. Many clerics and lay believers were subjected to harassment, including school and job discrimination, and some suffered arrest, trial, and imprisonment or exile. While the virulence of official antireligion has abated somewhat since the removal of Khrushchev, Fletcher and Lowrie suggest—somewhat differently than Bociurkiw—that because of the exacerbated antireligious policies of the state between 1959 and 1964, the situation of religion in Soviet society has been worsened, perhaps irreversibly.

The second major theme—the tenacity of religion in the USSR—is found in the essays of Bociurkiw and Kline. The former, basing his observations on recent Soviet sociological investigations, including the distribution of questionnaires and research expeditions to regions traditionally populated with Orthodox and sectarian believers, indicates that the extent of religious belief is larger than might be expected after five decades of state opposition and that grounds exist for thinking that the number of believers exceeds the estimates of these surveys. Kline discloses the existence of a religious orientation outside of organized religious groups. Relying chiefly on literary sources, but citing the works of sculptors and painters as well, he points to numerous religious allusions in the imaginative works of key members of the creative intelligentsia.

These five articles, then, attempt to provide a background against which the particular studies in section 3 will be more fully comprehensible. Together they indicate that while the state has persisted in its opposition to religion, the situation has not been one of undifferentiated or unrelieved warfare.

A.Q.B.

4

RELIGION AND ATHEISM
IN SOVIET SOCIETY

From the very inception of the Soviet regime, its attempts to cope with the problem of religion in the USSR have been hampered by its dogmatic assumptions concerning the nature, roots, and social functions of religion. Derived from Marx and Engels in a rather simplified Leninist version, the Bolshevik notion of religion reduced it to a socially harmful "illusion" born of men's ignorance and their fear of the natural and social forces controlling their existence. Equated with a "spiritual moonshine, in which the slaves of capitalism drown their human image," religion was viewed as a psychological tool used by the exploiters to keep the oppressed classes docile, apathetic, and incapable of overthrowing the seemingly providential status quo. In their service the ruling classes employed the greedy clergy, who perpetrated "frauds" upon the credulous masses, justifying and sweetening the unhappy lot of the latter with the promise of imaginary happiness in the next world. Not answering any universal human need, not rooted in any eternal religious sentiment, religion was destined to share the fate of the class system, private property, and exploitation. Through a combination of systematic scientific–atheistic education and the operation of social–economic forces

This is a revised and expanded version of an article first published in *Survey*, July 1966, pp. 62–71.

Bohdan R. Bociurkiw

liberated by the proletarian revolution, the toiling masses were to liberate themselves fully from "religious prejudices."[1]

The nearly fifty years of antireligious struggle and social engineering which were expected to eliminate the "social roots" of religion in the USSR, failed to emancipate the masses from "religious illusion." Since the launching of the First Five-Year Plan, this moment of deliverance has seemed to be just over the horizon, as the Soviet Union evolved through economic and social upheavals, the purges, and the war into an increasingly complex industrial and literate society under an apparently all-powerful dictatorship. To be sure, by the end of the thirties *organized* religion had been almost completely suppressed throughout the country, but for all its massive efforts in atheist indoctrination the regime could not destroy religious *beliefs* in a large section of the population. Pragmatist that he was, Stalin drew a lesson from the failure of the antireligious campaign when the German attack on the USSR made it imperative to mobilize all human and material resources for the country's war effort. Limited concessions were granted to the Russian Orthodox church and to other religious groups which could be utilized for the purposes of the Kremlin's domestic and foreign policies. Under this precarious and short-lived modus vivendi between the atheist regime and "patriotic" religious groups, organized religion experienced a significant, though partial, revival. Indeed, the churches even managed to recapture some of the ground they had lost among the younger generation.

In seeking to explain the tenacity of "religious survivals" in postwar USSR, Soviet theoreticians have not only been constrained by the narrow Leninist frame of reference but have also been compelled to maintain the fiction that with the construction of socialism such sources of "religious illusion" as fear, insecurity, dependence, exploitation, and alienation, have been eliminated in Soviet society. Consequently, they have found it necessary to fall back on such rationalizations as "ideological lag," "external capitalist influence," "the war," and, above all, the "neglect" or "inadequacy of antireligious propaganda" and the persistent "activities of churchmen

1. See a collection of Lenin's principal writings on the problem, V. I. Lenin, *O religii* [On religion] (Moscow, 1955). For a discussion of Lenin's views see Bodhan R. Bociurkiw, "Lenin and Religion," in Leonard Schapiro and Peter Reddaway, eds., *Lenin: The Man, The Theorist, The Leader. A Reappraisal* (London: Pall Mall Press, 1967), pp. 107–34.

and sectarians."[2] However, as the post-Stalin thaw slightly relaxed the dogmatic framework of Soviet philosophy, cautious voices began to appear in scholarly exchanges, criticizing the limitations of the official view of religious phenomena in Soviet society.

The most serious challenge appeared in an article by P. P. Cherkashin published by *Voprosy filosofii* in June, 1958, in which the author asserted the continued existence in the USSR of certain epistemological and social roots of religion.[3] The epistemological base of religion, he suggested, will remain even under communism, as this base derives from the inescapable contradictions "between the attained relative truth and absolute knowledge, between the objective content and the subjective form, between direct, emotional contemplation and the abstract logical work of the mind."

The vitality of religious survivals in the USSR, wrote Cherkashin, must also be explained by certain shortcomings in socialist society—its inequality in rewards, its marginal injustice and coercion. "Real contradictions and difficulties of our society may painfully affect the fate of an individual person, especially one not firmly tied to the collective . . . . In our circumstances, there may be 'failures' and 'fortunates' not only in family life. Personal plans may be drastically changed or shattered by unforeseen circumstances, unexpected events in the life of the country, some shift or other in economics or politics, not to mention the war. . . ."

Moreover, Cherkashin pointed out, religious survivals feed on "certain features of our life" which "simply contradict" socialist principles. Among such features he listed "errors in the direction of agriculture, which were absolutely unnecessary in the history of our society," a seemingly all-powerful bureaucratism with its "isolation from the masses, disregard of their needs and interests," and, in the past, the excesses of Stalinism with its "most crude violations of socialist legality." Finally, Cherkashin notes that Soviet society, especially the rural population, "has not yet fully overcome the dependence of man's activities on the play of elemental natural

2. N. I. Gubanov, "O prichinakh sushchestvovaniia religioznykh perezhitkov v SSSR" [On the reasons for the existence of religious survivals in the USSR], *Nauka i religiia* [Science and religion] (Moscow, 1957), pp. 50–67; *Kommunist*, no. 4 (1957), p. 57; I. P. Tsameriian, ed., *Osnovy nauchnogo ateizma* [The foundations of scientific atheism] (Moscow, 1961), pp. 421–31.

3. P. P. Cherkashin, "O sotsialnykh korniakh religii" [On the social roots of religion], *Voprosy filosofii* [Problems of philosophy], no. 6 (1958), pp. 29–41.

forces," and that this condition also contributes to the survival and revival of religious sentiments among the people.

This attempt to reduce the dogmatic element in the official notion of religion, while carefully confined to the Marxist frame of analysis (criticism of religion is a criticism of the society begetting religion), concealed broader implications for Soviet religious policy. As the latter soon took a sharp leftward turn, Cherkashin's article came under attack from the party Central Committee in July, 1959, for its "incorrect conclusion that the very same reasons which nourish religious prejudices in capitalist countries operate also in a socialist society."[4] Shortly afterwards, a *Pravda* editorial (August 21, 1959) restated in familiar terms the official interpretation of the reasons for the continued existence of religious survivals, stressing in particular such "subjective" factors as the weakening of antireligious propaganda, machinations, and violations of Soviet law by the "servants of religion," and the "laxity of organizations called upon to supervise the strict observance of Soviet legislation on religious cults."

The increasingly violent antireligious campaign extending from 1959 to 1964 and aimed at the "final and complete uprooting of religious prejudices" in Soviet society, represented a major test of the regime's thinking on religion.[5] On the surface, it produced results which could hardly fail to impress the party's ideological high priests. By 1965, the number of registered religious congregations in the USSR had been reduced by at least half of the 1954 total;[6] some denominations, in particular Judaism, lost most of their legal facilities for worship. Of the eight Orthodox theological seminaries reopened since the war, only three survived, their enrollments greatly reduced. At least two-thirds of the Orthodox monastic institutions had been closed.[7]

4. *Voprosy ideologicheskoi raboty* [Problems of ideological work] (Moscow, 1961), pp. 280–81.

5. See Lowrie and Fletcher, "Khrushchev's Religious Policy, 1959–64," chapter 7 below.

6. According to N. Eshliman and G. Iakunin, the two Moscow diocesan priests who, in December 1965, addressed petitions to Patriarch Aleksy and N. V. Podgorny, protesting against continuing state interference with the church, "no less than ten thousand churches" were closed between 1961 and 1964 (*A Cry of Despair from Moscow Churchmen* [New York, 1966], p. 45). A much lower figure was cited by a recent Soviet source which admitted that "about 30 percent of all religious congregations ceased to exist in the USSR during 1960–65" (E. I. Shekhterman, *Vera ili znanie* [Faith or knowledge] [Alma-Ata, 1967], p. 249). According to *Spravochnik propagandista i agitatora* [Reference book for propagandist and agitator] (Moscow 1966), p. 149, the Russian Orthodox church has 7,500 operating churches.

7. Eshliman and Iakunin claim that a much larger number of monasteries ("about one hundred") were closed during Khrushchev's antireligious campaign (*A Cry of Despair*, p. 45).

Under new laws and regulations severely curtailing the scope of ecclesiastical activities and discouraging laymen from openly performing religious rites, the number of church baptisms, marriages, and funerals had been drastically reduced, especially in large cities.[8] "New Soviet rites" were said to have displaced church feasts and rituals for all but the most "backward" elements of the toilers. In time-honored fashion these fruits of administrative repression were now advertised as the "inevitable" effect of "objective" forces at work in Soviet society.

Since Khrushchev's fall the self-congratulatory mood characteristic of the early 1960s has slowly been displaced by a critical reappraisal of the situation on the "antireligious front." Apart from the harm it had done to the Soviet image abroad, the "assault on heaven" was found to have hardly reduced the number of believers in the country. Deprived of legal facilities for worship, the embittered faithful have been increasingly resorting to underground religious practices or to replenishing the prohibited religious groups. For the authorities, this has magnified the problem of policing religious activities and has revived the specter of a religious underground evolving into a center of active political opposition to the regime. Religious persecution served to intensify eschatological tendencies among the believers, alienating the more fundamentalist, the more aggressive, and, significantly, the younger elements from their submissive leaders, who were suspected of "selling out" to the Godless authorities.[9]

8. Among the consequences of these measures has been the spread of rites performed in absentia or by proxy in a manner reminiscent of the late thirties.

9. The most significant split on this issue occurred among the Evangelical Christians-Baptists in 1961, when the more uncompromising elements of this church (the *initsiativniki*) repudiated their leadership and subsequently formed an "illegal" center of their own—the Council of Churches of Evangelical Christians-Baptists. See Michael Bourdeaux, *Religious Ferment in Russia: Protestant Opposition to Soviet Religious Policy* (London, 1968); A. I. Klibanov and L. M. Mitrokhin, "Raskol v sovremennom baptizme" [Schism within the contemporary baptist movement], *Voprosy nauchnogo ateizma* [Problems of scientific atheism] (hereafter *VNA*) no. 3 (1967): pp. 84–110; *Voprosy istorii religii i ateizma* [Problems of the history of religion and atheism] (hereafter *VIRA*) 11 (Moscow, 1963): 102–11; *Ezhegodnik muzeia istorii religii i ateizma* [Yearbook of the museum of the history of religion and atheism] (hereafter *Ezhegodnik*) no. 7 (Moscow-Leningrad, 1964): pp. 117–21. Similar tendencies are evident within the Russian Orthodox church, as illustrated by a series of protests circulated by clergy (Eshliman, Iakunin, Archbishop Ermogen) and lay believers (the Pochaev-believers, Talantov, Levitin-Krasnov, and others). According to Eshliman and Iakunin, eight bishops, headed by Archbishop Ermogen of Kaluga, appealed to the patriarch in the summer of 1965, deploring his overly docile attitude toward the civil authorities. (*A Cry of Despair*, pp. 56–57.)

As for the much publicized *oktiabriny*—"Komsomol weddings," "civil funerals," "consecrations into workers," and the like—these synthetic new rites admittedly failed to match the popular appeal, the emotional and aesthetic qualities of the religious ceremonies they were supposed to replace, although the small number of elaborate "Wedding Palaces" (*dvortsy brakosochetaniia*) did become popular, largely because they represented some improvement over the dreary bureaucratic routine of the *Zags* offices.

Symptomatic of the new self-critical mood in official circles was a postmortem on the Khrushchevite antireligious campaign conducted in the pages of the chief atheist journal, *Nauka i religiia*. Those participating in the discussion admitted the self-defeating nature of vulgar misrepresentations of religion, concentration on priestly "frauds" and "immorality," insults to believers, and the widespread reliance on intimidation and coercion in closing churches and dissolving religious congregations. "There can be no doubt," admitted a Minsk lecturer, V. Ivanov, "that the violations of the legislation on cults [by the atheists] and the offending of religious sentiments of the believers contribute to the existence of religious survivals." "We must all firmly assimilate one truth," declared a journalist, M. Morozov, that "in their great majority the believers in our country are honest Soviet men, toilers just as we atheists are, and one should treat them with respect."[10]

A most significant contribution came from a Lvov atheist, G. Kelt. Writing in *Komsomolskaia pravda* (August 15, 1965), she reminded fellow *antireligiozniki* that religion "cannot be abolished in one day," as it is not "an idle invention" but represents "a historical phenomenon which has existed over thousands of years." She goes on: "And today we are again lulling ourselves: 'many believers in our country had left the church and religion.' This is self-deception. One thing is true, that in the greater part of the territory of the Soviet Union there are no churches and no servants of religion. But there are believers. If not Orthodox, then sectarians of all possible shades. . . . The closing of a parish does not make atheists out of the believers. On the contrary, it intensifies the people's attraction towards religion and, in addition, embitters their hearts."

The writer concluded that "a naked, purely negative, bookish-

10. *Nauka i religiia* [Science and religion], no. 10 (1965), pp. 3–8, 11; no. 11 (1965), pp. 7–9; no. 12 (1965), pp. 5–6, 30–34.

oratorical atheism" would not succeed unless it countered religion at the aesthetic and emotional levels as well. What is needed, she suggested, is a substitute for the church: "a ritual center," a "shrine dedicated to the apotheosis of the genius of Man" combined with a "new ritual that would replace church liturgy."[11]

In line with the official criticism of the Khrushchevite "subjectivism" and "impulsive, superficial [ways of] solving the party and state problems," the authoritative *Voprosy nauchnogo ateizma*—the organ of the party's new Institute of Scientific Atheism—called in 1967 for "a scientific explanation of the nature of religion." "Deviating from this principle is a subjectivist conception which ultimately reduces the essence of religion to the deception of simpletons by charlatans and finds the causes for the existence of religious survivals in our country in alien ideological influence and the resourcefulness of churchmen, on the one hand, and in the shortcomings of atheistic propaganda, on the other hand. Such a conception leads to erroneous practical conclusions, revives efforts artificially to speed up the overcoming of religiousness, and encourages administrative methods in atheistic work."[12]

A "scientific materialistic" approach to religion must recognize that there still are "objective social factors" underlying "religious survivals" in Soviet society, such as "essential differences between the city and the village, between intellectual and physical work," and other "remnants of the old way of life," as well as alienation of individuals from the "collective," "weak social ties" of housewives and the like.[13]

Prescriptions for the elimination of "religious survivals" offered in the Soviet official media during recent years have suffered both from a general tendency to reduce religious phenomena to the plane of ideology and habit, reenforced by the pressure from one's "micro-environment," and from a reluctance to probe into the psychological and emotional roots of religiousness. Proposed substitutes for religious rites and calls for more elaborate antireligious campaigns appear, however, to misjudge the nature of Soviet society. Despite

11. For discussion preceding and following the publication of Kelt's article, see *Komsomolskaia pravda*, 29 May and 24 September 1965.
12. V. I. Evdokimov, "XXIII Sezd KPSS i voprosy ateisticheskoi raboty" [The 23rd congress of the Communist party of the Soviet Union and the problems of atheistic work], *VNA* 3 [1967]: 8.
13. Ibid., pp. 8–15.

the party's repeated reindoctrination drives, Soviet society has been growing increasingly secular, at least in the ideological sense. The combined effect of the contradictions between the official theory and practice, of the bureaucratization of the system and the *embourgeoisement* of the Soviet elite, and of the rising level of education and sophistication, has been the progressive erosion of the political myth with its replacement by a monotonous public ritual and holiday rhetoric.

Not the least important reason for the failure of the recent atheist campaign was its inability to overcome indifference among the party and Komsomol rank-and-file to the cause of antireligious struggle. The prevailing view appears to be that religious survivals are common only among the older generation or the less enlightened stratum of the population, where they do not pose any real threat to the regime and society and where they would eventually fade away in the process of social and economic change. A militant antireligious campaign, it is thought, would at least arrest, if not actually reverse, this process. Significantly, a poll conducted in 1961 by *Komsomolskaia pravda*'s Institute of Public Opinion revealed that the majority of Soviet youth consider adherence to religion among the least of "social evils."[14]

A 1965–66 survey of the circulation of antireligious literature in representative libraries of the Leningrad oblast revealed a relatively low level of public interest in the broad category of literature ciassified as "atheistic," as illustrated by the following tabulation.[15]

| | Read atheistic literature | | |
Occupation	Regularly	Occasionally	Never
Teachers	12.5%	70.8%	12.5%
Government employees and cultural workers	18.9	56.8	16.2
Engineers and technicians	8.0	55.2	33.3
Students	4.5	58.9	35.3
Workers	5.7	42.0	47.1
Pensioners, housewives, invalids	7.6	44.3	43.0
Community service employees	4.1	40.8	42.9

14. See B. Grushin and V. Chikin, *Ispoved pokoleniia* [The confession of a generation] (Moscow, 1962), pp. 148–50.

15. V. D. Kobetsky, "Metodika izucheniia chitatelskogo sprosa na nauchno-ateisti-cheskuiu literaturu" [Methods for studying readers' demand for scientific-atheistic literature], in *Konkretnye issledovaniia sovremennykh religioznykh verovany* [Factual research on contemporary religious beliefs] (hereafter *Konkretnye issledovaniia*), (Moscow, 1967), p. 93. It must be noted that the term "read" in the table refers in fact to the *borrowing* of atheistic works from public libraries.

Many industrial workers tend to agree with the believers' argument that their religious convictions are a private matter which must not be held against them in the allocation of jobs and benefits.[16] Indeed, among the Soviet intelligentsia—the social stratum least represented among overt believers—professional *antireligiozniki* have recruited remarkably few collaborators, while gaining themselves the reputation of "a sort of an atheist sect," which has "assimilated from its opponent the worst features of intolerance and fanaticism."[17]

The decline in militant atheism within the politically vocal strata of the Soviet population cannot be dissociated from changes in the overt attitudes of religious organizations towards the regime. Since the 1920s, after a period of open conflict and unsuccessful attempts to secure an equitable compromise with the regime, the Russian Orthodox church and most other religious groups not only had to pledge their loyalty to the new system but also to accept far-reaching governmental control over their activities and to give unconditional support to Soviet policies. Though it was not until the crisis of the the last war that the Kremlin saw fit to acknowledge the "patriotic attitude" of religious groups, ever since the late twenties these groups have been conspicuously loyal, to the extent of endorsing the regime's manifestly false claim that it had never persecuted religion or clergy but only "criminals hiding behind the cloak of religion." In nearly every religious group there were some who found the political and moral price of legality too high, and rather than compromise chose to withdraw into the religious underground; some simply discontinued church attendance and participation in religious rites performed by "legal" clergy.

Changes in the sphere of organized religion in the USSR are not confined to the realm of church-state relations. The institutional power of religion and the scope of religious activities drastically declined under the combined impact of a hostile political environment and social change. The most dramatic change in fortunes was that of the Russian Orthodox church.[18] The range of ecclesiastical activities

16. *Voprosy formirovaniia nauchno-ateisticheskikh vzgliadov* [Problems of the formation of scientific-atheistic views] (hereafter *VFNAV*), (Moscow, 1964), p. 43; *Nauka i religiia*, no. 2 (1966), pp. 2, 7.

17. G. Kelt in *Komsomolskaia pravda*, 15 August 1965; cf. *Nauka i religiia*, no. 5 (1962), p. 12.

18. For the impact of these conditions on Judaism, see Zvi Gitelman, "The Communist Party and Soviet Jewry: The Early Years," chapter 15 below.

was reduced to little more than worship and the administration of rites within the walls of the church.

The church's revival since the war has been strictly controlled and restricted in line with considerations of political expediency. Neither the total number of open Orthodox churches (which declined from some fifteen thousand in 1948 to eleven thousand in 1961, and may now be fewer than eight thousand),[19] nor their geographical distribution are indicative of the actual strength or local density of Orthodox believers. An examination of the geographical distribution of the Orthodox church in the USSR shows that the ratio of active churches to the population decreases sharply as one moves from west to east. The most "churchly" areas are those annexed to the USSR since the last war, followed by the territories which experienced a resurgence of religious life under enemy occupation, and the provinces which were threatened by the Germans (and where the Soviet authorities were prepared to grant some concessions to believers); the least "churchly" areas lie beyond the Urals. It is worth noting in this connection that in 1961 the *majority* of all active Orthodox churches and monasteries was located in the Ukrainian SSR (containing only 20 percent of the total population) and that the Republic's three former Uniate oblasts (Lvov, Ternopol, Ivano-Frankivsk, with 2 percent of the total population), accounted then for some 20 percent of all Orthodox churches operating in the USSR.[20]

Some light has been shed on the changes in the denominational structure and social base of organized religion by a series of surveys conducted since 1959 under the auspices of the Academy of Sciences, the Academy of Social Sciences, and individual institutions of higher learning in individual oblasts (especially Voronezh, Lipetsk, Riazan, Tambov, Penza, and Leningrad) and in the Ukraine, Belorussia, and Kazakhstan.[21]

The Russian Orthodox church has remained by far the largest (and, *politically*, the best-adapted) religious group in the country, but

19. *Nauka i religiia*, no. 11 (1962), p. 60; V. K. Tancher, *Osnovy ateizmu* [Foundations of atheism] (Kiev, 1961), p. 181.

20. Tancher, ibid., p. 181. Similarly of some two thousand sectarian congregations officially registered in the USSR in 1957, the majority was located in the Ukraine (*Nauka i religiia* [Moscow, 1957], p. 396); *Pravoslavnyi visnyk* [Orthodox herald], no. 7 (1957), p. 215; *Komsomolskaia pravda*, 7 February 1962; *Krokodil*, no. 5 (1963), p. 3.

21. Accounts of these investigations appeared in *VIRA* 9 (1961), 10 (1962), 11 (1963); *VNA* nos. 1, 2 (1966), 3, 4 (1967); *Konkretnye issledovaniia; Nauka i religiia*, nos. 1, 7 (1968); *Liudyna i svit* [Man and the world], nos. 5, 7, 8 (1967); and several Soviet learned journals.

much of its present institutional strength derives from the annexation of the Orthodox churches in the new Soviet territories in the west, as well as from the forcible conversion of the Uniates in the western Ukraine. On the other hand, the Moscow patriarchate has lost some of the faithful to the underground "Truly Orthodox Christians" and its flock has been persistently raided by the Baptists and other "Western" sects. The Old Believers and such old native sects as the *Dukhobory, Molokane, Subbotniki, Malevantsy, Izrailitiane* (Old and New), *Khlysty,* and *Skoptsy* have been rapidly declining in strength.

In contrast, the newer sects of Western origin—the Evangelical Christians-Baptists, the Adventists, as well as the banned Pentecostals and Jehovah's Witnesses, have been enlarging their following.[22] While the locus of Orthodoxy's organized strength has shifted to the countryside, the "Western" sects have developed a strong urban base, invading some newly industrialized areas only weakly covered by the Orthodox organization. Among the sects, the Baptists appear to be the strongest and most dynamic group. They have the advantage of a less institutionalized structure (which makes them less vulnerable to Soviet restrictions and pressures), and have successfully combined an intense missionary zeal with considerable ingenuity in adapting their message and style of operation to the changing social environment. The old sects of Russian origin were on the whole unable to adapt themselves to the new conditions; their withdrawal from the world into closed, self-sufficient communes became impossible in the thirties, with the collectivization of agriculture and the increasingly totalitarian nature of the regime.

After almost half a century of exclusion from public life and school, of the banning of religious instruction of young people under eighteen, and of administrative discrimination against known believers in all walks of Soviet life, all religious groups have been facing for years the specter of their gradual "withering away" in the absence of a large influx of young believers. According to a 1963 official estimate, approximately 70 percent of the overt believers were then over

22. See *VIRA* 9 (1961): 9–94, 161–88; no. 10 (1962): pp. 170–71; no. 11 (1963): pp. 69–71; *Ezhegodnik* no. 5 (1962): pp. 63–67; *Stroitelstvo kommunizma i dukhovny mir cheloveka* [The building of communism and the spiritual world of man] (Moscow, 1966), pp. 218–19; and, in particular, F. Fedorenko, *Sekty, ikh vera i dela* [Sects, their faith and works] (Moscow, 1965).

forty years of age.[23] The average age of members of religious congregations in the USSR varies considerably, however, in different regions (in the newer Soviet territories the age structure of believers comes closer to that of the general population) and among the different denominations. While the published Soviet data are inconclusive and restricted to sectarian groups only, they suggest that the Old Believers and the native Russian sects have been on the whole far less successful in rejuvenating their ranks than the Western sects.

Surveys conducted in the Ukraine in 1963–65 reveal also that sectarian (primarily Baptist) membership is generally younger than that of the Orthodox church; while 80 percent of the latter believers were over fifty years of age, only 53.2 percent of the sectarians fell into this age group.[24] Among new members joining the Evangelical Christians-Baptists in a series of urban centers, nearly one-third were young people. Surprisingly, the youngest membership recorded for any religious congregation belonged to an illegal congregation of the "Truly Orthodox Christians" in the early fifties. Little information is available on the age composition of the Orthodox believers. Observations conducted in the Penza oblast in 1963 revealed that over three-fourths of the regular churchgoers consisted of the over-forty age group, though at the 1963 Easter service in Penza approximately one-third of the congregation was identified as children and youth.[25]

Undoubtedly women (who accounted in 1959 for 55 percent of the total population) constitute a large majority of overt believers. A 1961 estimate placed the proportion of women in religious congregations at about 70 percent. It should be noted, however, that men are professionally and socially more vulnerable than women, many of whom do not hold jobs. In Orthodox churches some of the auxiliary functions once reserved for men only have now been opened to women. In terms of their educational and occupational characteristics, members of religious groups seem to come primarily from the less educated strata of Soviet society. Except, again, in the new western oblasts, such overlapping categories as housewives, peasants, unskilled workers, and those over working-age represent the over-

---

23. L. F. Ilichev in *Kommunist*, no. 1 (1964), p. 30.
24. *Konkretnye issledovaniia*, p. 139.
25. *Ezhegodnik* no. 7 (1964): p. 115. Of the 83 "activists" in the Michurinsk congregation (Tambov oblast) of *Istinno pravoslavnye khristiane* [Truly orthodox Christians], forty-four were under thirty and only twelve were born before the Bolshevik Revolution (*Ezhegodnik* 8 [1965]: p. 96).

whelming majority of the registered sect members and regular churchgoers.[26]

The official interpretation of the composition of religious congregations has persistently stressed the causal relationship between "religious superstitions" and low levels of education and skill, seclusion from the collective productive process, and limited access to the communication and artistic media. Inevitably, it is claimed, as the general level of education rises, as women are liberated from drudgery and alienation and drawn into the productive collective, as the uses of leisure become more organized and cultured, religion will gradually lose its hold on the less politically mature strata of the population.[27]

Apart from some success attained by individual religious groups in recruiting younger (and usually better educated) members, the influx of pensioners into the ranks of religious congregations tends to upset such a simple correlation. Including people of professional and white-collar-worker backgrounds, pensioners have come to play an increasingly important role in the administration of local congregations. In the Penza oblast, of 681 members of Orthodox groups in 1962, 225 were pensioners, of whom 144 had previously been decorated with orders and medals.[28] Idleness and age alone do not seem a sufficient explanation here. One must also take into account the relative invulnerability of individuals once they have retired from posts which are, as a rule, closed to known believers; there is the temptation to reactivate one's beliefs at this stage.

This brings us to the question of the actual spread and intensity of religious beliefs in Soviet society. No one knows with certainty how many believers there are in the USSR. Apart from the alleged findings of the abortive 1937 census, no credible statistics have been collected.[29] The occasional local surveys conducted by Soviet institu-

26. V. Iu. Kelembatova in *Narodnia tvorchist ta etnohrafiia* [Folklore and ethnography], no. 4 (1961), pp. 27–33; G. T. Utkin in *Kratkii nauchno-ateistichesky slovar* [Short scientific-atheistic dictionary] (Moscow, 1964), pp. 451–52; Tancher, *Osnovy ateizmu*, pp. 317–30; *Kommunist*, no. 1 (1964), p. 39; *Konkretnye issledovaniia*, pp. 77, 146–47, 212–14.

27. See I. A. Kryvelev, "Preodolenie religiozno-bytovykh perezhitkov u narodov SSSR" [Overcoming religious survivals in daily life among the peoples of the USSR], *Sovetskaia etnografiia* [Soviet ethnography], no. 4 (1961), pp. 30–44.

28. *VFNAV*, pp. 13–15.

29. Cf. N. S. Timasheff, "Urbanization, Operation Anti-Religion and the Decline of Religion in the USSR," *The American Slavic and East European Review*, April 1955, p. 232.

tions suffer from dilettantism and ideological bias, and from the understandable reluctance of the unknown proportion of believers to identify themselves as such. According to the director of the Institute of Scientific Atheism in Moscow, recent surveys conducted in several areas of the USSR reveal that "in some cases" believers constitute up to 15 percent of urban dwellers and up to 30 percent of the rural population.[30] An even higher proportion of believers was identified by surveys of large samples of the population in a number of areas: in Kazan 21 percent of that city's adults were listed as believers (81 percent of this group were women) and an additional 7.2 percent were listed as "waverers"; in Voronezh oblast 7.9 percent of the urban and 15.6 percent of the rural adult population were believers, with an additional 17.1 percent "waverers"; and in Kaluga oblast 39.7 percent were believers and 12.9 percent "waverers."[31]

Another index, however imperfect, of the extent of religious sentiments in society has been the degree to which births, marriages, and deaths have been accompanied by the corresponding religious rites. The published data for the Riazan and Penza oblasts, while restricted to the Orthodox church, suggests that a much greater proportion of the population resorts to these rites than has usually been asserted by Soviet spokesmen. That large numbers of young people are clearly involved in these practices—in spite of the shortage of churches and clergy and the virtual impossibility of escaping official detection— also tends to show that the common association of religion with old age may not correctly reflect the real situation.

Thus, in the Riazan oblast, where of the prerevolutionary total of 991 churches only 61 were operating in 1960 (one church for twenty-four thousand inhabitants), 60 percent of all children born in 1960 were baptized in church. In the same year, 15 percent of all marriages and 30 percent of all funerals were performed according to the Orthodox rite. In the Penza oblast, in which only thirty-four churches (against 924 before 1917) remained open in 1962 (one church for forty-four thousand inhabitants), the figures for church baptisms, marriages, and funerals were 48.5, 6.4, and 20.9 percent, respective-

30. A. Okulov in *Nauka i religiia*, no. 8 (1967), p. 16.

31. Ibid., p. 18; *VNA*, no. 4 (1967), p. 134; and V. D. Pechnikov in *Vestnik moskovskogo universiteta* [Moscow University herald], no. 4 (1968), pp. 60–69. In 1964, some 11 percent of the adult population of the Voronezh oblast attended Easter services (*Konkretnye issledovaniia*, p. 148).

ly.[32] A recent survey of Leningrad and Moscow workers and students revealed that 47 percent of the sample baptized their children and only 35 percent denied doing this. On the whole, according to an authoritative Soviet source, "in a whole series of oblasts 40 to 50 percent of all newborn were submitted to baptism at the end of the 1950s and in the beginning of the 1960s."[33]

Such widespread resort to religious ceremonies, along with the retention of icons in the majority of households investigated, has been officially ascribed to pressure and even threats on the part of "fanatical" grandparents and other relatives.[34] The important fact remains that rather than submit to powerful antireligious pressures from outside and fight ideological battles at home, many young people place family loyalty above ideological principle. The survival of the family, despite all attempts to transform it into another level of control, has doubtless been the major factor in ensuring a considerable degree of continuity of religious beliefs and practices in Soviet society.[35] Notwithstanding their exposure to heavy doses of antireligious propaganda in school, youth organizations, and the army, many young adults in today's USSR are evidently willing not only to tolerate "religious survivals" among the older generation but also to charge their believing grandparents with the care and upbringing of the youngest generation of Soviet citizens.

By all accounts, organized religion in contemporary Soviet society represents only the visible and politically least vulnerable part of a much larger body of actual believers. These appear in varying percentages in all social strata and age groups and range from those totally devoted and prepared to bear witness to their faith, to the "utilitarian believers" careful to light the proverbial candles to both

32. *VIRA* 11 (1963): 67, 73, 80–82. The performance of Orthodox rites by the population in the Riazan oblast had increased two to threefold during the 1950s. *VFNAV*, pp. 11–13.

33. *Konkretnye issledovaniia*, p. 57; *Stroitelstvo kommunizma i dukhovny mir cheloveka*, p. 221.

34. A 1966 survey conducted in Cherkasy, the Ukraine, showed that 97 percent of the parents who baptized their children were not churchgoers. Of these, 52 percent were motivated to baptism by family pressure, and 34.2 percent by respect for tradition (*Liudyna i svit*, no. 8 [1967], pp. 30–32).

35. Thus a recent survey in the Ukraine revealed that nearly 61 percent of believers embraced religion as a result of family upbringing, over 26 percent became religious as a result of personal misfortunes, and less than 9 percent were won over to religion by "religious propaganda." As for the attractions of religion, 26.4 percent of believers cited the church's moral teachings, 21.8 personal salvation, 19.4 consolation in grief, and 6 percent aesthetic qualities of religious rites (*Liudyna i svit*, no. 2 [1967], pp. 28–31).

God and Devil.[36] The majority of those born since the 1917 revolution (especially in urban areas) are probably indifferent to religion, but have by no means become converts to militant atheism. While greater urbanization will probably bring a further decline in the number of believers in the USSR, it would seem that as Soviet society comes of age, as it begins to shed the straitjacket of totalitarian controls, it will become more tolerant of religious sentiments in its midst. At the same time, however, the process of secularization at work in Soviet society fosters the attrition of the political faith which has provided the regime with its claim to legitimacy, its raison d'être. In the long run this process may yet prove to be a greater danger to the survival of the dictatorship than religion itself.

36. To this writer's knowledge, the most extensive survey of the relative spread of religion and atheism among the Soviet population was conducted during 1964–66 in the Voronezh oblast, which covered a sample of 37,519 adults. The following table shows the distribution of the population in terms of their attitudes towards religion:

Attitude towards religion	% of urban adults	% of rural adults
Convinced believers	7.9	15.6
Wavering	7.2	17.1
Indifferent	25.5	27.7
Atheists	59.4	39.6

By occupational groups the distribution was as follows:

Occupational group	Convinced Believers	Wavering	Indifferent	Atheists
Intellectual workers (with university degrees)	0.6%	0.9%	10.5%	88.4%
Employees (without university education)	1.0	2.8	18.7	77.5
Highly skilled workers	1.0	1.5	41.2	56.3
Skilled workers	5.4	10.9	26.9	56.8
Unskilled workers	22.2	21.7	35.7	20.4
Skilled kolkhoz workers	1.3	5.0	23.1	70.6
Kolkhoz peasants	10.7	20.6	29.5	39.2

Source:
Tables based on M. K. Tepliakov in *VNA*, no. 4 (1967), pp. 134–37.

5

THE LEGAL STATUS OF RELIGION
IN THE SOVIET UNION

According to Marxian theory any legal system is simply an expression of the class structure of a given country in a given historical period. It serves the needs of the ruling class of the moment. Accordingly, all legislation in the Soviet Union, including that in the area of religion, cults, and religious observance, has been intended to meet the needs of the regime and the new society it is building. Almost every Soviet handbook for antireligious work reflects this concern by its divisions: (1) excerpts from the writings of Marx, Engels, and Lenin (as well as those of the current leader); (2) pronouncements and resolutions of the Communist party on religious matters; (3) relevant governmental legislation.

Understandably, the writings of the theoreticians of communism serve as the ideological basis for both the party and the government. But in religion, as in other areas, Marxian theory as such tends to be modified by concrete experience and local interpretation. These differences notwithstanding, the normative influence of the theoreticians on legislation has been great indeed, and for a full understanding of the legal framework within which religious life exists one must be familiar with their work.[1]

1. References to religion are to be found in various works of Marx, Engels, Kautsky, Plekhanov, Lenin, and other Marxist writers. References pertinent to this study may be found in the following works: Karl Marx, *Kritik der Hegelschen Rechtsphilosophie:*

Joshua Rothenberg

Another requirement for proper understanding is awareness of the dual agencies through which power is exerted in the USSR: the Communist party and the Soviet government. It is virtually impossible to give a brief and accurate characterization of the relationship between the two; formally, only government legislation has legal validity, though party pronouncements usually formulate general policy and indicate the nature of legislation to be enacted. Practically speaking, however, there is little contradiction between the two, and both are binding at all levels, as the present study will undertake to demonstrate.

Legislation on Religion

The first official act of the Soviet government touching religion was the "Declaration of the Rights of the Peoples of Russia" (*Deklaratsiia prav narodov Rossii*) of November 2, 1917,[2] abolishing all national-religious privileges and restrictions. The declaration was aimed mainly at the Russian Orthodox church, the state church of the Russian empire. It abolished the church's preeminent position and equalized the legal status of all religious cults in the Soviet Union. Several minority groups had previously suffered national *and* religious persecutions and restrictions, for example, the Armenians and the Jews. The use in the declaration of the phrase "national-religious" suggests that its authors were fully aware of the close relationship in some minority groups between their "national" and "religious" identities, with the result that restrictions in one area affected the other. Interestingly enough the expression "national-religious" did not appear in official declarations after this early period. The reason for this is that such a term tended to support the claims of several minority groups that their religious practices and customs were in many ways inseparable from their national customs. Official Soviet policy recognized national and cultural identity, but realized that the "national-religious" expression could prove to be a handicap in the struggle to eliminate religious survivals.

Fruehe Schrifften (Stuttgart, 1962), p. 488; Karl Marx, *Das Kommunistiche Manifest* (Vienna, 1921), p. 41; V. I. Lenin, "Sotsializm i religiia" [Socialism and religion], in *Sochineniia* [Works], 4th ed. (Moscow, 1947), 10: 65–69; idem, "ob otnoshenii rabochei partii k religii" [On the relation of the workers' party to religion], ibid., 15: 371–81; idem, "klassy i partii v ikh otnoshenii k religii i tserkvi" [Classes and parties in their relations to religion and the church], ibid., 15: 382–90.

2. F. Garkavenko, ed., *O religii i tserkvi; sbornik dokumentov* [On religion and the church, a collection of documents] (Moscow, 1965), pp. 95, 119.

Towards the end of 1917 several legislative acts directly concerning religion were announced. On December 11, 1917, an ordinance (*postanovlenie*) was issued over Lenin's signature ordering all religious organizations to transfer their "schools, seminaries, academies, lower, intermediate, and higher schools and institutions" to the People's Commissariat of Education.[3] A few days earlier a decree had been issued that nationalized all land, including that of the church.[4] (Religious educational institutions and monastic lands were extensive.)

On December 18, the Council of People's Commissars announced the decree "On Civil Marriages, Children, and Civil Acts Registry" (*O grazhdanskom brake, o detiakh i o vedenii knig aktov sostoianiia*), the principal provision of which was to limit legal validity to civil marriages.[5]

By an order (*prikaz*) of the People's Commissar of Public Welfare (*narodny komissar gosudarstvennogo prizreniia*) of January 20, 1918, the apportionment of state funds for the upkeep of churches, clergy, and the conduct of religious ceremonies was stopped.[6]

The first comprehensive legal act concerning religious life was issued January 23, 1918, in the form of a decree of the Council of People's Commissars. The decree, in its final form, was entitled "On the Separation of Church from State and School from Church."[7] It established a completely secular state and granted to every citizen the right to profess any religion or no religion. Any indication of religious affiliation or nonaffiliation in official documents was barred (par. 3). The teaching of "religious dogmas" was prohibited in all state schools and in all private educational institutions where general subjects were taught. Citizens were free to study and teach religion only privately (par. 9). The churches and other religious associations were denied the right to own property and did not enjoy the rights of a legal entity.

3. Ibid., p. 119.
4. Ibid.
5. Ibid.
6. Ibid., pp. 119–20.
7. *Ob otdelenii tserkvi ot gosudarstva i shkoly ot tserkvi* [On the separation of church from state and school from church]. In *Sobranie uzakoneny i rasporiazheny raboche-krestianskogo pravitelstva RSFSR* [Collection of laws and decrees of the government of workers and peasants of the RSFSR], no. 18, 26 January 1918; reprinted in *O religii*, p. 96. English translation in Appendix, section 2, below.

The preparation and publication of this decree has an interesting and perhaps little-known history. In fact it was printed two days earlier, January 21, in the government daily

The decree of January 23, 1918, was to serve as the guide in religious policy for many years. The deprivation of property rights, the loss of the status of a legal entity, and the prohibition of religious instruction in schools were all widely enforced and seriously curtailed most church activities as these had existed up to that time. Two paragraphs of the total of thirteen proved to be especially significant in ensuing years, primarily because they permitted considerable latitude in interpretation. Paragraph five states that "the free performance of religious observances is guaranteed insofar as they do not disturb public order and are not accompanied by encroachments upon the rights of other citizens." This vague clause provided almost unlimited opportunity for restricting the exercise of the right to religious observances, in and outside houses of prayer. Paragraph thirteen reads: "All property of the church in Russia and of religious associations is declared to be the property of the people. Buildings and objects earmarked for religious observances may be given for the free use of the respective religious associations by special decision of the local or central state authorities." The state thereby became the owner not only of the buildings belonging to religious groups, but also of all objects contained in them. The cults were thus in the position of having to lease their property from the state.

Four weeks after the publication of the decree (February 18, 1918) an ordinance was issued by the State Commission of Education which declared that "the state is neutral in matters of religion . . .and

Izvestiia under a quite different title: "On Freedom of Conscience, the Church and Religious Associations." On December 11, 1917, the Council of People's Commissars had nominated a committee to draft the text of the decree. The members of the committee were A. V. Lunacharsky, P. I. Stuchka, P. A. Krasikov, M. A. Reisner, and an unnamed clergyman. Lenin was not satisfied with the text of the decree as drafted by this group and made many revisions, "putting teeth in it," as Soviet historians have since evaluated the changes. The first text had traces of "revolutionary romanticism." (One of the members of the drafting committee, Lunacharsky, had been attacked by Lenin some years before for his attempts to reconcile religious ideas with Marxian teachings.) It was Lenin who changed the title of the published decree from "On Freedom of Conscience..." to "On Separation of Church from State. . . ." The basic tenet of the decree was, in Lenin's opinion, not freedom of conscience but the separation of the church from the state on the terms outlined in the decree. A facsimile of the first text of the decree with an added handwritten note by Lenin is reprinted in the publication of the Soviet Academy of Science, *Voprosy istorii religii i ateizma* [Problems of the history of religion and atheism] (hereafter *VIRA*), 5 (Moscow, 1958): 16. Lenin added the second half of the last (thirteenth) paragraph of the decree that made the state the legal owner of all religious buildings and objects. The changed text with Lenin's additions was published two days later in *Gazeta raboche krestianskogo pravitelstva RSFSR* [Newspaper of the government of workers and peasants of the RSFSR], no. 15, 23 January 1918. (See also *VIRA* 5 [1958]: 154, and *O religii*, pp.119–20).

hence it follows that the government cannot take upon itself the religious education of children." It reiterated the earlier prohibition of the "teaching of religious beliefs" in all schools under the supervision of the Commissariat of Education.[8]

It must be stated that there were ambiguities and contradictions in the policy toward religion followed by the party in its first year in power. This can be explained in terms of the events of the period. The Civil War was at its height and the anti-Bolshevik forces made good use among believers of communist attitudes towards religion. There was considerable hostility towards the new regime on the part of large segments of the clergy and the faithful of the Orthodox church, and to a lesser degree, on the part of the other minority religions. In these circumstances, the regime's need for maximum popular support gave rise to a checkered pattern which included both stern measures and concessions; the interpretation of the decrees changed with the time and the place.

The constitution of the Russian Soviet Federated Socialist Republic (RSFSR), adopted by the Fifth Congress of Soviets on July 10, 1918, included elements of this ambiguity. On the one hand article 65g relegated members of the clergy to the category of second-class citizens, along with "capitalists, merchants, former members of the police, criminals, and imbeciles." They could not hold public office, and even the right to vote was denied them. (This restriction gave rise to other limitations in matters of food rations, housing, etc.) On the other hand, article 13 stated: "To secure for the workingman true freedom of conscience, the church is separated from the state and the school from the church, and *freedom of religious and antireligious propaganda is recognized as the right of every citizen.*"[9] (In the "Stalin" constitution of 1936 this formula was altered to retain the right to profess religion but not to propagate it.)

It was seven months later before a detailed "ordinance-instruction" to carry out the decree of January 23, 1918, was ready. On August 24, 1918, the People's Commissariat of Justice issued the "Ordinance for Carrying out the Decree on the Separation of Church from State and School from Church."[10] This ordinance-instruction enumerated the

8. *O religii*, pp. 99–100.

9. *Istoriia sovetskoi konstitutsii v dokumentakh, 1917–1956* [History of the Soviet constitution in documents] (Moscow, 1957), pp. 145, 155. Emphasis added.

10. *VIRA*, 5 (1958): 11. This instruction was in force until 1929, when a new one was introduced.

churches and cults that were included in the provisions of the decree. (*Churches:* Russian Orthodox, Old-Believers, Georgian, Catholic, and Protestants of all denominations. *Cults:* Judaism, Mohammedanism, and Buddhism. It was also to be applied to cults and beliefs not mentioned specifically.)

The main provisions of the instruction were as follows: the property of all religious cults was to be turned over to the local soviets of workers' and peasants' deputies; all funds were to be confiscated; an inventory of all properties had to be submitted, and the property could then be returned to the worshippers for their use free of charge, provided that at least a group of twenty persons would assume the responsibility for the property and its upkeep.[11] (Church properties not used specifically and exclusively for religious purposes, such as hospitals, hotels, landed estates, candle factories, fisheries, and the like were to be taken over without the right to lease. This "confiscation of church or religious properties" was to be "completed not later than two months" after the date of publication of the instruction.)

The *dvadtsatka*, or group of twenty, was charged with making all repairs and paying all expenses necessary to maintain the property. In case of "abuses and embezzlement" the property was to be returned to the local soviet. If no group of twenty was willing to take responsibility for the property, three separate notices offering it to the public for religious use were to be placed in the press by the local soviet, and a notice to this effect was to be posted on the door of the house of prayer. After one week the soviet was to send information about the vacant building to the Commissariat of Education with suggestions as to its future use. After receiving an answer from the commissariat the local soviet was to proceed with the closing. The application of subtle pressure at various stages of this procedure, particularly on the members of the *dvadtsatka*, came to be a routine method of securing the closing of a church.

Side by side with these strictures, the instruction formulated certain rights that had not previously been specified, although in practice these rights were not unambiguous. For example, concerning the right to build new houses of prayer, the procedure required that the responsible *dvadtsatka* deposit an unspecified sum of money in the

---

11. This was the first time that the *dvadtsatka* or "group of twenty," the basic unit of religious associations, was introduced. Still in use today, the group's functions and responsibilities have been elaborated in greater detail over the years.

state treasury as a guarantee that the building would be completed. This provision, in reality, left ultimate control in the hands of the authorities since they could set the amount of money required.

Further items of interest included were as follows: (1) Religious instruction was forbidden in all state, public, or private educational institutions; an exception was made in the case of theological seminaries. (2) All records of religious groups (for births, marriages, deaths, and so forth) were to be turned over to the local soviets, though clergymen were permitted to make copies of these records and to continue keeping such accounts so long as no fees were exacted and with the understanding that such records had no legal validity. (3) Public processions could be held, but only with the advance permission of the local authorities. (4) All religious services and religious objects were banned from public buildings.

With these detailed instructions in hand, local authorities began to implement the January 23 decree. In many areas the disestablishment was accomplished with excessive zeal, with the result that on January 3, 1919, a circular letter was issued which pointed out the "mistakes" made by many in the interpretation and application of the instruction. This "Circular on the Problem and the Separation of Church and State,"[12] from the Eighth Department of the People's Commissariat of Justice, began as follows: "Recent reports received from various places reveal that not all local officials correctly understand the tasks of the Soviet authorities concerning the separation of church and state." From the admonitions of this circular it is clear what excesses had been committed. For example, it said that a house of prayer was to be closed *only* if a group of twenty could not be found to assume responsibility for it, or if the local soviet, because of a *genuine* need for suitable quarters for public use and for "satisfying the demands of the working masses," should decide to close it. (The implication as to what had been going on here is clear.)

The circular declared it inadmissible to strip religious objects of their ornamentation when such objects had been transferred to a group of citizens for religious use. Likewise, making revolutionary banners and decorations from these ornaments was described as both

---

12. *Tsirkuliar po voprosu ob otdelenii tserkvi ot qosudarstva.* In *VIRA* 5 (1958): 34 (where the date of the circular is given as January 3, 1919); also in *O religii*, p. 100 (where the date is given as December 1918).

illegal and inexpedient, since this offended the feelings of religious believers and destroyed the artistic worth of the objects.

Ministers and priests suspected of counterrevolutionary activities were not to be searched or arrested while performing religious rites, unless such action was absolutely indispensable. When searches had to be conducted in houses of worship, a representative of the religious group should be present and a correct attitude toward the religious feelings of believers maintained. Ridicule and humiliation of clergymen should be avoided. Similarly, unseemly forced labor, such as cleaning streets, was not to be administered to clergymen, since such punishments were apt to anger believers and cause them to regard the clergyman as a martyr. It was also said to be inadmissible to prohibit ministers of a cult from giving sermons, even on religious topics, in their houses of prayer.

These practices were widespread and had even aroused the anger of nonreligious people in many instances. Consequently the circular warned that religious prejudices and the obscurantism of superstition were not to be fought "with the aid of punishment but with an improved educational system, propaganda of communism, and with the organization of the economy on communist principles" (par. 12).

Although the January 23 decree and the August 24 instruction provided the essential legal framework for religion in the early years of Soviet rule, the new regime could not limit itself exclusively to these edicts, if only because they did not solve all the legal problems that subsequently arose. As a consequence, it was necessary from time to time to issue decrees to clarify one or another problem. One important question which might serve to illustrate this trend is that of the right to give religious instruction; this right remained unclear for many years and varied from republic to republic. The Commissariat of Public Education issued a circular (March 3, 1919) stating that, "teaching religious doctrines to persons below the age of eighteen *is not permissible.*"[13] This circular clearly contradicted the corresponding provision of the decree of January 23 issued by the Council of People's Commissars which stated that religious subjects might be taught and studied *in a private manner.* Two years later (April 23, 1921) the Commissariat of Public Education issued an explanation

13. P. V. Gidulianov, *Tserkov i gosudarstvo po zakonodatelstvu RSFSR* [Church and state in the legislation of the RSFSR] (Moscow, 1923), p. 27, as quoted in J. S. Curtiss, *The Russian Church and the Soviet State, 1917–1950* (Boston, 1953), p. 76. Emphasis added.

of its circular in which it stated that what it really meant was that "religious teaching outside of religious institutions, i.e., seminaries, should not assume the form of regularly functioning educational institutions."[14] In 1924 still another explanation was given: persons below the age of eighteen could receive religious instruction only at home. "At home" might mean either in the home of the child, or of a clergyman or other instructor. The instruction, however, should not assume the proportions of a regular class of instruction and the group therefore could not include more than three children.[15] This ruling applied to the RSFSR only, for in the Ukrainian Republic the regulations were stricter.

Within the People's Commissariat of Justice it was the eighth division which was in charge of religious affairs. Its main function was to enforce the "separation of church from state." In 1919 the first issue of its journal *Revoliutsiia i tserkov* (The revolution and the church) appeared. It contained legislative acts, administrative orders, and pertinent documents, as well as numerous articles interpreting these and outlining official policies on religion.

After the publication of the instruction for implementation of the January 23 decree "liquidation sections" of the eighth division (later the fifth division) were established and attached to the executive committees (*ispolkom*) of the city and district (*oblastnoi*) soviets. The task of these sections was to nationalize the property and confiscate the liquid assets of all the religious organizations in the country.

Legislation, as has been said, was not the government's sole policy-guide. Party pronouncements also played an important role. The program of the Communist party adopted at the Eighth Congress in March, 1919, stated in paragraph thirteen that the party was not satisfied to let matters rest with the separation of church from state and school from church, measures that "even the bourgeois democracies have included in their programs, although they have not realized them." It spoke of the need for well-planned, scientific antireligious propaganda, disseminated with all due regard to avoid offending the feelings of believers, as this would only lead to an

14. P. V. Gidulianov, ed., *Otdelenie tserkvi ot gosudarstva: polny sbornik dekretov RSFSR i SSSR: instruksy, tsirkuliarov, i.t.d., s raziasneniiami v-ogo otdela NK iustitsii RSFSR* [The separation of church from state; complete collection of decrees of the RSFSR and the USSR; instructions, circulars etc. With interpretations of the fifth department of the People's Commissariat of Justice of the RSFSR], 2d ed. (Moscow, 1924), pp. 207–8.

15. Ibid., pp. 203–5, 369–70. See also *O religii*, pp. 105–9.

increase of religious fanaticism.[16] A resolution adopted at the congress, while warning against counterrevolutionary propaganda in the guise of religious preaching, was nonetheless very explicit about restrictions of religious freedom or the use of force, saying that those who violated these precepts should be severely punished.[17]

The Tenth Party Congress (March, 1921) charged the Committee for Political Education (*Glavpolitprosvet*) of the Commissariat of Education with organizing and conducting antireligious propaganda on a massive scale.[18] To this end the commissariat was to initiate the publication of books and periodicals, as well as to organize public lectures, utilizing "all the methods of contemporary technology."[19] The Central Committee of the party subsequently issued an ordinance, "On the organization of antireligious propaganda and on the violation of paragraph thirteen of the program."[20] In addition to refusing party membership to anyone fulfilling any religious function this ordinance called upon all party members to participate actively in antireligious activities. Continued civil strife in the country accounted for the section of the ordinance in which communists were counselled not to push the program unduly, but rather to prepare themselves in depth. It is interesting to note that the document stresses the need to "avoid anything that would make any given nationality think, and our enemies say, that we are persecuting people because of their faith" (par. 10).

The end of the period of War Communism and the inauguration of the New Economic Policy saw a further elaboration of this element of caution. In 1922 the party issued "Directives of the Central Committee of the Communist Party to the Soviet and Party Organs

16. *KPSS v resoliutsiiakh i resheniiakh sezdov, konferentsy i plenumov Tsk* [The Communist party of the Soviet Union in the resolutions and decisions of the congresses, conferences and plenums of the Central Committee] 7th ed., 3 vols. (Moscow, 1954): 1: 420–21. Reprinted in *O religii*, p. 56.

17. *O politicheskoi propagande i kulturno-prosvetitelnoi rabote v derevne* [On political propaganda and cultural-educational work in the countryside]. In *O religii*, pp. 46–57.

18. The *Glavny politiko-prosvetitelny komitet narkomprosa RSFSR* [Chief committee of the Narkompros (People's commissariat for education) of the RSFSR for political education] was in existence from 1920 to 1930.

19. Paragraph six of the resolution, *O glavpolitprosvete i agitatsionno-propagandistskikh zadachakh partii* [On the Glavpolitprosvet (Central administration of political education) and the agitational-propaganda tasks of the party], in *KPSS v rezoliutsiiakh*, 1:551; reprinted in *O religii*, p. 57.

20. *O postanovke antireligioznoi propagandy i o narushenii punkta 13 programmy.* In *Izvestiia TsK RKP (b)* [News of the Central Committee of the Russian Communist Party (Bolshevik)], no. 33 (Moscow, 1921), pp. 32–33; reprinted in *O religii*, pp. 57–60.

on the Question of the Attitude towards Sects and Policy in Relation to Religious Groups in General."[21] This document stresses the need to be "especially thoughtful in carrying out all kinds of measures that touch upon the religious views of the broad masses of the peasantry" while at the same time being careful not to neglect their scientific antireligious education. The directives took cognizance of the role played by sectarian communes in alleviating the acute food shortages of the time. Party members were reminded that "the present period is not at all opportune for pressing the antireligious struggle."

Another party resolution "on propaganda, the press and agitation" concerned itself mainly with the state of antireligious work among the national minorities.[22] This resolution, passed by the Twelfth Party Congress in 1923, said that the New Economic Policy had fostered the growth of bourgeois and clerical-national sentiments among the minorities. Thus vigor was detected in such movements as Pan-Islamism, Pan-Turkism, and Zionism, as well as Catholic activity among Poles and Baptist influence on Latvians and Estonians. The resolution called upon the communists among these minorities to organize antireligious programs aimed at them. Another resolution of the same congress, "On the Organization of Antireligious Agitation and Propaganda," repeated the now-familiar cautionary note concerning crude tactics and advocated the incorporation of good programs of antireligious instruction in the schools.[23] The problem of the need for prudence and education in the villages and among minorities was further discussed in a resolution of the Thirteenth Party Congress (May, 1924), "On the Work in the Villages."[24] It stated that "administrative measures, such as the closing of churches, mosques, synagogues, and houses of prayer," especially in the eastern areas, would prove to have a harmful effect.

In 1925 the Commissariat of Internal Affairs issued a circular on the question of religious ceremonies in the homes of believers. It

21. *Direktivy TsK RKP sovetskim i partynim organam po voprosu ob otnoshenii k sektam i politiki v otnoshenii religionznikh grup voobshche.* In *Spravochnik partynogo rabotnika* [The party worker's handbook] (Moscow, 1922), pp. 93–94; reprinted in *O religii*, pp. 61–63.

22. *O propagande, pechati i agitatsii.* In *KPSS v rezoliutsiakh*, 1: 741–42. See also *O religii*, pp. 63–64.

23. *O postanovke antireligioznoi agitatsii i propagandy.* In *KPSS v rezoliutsiakh*, 1: 743–45; reprinted in *O religii*, pp. 64–67.

24. *O rabote v derevne.* In *KPSS v rezoliutsiakh*, 2: 53; reprinted in *O religii*, p. 68.

stated that the "performance of religious ceremonies within the homes of believers, like that of religious ceremonies in church, is permitted without hindrance, without special permission."[25] Reiterated in subsequent legislation, this provision is apparently still in force, although in practice it has often not been respected.

1929-41

As the 1920s drew to a close, the regime felt that it had sufficiently consolidated its position to be able to proceed with the implementation of new programs. The five-year plans, designed to achieve a purely socialist economy, were introduced in place of the New Economic Policy. In the area of religion, too, the often hesitant and ambiguous policies of the 1920s were replaced by more forceful and aggressive measures. An early expression of this reorientation was the substitution, in the spring of 1928, of the term "antireligious education" for "nonreligious education" in official documents. This change was followed in 1929 by a directive of the Commissariat of Education to make corresponding changes in the methods of instruction to be employed.[26] Likewise, the increased importance accorded to matters of religion and religious cults was emphasized by the establishment, on April 8, 1929, of a standing committee on affairs of cult, attached to the Presidium of the All-Union Central Executive Committee (headed by P. G. Smidovich).

This adjustment of religious policy was made concrete in two documents. They were the "Decree on Religious Associations" (*O religioznykh obedineniiakh*) of April 8, 1929,[27] and the "Instructions of the People's Commissariat of the Interior" of October 1, 1929, subtitled "On the Rights and Obligations of Religious Associations" (*O pravakh i obiazannostiiakh religioznykh obedineny*), which clarifies and supplements the April law.[28] These two documents suggest that

25. Gidulianov, *Otdelenie*, 1926 rev. ed., pp. 55–56. This book includes many illuminating cases of litigation on religious matters.

26. M. Enisherlov, ed., *Voinstvuiushchee bezbozhie v SSSR za 15 let (1917–1932)* [Militant atheism in the USSR in the past fifteen years] (Moscow, 1932), p. 236.

27. Ordinance (*postanovlenie*) of the All-Russian Central Executive Committee of the Soviets and the Council of People's Commissars; in *Sobranie uzakoneny i rasporiazheny raboche-krestianskogo pravitelstva RSFSR*, no. 35 (1929), text no. 353; amendments in no. 8 (1932), text no. 41 II 6. English translation in Appendix, section 2B, below.

28. N. Orleansky, comp., *Zakon o religioznykh obedineniiakh RSFSR i deistvuiushchie zakony, instrukstii s otdelnymi kommentariiami* [The law on religious associations of the RSFSR and laws and instructions in force, with individual commentaries] (Moscow, 1930). English translation in Appendix, section 2C, below.

the regime now believed that the 1918 laws, which had regulated religious life in the country prior to 1929 (the decree of January 23, 1918, and the instruction of August 24 of that same year), had not sufficiently provided for many aspects of religious activity, leaving some area in which believers could maneuver. Consequently, it was decided that new directives, more all-inclusive and more detailed, were required.

The two acts of 1929 remain in force today and still define most of the rights and duties of Soviet citizens in religious matters, as well as the status, rights, and responsibilities of recognized religious cults and religious organizations. For this reason it is necessary to discuss these measures at some length—first in general, then by individual topics, and finally in regard to certain implications which they held for religious communities. According to the provisions of these enactments citizens have the right to form and to belong to two kinds of religious organizations. Members of a cult, denomination, sect, or doctrine who are eighteen years of age and over may form "religious societies" or "groups of believers." Believers who have formed a religious society or group may perform religious rites, arrange prayer or general meetings of believers, manage religious property, and conclude civil transactions connected with the management of religious property and the performance of religious rites.

The law and the instruction also enumerated many activities *not* permitted to the societies or groups, thereby restricting them to the performance of purely religious rites and ceremonies. (For instance, it was made illegal to give material help to other members of a religious organization, to establish libraries, reading rooms, or dormitories for the poor, and to organize group excursions.) Religious societies, but *not* groups of believers, may receive, free of charge, under contract from the local soviet, special prayer buildings and objects intended exclusively for the cult. Both religious societies *and* groups of believers, however, may use for prayer-meetings premises left to them by private persons or obtained from the local soviets by lease. The contracts for the use of such premises are to be concluded by individual believers under their personal responsibility.

No person is permitted to belong to more than one religious organization; those who do may be prosecuted in accordance with the criminal code. The activities of a clergyman are to be restricted to the area where the members of his congregation reside and where his prayer house is located. Moreover, a clergyman may undertake these activities only after he has submitted appropriate information about himself to the registration agency (the local committee on religious affairs).

Registration. A religious society or a group of believers must submit an application for registration and a list of its founders. Within one month the registration agencies must register the group or inform the petitioners of the denial of registration. Paragraph 46 of the instruction stipulates that the registration must be denied "if the religious association's methods and forms of activity are contrary to the laws in effect, threaten the public order or safety, or provoke discord or hostilities among the nations."

Collection and expenditure of funds. Members of a religious society or group may collect voluntary donations inside the prayer building. Outside the building, voluntary donations may take place only among persons who are members of the given religious association (unless special permission has been granted). Religious associations may not establish compulsory membership fees or introduce membership cards. The funds collected may be spent only in connection with the maintenance of religious property, the performance of religious rites, the remuneration of clergymen, singers, and watchmen, and the activities of the executive bodies of religious societies or groups. Any kind of religious property, whether donated or purchased with voluntary donations, shall be included in the inventory of religious property, to be kept on record with the civil authorities; it thus becomes state property and a part of the existing lease agreement.

Executive bodies. Such bodies are elected by open ballot at general assemblies of the members. A religious society elects an executive body of three members, a group of believers elects one representative. The registration agencies have the right to remove individual members from the executive bodies. Religious conferences and conventions may elect their own executive bodies for the execution of their decisions. All transactions concerning the management and use of religious property must be made exclusively by the individual members of the executive bodies, and not by the executive body itself since executive bodies do not enjoy the rights of legal entities. They may not acquire property by purchase, or rent premises for prayer meetings, or conclude any kind of contracts or transactions. A religious society or group may elect, at a general assembly, an auditing committee of not more than three members for exercising control over religious property and funds received from voluntary contributions.

Meetings and conventions. Prayer meetings in prayer buildings or in buildings especially adapted for this purpose and considered satisfactory as to technical and sanitary conditions, may be arranged without notification to or permission from the authorities. Prayer meetings in premises which are not especially adapted for this purpose (that is, private homes or apartments) may be arranged but only with permission for each separate meeting. A religious society or group, however, may notify the authorities in advance of a series of prayer meetings to be held within a period of no more than one year. *Believers who have not formed a society or group must notify authorities regarding each prayer meeting separately* (par. 22 of the instruction). An application must be filed and written permission must be obtained for general assemblies of religious societies or groups. Religious societies and groups and their executive bodies, as well as the executive bodies of religious conventions and conferences, may initiate and organize the convocation of a religious convention or conference (par. 28). Permission for such conventions and conferences may be granted by the committee for religious matters concerned (local committees for a local convention, a republic committee for a republic convention, and the Committee for Religious Affairs of the Council of Ministers for an all-Russian or all-Union convention or conference). Permission shall be denied if the meeting, convention, or conference conflicts with the laws in effect, threatens the social order and safety, or provokes discord and hostility among the nations (par. 31).

Processions and ceremonies. Religious rites and ceremonies or the display of objects of cult in public institutions and enterprises is prohibited, with the exception of religious rites for dangerously ill persons in isolated rooms of hospitals and of religious ceremonies in cemeteries and crematoria. *Any kind of religious ceremony may be performed within the family home or apartment without the permission or notification of the authorities.* Permission is not required for religious processions around the prayer building if they are an integral part of the religious service. Otherwise, permission for religious rites or processions outside the prayer building must be obtained from the executive committee of the local soviet. Permission is not required for religious services connected with a funeral.

Reporting. A list of the executive bodies and auditing committees, together with data on the clergy or preachers, shall be submitted within seven days of the request to the registration agencies to organize a group or society. A religious society must submit a list of all its members according to the established form. By January 1 of each year a report shall be submitted on changes in the list of members of the society or group. If the provisions on the submission of data or reports are continuously violated, the registration agency may require the removal of the members of the executive body and the election of new members.

Surveillance. The activities of the religious societies and groups are subject to the surveillance of the committees for religious matters. These committees, as well as other authorities "whose duty it is to safeguard the revolutionary order and safety," may send their representatives to each assembly or meeting of a religious society or group for the purpose of "watching over order and safety." They "are obliged" to adjourn the assembly under certain conditions enumerated in the instruction, for example, when there is any deviation from the agenda submitted by the organizers of the assembly. Routine inspections of religious societies or groups may be performed at any time by the committees for religious matters.

Liquidation. A religious society or group may be liquidated by a decision of the general assembly of the society or group. In the event of the disclosure of deviations from the rules established for the association, the registration agency shall demand the correction of the defects. If the religious society or group refuses to correct the defects, or if it violates the laws under which it operates, the city or district committee for religious matters may ask the committee for religious affairs of the Council of Ministers to liquidate the society or group. A decision to liquidate a society or group may be appealed before the Council of Ministers within two weeks from the date of the delivery of the decision. The liquidation is suspended until the decision on the appeal is handed down. The contract of lease of religious property may be annulled by a decision of the committee for religious affairs of the Council of Ministers at the request of the respective city or district committee. The contract may be annulled if the religious society or group has not observed the orders of the authorities on reregistration, renovations, and the like, as well as when the prayer building is needed for state or public use (par. 64).

Certain additional comments must now be made and conclusions drawn concerning the two legislative acts of 1929. The laws made provision for two types of registered religious organizations: the religious societies which number "not less than twenty members," and the religious groups or groups of believers which number less than twenty. The specific legal status of the religious groups is relatively unclear. What their rights are and how they differ from religious societies (other than in the number of members) is somewhat difficult to determine. Both societies and groups are recognized "religious units." Both must be registered by the committee for religious affairs at the city or area (*raion*) soviet (pars. 4, 5, and 6), though the forms to be submitted are different. A religious society elects an executive body of three members, whereas a group of believers has only one representative.

The most important difference seems to be that only a religious society, and not a group of believers, may be granted permission by the city or district soviet to use "special" prayer buildings and objects of cult free of charge (par. 10). "Special buildings" refers to existing church buildings. The law recognises a second category of building: "Other premises left to them by private persons or leased to them by the local soviet." Buildings in this second category can be leased to groups of believers as well.

A more serious difference exists between these two types of registered religious organizations than is defined by the law. There is ample evidence that the right to establish a group of believers has seldom been granted. Certainly in recent years the provision which makes this possible seems to be a dead letter. In a "Summary of Information Relating to the USSR" submitted to the United Nations by the Soviet government in 1959, the portion dealing with conditions under which religious associations may be formed says nothing about groups of less than twenty members.[29]

It is reasonable to assume that two other provisions of the instruction are either not widely known or believers are not allowed to take

29. United Nations, Commission on Human Rights, Subcommission on the Prevention of Discrimination and the Protection of Minorities, "Study of Discrimination in the Matter of Religious Rights and Practices," conference room paper no. 35, January 30, 1950. This is a summary of information relating to the Union of Soviet Socialist Republics by special reporter Areot Krishnaswami.

advantage of them. Paragraph 22 states that "believers who have not formed a society or group must notify authorities regarding each separate prayer meeting." This implies *the right of a nonregistered group to exist and to hold religious services.* Paragraph 34 permits "the performance of religious ceremonies, such as prayers, requiem masses, baptisms, the bringing in of icons and the like," in the home or apartment of believers *without notification to or permission from the authorities.* There are no specific restrictions as to the number of persons allowed to participate in such rites. Despite this provision, prayer meetings in homes have been subject to disciplinary action, and for this reason are usually held clandestinely.[30]

Although the law emphasizes that religious societies do not enjoy the rights of legal entities, some of its provisions seem to contradict this. For example, legal acts are normally executed by individual members of the executive bodies with the exception that prayer houses and objects of cult are obtained under contract not by individuals but by the whole group. This contractual capacity would seem to endow the group with quasi-legal status. It may be that this exception was made because it was impossible or impractical to deal with individuals in such cases, if only because Soviet civil law does not envisage a contract of lease without compensation. Article 152 of the civil code of the RSFSR (and comparable articles in the codes of the other Soviet republics) states: "under the contract of lease of property, one party (lessor) undertakes to assign property for temporary use by the other party (lessee) for a definite compensation."[31] Cases that have come before Soviet courts illustrate the problems involved in dealing with individuals.[32]

30. In the early years of Soviet rule, several "test cases" in this area resulted in the decision to uphold the separation decree. In each case the fifth division of the Commissariat of Justice declared that Soviet citizens may conduct their prayer meetings in their own homes without hindrance, provided they have submitted to the authorities information on the time and place of such meetings. For details of these decisions see Gidulianov, *Otdelenie*, p. 10.

31. In addition, in regard to nationalized buildings (which would include religious buildings) articles 159, 161, 163, and 164 of the civil code provide that all capital and current repairs must be made by the lessee, as well as payment of all taxes, insurance, and other assessments. V. Gsovsky, *Soviet Civil Law* (Ann Arbor, 1949), 2: 119.

32. As an example the case of Iarolan vs. the Iranian Jewish Synagogue may be cited. On January 15, 1938, the People's Court of the Korov District in Tbilisi found against the Iranian Jewish Synagogue and awarded the plaintiff, Sarkis Iarolan, three hundred rubles for injuries sustained while making matzos, as well as eighty rubles a month until he attained his majority. The president of the Supreme Court of the USSR found that the case had to be thrown out because the synagogue, as a religious association, had no rights as a

The law and the instruction of 1929 are phrased so as to enable the authorities to curtail or halt the normally permitted activities of a religious association whenever they deem it expedient. Paragraph 46 of the instruction provides that a society's registration must be denied when the forms of its activities do not conform to existing laws or when they threaten public order or safety. This broad clause can be interpreted to include almost any activity, if the authorities so desire. Equally broad is the right, even the obligation, of the local committees for religious affairs to adjourn religious assemblies when, for example, they deviate from the agenda submitted by the organizers of the assembly. (In effect this means that almost any meeting could be broken up.) Also, associations can be dissolved if they violate the pertinent laws. In every case *the interpretation of what the law means is in the hands of the authorities.*

A further complication is that in the Soviet Union the judiciary has often, in varying degrees, been subordinated to the agencies of the party and the state. As a result the country several times has experienced almost complete disruption of legal procedure. The atmosphere of uncertainty about law in general which this condition has engendered has frequently led to wide divergence in the interpretation of statutes and, occasionally, to complete disregard of them,

The closing of prayer houses when the local authorities have deemed it necessary to put a building to other use, pursuant to the needs of the state, has often been employed. In this event the law grants the religious association the right to lease or build a new building, but the exercise of this right, too, is dependent upon the discretion of the authorities. Many buildings have been condemned as unsafe, and the law states "that the decision of the technical committee stated in the examination document is binding and subject to execution" (par. 49). No appeal is possible in such a case. In the event of a fire which renders a prayer house unusable, it is up to the authorities to decide whether to use the insurance payments for the restoration of the building or for the "social and cultural needs of the community."

Any member of a *dvadtsatka* (in Soviet parlance, the "religious

---

juridical person under the laws in force and could not therefore be a defendant. He directed that in rehearing the case, specific individuals, members of the executive organ of the given religious association, had to be brought to trial as defendants. In *Sovetskaia iustitsiia*, nos. 15–16 (1939), p. 70, as quoted in John N. Hazard & Morris L. Weisberg, *Cases and Reading on Soviet Law* (New York, 1950), pp. 137–38.

activists" of a group) may withdraw from the association at any time. Since such a withdrawal leaves the number of responsible members at less than twenty, the contract of lease is liable to annulment. If new members volunteer to replace those who have withdrawn, registration must be accomplished all over again and a new contract drawn. If the authorities are determined to harass the members of the *dvadtsatka*, they have several means of doing so—job placement and advancement, assignment of living quarters, educational facilities for the members' children, and so forth.

In addition, other pressures may be placed on the *dvadtsatka* members, such as the invocation of paragraph 29d, the law which imposes on the signing members the responsibility for compensating the state for any damage done to the property occupied. The threat of exorbitant indemnities for real or imagined damage is known to have been effective in obtaining the withdrawal of members. If such pressures fail, paragraph 14 of the law and paragraph 13 of the instruction give the authorities the right to remove individual members from the executive board of an association.

Though fundamental, the law and the instruction of 1929 were not the only legislative acts in the late twenties which signified a harsher environment for religion. An obvious target was the clergy. In a decree issued in 1928 the income tax paid by clergymen was to be levied on all sources of income "on the basis of information available to the fiscal authorities."[33] In large measure this decree left the clergy open to the whims of the appropriate *finotdel* (fiscal department). Prohibitive taxes were also levied on their homes and rents were raised drastically. Many were evicted from their quarters in municipally-owned buildings if their income (based on the arbitrary fiscal information noted above) was over three thousand rubles per year.[34] Also, food in cooperative stores could only be sold to clergymen if a special deposit had been paid in advance. These anticlerical measures appear to have boomeranged, however. In the face of the sympathy gained by clergymen among believers, the presidium of the Central Executive Committee of Soviets was forced to request "the uncon-

33. *Sobranie zakonov i rasporiazheny raboche-krestianskogo pravitelstva SSSR* [A collection of laws and decrees of the government of workers and peasants of the USSR], no. 24, May 1928.

34. *RSFSR: sobranie uzakoneny*, no. 33, 1929, as quoted in Orleansky, *Zakon o religioznikh obedineniakh RSFSR*, pp. 58, 60. Also published in *Pravda*, 3 January 1930, and *Izvestiia*, 6 June 1930.

ditional elimination of additional restrictions on the disenfranchised and their families, such as expulsion from their homes and towns; wholesale deprivation of medical aid; prohibition of building; expulsion of their children from schools; and other deprivations."[35]

Another target was the religious calendar. In August, 1929, the Council of People's Commissars of the USSR ordered the introduction of the continuous work week, according to which the day of rest fell on various days of the week. The change was promoted in the name of more efficient production. The All-Union Trade Council exposed another view in voicing the hope that "this measure will inevitably lead to fundamental changes in the old tradition of life . . . and facilitate a more successful struggle against religion and other survivals of the old way of life."[36] The observance of the religious day of rest and of religious holidays was made even more difficult by the decree of November 15, 1932, by which one day's unauthorized absence from work (*progul*) could be punished by the deprivation of the right to ration cards and to the use of housing facilities belonging to the enterprise concerned.[37]

The antireligious measures of the interwar period were, in many areas, properly understood as to their intent, but implemented in a way which was often counterproductive. Hence, evoking memories of the Commissariat of Justice's Circular Letter of January 3, 1919, the Sixteenth Party Congress (1930) passed a resolution which constituted a clear case of the party intervening in the administration of the laws on religion.[38] Section six spoke of "some completely inadmissible distortions of the party line in the sphere of the struggle against religious prejudices." Foremost among these distortions was the "administrative closing of churches without the acquiescence of the overwhelming majority of the villagers, which action usually leads to the strengthening of religious prejudices." Section seven prescribed the abandonment of such practices, which were "fictitiously disguised as the public and voluntary wish of the population." Henceforth the decisions of village meetings concerning the closing of churches were to be confirmed by the regional executive committee of soviets.

What was undoubtedly one of the most important changes in law

35. *Izvestiia*, 23 March 1930.
36. The seven-day week was adopted once again in 1941.
37. *SSSR: sobranie zakonov*, no. 475, 1932.
38. *Pravda*, 15 March 1930.

pertaining to religion emerged in the framing of constitutional provisions in this regard. The Constitution of the Russian Republic (RSFSR) of 1924 had contained the provision (article 4) which stated that "freedom of religious and antireligious propaganda is recognized for all citizens."[39] Similar provisions had been included in the constitutions of the other republics. But in May, 1929, the Fourteenth Congress of Soviets amended this provision; the wording was changed to "freedom of religious worship and freedom of antireligious propaganda are recognized for all citizens." In 1936 this new text became article 124 of the "Stalin Constitution."[40] The use of the word "freedom" before both "religious" and "antireligious" activities was meant to create the impression that the state was "neutral" on the question of religion.

This was not the case, of course, as freedom of antireligious propaganda continued to be officially sanctioned and religious propaganda was now illegal. This proposition—that atheists have the right to conduct propaganda but believers do not—is the fundamental fact of the condition of religious associations in the Soviet Union. It has given the atheists not only freedom of action but a legally recognized privileged position.

For the sake of completeness it should be noted that article 135 of the new constitution granted the right to vote and to be elected, to all citizens of the Soviet Union, including members of the clergy. It thus disposed of the category of *lishentsy* (citizens deprived of rights) that had been established by the constitution which was adopted by the Fifth Congress of the Soviets on July 10, 1918.

1941–59

The outbreak of Soviet–German hostilities in June, 1941, substantially altered the situation of all religious organizations. The Russian Orthodox church achieved something of a preeminent position among the churches, reminiscent of its prerevolutionary status.

39. V. Gsovsky, "The Legal Status of the Church in Soviet Russia," *Fordham Law Review* 8 (1939): 1–28. See also U.S. Senate, Committee on the Judiciary, *Church and State Under Communism*, 88th Cong., 2nd sess., 1964, vol. 1, *The USSR*.

40. *Konstitutsiia soiuza sovetskikh sotsialisticheskikh respublik* [Constitution of the Union of Soviet Socialist Republics] (Moscow, 1959), p. 26. Article 124 of the Constitution states: "In order to ensure to citizens freedom of conscience, the church in the USSR is separated from the state, and the school from the church. Freedom of religious worship and freedom of antireligious propaganda are recognized for all citizens." See text in Appendix, section 1.

These altered circumstances were in no way reflected, however, in new or altered legislation. The *Zhurnal moskovskoi patriarkhii* (Journal of the Moscow patriarchate) published the particulars of the concessions granted the Orthodox church, but the only official government announcement of any change was that of the decision to establish a separate Council for the Affairs of the Russian Orthodox Church under the Council of Ministers. The government did not admit that the Orthodox church was receiving preferential treatment; indeed, it stated emphatically that "the creation of the Council for the Affairs of the Russian Orthodox Church bears testimony to the equality of all religions in the Union of Soviet Socialist Republics."[41] As if to lend credence to this statement, a separate council for all other religious cults was established soon after.

The duties and responsibilities of the two councils were outlined as follows:

The Council for the Affairs of Religious Cults and the Council for the Affairs of the Russian Orthodox Church shall be responsible for liaison between the government of the USSR and the leaders of religious associations (of the corresponding cults) on questions affecting those cults and requiring action by the government of the USSR.

The Council for the Affairs of Religious Cults and the Council for the Affairs of the Russian Orthodox Church shall:

(a) carry out the preliminary examination of questions raised by ecclesiastical boards or leaders of religious communities (cults) requiring action by the government of the USSR;

(b) draft laws and regulations on questions relating to religious cults, instructions and directives, and submit them to the government of the USSR for consideration;

(c) supervise the application in correct form and in due time throughout the territories of the USSR, of government laws and regulations relating to religious cults;

(d) submit conclusions on questions relating to religious cults to the government of the USSR;

(e) provide for the general registration of churches and houses of worship.

Representatives of the Council for the Affairs of Religious Cults and the Council for the Affairs of the Russian Orthodox Church of the Council of Ministers of the USSR shall be attached to the Council of Ministers of the Union and Autonomous Republics and the regional executive committees.[42]

41. United Nations, Commission on Human Rights, "Study of Discrimination in Religious Rights and Practices," p. 18.

42. Extract from order no. 628 concerning religious councils, confirmed by the Council of People's Commissars of the USSR on May 29, 1944, in ibid., p. 18. Additional information on these bodies in their historical growth will be found later in this chapter, in the section entitled "Administration and Supervision of the Laws on Religion."

Walter Kolarz maintains that in September, 1943, the Russian Orthodox church was recognized as a legal person. He further says that in 1945 this recognition was accorded legal form and extended to all religious groups in the country.[43] Neither of these opinions is literally correct. The most that can be said is that in actuality the Soviet government tacitly, and without any changes in law per se, restored a number of privileges to the Orthodox church, among them de facto (but not de jure) status as a legal entity. The proof of this is the fact that the terms of this agreement—which from our present perspective proved temporary—were never published in either the Soviet press or the *Sobranie uzakoneny* (Code of laws).

Wartime conditions, coupled with these changes in governmental policies, resulted in a marked increase in religious observance. Apparently the extent of this revival was both unexpected and a matter of some concern for the authorities. As early as 1944 the party felt constrained to reiterate its fundamental attitude towards religion and to call for the renewal and strengthening of "antireligious work through all means of scientific enlightenment, by using all media of communication—the spoken word, printed materials, the radio and films."[44]

Several official pronouncements of the early postwar period also seem to stem in part from the party's concern at the extent of religious observance thirty years after the Revolution. The most important of these pronouncements appeared on July 7, 1954, in a party ordinance entitled "On the Great Deficiencies in Scientific-Atheistic Propaganda and the Means of Improving It."[45] Decrying the widespread neglect of this critical aspect of ideological work, the ordinance told how religious organizations had "increased their activities and adroitly adjusted to contemporary conditions." As a result one could observe "a rise in the number of citizens observing religious holidays . . . as well as an increase in pilgrimages to holy places." All of this resulted in serious harm, not least of all to the national economy. The ordinance scored the opinion of many in

43. Walter Kolarz, *Religion in the Soviet Union* (New York, 1961), p. 52. Kolarz also states that since World War II church property as such has been recognized. The present writer has nowhere found substantiation of this statement.

44. *Sputnik agitatora* [The agitator's companion], nos. 19–20, 28–29, 1944. Reprinted in *O religii*, pp. 69–71. Ordinance *Ob organizatsii nauchno-prosvetitelnoi propagandy* [On the organization of scientific-educational propaganda].

45. Reprinted in *O religii*, pp. 71–77.

both party and government who felt that with the liquidation of the class base of the church and the suppression of its counterrevolutionary activities atheistic propaganda would be suspended. Citing what it called "deplorable conditions" the Central Committee ordered a "widening, strengthening and deepening" of antireligious propaganda. Specific measures were outlined and the government agencies responsible for concrete action were indicated, among them the Ministry of Culture, which was to organize lectures and courses of instruction in atheism in all schools and institutions of higher education. Indeed, all courses were to be "saturated with atheistic content."

This ordinance had subsequently to be qualified, as had been the case on previous occasions. Perhaps reflecting the confused political conditions following Stalin's death on November 10, 1954, the Central Committee issued another ordinance, "On the Mistakes in the Conduct of Scientific–Atheistic Propaganda Among the Population."[46]

The Central Committee criticized those who, instead of conducting antireligious propaganda as ordered, chose to insult clergy and believers: "such actions are contrary to the numerous instructions of the party on the inadmissibility of insulting the feelings of religious believers." It said that some citizens who were still under the influence of religion nonetheless were "honorably fulfilling their duties to the homeland" and that it was "stupid and harmful" to keep them under political suspicion simply because of their beliefs. Finally, it repeated the admonition to avoid administrative measures which "only strengthen and even increase religious prejudices," and maintained that insults and anecdotes about clergymen could never replace scientific propaganda and personal solicitude for believers.

With this ordinance a relatively new element was introduced into party instructions on religion, namely, that believers were not enemies of the regime, but unfortunates obsessed with superstition, harmful primarily to themselves. The state and healthy citizens, interested in the well-being of all the populace, should help these people overcome their weakness, much as they would come to the aid of an alcoholic or a drug addict.

46. *Pravda*, 11 November 1954. Reprinted in *O religii*, pp. 77–82. For further details of this call for moderation see Donald A. Lowrie and William C. Fletcher, "Khrushchev's Religious Policy," chapter 7 below.

1959–67

The Twenty-second Party Congress in 1960 adopted a resolution, "On the Tasks of Party Propaganda in Present-day Conditions,"[47] in which party organizations were reproved for occasionally taking "a passive, defensive position towards idealistic religious ideology, which is hostile to Marxism–Leninism." In conjunction with this resolution, the program passed by the congress reiterated the need to "educate people in the spirit of a scientific–materialistic worldview." In his report, Khrushchev said that Soviet education aimed at freeing men from religious prejudices and superstition, which prevent a full utilization of man's creative powers. He called for a well-prepared and all-encompassing system of scientific–atheistic education, giving special attention to children and adolescents.[48]

In June, 1963, a plenary session of the party's Central Committee described as the duty of all party members a "stubborn fight against religious survivals" and "the development of scientific–atheistic work."[49] Shortly thereafter the Ideological Commission of the Central Committee of the party issued a lengthy and important document entitled "On Measures to Strengthen Atheistic Education of the People." The Central Committee adopted the document and instructed the lower echelons of the party to take appropriate action.[50] An Institute of Scientific Atheism at the Academy of Social Sciences of the Communist Party was established whose job was to "coordinate and direct all scientific work in the field of atheism" being done by the various institutes of the Academy of Sciences of the USSR and by all institutions of higher education and establishments of the Ministry of Culture of the USSR. These organizations were to "take up the problem of a more active participation of academic institutions . . . in the working out of scientific approaches to the problems of atheism." A special publication, "Problems of Scientific Atheism," was to be published twice a year, and a compulsory course on the fundamentals of scientific atheism was to be introduced in the

47. *O zadachakh partynoi propagandy v sovremennykh uslovihakh*, in *Materialy XXII sezda KPSS* [Materials of the 22d Congress of the CPSU] (Moscow, 1961), p. 412. Reprinted in *O religii*, pp. 82–83.

48. *Materialy*, pp. 111–12.

49. *Plenum tsentralnogo komiteta kommunisticheskoi partii sovetskogo Soiuza 18–21 iunia 1963* [Plenum of the Central Committee of the Communist Party of the Soviet Union, June 18–21, 1963] (Moscow, 1964). Cited in *O religii*, p. 84.

50. *Partynaia zhizn* [Party life], no. 2, 1964. Reprinted in *O religii*, pp. 85–92.

universities. A long list of measures to be introduced from the kinder-
garten level up was given.

With regard to the enforcement of existing legislation the commission said: "In order to restrict the unlawful activities of the
clergy and believers (individuals and groups), control must be increased to shield children and adolescents from the influence of
clergymen, as well as insuring that parents do not force their children
to practice religion."[51] The journals *Sovet deputatov trudiashchikhsia*
(Council of workers' deputies), *Sotsialisticheskaia zakonnost* (Socialist legality), and *Sovetskoe gosudarstvo i pravo* (The Soviet state and
law) were instructed to give a systematic illumination of the problem
of legislation in regard to cults and their application in practices.
Likewise, the control committees for enforcing legislation on cults at
the *raiispolkom* and *gorispolkom* levels were to become more actively
engaged in these problems.

It is clear that party concern over the extent of "religious survivals" throughout the fifties and sixties stemmed largely from its
surprise at the way in which religion sprang back during the war. As
late as 1964, L. Ilichev asserted in his article "The Formation of a
Scientific World-Outlook and Atheistic Education"[52] that the increased influence of the churches, especially of the "Western sects"
(that is, the Baptists), was a result of the policy shift of 1943–44,
when the church strengthened its position as a consequence of "a
retreat from the Leninist legislation on religion, allowing the
churches unwarranted relief from taxes and supplying them with
construction materials and greater freedom in managing their
activities."

As stated at the outset, party pronouncements play a critical role in
the formation and interpretation of legislation on religion. This observation was again vindicated by events in the 1960s. In this connection one must first examine the criminal code of the RSFSR,
which was adopted by the Supreme Soviet of that republic on July 25,
1962. It includes several articles related to religious matters (ana-
logues of which soon appeared in the codes of all the other Soviet

51. For further information on the implementation of this exhortation see Lowrie and
Fletcher, "Khrushchev's Religious Policy," chapter 7 below.
52. L. Ilichev, "Formirovaniia nauchnogo mirovozzreniia i ateisticheskoe vospitanie",
Kommunist, no. 1, 1964.

republics).[53] Article 142 stated that violations of the laws on the separation of church from state and school from church shall be punishable by corrective work for a period of up to one year or a fine of up to fifty rubles. (In March, 1966, this article was amended to provide harsher punishment.) Article 143 was adopted from the older code (article 127); it provides punishment for interference with religious observances "unless the observances disturb public order and are accompanied by infringement upon the rights of citizens." The only change in this article is that, whereas formerly the sentence was corrective work for a period of up to six months, in the new code the alternative of "public reprimand" was added. This alternative obviously broadens the punitive character of the article and makes its restrictive power on persons who violate the rights of religious observance potentially weaker.

Article 227 of the code makes punishable "infringements upon the person and the rights of citizens under the appearance of performing religious rites." This article defines such offences as "the organization or leading of a group, the activities of which, under the appearance of preaching religious dogmas or performing religious rites, are connected with inflicting harm on the health of the citizens, or with other encroachments upon the person or rights of citizens, or with inciting citizens to refuse to participate in civic activities or to perform their civic duties, or with drawing minors into such a group." Such activities shall be punishable by confinement for a period of up to five years, or deportation for such a period, with or without confiscation of property. Punishment is lighter for those who merely promote such activities, or in cases where the public danger from such activities is less. This article aims principally at members of fanatical sects whose beliefs entail self-mutilation (for example, the *skoptsy*) or withdrawal from society (for example, the Old Believers). It can be applied, however, against almost any group, since both circumcision and baptism by immersion have been legally construed as harmful to health. In theory, even refusal to take part in atheistic activities, such

---

53. *Ugolovnoe zakonodatelstvo soiuza SSSR i soiuznykh respublik* [Criminal legislation of the Soviet Union and the Union republics], (Moscow, 1963), pp. 123, 142. See also Harold J. Berman, *Soviet Criminal Law and Procedure, the RSFSR Codes* (Cambridge, Mass., 1966), pp. 141ff. and *Church and State Under Communism*, p. 39. The English text of the relevant articles of the criminal code of the RSFSR appears in the Appendix, section 3, below.

as courses of instruction in schools, can be interpreted as refusing to participate in civic activities.

In addition to the foregoing articles which deal explicitly with religious matters, there are others which can be invoked against religious activity as well. Article 70 of the code prescribes stiff punishment for "incitement or propaganda for the purpose of undermining or weakening the Soviet government" and for the "dissemination, for the same purpose, of slanderous fabrications discrediting the Soviet political and social order, or the dissemination, for the same purpose, of literature containing any such material."[54]

Article 74 of the criminal code is entitled "Infringement of national and racial rights of equality," and specifies that "direct or indirect limitation of rights, or the establishment of direct or indirect privileges on the ground of race or nationality" is punishable by deprivation of freedom.[55] This is based on the 1927 code of the RSFSR which prohibited "propaganda or agitation aimed at arousing national or religious enmities or dissension" and the "dissemination, manufacture, or possession of literature of such nature,"[56] except that in the new code the reference to "religious enmity" has been deleted.

Another relevant legislative act, which is neither part of the criminal code nor exclusively concerned with religion, is an edict of the presidium of the Supreme Soviet of the RSFSR, "Strengthening the Fight Against Persons Avoiding Socially Useful Work" (May 4, 1961), the so-called antiparasite law. This edict can easily be applied to members of religious cults and ministers of religion whose work is, by Soviet definition, not socially useful. P. B. Taylor aptly describes the decree as "a multi-purpose control that embraces prostitutes and poets, as well as monks and mullahs."[57] Any person who leads a "parasitic way of life" can be forcibly resettled in special designated areas for a period of from two to five years, or he can be assigned to hard labor for that period. This can be accomplished either by court order or by the decision of the collective of workers of any area,

---

54. *Ugolovnoe zakonodatelstvo*, p. 108.
55. Ibid., 109.
56. *Ugolovny kodeks RSFSR* [The criminal code of the RSFSR], (Moscow, 1953), p. 23.
57. Pauline B. Taylor, "Sectarians in Soviet Courts," *Russian Review*, July 1965, p. 286.

subject to final approval by the local soviet.[58] While the edict has not been widely applied, it clearly could be invoked to place most clergymen outside the law at any time.

In July, 1964, the authoritative organ *Sovetskoe gosudarstvo i pravo* published an article by Iu. T. Milko which was indicative of these new legal trends on religious affairs. The title of the article itself is significant: "Scientific–Atheistic Propaganda and the Juridical Struggle Against Crimes of Churchmen and Sectarians."[59] Because of the journal in which it appeared, this article is equivalent to an authoritative legal interpretation. Milko began by stating that the Soviet government not only refrains from interfering in the life of religious groups, but "actively defends this freedom and accords it the protection of law." Similarly, it is not religion or clergymen that the government is fighting but rather their infractions of the law: "The determination of the offense should be based not on the fact that the guilty party belongs to a religious association but on the substance of his criminal activity." He then enumerated the articles of the code which should be invoked in particular cases.[60] Special attention was given to article 70 (on anti-Soviet propaganda) which, in his opinion, was too seldom applied to religious offenses. It ought to be applied not only to those who use unregistered religious groups to commit crimes such as taking advantage of the religious prejudices of believers; the same treatment should be given to members of legal or registered groups.[61] He stated that leaders of the latter have preyed upon their members "to promote anti-Soviet ideologies." On the question of what constitutes anti-Soviet ideological activities, the author said this must be decided by the courts in each particular case, though it is obvious that "anti-Soviet ideology" could include almost any sort of religious belief, since religious and communist ideologies are inherently opposed.

Milko also adduced examples of particular offenses which could be cited as infractions of article 227. Prohibition of attendance at

58. *Sovetskaia iustitsiia* [Soviet justice], (Moscow, 1961), no. 10, p. 25.

59. Iu. T. Milko, "Nauchno-ateisticheskaia propaganda i ugolovno-pravovaia borba s prestupleniami tserkovnikov i sektantov," *Sovetskoe gosudarstvo i pravo* 7 (1964): 67–75.

60. In the earlier criminal code several articles were applied to similar offenses: article 59 (arousing religious enmity), article 122 (religious instruction), article 124 (compulsory collection of funds), article 125 (assumption of the rights of a legal entity), and article 126 (performing religious rites in public institutions). See V. Gsovsky, *Soviet Civil Law*, 2: 336ff.

61. *Sovetskoe gosudarstvo i pravo*, p. 65.

movies and other cultural activities, as well as the prohibition of racial or religious intermarriage, while not done with the purpose of weakening the government, are nonetheless fostered by religious fanaticism and thereby violate this article. Article 227 originally defined a criminal act as organizing or leading activities, under the guise of religious preaching, which entail damage to health or sexual licentiousness.[62] The version of the article adopted in 1962 deleted the words "sexual licentiousness" and added the broader prohibition of "encroaching upon the person or rights of citizens, or with inciting citizens to refuse participation in civic activities or performance of civic duties."[63] Milko offers examples of what constitutes "doing harm to the health of a believer": "zealous prayer or long fasts, or refusal to receive medical help, and the results of making sacrifices in expiation of sin."

Commenting on the antiparasite law, Milko observed: "The mere fact of anticivic activities by a leader of a religious sect is not yet sufficient basis for his administrative deportation. The application of the measure is possible only when a warning has been given him by the proper administrative organs and he has not taken up decent employment in the prescribed time." If this qualified the law somewhat, Milko also admonished the courts not to "apply administrative punishment when there are grounds for criminal prosecution."[64]

This antiparasite law was amended in 1965, partly because it was ambiguous, but primarily because Soviet jurists felt that it undermined both the prestige of the courts, by creating in effect additional courts, and the validity of the criminal code, by its very ambiguity. The amendment was passed by the presidium of the Supreme Soviet of the RSFSR in September, 1965.[65] The principal modifications are as follows: (a) the competent forum to apply the law shall be the executive committee of the *raion* or city soviet within the oblast, krai, or autonomous republic concerned; (b) the previous sanction of exile by order of the *raion* or city people's court shall be retained for

62. *Zakony RSFSR i postanovleniia verkhovnogo soveta RSFSR priniaty na tretei sessii verkhovnogo soveta RSFSR* [Laws of the RSFSR and ordinances of the Supreme Soviet of the RSFSR enacted at the third session of the Supreme Soviet of the RSFSR] (Moscow, 1960), p. 142.

63. Taylor, *Sectarians in Soviet Courts*, p. 284.

64. Milko, "Nauchno-ateisticheskaia propaganda," pp. 74–75.

65. R. Beerman, "The Anti-parasite Law of the RSFSR Modified," *Soviet Studies*, January 1966, p. 387. For the English text of the antiparasite law, as amended, see Appendix, section 5, below.

Moscow and Leningrad only; (c) the law shall contain no provision for confiscation of property as part of the punishment. A new defini- tion of an idler is given: "an able-bodied adult who persistently refuses to work in an honest way and who is leading an antisocial, parasitic life." Despite these amendments it is still doubtful whether the law is compatible with the Soviet constitution and Soviet legal structure.

On March 24, 1966, the Soviet government made further changes in its religious legislation with the publication of three new acts. The first of these, an ordinance "On the application of Article 142 of the RSFSR Criminal Code,"[66] enumerated six kinds of violations of the laws on the separation of church from state and school from church which were subject to punishment under this article. Three of these are merely a reiteration of old provisions (paragraphs 1, 2, and 5), but the remainder contain new elements worthy of examination.[67] Paragraph 3 makes culpable "the commission of fraudulent actions for purposes of inciting religious superstition among the masses of the population"—a vague wording that can be broadly interpreted. The paragraph could be an echo of old slogans, but it is more likely the regime's response to the troublesome activities which have recent- ly characterized some of the religious sects.

Paragraph 4—"the organization and conduct of religious meetings, processions, and other cult ceremonies disturbing public order"— significantly alters previous legislation. Whereas previous legal pro- vision withdrew protection of the law for religious rites only if their performance violated public order, the new ordinance makes such performance *in itself* a criminal offense. Since the meaning of the phrase "disturbing public order" is dependent on the interpretation of local Soviet authorities, who by their own admission are opposed to the very existence of these observances, this change can only be construed as unfavorable to religionists.

Perhaps in part to offset such restrictive and (poorly defined) provisions, paragraph 6 has strong "liberal" overtones that might be of great importance to religious believers. It designates as unlawful and punishable under article 142 "the refusal to hire citizens for work,

66. "O primenenii stati 142 Ugolovnovo Kodeksa RSFSR," *Vedomosti verkhovnogo soveta RSFSR* [Bulletin of the supreme soviet of the RSFSR], no. 12, 24 March 1966, ordinance 21. For the English text see Appendix, section 3A, below.
67. For full discussion of these acts see Joshua Rothenberg, "The Status of Cults," *Problems of Communism*, September/October 1967, pp. 119–24.

or to admit them to educational institutions, the dismissal from work or expulsion from educational institutions, the deprivation of citizens' privileges and benefits that have been established by law, as well as other substantial limitations of the rights of citizens, because of their attitude toward religion." This is essentially a negative restatement of a legal right granted by the Soviet constitution and by previous legislation. The publication of explicit legal prohibition of such discriminatory practices is, however, not only confirmation of their occurrence but of potential benefit to religious believers.

The second legislative act issued in March, 1966, also relates to article 142 of the criminal code, but its scope and significance are relatively minor.[68] It concerns recidivism, making punishment in such cases harsher by changing it from "correctional work" to "deprivation of freedom" and by lengthening the maximum sentence from one year to three years. The third act of March, 1966, determines administrative responsibility for punishment of violations of various established rules concerning religious cults.[69] Apparently, the offenses enumerated in this act were not considered important enough to warrant prosecution before the court under criminal law.

The offenses to be punished administratively are: (1) failure to register associations with the proper authorities; (2) violation of the rules established by legislation on organizing and conducting religious meetings, processions, and ceremonies of cult; (3) the organization and holding of special meetings of children and youth, the organization of work, literary and other circles and groups "having no relation to the observance of cult." The punishment for all these offenses is a fine of up to fifty rubles imposed by administrative commissions of the county (*raion*) or city soviets.

This brings the survey of Soviet legislation concerning religion down to the present. Before offering certain general conclusions on these laws, it would be relevant to discuss briefly the administrative structure that has been created to implement this legislation.

68. "Ukaz Prezidiuma Verkhovnogo Soveta RSFSR o vnesenii dopolneii v statiu 142 ugolovnovo kodeksa RSFSR," *Vedomosti verkhovnogo soveta* [Order of the presidium of the Supreme Soviet of the RSFSR on implementing article 142 of the criminal code of the RSFSR], no. 12, 24 March 1966, ordinance 390. For English text see Appendix, section 3A, below.

69. "Ukaz prezidiuma verkhovnogo soveta RSFSR 'Ob administrativnoi otvetstvennosti za narushenie zakonodatelstva o religioznykh kultakh'" [The decree of the Supreme Soviet of the RSFSR "On administrative responsibility for violations of the law on religious cults"], *Vedomosti verkhovnogo soveta*, no. 12, 24 March 1966, ordinance 219. For English text see Appendix, section 3A, below.

Administration and Supervision
of the Laws on Religion

Information on the administration of the laws on religion is not as
readily available as that pertaining to other branches of the legal
structure. Most of what is included here has been deduced from indirect Soviet sources, such as references in books, articles, and newspapers; as such, the information is not definitive. Primary attention
will be given to most recent practice.

General supervision in the implementation of existing legislation
is vested in the state procurator (*prokuror*), now a very important
office in the Soviet Union. (The authority and power of this official has
increased constantly since the beginning of the post-Stalin period.) It
is his responsibility, also, to see that the laws on religious matters
are correctly implemented and that violators of these laws are
prosecuted.

Two agencies are directly responsible for the administration and
supervision of organized religious life: the Council for the Affairs of
Religious Cults (this is under the Council of Ministers of the USSR,
which is a central agency but also has a network of local representatives); and the local soviets. Considering the latter first, the local
soviets exert their control over religious life in their general capacity
of the highest administrative body at the local level, but also more
directly through specially designated committees or sections for
religious affairs.

According to the law and the instruction of 1929 (still in force),
the committee (later section) for religious matters of the city or
county soviet (*gorsovet* or *raisovet*) is to serve as the agency of registration for local religious associations. The religious sections of the
soviets, therefore, act as the lessors in contracts of lease of religious
property. In addition, these sections, (in conjunction with the representatives of the Council for Religious Cults) exercise control over
the activities of the congregations, their elected bodies, and their
clergymen. Religious associations must submit to these sections lists
of their members, information about their clergymen, financial
accounts, and reports about practically all aspects of the organization. If desirable, the section may petition the higher echelons of
power for closing a house of prayer, and they may, in certain cases,
dissolve the contract of lease with the religious association.

The second agency directly responsible for the administration and control of religious matters is the Council of Ministers of the USSR. This agency is the direct heir of the Standing Committee on the Affairs of Cults, established in 1929, and its successors, the Council for the Affairs of the Russian Orthodox Church and the Council for the Affairs of Religious Cults, both formed in 1943–44. The present council is, in effect, a merger of these last two, accomplished in January, 1966.

According to the law of 1929 the administrative prerogatives of the Standing Committee included: (a) the establishment of the forms of application, registration and reportage to the local authorities on religious matters, and the manner and the time of their submission (pars. 6, 8, 63); (b) the granting of permission for all-Union and RSFSR religious conventions and congresses (par. 20); (c) the control of nationalized objects of cult (par. 25); (d) and, in conjunction with the council of ministers of the republic or autonomous region, the annulment of the contract of lease on a religious building, either on its own initiative or upon the representation of a local committee on religious matters (pars. 36, 43, 51).

The instruction issued somewhat later by the Commissariat of the Interior amended certain provisions of the law and further elucidated procedural matters, especially in regard to the annulment of the contracts of lease. According to the instruction, the Standing Committee, at the request of the local committee on religious matters, makes the final decision on the liquidation of a religious society or group, which decision may be appealed to the Council of Ministers (par. 62), and on the annulment of a contract leasing prayer buildings and religious property (par. 63). It should be noted that the two actions are *not identical*, as is frequently assumed. The functions of the Standing Committee were formulated again at the time of its reorganization and division into two councils in 1944. (See notes 43 and 44 above.)

The evolution which resulted in the present Council of Affairs of Religious Cults has made it the most authoritative agency concerned with the administration of legislation. As the representative of the Soviet Union at the Commission on Human Rights of the United Nations remarked in 1959 in his report, the then dual councils "have representatives in regions, territories and republics to maintain liaison between state agencies and local religious organizations, to carry out the registration of religious communities and the official transfer of church buildings, both to existing and to newly-organized religious communities."[70] Precisely what relation these deputies of the councils have had to the religious sections of the local soviets is not clear. The report seems to indicate, however, that the council's representatives have assumed certain prerogatives previously held by the local soviets, such as the registration of religious communities and the transfer of prayer buildings. This would suggest that by 1959 the councils had come to overshadow the local soviets. As is clear from the report, many functions still remained in the hands of the local state agencies, as the first responsibility of a council representative was "to maintain liaison between state agencies and local religious organizations."

Early in the 1960s however, according to the open letter of two Russian priests to the chairman of the presidium of the Supreme Soviet, the representatives of the councils renounced their prerogative of being the "liaison between state agencies and religious organizations" and assumed the functions of principal supervisors of local religious organizations.[71] Documentary evidence exists to support this charge and suggests that the change came as part of the new campaign levelled against religion.[72] The representatives of the councils were also accused of acting at this time contrary to existing Soviet laws on religious matters by giving oral and telephone orders which they were unwilling to confirm in writing, thus instituting a new kind of "oral legislation" or legislation by telephone.[73]

In October, 1964, Khrushchev fell from power. Incomplete evidence suggests that some amelioration of the antireligious campaign and regularization of legal procedures then occurred.[74] One procedural alteration has been the amalgamation, in January, 1966, of the two councils into a single Council for the Affairs of Religious Cults. What this signifies is not yet clear, although writing in

---

70. United Nations, Commission on Human Rights, "Study of Discrimination in Religious Rights and Practices,"p. 17. Milko, in "Nauchno-ateisticheskaia propaganda," stated that "control over the observation of legislation on religious cults is entrusted to the executive committees of the local organs of authority [soviets], the two councils for religious matters at the Council of Ministers and also their representatives in the localities," pp. 74–75.

71. Letter of two Russian Priests to the chairman of the Presidium of the Supreme Soviet. Text in *Religion in Communist-Dominated Areas*, published by the National Council of Churches, 15/31 May 1966.

72. See Appendix, section 5, below.

73. See footnote 72 above.

74. See "Khrushchev's Religious Policy," chapter 7 below.

Izvestiia in August, 1966, the new chairman, V. A. Kuroedov, declared that as a result of the merger "the role and responsibility of the Council in the control over the legislation on cults had been significantly increased and corresponding rights granted to it."[75]

Besides these two basic agencies (the Council for the Affairs of Religious Cults with its local representatives, and the local soviets), there are several other institutions which in one way or another exercise influence or control in religious matters. One of these is the Ministry of Public Order of the respective republics which acts through its subordinate departments and through the militia. The militia has wide powers for the maintenance of public order and has the authority to impose fines by administrative decision, and to detain persons and to conduct preliminary investigations in many types of suspected crime.[76]

Religious associations are always under the surveillance of the local militia. Paragraph 57 of the 1929 instruction charged the militia with the responsibility of seeing to it "that no forcible activities against persons are committed, no property demolished or abused, or other illegal activities performed during [religious] processions and ceremonies." The local militia also functions in close cooperation with the local executive committees of the soviet, but whether—in case of conflict in religious matters—the militia is primarily the agent of the Ministry of Public Order or of the local soviet is not clear.

That such conflict would be rare seems certain because of the commanding role the Communist party assumes in Soviet society not only in economic and political affairs but also in religious matters; this is especially so because the party is the sole interpreter of acceptable ideology and the chief protector of society against ideological enemies. For every *gorsovet* (city soviet) there is a *gorkom* (city party committee), and for every *obsovet* (district soviet) there is the powerful *obkom* (district committee of the party). Attempts to define the lines of demarcation between the authority and powers of the lower-level agencies of the Soviet government and those of the Communist party have been made, but without final success. The general assumption is that the party apparatus has the responsibility of *supervising* and *controlling* the state apparatus. Since the areas of

75. *Izvestiia*, 30 August 1966.
76. Leonard Schapiro, *The Government and Politics of the Soviet Union* (New York, 1965), p. 160. Also, Berman, *Soviet Criminal Law*, pp. 65–68.

activity and the responsibilities of the two authorities are ill-defined and constantly overlapping, in practice the local party committees have all too often assumed more extensive powers than simply ones of "control." Jerry F. Hough, in his study, "The Soviet Concept of the Relationship Between the Lower Party Organs and the State Administration,"[77] relates a case in which a party *obkom* removed a *prokuror* (district prosecutor). Hough concludes that the Russian word *kontrol* implies more than its English equivalent, and includes some form of "checking" (to which might be added, "correcting").[78]

In matters of religion the "control" of lower party organs over other state agencies is probably even more pronounced than in the economic field, if only because of the more immediate ideological involvement. But moving from ideology to practical politics, it would seem certain that the closing of a house of prayer would not be done without the knowledge and approval of the local party committee, which decides whether it is expedient and safe to do so.

Still another powerful agency with points of supervision and control in religious affairs is the security police, known until recently as the KGB (*komitet gosudarstvennoi bezopasnosti* [Committee of state security]). There is clear evidence that the KGB, in addition to its special departments or sections for religious affairs, both on the central and local levels,[79] has in its employ secret agents and informers, who have infiltrated the executive bodies of religious associations and seminaries. This would certainly be a logical step for these guardians of state security, since it is clear that the regime considers religious cults to harbor actual or potential enemies. Certainly the KGB is responsible for the detection and preliminary investigation of all crimes against the state. A number of the articles of the criminal code, as pointed out earlier, refer to activities deemed criminal, to which religious believers and religious organizations would be specifically subject.

As noted earlier, the Commissariat of Justice has also been closely

77. *Slavic Review*, June 1965.

78. In fact, the functions of a *prokuror* (procurator) are more diverse and larger in scope than those of a prosecutor. The *prokuratura* in the Soviet Union has become a powerful judicial institution with vast prerogatives. (See, for instance, Berman, *Soviet Criminal Law*, pp. 17, 67–78.)

79. Walter Kolarz reports that the first head of the Council for the Affairs of the Russian Orthodox Church, G. Karpov, was a former chief of the religious section of the secret police and his superb knowledge of the intricacies of the Russian Orthodox church was a result of his long former experience in this field.

associated with the implementation of religious laws. It issued the instruction for carrying out the Decree of Separation of the Church from the State (August 24, 1918), and the instruction for the Law on Religious Associations of 1929. The eighth division of the Commissariat, whose function was to liquidate the bonds between church and state, published the periodical *Revoliutsiia i tserkov* which became the medium for expressing the regime's attitude on religious matters and publishing all pertinent official documents and legislation. The liquidation sections of the eighth division were attached to the executive committee of the provincial soviets. The eighth division (later the fifth division) had the power to authorize the requisitioning of churches. These functions of the Commissariat of Justice were later transferred to the Commissariat of the Interior.

Several ministries have jurisdiction over particular matters relating to religion, most importantly the Ministry (formerly Commissariat) of Public Education, which has issued circulars and instructions on the problems (and the legal aspects) of religious instruction for children. One of these circulars (Circular of the Commissariat of Public Education, March 3, 1919) even contradicted the basic law of January 23, 1918, by insisting that "teaching religious doctrines to persons younger than eighteen years is not permissible." (The law said that such instruction is permissible when given privately.) The commissariats (later ministries) of education of the republics have issued various, often contradictory, instructions and orders.

By way of summary, the evidence available suggests that minor decisions on religious matters are made by four agencies: (1) the local representative (plenipotentiary) of the Council for the Affairs of Religious Cults; (2) the local executive committee for the soviet and its religious section; (3) the local party Committee; and (4) the local security agencies (militia and/or a representative of the KGB).

In general, the local party Committee coordinates and arbitrates differences of opinion. (The individuals who represent the above agencies are, as a rule, all members of the party.)

More important decisions, such as those pertaining to the closing of important churches or holy places, or to the holding of religious conferences would be made at the center by the Council of Ministers of the USSR after receiving the opinion of the district committee of the party (*obkom*) and the Council for the Affairs of Religious Cults. Questions of highest priority in religious matters are decided by the

Central Committee of the Communist party and its ideological commission, which then issue authoritative instructions to be implemented all down the line through the multiple agencies of administration.

Conclusions

Viewed over fifty years, the general tendency in Soviet legislation on religious matters has been an *increase* in restrictions and control over organized religious life in the country. The comparatively liberal decree of January, 1918, is still in force, except where it has been superseded by later legislation, particularly the extensive and harsh law of 1929. In that same year a constitutional amendment replaced *freedom to propagate* religious beliefs by *freedom to practice* religion; this change was retained in the constitution of 1936 which remains in effect today. The articles of the criminal code of 1960 and the amendments of 1962 pertaining to religious matters are stricter and more inclusive than the corresponding articles in the previous codes. The enactments of March, 1966, are somewhat puzzling. Their relationship to previous religious legislation is not clear; much of what they contain is a repetition of old laws, and the new provisions are vague and arbitrary. Codification of the laws on religious matters and clarification of their meaning are urgently needed. Until then, their interpretation at a given moment remains the key.

Soviet policy in regard to religion has not necessarily followed legislation, and has not always been synchronized with changes in legislation. Short "liberal" intervals in a generally restrictive policy were not accompanied by corresponding legislation. This was true of the great detente in antireligious policies during the "Great Fatherland War." The existing legal framework has not prevented the Soviet regime from using the law alternately for relaxation and restriction.

Soviet legislation and the administration and observance of existing laws have always been the weakest links in the state's chain of functions. The laws were often violated, their very existence being unknown to most citizens and their validity problematic. At present, however, an equitable application of the law and a general esteem for legality seem to be on the increase. In spite of the fact that widely accepted concepts of the law, such as *lex retro non agit* (laws do not apply retroactively), and *nulla poena sine lege* (no punishment without law) are violated from time to time, there has been in the Soviet

Union a growing tendency both to espouse Western notions of law and to adhere more faithfully to "socialist legality."

In contrast to this general pattern, respect for existing laws on religious matters is hardly discernible. Both the decree of January, 1918, and the law and instruction of 1929, although still in force, are often disregarded. Their very existence is not well known, seemingly by design, and their validity is at many points doubtful.

In one sense a return to "Leninist legislation" would, in religious matters, be a return to a more liberal policy. Such a move would have to consider Lenin's observation that "Everyone must be perfectly free not only to belong to whatever religion he pleases, but he must be free to disseminate his religion and to change his religion."[80]

Obviously the notion of separation of church and state in the Soviet Union differs from that of many other countries by virtue of the professed desire of the Soviet regime to erase religious beliefs from the consciousness of the Soviet people.

Although official documents of the party were usually careful to delineate the division of authority between state and party, in practice this division has been all but lost. The peculiar status of the party was officially recognized in the 1936 constitution, which stated that the party "represents the directing core of all organizations of the toilers, both voluntary and state" (par. 26). The official program of the "directing core" clearly states that it is not neutral in matters of religion. The party retains ultimate control over both the formulation and the administration of the law. In the past this has proven to be very disruptive of the civil order.

Soviet legislation in general and its religious legislation in particular has always been characterized by a wealth of ambiguities which lend themselves to widely divergent interpretations. In some cases the ambiguities seem intentional, aimed at permitting both central and local authorities to maneuver to their best advantage.

Existing Soviet legislation, discriminatory and restrictive though it is, would still suffice to permit believers to practice their religion— within limitations—provided the administrative authorities would not use the powers at their disposal to implement the law more strictly than is called for. Even the harsh laws of 1929 allow for very small groups of persons to register and to conduct prayer services, but in practice such groups, even of legally recognized religions, are

80. V. I. Lenin, "To the rural poor," in *Selected Works* (New York, 1943), 2: 284.

frequently denied this right and forced to lead an illegal religious life.

The greatest single area of potential interpretation of the law to the disadvantage of believers seems to be vested in the criminal code and in legislation covering offences under administrative jurisdiction. The recent admonition, cited above, for officials to make greater use of articles 227 and 70, is a disturbing sign.

It is not impossible that the greater concern for legality, noted of late, will ultimately be reflected in the religious field. Pragmatically, undue repression of religion has often led to uncontrollable underground religious organizations. Also, there is an emerging public opinion which frequently finds the harsh restrictions on religious believers unjust, or at least unnecessary. Finally, the exigencies of the struggle within the communist bloc may impel the Soviets to restrain their antireligious programs; foreign communists have usually reacted unfavorably to repressions in this area, preferring proper legal procedures and more educational approaches.

Accordingly, the time may now be propitious for demands to be made of the regime at least to respect the existing laws on religion. A prominent jurist, A. Anashkin, recently made just such a plea.[81] Although there seems little hope for any genuine tolerance of religion, given the party's understanding of the nature and content of its ideology in this area, one can hope for an increase of respect for the legal process and the rights of the individual.

81. G. Anashkin, "O svobode i sobliudenii zakonodatelstva o religioznykh kultakh" [On freedom and the observance of the laws on religious cults], *Sovetskoe gosudarstvo i pravo*, no. 1, 1965. (Mr. Anashkin was recently removed from his position on the Supreme Court of the USSR.)

6

THE ORIGINS OF SOVIET ANTIRELIGIOUS ORGANIZATIONS

An intriguing chapter of Soviet history which has not yet been adequately explored is the emergence of the antireligious movement in the first decade after the Revolution. Though a relatively minor feature of the turmoil of those times, this movement has its own turbulent development which gains in significance when viewed in the larger context of surrounding events. In this study the prehistory of the movement will be traced mainly through early governmental decrees concerning religious affairs, party pronouncements regarding antireligious propaganda, and the often intensive but generally uncoordinated and even contradictory efforts at carrying out one or the other.

The antireligious movement, when it finally took shape, was essentially a propaganda undertaking. As such one might logically expect it to have taken its cues from party pronouncements on the subject. Yet its relationship with the party was not a simple one, and the process through which the party gradually assumed direction of it was also complex. The predominantly ad hoc character of antireligious activities in the first years of Soviet power began to change in the early twenties, reflecting similar shifts in the political and social realms. The year 1922 saw the emergence of several approaches to the task of combating religion. This diversity was soon manifested in sharp public discussion of policy and a contest for the leadership of

Joan Delaney

the movement then in the process of being formed. The dispute was formally settled by party intervention only after strenuous intramural debate which overflowed into the central press and which involved, at least implicitly, important party officials.

This study will be limited to the formation of the antireligious movement, with focus on the crucial debate which took place between 1923 and 1926, a debate which culminated in explicit party approval of one faction over all others and coincided with other important events of great political significance. The party's ultimate decision was important for several reasons. First, it established an official policy in an area where the party had previously abstained from direction. Second, this policy constituted a middle course between the various opinions, since the approach which the party supported was neither the short-range shock technique of the left, which sought to destroy religion forcibly, nor the liquidationist position of the right, which held that religion would die of itself. (This via media approach to controversial problems characterized many party decisions in the years when Stalin was consolidating his position.)[1] Third, the norms enunciated in 1926, while often ignored in practice, remain, in principle, and are regarded with particular interest today. Indeed, the period of the mid-twenties is now under intensive study by Soviet antireligionists, whose research frequently results in new insights and conjectures touching present and future policy in the area of religion.

In the immediate postrevolutionary period a coordinated propaganda campaign against religion as such was not pressed. Instead, the struggle was bound up almost totally with the struggle against counterrevolution, its prime task being to expose the reactionary role of the church and to implement the January, 1918, government decree of separation of church from state and school from church.[2]

1. An interesting parallel is to be found in events in the literary field in the mid-twenties. Amid a profusion of approaches to building a new literature, one particularly militant group controlling the All-Union Association of Proletarian writers (VAPP), demanded party confirmation of its stand. The matter was thrashed out in the press from 1923 to 1925, after which time the Politburo published a resolution "On the Policy of the Party in the Field of Belles-Lettres." Moderate though the statement was, it marked a decisive step: party entrance into an area where it had previously abstained from pronouncements. This entire sequence of events is discussed thoroughly in Edward J. Brown, *The Proletarian Episode in Russian Literature, 1928–1932* (New York, 1953).

2. V. L. Andrianova and S. G. Rutenburg, "Antireligiozny plakat pervykh let sovetskoi vlasti" [The antireligious poster in the first years of Soviet power], *Ezhegodnik muzeia istorii religii i ateizma* [Yearbook of the Museum of the History of Religion and Atheism] 5 (1961): 190.

Execution of this government decree was supervised by a special commission attached to the party's Central Committee, which also functioned as the party organ for directing antireligious propaganda. This commission was then, and for many years thereafter, headed by Emelian Iaroslavsky, who in the next two decades was to become the leader and chief promoter of the antireligious movement.[3]

Actual implementation of the separation decree was primarily the responsibility of the eighth division of the Commissariat of Justice, headed by P. A. Krasikov. Also a member of Iaroslavsky's commission,[4] Krasikov later recalled how Lenin had counseled him to link the work of his division with that of antireligious propaganda.[5] The journal *Revoliutsiia i tserkov* (The Revolution and the church) was published by the eighth division and edited by Krasikov. Until 1922 it was the only antireligious periodical with national distribution. Though essentially devoted to matters concerning the separation decree, it also carried solid propaganda pieces by Krasikov, Lunacharsky, and others. It was published from 1919 to 1924,[6] in relatively small printings of thirty to forty thousand. Because of the unsettled conditions of the time, it appeared at irregular intervals. In any case, *Revoliutsiia i tserkov* was not basically an organ of mass appeal, despite Krasikov's testimony to Lenin concerning its popularity.[7]

Other antireligious operations of the eighth division included organizing lectures and debates in which such men as Iaroslavsky, Lunacharsky, and Krasikov took leading parts. It also supervised the production of propaganda posters and in this involved such prominent figures as the poets Maiakovsky and Demian Bedny. These posters, together with sporadically distributed leaflets,[8] were designed for mass distribution.[9]

Another department of the new government which early concerned

3. S. N. Savelev, "Em. Iaroslavsky i preodolenie anarkhistskikh vliiany v antireligioznoi rabote v SSSR" [E. Iaroslavsky and the overcoming of anarchistic influences in antireligious work in the USSR], *Ezhegodnik* 7 (1963): 37.

4. Ibid.

5. M. I. Shakhnovich, "V. I. Lenin o preodolenii religii" [V. I. Lenin on overcoming religion], *Ezhegodnik* 5 (1961): 18.

6. For one year, 1921, it was replaced by a wall newspaper of the same name, which had lively links with the countryside. See N. A. Krylov, "Iz istorii propagandy ateizma v SSSR (1923–1925)" [From the history of atheistic propaganda in the USSR (1923–1925)], *Voprosy istorii religii i ateizma* [Problems of the history of religion and atheism] (hereafter *VIRA*) 8 (Moscow, 1960): 175.

7. Shakhnovich, "V. I. Lenin."

8. *Nauka i religiia* [Science and religion], no. 3, November 1959, pp. 73–74.

9. Andrianova and Rutenburg, "Antireligiozny," pp. 192–94.

itself with antireligious measures was *Narkompros* (People's Commissariat for Education), which in its battle to ensure the totally "secular school" pressed the implementation of the second half of the separation decree, the separation of school from church. The All-Russian Teachers' Union provided formidable opposition to the removal of religious instruction from the curriculum, even to the point of calling teachers' strikes in four cities at the end of 1917 and the beginning of 1918. A rival teachers' organization, linked to *Narkompros*, was quickly formed (the All-Russian Union of Teacher-Internationalists, established in December, 1917) to promote teacher cooperation in removing all religious influence from the schools.[10] This cooperation was also stressed in the decrees of the Eighth Party Congress in March, 1919,[11] and in the numerous post-Congress teachers' conferences at which Lenin, Lunacharsky, Krupskaia, and others interpreted and promoted the Congress' decisions.[12]

The first major party initiative concerning antireligious propaganda was contained in article thirteen of the party program adopted at the Eighth Congress. This formulation was to be significant in shaping the goals of the antireligious movement in the next decade, when it came to exist as a separate entity with long-range goals of its own. Not satisfied with the government's separation decree, the party declared its intention of removing the conditions which, according to Marxist theory, had given rise to religious belief: "The party aims at the complete destruction of the link between the exploiting classes and the organization of religious propaganda, while assisting the actual liberation of the working masses from religious prejudices and organizing the widest possible scientific-educational antireligious propaganda. At the same time it is essential to avoid carefully any injury to the feelings of believers, which leads only to the strengthening of religious fanaticism."[13]

These proposals, however, were not systematically implemented for some time after the adoption of the program. Such a plan of action would seem to demand a complex central propaganda appara-

10. P. G. Ryndziunsky, "Borba za preodolenie religioznykh vliiany v sovetskoi shkole (1917–1919 g.)" [The struggle to overcome religious influences in Soviet schools (1917–1919)], *VIRA* 3 (Moscow, 1956): 67–73.

11. *Kommunisticheskaia partiia sovetskogo soiuza v rezoliutsiiakh i resheniiakh* [The Communist party of the Soviet Union in resolutions and decisions] (hereafter *KPSS*), 7th ed. (Moscow, 1954), pt. 1, p. 551.

12. Ryndziunsky, "Borba za predolenie," p. 84.

13. *KPSS*, pp. 420–21.

tus closely supervised by the party command. In 1919 such a structure did not exist and the matter of antireligious propaganda was still far down on the agenda. As the multiple pressures of civil war and the struggle to stabilize Bolshevik power in chaotic conditions began to lessen, the need to give some attention to the finer points of ideology became more apparent. Both government and party made gestures toward meeting this need through education. In November, 1920, *Narkompros* expanded its operations through the creation of *Glavpolitprosvet* (Central Administration of Political Education), which was placed under Krupskaia's direction. Lenin assigned as its goal the "education of true communists, able to defeat falsehood and prejudices."[14] Even before the end of the period of War Communism, *Glavpolitprosvet* set about establishing schools, courses, rural reading-rooms, workers' universities, and other educational-propagandistic centers.[15]

Thus, as the country emerged from civil war, the task of communist education came more sharply into focus. This was the meaning of the stronger and more explicit mandate to *Glavpolitprosvet* from the Tenth Party Congress in March, 1921, with its special directives concerning antireligious propaganda, for which the agency was enjoined to make the widest possible use of mass media.[16] It was Krasikov who, in the name of the Moscow party organization, introduced an amendment to this resolution to strengthen the importance of antireligious propaganda.[17] The Eleventh Party Congress in March of 1922 reiterated the responsibility of *Glavpolitprosvet*, especially in the publishing field.[18]

Still, the resolutions taken in these congresses were not widely translated into action insofar as they concerned organized antireligious propaganda. In spite of official encouragement and a few sporadic attempts, no large-scale organized effort was made to implement article 13. This was chiefly because antireligious propaganda was far down the list of the party's urgent tasks. Furthermore, in the minds of many party functionaries such propaganda seemed

14. V. I. Lenin, *Polnoe sobranie sochineny* [Complete works], 4th ed. (Moscow, 1962), 31:343.
15. N. A. Nistratova, "N. K. Krupskaia o borbe s religioznymi perezhitkami" [N. K. Krupskaia on the struggle with religious survivals], *Ezhegodnik* 5 (1961): 35.
16. *KPSS*, p. 551.
17. Shakhnovich, "V. I. Lenin," p. 18.
18. *KPSS*, p. 644.

limited to church-state separation. When this had been accomplished the need for propaganda was no longer felt to be as urgent.

The year 1922 proved to be a turning point in this as in many other areas of Soviet life. Before the turning point was reached there was one more, perhaps climactic example of the ad hoc mode of operation in the antireligious field—the seizure that spring of church valuables to pay for food imports necessitated by famine. This was, of course, an extraordinarily delicate operation. Throughout 1921 the church had profited by several months of relative calm in which it had strengthened its position. The government was weak, and faced with countless problems within the country; it was unable to afford a step which would arouse vigorous popular opposition. Yet the unrest caused by poor economic conditions was at least as dangerous. A bold plan, therefore, was formed for a lightning campaign to gather in the church's movable property before resistance could organize itself.

The Trotsky archive provides fresh information on the inner workings of this project. Early in 1922 a carefully organized and at first highly secret plan was prepared for systematically tapping this resource. The mastermind and head of the secret commission in charge of this project was Leon Trotsky. In a letter to Lenin dated January 30, 1922, Trotsky said that the necessary political groundwork for action was already being prepared, but that the project had to be discussed with the utmost caution to avoid being reported in the foreign press.[19]

A subsequent communication from Trotsky to the other members of the Politburo indicated that a conflict of authority had arisen in the Moscow phase of the operation through the appointment of overlapping commissions by the All-Russian Central Executive Committee (VTsIK). Trotsky peremptorily demanded that a new secret commission be set up, drawing chiefly on his already-existing commission for its membership, and that it be empowered to coordinate secretly all aspects of the matter—political, organizational, and technical. The actual seizure had to begin in March and be completed in the shortest possible time. The new secret commission, to be chaired by Trotsky's lieutenant, Sapronov, was to operate under cover of the more public *Pomgol*, the commission for aiding the hungry.[20]

19. Trotsky Archive, Houghton Library, Harvard University, Cambridge, Mass., T-728.
20. Ibid., T-736.

The operation could in some ways redound to the benefit of anti-religious propaganda, since the clergy's resistance in the face of acute hunger could be used to discredit them. But this was still a far cry from the program of constructive atheistic education envisioned by such men as Iaroslavsky. It is noteworthy that, despite his chairmanship of the special party commission charged with implementing the separation decree and organizing antireligious propaganda, Iaroslavsky's name does not appear on the list for Trotsky's commission.[21] Why this expert antireligious propagandist was not called upon to serve on that commission during the seizure of church valuables, when management of public opinion was of such importance, is a matter for speculation. It would be helpful to know the precise views of the rival group in Moscow to which Trotsky referred and whether Iaroslavsky was a member. Even without these pieces of information, there is reason to suspect that at this time or very soon thereafter, these two men began to contend for first place in antireligious affairs, in a rivalry which was to bear on the future of the movement.

There is evidence to this effect in Trotsky's autobiography. Writing some years later, he recalled that in the summer of 1922, antireligious propaganda was one of some dozen tasks which Lenin had entrusted to him unofficially, asking him not to let it out of his sight. Trotsky reports with relish that Lenin, while convalescing after his stroke of May 26, was upset to learn of Stalin's effort to revive the antireligious propaganda apparatus and to move it away from Trotsky. "Iaroslavsky, I think in the guise of my deputy, was pushed forward to take charge of antireligious propaganda."[22] This episode was, of course, remembered by Trotsky in exile, by which time he had cause to detest Iaroslavsky. Certainly there was a real difference of opinion between the two men concerning the importance of antireligious propaganda, as will be seen later. More significant, however, is the intriguing likelihood that Iaroslavsky's omission from Trotsky's secret commission was part of a larger, political rivalry—one between Trotsky and Stalin—which had not

21. In his letter to the Politburo Trotsky lists as members of the original commission Bazilevich, Galkin, Lebedev, Unshlikht, Samoilova-Zemliaka (sic), Krasikov, Krasneshchekov, and Sapronov. For the new secret commission he names Sapronov (chairman), Unshlikht, Medved, Samoilova-Zemliaka, and Galkin.

22. Leon Trotsky, *My Life*, (New York, 1930), p. 476.

yet come into the open. (This possibility will also be discussed below.)

Meanwhile, a shift in antireligious propaganda did occur in 1922, which might correspond to the "renewing" of the apparatus resented by Trotsky. In addition to the denigration of church and clergy occasioned by their resistance to the seizure of church valuables, another trend became apparent. In its larger scope it represented an attempt to move away from immediate attacks on the class ties of religion and its allegedly counterrevolutionary character toward the "scientific-educational" propaganda prescribed in the 1919 statement. This new trend manifested itself especially in the field of journalism, where it came to be identified with Iaroslavsky.

The importance of journalism was stressed in a programmatic article of Lenin's in 1922 on the meaning of militant materialism.[23] Appearing in an early issue of a new Marxist journal, the essay prodded the editors toward a more militantly atheistic stand. Lenin insisted that their publication should act as a goad to the existing state institutions charged with antireligious work, which, bogged down in Russian bureaucracy, was being carried on "extremely laxly, extremely unsatisfactorily." This journal's propaganda, he continued, must act to correct and to enliven the work of the state institutions concerned. If, as certain documents indicate, Lenin had acted to restrain antireligious initiatives the previous year and had stressed careful planning for a scientific campaign against religion,[24] he now seemed to feel that the time had come for accelerated activity.

Despite Lenin's urging, *Pod znamenem marksizma* did not become the leader in antireligious journalism, on either the specialized or the mass-consumption level. In the antireligious field as a whole, literature for the masses was in short supply. The non-party publishing house *Ateist* (The Atheist), established in 1922, specialized, according to a later criticism, in translations of the works of bourgeois atheists, often published with an un-Marxist commentary.[25] Other publishing

23. Lenin, "O znachenii voinstvuiushchego materializma," *Pod znamenem marksizma* [Under the banner of Marxism] 33 (1962): 203.
24. Cf. "Sokrovishchnitsa bessmertnykh idei. Dva novykh dokumenta V. I. Lenina" ["Treasury of immortal ideas. Two new documents of V. I. Lenin"], *Nauka i religiia*, no. 10, 1965, pp. 2–4.
25. L. Dunaevsky, "Nauchno-issledovatelskaia rabota v oblasti voinstvuiushchego ateizma za 15 let" [Scientific study in the field of militant atheism over 15 years], in *Voinstvuiushchee bezbozhie v SSSR za 15 let* [Militant atheism in the USSR over 15 years] ed. M. Enisherlov et al. (Moscow, 1932), p. 433.

efforts included collections such as the Moscow party committee's *Kommunizm i religiia* (Communism and religion) and separate articles and brochures by stalwarts of antireligious propaganda. A few issues of several antireligious newspapers appeared in Moscow and Petrograd, among them *Nauka i religiia* (Science and religion) edited by the former priest and zealous propagandist, Mikhail Gorev (Galkin). But neither their appeal nor their usefulness was sufficient to insure them a long life.[26] Then, at the end of 1922, came a major event in antireligious journalism: the appearance of a newspaper which was to function both as reading for the masses and as a guide for the propagandist. It was also to serve as the organizational point for the coming movement. On December 21, 1922, the first number of the weekly newspaper *Bezbozhnik* (The godless) appeared in Moscow, replacing Gorev's publication. Soon it was playing a central role in antireligious propaganda and operating with considerable success among that more recalcitrant group, the peasantry. Its editor was Emelian Iaroslavsky.[27]

At this same time Iaroslavsky was involved in other antireligious activities which helped his journalistic undertaking. He organized a "circle for the study of the history of religion" in the communist Ia. M. Sverdlov University in Moscow.[28] His students put their studies into immediate practice by lecturing and writing and by aiding in the preparation of Iaroslavsky's first antireligious book, *Kak rodiatsia, zhivut, i umiraiut bogi i bogini* (The birth, life and death of the gods and goddesses), which was first published in 1923. Iaroslavsky's other antireligious classic, *Bibliia dlia veruiushchikh i neveruiushchikh* (The Bible for believers and non-believers), written at the same time, began to appear serially in *Bezbozhnik* in December, 1922.[29]

Other modes of antireligious propaganda initiated at this same time were of a less sophisticated character. The Komsomol Christmas of 1922, the first major Komsomol antireligious project, which resulted from resolutions taken two years earlier, was poorly conceived and ill-prepared, an inauspicious event from both a practical and a theoretical point of view. A Komsomol directive, received by

26. Krylov, "Iz istorii propagandy ateizma," pp. 173–75.
27. Savelev, "Em. Iaroslavsky," p. 37.
28. Ibid.
29. M. M. Sheinman, "Propagandist ateizma Em. Iaroslavsky" [E. M. Iaroslavsky; propagandist of atheism], *VIRA* 6 (Moscow, 1958): 101,

the local branches at the last minute, instructed them to "put on mass carnivals portraying the ancient pagan gods, prototypes of Christ, and to introduce elements of satire through the portrayal of political and everyday occurrences." The general theme was to be a review of deposed gods.[30]

The campaign got completely out of hand, and official reaction was quick in coming. Very early in 1923 the party Central Committee dispatched a circular concerning future antireligious campaigns, particularly those held at Easter. "On holidays hold popular lectures of antireligious content, as well as spectacles, movies, and plays; refrain from holding street processions. Take all steps to avoid giving offense to religious feelings, shifting the weight of the work to a scientific explanation of the origin of religious holidays, especially of Easter."[31] On January 27 a meeting of the Komsomol central committee took stock and ordered a more thorough preparation for the Easter campaign, utilizing the resources of *Narkompros*. A special literary commission was chosen, made up of Iaroslavsky, Skvortsov-Stepanov, and Krasikov. Recommended literature included Iaroslavsky's *Bibliia* and the antipaschal issue of the newspaper *Bezbozhnik*. Antireligious circles helped prepare speakers for the holiday programs. During subsequent campaigns Iaroslavsky, writing in *Bezbozhnik*, continued to give practical advice in answer to readers' questions about methods of coping with religious celebrations and creating substitutes for them.[32]

The Christmas fiasco of 1922 had given clear notice of the need for better preparation and above all for more centralized planning and control in antireligious propaganda. Almost simultaneously with the Komsomol Easter of 1923 the party took official note of this new, more serious approach to the matter. The Twelfth Party Congress in April of that year devoted a great deal of attention to questions of propaganda, the press, and agitation, and a special section of its resolutions was entitled "O postanovke antireligioznoi agitatsii i propagandy" (On the regulation of antireligious agitation and propaganda).[33] This new emphasis manifested an increasing concern with

30. A. Vakurova, "Komsomol na antireligioznom fronte" [The Komsomol on the antireligious front], in *Voinstvuiushchee bezbozhie*, p. 305.
31. *Kommunisticheskaia partiia i sovetskoe pravitelstvo o religii i tserkvi* [The Communist party and the Soviet government on religion and the church], (Moscow, 1959), p. 76.
32. Vakurova, "Komsomol," pp. 306–7.
33. *KPSS*, pp. 743ff.

ideology and political education to counteract the retreat on the economic front (that is, the New Economic Policy) and the general disorientation of a country in the grip of numerous fundamental changes.

The party's task was "to make worker and peasant alike into practical instruments of revolution, armed with the methods of the Marxist approach to the concrete questions of revolutionary construction."[34] The resolution on antireligious propaganda pointed out that the revolutionary process had not yet eradicated the conditions which, according to Marxism, permitted the existence of religion; and that under these conditions it was necessary to carry on propaganda systematically and in depth, so as to convince workers and peasants of the incompatibility of religion with their interests. Coarse methods and crass mockery were to be avoided, since they were offensive to the feelings of believers and tended to strengthen their fanaticism. The party called instead for a serious and scientific approach, always adapted to the audience in question. It said that it could cope with its responsibilities in this direction:

provided that in the very near future it succeeds in setting up an extensive program of training for antireligious agitators and propagandists. This program, moreover, must draw upon all the resources of the state and party, beginning with the communist universities. Special courses on the origin, development, and history of religion, religious beliefs, cults, and church organizations must . . . be offered. These courses should be linked up with the study of human society and the struggle between the exploiting and the exploited classes, and the exposure of the historically demonstrable connections between capitalism and religious propaganda. . . . In addition to incorporating antireligious education into the general system of communist education in the schools, special antireligious circles and seminars must be sponsored, both in the schools and outside them. This work should be conducted under competent party direction at all times.

The organization of systematic antireligious propaganda and agitation is one of the best means of spreading party influence among the broad mass of the workers. But the party must not forget that all our antireligious agitation and propaganda will fail to affect the masses until the program of urban and rural education in the spirit of the scientific-materialistic natural sciences moves off dead center, that is, until the overwhelming majority of the rural population ceases to be illiterate. The proper organization of the school, the preparation of teachers, the creation of a broad network of institutions of political education (especially village reading-rooms), the supplying of the village with Soviet newspapers and books, the complete liquidation of

34. Ibid., p. 730.

illiteracy—all these things, in conjunction with the successes of Soviet agriculture and industry, will create conditions in which the religious prejudices in the minds of tens of millions of citizens of the various republics can finally be eradicated.[35]

An ambitious program indeed, that could not immediately be implemented in anything like the manner outlined. It would be revealing, perhaps, to know on what initiative and under what authorship this resolution entered the proceedings of the party congress. In retrospect, it reads almost as a charter for the atheistic organization which was then taking embryonic form around Iaroslavsky's newspaper *Bezbozhnik*, the body which would eventually grow into the *Soiuz voinstvuiushchikh Bezbozhnikov* (League of the the Militant Godless, or SVB).

The year 1923 marks the actual beginning of the movement's history. It was by no means a story of constant upward progress. Though the Twelfth Party Congress resolutions would seem to have smoothed the way, the party as a whole still took no observable interest in antireligious activity. Yet not long after this congress a movement did emerge, accompanied by radical disagreement concerning its every phase: form, content, and method of propaganda, as well as—or perhaps most of all—the leadership of such activity. If the 1923 resolution was totally in harmony with the view of propaganda in depth continually propounded by Iaroslavsky, not all of those in the field agreed. Neither then nor for many years thereafter was there unanimity among those interested on the policy to be pursued against religion. In actual practice propaganda and agitation often took on extremely crude aspects and pursued a very short-range course. In fact, Iaroslavsky's organization, at first called *Obshchestvo druzei gazety 'Bezbozhnika'* (Society of Friends of the Newspaper Bezbozhnik, or ODGB), was hardly spawned when its president entered into heated and prolonged public debate with another antireligious faction, grouped around another periodical, a debate which the party itself was eventually called in to settle. That no such decision was handed down until the question of leadership in the party itself had been virtually eliminated by Stalin's consolidation of power is significant.

The antireligious debate, which lasted from 1923 to 1926, began against the background of great restiveness in the country and the

35. Ibid., p. 745.

party. In the summer of 1923 strikes and economic difficulties beset the land, and a demand for freedom of discussion and an opposition to bureaucracy led by Trotsky broke out in the party. It was not a time for creating additional factions among the populace, but rather one of rallying and unifying by any means possible. In early June the central soviet of trade unions warned all local organizations not to allow any deviations from the Twelfth Party Congress line on antireligious propaganda. The newspaper *Bezbozhnik* carried repeated warnings of this nature, and on May 27 Iaroslavsky wrote of the need to improve relations between believers and nonbelievers among the workers, avoiding coercion in religious questions.[36]

The approach was to be positive and enlightened. The basic forms to be used were lectures, papers, and discussions. That summer the Moscow party committee stressed the preparation of rural antireligious workers. There was a drive to enlist the aid of nonparty specialists. Seminars in Moscow and Petrograd and other areas became methodological centers which worked out programs for discussion circles and individual lecturers.[37] Public debates were common, but the party warned of the need for caution.[38]

The newspaper *Bezbozhnik* had quickly widened its sphere of influence by means of a net of correspondents and readers throughout the country, but it now also had a rival publication which followed a propaganda line in most ways directly opposed to *Bezbozhnik's*. Beginning on January 4, 1923, a monthly journal of mass circulation, also called *Bezbozhnik*, began to appear in Moscow. Aimed especially at city readers, it did not spare crudity or "strong words," as one of its editors observed, to disabuse its readers of their beliefs.[39] With its third issue the title was changed to *Bezbozhnik u stanka* (The godless at the workbench), in order to define its readership and defend its policy, which was deemed too harsh for a rural audience. Its editor was M. M. Kostelovskaia, then secretary of the Moscow party committee. Around this new, hard-line journal there gathered those who held that atheistic propaganda should focus on exposing

36. N. A. Chemerissky, "Iziatie v 1922 g. tserkovnykh tsennostei dlia pomoshchi golodaiushchim" [The confiscation in 1922 of church valuables in aid of the starving], *VIRA* 10 (Moscow, 1962): 209.

37. Krylov, "Iz istorii propagandy ateizma," pp. 168–69,

38. Ibid., p. 180.

39. Savelev, "Em. Iaroslavsky," pp. 38, 40.

the class role of religion, and that the natural-science approach was mere "enlightenment" (*prosvetitelstvo*).[40]

The new publication did not have long to wait for a reaction from the party organ concerned with antireligious propaganda. The commission of the Central Committee concerned with the separation decree came out against the new journal on February 20, 1923. It called the attention of the Central Committee to the fact that the journal put out by the Moscow party organization "totally contradicts the line taken by the antireligious commission on the question of antireligious propaganda" and declared that it considered the publication "totally inappropriate and even harmful." The antireligious commission therefore requested that the Central Committee merge the journal with the newspaper *Bezbozhnik*.[41]

Since Iaroslavsky was head of the commission, a power play may be suspected. The interesting fact is that nothing was done for at least three years. Even though he held office in several key bodies, Iaroslavsky apparently was not able to rally enough support or interest in the Central Committee to counter the opposition view and the influence of the Moscow party secretary.

Meanwhile, both the newspaper and the journal began to organize supporting groups. The group around *Bezbozhnik u stanka* formed the Moscow Society of Godless in the fall of 1923. The next summer followers of *Bezbozhnik* sent resolutions to its editorship demanding unification. On August 28, 1924, the founding meeting of the ODGB was held, at which a temporary constitution was adopted and the presidium of its central soviet chosen, with Iaroslavsky at its head. Cells were organized in various parts of the country, despite opposition in some places, notably the Ukraine, and in the Red Army.[42] On April 19, 1925, a congress of the ODGB and correspondents of the newspaper *Bezbozhnik* met to settle methodological questions. In June, the group became the League of the Godless (the adjective

---

40. Ibid., pp. 37–38.
41. Ibid., p. 39.
42. V. Shishakov, "Soiuz voinstvuiushchikh bezbozhnikov (1925–1931)," in *Voinstvuiushchee bezbozhie*, pp. 324–25, 328; also, G. Struchkov, "Antireligioznaia rabota v Krasnoi Armii" [Antireligious work in the Red Army], ibid., p. 418. The resistance in the Ukraine is generally attributed to a reaction against excesses in the carrying out of the first Komsomol Christmas. It is worth noting, however, that the chairman of the Ukrainian Sovnarkom was Trotsky's long-time friend, Christian Rakovsky. The other pocket of resistance, the Red Army, was of course still totally in Trotsky's command.

"militant" was added at the organization's second congress in June 1929),[43] forming the first all-union atheistic society.[44]

By this time the debate on content and method had boiled over into the central press. It had first appeared in print with an article by S. Polidorov, one of the chief staff members of the journal *Bezbozhnik u stanka*, which appeared in *Sputnik Kommunista* [(The communist's companion) 1924, nos. 2–3], the organ of the Moscow party committee. Polidorov's article, "Antiklerikaly i bezbozhniki: Dve linii v antireligioznoi propagande" (Anti-clericalists and atheists; two approaches in antireligious propaganda) pointed to the two tendencies in antireligious propaganda evident during 1923 and 1924, which, he said, should be brought into the open and the differences submitted to discussion before the party. The immediate focus of his attack was the allegedly permissive attitude of the Iaroslavsky faction toward renewal-minded sectors of Orthodoxy and the schismatic "Living Church." This faction was labeled as anticlerical, because its enmity was said to be directed at the oldline clergy only, while Polidorov claimed for his camp the distinction of being genuinely godless.

But the differences were even broader, extending to other matters of content and method as well. As has been noted, the simple, direct, life-related approach with a sharp cutting edge was the method advocated by the Moscow party committee. Polidorov considered Iaroslavsky's method of complicated comparisons with myths of other more ancient religions, religions which had hardly been studied by Marxist scholars, to be ineffectual and useless. Propaganda should take facts from the religious life of the present, not the past. He maintained that the evidence showed which approach was the correct one.[45]

Prompt replies to Polidorov's salvo were given in *Bezbozhnik* by Gorev, now associated with Iaroslavsky, and in *Sputnik Kommunista* by Iaroslavsky himself, in an article entitled "Marksizm i anarkhizm" (Marxism and anarchism). The discussion then moved to the pages of *Pravda*. On January 25, 1925, Kostelovskaia published an article there entitled "Ob oshibkakh v antireligioznoi propagande" (On mistakes

43. Shishakov, "Soiuz voinstvuiushchikh," p. 334.

44. Ibid., p. 326. There were local organizations earlier. The oldest is reported to be that founded in Voronezh in 1921. Cf. ibid., 324.

45. Savelev, "Em. Iaroslavsky," pp. 38, 40.

in antireligious propaganda), which was quickly answered, also in
Pravda, by Iaroslavsky's "O metodakh antireligioznoi propagandy"
(On methods of antireligious propaganda). In his articles Iaroslavsky
rejected any "impoverishment of content of scientific-atheistic propaganda" and criticized the other side's superficiality and essential
frivolity of approach.[46]

To support his point—this was a technique which had only
recently come into use—he invoked the authority of Lenin. In 1909
Lenin had indicated the necessity of explaining the source of faith
and religion among the masses in materialist terms. "Therefore,"
asserted Iaroslavsky, "we will continue the work of studying religion,
and we advise our comrade antireligionists not to let the names of
vanished gods and goddesses frighten them, but search behind them
for the social structure which produced them, the social relationships which produced faith in these gods."[47] In reply to Kostelovskaia's implication that his work was not even Marxist, Iaroslavsky
again appealed to Lenin, this time to the 1922 article, "O znachenii
voinstvuiushchego materializma" (On the significance of militant
materialism) where Lenin sanctioned the use of bourgeois criticisms
of religion.[48]

In contrast, the propaganda of *Bezbozhnik u stanka* consisted in
large part of priest-baiting and mockery of religious practices, while
the program of studies it organized for a beginning workers' circle
included such titles as "Religion and the Class Struggle" and "Religion and the State," shunning any attempt at a scientific explanation
of the origin of the world or of man. In fact Kostelovskaia held that
science and religion could coexist peacefully. Indeed, she maintained,
the effect of introducing science into the picture was to refine
religious belief and enable it to adapt to scientific discoveries and
theories, thus rendering it more dangerous than ever.[49]

Kostelovskaia and Iaroslavsky disagreed sharply on other points
as well. The latter linked antireligious propaganda and moral
behavior by demanding of the members of ODGB abstention from

46. Ibid.
47. Ibid., pp. 40–41.
48. Ibid., p. 42.
49. Ibid., pp. 43–44. It is most interesting that this view was decisively defeated as a
premise of antireligious propaganda in the mid-twenties, since today's propagandists
frequently are found warning against a "refined" type of religion which claims to be able
to coexist with science.

intoxicants in the interests of more effective propaganda, and in general stressed the need for personal example. Kostelovskaia scoffed at this "asceticism," which she claimed smacked of sectarianism or Tolstoyanism. Iaroslavsky also included in his moral code the insistence that the *bezbozhniki* should in no way practice religion, a matter which some propagandists, strangely enough, considered a private concern.[50]

The two editors differed strongly on the degree of party participation needed in antireligious propaganda. Iaroslavsky, defending the distinctions he made between different factions within the Orthodox church, insisted that the political attitudes of such groups toward Soviet power had to be considered. Kostelovskaia answered that politics was one thing and antireligious propaganda another, and that the party, not the government, stood at the head of antireligious propaganda. Iaroslavsky buttressed his position with Lenin's 1922 demand for antireligious propaganda to supplement and correct the work of state institutions, thus implying a cooperation between state and party in the matter.[51]

Furthermore, there was disagreement on who should carry on the propaganda. Kostelovskaia, holding that the young worker was not totally irreligious, demanded that the organizers of antireligious propaganda in rural areas should be workers from the masses, who must "prepare for the village an antireligious dictatorship." Her view that the antireligious propagandist must be a party member was directly opposed to Iaroslavsky's contention that party and nonparty people must be brought into close cooperation in this as in other matters, and that antireligious activity was in its way a step to *partynost* (identification with the goals of the party program). On this point there was confusion in the ranks of Iaroslavsky's ODGB. Talk of the necessity of party membership, according to one writer, "hindered the growth of the League of the Godless as a mass organization."[52]

In sum, then, this running battle involved basic disagreements about whether the business at hand was the immediate destruction of a relatively limited and superficial phenomenon or the reconstruction

50. Ibid. Savelev observes that Kostelovskaia in effect turned over questions of morality to churchmen and preachers.
51. Ibid., p. 45.
52. Ibid., pp. 45–46.

of a worldview by long-term education. The former view led to a hard-line policy which gave no quarter to religious belief, while the latter, no less determined, was at the same time more patient and more pragmatic in attaining its goals. Furthermore, the hard-line faction wanted antireligious propaganda to be exclusively a party undertaking, while Iaroslavsky's program called for a broader base. Both sides insisted that their views were the only correct ones, and both openly demanded that the matter be settled by the party.

In addition to these positions of the center and the left ("leftist deviation" as the latter came to be called) there was a rightist position made up of those who resisted any party activity on the religious front at all, on the grounds that religion would die out of itself if ignored. Part of this attitude, the *samotek*, or liquidationist, theory may have been a reaction to excesses in the struggle against religion—administrative measures or over-enthusiastic propaganda. Whatever its cause, insofar as it was localized, this opposition was centered in the Ukraine. In 1925 a book published there openly advocated the liquidation of atheistic propaganda as an independent part of the party program of political education.[53] Some Ukrainians even managed to interpret the pronouncements of the Thirteenth Party Congress on the use of materialistic explanations of nature and social life as a signal for abandoning any criticism which approached religion from the point of view of class associations.

Another stubborn source of resistance to active propagandizing against religion was to be found in the teaching profession. Teachers and school directors seemed perennially prone to support the *samotek* theory in practice by adopting a policy of "nonreligious" rather than antireligious education.

This indifference of the right could hardly be overcome through issuing decrees. Iaroslavsky struck out against the liquidationist position in a new monthly methodological journal, *Antireligioznik* (The antireligious worker) in an article entitled "Nado li organizovyvat vsiudu soiuz bebozhnikov?" (Should leagues of the godless be organized everywhere?).[54] Despite these early efforts, however, the problem was to be with him and his organization for a long time to come.

53. Ibid., p. 47. The book was a collection of articles, entitled *Puti antireligioznoi propagandy* [The paths of antireligious propaganda], edited by Viktoriia Ulasevich.
54. Ibid., p. 48.

Iaroslavsky thus faced opposition from both the right and the left in his stand on antireligious propaganda, though obviously the left offered much more vigorous opposition. The open debate stormed on for two years. At last, however, the party Central Committee, which had remained officially aloof during the extended quarrel, stepped in and confirmed Iaroslavsky's central position. A special conference on antireligious propaganda was organized in connection with the Central Committee on April 27–30, 1926, to consider the disputed questions. Present were twenty-five leading party workers from regional party organizations and thirty from Moscow. The theses accepted at that meeting, and subsequently confirmed by the Central Committee, were prepared by the central soviet of the League of the Godless and the editorial staffs of the newspaper *Bezbozhnik* and the journal *Antireligioznik*.[55] Since Iaroslavsky was president of the League and editor of both periodicals, it is no surprise to find in the theses a summary of the principles he had been defending over the past several years. In regard to the leftist deviation it was said that:

The underestimation of the significance of the subjective side of religion . . . and the attempt to limit our task to mere exposure of religion as a method of enslaving the workers, ultimately leads to a narrowing of the scope of antireligious propaganda and reduces it to a superficial mass-rally sort of agitation. This in turn permits the growth of those oversimplified mechanistic, unscientific, and often idealistic interpretations of religion as something invented by the ruling classes and the priests. Furthermore, such a limitation of our work deprives us of achieving the broadest impact of our ideological influence, especially among the proletarian masses where religious sentiments are far from extinct. Following this course we would be forced to hit "the peaks of the masses" only. This type of "proletarian aristocracy" is politically very dangerous.[56]

The deviation of the right was also denounced:

According to the "liquidationist" view, antireligious propaganda should be divorced from the concrete questions of class struggle which are met in everyday life and politics. This view holds that such propaganda should be liquidated and replaced by mere "enlightenment," the simple dissemination of knowledge from the natural sciences. Such a deviation is equally harmful, since it is well-known that no "culture," no system of education is of itself capable of saving man from the opium of religion.[57]

55. Ibid., p. 49.
56. *Antireligioznik*, no. 8, 1926, p. 65.
57. Ibid.

The theses further stressed the importance of understanding the milieu of the believer and of adapting propaganda to it. An entire section considered the problem of propaganda among national minorities, with stress on understanding national religious nuances. The practical conclusions underscored a key principle which had been advanced by Iaroslavsky in his fight with Kostelovskaia: antireligious propaganda could not and should not be considered the responsibility of the party alone. A large group of Bezbozhnik activists—peasants and workers—should be created around the party to promote the work.[58]

Thus, Iaroslavsky seemed to have won a total victory. He had apparently defeated the "assault" mentality of the left and convinced the party that conquering religion was a slow, serious process, one that demanded and deserved the party's full cooperation. The central coordination at which Iaroslavsky aimed, however, was not ultimately attained until the Second Congress of the League of the Militant Godless in 1929.[59] But the theoretical question as to the line antireligious propaganda was to take had been resolved. The creation of an ideal organization for promoting this line seemed now to be only a matter of time, tenacity, organizational skill, and sheer power, all turned toward overcoming resistance and apathy.

Points of particular significance here, however, are the "why" and "how" of this victory in the spring of 1926. Why had Iaroslavsky been unable to muster the support he wanted early in 1923? What had happened to enable him to obtain it three years later? The sparse and conflicting nature of the evidence makes any answer largely conjectural. Still, a brief look at the political developments of the period and Iaroslavsky's relationship to them suggests some possible readings. Iaroslavsky's overriding concern on the antireligious front was the central coordination of propaganda in reliable hands—his own—where it would be treated with proper seriousness and where it might be used, in the words of the resolution of the Twelfth Party Congress, as a powerful "means of spreading party influence among the wide mass of the workers." Eventually he achieved a structure which had a virtual monopoly on atheistic propaganda, a structure closely linked to the party but extending its lines far beyond it. What-

58. Ibid., p. 69.
59. Shishakov, "Soiuz voinstvuiushchikh," p. 328.

ever other shades of meaning it may have, the story of this organization's rise and success is, to a significant degree, a paradigm and a function of what was happening in the larger arena of the party: bureaucratization and the centralization of power under Stalin. It is in the relationship of the smaller picture to the larger that the explanation of the above puzzle may be found.

One consequence of the civil war which gradually became apparent was the consolidation of power in the hands of the top leadership. Yet very soon opposition to excessive centralization and bureaucratic control made itself heard. The first major phase of this dispute came with the rise of the Worker's Opposition in 1920. This group's demand for the control and management of industry by the trade unions was dealt with at the Tenth Party Congress in March of 1921. The resolution "On Party Unity" prepared the way for the party purge of 1921–22 and laid the foundation for the future monolithic party. Stalin was to use the resolution well as he gradually rid himself of every audible source of dissent. In the meantime, in a relatively inconspicuous way, he consolidated himself in positions which allowed him to build his own machine, an organization within an organization. It is through this inner organization that Iaroslavsky enters the picture.

An old Bolshevik reared in the Trans-Baikal region among political deportees, Iaroslavsky was already a professional revolutionary of long standing in 1917.[60] In July of that year he was one of a number of Siberian exiles who made their way back to Moscow and helped prepare the October Revolution. A member of the Moscow military-revolutionary committee in October[61] and later the first commissar

60. His true name was Minei Izrailovich Gubelman. A eulogy delivered at a general meeting of the Academy of Sciences shortly after his death on December 4, 1943, describes him as the son of a peasant in Chita, Zabaikal province, a furrier who later became a teacher. His mother was a fisherman's daughter. In 1898 he organized the first Social Democratic circle among workers on the Trans-Baikal railroad. In 1901 he went abroad, where he met leading revolutionaries. After his arrest in Chita in 1902 for illegal printing, he became an underground, professional revolutionary, traveling about the country doing organizational work. His extensive work in Iaroslavl led him to settle on the pseudonym Iaroslavsky. He was a delegate to the Fourth and Fifth Bolshevik Congresses. His fourth arrest, in July 1907, interrupted his activities for some time. He was sentenced to seven years' hard labor, following which he was exiled to Iakutsk, from which he traveled to Moscow in 1917. See I. I. Mints, "Akademik Emelian Mikhailovich Iaroslavsky" [Academician Emelian Mikhailovich Iaroslavsky], *Obshchee sobranie AN SSSR 14–17 fevr. 1944 goda* (General Meeting of the Academy of Sciences of the USSR, Feb. 14–17, 1944], (Moscow–Leningrad, 1944), pp. 147–57.

61. Sheinman, "Propagandist ateizma," pp. 75–76.

of the Kremlin,[62] in 1918 Iaroslavsky was a left communist and at the Eighth Party Congress in 1919, as part of the military opposition, he was ranged opposite Stalin.[63] During 1919 he was dispatched to do agitational work in the interior.[64] In 1921 he was recalled to Moscow where he became involved in the central party organization in what can be seen retrospectively as a direct relationship to Stalin. This came about through efforts to regularize the party's central machinery following Sverdlov's death in 1919. Three new organs were set up by the Central Committee for this purpose: the Politburo, the Orgburo, and the Secretariat. Stalin shortly assumed practical direction of the six-member Secretariat. In 1920 the Ninth Party Congress passed a resolution to add three full-time members to this body. These new members, however, soon disgraced themselves by taking a position against Lenin and with Trotsky in the 1920–21 dispute over trade unions. As a result they were replaced at the Tenth Party Congress by Molotov, Mikhailov, and Iaroslavsky, who also were made members of the Central Committee. Concerning these appointments, E. H. Carr has observed: "It is perhaps worth noting that the three dispossessed members of the Secretariat were to become Stalin's enemies and two out of the three new members his staunchest supporters. For the first time Stalin's hand may with plausibility be discerned in crucial party appointments."[65] The fact that Iaroslavsky was one of the two implies that in 1921 he was already a Stalin man, to a degree. But when and how this alliance took place the record, unfortunately, so far does not reveal.[66]

On April 4, 1922, Stalin became general secretary. It was from this vantage point that later, after the demise of Lenin, his drive for

62. V. Ruban, *Emelian Iaroslavsky v "Pravde" 1918–1919* gg. [Emelian Iaroslavsky in *Pravda*, 1918–19], (Kiev, 1959), p. 4.

63. Jan M. Maijer, ed., *The Trotsky Papers, 1917–1922* (The Hague, 1964), vol. 1, *1917–1919*, pp. 300–301, n. 7.

64. Ibid., p. 308, n. 1.

65. E. H. Carr, *The Bolshevik Revolution, 1917–1923* (London, 1950), 1: 204.

66. It is known that both Stalin and Iaroslavsky were at the Tammerfors Bolshevik Conference in December of 1905. Long after the fact, Iaroslavsky wrote: "It was my great fortune to be present at this Conference, which was attended by Lenin and Stalin, and to work with Comrade Stalin on the commission for drawing up the political resolution" (E. Iaroslavsky, *Landmarks in the Life of Stalin* [Moscow, 1940], p. 47. The bias of this work is so great as to minimize its reliability. Had there been any other open connection between them, however, Iaroslavsky would doubtless have mentioned it. The fact that Iaroslavsky went to the provinces in 1919, after his left Communist stance, and returned to Moscow in 1921 to become a member of the Central Committee and immediate supporter of Stalin allows the conjecture that his return depended to a degree on this support. But there is, of course, no direct evidence for this supposition.

power was launched. It is surely not amiss to see him, even at this stage, building his apparatus. The Secretariat was certainly not his only base of operation. And it is to be noted how often, as Stalin assumed control over one party organ after another, Iaroslavsky appeared there in some capacity. Among the official contacts between them, apart from the Secretariat, two others are worth noting. From 1919 Stalin had been Commissar of the Workers' and Peasants' Inspectorate (*Rabkrin*), set up by Lenin in the hope of cleansing every branch of the administration of inefficiency and corruption. However partial its success, it gave Stalin an admirable opportunity to keep an eye on the entire party administration, from top to bottom. Besides this, in 1920 the Central Control Commission was formed, attached to the party Central Committee. It was intended to serve as a tribunal for exposing bureaucratic malpractice within the party. However, as reformulated at the Tenth Party Congress in 1921, the commission's role was, through its regional and local branches, that of "strengthening the unity and authority of the party."[67] The Eleventh Party Congress in 1922 further strengthened the Commission's control over local bodies.[68] Since the General Secretariat was the coordinating link between the Central Control Commission and the Central Committee, Stalin came to dominate the commission and in effect—though it was not immediately apparent—was assured of having the party's entire control apparatus in his hands.

An indicator of the growing control exercised by Stalin through these two bodies was the fact that Iaroslavsky was given responsible positions in each. From 1923 the latter worked as a member of the college of the People's Commissariat of *Rabkrin* and as secretary of the Central Commission, and was beginning to be openly known as a Stalin man.[69] In addition, Iaroslavsky came to hold other positions; he was a member of the Central Executive Committee of the Congress of Soviets of the USSR, a deputy to the Supreme Soviet, and sat on the editorial boards of the chief party organs, *Pravda* and *Bolshevik*.[70] In such positions he must have been an invaluable lieutenant for a a rising dictator.

The question to be asked, at this juncture, is how this relationship of Iaroslavsky and Stalin affected the antireligious movement. To

67. *KPSS*, p. 533.
68. *KPSS*, p. 636.
69. E. H. Carr, *The Interregnum, 1923–1924* (London, 1954), p. 313.
70. Sheinman, "Propaganda ateizma," p. 76.

put it another way, how did their connections serve the ends of each? Versatile and productive though he was in a variety of fields, there seems no doubt that Iaroslavsky was especially partial to work in the antireligious field. An intellectual, a revolutionary, and an organization man, he devoted a generous share of his abilities to the struggle against religion. The reasons for this are probably a blend of the early background of the man, his conviction about the need to eradicate religion if the revolution was to prosper, and a canny opportunism which saw leadership of the antireligious movement as a promising fulcrum for personal power. At any rate, he clearly regarded the extirpation of religion as a prerequisite for the establishment of socialism, and never wavered, it would seem, in his efforts to publicize his views on why and how this must be accomplished.

A historian himself, Iaroslavsky firmly held to the long-range view of religion and its socio-historic causes. Rejecting the view of religion as a mere "deception of the priests," he also rejected administrative measures against religion. In his view it could only be eliminated by propaganda based on the achievements of science. To this end he wrote numerous antireligious works.[71] The very single-mindedness and persistence of Iaroslavsky's work in the movement indicates that this role, whether or not it depended totally on his own initiative, was to his liking and advantage. On the other side, Stalin was not one to overlook a potential instrument of control, in this case the movement itself, which could be secured only by keeping it out of the hands of a rival and placing it in those of a trusted subordinate.

These considerations touching Iaroslavsky, Stalin, and the larger political background throw considerable light on the development and fate of the antireligious movement. It seems likely that Stalin did indeed use Iaroslavsky in 1922 to take control of antireligious propaganda from Trotsky.[72] It is also plausible to see a direct relationship between Stalin's rise to power and the success of Iaroslavsky in his endeavors.

71. Ibid., p. 87.
72. In spite of the rivalry indicated by Trotsky, Deutscher is probably not correct when, in describing Trotsky's numerous occupations, he says: "He led, for instance, the Society of the Godless before Iaroslavsky took over its direction. He led it in a spirit of philosophical enlightenment which was least likely to produce those excesses, offensive to the sentiment of the believers, which marred the Society's work under Iaroslavsky" (Isaac Deutscher, *The Prophet Unarmed. Trotsky: 1921–1929* [London, 1959], p. 28.) Deutscher bases this observation on Trotsky's role in the 1922 gathering of church valuables, and seems to be under the impression that the Society existed at that time.

Iaroslavsky's role in the denunciation of Trotsky is a matter of record and was considered by the latter as decisive in Iaroslavsky's career.[73] Another question relevant to the antireligious movement pertains to the rivalry between the two men. Was there, besides the political consideration, a real disagreement between them on the actual conduct of antireligious propaganda? If his writings are an indication, Trotsky's attitude toward religion differed markedly from Iaroslavsky's, if only because the subject occupies almost no place there. One brief article, which appeared, significantly, in *Pravda* in July of 1923, may be taken to sum up Trotsky's views on the degree of religion's hold on the masses, as well as on the usefulness of antireligious propaganda.

Religious sentiments among the Russian working class are almost non-existent. In fact, they never existed. The Orthodox church was a bureaucratic organization and a domestic ritual. It never penetrated deeply into the people's consciousness, nor did it manage to relate its dogmas and canons to their inner experience. The reason was . . . the lack of culture in Old Russia, and this was true of the church as well. Therefore, having awakened to culture, the Russian worker is easily freed from his purely external links to the church. True, it is a more difficult matter with the peasantry, but not because he is more deeply involved in the church's teaching—there is no indication of that—but because his stagnant and monotonous environment is closely allied to the stagnant and monotonous ritual of the Church.[74]

Religion, thus, is a matter of custom, and its ritual relieves the otherwise bare expanses of life. How is it to be extirpated? "Antireligious propaganda is not enough." Of course it is necessary, he concedes, but it reaches only a minority, the most thoughtful. The vast majority are unaffected by antireligious propaganda simply because they do not think. For them he proposes that the cinema, which supplies all that the church has offered, can be an effective replacement for religion. Furthermore, it might be a source of revenue for the government.

A comparison of Trotsky's views (expressed in *Pravda* at the very

73. Trotsky, *My Life*, p. 492. It is appropriate to note here that the opposition of views between Trotsky and Iaroslavsky existed in areas other than the antireligious movement; for example, in the literary field. When the leaders of VAPP, the most militant of the literary proletarians, began publication of the journal *Na postu* [On guard], in August, 1923, listed among the journal's collaborators was Emelian Iaroslavsky (Brown, *The Proletarian Episode in Russian Literature*, pp. 19, 248, n. 77).

74. "Vodka, tserkov i kinematograf" [Vodka, the church and the cinema], *Sobranie sochieneny* 21 (Moscow–Leningrad, 1927): 22–26. Reprinted from *Pravda*, no. 154, 12 July 1923.

time when the factional quarrel concerning antireligious propaganda was mustering strength), with those of the rival parties reveals at least two facts. First, Trotsky and Iaroslavsky were in basic disagreement on the tenacity of religion's hold on the people and, consequently, on what should be done about it. Second, while on the question of religion's influence Trotsky's position largely coincides with that of Kostelovskaia and her camp, on the manner of dealing with religion he differs. In fact, judging by the statement above, Trotsky's position is basically "liquidationist," and therefore akin to the attitude prevalent in the Ukraine, where the party was dominated by his long-time friend Rakovsky.

The struggle for leadership between Iaroslavsky and the *Bezbozhnik u stanka* group probably cannot be regarded as simply another aspect of the Trotsky-Iaroslavsky opposition. The Moscow party secretary who headed the leftist faction may well have had support higher up, but without further information there is no reason to link this faction with Trotsky. The rightist position, based in the Ukraine and especially strong in the teachers' union, by its very nature offered no candidate to lead the movement, but rather resisted any leadership whatsoever.

The controversy had raged for two years before the SVB was founded. However, the SVB quickly gathered strength and by the end of 1925 began to look like a mass movement, viable and potentially useful, especially in the sensitive rural areas, where *Bezbozhnik u stanka* had antagonized the populace. Iaroslavsky's way was presumably being made easier. For, returning to the purely political, if Iaroslavsky's success is to be linked with Stalin's rise and Trotsky's decline, the obvious fact is that in February, 1923, when Iaroslavsky first appealed for party support for his antireligious program, the struggle for power had not yet broken into the open. Lenin was still alive, though ailing, and Trotsky was still powerful; Stalin had a distance to go before his authority could be absolutized. By 1925, however, Stalin was in a position to show judicious support to the movement, and by the spring of 1926 he could act decisively. Throughout 1925 Stalin had been involved in political moves of the first magnitude. He had broken with the triumvirate consisting of himself, Zinoviev, and Kamenev, which had first displaced Trotsky. Next he had moved into a new alliance with Bukharin, Rykov, and Tomsky, who emerged as spokesmen for the newly forming right wing in the party and the Politburo, while Zinoviev and Kamenev headed the new left wing.

At this juncture the factions froze into opposing positions on almost every phase of party policy. Very likely it was this conjunction of facts which precipitated the party's entry into such fields as antireligious activity, where it had previously withheld confirmation of any one group. Its entrance, as has been pointed out, was on the middle ground. But if in the mid-twenties Stalin still behaved as a man of moderation who threw his weight behind the middle-of-the-road settlement, he was nonetheless heading in the direction of total control. Meanwhile, Iaroslavsky's position in the antireligious movement between right and left corresponded to Stalin's current style. The principles of the 1926 resolution on antireligious propaganda were destined to be partially qualified in the near future. Indeed, they reasserted themselves in their original form only in the late thirties, shortly to be suspended again by wartime needs. Nonetheless, today they seem once again to have been reinstated as norms of antireligious work, and the leftist and rightist deviations are both again cited as perennial dangers.

This entire early period is now being singled out for study. Motivated by concern over the persistence of religion after a half-century of official atheism, today's Soviet antireligionists are re-examining and utilizing the past. Current trends toward using various academic disciplines, notably the social sciences, to study and combat the phenomenon of religion seek and find support in the theories of Iaroslavsky. The relative effectiveness of the SVB organization, through which he attempted to coordinate and direct antireligious efforts, makes a study of its formative period relevant. Students of the Soviet religious situation, past and present, may find it worthwhile to acquaint themselves with this reevaluation.

7

KHRUSHCHEV'S RELIGIOUS POLICY
1959-1964

The late fifties and early sixties saw a renewed commitment to the atheistic tenets of communist ideology in the Soviet Union. If the postwar Stalin years were ones of detente between church and state, the consolidation of power in the hands of Khrushchev resulted in a unilateral withdrawal of the government from the modus vivendi which had been worked out during the war. The state, despite the continued cooperation of the church, now attempted to breathe new life into the doctrine that religion must disappear with the demise of capitalism. The antireligious campaign of the early sixties revived and, in some respects, intensified the policy of the prewar period.

The 1959–64 campaign was not without precedents in the mid-fifties. Khrushchev himself had issued a call for moderation on November 10, 1954, which effectively terminated the "Hundred Days" campaign.[1] Inasmuch as that abortive campaign against religion seems to have been associated with Malenkov,[2] it is probable that the irenic tenor of this statement represented a tactic in the struggle for power, rather than an accurate index of Khrushchev's

1. *Pravda*, 11 November 1954; reprinted in *Kommunisticheskaia partiia i sovetskoe pravitelstvo o religii i tserkvi* [The Communist party and the Soviet government on religion and the church] (Moscow: State Publishing House for Political Literature, 1959), p. 106.
2. Helene and Pierre Lazareff, *The Soviet Union after Stalin* (London, 1955), p. 202. See also Joshua Rothenberg, "The Legal Status of Religion in the Soviet Union," chapter 5 above.

Donald A. Lowrie and William C. Fletcher

own approach to the religious question.[3] In his Central Committee report at the Twentieth Congress in 1956 there was a hint of what the future might hold:

> But it would be wrong to think that the survivals of capitalism in the minds of people have already been wiped out. Unfortunately, in our fine and industrious Soviet family one can still meet people who do not participate in productive labor and do not perform useful work for the family or for society. One can also meet people who maliciously violate the rules of the socialist community. It is impossible to stamp out these ugly manifestations merely by administrative measures, without the participation of the masses themselves.[4]

There was no explicit reference to religion in this statement, although the phrase "survivals of capitalism" might raise the issue in the minds of those well-versed in party semantics. In his report to the Twenty-first Congress in 1959 Khrushchev's treatment of capitalist survivals was even less pointed.[5]

But the campaign was definitely taking shape. In the "building of communism" discussions at the Twenty-first Congress a renewal of antireligious effort could be foreseen.[6] In fact, it was rumored that a secret resolution was adopted by the congress calling for the elimination of all religion from the USSR during the seven-year plan then under discussion.[7]

Certainly there is evidence that the Russian Orthodox church correctly read the portents. In December, 1959, it moved to defend itself by excommunicating recent clerical defectors to atheism,[8] and early in 1960 its leaders gave dire warning of troubles to come.[9] Im-

3. G. D. Embree, *The Soviet Union Between the 19th and 20th Party Congress, 1952–56* (The Hague, 1959), pp. 106–7; Konrad Kellen, *Khrushchev: A Political Portrait* (New York, 1961), p. 131.

4. Translation from Leo Gruliow, ed., *Current Soviet Policies*, vol. 2 (New York, 1957), p. 54.

5. Ibid., 3: 54.

6. Constantin de Grunwald, *The Churches and the Soviet Union* (New York, 1962), pp. 61–64; cf. "A Program for an Atheistic Society," *Nauka i religiia*, September 1961, translated in *Joint Publications Research Service* (hereafter *JPRS*), 10, 899, no. 5 (11 January 1961), p. 6.

7. Donald A. Lowrie, "The Russian Church at New Delhi," *Christian Century*, 1 November 1961, p. 1299.

8. "Vypiska iz postanovleniia sviateishego patriarkha i sviashchennogo sinoda no. 23, 30 dekabria, 1959 goda" [Excerpt from ordinance no. 23 of his holiness, the patriarch, and the holy synod, Dec. 30, 1959], *Zhurnal moskovskoi patriarkhii* [Journal of the Moscow patriarchate] (hereafter *ZHMP*), February 1960, p. 27.

9. I Khiberin, "Tezoimenitstvo sviateishego patriarkha Aleksiia" [The nameday of his holiness, Patriarch Aleksy], *ZHMP*, April 1960, pp. 19–20.

mediately thereafter the nascent antireligious campaign broke into the open in unmistakable terms.

On January 10, 1960, the Central Committee issued a call for more antireligious propaganda.[10] On January 27 *Pravda* announced that the Society for the Dissemination of Political and Scientific Knowledge, which, among its other duties, bore sole responsibility for antireligious propaganda, had held a congress attended by Brezhnev, Kosygin, Mikoyan, Suslov, and others of the top leadership.[11] Two days later, the first secretary of the Moldavian party's central committee demanded that "the Council of Ministers and local party and governmental organs must not let a single violation of Soviet legislation by the clergy go unpunished."[12] On February 18 his counterpart for Belorussia stated: "Certain churchmen have become so bold as to begin violating Soviet laws. In this, they have been encouraged by our officials in charge of ecclesiastical affairs, who, incidentally, far from being controllers of the activities of the churchmen, have in some cases virtually become their assistants."[13]

Three days later *Izvestiia* announced that G. G. Karpov, the chairman of the Council for the Affairs of the Russian Orthodox Church since that Council's inception, had been replaced by V. Kuroedov.[14] Concurrently, Metropolitan Nikolai, who had occupied a position in the Orthodox church similar to that of Karpov for the state, was replaced by Bishop Nikodim.[15] The removal of the two men who had come to symbolize the regime's policy of the forties was the first concrete evidence of a change in policy.

At the Twenty-second Congress of the party in 1961 Khrushchev openly gave his support to the antireligious campaign which by then was well under way.

The battle with survivals of capitalism in the consciousness of the people, the changing by our revolution of the habits and customs of millions of people built up over the centuries, is a prolonged and not a simple matter. Survivals of the past are a dreadful power, which, like a nightmare, prevail over the

---

10 A. Hakimoglu, "Forty Years of Anti-Religious Propaganda," *East Turkic Review*, no. 2 (December 1960), p. 69.

11. *Pravda*, 27 January 1960.

12. *Sovetskaia Moldaviia* [Soviet Moldavia], 29 January 1960, quoted in Boris Iwanow, ed., *Religion in the USSR* (Munich, 1960), p. 214.

13. Ibid., p. 215, quoting *Sovetskaia Belorussiia* (Soviet Belorussia), 18 February 1960.

14. *Izvestiia*, 21 February 1960.

15. "Opredeleniia sviashchennogo sinoda [Decisions of the holy synod], *ZHMP*, July 1960, p. 6, October 1960, p. 4.

minds of living creatures. They are rooted in the modes of life and in the consciousness of millions of people long after the economic conditions which gave birth to them have vanished. . . . Communist education presupposes emancipation from religious prejudices and superstitions, which hinder individual Soviet people from fully developing their creative powers. A well thought-out and well proportioned system of scientific atheist propaganda is necessary, which would embrace all strata and groups of society, to prevent the spread of religious attitudes, especially among children and juveniles. . . . The interests of building communism require that questions of communist education stand at the center of the attention and activity of each party organization, of all communities.[16]

Further elaboration on precisely what was intended was provided by the chief antireligious journal, *Nauka i religiia* (Science and religion), in April, 1962: "During the period of the personality cult, all churches, and the Orthodox church in particular, received a number of privileges which contradicted Lenin's decree on the separation of Church and State. . . ."[17] To correct this, the Council for the Affairs of the Russian Orthodox Church, which hitherto had been defined as a "means of contact between the government and the patriarchate," in 1961 was officially redefined as a supervisory organ for insuring the observance of Soviet laws by the church.[18] In March, 1963, *Nauka i religiia* noted that "several new stipulations concerning religious cult have recently been adopted," and defined the new laws in terms which considerably increased restrictions on religious activity, particularly with regard to participation in secular activities such as cinemas, plays, and clubs.[19] But this seems not to have been enough. At a closed meeting of the Central Committee of the party in June, 1963, Ilichev demanded more antireligious propaganda,[20] and in January, 1964, speaking officially as the chairman of the ideological section of the Central Committee, he put forth a fourteen-point program for a vastly expanded antireligious campaign.[21]

16. *Pravda*, 18 October 1962.

17. Nadezhda Teodorovich, "Increasing Pressure on the Moscow Patriarchate," *Bulletin of the Institute for the Study of the USSR*, October 1962, p. 47, quoting *Nauka i religiia*, April 1962, pp. 48–49.

18. Thomas E. Bird, "The Party, the Patriarch and the World Council," *Commonweal*, 13 April 1962, p. 55, citing *Sputnik ateista* [The atheist's companion].

19. E. Rozenbaum, "Decree on Freedom of Conscience," *Nauka i religiia*, March 1963, translation in *Religion in Communist-Dominated Areas* (*RCDA*), 17 June 1963, pp. 110–11.

20. L. F. Ilichev, "Primary Tasks of the Party Regarding Ideological Work," *Bakinsky rabochy* [The Baku worker], 19 June 1963, translated in *RCDA*, 19 August 1963, p. 152.

21. *Partynaia zhizn* [Party life], February 1964, pp. 22–26.

From the beginning the campaign of the sixties enjoyed explicit support by the highest levels of the regime. This represented a marked departure from prewar antireligious efforts. None of the former campaigns had had the explicit support of the top levels of party or government, but were conducted by functionaries well down in the ruling hierarchy. To be sure, Stalin on occasion had supported antireligious activity in informal interviews,[22] but none of these earlier efforts had anything like the measure of serious support which top-level officials now gave to the activities of the atheistic propagandists.

Antireligious Propaganda

Although there has perennially been some antireligious propaganda in the USSR, special campaigns against religion have always been accompanied by a radical increase in this propaganda. The campaign of the sixties was no exception. The Soviet state possesses a large and well-organized capability for propaganda, and it was quickly mobilized in support of the campaign.

At the beginning of the campaign, the Society for the Dissemination of Political and Scientific Knowledge had a membership of about eight hundred thousand.[23] Its scientific-atheistic section, created after the war, was a revival of the prewar nationwide network of local, provincial, and regional branches of the League of Militant Godless and many of its functionaries had experience from the prewar antireligious campaigns.[24]

Massive attempts were made to saturate the entire educational system with atheism, with the aim of making "scientific atheism" a required subject in every class in every school.[25] Scientifically-prepared texts and other teaching materials were prescribed for each grade. In addition to actual courses in atheism, every other subject in the curriculum was, ideally, to be taught from the atheistic viewpoint. Hundreds of special texts outlining the atheistic method

---

22. For example, see his statement of 9 September 1927 in *Sochineniia* [Works] (Moscow, 1947), 10: 132–33.

23. *Pravda*, 3 April 1959, and 27 January 1960.

24. Walter Kolarz, *Religion in the Soviet Union* (New York, 1962), p. 16.

25. K. Kindrat and S. Martseniuk, "The Sacred Cause of Educators," *Nauka i religiia*, September 1961, translated in *JPRS* 10899, no. 5, p. 40; "V institute nauchnogo ateizma" [In the institute of scientific atheism], *Politicheskaia samoobrazovanie* [Political self-education], April 1965, p. 143; A. Valentinov, "The Primer of Materialism—Notes of a Propaganda Worker," *Komsomolskaia pravda*, 14 June 1963.

of teaching algebra or agriculture or the history of engineering were
to be made available to teachers.[26] Teachers were constantly reminded that it was not sufficient that every student should leave school a
nonbeliever; the ideal was to turn every student into a propagandist
of atheism.[27]

Perhaps because such efforts were not sufficiently effective,
special schools of atheism were ordered to be established. Ilichev's
order of 1964 for increased university preparation in atheism had
been anticipated as early as 1959 by the creation of two universities
of atheism.[28] This was the situation by 1964, according to the report
of *Nauka i religiia*:

A long-cherished dream of scientists, lecturers and propagandists has been
realized. In the Academy of Social Sciences of the Central Committee of the
Communist party, an Institute of Scientific Atheism has recently opened its
doors. This is to be the research and methodological center for all the
atheistic work in the country. The new institution is intended to "direct and
coordinate scientific research and to prepare highly qualified leaders." The
Institute has two divisions: "Theory of scientific atheism and criticism of
modern religious ideology," and "Organization of atheistic education."[29]

Schools of atheism were also established at the local level by en-
listing the "Houses of Culture" in the campaign.[30] For example, in
Tbilisi in 1964 lectureships in scientific atheism were instituted and
very soon there were as many as thirteen such lectureships in the city.
An increase in the number of public meetings was reported, and
there were seven local atheistic people's universities, including "a
very successful university of atheism in one of the city's great
factories."[31]

In October, 1964, a section for the education of children and youth
in connection with the Central Soviet of the Pedagogical Society of
the RSFSR was announced. Among its students were "scientific"
workers, teachers in higher and middle, special and professional

26. For example, see V. S. Ovchinnikov, "Osnovy nauchnogo ateizma v tekhnicheskom
vuze" [The foundations of scientific atheism in the technical schools], *Voprosy
filosofii* [Problems of Philosophy], no. 7 (1961), pp. 141–44.
27. Valentinov, "Primer of Materialism."
28. T. Otto Nall, "The Hope for Religion in Russia," *Christian Century*, 4 March 1959,
p. 262.
29. "V dobry chas!" [It comes at a good time!], *Nauka i religiia*, September 1964, p. 53.
30. For example, *Partynaia zhizn*, no. 5 (March 1965), p. 80.
31. D. Gegeshidze, "Prisposoblivaiutsia . . ." [Adapting. . .], *Agitator*, no. 21, November 1964, pp. 46–47.

schools, workers in preschool institutions and Komsomol organizations. The basic task of the new section was the "study, comparison, and distribution of the best experience in atheistic education of children and youth."[32]

As in the prewar campaigns, publishing also played an important role in the campaign. With its thousands of titles per year and a total of over a billion printed volumes, the USSR claims to be the greatest book publishing concern in the world.[33] Atheistic books were issued in immense variety at this time, from serious volumes for college students, to beautiful children's books, as good from the viewpoint of scientific pedagogy as anything produced in the West. These were printed in nearly all the languages of the Soviet Union, skillfully adapted to the history and thought patterns of each group.[34] In addition, newspaper and magazine articles on atheism appeared almost daily and journals specializing in atheism were once again created[35] (their predecessors had been allowed to lapse in 1941).[36]

Considerable efforts were also devoted to increasing the number and improving the quality of atheistic lectures and talks (*besedy*). Nevertheless, one of the constant criticisms of atheist leaders was that the lectures in any given place were few and uninteresting. *Sovetskaia Moldaviia* (Soviet Moldavia) stated that on one large collective farm "only seven atheist lectures have been given in six months, and no individual work with believers is being conducted."[37] Poor attendance was often reported, since believers would not willingly attend atheist talks, and in many cases an audience was collected by announcing a topic of an entirely different nature, which, once the audience was seated, turned out to be the same old "godless" material.[38]

Some efforts were made toward the production of antireligious films, but here, too, the consensus seemed to be that sufficient utilization of this medium was still lacking.[39] Whereas the use of

32. *Nauka i religiia*, October 1964, p. 92.
33. *Politicheskoe samoobrazovanie*, April 1964.
34. *Christian Century*, 16 September 1964, pp. 1141–42; Teodorovich, "Increasing Pressure," quoting *Voiovnychy ateist* [The militant atheist], no. 4 (1962], pp. 62–63.
35. *Nauka i religiia*, *Voiovnychy ateist*, and *Liudina i svit* [Man and the world].
36. *New York Times*, 1 October 1941 and 7 October 1941.
37. *Sovetskaia Moldaviia*, 8 July 1964.
38. Ibid.
39. *Komsomolskaia pravda*, 31 August 1962; A. Baigushev, "Day against Night," *Literatura i zhizn* [Literature and life], 9 April 1961; "Protiv ravnodushnykh" [Against those who are indifferent], *Nauka i religiia*, June 1964, pp. 86–89.

antireligious films was a direct reversion to the prewar campaigns—none had been produced in the interim[40]—a fairly new vehicle of atheistic propaganda was television. According to *Agitator*, this proved very popular among the workers. "Prominent atheists, former believers, talented propagandists and agitators, appear on the screen in conversations around a table recounting their experiences in work with believers." The authorities seemed to have higher hopes for television than radio. Believers did not listen to atheist broadcasts, but television could well be more attractive, although it was not yet available to more than a small proportion of the population.[41]

Another aspect of the campaign was the propagation of communist substitutes for religious rites (much like the East German use of *Jugendweihe* to replace confirmation). For years the state had been uncomfortable with the apparent anomaly that, despite all their Marxist education, many young people preferred to be married in church rather than in the local office of the marriage bureau. The reason usually given was that the stately and beautiful ceremonies of an Orthodox service were more impressive and attractive. Hence the atheists stressed the need for some communist rite which would be equally attractive to young people. The first "palace of marriage" was opened in a former grand-ducal residence in Leningrad, with such personal touches as a corsage for the bride and recorded music. This experiment was copied in some other Soviet cities, although in somewhat less pretentious surroundings. Statistics on the success of this move are not available.[42]

Perhaps because of this persistent attachment of the people to the church, one of the Soviet atheists' most persistent efforts was directed against the rite of baptism.[43] Years of intensive propaganda in the press and radio criticizing baptism as unhygienic, preceded other, more direct action. Seizing upon the occasion offered by the widely publicized death of an infant after an Orthodox baptism (which is usually by immersion), the government passed a law making it a

40. *Trud* [Labor], 28 June, 1954; *Sovetskaia Rossiia* [Soviet Russia], 19 October 1958.
41. Gegeshidze, "Prisposoblivaiutsia . . .," p. 47.
42. See "Le nuove feste i e nuovi riti sovietici" [New Soviet feastdays and rites], *Russia Cristiana*, no. 67–68, 1964; and Nikita Struve, "Pseudo-Religious Rites Introduced by the Party Authorities," in William C. Fletcher and Anthony J. Strover, eds., *Religion and the Search for New Ideals in the USSR* (New York, 1967), pp. 44–48.
43. William C. Fletcher, "Soviet Society and Religion: A Trip Report," *Communist Affairs*, June–August 1963, p. 11.

crime to cause a threat to health under the guise of religion.[44] All this apparently made little difference in the number of children baptized. Even in cases where parents feared to have their child baptized, grandmothers would take the infants to the priest.[45] Then a new ruling forbade a priest to baptize a child without the written consent of its parents,[46] and this was followed by the requirement that the father present a written permit which he previously had to have executed through the local police, giving his own name and residence. In some localities, consent of his place of employment was required.[47]

In common with similar prewar practice (1935), such stipulations put the parent on record as contravening the norms established by the party, and, worse, as a believing Christian.[48] Until this restriction was applied, it was reliably estimated that despite all the atheistic pressure, 80 percent of all children received baptism. The threat to the father's position involved in the new regulations may have reduced the number of baptized children, but as yet no reliable statistics are available.[49]

A substitute for the Christian baptismal ceremony was concurrently introduced. It was called the "name-giving ceremony," at which the child was presented with a medal with its name on one side and a picture of Lenin on the other. Under the new regulations, baptism became so difficult and dangerous for parents that some felt obliged to accept the new rite.[50] The following is from the "commemorative certificate" which is given at such ceremonies:

When you are grown, read these precepts and always follow them.

Remember that you are a citizen of the Great Motherland—the Union of Soviet Socialist Republics—the country of freedom and happiness, where man is a friend, comrade, and brother to man.

44. Article 227, *Ugolovny kodeks RSFSR* [Criminal code of the RSFSR] (Moscow, 1964), p. 91.

45. P. Darmansky, *Pobeg iz tmy* [Flight from darkness], (Moscow, 1961), p. 65; Iu. Rozenbaum, "Takoi zakon est" [There is Such a Law], *Nauka i religiia*, April 1964, pp. 83–85, and September 1964, p. 89; *New Statesman*, 2 May 1959, p. 596.

46. Rozenbaum, "Takoi zakon est," pp. 83–85.

47. Ibid.

48. Ibid.

49. *Komsomolskaia pravda*, 17 June 1961; *Literaturnaia gazeta* [Literary Gazette], 28 November 1961; V. Zelenchuk, et. al., "Novaia zhizn—novie prazdniki i obriady" [New life—new holidays and rites], *Kommunist Moldavii* [The Moldavian Communist], February 1965, pp. 22–26; Walter Kolarz, "Religion and the Russian Peasant," *Listener*, 30 June 1960, p. 1127.

50. *Izvestiia*, 20 December 1964.

Guard the Motherland as the apple of your eye, increase her wealth and glory.

Walk firmly on the path of life indicated by the great Lenin. Be honorable, diligent, and orderly in great and small matters. Respect parents and elders.

Support the honor of the collective, in which you learn and labor.

Remember, man's fortune is in joyful labor for the glory of one's people, the battle for the beautiful future of mankind—communism![51]

Similarly, there were concerted efforts to discourage the observance of religious holidays. This was motivated not only by ideological considerations, but also as an attempt to increase productivity—one collective farm reportedly lost thirty thousand man-days per year because of such festivals.[52] Apparently religious observances were primarily a rural problem,[53] but the cities do not seem to have been entirely free of such interruptions in planned working schedules. As early as 1954, *Trud* reported: "It is possible to determine all the religious festivals without looking at the church calendar from the flood of applications requesting a few days' leave in the country."[54]

The economic factor can by no means be considered the only motivation, for the state also attempted (with questionable success) to supplant certain religious holidays with secular ones. One writer reports with obvious discouragement: "Lately many cities and villages have been celebrating 'Russian Winter.' This holiday coincides with Shrove Tuesday and was apparently intended to replace that holiday. But it has not replaced it! We have missed something here. Something of the popular tradition has escaped us, and we have bureaucratized a gay festival. And as for Easter, no counterweight at all has been found. Also, some places celebrate a harvest holiday, but it is quite pale."[55]

One of the most persistent efforts of the new campaign was to encourage individual, person-to-person propaganda for atheism. This approach had been recommended before the war, but was not

51. N. Riabinsky, "New Times—New Rituals," *Sovetskie profsoiuzy* [Soviet trade unions], no. 19, October 1965, p. 34.

52. M. Lapshin, "Tsena propagandy" [The price of propaganda], *Molodoi Kommunist* [The young communist], December 1963, pp. 20–21.

53. P. A. Nikitin, ed., *Nash opyt vospitaniia iunykh ateistov* [Our experience in the education of young atheists] (Moscow, 1962), p. 5; *Sovetskaia Rossiia*, 8 October 1960.

54. *Trud*, 29 June 1954.

55. Iu. Feofanov, "Persistently, Flexibly, Intelligently!" *Sovet Deputatov Trudiashchikhsia* [Council of Workers Deputies], October 1960, translation from *Current Digest of the Soviet Press* (*CDSP*) 12, no. 51 (18 January, 1961): 37–38.

energetically implemented then.[56] But perhaps in part because Baptists and others had proven the effectiveness of this form of persuasion in the postwar period,[57] individual work with believers was heavily emphasized during the campaign of the sixties.[58] It was even endorsed at the plenary session of the All-Union Komsomol Central Committee in 1961: "In order to root out the monstrous survivals of capitalism, Komsomol organizations must conduct thorough-going individual work with each young person, aggressively, energetically, and flexibly fighting the influence of bourgeois ideology and strengthening scientific atheistic propaganda."[59]

Pravda gave a clear exposition of the ideal approach to this work the following year:

Friendly and intimate conversations of leading comrades with believers after working hours are seldom used and atheist propaganda in the homes of workers is weak. . . .

But the most important thing is to reach each man, to learn about his state of mind and his needs and demands, to show an attentive attitude toward him, and to bring timely help to those people who are beset by troubles or those who fall into misery. It is necessary to go fearlessly to the believers, help them to separate themselves from the inconclusiveness of religious ideas concerning nature and life.[60]

According to *Sputnik ateista* (The atheist's companion), the individual approach was "the most important and effective method"[61] available to the antireligious worker.

The agitator must establish contact with the believer, with his family and surroundings. . . . Once contact is established, the agitator should take the second step—in the course of conversation drop a word to start doubt in the believer's mind about the truth of religious dogmas, open his eyes to the contradictions and falsehoods in the Bible. . . . But this is still not enough. Every atheist agitator has a "maximum program." This is to steer the be-

56. B.V., "Iz opyta raboty sredi veruiushchikh" [From experience of work among believers], *Antireligioznyk* [The antireligious worker], October–November 1940, p. 70.

57. *Washington Post*, 14 August 1962; *VIRA* 9 (Sovremennoe sektantstvo [Contemporary sectarianism]), (Moscow, 1961): 30.

58. *Pravda*, 7 October 1963; *Kommunist Belorussii*, September 1964, p. 54; Feofanov, "Persistently, Flexibly, Intelligently!"; E. F. Muravev and Y. V. Dmitrev, "Atheism and Religion in the USSR," *Voprosy filosofii*, March 1961, translated in *Soviet Review*, no. 2 (July 1961], p. 54.

59. *Krasnaia zvezda* [Red Star], 22 November 1961, quoted by D. Konstantinow "Soundings in Unfamiliar Waters," *Bulletin of the Institute for the Study of the USSR* 9, no. 5 (May 1962): 38.

60. *Pravda*, 26 September 1962, translated in *RCDA*, 5 November 1962, pp. 3–5.

61. *Sputnik ateista* (Moscow, 1966), p. 439.

liever away from his religious organization and to isolate him from religious propaganda. After this, the believer often . . . breaks with religion.[62]

Nauka i religiia reported in 1964 that in the Moldavian town of Beltsy "believers' families are known to atheists, and agitators visit their homes." In another area eight hundred agitators were constantly at work in sectarian families.[63] Clearly, there were many such programs launched, but it is not clear what degree of success they achieved.

Another major thrust of the propaganda campaign was directed at women, probably because they constituted the majority of believers attending church services.[64] In part this condition may be due to the "missing generation" of men caused by the casualties of World War II,[65] but the more important reason is undoubtedly that women risk less than men by church attendance. A man might lose his job for being seen in church. Some women have such heavy duties in their homes that they do not hold outside jobs, and hence local atheists are unable to harrass them at their work.[66]

This special concern over women also sprang from the influence of women on their children: "Since a large porportion of people who are still believers is women, this is the most important field for atheistic propaganda today—spinsters, widows and mothers. Believing mothers are most important, since they always try to inject religion into their children."[67]

Considerable attention was also devoted to the role which the family plays in forming the religious consciousness of the future citizens.[68] "The family is the most important channel through which the churches seek to disseminate their influence upon the young."[69] Accordingly, some of the strongest statements made during the cam-

62. *Sovremennoe sektantstvo*, pp. 198–200.

63. "Ateisty Moldavii obmenivaiutsia opitom" [Moldavian atheists share experiences], *Nauka i religiia*, July 1964, p. 6–7.

64. Muravev and Dmitrev, "Atheism and Religion in the USSR," p. 48.

65. Nathaniel Davis, "Religion and Communist Government in the Soviet Union and Eastern Europe" (Ph.D. dissertation, Fletcher School of Law and Diplomacy, 1960), p. 404.

66. Ibid., p. 88.

67. *Muskovskaia pravda* [Moscow *Pravda*], 26 June 1964.

68. *Uspekhi sovremennoi nauki i religiia* [Contemporary science's successes and religion] (Moscow, 1961), p. 32; I. D. Pantskhav, ed., *O nekotorykh osobennostiakh sovremennoi religioznoi ideologii* [Some peculiarities of contemporary religious ideology] (Moscow, 1964), p. 288; "How Many Children Believe in God?" *Nauka i religiia*, February 1963, translated in *RCDA*, 20 May 1963, p. 75.

69. Muravev and Dmitrev, "Atheism and Religion in the USSR," p. 49.

paign advocated the invasion of the family by antireligious propagandists, demanding that when necessary, workers go into people's homes to drive out their belief in God.[70]

This invasion of privacy was reflected in numerous protests which found their way to the West during the campaign. According to one of these documents: "Madame X gives her children a religious upbringing . . . she and her children have been cruelly persecuted." An atheist agent visited her home, tore the icons from the wall, confiscated her passport and attempted to take the children away, remarking that nowadays there are special boarding schools to isolate children from believing parents. "Madam X has since vanished without a trace." Another mother persisted in taking her children to church, although on several occasions she was summoned to an interview with the principal of her children's school. He warned her, "We shall persecute you for taking your children to church . . . and put your children into a boarding school to prevent your crippling them further." At last report the mother had been informed that the city health department was arranging her transfer to a mental hospital and that the children would be placed in a state boarding school.

Forcible Measures Against Believers

The antireligious campaign did not consist only of propaganda measures. The direct use of force was widely applied, and if the massive brutality of the prewar period was not emulated, many of the individual measures introduced were more severe than their precedents had been. A particular example of the ways in which the campaign of the early sixties reached an unprecedented level of intensity was the effort to curtail religious influences on children. In the thirties antireligious work among children was for the most part confined to rather desultory attempts to produce propaganda materials suitable for the young.[71] Beginning late in 1961, however, children under eighteen years of age were forbidden to attend Baptist worship services,[72] and by the fall of 1963 this restriction was being applied in

---

70. F. Oleshchuk, "Doiti do kazhdogo veruiushchego" [Go to each believer], *Sovietskie profsoiuzy*, no. 17 (September 1962), pp. 33–34.

71. Leopold L. Braun, *Religion in Russia, from Lenin to Khrushchev* (Paterson, N.J., 1959), p. 34; Basil A. Maloff, *The Cross versus Communism behind the Iron Curtain* (Washington, D.C., 1952), p. 23.

72. *Slavic Gospel News*, June 1962, p. 9; Fletcher, "Soviet Society."

Orthodox churches as well.[73] In 1963 the Central Committee of the
Komsomol urged that services not be allowed to begin if children
were present in the church.[74]

According to the booklet, *Freedom of Conscience in the USSR*,
"The law categorically forbids attracting minors into religious
societies. This means that persons under eighteen years of age may
not be members of religious organizations, and do not have the right
to participate in church services or religious ceremonies of any
kind."[75]

These measures are without parallel in Soviet history; the most
that was ever done in the thirties was to claim that it was illegal for
parents to force children to go to church against their will.[76]

Similarly, priests were categorically denied the right to give religious instruction to children. In 1961 attention began to be drawn to
Soviet legislation prohibiting clerics from conducting special work
among children,[77] and in 1962 one authoritative source stated:
"Many such preachers are breaking the law . . . they teach children
the catechism. . . ."[78] This emphasis continued throughout the campaign.[79] The restrictions sought were actually more severe than the
regulations introduced in the Stalin era (which were still officially in
force), when priests had not been allowed to teach religion to children in groups larger than three; at no time was such permission
denied entirely, and priests had always been allowed to teach the
catechism at the invitation of the parents.[80]

The most conclusive of the indications that the campaign of the
sixties was more serious than any previous attack on religion were
the several known cases reported in the Soviet press in which parents
guilty of teaching religion to their children were denied parental

73. *Recent Developments in the Soviet Bloc.* Testimony of Paul B. Anderson to the U.S.
Congress, Subcommittee on Europe of House Committee on Foreign Affairs. 88th Congress, 2nd sess., Part I: *Recent Trends in Soviet and East European Literature, Arts, Human
Rights (Law and Religion), and the Younger Generation,* Washington, D.C., 1964, pp. 94–
102, 115–24.
74. *Christian Century,* 16 September 1964, p. 1142.
75. American Committee for Liberation, *The Beleaguered Fortress* (New York, 1963),
p. 16, quoting the booklet, *Freedom of Conscience in the USSR.*
76. *Komsomolskaia pravda,* 26 February 1937, and 20 April 1938.
77. *Uspekhi sovremennoi,* p. 26.
78. Donald A. Lowrie, "Eastern Christians under Duress," *Christian Century,* 21
November 1962, p. 1424, quoting *Nauka i religiia,* May 1962.
79. *Christian Century,* 16 September 1964, p. 1140.
80. See the Decree of 1929, in P. V. Gidulianov, *Otdelenie tserkvi ot gosudarstva*
[Separation of church from state] rev. ed. (Moscow, 1926), pp. 3–11.

rights and their children were removed to atheistic state boarding schools.[81] These reports were dramatically confirmed by the thirty-two Christians from Siberia who sought asylum at the American Embassy in January, 1963. Among the documents they left at the Embassy were several letters written by their own children from state boarding schools.[82] This, too, was a measure without precedent in Soviet antireligious history. It echoed a practice of czarist times which had been roundly condemned by all, including the communists themselves.[83]

Denial of parental rights was given ideological justification in 1962 at a Komsomol congress, when it was explained that freedom of conscience does not apply to children, and no parent should be allowed to cripple a child spiritually.[84] Legal grounds were supplied in an article in an authoritative legal periodical, which explained that the state, because it grants parental rights, has the power to withdraw them, in some cases even before the case has been brought to the courts.[85] (A local ruling of 1964, incidentally, stipulated that parents who have been deprived of parental rights must still provide for the support of the children.)[86]

But parents and children were not the only ones who suffered from coercive antireligious measures. Individual believers encountered repressions of a direct nature. Official denials of discrimination on the basis of religious belief are numerous, of course, especially for foreign audiences. In response to a letter inquiring about the status of a state employee who was "a believer," *The Soviet Weekly* in London published this statement: "No Soviet employer, government or otherwise, would dare ask a prospective employee to state whether he has religious beliefs or what these beliefs are. Religious beliefs are the personal concern of the individual. It would be illegal and, indeed, punishable by imprisonment, for anyone to withhold a job on the

81. *Selskaia zhizn* [Rural life], 14 June 1962, and 20 June 1962; *Izvestiia*, 28 June 1962; *Turkmenskaia iskra* [Turkmen spark], September 1962, translated in *RCDA*, 18 March 1963, pp. 12–13; *Voiovnychy ateist*, January 1962, p. 14, and February 1962, p. 19, cited in Teodorovich, "Increasing Pressure," p. 11; cf. *Pravda*, 3 October 1964.

82. *Newsweek*, 14 January 1963, p. 32, and 28 January 1963, pp. 45–46; George Bailey, "Religion in the Soviet Union," *The Reporter*, 16 July 1964, p.28.

83. Emelian Iaroslavsky, *O religii* [On religion] (Moscow, 1957), p. 186.

84. *Izvestiia*, 17 April 1962.

85. A. Pergament, "Roditelskie prava" [Parental rights], *Sovetskaia iustitsiia* [Soviet justice], no. 21 (1962), pp. 6–8.

86. *Kazakhstanskaia pravda* [Kazakhstan *Pravda*], 24 June 1964.

grounds of the applicant's religion. It is, therefore, quite possible for a religious person to work for any Soviet organ."[87]

It seems difficult, however, to reconcile this bland assurance with an earlier statement by an official attached to the Council of Ministers: "It is impossible for us to give responsible positions to men whose philosophical convictions are diametrically opposed to ours and could not, therefore, sincerely cooperate with us in pushing our program forward."[88]

In fact, workers have been demoted or discharged, and students barred from examinations, when it became known that they practiced a religion. Komsomol members formed patrols to follow and expose people who attended church services,[89] and guards were often posted at the doors of churches.[90] *Pravda* noted the case of a Baptist student who had been expelled from a secondary vocational school,[91] and *Nauka i religiia* reported two such cases in Stavropol. E. R. Androsova was excluded from the Pedagogical Institute "because she believed in God." Since all *teachers* at all levels are required to teach atheism, such action is perhaps understandable, however much it might conflict with Soviet assurances that religion is free. But this would not apply to the Baptist *student*, Nina Ivleva, who was expelled from the Agricultural Institute in Stavropol "for belief in God."[92]

Believing workers frequently suffered discrimination. "The Red Booklet of a Shock Worker" is a distinction awarded for outstanding effort, but in at least one case, when his Baptist affiliation came to light, a workman was forced to give up the "Red Booklet" that had been officially awarded him. In another case a certificate of honor conferred on a worker by both the party and his trade union was withdrawn because "an advocate of religious views is unworthy of such a certificate." In a Stavropol factory the workmen elected a Baptist to the local soviet, but the administration refused to accept his nomination. Another worker applied for a better apartment, and the local soviet was on the point of approving the request, when it was discovered that he was a believer. The application was refused

---

87. *Religious Digest*, June 1965.
88. de Grunwald, *The Churches and the Soviet Union*, p. 66.
89. *Leninskaia smena* [The Lenin generation], 20 September 1959.
90. *Uchitelskaia gazeta* [Teachers' gazette], 30 November 1963.
91. *Pravda*, 3 October 1964.
92. M. G. Mikhailov, "Stavropolskie vstrechi" [Meetings in Stavropol], *Nauka i religiia*, April 1965, p. 20.

"because of his religious convictions."[93] Similar discriminatory measures in allocation of living space have long been applied to priests, of course.[94]

Rigorous purging of believers from party organizations was also called for. One Soviet author complained: "What kind of measures do the Komsomol organizations take when it becomes known that a member of the Komsomol has taken part in a religious ceremony? At best the 'culprit' is tried at the meeting or is excluded from the Komsomol. Other forms of influencing people are hardly ever used."[95] Pressures are known to have been exerted against new party members, in some cases merely because their parents were religious.[96] Even some high Soviet officials were ousted from their posts on religious grounds. The party organ of Uzbekistan, for example, announced that the Minister of Trade of the Kara-Kalpak ASSR was dismissed because he was a practicing Moslem.[97]

Direct action against believers—arrest, trial, imprisonment or exile—was also introduced in some cases. In order to facilitate such action a new legal provision was created.[98] Article 227 of the criminal code of the Russian Republic prescribes a penalty of five years in prison or exile for religious activity which is "harmful to health," which "prompts citizens to nonparticipation in social activity or nonfulfillment of civil duties," or which entices minors into a religious group.[99] This compares unfavorably even with the law of 1923 which, at the height of the early struggle with the church, carried a maximum penalty of three years, and that only if the religious activity advocated forcible overthrow of the government or passive resistance to its acts.[100]

This new regulation was widely utilized. The Soviet press continually carried stories of religious people sentenced to prison, including many monks and at least three bishops.[101] The numerous

93. *Sovetskaia Rossiia*, 26 May 1965.
94. Darmanky, *Pobeg iz tmy*, p. 106.
95. N. Sviridov and G. Marchik, "For the Effectiveness of Ideological Work," *Molodoi Kommunist*, August 1962, translated in *RCDA*, 5 November 1962, p. 2.
96. *Partynaia zhizn Kazakhstana* [Kazakhstan party life], December 1964, p. 46.
97. *Pravda vostoka* [*Pravda* of the East], 22 October 1964.
98. P. Talanov and I. Okunev, "Garantia svobody sovesti" [Guarantees of freedom of conscience], *Nauka i religiia*, May 1963, pp. 45–48.
99. *Ugolovny kodeks RSFSR*, p. 91.
100. Gidulianov, *Otdelenie*, pp. 30–31.
101. *Uspekhi sovremennoi*, pp. 20–21; *Literaturnaia gazeta*, 10 April 1962; *Sovetskaia Rossiia*, 21 June 1960; American Committee for Liberation, *Beleaguered Fortress*, p. 14.

propaganda attacks against high prelates[102] were distinctly reminiscent of Stalin's campaign of 1937–38,[103] although arrests were
apparently more subtle than before. Sometimes in place of actual
arrest, churchmen were confined to mental institutions, an action
which effectively removed them from society without risking the
possibility of a popular protest in the wake of a court trial.[104] The
fear of such action seems to be reflected in the following excerpt from
a letter of a Russian Baptist: "Now, brother, I want to inform you
that I anticipate some sickness pretty soon and shall not be able to
write to you. If it is God's will, you will know more about it later, if
the Lord prolongs our life."[105]

Pressure on the Churches

While party doctrine is concerned with religion as an ideological
phenomenon, the focus of state antireligious action has been the
visible, institutional expression of religion in society. In this regard,
the campaign of the sixties paralleled its prewar predecessors, exacting a heavy toll on the churches. One theological seminary after
another was closed. Of the eight Orthodox seminaries and two academies permitted to open after the war, five of the seminaries were
closed.[106] Not only was the number of theological seminaries reduced, the number of students in those still functioning was similarly
reduced.[107] Young men who made known their intention to enter a
seminary could be quickly called up for military service or subjected
to concentrated antireligious propaganda in which the threat of
reprisal against their families was not far below the surface.[108]
Inasmuch as a priest was required to recommend a candidate in his
application to a seminary, this was another point at which pressure
could be exerted.[109]

102. See the list in Nadezhda Teodorovich, "The Episcopacy and the Diocesan Network of the Moscow Patriarchate," *Bulletin of the Institute for the Study of the USSR*, June
1961, p. 52.

103. For example, *Izvestiia*, 22 and 23 November 1937.

104. Nikita Struve, *Christians in Contemporary Russia* (London–New York, 1967),
p. 305.

105. *Slavic Gospel News Bulletin*, January–March 1962, p. 11.

106. Michael Bourdeaux, *Opium of the People* (London, 1965), p. 95; Struve, *Christians
in Contemporary Russia*, pp. 310–11.

107. D. Konstantinow, "The Orthodox Church, the Regime, and the People Today,"
Bulletin of the Institute for the Study of the USSR, February 1962, pp. 46–47.

108. Muravev and Dmitrev, "Atheism and Religion in the USSR," pp. 49–50.

109. Lowrie, "The Russian Church at New Delhi," *Christian Century*, 1 November
1961, p. 1299.

Similar attrition was evident in monastic institutions.[110] Prior to the new campaign, it had been possible for some groups of monks to register themselves officially as a collective economic unit or *artel*, providing themselves with the facilities for common life without registering themselves as the monastic community which in fact they were. Very early in the campaign this practice came to the attention of the authorities, and efforts were made to "unmask" these false kolkhozes.[111] But pressure against monastic communities was not confined to the unregistered monasteries. The number of properly registered monasteries also decreased. Although unreliable figures from the patriarchate claimed, at times, as many as ninety monasteries,[112] sixty-nine or seventy active monasteries was the figure most often cited before the campaign.[113] In its application for membership to the World Council of Churches in 1961, the Moscow patriarchate had reduced this figure to forty,[114] and in 1962 a Soviet source gave the figure as thirty-two.[115] This decline seems to have continued during the course of the antireligious campaign.[116]

Several different methods were used in closing monasteries. Sometimes "legal" measures were used. A monk's passport could be confiscated, and he could then be sentenced to expulsion for breaking the passport law. The abbot of the famous Pochaev monastery was so expelled, and police refused to permit the naming of his successor, leaving the institution leaderless. On another occasion there was a case in which a group of monks was seized in the monastery, driven several hundred miles in a truck, and left by the roadside with the warning never to return. Still others were declared to be mentally unsound and committed to a mental hospital. It was reported that of 140 monks formerly living in Pochaev, by 1964 only 10 remained. Taxi drivers bringing pilgrims to the monastery were arrested and their licenses revoked. Police cut all the wires bringing electric current to the monastery. All this harrassment, instead of simple closure of the

---

110. Struve, *Christians in Contemporary Russia*, pp. 302–10.

111. *Izvestiia*, 24 January 1960.

112. George C. Guins, *Communism on the Decline* (The Hague, 1956), p. 225.

113. S. D. Bailey, "Religious Boom in Russia," *Christian Century*, 12 March 1958, p. 305; Patricia Blake, "Alliance with the Unholy," *Life*, 14 September 1959, p. 114; Joseph H. Jackson, *The Eternal Flame; The Story of a Preaching Mission in Russia* (Philadelphia, 1956), p. 64.

114. *Time*, 5 May 1961, p. 57.

115. N. I. Iudin, *Pravda o petersburgskikh "sviatyniakh"* [The truth about the Petersburg "shrines"] (Leningrad, 1962), as translated in *RCDA*, 24 June 1963, p. 117.

116. Struve, *Christians in Contemporary Russia*, pp. 302–310.

monastery, was evidently due to the fact that for generations it had been a popular place of pilgrimage, and had to be preserved to prove to visitors that the monastic life is still permitted.[117] It should be noted, however, that such factors were not sufficient to preserve the even more famous Pecherskaia monastery in Kiev.[118]

Pressure was exerted against church services as well. As has been noted, it was dangerous for almost any worker to go to church, for fear his attendance might be reported and sanctions applied to him. At practically every service there were government agents to report on the sermon, and pressure was applied against any priest who broached anything but the most simple religious topics, as interpreted by a hostile listener.[119] Police orders forbade any procession outside the church building, even the climactic Easter procession at midnight. Sometimes tanks and trucks were sent to drive around the church building to drown out singing, and in many instances the services were invaded by unruly intruders who would make noise and jostle the worshippers.[120] If the lack of sufficiently large quarters led to overcrowded services, the state could object to the services on the grounds of the sanitation code,[121] or churches could be closed for failing to carry out repairs,[122] even when the state made it impossible for the church to obtain the necessary repair materials.[123]

Radical changes were introduced in the internal government of at least two of the churches early in the campaign. In 1960 the Baptist leadership issued an instruction discouraging preaching and proselytizing in the churches, and raising the minimum desirable age for baptism to thirty.[124] A widespread protest movement among the rank-and-file Baptists resulted.[125] The following year the Moscow patriarchate transferred the conduct of all parish affairs to a lay

117. Comité d'Information sur la Situation des Chrétiens en l'Union Sovietique, *Situation des Chrétiens en l'Union Sovietique* (Paris, 1964), pp. 42–43; A. E. Levitin, *Zashchita very v SSSR* [Defense of the faith in the USSR] (Paris, 1966), pp. 10–62.

118. Levitin, *Zashchita*, passim.

119. *Christian Century*, 16 September 1964, p. 1142.

120. American Committee for Liberation, *Beleaguered Fortress*, p. 11; *Washington Post*, 14 August 1962.

121. *Partynaia zhizn Kazakhstana*, December 1964, p. 46.

122. *Current Developments in the Eastern European Churches*, May 1964, p. 15.

123. Ibid., 14; A. Valentinov, "Soviet Legislation on Cults," *Nauka i religiia*, October 1961, translated in *JPRS* 11797, no. 8 (29 December 1961), p. 48.

124. Bailey, "Religious Boom in Russia"; *Uspekhi sovremenoi*, p. 288; Muravev and Dmitrev, "Atheism and Religion in the USSR," p. 53.

125. See Fletcher and Strover, *Religion in the USSR*, pp. 62–75. See also Michael Bordeaux, *Religious Ferment in Soviet Russia* (New York, 1968).

executive committee, from which the priest was specifically ex-cluded.[126] Even though according to the regulations of 1945 the government had full control over the appointment and removal of priests,[127] it apparently was felt that more control over the life of the local church was needed, for this new ruling made the priest, in effect, merely the employee of the local church council.

The state then proceeded to assume full control over the local church council: "The right to remove individuals from membership in the executive organ or revision committee of a religious society is the exclusive prerogative of the executive committees of local organs of state power."[128] These changes in the ecclesiatical constitutions are difficult to reconcile with the all-union constitutional principle of the separation of church and state, and have lately been subject to serious challenge on precisely these grounds.[129]

A large number of churches were closed during the campaign. Considerable attention was devoted to publicizing the legal grounds on which churches could be closed,[130] but in a great many instances legality was dispensed with and churches were closed simply by fiat, by the use of "administrative measures."[131] Any calculation of the number of churches closed is hampered by the lack of accurate statistics on the number of churches operating in the USSR after World War II. In its application for membership to the World Council of Churches in 1961, the Russian Orthodox church claimed twenty thousand churches,[132] and although this figure is lower than the twenty to thirty thousand which had been variously claimed during the fifties, the argument of one careful researcher suggests that even this figure is inflated.[133]

---

126. *ZHMP*, August 1961, pp. 15–17.

127. Nicholas Zernov, *Eastern Christendom* (New York, 1961), p. 218.

128. Valentinov, "Soviet Legislation," p. 46. See also A. A. Bogolepov, "The Legal Position of the Orthodox Church in the Soviet Union," chapter 9 below.

129. See the documents of the Eshliman–Iakunin controversy in *RCDA*, 15/30 June 1966, pp. 89–105, and 15/31 August 1966, pp. 126–129.

130. Valentinov, "Soviet Legislation," p. 50; *Nauka i religiia*, June 1964.

131. Valentinov, "The Primer of Materialism," p. 165.

132. *Time*, 5 May 1961, p. 57.

133. Nathaniel Davis gives the following summary of data: "There is a great discrepancy between the approximate figure given above [5–6,000] and the figure of 20,000 to 30,000 Orthodox churches which is given informally by officials of the Moscow Patriarchate. The Patriarchate's figures are open to question, however, on several grounds. In 1945–1946, four figures were given by sources at the Patriarchate: 20,000 [Kathleen Lonsdale, ed., *Quakers Visit Russia* (London, 1952), p. 138, and J. Jousselin, *Reforme*, 31 August 1946], 23,000 [Matthew Spinka, *The Church in Soviet Russia* (New York, 1956), p. 119], 25,000

During the campaign of the sixties the Soviet press presented lower estimates: "In 1941 there were nearly 4,000 Orthodox churches, in 1948 there were more than 15,000. Most of these churches were opened in the occupied territories where the clergy collaborated with the Nazis. However, some of the new Orthodox churches were registered on free (unoccupied) Soviet territory. Since 1948 few new churches have been opened."[134] Interestingly enough, this figure coincides fairly closely with the estimate made by G. G. Karpov in 1945, when he stated that there were sixteen thousand churches.[135]

There were numerous claims in the Soviet press of large numbers of churches closed. As early as 1961 approving note was made of five hundred churches closed in two areas alone.[136] In 1963, the figure of

[John S. Strohm, *Just Tell the Truth* (New York, 1947), p. 175], and 30,000 [Metropolitan Nikolay, as quoted by *The New York Times*, 28 November 1945]. Round numbers in this range have been given whenever the question has been asked of Patriarchate officials ever since that time. [1947—29,000, John S. Curtiss, *The Russian Church and the Soviet State, 1917–50* (Boston, 1953), p. 305; 1947—25,000, P. Fontanieu, 'Le probleme Religieux en l'URSS,' *Christianisme Sociale*, January–February 1955, p. 60; 1950—20,000, Robert Tobias, *Communist–Christian Encounter in East Europe* (Indianapolis, 1956), pp.225, 271; 1951—over 20,000, *Soviet News*, 21 August 1951; 1951—25,000, Gary MacEoin and Akos Zambory, *The Communist War on Religion* (New York, 1951), p. 11; 1951—20,000 buildings, 30,000 congregations, Tobias, *Communist–Christian Encounter*, p. 276; 1952—22,000, Corliss Lamont, *Soviet Civilization* (New York, 1952), p. 1952; 1952—25,000, N. S. Timasheff, 'Urbanization, Operation Antireligion and the Decline of Religion in the USSR,' *The American Slavic and East European Review*, SIV, 2 (April 1955): 233; 1954—20,000, A. S. Horsely, *The Sunday Times*, London, 12 December 1954; 1954—25,000, *Newsweek*, 18 October 1954; 1955—20,000, Jackson, *The Eternal Flame*, p. 64; 1956—20,000 parishes, Paul B. Anderson, 'Churchmen Visit Russia,' *Christian Century*, 18 April 1956; p. 186; 1956—22,000 churches, S. H. Steinberg, ed., *The Statesman's Year Book, 1958*, p. 1464.] Even though the Orthodox Church claims to have taken over the bulk of some 3,000 Uniate parishes in the Western Ukraine during 1946 [*ZHMP*, October 1948, p. 9; so also Estonia, *ZHMP*, April 1945, 3; also true of Transcarpathia, 1945], there has been no discernible reflection of this change in the statistics given by Orthodox officials. In fact, there seems to have been a tendency to scale down the claimed number of churches between 1946 and 1950. Moreover, the *Journal of the Moscow Patriarchate* avoids giving any church statistics in writing [exception: a Finnish bishop gave 22,000, and *ZHMP*, August 1957, published the whole speech]. Soviet government officials concerned with Orthodox affairs have also avoided giving exact figures in recent years, and when asked by foreigners, sometimes preface their reply with 'According to the Orthodox. . . .' This is an odd necessity if one recalls that a principal function of these officials is to receive reports and maintain records, and that their permission is necessary for every single church opening. The imprecision of ecclesiastical and official statistics can only be explained by a policy of withholding information" ("Religion and Communist Government," pp. 359–62).

134. A. Veshchikov, "Milestones of a Great Journey," *Nauka i religiia*, November 1962, translated in *RCDA*, 24 December 1962, p. 2.

135. *New York Times*, 7 June 1945.

136. *Pravda*, 7 October 1963; Teodorovich, "Increasing Pressure," pp. 45–46; cf. S. Ivanov, "Kak my organizuem nauchno-ateisticheskuiu propagandu" [How we organize scientific-atheistic propaganda], *Kommunist Moldavii*, July 1961, pp. 52–57.

11,500 was given by the antireligious press and was confirmed by representatives of the Orthodox church.[137] Estimates of the total number of churches closed range from one-half of those operating before the campaign[138] to ten thousand that were closed.[139]

Such figures are comparable to the number of churches closed during the worst prewar periods, 1928–32 and 1936–38.[140] Even if they are reliable, these estimates of reductions in the number of functioning churches do not necessarily imply a corresponding decline in the vitality of religion or even of functioning religious communities. One atheist commentator reminded her readers: "Withdrawal of registered status frequently results in a mere increase in the number of unregistered but functioning religious societies and groups. Consequently, the copying of figures from one column into another cannot be passed off as an indication of the success of atheistic efforts."[141]

Nonetheless it seems evident that this particular aspect of the campaign considerably increased the pressure on religious people in the USSR. It successfully reversed the growth trend in the life of the institutional church which had developed after World War II, and constituted a return to the situation which prevailed in the Stalin era before the relaxation of the wartime and postwar Stalin era.

Conclusions

The fall of Khrushchev by no means marked the end of the antireligious campaign. Certain features were made less harsh, and in particular the closing of churches apparently was greatly diminished or ceased entirely. There appeared to be some confusion at the center, if only because conditions in local areas varied greatly, with some areas enjoying considerable relaxation of antireligious efforts while others experienced no surcease whatsoever, apparently due to the attitudes of individual local and regional leaders. There was no significant decrease in the amount of energy devoted to antireligious propaganda, and forcible measures were still applied, on a reduced scale in some regions, but, in others, on at least as great a scale as

137. Testimony of Paul B. Anderson, in *Recent Developments*, p. 99.
138. *Commonweal*, 15 November 1963, p. 211.
139. Struve, "Christians in Contemporary Russia," p. 300.
140. William C. Fletcher, *A Study in Survival: The Church in Russia, 1927–1943* (New York, 1965), pp. 45–46, 80–83.
141. Valentinov, "Soviet Legislation," p. 51.

before. Legal stipulations restricting religious activity have not been rescinded, and, in some cases, may even have been intensified.[142]

This is not to say that the fall of Khrushchev was without benefit to those individuals and institutions who were the objects of the campaign. In general, it seems that the momentum was broken by his removal. Where the campaign of the sixties had been steadily increasing in intensity during the last five years or more of the Khrushchev period, this pattern did not continue after his fall.

It is beyond the scope of this paper to evaluate fully post-Khrushchev developments in the antireligious field, particularly the significance of the events of 1966 and 1967, when serious protest movements among the Baptists and Orthodox came to light. An already complex picture promised to become far more complicated as portions of the believing populace sought to resist and reverse the restrictions which had been applied in the campaign of the sixties.[143] Significant as these and other post-Khrushchev developments are, however, they must await further clarification before they can be properly evaluated.

It does seem evident, however, that the antireligious campaign conducted during the Khrushchev era has permanently altered the religious situation in the USSR. The party and the Soviet government undertook such a deep commitment to antireligious positions that a reversal could only be effected by radical revision of policy and procedure. And even if such revision were to occur, the churches have been too gravely weakened by the campaign to resume that position they enjoyed prior to it. What had been normative for the fifteen years following the war seems to have been altered beyond recall. In the future former procedures will have to be replaced by new modes of conduct and understanding, on the part of the church, on the part of the state, and on the part of observers in the West.

The campaign of the sixties left a situation which is anything but stable. If the antireligious efforts of the state are again increased, it would seem that the churches must expect further losses. Alternatively, if religious people find the means to effect a reversal of the antireligious policies of the Khrushchev era, something approaching

142. See Joshua Rothenberg, "The Legal Status of Religion in the Soviet Union," chapter 5 above.
143. See the Eshliman–Iakunin documents in *RCDA*.

genuine freedom of religion may eventually be attained. At the moment the situation is still unclear, and no definite commitment has been made in either direction.

8

RELIGIOUS THEMES
IN SOVIET LITERATURE

One may distinguish two pseudoreligious alternatives to traditional
religion among Soviet intellectuals today: doctrinaire Marxism–
Leninism, in its cosmological and "historiosophical" aspects (current
among a dwindling group), and "technological Prometheanism"
(current among a larger, and perhaps growing, group).[1] There is also
evidence of the existence and growth of a third alternative—a genuinely religious one.

This evidence is drawn from three kinds of sources: (1) literary
works, in both prose and verse, published in recent years in the
Soviet Union; (2) works written in the Soviet Union but published
only abroad; (3) works as yet unpublished, which circulate in the
Soviet Union in manuscript, typescript, or mimeographed form.

After examining this evidence, I shall add a few comments at the
end of this chapter on religious themes in music and the plastic arts,
where, of course, the evidence is both less clear and harder to come
by.

I

The younger Soviet intellectuals, writers in particular, who are now
turning to religion (whether ecclesiastical or nonecclesiastical) find

1. See G. L. Kline, *Religious and Anti-Religious Thought in Russia* (Chicago, 1968),
pp. 164–68.

George L. Kline

inspiration for this radical shift in three major Russian poets of the twentieth century: Anna Akhmatova (1888–1966), Boris Pasternak (1890–1960), and Marina Tsvetaeva (1892–1941).

Both Tsvetaeva and Akhmatova were devoutly Orthodox throughout their lives; Pasternak came to Christianity relatively late. (Akhmatova's funeral, like Pasternak's, was conducted in the Orthodox rite, but, unlike Pasternak's, was public, was announced in the Soviet press, and was immediately reported abroad.) Both Tsvetaeva and Akhmatova were under a cloud for many years, and remained virtually unpublished from the 1920s until 1961. That year saw the publication in Moscow of small volumes of selected poetry of all three poets; but all religious poems had been carefully excluded from these volumes. Four years later large volumes (seven to eight hundred pages) of the poetry of all three were published.[2] These volumes included a smattering of the explicitly religious poems as well as many poems with an implicit religious symbolism or lexicon. It is from these poems that examples of religious themes in Tsvetaeva and Pasternak will be drawn.[3] (Akhmatova will be omitted because she wrote relatively few religious poems, although many of her love poems contain religious allusions or suggestions, and poems like "Lot's Wife" have both a biblical setting and Old Testament rhetoric.)

The first selection is from one of Tsvetaeva's poems to Alexander Blok, written immediately after his death in 1921.[4] (Blok's early verse, which exhibits a religious symbolism and mysticism, has frequently been reprinted in the Soviet Union, although official stress has been laid upon his "mystical-revolutionary" poem of 1918, "The Twelve.")

> Други его—не тревожьте его!
>
> .   .   .   .
>
> Было так ясно на лике его:

2. All three volumes were printed in editions of forty thousand, and were sold out immediately. It is almost impossible to find any of them in the Soviet Union today. And, as of late 1969, none of them has been reprinted.

3. The selections offered here are not intended as an anthology—even in miniature—of the religious poetry of either Tsvetaeva or Pasternak, but only as evidence that some of the religious poetry of both poets is currently available to Soviet readers. Many of the explicitly Christian poems of the two poets are not included, because they have been published only abroad.

4. Russian poetry will be quoted in the original, followed by an English translation which, unless otherwise identified, is my own. Most of the poems quoted here have not previously been translated into English.

Царство мое не от мира сего.

.   .   .   .

У навсегда Повелевшего: быть!
Хлеба достанет его накормить![5]

(1921)

Friends of his, trouble him not!

.   .   .   .

His countenance has spoken clearly:
"My Kingdom is not of this world."

.   .   .   .

He who gave the eternal command: "Exist!"
Will have bread enough to nourish him!

In her earliest poems, Tsvetaeva (like Akhmatova, though more defiantly and less repentantly) often referred to her own "sinfulness":

Буду грешить—как грешу—как грешила: со страстью!
Господом данными мне чувствами—всеми пятью!

.   .   .   .

Вы, сопреступники!—Вы, нежные учителя!
Юноши, девы, деревья, созвездия, тучи,—
Богу на Страшном суде вместе ответим, Земля!

(1915)[6]

I shall sin—as I now sin—as I have sinned: with passion!
With all five of my God-given senses!

.   .   .   .

You, fellow-criminals!—You, tender teachers!
Young men, maidens, constellations, trees, and clouds,—
Earth, we shall make answer together, before God, at the
Last Judgment!

But Tsvetaeva's typical religious poems are hymns of gratitude or celebrations of the wonders of creation:

Благословляю ежедневный труд,
Благословляю еженощный сон.
Господнию милость—и Господен суд,
Благой закон—и каменный закон.

(1918)[7]

5. Marina Tsvetaeva, *Izbrannye proizvedeniia* [Selected works], (Moscow and Leningrad, 1965), pp. 98–99. Here and in all other quotations from Soviet sources I have resisted Soviet "orthographic atheism," restoring capital letters to words which refer to Deity (in the present case Повелевшего). In the Tsvetaeva volume the words Бог [God] and Божий [God's] occur at least a dozen times written with a small letter. There are also more than half a dozen instances of small-letter Господь [Lord] and Господний [Lord's].

6. Tsvetaeva, *Izbrannye proizvedeniia*, pp. 71–72.

7. Ibid., p. 128.

I bless the work of every day,
I bless the sleep of every night.
The Lord's mercy—and the Lord's judgment,
The kindly law—and the law as hard as stone.

There is an almost pagan strand in her hymns of Christian gratitude:

Благодарю, о Господь,
За Океан и за Сушу,
И за прелестную плоть
И за бессмертную душу,

И за горячую кровь,
И за холодную воду.
—Благодарю за любовь.
Благодарю за погоду.
                                    (1918)[8]

I thank Thee, O Lord,
For ocean and dry land,
For glorious flesh
And an immortal soul,

For hot blood,
And chill water.
—I thank Thee for love.
And I thank Thee for weather.

One of Tsvetaeva's most perfect short poems is a concise evocation of the power and glory of God, reminiscent of the book of Job:

Все великолепье
Труб—лишь только лепет
Трав—перед Тобой.

Все великолепье
Бурь—лишь только щебет
Птиц—перед Тобой.

Все великолепье
Крыл—лишь только трепет
Век—перед Тобой.
                                    (1921)[9]

8. Ibid., p. 139.
9. Ibid., p. 173. My translation of this poem has appeared in *Arroy*, the Bryn Mawr-Haverford literary review, May, 1969.

The massed magnificence of trumpets
Is only a murmur of grasses
Before Thee.

The massed magnificence of tempests
Is only a twitter of birds
Before Thee.

The massed magnificence of wings
Is only a flutter of eyelids
Before Thee.

Only one of the poems in the 1965 Moscow edition refers directly to the passion of Christ:

—Отче, возьми в назад,
В жизнь свою, Отче!
.　.　.　.　.　.

Ревностью взор разъят,
Молит и ропщет . . .
—Отче, возьми в закат,
В ночь свою, Отче!

Празднуя ночи вход,
Дышат пустыни.
Тяжко—как спелый плод—
Падает: "Сыне! . . ."
(1921)[10]

"Father, take me back
into Thy life, O Father!"
.　.　.　.　.　.

Torn by jealous stares,
He prays and murmurs:
"Father, take me into thy
Sunset, into Thy night, O Father!"

The desert breathes
To celebrate night's coming.
The word falls heavily, like a ripe
Fruit: "My Son!"

10. Ibid., p. 172.

Another Tsvetaeva poem with explicitly religious language appeared in print for the first time in the 1965 Soviet edition. It includes the lines:

> Лишь только б мои два локтя
> Всегда утверждали:—*Даст*
> Бог! *Есть* Бог!
>
> (1933–35)[11]

> But only let my two elbows
> Proclaim forever:
> God *will provide*! God *exists*!

Tsvetaeva's influence on the younger Soviet poets is clear and strong, and includes her religious orientation. (This is particularly true of Joseph Brodsky, to whom we shall return.) But the influence of Pasternak is probably even stronger, one reason being that he was still alive and active while even the youngest generation of contemporary Soviet poets was growing up. Tsvetaeva had died while most of them were still children (Brodsky, for example, was only a year old).

Pasternak, as noted, came to Christianity relatively late, and expressed an avowedly religious viewpoint in his work only during the last decade of his life. But the younger Soviet poets are impressed by the seriousness and freshness of what one Western critic has called his "re-invented Christianity." And they respect, even when they do not accept, his view of Christianity as a religion which fuses "sacrificial love" and "creative freedom"—Lara and Iury, "life" and "poetry." *Dr. Zhivago* and the full cycle of Zhivago poems remain unpublished in the Soviet Union, although in mid-1967 Harrison Salisbury reported from Moscow that *Dr. Zhivago* was scheduled for inclusion (late in 1968 or early in 1969) as the final volume of a six or seven-volume edition of Pasternak's collected works.[12] A few of the relatively nonreligious Zhivago poems are included in the 1965 edition, under the antiseptic title "Poems from a Novel." Nowhere

---

11. Ibid., p. 301. The poem is about Tsvetaeva's writing desk, and the elbows referred to are the poet's elbows, propped on the desk as she writes.

12. *New York Times*, 16 July 1967. As of late 1969 this report seems, in retrospect, highly premature, since even the *first* volumes of Pasternak's "collected works" have not yet appeared in the Soviet Union.

in his long and sympathetic introduction does Andrei Sinyavsky (at the time the book went to press he had not yet been publicly unmasked as Abram Tertz) refer by name to *Dr. Zhivago,* or to religious motifs in Pasternak's work.

One of Pasternak's earliest poems, which appears in the 1965 Soviet edition, contains religious references of a generalized "symbolist" nature.

> И, как в неслыханную веру,
> Я в эту ночь перехожу,
>
> . . . . . .
>
> Где пруд, как явленная тайна,
> Где шепчет яблони прибой.
> (1912–14)[13]

> I wade into this night as though embracing
> A new faith, a creed utterly unknown.
>
> . . . .
>
> This pond is like a mystery laid open,
> This blooming apple-tree—a surge of spray.

Almost twenty years later Pasternak made a similar affirmation in the poems "Spring Again" (Опять весна) and "Pines" (Сосны). (The lines quoted below are also quoted by Sinyavsky in his introduction, at pp. 15 and 58, respectively.)

> Это поистине новое чудо,
> Это, как прежде, снова весна.
>
> . . . . . .
>
> В пруд и из пруда в другую посуду.
> Речь половодья—бред бытия.
> Опять весна (1941)[14]

> This in truth is a new miracle,
> This, as before, is spring renewed.
>
> . . . .
>
> From one pool to the next, as from one
>   vessel to another:
> A spring-swollen stream babbles in the
>   frenzy of existence.

13. Boris Pasternak, *Stikhotvoreniia i poemy* [Verses and poems], (Moscow and Leningrad, 1965), pp. 65f. My translation has appeared in *Boris Pasternak: Seven Poems* (Santa Barbara, Calif., 1969).

14. Ibid., p. 406.

И вот, бессмертные на время,
Мы к лику сосен причтены
И от болезней, эпидемий
И смерти освобождены.
Сосны (1941)[15]

And thus, immortal for a time,
We are part and aspect of the pines
Freed from diseases,
Epidemics, even death.

Two years later, in 1943, in a moving poem in memory of Marina Tsvetaeva, not published in the Soviet Union until 1965 (in the journal *Novy mir* [New World]), Pasternak declared:

У смерти очертаний нет.

Тут все—полуслова и тени,
Обмолвки и самообман,
И только верой в воскресенье
Какой-то указатель дан.

. . . . . .

Лицом повернутая к Богу,
Ты тянешься к Нему с земли,
Как в дни, когда тебе итога
Еще на ней не подвели.[16]

Death has no features.

There all's half-words and shadows,
Slips of the tongue and self-deceptions,
And it is only the faith in resurrection
Which can give us some kind of clue.

. . . .

With your face turned to God,
You stretch up toward Him from the earth
As in the days before the earthly
Summing up of all you were and did.

Religious themes are peripheral in the few Zhivago poems included in the 1965 Soviet edition of Pasternak's poetry. But the theme of life as sacrificial love is stated in two of them, "The Wedding" (Свадьба) and "Dawn" (Рассвет):

15. Ibid., p. 396.
16. Ibid., p. 568.

Жизнь ведь тоже только миг,
Только растворенье
Нас самих во всех других
Как бы им в даренье.
                              Свадьба[17]

For life too is only a moment,
Only a dissolving
Of ourselves into all others,
As though in gift to them.

Я ими всеми побежден,
И только в том моя победа.
                              Рассвет[18]

I am vanquished by them all,
And this is my sole victory.

Explicitly Christian symbolism is found in "Winter Night" (Зимняя ночь), a poem about Iury Zhivago's love for Lara:

На свечку дуло из угла,
И жар соблазна
Вздымал, как ангел, два крыла
Крестообразно.[19]

A distant draught tugged at the flame;
Temptation's fever
Spread angel-wings whose shadow swelled
To form twin crosses.[20]

Two of Pasternak's poems written between 1956 and 1959 exhibit both religious symbolism and specific Christian conviction. The first is called "When the Weather Clears" (Когда разгуляется). I quote its last three and a half stanzas:

Разлито солнце по земле.
Просвечивает зелень листьев,
Как живопись в цветном стекле.

17. Ibid., p. 435.
18. Ibid., p. 444.
19. Ibid., p. 440.
20. My translation of this poem appeared in the Columbia University *Forum*, Winter 1959, p. 23. It has been reprinted, with slight revisions, in the *Columbia University Forum Anthology* (New York, 1968), pp. 50–51, and in *Boris Pasternak: Seven Poems*.

В церковной росписи оконниц
Так в вечность смотрят изнутри
В мерцающих венцах бессонниц
Святые, схимники, цари.

Как будто внутренность собора—
Простор земли, и чрез окно
Далекий отголосок хора
Мне слышать иногда дано.

Природа, мир, тайник вселенной,
Я службу долгую твою,
Объятый дрожью сокровенной,
В слезах от счастья отстою.[21]

... sun spills on earth
Illuminating leaves
   Like stained glass windows

Where hermits, saints and tsars
Peer, under glinting crowns
   Of sleeplessness,
From church to eternity.

Remote in this far-reaching
Cathedral of the world,
   A choir allows me
The Echo of a note.

World's tabernacle, nature,
I kneel through your long service.
   A trembling hugs me;
I cry with happiness.[22]

The most openly religious of Pasternak's late poems (apart from the Zhivago cycle) is "In the Hospital" (В больнице). I quote its last four stanzas:

"О Господи, как совершенны
Дела Твои,—думал больной,—
Постели, и люди, и стены,
Ночь смерти и город ночной.
Я принял снотворного дозу
И плачу, платок теребя;
О Боже, волнения слезы
Мешают мне видеть Тебя.

---

21. Pasternak, *Stikhotvoreniia i poemy*, p. 456.
22. Translation by Michael Harari in *Boris Pasternak: Poems 1956–1959* (London, 1960), p. 39. By permission of Collins and Harvill Press.

Мне сладко при свете неярком,
Чуть падающем на кровать,
Себя и свой жребий подарком
Бесценным Твоим сознавать.

Кончаясь в больничной постели,
Я чувствую рук Твоих жар.
Ты держишь меня, как изделье,
И прячешь, как перстень, в футляр."[23]

"How perfect are your works,
O Lord," he mused, "men, wall,
Night city, death in the night
And beds in hospital.

I tug my handkerchief;
Tears worry a way through
The drowsy sedatives, O God,
And blur my sight of you.

It's pleasant, as the light
Gropes for my bed, to see
That both my life and self
Were your rich gifts to me.

I feel your warm hands hold me
Here in the ward, replace
Their handiwork, your ring,
Inside death's jewel case."[24]

As I have already noted, Sinyavsky's introduction does not refer directly to the religious themes in Pasternak's poetry. Sinyavsky does manage to say things, not often heard in public in the Soviet Union, about "absolute and eternal values." He writes that, for Pasternak, life is "something unconditional, eternal, absolute, an all-pervasive force, and a very great miracle." He speaks of Pasternak's "amazement at the miracle of existence,"[25] and adds that, for Pasternak, the "vitality of nature" is "all-conquering" and "saving" (спасительная). He asserts that Pasternak's art "bears witness to the significance of what is, to the greatness of life, to the immeasurable value of human

23. Pasternak, *Stikhotvoreniia i poemy*, p. 468.
24. Translation by M. Harari in *Pasternak: Poems 1956–1959*, p. 75. The more traditional and, I think, preferable rendering of ты and твой would be as "Thou" and "Thy" (or "Thine"). By permission of Collins and Harvill Press.
25. A. Sinyavsky, "Poeziia Pasternaka" [Pasternak's poetry], in Pasternak, *Stikhotvoreniia i poemy*, p. 15.

existence."[26] Finally, Sinyavsky mentions, without explicit reference to *Dr. Zhivago*, that in Pasternak's last works "what is contingent in the fate of his heroes has a providential character."[27]

Solzhenitsyn is a Soviet writer of the middle generation, half-way between Pasternak and, say, Voznesensky. There is evidence of religious concern in his celebrated novella, *One Day in the Life of Ivan Denisovich*, but he expresses his religious convictions more clearly in the superb short story, "Matryona's Home" (published in 1963 in *Novy mir*, but not reprinted in book form). Of the heroine, the narrator says:

... I didn't once see her say her prayers or even cross herself. But, whatever job she was doing, she began with a "God bless us," and she never failed to say "God bless you," when I set out for school. Perhaps she did say her prayers, but on the quiet, either because she was shy or because she didn't want to embarrass me.[28]

At the end of the story, after Matryona's death, he adds: "We had all lived side by side with her and never understood that she was that righteous one without whom, as the proverb says, no village can stand."[29]

The younger Soviet poets whose works appear in large editions have not touched upon religious themes *stricto sensu*, but they employ a certain amount of religious rhetoric and symbolism. In a poem written in 1965 Voznesensky uses the phrase *vechnaia pamiat* (literally "eternal remembrance"), which is from the Orthodox funeral service, and prominent at the beginning of *Dr. Zhivago*.

> Аминь.
>
> Убил я поэму. Убил, не родивши. К Харонам!
> Хороним.
>
> .   .   .   .
>
> вечная память,
> зеленые замыслы встаньте как пламень,
> вечная память,
> мечта и надежда, ты вышла на паперть?
> вечная память!
>
> Аминь.[30]

26. Ibid., p. 61.
27. Ibid., p. 45.
28. English translation by H. T. Willetts in P. Blake and M. Hayward, eds., *Half-way to the Moon: New Writings from Russia* (New York, 1964), p. 68. By permission of Holt, Rinehart and Winston and Weidenfeld and Nicolson.
29. Blake and Hayward, *Half-way to the Moon*, p. 91.
30. *Akhillesovo serdtse* [My Achilles' heart] (Moscow, 1966), pp. 5, 7.

Amen

I have killed a poem, killed it before it was
born. Take it to Charon.
Let us bury it.

. . . .

Eternal remembrance,
green projects, rise up like flame,
eternal remembrance,
dream and hope, have you gone begging?
Eternal remembrance!

Amen.

Boris Slutsky, famous for his (mostly unpublished) anti-Stalin
poems and poems critical of Soviet anti-Semitism, in 1962 published
a "Footnote to the Debate about Andrei Rublev" (the reference, of
course, is to the famous Russian icon-painter of the fifteenth century):

Нет, все не сунешь в схему.
И как бы ни совали,
Рублев,
   принявший схиму,
Неверов
   был едва ли.
Он на колени падал пред
В начале бывшим
    Словом,
. . . .
А спас его не волопас—
Начал труда носитель,
А просто:
   Спас,
    Спас,
Спас
(По нашему спаситель).[31]

No, not everything fits into a scheme,
however much you try:
Rublev, when he took the vows,
Was scarcely an unbeliever.

31. "K diskussi ob Andree Rubleve" [On the discussion about Andrei Rublev], *Yunost*,
[Youth], no. 2 (1962), p. 41.

He fell on his knees
before the Word—the one
that was in the Beginning.

.   .   .   .

He was saved not by a swineherd
—symbolizing Labor—
but quite simply
                     by the Savior.[32]

In some of Yevtushenko's recent poems there are Christian references, but so far as I can determine, nothing that could be called a Christian theme. Thus, his poem about European and American films, which claims that James Bond is presented as a kind of Christ-figure (!), ends with the phrase:

Шпион останется шпионом,
Христос останется Христом.[33]

A spy is still a spy,
and Christ remains Christ.

II

Of the younger Soviet writers, Andrei Sinyavsky (now serving a seven-year term at hard labor) is the most explicitly Christian, and closest to Russian Orthodoxy. His convictions are expressed indirectly in the novella *Liubimov* (translated into English as *The Make-peace Experiment*), in which the only victim of the strange bloodless revolution in the town of Liubimov is described as lying "on the ground with palms outstretched, as though he were Jesus Christ."[34] Like Sinyavsky's other fiction, this story and his volume *Thoughts Unaware*, have been published—in Russian and in translation—only abroad.

The prayers of the village priest Ignat, at the very end of the story, have great poetic as well as religious power (and a splendid Old Church Slavonic flavor).

32. English translation by Max Hayward in Blake and Hayward, *Half-way to the Moon*, p. 148. By permission of Holt, Rinehart and Winston.

33. "Zapadnye kinovpechatleniia" [Impressions of Western films], as read at Lincoln Center, New York, 17 December 1966.

34. "Liubimov," in *Fantasticheski mir Abramo Tertsa* [The fantastic world of Abram Tertz] (New York, 1967), p. 328.

"Отче наш, возвесели души ранее удрученных до конца бурями житейскими
. . . . Отче наш, утеши их в лоне Твоем, яко же мать утешает чады своя."[35]

"Father, make glad the souls of those who lose heart in the face of life's
storms. . . . Father, comfort them in Thy bosom, as a mother comforts her
children."

There follows an almost Dantesque catalogue of the violent deaths of
those for whom Ignat prays:

"Спаси, Господи, скончавшихся в тяжких мучениях, убиенных, погребенных
живыми, поглощенных землею, волнами, огнем, растерзанных зверями,
умерших от глада, мраза, с высоты падением, и за скорби кончины их даруй
им вечную радость Твою . . . Отче наш, упокой всех одиноких, сирых,
нищих, неимущих ближнего, молящегося за них."[36]

"Save, O Lord, those who have perished in grievous torment, slaughtered,
buried alive, swallowed up by the earth, by waves, or by fire; torn by wild
beasts; starved, frozen, or fallen from great heights; and give them, in
return for the grief of their endings, Thine eternal joy. . . . Father, console
all those who are lonely, the orphaned, the poor, and those without a friend
or relative to pray for them."

Finally, there is the prayer for sinners of various kinds:

"Отче наш, умилосердися над уязвленными гибельным неверием. Отче наш,
тяжки их грехи, но сильнее милость Твоя. Отче наш, прости скончавшихся
без покаяния. Отче наш, спаси погубивших себя в помрачении ума. Отче наш,
очисти их ради верных, вопиющих Тебе день и ночь. Отче наш, ради незло-
бивых младенцев прости их родителей. Отче наш, слезами матерей искупи
грехи их чад."[37]

"Father, have mercy on those wounded by ruinous unbelief. Father, their
sins are grievous, but Thy mercy is greater. Father, forgive those who have
died without repenting. Father, save those who, their minds beclouded, have
destroyed themselves. Father, purify them for the sake of those faithful ones
who raise their voices to Thee day and night. Father, forgive the parents for
the sake of their gentle babes. Father, let the tears of the mothers atone
for the sins of their children."

In *Liubimov* it is not altogether clear where Sinyavsky's own
sympathies lie. But his *Thoughts Unaware*, first published in Russian

35. Ibid., p. 393.
36. Ibid.
37. Ibid., p. 394. Cf. also the English translation of the prayers by Manya Harari, in
The Make-peace Experiment (New York, 1965), pp. 186–88.

in New York in 1966, makes his own position crystal clear. There he devotes many pages to religious meditation and theological speculation. His purpose is plainly stated: "We have had enough talk about man. It is time to think of God."[38] Sinyavsky adds that, because of technological progress and the "comfort" of city life, "belief in God has ebbed." He asks rhetorically: "Can I catch sight of the Lord God in a world where, at every step, I encounter man? God's voice sounded in the wilderness, in silence, but silence and the wilderness are precisely what we lack. We have drowned out everything and filled it up with ourselves and we are amazed that God does not appear to us."[39]

In another section Sinyavsky states the reason for his religious belief. It is very simple: "One should believe not on the strength of tradition, not from fear of death, not 'just in case', not because someone commands it, or something frightens you . . . not in order to be saved, and not for the sake of non-conformity. One should believe for the simple reason that—God exists."[40]

Sinyavsky contrasts the isolated particularity of contemporary, secularized city-dwellers with the sense of being at home in the universe that once characterized devout peasants, for whom even the "monotonous ritual" of eating took on a universal meaning: "Observing fasts and holy days, man lived according to a calendar of universal history which began with Adam and ended with the Last Judgment."[41] The peasant "maintained a constant tie with the whole immense creation and died in the depths of the universe, in the bosom of Abraham. But we, having read our thin newspaper, die alone, on our narrow . . . sofa." Even in crossing himself before his meals the peasant "by this reflex gesture unites himself with earth and heaven, with past and future."[42] Modern men, lacking such rituals, have lost the meaningful bond between themselves and the world which these rituals symbolize.

Sinyavsky has a strong sense, akin to that in Tsvetaeva and Pasternak, of the wonder and glory of creation. In *Liubimov* the expression of this sense is poetic: there he refers to the "magic crystallography of

38. *Mysli vrasplokh* (New York, 1966), p. 87.
39. Ibid., p. 85. An English translation, under the title "Thought Unaware," appeared in the *New Leader* 48, no. 15 (1965): 16–26. The translations given here are my own.
40. Ibid., p. 110.
41. Ibid., p. 83.
42. Ibid., p. 84.

each of God's snowflakes, fluttering like . . . miniature humming-birds."[43] In his aphoristic writings, Sinyavsky says that if we took the "divine cosmogony" seriously, each tiny flower would make us swoon with astonishment, as we realized that "in each seed, each speck of dust, the future [flower], with its twelve petals, is already present."[44]

But in the same work Sinyavsky's vision is sometimes conceptualized almost to the point of a philosophical theology (and thus becomes more remote from the poetic vision of Tsvetaeva and Pasternak). "The laws of nature," Sinyavsky declares, "are a miracle, extended in space and time. Thanks to them, snowflakes, mammoths, sunsets, and other masterpieces of creation can exist for a more or less extended period, can periodically arise and develop, following a definite tradition (the tradition of the conservation of energy, the tradition of the earth's gravitation, etc.). This tradition can be broken by a new miracle. . . ."[45]

Of God, Sinyavsky speaks in Kierkegaardian paradoxes (although he nowhere refers to Kierkegaard): "[God] is unknowable and everywhere known; inaccessible and closer than what is closest; cruel and kind; absurd, irrational and logical in the extreme."[46] Similarly, Christianity is "a religion of the greatest hope, born of despair; the religion of a chastity affirmed in the sharpest consciousness of one's sinfulness; a religion of the resurrection of the flesh in the midst of stench and corruption."[47]

Heresy, he says, "is today not so dangerous as drying out at the roots. O Lord! Better that I err in Thy name than that I forget Thee."[48]

Sinyavsky is one of the very few contemporary Soviet writers to comment on the historical church:

The Church cannot fail to be conservative, so long as it wishes to remain faithful to tradition. . . . But besides the desire to safeguard an ancient sanctity, to keep the Testament, the Church invariably "lags behind life" in order that, remaining outside of time, it may bring us the fragrance and flavor of eternity. With its fixed forms, the archaic character of its liturgy is like the sky, which shows no tendency to develop at the speed of history.

43. "Liubimov," in *Fantasticheskii mir Abrama Tertsa*, p. 359.
44. *Mysli vrasplokh*, p. 124.
45. Ibid.
46. Ibid., p. 132.
47. Ibid., p. 141.
48. Ibid., p. 139.

Even the Church's stagnation is that of "an undecaying mummy which awaits the hour when it will hear the command: 'Arise and go forth!'"[49]

Valery Tarsis, who is much older than Sinyavsky, used occasional religious symbolism in his early story, "The Bluebottle Fly." For example, the narrator remarks that "the pine has even thrown out its dead limbs to receive my body in crucifixion."[50] But Tarsis does not touch upon explicitly religious themes until the semiautobiographical story "Ward 7." Of its hero he writes:

Almazov thirsted for action, he saw it as sacramental. His duty as a writer was to speak new words, and his worst fear was of uttering words which failed to become acts, failed to become God transfiguring our wretched, terrifying, bankrupt world.

He had searched for years. . . . There were many gods but never the one God, no one knew Him, least of all himself—and he longed with an insane intensity to find Him, to be guided to Him out of his dark night.[51]

Among his spiritual companions Almazov numbered such "doomed seekers" as Plato, Pascal, his "beloved Pasternak," and "above all, Dostoevsky, who of all men had drawn closest to God but had not had time to finish saying what he knew of Him."[52] Of his experience in the Soviet mental hospital, Almazov writes: "I saw it as truly as I see the sky, of which scientists deny the existence, as they deny God, but which poets and prophets have sung, as they have sung God, ever since the human voice has been heard on earth."[53]

In public statements since his emigration from the Soviet Union to Greece, Tarsis has made it clear that he is a believing Christian, and that he has for many years known and valued the works of such religious thinkers as Vasily Rozanov (1856–1919) and Nicholas Berdyaev (1874–1948). He reports that while in the Soviet Union he regularly received their books from abroad.

The first issue of the mimeographed underground literary journal

49. Ibid., p. 137.
50. *Skazanie o sinei mukhe* (Frankfurt am Main, 1963), p. 78. See also the English translation by Thomas Jones, *The Bluebottle* (New York, 1963), p. 108.
51. *Palata No. 7* (Frankfurt am Main, 1966), pp. 37–38; *Ward 7*, trans. Katya Brown (New York, 1965), p. 35. By permission of Collins and Harvill Press.
52. *Ward 7*, p. 36.
53. Ibid., p. 157. The Russian expression "chelovecheskoe slovo," here translated as "human voice," could also be rendered as "human language."

Feniks ([The Phoenix] Moscow, 1961) was reproduced in full in the emigré journal *Grani* ([Boundaries] no. 52, 1962). Several of its poems touch on religious themes.

Iu. Galanskov's "Manifesto of Man" uses simple but striking Christian imagery:

И вдруг—
словно грома раскаты
и словно явление миру Христа—
восстала
растоптанная и распятая
человеческая красота.
Это—я,
призывающий к правде и бунту.

. . . .

И пусть мне ворон выклевывает
на мраморе тела
крест![54]

And suddenly
like peals of thunder
like the appearance of Christ to the world—
human beauty,
trampled on and crucified,
rose in revolt.
It is I,
summoning you to truth and rebellion.

. . . .

And let the raven carve out
a cross
on the marble of my body!

Two of the women poets represented in *Feniks* deal even more directly with religious themes. A. Onezhskaia declares, simply:

Вопреки всем правдам и неправдам
Верила в распятье на кресте.[55]

Despite all truths and lies
I believed in the crucifixion on the cross.

---

54. "Chelovechesky manifest," in *Grani*, no. 52 (1962), pp. 153, 154. In 1967 Galanskov was sentenced to several years in exile.
55. *Grani*, no. 52 (1962), p. 142.

Natalia Gorbanevskaia offers an apocalyptic vision of "Mushroom Rain" (a by-product of atomic explosions). Her poem includes the lines:

> Боже! Господи! Где ж Ты!
> Рваная, мокрая изнанка облаков.
> Боже! Господи! Где ж ты!
> И каков?
>
> Лика Твоего в хаосе
> не обнаружу. . . .
>
> .   .   .   .   .
>
> Ах— вот и грибы
> стосаженные выросли.
> Не сберегли мы, Господи, Твоея милости.[56]

> My God! My Lord! Where art Thou!
> I see the tattered, wet seamy side of clouds.
> My God! My Lord! Where art Thou!
> And what art Thou?
>
> I cannot see Thy face
> In the chaos. . . .
>
> .   .   .   .   .
>
> Mile-high mushrooms have
> sprung up there.
> O Lord, we have not treasured up Thy mercy.

In a 1961 volume entitled *Sovetskaia potaennaia muza* (The secret Soviet muse), Boris Filipoff brought together a number of poems, some written as early as the 1920s, that have not yet been published in the Soviet Union. Several of the poems by Alexander Kotlin, dating from the 1930s and 1940s, make copious use of religious imagery. His wartime poem, written in 1942, about the burial of German soldiers, along with Russian soldiers and civilians, contains the lines:

> Безымянными полнится наша страна,
> А Господь разберется в их именах.[57]

> Our land is filled with nameless dead,
> But the Lord will know their names.

In another poem of the same year, entitled "In a Strange Land," Kotlin writes:

56. Ibid., p. 166.
57. "Voina" [War], in *Sovetskaia potaennaia muza* (Munich, 1961), p. 47.

Нет человеку других дорог,
А в небе высоком жестокий Бог.[58]

Man has no other road,
And a cruel God is in the high heaven.

In an untitled and undated poem appearing in the same volume, a poet identified only by the initials "V.R.," exclaims:

Бог поможет отыскать мне родину,
Ту, которую я потерял!

. . . . . .

Вся Россия— это Божье зарево,
Золотой раскольничий костер![59]

God will help me to find a homeland,
the one which I have lost!

. . . . . .

All of Russia is a divine glow,
A golden blaze of the Old Believers!

The last line refers, of course, to the practice of the Old Believers in the late seventeenth century of burning down their own churches and immolating themselves in the flames, rather than submit to the authority of the Orthodox church.

Svetlana Allilueva, Stalin's daughter, has revealed that she was converted from Marxist atheism to Orthodox Christianity in Moscow in the early 1960s, and was even baptized by an Orthodox priest. So far as one can judge from the writings which she has published since seeking refuge in the West, her religious beliefs, though undefined and elusive, are perfectly sincere.

The most important of the younger poets whose work reveals a definite religious content is Joseph Brodsky of Leningrad.[60] His work exhibits at least three religious themes: (1) the "Christian existentialist" theme—joy and gratitude for each precious moment of existence; (2) the "passion" or "crucifixion" theme—religious suffering and redemption; (3) the theme of "Christian culture"—the

58. Ibid., p. 53.
59. Ibid., p. 27.
60. Only two of Brodsky's many religious poems have been published in the Soviet Union: his "Verses on the Death of T. S. Eliot" and an untitled poem which begins "V derevne Bog zhivet ne po uglam" [In villages God lives not out of sight] appeared in *Den poezii* [The day of poetry] (Leningrad, 1967), pp. 133–35. My translation of the Eliot poem has since appeared in the *Russian Review* 27 (1968): 195–98.

relation of Christianity to culture in the modern world generally
and in the Soviet Union in particular. I shall quote portions of three
poems which illustrate, respectively, each of these themes and conclude with excerpts from Brodsky's long poem to John Donne,
which combines all of these themes with the theme of the poet's fate
and mission in the world.

The first poem, "January 1, 1965" (1 января 1965 года), is often
referred to as Brodsky's "Christmas poem" (in the Orthodox
calender Christmas falls on January 7th; New Year's day, however,
is the time when Soviet citizens exchange gifts):

> Волхвы забудут адрес твой.
> Не будет звезд над головой.
> И только ветра сиплый вой
> расслышишь ты, как встарь.
>
> . . . .
>
> . . . поздно верить чудесам.
> И, взгляд подняв свой к небесам,
> ты вдруг почуствуешь, что сам—
> чистосердечный дар.
>
> 1 января 1965 года (1965)[61]

> The Wise Men will unlearn your name.
> Above your head no star will flame.
> One weary sound will be the same—
> the hoarse roar of the gale.
>
> . . . .
>
> It's far too late for miracles.
> But suddenly, lifting your eyes
> to heaven's light, you realize:
> your *life* is a sheer gift.

The second poem, "Adieu, Mademoiselle Véronique" (Прощайте,
мадмуазель Вероника), involves an untranslatable play on the
Russian words *kreslo* ("armchair") and *krest* ("cross"). The armchair, indeed, becomes a kind of cross which the poet must bear.

III

> . . . .
>
> Через двадцать лет я приду за креслом,
> на котором ты предо мной сидела
> в день, когда для Христова тела

---

61. The full Russian text appears in *Novy zhurnal* [New Review], no. 95 (1969), p. 52.

завершались распятья муки—
в пятый день Страстной ты сидела, руки
скрестив, как Буонапарт на Эльбе.
И на всех перекрестках белели вербы.
Ты сложила руки на зелень платья,
не рискуя их раскрывать в объятья.

.   .   .   .

VII

.   .   .   .
. . . волшебный фонарь Христовой Пасхи
оживляет под звуки воды из крана
спинку кресла пустого, как холст экрана.

VIII

.   .   .   .
. . . в сумме своей наших дней объятья
много меньше раскинутых рук распятья.

IX

.   .   .   .
но если только не ложь, что Лазарь
был воскрешен,—то я сам воскресну.
Тем скорее, знаешь, приближусь к креслу.

(1967)

III

.   .   .   .
I shall come, in some twenty years, for the armchair
that you sat on, facing me, when, for Christ's body,
the cross's torments at last were ended—
you sat, on that fifth day of Holy Week, folding
your arms, like Napoleon exiled on Elba.
Palm fronds glowed golden at every crossing.
You laid down your arms on your grass-green garment,
avoiding the open-armed risk of passion.

VII

.   .   .   .
. . . the magic lantern of Christ's own passion
at the sound of drops from the dripping faucet,
lights up the back of the empty armchair
as though it were meant for a movie screening.

VIII

. . . .

The sum total of all of today's embraces
gives far less of love than the outstretched arms of
Christ on the cross.

IX

. . . .

but if only it isn't a lie they've told me,
and old Lazarus rose from the dead in truth, then
I too shall rise, rushing for that armchair.

. . . .

In similar fashion, the third poem, "A Stopping Place in the Desert" (Остановка в пустыне) moves from a visual experience to reflections on things of the spirit. Here Brodsky's point of departure is the destruction of an Orthodox church not far from his home.

Теперь так мало Греков в Ленинграде,
что мы сломали Греческую церковь,
дабы построить на свободном месте
концертный зал. В такой архитектуре
есть что-то безнадежное.

. . . .

. . . .

. . . И как-то в поздний час
сидел я на развалинах абсиды.
В провалах алтаря зияла ночь.
И я—сквозь эти дыры в алтаре—
смотрел на убегавшие трамваи,
на вереницу тусклых фонарей.

. . . .

. . . Одно,
должно быть, дело нацию крестить,
а крест нести— уже совсем другое.

. . . .

Сегодня ночью я смотрю в окно
и думаю о том, куда зашли мы?
И от чего мы больше далеки:
от православья или эллинизма?
К чему близки мы? Что там, впереди?
Не ждет ли нас теперь другая эра?
И если так, то в чем наш общий долг?
И что должны мы принести ей в жертву?

Остановка в пустыне (1966)

So few Greeks live in Leningrad today
that we have razed a Greek church, to make space
for a new concert hall, built in today's
grim and unhappy style.

. . . .

So, in the end, I sat—late that same night—
among fresh ruins in the church's apse.
Night glimmered through the altar's gaping holes.
And through these open altar-wounds I watched
retreating streetcars as they slowly swam
past phalanxes of deathly-pale streetlamps.

. . . .

It is one thing to bring a folk to Christ;
to bear His cross is something else again.

. . . .

Tonight I stare into the window's void
and meditate upon that point to which
we've come, and ask myself: from what are we
now most remote—the world of ancient Greece,
or Orthodoxy? Which is closest now?
What lies ahead? Does a new epoch wait
for us? And, if it does, what duty do we owe?—
What sacrifices must we make for it?[62]

Elsewhere I have commented in some detail on Brodsky's "Elegy for John Donne" (Большая элегия Джону Донну);[63] here I will note only that Brodsky combines one of Donne's conceits—the human soul as a thread upon which heaven and earth are strung together like beads—with the image of falling snow, to form the strikingly original image of snowflake-needles stitching body to soul and earth to heaven.

Джон Донн уснул, уснуло все вокруг.
Уснули стены, пол, постель, картины,

. . . .

Спят ангелы. Тревожный мир забыт
во сне святыми—к их стыду святому;
Геенна спит и Рай прекрасный спит.
Никто не выйдет в этот час из дому.
Господь уснул. Земля сейчас чужда.

62. My translation of the full poem appeared in *Unicorn Journal* 2 (1968): 28–30.
63. See the *Russian Review* 24 (1965): 341–53.

Глаза не видят, слух не внемлет боле.
И дьявол спит. И вместе с ним вражда
заснула на снегу в английском поле.
Спят всадники. Архангел спит с трубой.
И кони спят, во сне качаясь плавно.
И херувимы все— одной толпой,
обнявшись, спят под сводом церкви Павла.

. . . .

"Не та ль во тьме прикрыла взор рука,
которая повсюду здесь маячит?
Не ты ль, Господь? Пусть мысль моя дика
но слишком уж высокий голос плачет."
Молчанье. Тишь.—"Не ты ли, Гавриил,
подул в трубу, а кто-то громко лает?
Но что ж, лишь я один глаза открыл,
а всадники своих коней седлают.
Все крепко спит. В объятьях крепкой тьмы.
А гончие уж мчат с небес толпою.
Не ты ли, Гавриил, среди зимы
рыдаешь тут, один, впотьмах, с трубою?"

"Нет, это я, твоя душа, Джон Донн.
Здесь я одна скорблю в небесной выси

. . . .

Ты видел: жизнь, она как остров твой.
И с Океаном этим ты встречался:
со всех сторон лишь тьма, лишь тьма и вой.
Ты Бога облетел и вспять помчался.
Но этот груз тебя не пустит ввысь,
откуда этот мир—лишь сотня башен
да ленты рек, и где, при взгляде вниз,
сей страшный суд почти совсем не страшен.
И климат там недвижен, в той стране.
Оттуда все, как сон больной в истоме.
Господь оттуда— только свет в окне
туманной ночью в самом дальнем доме.

. . . .

Подобье птиц, он спит в своем гнезде,
свой чистый путь и жажду жизни лучшей
раз навсегда доверив той звезде,
которая сейчас закрыта тучей.

. . . .

Подобье птиц, и он проснется днем.
Сейчас лежит под покрывалом белым,
покуда сшито снегом, сшито сном

пространство меж душой и спящим телом.

.   .   .   .

Ведь если можно с кем-то жизнь делить,
то кто же с нами нашу смерть разделит?
Дыра в сей ткани. Всяк, кто хочет, рвет.
Со всех концов. Уйдет. Вернется снова.
Еще рывок! И только небосвод
во мраке иногда берет иглу портного.
Спи, спи, Джон Донн. Усни, себя не мучь.
Кафтан дыряв, дыряв. Висит уныло.
Того гляди и выглянет из туч
Звезда, что столько лет твой мир хранила.
                                              (1963)[64]

John Donne has sunk in sleep . . . All things beside
are sleeping too: walls, bed, and floor—all sleep.

.   .   .   .

The angels sleep. Saints—to their saintly shame—
have quite forgotten this our anxious world.
Dark Hell-fires sleep, and glorious Paradise.
No one goes forth from home at this bleak hour.
Even God has gone to sleep. Earth is estranged.
Eyes do not see, and ears perceive no sound.
The Devil sleeps. Harsh enmity has fallen
asleep with him on snowy English fields.
All horsemen sleep. And the Archangel, with
his trumpet. Horses, softly swaying, sleep.
And all the cherubim, in one great host
embracing, doze beneath St. Paul's high dome.

.   .   .   .

"Has not that Hand protected my dull eyes,
that Hand which looms up here and in all times?
Is it not thou, Lord? No, my thought runs wild.
And yet how lofty is the voice that weeps."
No answer. Silence.—"Gabriel, hast thou
not blown thy trumpet to the roar of hounds?
But did I stand alone with open eyes
while horsemen saddled their swift steeds? Yet each
thing sleeps. Enveloped in huge gloom, the hounds
of Heaven race in packs. Oh Gabriel,
dost thou not sob, encompassèd about
by winter dark, alone, with thy great horn?"

64. "Bolshaia elegiia Dzhonu Donnu" in Brodsky, *Stikhotvoreniia i poemy* (New York, 1965), pp. 130, 131–32, 133, 134, 135–36.

"No, it is I, thy soul, John Donne, who speaks.
I grieve alone upon the heights of Heaven. . . .

.   .   .   .

Thou sawest Life: thine Island was its twin.
And thou didst face the ocean at its shores.
The howling dark stood close at every hand.
And thou didst soar past God, and then drop back,
for this harsh burden would not let thee rise
to that high vantage point from which this world
seems naught but ribboned rivers and tall towers—
that point from which, to him who downward stares,
this dread Last Judgment seems no longer dread.
The radiance of that Country does not fade.

From there all here seems a faint, fevered dream.
From there our Lord is but a light that gleams,
through fog, in window of the farthest house . . . ."

.   .   .   .

Like a wild bird, he sleeps in his cold nest,
his pure path and his thirst for purer life,
himself entrusting to that steady star
which now is closed in clouds. . . .

.   .   .   .

Like a wild bird, he too will wake at dawn;
but now he lies beneath a veil of white,
while snow and sleep stitch up the throbbing void
between his soul and his own dreaming flesh.

.   .   .   .

For though our life may be a thing to share,
who is there in this world to share our death?
Man's garment gapes with holes. It can be torn
by him who will, at this edge or at that.
It falls to shreds, and is made whole again.
Once more 'tis rent. And only the far sky,
in darkness, brings the healing needle home.
Sleep, John Donne, sleep. Sleep soundly, do not fret
thy soul. As for thy coat, 'tis torn; all limp
it hangs. But see, there from the clouds will shine
that Star which made thy world endure till now.

III

The number of religiously significant works by Soviet poets and prose
writers published neither in the Soviet Union nor abroad, but nevertheless available in manuscript to Western students, is not large.

Such works are usually published in the West within a year or two of their arrival. However, one of the young "Leningrad poets" has written a powerful short poem about a huge tree (perhaps a redwood?) which has not yet appeared in the West and deserves to be quoted in full:

Воздвигнутый в честь сотворенья вселенной,
Аккумулятор воли растения
Хранит в тайниках древесины
Нуклеин дохристовых распятий.
Полон святости нерукотворной
Биохрам от корней до купола.
Тих и светел в белой колыбели,
Внемли дереву Бога, ребенок.

Erected in honor of the creation of the universe,
This storage battery of vegetative will
Preserves in the recesses of its wood
Nucleic acids of pre-Christian crucifixions.
Filled with a holiness not made by hands,
It is a bio-temple, root to crown.
Calm and radiant in your white cradle,
Child, take God's great tree unto yourself.

It seems likely that there is considerable poetry of this quality in the Soviet "cultural underground." We can only hope for its early emergence into the daylight of print.

IV

Religious themes are not limited to literature. Some of the recent drawings and sculpture of Ernst Neizvestny embody these themes; Neizvestny's Moscow studio is jammed with stylized, somewhat abstract crucifixes. Many of the self-portraits of Zverev are Christ-like figures, crowned with thorns. Such works have been known to a small circle for many years, but they have not yet been publicly shown in the Soviet Union.

Two recent public events and two publications are worth noting. In July, 1966, a large collection of "monuments of ancient Russian culture" was exhibited at the Manège on Red Square. In addition to a few delightful specimens of folk-art, the exhibit consisted mainly of paintings of Russian churches—hundreds of them. The paintings were by many different hands, and had been done at various times, from the 1920s to the 1960s. Most of them were competent rather than outstanding, artistically speaking, but as a group they provided a superb sampling of Russian church architecture. This unprecedented collection was warmly received by the Soviet public.

In August, 1966, a public recital of Russian Orthodox church music was given in Moscow and, although the event was not announced in the press or on the usual wall-posters, the hall was packed.

At about the same time a Russian translation (from Polish) of a collection of biblical tales by Kosidorowski was published, and immediately sold out. O. Chaikovskaia's *Protiv neba na zemle* (Against heaven on earth), which came out in Moscow in the same year, is, as Albert Todd has pointed out, "a remarkably straightforward account of the religious legends and traditions of Holy Russia."[65]

These may be no more than straws in the cultural wind, but they all seem to point in the same direction, as do the religious allusions collected and presented here from a variety of works in poetry and prose produced in the Soviet Union. Tarsis has revealed the existence in the Soviet Union of a religiously-oriented literary and cultural group known as *Smog*—the name is an acronym formed from the initials of the Russian words *smelost* ("daring"), *molodost* ("youth"), *obraz* ("image" or "icon"), and *glubina* ("depth"). (*Smog*, of course, is also the Russian word for "I [or he] was able.")[66]

Just how influential this or other such groups may be is difficult to estimate. But it seems clear that there has been, especially in the last dozen years, a definite turn toward religion on the part of many of the most sensitive and creative young Soviet intellectuals. And this in itself is something both new and significant.

65. "The Spiritual in Recent Soviet Literature," *Survey*, no. 66 (1968), p. 94. Reprinted in M. Hayward and W. C. Fletcher, eds., *Religion and the Soviet State: A Dilemma of Power* (New York, 1970).

66. See also the "Smog Manifesto" printed in *Grani*, no. 61 (1966), pp. 14–15, which lists among the spiritual mentors of the Smog group Rublev, Dostoyevsky, Tsvetaeva, Pasternak, and Berdyaev.

III

RELIGIOUS GROUPS IN THE SOVIET UNION

INTRODUCTION

The first impression made by the articles grouped together in this section is that of the variety in the organized religious life in the USSR. Specialists in the field may be aware that the dozen or so communities discussed constitute but a small part of the total number of religious divisions or associations. But many readers—including, perhaps, some scholars of Soviet affairs who specialize in subjects other than religion—will probably find here a larger and more variegated picture of religion in the Soviet Union than they have known, and certainly than they would expect to find, judging by most studies on the subject to date.

A second impression, less immediate or obvious, but one which steadily emerges from a careful reading of these articles, is the number of different ways in which the phenomenon of religion in the USSR can be observed. These differences stem partly from the specific focus of *interest*—a limited subject, as in Zvi Gitelman's article on the Jewish members of the Communist party; a brief time-span, as in Andrew Blane's essay on a single year in the life of the Protestant sects; or both together, as in Bernhard Wilhelm's study of the relations between the Moslems and the state in the last years of Stalin's rule. But these variations arise even more from the particular *angle* of focus: together, the essays in this section reflect the concerns and methodologies of law, history, ecclesiology, political science, sociology, and ethnology.

The multiplicity of subject matter and approach notwithstanding, one theme runs like a thread throughout this section, namely, the formative role which the Soviet state has played in organized religious life. The particular hue of this thread, whether light or dark,

varies with each religious body studied. Furthermore, the essays by
political scientists (Vardys and Gitelman), and those by clergymen
(Melia and Krikorian), afford pronounced contrasts in shading. In
the first group the role of the state or the Communist party is both
crucial and dominant; in the second group the influence of these
political forces is critical, but less central, because ecclesiastical interests come to the fore. Apart from such nuances, an unmistakable
characteristic of all the articles is the enormous importance of the
church–state problem.

These twelve essays, taken together, create a fresh perspective
which both affirms and alters generally-held viewpoints. As a unit
they argue forcefully that the encounter between church and state in
the USSR has been complex and variegated, not monolithic or uniform. General trends certainly abound, and the various religious
groups have shared much in their efforts to adapt to and survive under
a regime which persistently has been more antireligious than secular
in character. Likewise, all of the religious communities have suffered
the disruptions and dislocations that have accompanied the tumul-
tuous decades of the Soviet era—war, revolution, civil war, industrialization and collectivization, war again, and the frenzied efforts to keep
pace in an age of rapid change and intense international competition.
All the groups discussed here have experienced antireligious attack,
direct and indirect, ideological and administrative, and in certain
periods—the early thirties and the early sixties—simultaneously; all
have also known periods of reprieve by and rapprochement with the
state, especially during the "Great Fatherland War."

One interesting example of such common experience which has
not previously been pointed out is the "Living Church" movement
of the 1920s—the rise of schismatics who, in the name of "modernization" or "adaptation" to new realities, actively sought, with the
opportunistic support of the Soviet regime, to wrest control from
established religious authorities. The rise of the Living Church movement in the Russian Orthodox church has been widely discussed, but
no studies have shown, as the present ones do, that a similar phenomena arose within the Georgian Orthodox and Armenian churches,
as well as among the Moslems and the Jews.

At the same time, fully as striking as the common aspects are the
unique features in the encounter of the various religious groups with
the state, whether this encounter is experienced singly or in concert

with other religious communities (and in contrast to the life of the Russian Orthodox majority). Peculiarities of character in some communities have created a number of these differences. Distinct community character seems to have made the Mennonites (Epp), the Siberian tribes (Gapanovich), and to a lesser extent the Jews (Gitelman), particularly vulnerable to the erosion of the social engineering that accompanies industrialization and collectivization. The fusion of ethnic or national identity with religious affiliation among the Georgians (Melia), the Armenians (Krikorian), the Moslems (Wilhelm), the Jews (Gitelman, Rothenberg), and to some degree the Baltic peoples (Vardys, Veinbergs), has complicated their relations with the Soviet state. This same state, though multi-national and antireligious in theory, has in fact frequently been Great Russian and even Orthodox, at least in interchurch affairs. For the Roman Catholics (Mailleux, Vardys), the Moslems (Wilhelm), and the Jews (Rothenberg), the existence of a close politico-religious tie with a center outside the USSR has added elements of distrust and strain to their dealings with the Soviet government.

Historical particularities which antedate the advent of Soviet power have also played a part in creating variant patterns of church–state relations within the USSR. The two-pronged drive in Georgia for national independence and an autocephalous church began well before 1917 (Melia); the sizeable and influential Armenian diaspora, the existence of which greatly affected that church's fate, also dates from before the Revolution (Krikorian); the Mennonites knew privilege (Epp) and the Baptists encountered hardship (Blane) for long years under the czars; a considerable number of Jews were active participants in the revolutionary movement (Gitelman); and the Baltic lands and large portions of White Russia and Little Russia entered the Soviet orbit after two decades of independence or semi-independence (Mailleux, Vardys, Veinbergs). Finally, even geography seems to have introduced special features into the overall picture of church–state relations, as is indicated by the essay on the tribes of Siberia (Gapanovich).

Every bit as important as the contributions of these articles to the general picture of church–state relations in the Soviet Union is the unusual quantity of hard and not readily accessible information which they give about the various religious groups. To illustrate briefly: (1) Rothenberg, for the Jewish religious community, and

Veinbergs, for the Baltic Lutherans, give a wealth of data on the number of believers, religious leaders, and houses of worship, as well as considerable information about the types of religious rites and the degree of participation in them by the faithful. (2) Bogolepov analyzes the legal structure and institutional operation of the Russian Orthodox church in such informed detail that much light is shed both on the inner workings of this church and the interplay between a religious community and government agencies.

The cumulative result of the information and insights which these highly individual articles offer may well be to call into question many current generalizations about religion in the Soviet Union. But in so doing they also suggest lines of investigation for arriving at a new clarity which will be at once fuller and more authentic. At the most basic level the articles in this section reveal that religion in the USSR cannot simply be reduced to church–state relations; that critical as the role of the state has been and still is in the life of all religious communities this role cannot be properly understood apart from the larger framework of history and society. The implications of all this for the future of research in this area are clear. If we are to achieve a more informed synthesis, a series of specialized studies across a broad spectrum is indispensable. The chief value of these articles may lie in the fact that they raise more questions than they answer.

A.Q.B.

THE LEGAL POSITION
OF THE RUSSIAN ORTHODOX CHURCH
IN THE SOVIET UNION

I

The legal position of the Russian Orthodox church in the Soviet Union is officially defined by two kinds of acts: (1) decrees and orders of the Soviet government, and (2) decisions of the central authorities of the Russian Orthodox church itself. On close examination there is little difference between these two types of acts, since the decisions of the church authorities are published only with the prior agreement and permission of the state, or by its direct demand.

The basic government acts relevant to religion consist of the decree of January 23, 1918, "On the Separation of the Church from the State and the School from the Church," and the decree of the All-Russian Central Committee of the RSFSR of April 8, 1929, with subsequent amendments. (This latter law comprises a cumulative codification to that year of all basic decisions of the Soviet government concerning religious associations.) To these should be added the section of the Constitution of the USSR—introduced in 1936 and still in effect—"On the Basic Rights and Duties of Citizens" and in particular article 124 "On the Guarantee of Freedom of Conscience."[1] The most important regulation issued by the church authorities is "The Statutes of the Russian Orthodox Church," adopted in 1945

1. For the English text of basic Soviet laws on religion, see Appendix.

Alexander A. Bogolepov

and amended in 1961.[2] In addition to these governmental and ecclesiastical laws, the life of the church is regulated by direct administrative measures because state law grants extraordinarily broad discretionary powers to the governmental organs responsible for the
supervision of religious institutions. Consequently, the activity of
the Orthodox church is complicated at almost every point by its
lack of independence from the institutions of the state administration; and since in the Soviet Union there are no organs of legal control over the activities of the administration, it is impossible to avoid
the arbitrary character of this supervision.

Regardless of the rhetoric about legality in absolutist political
systems—whether of autocratic monarchies or revolutionary dictator-
ships—precise observance of the law therein is not possible. Independent courts, local self-governing political organs or social groups (in
which category the church would fall), as well as recognition of the
inalienable rights of persons—all of these would limit the authority and
the freedom of action of the ruling power, infringing on its absolute
character and upsetting its prescribed order. Understandably, then,
expediency prevails over conformity with the law. A complaint to the
highest administrative organs rarely achieves the desired goal, and
the lower administrative organs for the most part comply willingly
with the orders of these higher organs, implementing even those
orders which go beyond the power of existing law.

In the Soviet Union dialectical materialism and atheism are considered to be the indispensable ideological bases for the construction
of communism. Materialism is the doctrine which is intended to
replace religion in the consciousness of the people. This explains the
Soviet regime's antipathy to religion and its efforts to direct the activities of religious institutions into channels of state policy. It also
explains why arbitrary actions on the part of Soviet administrative
organs have come to be a normal part of the life of the Russian
Orthodox church.

The supervision of all religious associations was initially entrusted
to special divisions or departments of the People's Commissariat of
Justice, and subsequently to the People's Commissariat of Internal
Affairs. During World War II this system was altered by the establishment of two special institutions under what is now called the Coun-

---

2. *Polozhenie ob upravlenii russkoi pravoslavnoi tserkvi* [Decree on the administration
of the Russian Orthodox church] (Moscow, 1945).

cil of Ministers of the USSR: the Council for the Affairs of the Russian Orthodox Church (1943)[3] and, for all other religious bodies, the Council for the Affairs of Religious Cults (1944)[4]. In January, 1966, these institutions were merged into a single Council for Religious Affairs.[5]

From the outset the powers of the Council for the Affairs of the Russian Orthodox Church were defined very broadly. It was responsible for implementing governmental decrees concerning religion and was granted discretionary powers in numerous religious matters for which there was no prescribed law. In addition, this Council was entrusted with the reponsibility for working out new laws related to Orthodox church affairs as the need arose, and by this means was drawn into the law-making process. (Similar powers were granted to the Council for the Affairs of Religious Cults in regard to the other religious bodies.) Utilizing these broad powers, both councils began to issue instructions to their filial organs, which had been established under the governments of the union and the autonomous republics, as well as under the regional and district executive committees. The filial organs in turn issued instructional circulars to still lower administrative organs. These instructions and directives have played an enormous role in religious life in the USSR since World War II, and perhaps nowhere with greater effect than in the life of the Russian Orthodox church.

II

In Soviet Russia the struggle against religion began under the slogan of "the separation of church and state." In democratic countries this phrase has meant that the state favors no single religious group and does not interfere in any of their activities, but grants to all full freedom in internal affairs. In the communist world "the separation of church and state" has come to signify the denial of the property rights of all religious associations and the subordination of all of their activities to state control.

From the very beginning the plan of the Soviet government was most radical. It aimed at eliminating religion from human consciousness, and began by launching an "assault on Heaven" that was

3. *Izvestiia*, 8 October 1943.
4. *Izvestiia*, 1 July 1944.
5. For the announcement, see *Izvestiia*, 18 December 1965.

designed to destroy all religious organizations. To this end three types of measures were introduced.

First of all came the attempt to deprive the churches of their economic base. All religious property—churches, buildings, land, philanthropic and educational institutions—was taken from the churches and placed under the control of the state. The single economic source left for survival was the voluntary donations of parishioners, since even the establishment of any kind of obligatory membership dues was forbidden on the grounds that this would constitute a coercive measure.

The second means of attack was the sharp curtailment of all church activities. What was proclaimed as freedom of religion proved to mean only freedom of cult or freedom of divine worship. Religious associations were essentially confined to the houses of worship. After 1929, church organizations were also deprived of the right to carry on any kind of religious propaganda, whereas antireligious propaganda was granted the widest possible freedom. At the same time the churches were forbidden to engage in any philanthropic activity, to form social and cultural circles, or to organize under church auspices any kind of meetings other than divine services.[6]

The third antireligious measure, especially important for the Russian Orthodox church, was the destruction of the hierarchical structure. According to Soviet legislation all ministers of the cult were to have equal status. The central authority of the Russian Orthodox church did not have the right to issue instructions to diocesan bishops, who in turn were deprived of their authority over parish priests. The priests themselves were cut off from any official role in parish communities. All orders and punishments, even those purely ecclesiastical in character, were forbidden to the church on the grounds that they constituted compulsory measures. In these circumstances it is easy to imagine the difficulties and risks connected with the administration of the church, when any act of ecclesiastical authority could, by malevolent denunciation, incur prosecution whose consequences could be dire.

Soviet legislation reduced the church to small groups of believers— "groups of twenty"—entirely isolated in the conduct of their affairs and in no way attached to the hierarchy or connected with one

6. See Joshua Rothenberg, "The Legal Status of Religion in the Soviet Union," chapter 5 above.

another. The "groups of twenty" collected voluntary contr[...] and, at their discretion, distributed them, leased churches, and [...] and fired servants of the cult—priests, pastors, preachers, and sim[...] functionaries. These groups of believers could convene congresses and form executive committees for these gatherings, with special permission from the government for each occasion. The government also reserved for itself the right to bar individual persons from participation in these congresses and from membership on the executive committees. The collection of voluntary offerings for the setting up of congresses was permitted, but not the permanent establishment of a central fund by the religious associations.[7]

Now exempt from hierarchical control, the "groups of twenty" were placed under the supervision of the local organs of the Soviet government. A list of the clergy and the lay members of the executive and administrative bodies of the groups had to be "registered" with governmental authorities. But successful registration—which would seem a perfectly normal and inoffensive formality—depended upon the judgment of local officials. Registration could be denied if the methods and forms of the community's activity did not conform to existing Soviet law, or threatened the peace and security of society, or stirred national discord and enmity.[8] In fact these stipulations were only a camouflage, since the result of such extraordinarily broad conditions for registration amounted, in practice, to equating "registration" with permission to exist.

Having been reduced to small, unconnected groups of believers, the church—according to the intent of Soviet legislation—was supposed to disintegrate and die. In order to accelerate this process, a wide range of regulations was introduced concerning the closure of churches and the demotion of clergy to the status of citizens without rights. The closing of a church was legal if the building was required for state or civic needs, if the church group proved untrustworthy and anti-Soviet, or if the workers expressed this desire by means of

7. See the Decree on Religious Associations of April 8, 1929, of the All-Russian Central Executive Committee of the RSFSR, articles 20–22, and 54, in Appendix, section 2B, below.

8. See the Instruction of the People's Commissariat of Internal Affairs of the RSFSR of October 1, 1929, article 46, and the Decree of April 8, 1929, article 8, in Appendix, sections 2C, 2B, below.

nd the like.[9] The clergy, though deprived
to pay totally unreasonable taxes in com-
by other members of the so-called "free
lergy were not permitted to be employed in
cupy quarters in nationalized residences.
allowed to enroll in educational institu-
of many of these measures coincided with
mockery of religious faith, including
blasphemous articles published in the antireligious journals and
noisy disorders created in the churches by the League of the Militant
Godless during religious services.

As a result of the devastation introduced through these legal and
administrative measures, by 1941 there remained within the then-
existing boundaries of the Soviet Union fewer than 12 per cent of the
pre-1917 Orthodox parish churches (4,225 out of 46,457), and some
90 percent of the parish priests had been deprived of their posts.[11]
By revolutionary decree and without benefit of legal process many
leading bishops, clerics, and lay members of the church councils
had been liquidated. Almost all of the members of the hierarchy
served time in prison or in exile; most clerics, monks, nuns, and ordinary laymen who suffered arrest were doomed to an arduous life in
prison or exile, although some were subsequently freed. The persecution of believers during the first two decades of Soviet rule took
place on an unprecedented scale.

III

In the mid-twenties, together with other bishops, Metropolitan
Sergy (Stragorodsky) was imprisoned. Since he was the locum tenens
of the patriarchal throne, his arrest gravely weakened the existing
central church administration. In 1927, upon his liberation from
prison, Metropolitan Sergy sent out a formal encyclical to priests and
their flocks, summoning them, in Paul's words, to loyalty to the

9. See the Instruction of the People's Commissariat of Justice and of Internal Affairs of
April 27, 1923 and June 19, 1923 in P. V. Gidulianov, ed., *Otdelenie tserkvi ot gosudarstva, polny sbornik dekretov RSFSR i SSSR; instruktsii, tsirkuliarov, i t. d.* [Separation of
church from state, complete collection of decrees of the RSFSR and the USSR; instructions, circulars, etc.], rev. ed. (Moscow, 1926).

10. A. A. Bogolepov, *Tserkov pod vlastiu kommunizma* [The church under communist
rule] (Munich, 1958), pp. 10–14.

11. Paul B. Anderson, *People, Church, and State in Modern Russia* (New York, 1944),
p. 120.

Soviet government and to civic fidelity "not out of fear of punishment, but for conscience's sake" (Rom. 13:5). On these grounds he considered it possible to place the Orthodox church on a correct footing with the Soviet government and to secure for the church a legal and peaceful existence in the Soviet Union. He received in exchange permission to establish a central church administration through the formation of a Holy Synod comprised of bishops, selected by him and approved by the government. In this interplay the Soviet government at long last obtained the recognition and the promise of cooperation from the church which it had sought in vain from Patriarch Tikhon.

Nonetheless the persecution continued. Information about this persecution soon became known abroad and complicated the efforts of the Soviet government to strengthen its international position. As a result, the silence of the hierarchy became intolerable, and the Soviet government demanded that Metropolitan Sergy, as locum tenens, publicly declare that religious persecution was nonexistent in Russia. At this very time, as part of the introduction of the First Five-Year Plan, the compulsory collectivization of peasants into kolkhozes was in progress. Simultaneously, fresh efforts had begun to close churches and to banish priests, especially in the countryside. Clerics were classified as kulaks (wealthy peasants) and opponents of collectivization. Like kulaks, the clerics and their families were driven from their homes and exiled to distant places while their belongings remained behind.

The central administration of the church was deeply depressed by this turn of events, for not only did it threaten the welfare of clerics and their families, but it meant that village churches would be left without priests. In these circumstances, Metropolitan Sergy agreed to meet the demands which more than once had been made of him by the Soviet government; in so doing, however, he presented certain counterdemands. The Metropolitan insisted that the Soviet government immediately renounce the classification of clergy as kulaks and cease expelling them from their homes.[12] Sergy's demand was met, and the expulsion of the rural clergy was halted. On February 15, 1930, Metropolitan Sergy issued a written statement to newspaper

12. V. P. Vinogradov, "Eine Studie über die Arbeit von Prof. A. A. Bogolepov: *Die Kirche unter der Herrschaft des Kommunismus*," *Soviet Studies*, no. 9 (Munich, 1960), pp. 91–111.

correspondents. This asserted that the persecution of religion never had existed in the USSR, nor did it now, since according to the decree of 1918 on the separation of church from state "the confession of any faith is completely free"; "the closing of churches does not take place at the initiative of the government, but by the desires of the population"; and where the prosecution of the clergy occurred it had "not been for religious convictions but for civil crimes."[13]

Metropolitan Sergy readily learned of the misunderstanding and disturbance which his declaration evoked among certain circles abroad. Archpriest V. P. Vinogradov has reported the remark which Metropolitan Sergy made in his presence: "Is it really possible that the West does not understand that an Orthodox bishop in Russia could not possibly say freely what I said in my interview? Is it possible that they cannot infer from this statement the difficult position in which the supreme church administration finds itself in the Soviet Union?"[14]

Four days after his interview Metropolitan Sergy turned to the Soviet government with a new appeal for the curtailment of the oppression of the clergy, which he described as illegal and arbitrary. Among other things, Metropolitan Sergy pointed to the levying of taxes on members of the clergy which bore no relationship whatsoever to their activity (for example, taxes on agricultural products), to the establishment of labor norms exceeding all reasonable limits, and to the forbidding of priests to reside within the boundaries of their own villages. Although Metropolitan Sergy succeeded through his declaration of February 15, 1930, in softening the blows being levelled against the church, the Soviet government did not halt its persecution of religion. What was more serious, the interview of February 15, 1930, was to serve as a burdensome precedent in the future.

By 1935, for all practical purposes, the permission granted to Metropolitan Sergy to have a synod had lost its significance. The episcopal members of the synod had been gradually isolated from each other. Metropolitan Sergy's single remaining assistant was his vicar, Sergei (Voskresensky). Once again the bishops became subject to exile, and one after another the dioceses were left without a ruling bishop and so passed under the direct supervision of Metropolitan

13. *Izvestiia*, 19 February 1930.
14. Vinogradov, "Eine Studie," pp. 91–111.

Sergy. In 1937–38 a new wave of persecutions broke out, with the further closing of churches and the fresh persecution of clergy.

IV

In spite of the severity of the new persecution, the church survived. One of the leaders of the League of the Militant Godless regretfully admitted that religion remained very much alive.[15] In 1939 the persecution began to abate. During the war with Hitler, when the very foundations of the Soviet state were threatened, Stalin had to make use of the church. As a series of relatively isolated communities the Orthodox church was not capable of significant assistance; to be effective, the church needed a stronger and more unified organizational structure. The Soviet government could also see that through a centralized authority the state could more easily direct the activities of the whole church along the desired path.

In 1943 a convocation of the Council of Bishops was permitted, in which Metropolitan Sergy was elected Patriarch of Moscow and All Russia. When Sergy died in 1945, a *sobor* (council)—in which, with the permission of the government, both clerics and laymen participated—elected a new patriarch, Aleksy. This council also adopted the "Statutes of the Russian Orthodox Church." Clearly, the text of these statutes had been worked out on the basis of preliminary discussions between the church hierarchy and the Soviet government. The full text of the statutes was accepted by the council in the course of a single session and without objection from any quarter. In the person of G. G. Karpov, Chairman of the Council for the Affairs of the Russian Orthodox Church, the government was represented at the council and approved its action.

The new statutes introduced substantive changes in two respects: (1) a hierarchical church structure was reestablished, and (2) the church's financial basis was improved through the creation of a centralized system of funding. The new regulations created a conciliar facade behind which arose a structure with the centralized direction of church affairs in the hands of a single personage. The ruling bodies which were to comprise this decorative conciliar system were the local council, the Council of Bishops, and the Holy

---

15. F. N. Oleshchuk, *O preodolenii religionznykh predrassudkov* [On overcoming religious prejudices] (Moscow, 1941), p. 37.

Synod; the single personage in whom real power resided was, of course, the patriarch.

The patriarch now occupied the highest position within the church government. He alone was vested with broad powers in matters of ecclesiastical government, with the organs of the administration subordinated to him. The orders of the higher ecclesiastical bodies to the lower were no longer to be regarded as compulsory measures. The extent of the patriarch's authority was first of all evident in his relations with the episcopate: he had authority to appoint diocesan bishops at will, to transfer them from one diocese to another, to supervise their activities, and to award them titles and the highest ecclesiastical honors.

The Holy Synod, consisting of six bishops, did not have explicitly designated responsibilities independent of the patriarch; rather it was to be his consultative organ. The agenda of the Holy Synod depends upon the patriarch, and he is free to submit for the consideration of the Synod matters which, according to the statutes, are under his personal jurisdiction. Accordingly, the sphere of the Synod's activities can be enlarged or reduced in conformity with the patriarch's wishes. In practice, after 1945, these activities were extended. The appointment and transfer of bishops, a function which could be performed by the patriarch alone, were usually discussed by him with the Synod and published as its decisions; other, more important, problems have also been submitted for the consideration of the Synod. Of course, all decisions have had to conform to the views of the patriarch.

The council of the ruling bishops likewise had no definite powers or rights of initiative. Also, its sessions could take place only with the prior permission of the government. Under existing circumstances, however, it has not always been possible to call a council of bishops. The opinions of the bishops have sometimes been requested by telegraph, with their written replies treated in the same manner as votes at a session. In its turn, the local council, although it consists of bishops, clergy, and laymen, cannot be considered truly representative of the whole church. The method of selecting the clerical and lay delegates was not defined. The membership of the council had to be examined by governmental authorities, just as the membership of any other meeting for religious purposes would be; this means, practically speaking, that the council can consist only of persons who have been allowed by the Soviet government to take part in it. The local council is thus called at the will of the patriarch and with governmental permission. It has neither definite powers nor independent initiative, and can only act upon questions presented to it. The chief function which belongs exclusively to the local council is the election of a new patriarch. Historically speaking, from 1945 until 1968 the council of bishops was convoked rarely—most significantly in 1961—and the local council was not convened a single time.

Just as the central administration was now based upon the authority of the patriarch, so the administration of a diocese was built upon the authority of the bishop. The bishop governs the diocese personally, although he may use the assistance of a "diocesan council," consisting of three to five priests chosen by himself. The diocesan council has to review for his decision such matters as he sees fit to direct to it for preliminary investigation. Therefore, the diocesan council is no restriction upon the bishop. Laymen have no part in diocesan administration. There is at present no additional information available about the activities of these diocesan councils.

Of particular importance in the new regulations was the transformation of the "groups of twenty" into parish communities. Now, in place of the "groups of twenty," the parish meeting came to the fore, with the right to elect a four-member parish council and an auditing commission. The parish priest was no longer to be the hired executor of church rites and activities. He was now appointed by the diocesan bishop "for the spiritual guidance of believers and for the administration of the clergy and the parish,"[16] and became ex officio "the responsible chairman of the parish council" with the authority to guard the legality of its activities. In the event of illegal activity on the part of the parish council or any of its individual members, the parish priest was obliged to report the matter to the diocesan bishop and then, with the consent of the commissioner of the Council for the Affairs of the Orthodox Church, he could propose that the parish community replace the guilty members.[17]

The most immediate and truly important result of the alteration of parish government was the improvement of the financial position of the church. The parish council remained the basic organ for the collection of church funds, but—according to the new statutes of

16. *Polozhenie*, art. 35.
17. Ibid., art. 46.

1945—there was now added to the existing system of donations during church services certain other "voluntary donations" for candles, prosphora, and the like—contributions of an unspecified amount.

Another change was the increase established in required payments. To the regular expenses of upkeep for the houses of worship and support of the clergy were now added special contributions for the diocesan and patriarchal administrations and for the maintenance of religious schools, that is, the seminaries and academies. The reestablishment of the hierarchical structure made it possible not only to impose these contributions, but also to define their amount and frequency. Although the parish council controlled parish property, it did so "under the direct guidance" of the parish priest, whose signature was required with that of the treasurer on all checks.[18] The parish priest in his turn had to carry out the instruction of the diocesan bishop in directing the life of the parish, and had to present to the bishop semiannual reports on the parish and its monetary expenditures.[19] The diocesan bishop, finally, was required to carry out the directives of the patriarchal administration. Through the diocesan bishops, then, the patriarchal administration could exercise its authority over the priests and the parish councils, establish the size of the contributions required, and create a centralized administration for church finances. What had formerly been forbidden was now made possible, namely, the formation of a central treasury for church finances.[20]

In effect the "groups of twenty" were now formed into parish communities and were organically incorporated into the structure of the general church system. What from the point of view of Soviet law had only been dispersed communities of believers were now reconstituted into a unified whole.

The church was granted still other privileges. Religious schools for the preparation of clerics were opened: six seminaries and two theological academies. The monthly publication of the official church organ, the *Zhurnal moskovskoi patriarkhii* (Journal of the Moscow patriarchate) was begun, and the Church was granted the use of

18. Ibid., art. 44.
19. Ibid., art. 45.
20. A. A. Bogolepov, *The Statutes of the Russian Orthodox Church, 1945* (New York 1959), pp. 3, 14–16.

state-owned enterprises for the production of candles, censers, chalices, and other objects of cult.

Certain limitations previously introduced continued to lie heavy upon the church. Although the hierarchical structure of the Church had been reestablished (with the diocesan bishops subject to the patriarch, and the parish priests subject to the diocesan bishops), the government retained control over the composition of the clergy. All members of the clergy—patriarch, bishops, and parish priests—were permitted to exercise their religious functions only after the registration of their stamp and seal by the proper civil authorities. This registration, demanded of each new cleric, was of an individual and nontransferable character which, for all practical purposes, represented confirmation of his appointment by the secular authorities.[21]

Freedom of religious activity also remained limited, as before, to the conduct of divine services within church buildings. Only funeral processions to cemeteries and visitations by priests to those critically ill in hospitals or in prisons were permitted in public places. As had previously been the case, all religious propaganda outside of houses of worship and any organization of schools for the teaching of religion to children were categorically forbidden. Engagement in philanthropic or cultural activities, and the formation of circles or groups under church auspices were still prohibited. The decree concerning the closure of churches still remained in force. And in practice persons openly belonging to a religious confession were, as before, not permitted to occupy any significant post; such posts were open exclusively to members of the Communist party or to unions associated with it.

Although important concessions had been granted, the struggle of the Communists with religion was not curtailed; it only assumed new forms. The development of antireligious propaganda, with the goal of total elimination of religion from public life, remained. The Communists hoped to overcome the church with ideological warfare, while not allowing the church to defend itself with similar weapons. All of this comprised a transition from a violent, open struggle against religion to a "cold war" carried on under cover of a truce.

V

The change in legal conditions, nevertheless, did make it possible for

21. *Polozhenie*, art. 16, 26, 48.

the Orthodox church to strengthen itself organizationally and finan-
cially. The impoverished people generously sacrificed for the sake of
the church. By the beginning of the 1950s, the number of dioceses
had reached seventy-two, and the monasteries totalled eighty-nine.
And taking into account the approximately six thousand parishes
added in the regions annexed to the USSR after the war, the total
number of parishes and churches, according to official estimates, had
grown to between twenty- and twenty-two thousand.[22]

In light of the improved wartime situation, the locum tenens of the
patriarchal throne, Metropolitan Sergy, considered it necessary to
restate the basic position which he had taken in his dramatic interview twelve years earlier. This was done in 1942 in the book, *Pravda
o religii v Rossii* (The truth about religion in Russia).[23] His successor,
Patriarch Aleksy, developed this idea in even greater detail in *Russkaia
Pravoslavnaia Tserkov* (The Russian Orthodox church), published in
Moscow in 1958. By now this position had become the official ideology of the Moscow patriarchate. It was an effort to present the
church's position in Russia in a favorable light, based exclusively on
the formal provisions of the Soviet constitution, along with avoidance of all questions about the existence of religious persecution and
acceptance of the Communist order on ostensibly religious grounds.

In a conversation with the representatives of the Novosti Press
Agency, Patriarch Aleksy confirmed, as Patriarch Sergy had before
him, that "all citizens of our fatherland have been guaranteed full
and unhindered freedom of conscience under the constitution."[24] "In
the light of this," continued the Patriarch, "our Russian Orthodox
church enjoys all the conditions necessary for fulfilling its sublime
mission according to the holy canons and to Orthodox tradition."[25]
As concerned the repeated persecution of believers by the state, the
patriarchal administration took a position similar to the government's, explaining that the legal persecution of believers occurred

22. *Russkaia pravoslavnaia tserkov* [The Russian Orthodox church] (The Moscow
patriarchate, 1958), pp. 40–41; *USSR Information Bulletin*, January 1949; Interview with
Archbishop Boris, *Newsweek*, 17 January 1952, p. 84; N. S. Timasheff, "Urbanization, Operation Antireligion and the Decline of Religion in the USSR," *The American
Slavic and East European Review*, April 1955, pp. 203–4; *One Church* (The Exarchate of
The Russian Orthodox Church in America, 1956), nos. 5–6.
23. *The Truth about Religion in Russia* (Moscow, 1942), p. 26.
24. *Zhurnal moskovskoi patriarkhii* [Journal of the Moscow patriarchate] (hereafter
ZHMP), 1967, no. 1, p. 5.
25. Ibid.

not because of their faith, but because of illegal activities which made them subject to punishment just as violations of civil law made other citizens subject to punishment. Soviet law includes many prohibitions and limitations on religious and church activities. Since violation of these laws is considered either on a par with theft and murder, both criminally punishable activities, or with infringements of the law punishable by administrative measures, the patriarchate had room, following the line of the Soviet government, to refute the rumors which reached the West about religious persecutions in Russia and even to declare such rumors false and slanderous.[26] Specific cases were said to invoke only general criminal punishment which had nothing at all to do with religion.

Patriarch Sergy had earlier requested the faithful to serve the Soviet Union not out of fear of punishment, but for love of country. After Sergy's passing, this expression of loyalty was further justified by the assertion that Soviet power was introducing into historical life many of the lofty moral principles which the church had always preached and continued to preach.[27] The hierarchs of the Russian church therefore came to recognize that Christians might actively participate in the construction of a classless, socialist society, free of exploitation, racism, and inequality, in which each member enjoyed equal rights and equal possibilities for individual development and active participation in the life of society as a whole.[28] The socialist system, according to this view, has concentrated in the hands of the government all the instruments and means of production to serve the public good, with the result that "the official forms of public assistance and state concern in the social welfare of the citizens are incomparably more effective in the socialist states than in the capitalist states."[29]

This, of course, amounts to ecclesiastical justification of the Communist system despite the latter's open struggle with religion. In this new formulation the tie of atheism and materialism with the Communist construction of society is clearly broken and communism is

---

26. *Russkaia pravoslavniia tserkov: organizatsiia, polozhenie i deiatelnost* [The Russian Orthodox church: organization, situation and activity] (Moscow, 1958), pp. 24–25.

27. *ZHMP*, 1955, no. 6, p. 27.

28. *ZHMP*, 1966, no. 10. A declaration of Metropolitan Nikodim at a press conference in Geneva on July 22, 1966.

29. Metropolitan Nikodim, "Dialogue with Roman Catholics," *One Church*, 1966, nos. 11–12, pp. 252–54.

accepted as a visionary theory rather than in the form in which it has appeared in historical reality. "I do not have the atheistic point of view of the Communist party," said Metropolitan Filaret of Kiev to members of the press, "but the party strives for the welfare of the people and for the just distribution of goods and the equality of all. There is nothing in this contradictory to Christian doctrine."[30]

Such an ideological development naturally pushed the church into close collaboration with the Soviet government. Under Patriarch Sergy the church had rendered aid to the government chiefly through defending the fatherland against Hitler. After Sergy the hierarchy attempted wholeheartedly to support the internal policies of the Soviet government, while unscrupulously justifying all its undertakings in international affairs. In particular, representatives of the Moscow patriarchate played a large part at international Communist conferences for "the defense of peace." Having set its course on good relations with the Soviet government, the supreme church administration saw in this policy the only possibility of preserving an open existence for the Orthodox church in the Soviet Union and of strengthening the church's role in international religious affairs.

VI

Under the "new religious policy" and side by side with the renewal of church activity, the deeply-rooted antipathy of the regime toward religion again flared up. N. S. Khrushchev, the Chairman of the Council of Ministers of the USSR, began a new persecution of religion toward the end of the 1950s.[31]

The agents of these antireligious measures was the Council for the Affairs of the Orthodox Church. The signal for the new onslaught was the replacement of G. Karpov by V. Kuroedov as the head of

---

30. *Informations Catholiques Internationales* (Paris), as quoted in *The Orthodox Church,* 1967, no. 3, p. 1. The representative of the Evangelical Christians-Baptists, N. I. Bovtunov, expressed himself in this same spirit: "I personally have never been nor attempted to be a Communist, but I travel hand-in-hand with sincere Communists because belief in God does not hinder us from travelling together toward desired goals. To believe or not to believe in God is a personal affair. The conscience of one leads him to believe in God, and he sincerely believes. The conscience of another does not lead him to believe in God, and so he does not believe. But this should not divide us. All who live on this earth must live only for a single dream—how to construct Communism throughout the world as quickly as possible." *Liudyna i svit* [Man and the world], 1966, no. 11 (Kiev) as quoted in *Religion in Communist-Dominated Areas* (hereafter *RCDA*), 1967, no. 5, p. 41.

31. See Donald A. Lowrie and William C. Fletcher, "Khrushchev's Religious Policy, 1959–1964," chapter 7 above.

this council.[32] In order to carry out the new attack against religion, all the discretionary powers of the administration which, though in force, had been laid aside, had first to be resurrected and broadened. Still not satisfied, the Council for the Affairs of the Orthodox Church then introduced new measures for matters not covered in earlier Soviet law.[33] But even this proved insufficient. Consequently, certain modifications were made in the Statutes of the Russian Orthodox Church which had directed the life of the church since their adoption in 1945.

Of the previous measures, chief use was made of the decrees on the registration and closure of churches. Here the new campaign unfolded rapidly.[34] Some fifty monasteries were liquidated, among them the Kievan Monastery of the Caves. Of the eight seminaries, only three were left open. By the end of 1965 some ten thousand churches had been closed, or one-half of those which had been in existence. With this mass closing of churches, it is obvious that the number of parishes and of clerics in parochial service sharply diminished.

The right of the administration to register new clerics came to be viewed as the right to remove them from service by the "withdrawal" of their registration. Sometimes, in order to facilitate dismissals, a "reregistration" was ordered, in which clerics who, from the government's point of view, were unsuitable would be denied a new registration. In this fashion those persons who for one reason or another were unsatisfactory to the government, in particular the insufficiently pliant, were weeded out of the church ranks. The threat of "withdrawal of registration" thus came to hang over the head of each priest. In the hands of the Council for the Affairs of the Orthodox Church this threat became a key weapon for coercing priests and bishops into compliance with the illegal demands of the authorities. The threat of "withdrawal of registration," as well as many unlawful orders of the atheistic authorities, were accomplished almost exclusively through simple oral directives.

The discretionary powers of administrative officials over religious life were even further broadened by several circulars issued by the

32. *Izvestiia*, 21 February 1960.
33. See Rothenberg, "Legal Status of Religion," chapter 5 above.
34. Nikita Struve, "New Ordeals for the Church in Russia," *St. Vladimir's Seminary Quarterly*, 1963, no. 4, pp. 172–77, 184.

Council for the Affairs of the Orthodox Church. These new measures went beyond all limits previously established by the highest organs of the state and were clearly aimed at "finding new means" to undermine the activities of the religious associations.[35]

As far as is possible to judge from the actions of commissioners of the Council for the Affairs of the Orthodox Church, these circulars prohibited the involvement of children and minors (those under eighteen years of age) in church services as singers, altar boys, or the like. In certain dioceses preschool and school-age children were not even permitted to receive holy communion in the churches. Without written permission from local authorities, clerics were forbidden to conduct requiem services at the cemeteries or rites in homes (with the exception of holy communion and the anointing of the sick). In addition, the parish councils were required to register all baptisms and weddings. Baptisms could be performed only in the church, and only with the consent of both parents who, at that time, had to present their passports.[36] The simultaneous closure of many churches often forced long and arduous trips on parents with newborn infants, and the requirement of presenting passports made it virtually impossible for anyone who worked in a Soviet institution to baptize his children covertly or to be married secretly in a religious ceremony in church.

The requirement of registration for baptisms or weddings appeared to be unexceptional. But persons whose religious convictions came unexpectedly to light by this means were subject to public ridicule as loafers and ignoramuses, at their place of work or study or through local newspapers and wall posters. Such persons could also become the object of various administrative reprisals. It is true that, according to the decree of the Supreme Soviet of the RSFSR of March 18, 1966, refusal to accept a person into employment or into an educational institution or, equally, to dismiss him from employment or from an educational institution, or in any way to limit his civil rights because of his religious convictions, was made punishable under article 43 of the criminal code.[37] To make the conditions for the employment of believers extremely difficult, or to make their dismissal relatively simple, other grounds could readily be found to

35. See Appendix, section 5, below.
36. See Lowrie and Fletcher, "Krushchev's Religious Policy," chapter 7 above.
37. The English text of this decree is in the Appendix, section 3, below.

indicate personal unacceptability—lack of qualification, a necessary cutback in the labor force, and the like.

To achieve greater success in the struggle with religion, the local organs for the supervision of religious associations were strengthened. As an aid to the local branches of the Council for the Affairs of the Orthodox Church, new "cooperating commissions" were introduced at the regional and district executive-committee levels. These commissions were created not by a decree of the highest state organs in the USSR, but by a circular sent out by the Council for the Affairs of the Orthodox Church. This circular was issued—as has now become customary—without publication in the Soviet Union. The text of the circular has since come to light abroad.[38] The cooperating commissions were to be formed by the local government executive committees. In addition to the vice-chairman or secretary of the local executive committee, the membership was to include "persons politically prepared" to exercise control over religious societies: deputies of local soviets, workers in cultural-educational institutions and in the organs of public education, propagandists, workers in village soviets, and other individuals drawn from local activists.[39]

The basic task of the cooperating commissions was an all-encompassing surveillance of persons who took part in religious associations. The commissions were to check closely on the observance of Soviet legislation by ministers of the cult, to expose any attempt to transgress Soviet law, and in proper time to report such activity to the local executive committee. They were also expected to bring to account ministers of the cult who illegally performed religious rites in the homes and apartments of believers and who received compensation without receipt to avoid declaring this for income tax. The commissions were also to verify the accuracy of the record of religious rites and to stop any baptism of children which did not have the agreement of both parents.[40] This new attempt to narrow the circle of believers by all means possible was so strong that the Council for the Affairs of the Orthodox Church extended its surveillance beyond clerics to all persons in any way connected with the Church.

The cooperating commissions are required to ascertain who attends church, who has his children baptized, who goes to confession,

38. *RCDA*, 15 April, 1967, pp. 58–69. See also the Appendix, section 5, below.
39. *RCDA*, 15 April 1967, pp. 58–69.
40. Ibid.

who requests a religious wedding or funeral, and who among the young comes under the influence of the ministers of the cult. This information is to be recorded in special lists which are useful for holding priests accountable in the violation of instructions, for ascertaining the negative influence of religious holidays on labor productivity, and for discovering means to curtail the influence of religion on particular individuals. All of this is a way of measuring the results of antireligious propaganda and the remaining number of believers in a given locality or within a specific group (parish, industrial plant, and the like). Believers thus identified are subjected to intense atheistic reeducation, frequently by means of "person-to-person anti-evangelism" (to use Paul B. Anderson's phrase).[41] This is a tortuous system of importunate and unavoidable interference in personal life. On the one hand, it consists of an insidious, but persistent, promise of various kinds of privilege to those who defect from religious faith; on the other hand, it involves the threat of administrative penalties, which are legitimized by the broad discretionary powers granted to Soviet administrators.

One of the most important tasks of the commissions "must be the seeking out of means and the introducing of concrete proposals aimed at limiting and weakening the activities of religious societies and ministers of the cult (within the framework of the law)" or, in other words, the preparation of new governmental decrees to apply fresh pressure on believers.[42] In these terms, the Council's secret circular defines in the clearest possible fashion the recent tactics of the Council for the Affairs of the Orthodox Church. The full text of this circular strikingly conforms to the information about the new wave of religious persecutions in Russia which reached the outside world long before the text of the circular itself.[43]

In such adverse circumstances it is not surprising that the regime has been able to find people who will serve as its agents within the church. Even Patriarch Aleksy himself has acknowledged the penetration of unworthy persons into the confines of the church.[44] A

41. Paul B. Anderson, "A Decade of Significance for Religion (1956–1966)," in Dennis Dirscherl, S.J., ed. *The New Russia* (Dayton, Ohio), 1968, p. 147.

42. *RCDA*, 15 April 1967, pp. 58–59.

43. Struve, *New Ordeals*, pp. 78ff; "The Open Letter of Two Moscow Priests, N. Eshliman and G. Yakunin," *St. Valdimir's Seminary Quarterly*, 1966, nos. 1–2.

44. *Messager de l'Exarchat du Patriarchat Russe en Europe Occidental*, 1961, nos. 38–39, pp. 68–69.

shocking reference to such a cleric is given in the recent "Open Letter" of the believers of the Korov diocese, in which they declare that all complaints to ecclesiastical and state authorities about the scandalous behavior of this priest have gone without results. To those complaining, the local commissioner of the Council for the Affairs of the Orthodox Church plainly stated: "These are just the kind of priests we need."[45] The appearance in Russia of clerics who feather their own nests by servility to the Soviet government can also be traced to the unfortunate interruption in the functioning of all theological schools from 1918 to 1944, to the requirement of a course in antireligion at the state schools as a prerequisite for admission to the seminaries, and to the whole coercive atmosphere in which young people grow up in the Soviet Union.

VII

The most grievous blow levelled against the Orthodox church in the new attack was the alteration of the statutes which had been adopted under Stalin in 1945. Khrushchev's church policy here was characterized by two aims: to increase the subordination to the atheistic state of the highest organ of church administration, the Holy Synod, and to separate the hierarchy from the lowest church unit, the parish.

According to the statutes of the Russian Orthodox church of 1945, the Holy Synod was to consist of three permanent members, the metropolitans of Krutitsk, Leningrad, and Kiev, and three temporary members, ruling bishops appointed annually in order of seniority of consecration. Except for the metropolitan of Krutitsk, the members of the Synod were resident in the locale of their appointment, which was usually away from Moscow. But as Patriarch Aleksy declared to a Bishops' council on July 18, 1961: "Now more and more questions have arisen demanding immediate attention, which in turn have required a speedy convocation of the permanent members of the Synod. . . . In existing circumstances this proved difficult; it was therefore expedient to have three readily available permanent members of the Holy Synod with authority to render decisions in urgent affairs."[46] For this purpose the membership of the Synod was enlarged to eight. Of residents in Moscow it now

45. *Vestnik russkogo studencheskogo khristianskogo dvizheniia* [Herald of the Russian student Christian movement], 1966, no. 82, 3–20.
46. *ZHMP*, 1961, no. 8, pp. 7–8.

included the chairman of the Department of External Relations and the Director of the Affairs of the Moscow patriarchate—both of episcopal rank. Together with the metropolitan of Krutitsk, these became a three-member collegium of the Synod who could make quick decisions on questions which, in the view of the government, could not be postponed. All three of these synodal members are church officials directly subject to the patriarch, actually belonging to the chancery of the patriarchal administration. From the point of view of the Soviet government, the smaller the membership of the Synod the easier it is to influence and direct it towards desired goals.

In reflecting on the reform of the Synod, what is striking is not only the great haste but also the unauthorized means by which the reform was accomplished. This reorganization of the Holy Synod was brought about by a change in part 2 of the 1945 statutes of the Russian Orthodox church. Since these statutes were adopted by a local council of the Russian Orthodox church, they could only be legitimately altered by a similar local council. But it is apparent that a change in the composition of the Synod was demanded so rapidly, that to consider convening a local council was not really possible. Nor could the matter be reserved for the convening of a council of bishops. This alteration in the legal constitution of the Holy Synod was made, at the request of the patriarch, by the Holy synod itself in a meeting of March 16, 1961. Four months later, on July 18, the change was submitted to a council of bishops for consideration. The council listened to the presentation, after which one of the members of the Synod moved "to dispense with further discussion and to confirm unanimously the decision of the Patriarch and of the Holy Synod." This was duly done.[47]

A month after the change in the membership of the Holy Synod, in a session of April 18, 1961, the Synod also altered part 4 of the 1945 statutes, which related to the parishes. These changes were quickly introduced into the various dioceses. This time the patriarch openly admitted that in April, 1961, the Council of Ministers of the USSR had directed, through the Council for the Affairs of the Russian Orthodox Church, that the regulations concerning religious communities and their economic activities needed to be revised to make them

47. Ibid., p. 9.

correspond to the legislation on cults (apparently the law of April 8, 1929, "On Religious Associations").[48]

This directive of the Soviet government which noted that the statutes of 1945 were out of harmony with the law of 1929, still extant and in force, might seem rather strange. There unquestionably was a lack of correspondence between them. But the statutes of the Russian Orthodox Church had been adopted only with the prior agreement and approval of the state. Their lack of correspondence with existing law was allowed by the Council of People's Commissars of the RSFSR as a special reward for the wartime service of the Russian church. In essence, the statutes of 1945 were a special law for the Russian Orthodox church. This lack of harmony was clearly evident to the Soviet government in 1945 when it permitted the working out and adoption of these statutes. But in the 1960s, in order to implement the new policy of curtailing church activity, some pretext was needed. Taking advantage of the unseemly circumstances, the Soviet government "directed" that the church authorities demand the alteration desirable to the government, but in such a way that it would appear to be a law initiated by the church itself. The patriarch and the Holy Synod had to fulfill the directive of the government quickly. Only after the new regulations had already begun to be introduced into parish life were they presented, on July 18, 1961, for the consideration of the Council of Bishops. The council unanimously confirmed the new regulations issued by the Holy Synod on April 18, 1961, and added, for the sake of decorum: "pending the convocation of a regular meeting of the Local Council of the Russian Orthodox Church."[49]

The new regulations for parishes brought an abrupt change in the status of the parish priest and of the parish council, as well as in the financial administration and organizational structure of the church at large. The basic principle of the reform was a sharp distinction between economic and spiritual affairs: all economic concerns were placed in the hands of the parish council, and all spiritual matters were entrusted to the priest. But the priest had no right to supervise or to control the economic activity of the council to insure that it corresponded with the spiritual interests of the church.

48. Ibid., pp. 11–14.
49. Ibid., p. 15.

According to the statutes of 1945, parish priests were appointed by the diocesan bishop. Now they were to be selected by the parish communities and the bishop could only bestow his blessing upon them. The conduct of divine services and church rites, as well as the spiritual guidance of the parishioners, were to be the exclusive functions of the priest. The "pastor of the parish" was recognized as "the responsible person before God and his bishop for the well-being of the religious life and moral health of the parish."[50] In matters pertaining to divine services or the mutual relations of clergymen, the parish council did not have the right to interfere. Lectors, cantors, and other church servants were to now be hired jointly by the priest and the parish council. In the event of disagreement, the issue was to be resolved by the diocesan bishop. The priest could no longer attend meetings of the parish council, even in the role of an ordinary parish member. And since he was now to have no relation to the financial administration of the parish, he no longer had the right to sign checks. If the priest required funds for the conduct of divine services or church rites, he was to present his request to the parish council. Apparently, in these instances, he could attend council meetings but had no right to vote.

The parish council was now to consist of a church warden, his assistant, and a treasurer, all to be elected at a general meeting of the parish. It was to be responsible for dispersing parish funds, both for the needs of the parish (for example, salaries of priests, workers, and church servants) and for the requirements of the higher organs of church administration. The new regulations emphasized in particular that funds to support the work of the diocesan bishop, the patriarchal administration, religious and educational institutions, and the pension fund were to be allocated by the parish councils only on a "voluntary basis." Moreover, allocations were to correspond to need and to available parish funds.

As a consequence, the amount of money assigned for the various needs was now to be set by the parish council itself without the necessity of following directives from the diocesan or the central church administration. This removal of the right of control over the activities of the parish council from the parish priest held serious consequences for the hierarchical structure of the church. It meant that

50. Ibid., p. 16.

those organs of church administration which previously stood over the priest (the diocesan bishop and the Holy Synod) and which, through the priest, had acted upon the local parish, were now similarly deprived of control over the parish and the activities of its council.

The parish council, however, was not entirely autonomous since it stood under the supervision of an auditing commission of three persons elected by the general meeting of the parish. If the auditing commission noted any shortcomings or mismanagement in the work of the parish council, it was to report this information to the local government organs responsible for the activities of religious associations. In this fashion the new regulations removed the parish council from the control of the central organs of the church and placed it exclusively under the control of local city and regional executives of the state.

By the special circular of the Council for the Affairs of the Orthodox Church this control was then converted into full subjection. The basic thrust of the circular was to ensure that the responsible leaders of the church community would "satisfy" the local executive committees rather than serve the spiritual interests of believers. The circular states: "It should be kept in mind that at present the 'groups of twenty' in all of the believing communities do not inspire special confidence,"[51] so that they can be entrusted with state property. To change this circumstance the circular first of all limited the number of members of a community who could enter into an agreement for obtaining a church building and lay the foundation for the organization of a parish. This number was no longer at least twenty, but was now not to exceed twenty. In this way a broad base of believers lost the right to participate in church activities.

Next, a review of the composition of all the "groups of twenty" was urged, with definite criteria to be established for persons permitted to be selected for a "group of twenty." "You should recommend" to the local executive committee of the community, stated the circular, that they "create a new 'group of twenty' composed of educated persons capable of managing the community (no fanatics), who would honorably fulfill Soviet laws and your suggestions and recommendations. When a satisfactory 'group of twenty' believers is

51. *RCDA*, 15 April 1967, pp. 58–69.

created, then sign the contract with them."[52] By this means the composition of the "group of twenty" was to be selected by the state
organs in charge of local supervision of the church with the basic
criterion for selection being the readiness of a believer to fulfill all
the "suggestions" and "recommendations" of the local branches of
the atheistic Council for the Affairs of the Orthodox Church. The
circular excluded in advance from any "group of twenty" those
persons most deeply involved in the life of the church: clergymen,
church servants, choir directors, wardens, janitors, furnacemen,
chauffeurs, bakers of altar-bread, bell-ringers, and the like.

A still more direct and outspoken order of this circular to the local
executive committees concerned the makeup of the parish council. "It
is desirable that you take part in the selection of members for the
executive organ and select those persons who adhere to our line."[53]

The impact of this recent parish reform on the life of the Russian
Orthodox church has been enormous: the central administration of
the financial affairs of the Church was shattered and the hierarchical
structure undermined since the lower church units—the parish communities—were separated from the church organs over them. A
return to the "groups of twenty" as they had existed before 1945 has
now taken place. The postwar line of retreat from the antireligious
policy of the twenties and thirties thus took a sharp turn at the end
of the fifties back towards its starting point. And the Council for
for the Affairs of the Orthodox Church did not hesitate to make this
return to the past especially onerous.

VIII

The new persecution of the church begun by Khrushchev called forth
bitter distrust on the part of the believers. At first, however, the
hierarchy staunchly supported the "new religious policy" of the
Soviet government, while clerics and laymen displayed their full
loyalty to the regime. But the unexpected removal of the privileges to
which the believers had become accustomed since World War II and
the progressive introduction of new limitations finally led to unprecedented protests.

No longer were these in the form of deferential appeals by the
patriarch to the Council of Ministers of the USSR. Such appeals

52. Ibid.
53. Ibid.

ordinarily resulted in oral promises from the government that administrative organs would not exceed legal boundaries—promises that, in the circumstances, had to satisfy the patriarchal administration.[54] This time—at least from 1965 on—the protests were openly voiced. And they came from bishops, priests, and even laymen.

Several bishops, headed by Archbishop Ermogen of Kaluga, courageously opposed the closing of churches in their dioceses and sent a declaration to Patriarch Aleksy stating that the regulation on the reform of parish administration adopted with such extraordinary haste in 1961 by the Council of Bishops contradicted canon and civil law, and that its implementation was leading to the dissolution of parish life. Following Archbishop Ermogen's protest, two Moscow priests, Father Nicholai Eshliman and Father Gleb Iakunin, on November 21, 1965, addressed an "Open Letter" to Patriarch Aleksy. They apparently had already been in communication with Archbishop Ermogen. Three weeks later, on December 15, these same priests sent a special "appeal" to the secular authorities—"to the Chairman of the Presidium of the Supreme Soviet of the USSR, N. V. Podgorny, to the Chairman of the Council of Ministers of the USSR, A. P. Kosygin, and to the General Procurator of the USSR, R. A. Rudenko." Copies of both the open letter to the patriarch and the appeal to the secular authorities, with an introductory explanation, were subsequently sent to all the bishops of the Russian Orthodox church.[55]

The appeal to the secular authorities was particularly remarkable. It constituted the first open protest by clerics of the Orthodox church against the increasing persecution of religious faith. This act ruptured the tactics of silence by the hierarchy. With their appeal the two priests took upon themselves the whole weight of a public stand which, in their opinion, should have been made long before by the highest church authorities.

In their appeal to the government, Fathers Eshliman and Iakunin protested the violation of Soviet legislation by the Council for the Affairs of the Orthodox Church and its local branches. They pointed in particular to: (1) the abuse of the law on the registration of clerics, (2) the illegal closure of churches, monasteries, and seminaries, (3) the

54. *ZHMP*, 1961, no. 8, p. 6.
55. The full text of these documents can be found in English translation in *St. Vladimir's Seminary Quarterly*, 1966, nos. 1–2.

prohibition of the conduct of church rites in homes without written permission of the Soviet authorities, (4) the obligatory registration by priests of the baptisms of infants, (5) the limitations placed upon the participation by children in church services, (6) the reduction in the number of members allowed on the parish council, and (7) the interference in the financial affairs of the religious associations.

In their open letter to the patriarch, the two Moscow priests listed the same violations of civil law and the arbitrary activity of the state organs which they enumerated in their letter to the leaders of the Soviet government. But in addition they emphatically declared to the patriarch that the demands of the state authorities contradicted church canons, pastoral reponsibility, and Christian conscience and they forcefully charged the hierarchy with total submission to these demands and to silent acquiescence in the activities of the "secular authorities."

In June, 1966, believers from the Kirov Diocese (formerly the Viatka Diocese), citing the letter of Fathers Eshliman and Iakunin, addressed an open letter of their own to Patriarch Aleksy.[56] With data from the Kirov Diocese they substantiated the patent illegality and arbitrariness of the activities of the state administration described by the two Moscow priests. Noting the fruitlessness of their complaints about the unworthy behavior of their local ruling bishop, they lamented with bitterness the fact that the Russian Orthodox church had no impartial or fair judges. They asked the patriarch to take steps to correct the circumstances which had come about and to initiate steps for the convocation of a local council of the Russian Orthodox church.

As far as is presently known, these protests have produced no ameliorating results for the Orthodox church. Archbishop Ermogen was deprived of his episcopal see and sent into retirement to the Zhirovtsy monastery. Both Moscow priests were suspended from their posts and even barred from performing divine services. In spite of the lack of visible results, these protests have become widely known and still reverberate in the minds of believers in the Soviet Union and in world public opinion, if only because their protests reflected an extraordinary courage and readiness to assume the obvious danger of severe reprisals. At the same time that the ruling hierarchy has remained silent about the persecution of religion in

---

56. *Vestnik russkogo studencheskogo khristianskogo dvizheniia*, 1966, no. 82, pp. 3–20.

Russia, these open protests from clerics and laymen offer witness to the beginning of a new era in the life of the Russian Orthodox church.

It is worth noting that Christian believers were the first citizens in the USSR who dared publicly to protest the hypocritical use of the liberal slogans of "freedom of conscience" and of "civil rights".[57] Their courage broke the ice. After their protests have come those of the Soviet intelligentsia: members of the Academy of Science, professors and scientific researchers (as in the case of Esenin-Volpin), and also writers (as in the cases of Sinyavsky and Daniel). All these later protests have reiterated the basic themes of the letter of the two Moscow priests: that the Soviet regime has violated its own law and abused its own administrative authority. They all confirm that "socialist legality" does not really exist in the Soviet Union, and that in the context of a continuing totalitarian structure this will never be allowed to exist.

57. A courageous protest against religious persecutions was also made by the Organizing Committee of the Evangelical Christians-Baptists (a church group which has broken off from the All-Union Council of Evangelical Christians-Baptists). It directed its own "Appeal" to the Soviet government as early as April, 1965, and its members likewise suffered repressive measures at the hands of the Soviet state. *RCDA*, 1966, no. 21; ibid., 1967, nos. 5, 10 15–16, and others. (For the protest movement among the Evangelical Christians-Baptists see Michael Bourdeaux, *Religious Ferment in Russia* [New York, 1968].)

10

THE GEORGIAN ORTHODOX CHURCH

This study will attempt to deal with the problem of the interdependence between the development of the Orthodox church of Georgia and the political and cultural destiny of the country, as well as with the present situation of that church. The church played a significant role in the unification of the Georgian territories and in the preservation of national selfconsciousness when the country was broken up and occupied by foreigners in the past. It might appear that our discussion of the Georgian church does not proceed beyond the question of the autocephaly of that church in the communion of Orthodox churches. But, apart from its role in the maintenance of the historical personality of the Georgian people, the quest for autocephaly is in itself a manifestation of the spirit of freedom; nations which have attained cultural and political maturity tend naturally to imbue their religious expression with their own individuality.

Clearly, nations can seek to achieve freedom in other areas and in other ways, with no regard for ecclesiastical matters whatever, but where Georgia is concerned the striving for ecclesiastical autocephaly has been one of the constants in its national history. Autocephaly was one area in which the concern of the church, nationalist sentiment, and even political considerations found common ground. An explanation of this is found in Professor N. Marr's book on the

Elie Melia

history of Georgia.[1] Another illustration is the open letter of October
11, 1907, sent to the viceroy of the Caucasus by the Georgian
nobility which, as in the other parts of the Russian empire, constituted
an officially recognized representative body. This letter requested the
reestablishment of the autocephaly of the church of Georgia and
cited the earlier suppression of autocephaly as one of the principal
causes for the decline of religious life in that country.

The Georgian Orthodox church prior to 1917

The region of Georgia ("Sakartvelo"[2] in Georgian, "Gruziia" in
Russian) which played a key role in the formation of the country is
called Kartli or Iveria (Iberia); it was under this last name that the
land was known to the classical Greek and Latin writers. Ancient
documents give the church of Georgia the name of the church of
Iberia, which name is still used today in Georgian ecclesiastical language, although the head of the church bears the title of Archbishop
of Mtskheta-Tbilisi, Catholicos and Patriarch of all Georgia. Mtskheta
was the capital until it was transferred to Tbilisi in the fifth century;
but Mtskheta, with its magnificent cathedral, Sveti Tskoveli ("life-
giving column"), situated not far from Tbilisi, remains the nominal
metropolitan see.

Christianity came to Georgia at an early date. In the list of the
fathers of the first ecumenical council, which met in Nicea in 325,
one finds the name "Patrophilos, Bishop of Pytionte," a city of the
Byzantine ecclesiastical district of Polemoniac Bridge. This city still
exists in Georgia under the name of Bitchvinta (*Pitsunda* in Russian).
The existence of a bishopric presupposes that a Christian community
had existed there for a considerable time prior to the council. Then
about the year 330, a woman by the name of Nina converted the
Queen of Iberia and then the King, and eventually the entire nation
was baptized. This story was told to the Latin historian Rufin by a
prince of the royal family of Iberia, Bacurios, a general in Palestine in
the service of Byzantium. Rufin left Palestine in 397 and included the
story in his *Ecclesiastical History*, written in 403.

The new ecclesiastical community was apparently canonically dependent on the metropolitan center of Caesarea in Cappadocia. Over

---

1. N. Marr, *Istoriia Gruzii: kulturno-istorichesky nabrosok* [The history of Georgia: a
cultural-historical sketch], (St. Peterburg, 1906).
2. Sakartvelo, or the country of the Kartvels or Kalduels (Chaldeans).

the centuries the canonical status of the church of Georgia underwent successive alterations. Maneuvering between Persia and Byzantium, King Vakhtang Gorgassal (449–99) obtained from the emperor of Byzantium a certain degree of autonomy for the church of Iberia, whose leader henceforth took the title of *catholicos*, a title common to the heads of churches situated outside the Byzantine Empire. Somewhat later the church of Iberia was united with the monophysite church of Armenia at the Council of Dvin (one of the Armenian capitals) in 506. This union lasted only a century and was denounced by the Georgians in 607, under Catholicos Kirion I. Western Georgia, which had been incorporated into the Byzantine Empire, remained faithful to Chalcedonian orthodoxy throughout this period. When the Byzantine emperor Heraclius, who conquered the Persians, took Tbilisi in 627, all vestiges of monophysitism were eliminated.

On returning to communion with the Orthodox churches, after a century of separation, the church of Iberia once again had to raise the question of its jurisdictional autonomy. This question had first arisen following the Arab invasions; this foreign presence had stimulated a growth of national self-awareness, an understandable result of the struggle for liberation. The result was the unification of the eastern and western Georgian lands into a single kingdom, and with it the unification of their ecclesiastical districts, including those in western Georgia which to that time had been dependent on the patriarchate of Constantinople.

Unification was effected according to the norms of the medieval feudal system, using a combination of alliances by marriage and adoption. Bagrat III was the first king of a united Georgia (d. 1014). Full ecclesiastical independence was achieved in 1057. (Ephrem the Less reports that at the Council of Antioch in 1057, presided over by Patriarch Theodosius, the question of the autocephaly of the church of Georgia was raised and settled.) Since that time the church of Georgia has been autocephalous except for the period between 1801 and 1917 when the Russian civil authorities unilaterally suppressed autocephaly without the confirmation of any ecclesiastical body, Georgian or Russian. The nature of this course of action automatically deprived it of any canonical validity.

It was also at this time that Georgia first lost all attributes of sovereignty. King Irakly II, pressured by the Turks and the Persians, and hoping to insure the survival of his nation, signed a treaty of protection with Catherine II of Russia (Treaty of Georgievsk, 1783). This pact stipulated that, in addition to retaining its own dynasty, army, currency, and administration, the autocephaly of the church of Georgia was positively guaranteed.

Despite Russian protection, however, in 1795 Georgia was invaded by the Persians, led by the energetic usurper Aga-Mohammed-Khan, and only his assassination in 1797 and the disorders which followed in Persia saved the country. The last king of Georgia, George XII, Irakly's son, urged the Russians to come to his aid. Paul I of Russia annexed the kingdom and, at the death of the Georgian king (October 28, 1800), named the monarch's son, David, governor of Georgia. Alexander I confirmed the annexation by a solemn decree dated September 12, 1801, but relieved Prince David of his recently acquired post.

It was at this time that the autocephaly of the church of Georgia was suppressed without legal process by a simple imperial decree. (In 1810 Catholicos Anthony II, one of the sons of Irakly II, was called to Russia, with the right to be seated in the Holy Synod in the eighth place among the numerous Russian bishops. The following year he was retired and not replaced.) The ancient autocephalous church was reorganized into the exarchate of Georgia with jurisdiction over the three provinces which had once formed the united kingdom of Georgia. This was the last officially recognized vestige of the territorial unity of the former kingdom of Georgia. The first exarch after the annexation was a Georgian, Archbishop Varlaam Eristavi; his fifteen successors were all Russians. But if the head of the exarchate was from that time on chosen from among the Russian bishops (as was the bishop of Sukhumi, formerly Abkhazi), the four other bishops of the exarchate were chosen from among the Georgians, and this preserved the possibility of a canonical restoration of autocephaly at the opportune time.

In 1900 there were four dioceses in the exarchate of Georgia: (1) Kartli-Kakheti, ruled by the exarch and assisted by two suffragans, the bishops of Gori and Alaverdi, with 576 parishes for 374,405 parishioners in all; (2) Imerethi, with 496 parishes for 478,290; (3) Gouria-mingrelia, with 352 parishes for 321,952; (4) Sukhumi (Abkhazi), with 103 parishes for 103,750 (the area had been largely converted to Islam). In all there were 1,527 parishes for 1,278,487 faithful. The clergy consisted of six bishops (of whom four were Georgians), 62 archpriests, 1,647 priests, 231 deacons, and 1,805 readers.

By 1913 the number of parishes had increased to 2,055. Also, there were within the exarchate twenty-seven monasteries with 1,098 monks and seven convents with 281 nuns. The seminary of Tbilisi, founded in 1817, had, in 1902, 177 students; the one in Kutaisi had 206. In addition there were six diocesan schools for boys and two for girls, with a high school program to insure the instruction of the children of clerical families. On January 1, 1899, the exarchate had 381 parochial schools of either one class (3 years) or two classes (four years), with 13,084 boys and 3,986 girls; in addition, there were 182 schools of basic literacy with 5,807 children of both sexes.

The official policy of russification was strongly opposed by most Georgians. More particularly, a Society for the Promotion of Education Among Georgians was organized in 1877. It counted as members most of the intellectual elite of the country. The society founded and subsidized schools, theaters and libraries; it created a historical museum and a library of manuscripts and old documents; it edited manuals; it gave out scholarships to Georgian students in Russian and European universities.

The complete Bible (in Georgian) was published in 1884 by the publisher Kheladzeen in 2,400 copies. The New Testament was published several times, the last three editions being 1879, 1904, and 1912.

The Georgian Orthodox Church Since 1917

Following the Russian revolution in February, 1917, Georgia once again became independent, quickly uniting all the former territories within its historical boundaries. This reestablishment of sovereignty was accomplished in several stages, which followed in rapid succession. In March, 1917, the provisional government of Russia created a special committee for Transcaucasia. Eight months later, following the Bolshevik coup d'etat in Russia, a Commissariat of Transcaucasia, based upon the national councils of each of the peoples of Transcaucasia, was created. On April 28, 1918, the Independent Federated Republic of Transcaucasia was proclaimed. On May 26, 1918, the independence of the Republic of Georgia was announced.

Soviet Russia recognized Georgia's independence in a treaty

signed on May 7, 1920. And although the General Assembly of the League of Nations, citing its fear of not being able to supply aid in the event of aggression, on November 16, 1920, rejected Georgia's request for admission, on January 27, 1921, the Supreme Council of the Allied Powers (England, France, Italy, Japan, and Belgium) recognized the Republic of Georgia de jure through a telegram from the French Minister of Foreign Affairs to his Georgian counterpart. Many other countries followed this example.

On March 25, 1917, while the provisional government still ruled in Russia, an assembly composed of the Georgian bishops, members of the clergy, and the laity, proclaimed the reestablishment of the autocephaly of the church of Georgia. A plenary council composed of representatives of the episcopate, the clergy, and the laity was held from September 9 to 17 of the same year, confirming this action and reorganizing the church of Georgia. The patriarch-catholicos was to be elected by a general council. He was to be assisted by a permanent council of the catholicate on which representatives of the clergy and laity would have seats. The episcopal sees were redistributed as follows: the metropolitan see of Mtskheta-Tbilisi (the see of the catholicos), with two auxiliary bishops at Gori and at Alaverdi; the metropolitan see of Kutaisi; the metropolitan see at Chkhondidi; and the Archbishopric of Bichvinta-Abkhazi.

Kirion II was duly elected catholicos, and his investiture took place at Mtskheta in the cathedral of Sveti Tskoveli, attended by large numbers of the nation's elite. In addition, there was an extraordinarily large gathering outside the church estimated at one hundred thousand. The catholicos had once more become the spiritual head of Georgia.

As early as March 27, 1917, the Russian provisional government, which until the convocation of a Russian constituent assembly was to assume the financial responsibility and administrative control of confessional organizations, published a law "concerning the judicial consequences attendant upon the reestablishment of the autocephaly of the ancient church of Georgia." On July 25 of the same year, this same government published "provisional rules concerning the situation of the church of Georgia in the Russian state." Nevertheless, on December 29, 1917, shortly after his election as head of the church of Russia, Patriarch Tikhon sent a letter of censure to "Bishop" Kirion refusing to recognize the autocephaly of the church of Georgia.

(Autocephaly was recognized by the patriarchate of Moscow only in November, 1943.)

A Georgian church council which met on June 17, 1920, confirmed Catholicos Leonid, who, through a personal privilege granted him by the preceding council, had succeeded with full rights to Catholicos Kirion II. The latter had died tragically in June, 1918. This Council also regulated relations with the restored Georgian state which had promulgated a decree of the separation of church and state. It sought to resolve the question of the transfer of the ecclesiastical schools to the state, to organize the budget of the church, and to establish the norms of maintenance of the clergy. This latter task was particularly urgent since the church not only had to surrender its schools without compensation, but also suffered from the new agrarian law which confiscated without compensation all pieces of land exceeding seven hectares.

The events which soon followed made these problems seem almost trifling. After an initial attempt which was repulsed in 1920, the armies of Soviet Russia again invaded Georgia early 1921. On February 25 Tbilisi fell and on March 17–18 the Georgian government was forced to embark at Batumi, whence it went into exile, first in Constantinople, then in Paris.

On July 11, 1921, Catholicos Leonid died in an epidemic and the council of the catholicate designated Metropolitan Ambrose as locum tenens. He was subsequently elected catholicos by a council which met at Guelati September 1–5, 1921. Since then all the catholicoi have been elected by councils limited in membership to bishops only.

Religious persecution began soon after the establishment of the Transcaucasian Soviet Federated Republic. On February 7, 1922, Catholicos Ambrose sent a letter of protest to the Inter-Allied Conference at Genoa, protesting both the campaign of religious persecution and national oppression. In February, 1923, Catholicos Ambrose, Archbishop Nasaire, and all the members of the council of the catholicate were arrested. Three charges were laid against them: (1) that the catholicos had sent a letter to the Genoa conference in 1922, (2) that historic treasures of the church had been concealed, and (3) that the seizure of precious objects by a government commission which planned to use these riches for famine relief had been obstructed. Archbishop Nasaire was assassinated during the trial. All the members of the council sided with the catholicos, who conducted himself in a most courageous manner, assuming complete responsibility for these actions which he justified as his official obligations and the tradition of the church in similar cases. He was sentenced to eight years in prison; the other accused received lighter sentences.

On August 27, 1924, a general uprising broke out all over Georgia, involving the active participation of most of the population, including the clergy. The uprising had been prepared by a Committee for Independence, together with representatives of all the political parties (with the exception of the Communist party), senior military officers, and university personnel. The insurrection was put down in a few days; only a few isolated groups managed to survive for a time in the underground. The number of victims of police repression, most of whom were shot, has been put at seven thousand.

The aggressive Ambrose (Khelaia) was freed before the completion of his jail sentence, but died on March 29, 1927. On June 21, 1927, Catholicos Christopher II (Tsitskishvili) was elected as his successor. On August 5 he sent an ironic letter to Ecumenical Patriarch Basil III whose reply,[3] addressing Christopher as "catholicos," indicated official recognition of his position by the prime see of the Orthodox world. Catholicos Christopher II imposed an accommodation with the established political order on the hierarchy, with instructions to respect this policy on pain of excommunication.

Christopher II was followed in the office of catholicos by: Callistratus (Tsintsadze), June 21–22, 1932 (d. February 3, 1952); Melkhisedek (Pkhaladze), April 5, 1952 (d. January 10, 1960); Ephrem II (Sidamonidze) who is reigning at present, having been elected on February 20, 1960, as the one hundred thirty-ninth head of the church of Georgia. Among these, Callistratus Tsintsadze enjoyed special popularity, echoes of which are still heard today, fourteen years after his death. This popularity emerges from the unanimous testimony of the Georgians who have visited the West, or, at least, of those who have shown some interest in matters of religion. His twenty-year reign coincided with the period of Stalinist terror, during which he had to make humiliating contributions to the regime (for example his effusive telegram to Stalin, congratulating him on his

---

3. *Orthodoxia* (official organ of the Ecumenical patriarchate), September 1927.

seventieth birthday,[4] and his anti-American declarations at the peace-movement congresses under Soviet sponsorship).[5] Without resorting to any spectacular measures, and owing only to his resolute personal traditionalism, Catholicos Callistratus was able to mitigate the rash reformist orientation of his predecessor, Christopher II, and hold the church of Georgia beyond the reach of the Living Church movement, which, for a brief time, enjoyed such success in Russia.

It was during these first twenty years of Soviet rule that the church, if not Christian faith, was greatly reduced in regard to the number of practicing believers taking an active part in parish life. Furthermore, the ecclesiastical organization which remained became largely a formal institution. No religious instruction or charitable work was tolerated nor, a fortiori, any form of witness to or active presence in the world.

The persecution may seem to have been somewhat less violent than in Russia proper, but the antireligious campaign was greatly facilitated in Georgia by the small number of believers and by the lack of well-trained priests and an intellectual elite truly integrated into the church.

The ideology of the revolutionaries was understandably anticlerical, given the intimate union between the czarist state and the church. If anything, this ideology affected Georgia more than it did Russia; in Georgia there were no intellectuals who, like Bulgakov, Berdyaev, and others, could reexamine their attitudes, see the philosophical flaws of Marxism, and return to religion. (The blind policy of russification pursued by the czarist government deprived the nation of an institution of higher education, indispensable for the training of men capable of this kind of objectivity. When such an institution was requested the petition was denied, even though the staff would have been readily available, as was demonstrated by the rapidity with which the university, opened in Tbilisi after the revolution, developed into an academic center of the highest caliber.) In general the clergy were not on a par with men of letters or scientists; their only training was in philosophy, theology, and history.

4. *Zhurnal moskovskoi patriarkhii*, [Journal of the Moscow patriarchate] (hereafter *ZHMP*), 1950, no. 1; the telegram was dated 20 December 1949.

5. *ZHMP*, 1950, no. 11, pp. 26–27; ibid., 1951, no. 12, pp. 18–19. For discussion of a similar development within Soviet Islam see Bernhard Wilhelm, "Moslems in the Soviet Union," chapter 12 below.

To be sure, there were some exceptions, such as the archpriest Corneille Kekelidze. Writers such as the famous Ilya G. Chavchavadze (d. 1907), scientists such as the archaeologist Euthymius Takaishvili (who died after the last war), and historians such as Jordania, Djanashvili, Platon Iosseliani, were believers whose faith was evident in their work. They were not, however, part of any movement for the vindication of the faith in the historical context of the time.

In 1943 the government of the Georgian SSR, copying its Russian model, normalized its relations with the Church and named a high official chargé d'affaires of the Orthodox church of Georgia. In November of that same year the reestablishment of communion between the churches of Russia and Georgia took place, with the patriarch of Moscow recognizing the autocephaly of the church of Georgia.[6]

The attitude of the Russian and other Orthodox churches towards the church of Georgia is complicated, but has had a great influence on the overall situation of the Georgian church since the Revolution. At first glance the attitude of the Moscow patriarchate seems somewhat ambiguous. The Georgian church had no representative at the Pan-Orthodox Conference, which was originally to be held at Rhodes in 1960, but which actually met in 1961. The official reason given by Georgian ecclesiastical circles was that the invitation had been received too late to obtain the necessary diplomatic visas. Other reasons suggest themselves in connection with the visit of Patriarch Aleksy of Moscow to Constantinople to discuss possible participation by the Russian church in the Rhodes conference. He laid down four conditions for such participation. It is definitely known that one of the four conditions *did* relate to the church of Georgia, but its precise nature has not been made public. This condition seems to have been that the ecumenical patriarch would not communicate directly with the patriarch catholicos of Georgia, but do this through Moscow. (If Patriarch Aleksy had asked for something favorable to the church it is highly unlikely that this would have been kept hidden.) It appears that the Russian church regretted having been induced by Stalin in 1943 to recognize the autocephaly of the Georgian church, and that this secret condition was a move to reduce the practical scope of that earlier decision. The condition had to be made secretly for fear of

6. *ZHMP*, 1944, no. 3, pp. 6–21; the decision of the synod was dated 19 November 1943.

arousing national feeling. The fact of such a move seems clear enough, since the Georgian church, which was absent from the first two Rhodes conferences (1961 and 1963), allowed the Russian church to exercise its proxy—a measure which was doubtless forced upon the Georgians.

If the Moscow patriarchate, in keeping with the attitude of the Russian church throughout the nineteenth century, was opposed to Georgian autocephaly, we could expect that it would attempt in numerous ways to induce the Greek churches to adopt a similar stand. Whether because of Russian pressure or their own neo-Byzantine reluctance to identify the offices of catholicos and patri-arch, the ecumenical patriarchate and the other Greek churches clearly tend to consider the church of Georgia merely as an autono-mous church (on a par with the churches of Finland and Czecho-slovakia) and not as an autocephalous church.[7]

The argument which sees this attitude as primarily a question of the pressure brought to bear by the Moscow patriarchate finds sup-port in the fact that Constantinople did recognize the Georgian church in the thirties, when relations between Moscow and the other churches were still unclear and even somewhat strained. As noted above, however, there are also elements of ambiguity in the position of the Russian church. At the Third Rhodes Conference, in the face of Greek uncertainty as to whether the Georgian church was auto-cephalous or autonomous, and consequently, whether it occupied the sixth or the twelfth place among the fourteen autocephalous churches,[8] the Russian delegation, in the person of Archbishop Basil Krivoshein, openly supported the Georgian bishop in his request for a better consideration for his church.

The title of the head of the church of Georgia also raises a prob-lem. He is officially called the patriarch-catholicos. The title "catho-licos" was given to the heads of churches situated outside the Byzantine Empire. The patriarchates of Russia, Romania, Serbia,

7. This tendency appeared at the time of the first Rhodes Conference in 1961. The Georgian church was invited to attend as an autonomous body with a corresponding number of delegates. For details, see the account of the Russian Archbishop Basil Krivo-shein, who attended the three pan-Orthodox conferences at Rhodes, in the *Messager de l'Exarchat du Patriarche Russe en Europe Occidentale*, 1964, no. 45, p. 7. This tendency appeared even more clearly at the third meeting (1964) when the Georgian delegate, Bishop Ilia of Chemokmedi, threatened to leave the conference. See ibid., 1965, no. 51 (July–September), pp. 138–40, again an account by Archbishop Krivoshein.

8. Ibid., p. 139.

Bulgaria, as well as of the Orthodox churches in Poland, Czechoslovakia, and, it seems, Finland, have at one time recognized the
patriarchal dignity of the catholicos of Georgia. This was particularly evident in the exchange of good wishes at Christmas and Easter.
On the other hand, the Greek-speaking churches tended to take
exception to an identification of the titles of patriarch and catholicos.
The question has ecumenical importance because the title of catholicos is also used by the heads of the Armenian church and the
Syrian church of India.

In August, 1962, a session of the Central Committee of the World
Council of Churches (WCC) was held in Paris. At this meeting
several churches from the USSR asked for admission to the World
Council. Catholicos Ephrem II came in person to support the candidacy of his church. Indeed, he was the only church head present at
this working session. His lonely posture must be seen in context. It
is to be recalled that when a Geneva secretariat delegation of the
WCC to the USSR visited the patriarch of Moscow and the catholicos of Armenia, it did not stop at Tbilisi. The actual isolation of the
church of Georgia was equally obvious at the pan-Orthodox conferences at Rhodes. At a reception held at the end of the Paris
session, but before the vote on candidacy, it became apparent that
there was a general unwillingness to take a final vote at the time, with
the majority preferring to postpone this action to allow for further
discussion. Nevertheless, all the candidacies were finally accepted.
That of the church of Georgia had been officially sponsored by the
church of Russia. Catholicos Ephrem II returned to the USSR by
plane on the morning of August 19, a Sunday, and moreover, the
Feast of the Transfiguration; the Russian church delegation stayed in
Paris to celebrate the feast day.

In all of this the ambiguities in the attitude of the Moscow patriarchate are of primary interest. Moscow extended the Georgian
church recognition of its autocephaly in 1943, sponsored its membership in the WCC in 1962, and also supported its claim for greater
prestige and influence at the Rhodes conference. Interpreting these
munificent gestures in the context of the negative historical attitude
of the Russian church toward the Georgian church, it seems reasonable to conclude that they were forced on the Moscow patriarchate
by the Soviet government for political purposes. Just as the Soviet
Union has three representatives in the United Nations, so also

multiple representation on pan-Orthodox councils and the WCC have their advantages.

The Georgian Orthodox church today

Having examined the historical situation of the church of Georgia, we will go on to an evaluation of the church's situation today. During the above-mentioned visit to Paris (August 6–9, 1962), the catholicos spoke with Georgian emigrés on several occasions. In addition to being at pains to justify his participation in peace movements sponsored by the Soviet government, he also attempted to update and correct statistics on the Georgian church published earlier that year in which it was stated that the church had seven bishops, 105 priests, eighty parishes, two monasteries and two convents, as well as a publishing house.[9] The catholicos said that there were in fact three monasteries (one with seven monks and two with only two or three men), but only one convent, this at Mtskheta, with a dozen nuns.

Another source of information, the official calendar of the church, lists fifteen historical dioceses. Ten of these have no incumbent, but this situation antedates the revolution by well over one hundred years. The incumbent bishops and their dioceses are (1) the Archbishop of Mtskheta-Tbilisi, Patriarch-Catholicos of all Georgia, Ephrem II (Sidamonidze), born October 11, 1896, old style; (2) the auxiliary to the patriarch-catholicos, Ilia Chiolachvili, Bishop of Chemokmedi; (3) Diocese of Urbnissi, Metropolitan David (Devdariani); (4) Diocese of Kutasi-Gelenati, Metropolitan Naum (Chavienidze); (5) Diocese of Sukhumi and Abkhazi, Bishop Roman (Petriashvili). A Metropolitan David with no indication of surname is mentioned as incumbent of the diocese of Manglissi; the diocese of Argveti also has as incumbent a Bishop David, with no family name. It may be that in these two cases Metropolitan David (Devdariani), the incumbent of the see of Urbnissi, is administering Argveti and Manglissi as well, or it may be that Bishop David (Burduladze), mentioned in the 1962 calendar, somehow figures in the list of 1966 as one of the unidentified Davids. At the end of the list, a Russian Bishop Zenob (Mazhuga) is included, a supernumary, "superior

9. *Service Œcuménique de presse et d'information*, no. 22, 15 June 1962. These statistics were taken from a letter written by Patriarch Ephrem II in applying for membership in the WCC. They are preceded by a brief survey of the history of the church.

of the Church of Alexander Nevsky at Tbilisi, with the title Tetrits-kharo."[10]

The liturgical calendar is the church's only regular publication. It appears every year and contains no substantive articles but gives: (a) a list of the seven ecumenical councils (a few lines for each); (b) a list of the autocephalous Orthodox churches and their incumbents; (c) a list of the fifteen historical dioceses of the church of Georgia and their incumbents; (d) a list of the ten local Georgian councils which have met since the reestablishment of autocephaly; (e) a list of the 139 heads of the church of Georgia and of the twenty-four catholicoi of western Georgia (up to 1795) and the nineteen Russian exarchs (1811–1917); (f) a few dates from the ancient history of the church up to the year 315. Previously, the forty-eight dedication feasts of the churches, with their dates and the towns or villages where these dedications took place were to be found at the end of the calendar. The calendars which appeared under the pontificate of Catholicos Callistratus also listed the kings of Georgia. The 1966 calendar was published in an edition of twenty-five hundred copies.

Credit must be given to Catholicos Ephrem II not only for re-opening several churches, but also for the publication of a New Testament in Georgian in 1963, in which the archaic language has been slightly modified to facilitate reading. The number of copies published is not given. In the same year one thousand copies of a 263-page prayer book were published; it briefly explained the significance of the major feast days. Finally, in 1964, the catholicos was able to open a school at Mtskheta, at the Sumtavro monastery, for men preparing for the priesthood. Ten students are currently enrolled.

In some respects the information available is ambiguous. In regard to the recently opened seminary, one would have to know more about the seminarians and the arrangements that led to the opening in order to say just how encouraging this sign is. Recent visitors to Georgia have reported that during the Khrushchev campaign of 1959–64 all of the measures taken by the government in Russia proper were also applied in Georgia, and in some cases even more harshly.

Although the Soviet government is committed to encouraging and

10. This information was first given in the 1962 calendar; he is the first Russian bishop to figure in the church of Georgia.

assisting "legitimate" expressions of nationality within its borders, in general religion is not considered a possible form of such expression. On the other hand, in the eyes of the world, the Georgian church is linked with the Georgian nation as a political and cultural entity. As a consequence, it seems that a compromise has been decided upon wherein the church is retained as a formal structure, but its influence on the life of the people—at least in the strictly spiritual realm—has been vastly curtailed and possibly almost eliminated. The prestige accorded the patriarch-catholicos in 1943 recognized the role the church could play in rallying the people to the defense of the country. In general, however, the regime is no more willing to allow the catholicos to play such a vital role in the life of the republic than it is to allow the patriarch of Moscow to portray himself as the guardian of Russia's national heritage.

Perhaps the greatest problem of the Georgian church is its isolation. For the most part the Russian church is not disposed to lend support. The same is more or less true for the other major Orthodox churches. The Georgian church claims the support of many Georgians abroad, but it does not have any overseas exarchates. The Russian church does, and this, in the view of many, has on occasion mitigated the Soviet government's attitude toward the domestic situation of the church. Indeed, there are no Georgian bishops living abroad, nor is there an organized diaspora, either ecclesiastically speaking or in terms of a community of people with strong national ties. This is in contrast to the case of the Armenians, whose overseas religious press is constantly probing the meaning of events within the Soviet Union and keeping records and statistics.[11] Finally, there is no Uniate Georgian church that evokes the concern of the Vatican, as is the case, for example, with the Lithuanians and certain Armenians.

Lacking support outside the country, there have been few effective barriers to combat the regime's program of reducing the church's influence in the realm of religion and culture. In the early sixties this program came close to realization.[12] It remains to be seen if the post-Khrushchev leadership will allow any alteration in the existing situation.

11. Many of the Georgians who left the country after the revolution were of that stratum of society which had been largely russified in the course of the nineteenth century.

12. See Donald A. Lowrie and William C. Fletcher, "Khrushchev's Religious Policy, 1959–1964," chapter 7 above.

11

THE ARMENIAN CHURCH
IN THE SOVIET UNION
1917-1967

To date there is no history of the Armenian church covering the period 1917–67.[1] The writings of Walter Kolarz and Derenik Pholatian[2] are less than adequate. Kolarz's work contains much false information and several misinterpretations, and Pholatian has written only a general summary. The present study aims at presenting a more complete and accurate survey of the subject.

Decline of the Church Under Georg V

In 1917 the October Revolution shook the foundations of the Russian Empire and opened a new era in history; it did not effect the destiny of Armenia, however, until November 29, 1920, when the self-governing Republic of Armenia (1918–20) was declared a Soviet Socialist Republic.[3] As of that date the Armenian Apostolic Orthodox church found itself in a new situation. Three weeks later, on

1. I have given a brief historical survey for the period 1917–57 in my *Patmutiun Hay Ekeghetsii* [History of the Armenian church] (Beirut, 1965), pp. 210–16.
2. Walter Kolarz, *Religion in the Soviet Union* (London and New York, 1961), pp.150–75; Terenig Poladian (Derenik Pholatian), "The Twentieth Century," in Malachian Ormanian, ed., *The Church of Armenia*, rev. ed. (London, 1955), pp. 76–85.
3. *HSKhH dekretneri ev hramanneri zhoghovadzu* [Collection of decrees and orders of the Armenian Soviet Socialist Republic] (Etchmiadzin, 1921), 1: 1; V. Parsamyan, *Noyemberian Yeghaphokhutiune Hayastanum* [The November Revolution in Armenia] (Erevan, 1932); C. Aghayen, *Hoktemberian revoliutsian ev hay zhoghovrdi azatagrume* [The October Revolution and the liberation of the Armenian people] (Erevan, 1957).

Mesrob K. Krikorian

December 17, 1920, the government of Armenia, by state decree, nationalized the cultural institutions (schools, archaeological and historical museums, libraries and printing establishments) together with their movable and fixed property.[4] On December 28 all real estate was nationalized[5] and on December 31 religious subjects and services were forbidden in schools.[6]

The catholicos of that time was Georg V (Surenian), a cautious, wise, and peaceful man. In spite of the events which quickly led the church towards deterioration and fatal deprivation, he did not undertake serious resistance; unlike the Russian or Georgian church leaders, he avoided violence and patiently waited for an improvement of the situation. Succeeding Matheos Izmirlian, he had been elected patriarch-catholicos of all Armenia on December 13, 1911, and installed on July 2, 1912.[7] In 1912–13, by his order, Armenians all over the world celebrated the fifteen hundredth anniversary of the creation of the Armenian alphabet and the fourth centenary of Armenian book-printing. During the First World War Georg V witnessed the genocide of two million of his people in western Armenia (eastern Anatolia).

The regulations of the congregation of Etchmiadzin, published in 1917, show that the monastery had governing councils and administrative bodies, an educational committee, a seminary (called "Georgian"), a library, a museum and printing-house, an inn, the cathedral, and, nearby, the churches of St. Hriphsime, St. Gayiane, Zoarthnots and Shoghakath.[8] When Armenia became part of the Soviet Union, these administrative bodies were suppressed, the seminary was turned into a public school, the library, the museum, and the printing-house were reorganized as scientific-cultural institutes (February 5, 1921),[9] and the seventh-century church of Zoarthnots was turned into a state museum. A year later, the newspaper *Khorhrdayin Hayastan* (Soviet Armenia), carried the following information about the Institute: "The library of Etchmiadzin, the adjacent art gallery, the press and the ruins of the church of

4. *HSKhH dekretneri*, 1:16; *Kommunist* (Erevan), 18 December 1920.
5. *HSKhH dekretneri*, 1:31.
6. Ibid., p. 43.
7. Krikorian, *Patmutiun*, p. 210.
8. *M(ayr) Ator S. Edchmiatsni miabanakan kanonadrutiun* [Regulations of the congregation of the mother see of Holy Etchmiadzin], (Etchmiadzin, 1917).
9. *Kommunist* (Erevan), 8 February 1921.

Zoarthnots, together with all its buildings, are subject to the jurisdiction of the scientific Institute of Etchmiadzin. The library now has 1,700 manuscripts, 50,000 printed books and the valuable historical archives of Etchmiadzin. The members of the Scientific Institute are: Seneqerim Ter-Yakabian (vice-president and director of the library), Thoros Thoramanian, Araqel Babakhanian (Leo) and others."[10]

The books and manuscripts of the library of Etchmiadzin which during the First World War had been transported to Moscow for safekeeping, were returned in April–May, 1922, in 140 cases, together with the library and museum of the Lazarian Institute (Moscow) and valuable paintings.[11] In 1939 the library collection of Etchmiadzin was moved to Erevan, capital of Armenia, and in 1959 it was housed in a magnificent palace, the *Matenadaran* (library), which was then made an institute of scientific research. At present it contains more than ten thousand Armenian manuscripts, about one thousand manuscripts in other languages, such as Persian, Syriac, Arabic, Turkish, Greek, Latin, Russian, Indian, and Ethiopian, and about five thousand fragments.[12] Apparently the museum of Etchmiadzin which contained collections of archaeology, arts, crafts, and numismatics, was also eventually nationalized on January 24, 1923.[13]

As Soviet rule became established in Armenia, the ideological struggle was intensified and atheism was propagated on a broad scale. In January, 1928, the first issue of the illustrated review, *Anastoats* (The godless) appeared, [14] and on April 12, 1928, all landholdings of the monastery in Etchmiadzin were divided among the peasants for collectivized cultivation.[15] Later, a collective farm named *Anastoats* (later called "Mikoyan") was organized on these grounds. On October 30, 1928, the first conference of the Union of Atheists of Armenia took place[16] and on November 29, 1929, an "antireligious

10. *Khorhrdayin Hayastan*, 2 February 1922.

11. Ibid., 13 May 1922.

12. L. Khatchikian, "Matenadarane antsealum ev Sovetaken ishkhanutian tarinerin" [The Matenadaran in the past and during the years of Soviet rule], *Banber Matenadarani* [Messenger of Matenadaran], no. 4, (Erevan 1958), p. 12; G. V. Abgarian, *Matenadaran* (Erevan, 1962), pp. 13–15.

13. *HSKhH* dekretneri ev oroshumneri hauakatsu [Collection of decrees and decisions of the ASSR] (1923), 1 : 14.

14. For the rise of the antireligious movement in the RSFSR and the Ukraine see Joan Delaney, "The Origins of Soviet Antireligious Organizations," chapter 6 above.

15. *Khorhrdayin Hayastan*, 15 April 1928.

16. Ibid., 1 November 1928.

university" was opened in Erevan.[17] Although Armenian public opinion abroad usually understands the term university (*hamalsaran*) in its narrow sense, it is used in this context to mean *lsaran*—an academic assembly or general course given over a period of several weeks or months.[18]

One of the policies of the Soviet government at this time was to encourage religious schismatic movements in order to weaken the church. In Russia itself a group of priests led by Archpriest Alexander Vvedensky organized the "Living Church" and in place of the patriarchate established a supreme church administration. Aided by the government, the schismatic Living Church group became very influential.[19]

Among Armenians a similar schismatic movement was created in 1925–26 in Tiflis, Georgia, which in the nineteenth century had been the center of Armenian intellectual activity. This movement described itself as the "Free Church Brotherhood" and promised to renovate the Armenian church. The leaders of the Free Church declared: "We are not separatists. We love our ancient and historical church and by our collective efforts intend to raise her up to the high standard of her vocation, to render her glorious and to leave on her altar only Jesus Christ so that by living words he may attract not only the old, but also the young."[20]

Under normal circumstances this declaration might have been convincing and even appealing to the public, but since the Free Church group came into existence at a time when the mother church was suffering, it did not find a widespread response. The stated aims of the Free Church Brotherhood were: (1) to raise the church to the high standard of her vocation and restore apostolic simplicity and Christian spirit; (2) to liberate the church from the monarchy of the celibate priesthood; (3) to adopt the living modern language instead of the classical Armenian, which is not understandable by the people; (4) to abolish the peculiar clerical dress and establish honest

17. Ibid., 1 December 1929.

18. Cf. Stefan Malkhasian, *Hayeren batsatrakan bararan* [Armenian explanatory dictionary] (Erevan, 1944–45), 2: 220, s.v. "lsaran," and 3: 22, s.v. "hamalsaran" ("audience for all or for many listeners").

19. Paul B. Anderson, *People, Church and State in Modern Russia* (London, 1944), pp. 64–65.

20. Yakob Ter-Yaruthiunian, *Mer npatake—Hayots ekeghetsakan barephokhutiune ev nran hasnelu midchotsnere* [Our aim—the reform of the Armenian church and the means to reach it] (Tiflis, 1926), p. 32.

means of income; (5) to propagate Christian literature and canon law among the believers so that they may become conscious Christians.[21]

For these purposes the Free Church decided to open religious courses, give public lectures, publish its own periodical, as well as religious-historical books and pamphlets, and to send out visiting preachers and choirs.[22] In fact, the leaders of the schismatic movement did issue several numbers of their journal, *Azat Ekeghetsi* (Free Church), and did organize some lectures, but they did not succeed in winning much sympathy, because they were regarded as agents of a foreign power. The only positive result which may be due to their influence was Catholicos Georg V's reforms of the strict canons on marriage.

In spite of pressures from the Soviet government of Armenia, Catholicos Georg V continued to carry on his work, and endeavored to keep the dioceses of Armenia, Georgia and Azerbaidzhan organized. A photograph taken in the twenties at Etchmiadzin provides the following jurisdictional picture:[23]

I. Armenia
  1. Diocese of Erevan
     Archpriest Yakob Khatchvankian, governor
  2. Diocese of Shirak (Leninakan)
     Archimandrite Isahak, prelate
     Vram Karaghuyumdchian, delegate
  3. Diocese of Siunig
     Bishop Artak Smbatian, prelate
  4. Qarabagh (autonomous province)
     Archimandrite Vrthanes, prelate

II. Georgia
  5. Diocese of Tiflis
     Archbishop Georg Cheorekchian, primate
     Stephan Malkhasian (a renowned philologist), delegate

21. Ibid., p. 29.
22. Ibid.
23. Apparently this photograph was taken at a meeting of the internal dioceses, therefore the sees of the diaspora (in the Middle East, Iran, India, Europe, the United States, and Latin America) must be added.

III. Azerbaidzhan
    6. Diocese of Baku
       Archbishop Mattheos, primate
       Isahak Amirian, delegate
IV. Russia
    7. Diocese of Astrakhan
       Archimandrite Grigoris, governor
    8. Nor Nakhidchean
       Archpriest P. Bedelian, governor
       Andreas Saltikian, delegate

The personnel of the Supreme Spiritual Council, the actual governing body of current affairs of the Holy See of Etchmiadzin, can also be determined from this photograph. The council was composed of the following members:

1. Catholicos Georg V, president
2. Archbishop Khoren Muradbekian, chairman
3. Archbishop Garegin Yovsephian, member
4. Archbishop Bagarat Vardazarian, member
5. Bishop Giwt, member
6. Archimandrite Ruben Manasian, chancellor

On May 9, 1930, Catholicos Georg V died at an advanced age, having gained the reputation of a reformer. He had augmented the number of days ecclesiastically permissible for marriage; permitted ordinary priests to remarry; eased the canons on marriage among relatives up to the fifth generation; declared civil divorces valid; accepted the new Gregorian calendar (replacing the Julian); and approved the use of the organ in church.[24] He used as his signature *Vshtali Kathoghikos*, "the sorrowful Catholicos," because he had seen the tragic genocide of his people in Turkish Armenia and the decline of his church in Soviet Armenia.

The Struggle for Survival Under Khoren I

Two years after the death of Georg V, on November 10, 1932, the chairman of the Supreme Spiritual Council, Archbishop Khoren (Muradbekian) was elected catholicos of all Armenia by the delegates

---

24. Krikorian, *Patmutiun*, p. 211; Georg Mesrop, *Hamarot patmutiun Hay Ekleghetsoy* [A brief history of the Armenian church], rev. ed. (Beirut, 1955), pp. 129–30.

of nine dioceses within Armenia and eleven abroad. He was consecrated on November 13, 1932.

During the years 1935–36, by order of the new catholicos, Armenians all over the world celebrated the fifteenth centenary of the Armenian translation of the Bible. In 1937, earnestly interested in the renovation of the church, he undertook a program of reformation and, by a special encyclical (no. 417, August 1, 1937), submitted it to the patriarchs of Cilicia (Antelias, near Beirut), Jerusalem, and Constantinople, as well as to all the other Armenian bishops and prelates, in order to gain the benefit of the opinions of all church leaders. Unfortunately his sudden death in 1938 brought the plans of this great pontiff to an end.

Four years before the catholicos' death the Moscow correspondent of the *New York Times* interviewed Khoren I in Etchmiadzin concerning the situation of the Armenian church in the Soviet Union.[25] The catholicos expressed gratitude to the Russians for offering peace, security, and assistance to the Armenians in their endeavor to rebuild their homeland. He said that he sometimes had difficulties with the Soviet authorities, but appreciated the readiness shown by the government to settle all problems with good will and on the basis of mutual understanding.

As Stalin's power increased, however, the situation in Armenia became unbearable. During the period from 1936 to 1952 the agents of Stalin and Beria carried out cruel purges throughout the Armenian Republic and exterminated hundreds of intellectuals, writers, artists, clergymen, and statesmen as "nationalists" or "reactionaries." On July 9, 1936, the capable first secretary of the Communist party of Armenia, Aghasi Khandchian, was killed by Beria in Tiflis;[26] in February, 1938, the brilliant Armenian poet Eghishe Djarents died in the prison of Erevan; and in April of that year various rumors reached the diaspora that Catholicos Khoren I had been strangled[27]

25. *New York Times*, 11 November 1934 (see the Armenian translation in *Yusaber* [The conveyor of hope], [Cairo], 6 December 1934).

26. V. Alazan describes Khandchian as an intellectual and a patriotic statesman: "After his tragic death, when Khandchian's purse was taken from his pocket and opened, there, instead of money, they found the splendid patriotic poem by Eghishe Djarents, 'Es im anush Hayastani' [Of my sweet Armenia], copied in the fine and pleasing hand of Khandchian" (*Grakan tert* [Literary newspaper] [Erevan], 30 March 1962, p. 3). See the official announcement of the news of Khandchian's death in *Khorhrdayin Hayastan*, 12 July 1936.

27. *Yusaber*, 9, 13 May 1938; and Kolarz, *Religion in the Soviet Union*, p. 156.

or poisoned [28] by the Communists or had died of a heart attack.[29] The reason given in these reports for the death of Khoren I was his resistance to the confiscation of church treasures and vessels and the properties of the monastery and museum of Etchmiadzin,[30] but it must be recalled that the museum had already been declared national property on January 24, 1923.[31]

A more widely accepted version of his death, told by travellers, asserts that the government had demanded from Etchmiadzin forty thousand rubles in taxes and, since the monastery was unable to pay that sum, had confiscated the sacred properties. Subsequently the the catholicos suffered a heart attack and on Palm Sunday, 1938, was found dead.[32] On April 10 he was buried by nuns in the Church of St. Gayiane, near Etchmiadzin.[33] The catholicos was a courageous and conscientious priest who worked hard to make the Armenian church stronger and more alive, and he will be remembered as a good shepherd.

After the death of Catholicos Khoren I the activity of the Armenian church stopped almost completely. All the churches were closed and most of the clergymen were either arrested or dismissed. The locum tenens was the former primate of Georgia, Bishop Georg Cheorekchian. The sexton was Archimandrite Mattheos Atchemian, who, "during the four years of the war and before that, together with the locum tenens, has defended and cared for the cathedral and the apartments of the catholicoi, and with the aid of a poor, old local priest has regularly day and night officiated at the services."[34] Archimandrite Atchemian was born in 1879 in the village of Van, western Armenia. He studied in the local school and later became a teacher. In 1917 he was ordained deacon and a year later celibate priest at the monastery of Aghthamar. In June, 1919, he came to Etchmiadzin, and served the surrounding parishes. He also spent five years working with the Armenian dioceses of Russia. In 1926 he was appointed

28. *Yusaber*, 9 May 1938.
29. Ibid., 15 April, 2 May 1938.
30. Ibid., 2 May 1938; Kolarz, *Religion in the Soviet Union*, p. 156.
31. "The Catholicos was too important a man to be assassinated over such a comparatively trifling matter as the question of the remnants of Armenian church property" (Kolarz, *Religion in the Soviet Union*, p. 156).
32. *Yusaber* (2 May 1938), Pholatian ("The Twentieth Century," p. 78), and Kolarz (*Religion in the Soviet Union*, p. 156), assign the death of the catholicos to April 6, 1938.
33. *Yusaber*, 13 May 1938.
34. Archbishop Artavazd Siurmeian, *Depi Hayastan* [To Armenia] (Beirut, 1946), p. 34.

abbot of the monastery of Geghard, but after three years returned to
Etchmiadzin and worked there until 1945.[35]

The Period of Reestablishment Under Georg VI

Towards the end of World War II a policy of religious toleration
was introduced in the USSR. During the war the clergy assisted the
Soviet government in its war effort. In Russia itself the parishes and
clergy raised funds and outfitted a tank column in the name of
Dimitry Donskoi, a saint and national hero of the Russian people,
who had defeated the Tartars.[36] Similarly, in Armenia the locum
tenens, Archbishop Georg, received approval from Stalin to outfit a
tank column in the name of the national hero David of Sasun.[37] He
collected money from the Armenian communities abroad, and presented the tank column to the Soviet army (March 18, 1944).[38] In
1944 he addressed an appeal to the Armenian people, exhorting them
to defend their country with patriotism. During the war the government authorized publication of national historical novels to inspire
the troops. In 1939 the epic of David of Sasun appeared in six
languages (Armenian, Russian, Georgian, Azerbaidzhani, Ukrainian,
Uzbek, and in 1939 Yiddish); during 1940–41 three novels of Raffi
were printed, and in 1944 the first volume of Derenik Demirchian's
Vardanang was published (the second volume came out in 1946).
This book narrated the struggle of Christian Armenians against the
Zoroastrian Persians in the fifth century.

At the end of the war, the relations of church and state were to a
certain extent friendly. Although Archbishop Georg's first attempt,
in 1941, to organize the election of a catholicos had failed,[39] in 1945
he succeeded in personally calling on Stalin. On April 19 the seventy-
six-year-old locum tenens was received at the Kremlin to discuss the
problems of the Armenian church.[40] His biography contains the
following account: "During his interview with J. V. Stalin concerning
the affairs of the Armenian Church, His Eminence, the locum tenens,
succeeded in acquiring legal recognition for certain permissions
which the Holy See (of Etchmiadzin) had had in the past, and to solve

35. Ibid., pp. 34–35.
36. Anderson, *Modern Russia*, p. 10.
37. *Sovetakan Hayastan*, 26 January 1943.
38. Ibid., 31 March 1944.
39. Siurmeian, *Depi Hayastan*, p. 12.
40. *Soviet War News*, 23 April 1945, and Kolarz, *Religion in the Soviet Union*, p. 160.

certain relevant important questions and problems."[41] Although there is no complete record of this important meeting, it seems that the main points of the discussion were: (1) reorganization of the dioceses within Soviet Armenia; (2) election of a new catholicos; and (3) the reopening of the seminary.

Ten days after this meeting the Soviet army entered Berlin and the Armenian division (no. 89, bearing the name Thamanean), under the command of General Nower Safarian, distinguished itself.[42] On May 8, 1945, the war ended and on May 31, Archbishop Georg was honoured with the "Medal for the Defense of Caucasia."[43]

At the end of 1944, with the cooperation of the supreme council, the locum tenens had already summoned delegates from all the Armenian dioceses in and outside the USSR for the election of a catholicos.[44] On June 16, 1945, the national-ecclesiastical general assembly was opened at Etchmiadzin. One hundred twenty-one delegates took part in the assembly: eighteen clergymen and fifty-nine laymen from the USSR, and sixteen ecclesiastics and twenty-eight laymen from the Armenian communities abroad. The non-Soviet citizens came from Syria, Lebanon, Egypt, Palestine, Iraq, Turkey, Persia, Greece, Bulgaria, Rumania, England, France, the United States, and later (on June 30) from South America too. The catholicos of Antelias (patriarch of Cilicia), Garegin I Yovsephian, and the patriarch of Jerusalem, Cyril, came in person, and from the Church of England, the Reverend Hewlett Johnson was present. Among the internal delegates were such renowned figures as Awetik Isahakian, "master poet," Martiros Sarian, the painter, Tigran Hakhumian, the poet and

41. *Erdchankayishatak T. T. Georg Z. Kathnoghikosi Keange ev gordzunevtiune* [Life and activity of blessed Georg VI Catholicos], (Etchmiadzin, 1955), p. 57.

42. *Sovetakan Hayastan*, 3 May 1945.

43. *Erdchankayishatak*, p. 53.

44. The Armenian diaspora was, and is, one of the main factors in effecting good relations between Etchmiadzin and the Soviet government. The Communists of Armenia themselves eventually realized that if they were to enlist the moral, cultural, and financial assistance of the diaspora in their endeavor to build a well-developed socialist republic, they would have to permit Etchmiadzin not merely to survive but to reestablish her various institutions, since for the Armenian diaspora a homeland without Etchmiadzin would be incomprehensible and unacceptable. In the seventeenth century, when Shah Abbas I (1586–1628) transported the Armenians to Ispahan, they cried that it was impossible for them to live without Etchmiadzin. They were partly satisfied when the Shah brought fifteen stones from Etchmiadzin and used them to build the new church of Khodchents at Ispahan, new Julfa (See M. Ormanian, *Azgapatum* [History of the Armenian nation] [Istanbul, 1913], 2: 2296–2304, 2325–29). (For the difficulties of a minority church without a diaspora, see Elie Melia, "The Georgian Orthodox Church," chapter 10 above.)

playwright, Ashot Abrahamian, the historian, and Erowand Shehaziz and Garegin Levonian, the philologists.[45]

The general assembly met seven times (from June 16 to 22). At the opening session speeches were delivered by the locum tenens, Archbishop Georg, by Catholicos Garegin of Cilicia, by Ivan Vasilevich Poliansky (1898–1956), president of the Council for the Affairs of Religious Cults, and Suren N. Yovhannisian, chairman of the Council for the Affairs of the Armenian Church. Poliansky's words were sensible and carefully phrased. The following is a portion of his speech:

Right honorable patriarchs, church-leaders and civil delegates, you, representing all of the Armenian church, are assembled at the Holy See of Etchmiadzin, the cradle of the Armenian church, which is sacred for all Armenian believers. During the long existence of the Armenian nation, which in the past has seen so many failures, sufferings, and injuries, the Armenian church has always stood by the people, has helped to revive its national autonomy, has reared its children in national consciousness, and has contributed to the nation's cultural advancement. The role of the Armenian church as guardian of national integrity cannot be regarded as ended now, particularly when the Armenian people are scattered all over the world.[46]

Yovhannisian's speech touched on the same points. He said: "In hard days of misfortune, the Armenian church has not abandoned the Armenian people. She has linked her destiny with that of the Armenian people and in time of political storms her best representatives have devotedly struggled for the nation's freedom, and have sacrificed their lives for the liberation and welfare of the homeland."[47]

During successive meetings the general assembly examined the work of the locum tenens, Archbishop Georg (1941–1945), the draft of a national-ecclesiastical constitution, the financial situation of the catholicate of Etchmiadzin, and the question of the renovation of the cathedral. On June 22, Archbishop Georg was unanimously elected catholicos of all Armenia, and on June 24 he was installed by the catholicos of Cilicia, Garegin Yovsephian. On July 1, ten archimandrites were consecrated bishop by the new catholicos.

Georg VI was ordained a celibate priest on June 20, 1913, and appointed prelate in charge of Nor Nakhidchevan. In June, 1916, he

45. Siurmeian, *Depi Hayastan*, pp. 54–56.
46. Kolarz, *Religion in the Soviet Union*, p. 162; *Soviet News*, 26 June 1945; *Erdchankayishatak*, p. 60; *Edchmiadzin* [Etchmiadzin], 1945, nos. 6–7, p. 10.
47. *Edchmiadzin*, p. 13.

returned to the catholicate and acted as a member of the governing synod and director of the library. In April, 1917, he was consecrated bishop, and for a period of about three years served as chairman of the financial council. In 1921 he was sent to Tiflis to take charge of the Armenian community and its churches there, and in 1922 he was elected primate of the diocese of Georgia. On November 17, 1925, he was elevated to the rank of archbishop and in 1927 was named a member of the Supreme Spiritual Council. On April 18, 1936, he was appointed locum tenens by Catholicos Khoren Muradbekian.

Catholicos Georg VI, during his reign of nine years (1945–54), revived the congregation and seminary of Etchmiadzin, reorganized the dioceses of Armenia and of the other Soviet republics, regularly published the review *Edchmiadzin* (Etchmiadzin) and the church calendar, and undertook to renovate the cathedral of Etchmiadzin. He also wisely and tactfully governed the Armenian dioceses of the diaspora, except those of Syria, Lebanon, and Cyprus, which are subject to the Great House of Cilicia at Antelias, near Beirut. He enthusiastically encouraged repatriation when the Soviet government embarked on a campaign (November 21, 1945) to induce Armenians living abroad to settle in Soviet Armenia. On November 27, the catholicos addressed a memorandum to the Big Three powers, demanding the return of the Turkish Armenian provinces to Soviet Armenia. From 1945 to 1949 about one hundred thousand Armenians returned home. In 1960, while attending the festivities of the fortieth anniversary of the Armenian Socialist Republic (1920–1960), Nikita Khrushchev declared: "It is indisputable that Soviet Armenia now is the magnet which is attracting to her the best sons and daughters of the Armenian people."[48] In 1961 the Soviet government renewed its decision concerning the repatriation of Armenians.

Georg VI also worked for the cause of peace. On August 5, 1950, he signed a peace manifesto at Tiflis, together with the Russian patriarch, Aleksy, and the Georgian patriarch, Callistratus.[49] On October 16, 1950, he was included in the Committee for the Defence of Peace, by the third peace conference of the USSR which

48. *Sovetakan Hayastani 40 tarin* [The 40 years of Soviet Armenia] (Erevan, 1961), p. 80.
49. *Erdchankayishatak*, p. 106, and Kolarz, *Religion in the Soviet Union*, pp. 106, 164.

assembled at Moscow.[50] He was called by the people the "patriotic catholicos."[51] He died on May 9, 1954, after having worked effectively for the reestablishment of the church in Armenia.

The New Era of the Church Under Vazgen I

On September 30, 1955, the national-ecclesiastical general assembly which gathered at Etchmiadzin unanimously elected Vazgen I (Palchian) the bishop of the Rumanian-Bulgarian diocese, successor to Catholicos Georg VI (although Cheorekchian in his will had suggested the name of the locum tenens of the patriarchate of Jerusalem, Bishop Eghishe Terterian).

Vazgen was born Levon-Karabet on September 20, 1908, in Bucharest. He studied in the local school, and majored in pedagogy and psychology at the University of Bucharest (1932–37). From 1929 to 1943 he served the Armenian parish school as assistant teacher and at the same time contributed to the cultural activity of the Armenian community there. On September 30, 1943, he was ordained celibate priest in Athens by Bishop Karapet (Mazlumian). Returning home, he studied theology and was elected prelate-in-charge for the diocese of Rumania, and in 1948 ruling prelate. In 1951 Catholicos Georg VI ordained him bishop. In 1955, at the age of forty-seven, he became the head of the Armenian church and on October 2, 1955, was consecrated catholicos of all Armenia.[52]

Whereas the catholicoi Georg V (Surenian) and Khoren I (Muradbekian) fought to preserve the very existence of the Armenian church, Georg VI began its reestablishment. Catholicos Vazgen I now continued this renewal and ushered in a new era in the church. Immediately after his consecration, on October 6, 1955, he elevated to the rank of bishop two members of the catholicate of Etchmiadzin, Vardan Ter-Sahakian and Eznik Aznavurian, and five archimandrites from the patriarchate of Jerusalem: Haykazun Abrahamian, now chairman of the Supreme Spiritual Council at Etchmiadzin; Shnork

50. *Sovetakan Hayastan*, 20 October 1950; *Erdchankayishatak*, p. 106; *Edchmiadzin*, 1952, no. 5. For the involvement of Moslem leaders in the Soviet peace movement see Bernhard Wilhelm, "Moslems in the Soviet Union, 1948–54," chapter 12 below.

51. On the gravestone of the catholicos this epitaph is inscribed: "Georg Z. hayrenaser Katkhoghios Amenayn Hayots" [Georg VI patriotic catholicos of All Armenia].

52. I have taken these biographical notes from my booklet *Vazgen Vehaphare* [The catholicos Vazgen] (Beirut, 1958). A lengthy biography of the catholicos was published in 1958 at Etchmiadzin, *Vazgen A. Hayrapet Hayots* [Vazgen I, catholicos of Armenians].

Kalustian, now patriarch of Constantinople; Serovbe Manukian, primate of the diocese of France; Pargew Vrthanesian; and Hayrik Aslanian. On October 23, he ordained as bishop two other members of the order of Jerusalem: Shawarsh Guyumchian, prelate of the diocese of Damascus, and Psak Thumayian, prelate of London. Because no blessing of chrism (*miuron*) had taken place since 1926, on October 8, 1955, the new catholicos, assisted by twelve bishops, consecrated chrism.

From February 10 to May 13, 1956, on the occasion of the election of a new patriarch for the Great House of Cilicia at Antelias, Vazgen I paid a visit to the Armenian communities of Lebanon (Beirut), Egypt (Cairo and Alexandria), Italy (Rome, Milan and Venice), France (Paris, Marseille, Lyon) and England (London and Manchester).[53] From May 16 to September 8, 1960, the catholicos was in the United States and South America and on his way back stopped at Lisbon and Paris.[54] Continuing his visitations, in the summer of 1961 Vazgen I visited the Armenian communities of Turkey and Vienna; in October–November 1963 the communities of Europe, the Middle East, and India; in January–February, 1965, Cairo and Addis Ababa; in July–August, 1966, Vienna; and in July, 1967, Geneva.

Catholicos Vazgen I also undertook a program of church renovation. He established a special committee to carry out repairs and reconstruction. Assisted by the committee of architects and by the Supreme Spiritual Council, he accomplished the repair of the cathedral of Etchmiadzin and renovated the churches of Hriphsime, Gayiane, Shoghakath, Geghard, Oshakan, Bdchni, and Payazit. As a result of his personal call on President Nikolai Bulganin, on January 23, 1957, he was given possession of, and subsequently refurbished, the Manthashian Palace of the catholicoi, which in 1914, had been seized by the Imperial Russian government. In virtue of this zealous activity, in October, 1962, the national-ecclesiastical general assembly which gathered at Etchmiadzin granted him the title of *Shinarar Kathoghikos* "Builder Catholicos."

Vazgen I has paid particular attention to the seminary of Etch-

53. A description of the catholicos' first tour was published in 1956 at Etchmiadzin, *Amenayn Hayots Kathoghikos T. T. Vazgen A-i ughevorutiun* [The voyage of Vazgen I, Catholicos of All Armenians].

54. A detailed description of His Holiness' second tour was published in 1963 at Etchmiadzin, *T. T. Vazgen A. Hayrapeti erkrord ughevorutiun* [The second voyage of Vazgen I Catholicos].

miadzin. During his reign enrollment has increased, academic standards have been raised, a special fund established, and some well-known teachers secured from the University of Erevan to lecture on Armenian history, literature, and language, and on foreign languages. Since 1956 candidates for the priesthood have also come from the diaspora. The main problem of Etchmiadzin remains the training of ordinands; although the seminary usually has about thirty students enrolled, few are being ordained. This lack of vocations can be attributed, at least in part, to the secular atmosphere in the country and the celibacy required of priests of higher rank.

Catholicos Vazgen's interests extend to cultural activity as well. He regularly edits the review *Edchmiadzin*[55] and the church calendar. Periodically, historical and philological books are also produced by the press of Etchmiadzin. In 1956 the synod of bishops, which met at Cairo, decided to publish an official translation of the Bible in modern Armenian. This program is now being realized in Etchmiadzin, and the New Testament will soon be ready.

The Present State of the Armenian Church

The catholicos of Etchmiadzin is the supreme head of the Armenian church.[56] The Armenian patriarchates of Jerusalem and Istanbul are local sees; the first takes spiritual care of Armenians in the Hashemite Kingdom of Jordan and in Israel, while the latter is responsible for the Armenians of Turkey.

The catholicate of Cilicia, presently occupied by His Holiness Khoren I (Baroyian), from 1929 to 1956 had the dioceses of Aleppo,

---

55. In 1958 the review *Edchmiadzin* was published in 3,500 copies of which 2,000 were circulated among the internal dioceses. At that time it was decided to increase the total number of copies to 5,000. See *Vazgen A. Hayrapet Hayots*, p. 42.

56. The supremacy of the Holy See of Etchmiadzin is historically demonstrable, despite the fact that since 1956 the authorities of the catholicate of Cilicia at Antelias have claimed a position of equal authority. The statement of Babgen Kiuleserian, a scholar and co-adjutor to Catholicos Sahak of Cilicia, which appeared in an official publication, is sufficient reply to these claims. Regarding the hierarchy of the Armenian church, Kiuleserian attests: "La première personne de la hiérarchie ecclésiastique, le chef suprême de l'Église est le patriarche d'Etchmiadzin, le catholicos de tous les Arméniens. Le patriarche d'Etchmiadzin partage la jurisdiction suprême de l'Eglise avec les patriarches de Constantinople, de Jérusalem, du catholicos de Cilicie, sans que ceci porte aucune atteinte à la primauté du siège d'Etchmiadzin et à l'unité hiérarchique de l'Église. Les trois derniers sièges sont d'origine postérieure, et ont été créés sous la pression des conditions politiques et historiques dans lesquelles se trouvaient l'Arménie et les Arméniens" (*L'Église arménienne* [Beirut, 1936], p. 37; cf. Jaques de Morgan, *The History of the Armenian People* [Boston, 1965], p. 127, n. 1).

Damascus, Beirut, and Cyprus. After 1956, when a crisis developed in the church, the authorities of Antelias joined to their catholicate the diocese of Greece and Iran, and organized a diocese in the United States of America. An opposite trend was manifested in Syria where the diocese of Damascus passed under the jurisdiction of Etchmiadzin. Moreover, half of the Armenians in Greece refused to accept the new arrangement. The dioceses of the catholicate of Etchmiadzin are as follows:[57]

   I. Armenia
     1. Diocese of Ararat
     2. Diocese of Shirak (Leninakan)
  II. Soviet Union (outside Armenia)
     3. Diocese of Georgia and Imeritia
     4. Diocese of Azerbaidzhan and Turkestan
     5. Diocese of Nor Nakhidchevan and the Northern Caucasus
 III. Diaspora
     6. Diocese of Iran
     7. Diocese of India and the Far East
     8. Diocese of Iraq
     9. Diocese of Egypt (including Ethiopia and the Sudan)
    10. Diocese of Greece
    11. Diocese of Bulgaria
    12. Diocese of Rumania
    13. Diocese of Western Europe (having its center at Paris)
    14. Diocese of the United States of America (including Canada, with New York as its center)
    15. Diocese of California (including Mexico, with its center at Los Angeles)
    16. Diocese of South America (Argentina, Brazil, Uruguay, and Chile)

The Armenian church has three monasteries, one at Etchmiadzin, a second in Jerusalem, and a third in Antelias. In Armenia itself there are numerous historic monasteries, but only that of Geghard is active. There are four seminaries run by the catholicates of Etchmiadzin and Antelias and by the patriarchates of Jerusalem and Istanbul. In addition to these, a new theological school, St. Nerses, opened at

57. *Edchmiadzin*, T962, pp. 26–27.

Evanston, Illinois, with the aim of training American-born Armenians for the churches of the USA. The seminary course, which was recently suspended with plans to reopen in New York, covers a program of seven years—four years for secondary general education and three years for theological and philosophical education and Armenian studies.

Since 1922, as a result of the establishment of the Soviet regime in Armenia, the catholicate of Etchmiadzin has been governed by new regulations. The former *Bolojenia* (1836–1917) is replaced by a temporary constitution and the Holy See is permitted a Supreme Spiritual Council which assists His Holiness. Since 1956 a synod of bishops has also participated in dealing with problems of the Armenian church.

Concerning interchurch relations, the establishment of the Soviet regime in Armenia did not effect the ecumenical relations of the Armenian church with other churches within or without the USSR. The Holy See of Etchmiadzin sent consultants to the Lausanne World Conference on Faith and Order in 1927,[58] and to Edinburgh in 1937. Archbishop Artavazd Siurmian and Archimandrite Shnork Kalustian attended the First Assembly of the World Council of Churches at Amsterdam as observers. In 1952 Archbishop Tiran Nersoyan and Bishop Derenik Pholatian were present at the Lund Conference as special consultants, and in 1954 they participated as observers in the deliberations of the Second Assembly of the World Council of Churches at Evanston, Illinois.[59]

In the summer of 1962, at the meeting of the Central Committee of the WCC in Paris, the Armenian and Georgian churches were officially accepted as member churches. In June–July, 1964, Catholicos Vazgen I appointed the Reverend Dr. Mesrob K. Krikorian permanent representative of the Holy See of Etchmiadzin to the World Council of Churches in Geneva, and since then the Armenian church has taken a more active part in the ecumenical movement. On March 30, 1967, Dr. Eugene Carson Blake, general secretary of the WCC, paid a visit to Etchmiadzin,[60] while His Holiness was invited to make an official visit to the Ecumenical Center at Geneva, July 10–13, 1967.

58. Theodik, *Amenun taretsoytse* [The almanac for everyone], (Paris, 1928), p. 627; Poladian, in *The Church of Armenia*, p. 79.
59. Poladian, in *The Church of Armenia*, p. 79.
60. *Ecumenical Press Service* (Geneva), no. 12, 6 April 1967; *Edchmiadzin*, April 1967, pp. 18–21; *Lraper* [The Herald] (New York), 13 May 1967.

Under the reign of Vazgen I, the ecumenical activity of the Armenian church has developed remarkably. During his voyages to the Middle and Far East, eastern and western Europe, the USA and South America, His Holiness has met many church leaders. From October 28 to November 9, 1965, the leaders of the Armenian Catholic and Protestant communities abroad—Patriarch Ignatius Batanian and the Reverend Yovhannes Aharonian, both from Beirut—visited Etchmiadzin for the first time and took part in the festivities for the tenth anniversary (1955–65) of the enthronement of His Holiness Vazgen I.

During the fifty years of Soviet rule, relations between the Armenian church and the state have undergone considerable evolution, from intense persecution to the present state of coexistence which is reasonably satisfactory. Of course, the church has had to make certain sacrifices and concessions. Despite these vicissitudes, the church continues to play an important role in the life of the Armenian people, both at home and abroad. For the future one is allowed to hope that the present Marxist–Christian dialogue begun in the West and parts of Eastern Europe may result in numerous benefits for both the church and the Armenian people in particular and the welfare of humanity in general.

12

MOSLEMS
IN THE SOVIET UNION
1948-1954

The position of Islam in the Soviet Union in the immediate postwar years, specifically 1948 to 1954, can be usefully compared and contrasted with that of the Russian Orthodox church. Moslem leaders, along with the Orthodox hierarchy, gave full support to Soviet policies as the price for the continued existence of their institutions and the practice of their faith. But as part of the surge of anti-cosmopolitanism and russification of the last years of Stalin, the Communist party and the Soviet government conducted an intensive campaign against Islam unlike anything experienced by the Orthodox.

Before exploring the events of this period, a survey of Soviet treatment of Islam up to and through the war years is in order. Four phases have been distinguished: (1) 1917–20—broad tolerance; (2) 1921–28—relative tolerance; (3) 1928–38—acute conflict; and (4) 1937–47—relaxation and compromise.[1]

1917–1920

On November 24, 1917, in an appeal "To all toiling Moslems of Russia and the East, whose mosques and prayer-houses have been destroyed, whose beliefs and customs have been trampled on by the

1. Vincent Monteil, "Essai sur l'Islam en URSS," *Revue des Études Islamiques* (Paris, 1953), p. 46.

Bernhard Wilhelm
---

czars and the oppressors of Russia," the Soviet government promised: "Your beliefs and customs, your national and cultural institutions are declared henceforth free and inviolable. Organize your
national life freely and without hindrance. This is your right. Know
that your rights . . . are protected by the entire might of the revolution
and its organs. . . . Support this revolution and its government!"[2]

Confronted with the dual character of Islam, both religious and
national, the Soviet leadership regulated from the outset the legal
position of Moslem religious organizations, as it did that of other
religious peoples, by the decree of January 23, 1918, on the separation
of the church from the state.[3] At the same time a special People's
Commissariat for Moslem Affairs was set up under Stalin's Commissariat of Nationalities.[4] Where the government was actively hostile
toward the Orthodox church, it did not encourage direct attacks on
Islamic institutions or communities. Lenin recognized that "such
people as the Kirghiz, Uzbeks, Tadzhiks, and Turkmens" were
"still under the influence of their mullahs" and had to be handled
with great care.[5] In October, 1920, Stalin warned:

If, for instance, the Daghestan masses, who are profoundly imbued with
religious prejudices, follow the communists on the basis of the *Shari'ah*,[6] it is
obvious that the direct way of combating religious prejudices in that country
must be replaced by indirect and more cautious ways.[7]

Most Moslems were, in fact, hostile or at least suspicious of the
newly established Soviet regime, particularly the Islamic peoples of
the northern Caucasus, because of their fear, based, Soviet sources
claim, on "slanderous rumors," that the regime would destroy the
rites, laws, and traditions by which they lived.[8] Stalin, therefore,
hastened, in November, 1920, to reassure the peoples of Daghestan
and the adjacent Republic of Transcaucasia:

2. *Sobranie uzakoneny i rasporiazheny raboche-krestianskogo pravitelstva rossiskoi
sovetskoi federativnoi sotsialisticheskoi respubliki* [Collection of statutes and decrees of the
worker-peasant government of the Russian Soviet Federative Socialist Republic] (Moscow, 1917–38), app. 2, p. 6.

3. N. A. Smirnov, *Ocherki istorii izucheniia islama v SSSR*, [Outlines of the history of
the study of Islam in the USSR] (Moscow, 1954), p. 132.

4. *Sobranie uzakoneny*, 17: 243.

5. V. I. Lenin, *Sochineniia* [Works], 4th ed. (Moscow, 1941–50), 29: 151.

6. The *Shari'ah*, the Moslem canon law, is a collection of religious statutes containing
the Koranic laws (with commentaries) which must in all circumstances guide the true
believer.

7. J. V. Stalin, *Works* (Moscow, 1952–55), 4: 375.

8. Smirnov, *Ocherki*, p. 135.

Daghestan must be governed in accordance with its specific features, its manner of life and customs. We are told that among the Daghestan peoples the *Shari'ah* is of great importance. We have also been informed that the enemies of Soviet power are spreading rumors that it has banned the *Shari'ah*. I have been authorized by the government of the Russian Soviet Federative Socialist Republic to state here that these rumors are false. The government of Russia gives every people the full right to govern itself on the basis of its laws and customs. The Soviet government considers that the *Shari'ah*, as common law, is as fully authorized as that of any other of the peoples inhabiting Russia. If the Daghestan people desire to preserve their laws and customs, they should be preserved.[9]

According to one commentator, "these declarations . . . knocked a serious weapon of anti-Soviet agitation out of the hands of the counterrevolution. . . ."[10] It does not seem that at the time the Moslem peoples took Stalin's words at their face value. They were further wooed by decrees (Turkestan, January 10, 1921; Azerbaidzhan, July 21, 1922) establishing Friday, the Moslem day of prayer, as the day of rest in predominantly Moslem regions,[11] and by the establishment of a special People's Commissariat for the *Shari'ah* in Daghestan.[12]

1921–1928

In 1920 the Commissariat of Nationalities was reorganized and the Commissariat for Moslem Affairs disappeared.[13] The policy of the party and the Soviet state in relation to Islam took on a more hostile character as their authority strengthened in Moslem areas, but nevertheless the general approach remained cautious and relatively tolerant.

One tactic the Communists now employed was concurrently in use against the Orthodox church. In Daghestan there were some forty thousand Moslem religious leaders and officials. To divide and disorient this group the party encouraged a "progressive" pro-Soviet schism, advocating a revision of the *Shari'ah*. In 1923, the schis-

9. Stalin, *Works*, 4: 409.
10. Smirnov, *Ocherki*, p. 136.
11. P. V. Gidulianov, ed., *Otdelenie tserkvi ot gosadarstva; polny sbornik dekretov RSFSR i SSR; instruktsy, tsikuliarovi t.d.* [The separation of church and state: A complete collection of the decrees of the RSFSR and the other republics; instructions, circulars, etc.], revised ed. (Moscow, 1926), pp. 61–62.
12. Walter Kolarz, *Russia and Her Colonies* (New York, 1952), p. 198.
13. *Sobranie uzakoneny*, 39: 206.

matics held a congress and sent a message of allegiance to Lenin:
"The Congress . . . greets thee, leader of the great army of the toilers,
liberating the whole world from the chains of slavery and disgrace.
We believe in the victory of the army. . . . We believe that Islam will
be freed from oppression with its help. . . . We shall help thy army."[14]

This movement lost much of its appeal when the Commissariat for
the *Shari'ah* was abolished, the religious schools liquidated, and, in
1925–26, the registration of births, deaths, and marriages transferred from the Moslem to the Soviet authorities.[15] From the first,
limitations had been placed on the *Shari'ah* courts; now these were
"finally liquidated" and "the Soviet government began a decisive
struggle against the *Shari'ah*."[16]

Concerning propaganda, one writer said: "after the victorious
conclusion of the civil war and the defeat of the interventionists, with
the transition to peaceful construction . . . tasks of ideological
struggle were posed with special sharpness and force," with particular attention to "the struggle to overcome religion," including
Islam.[17] The speeches of Sergei Kirov, party plenipotentiary in the
Caucasus, in particular "played a great role in unmasking the class
essence of Islam and its code of laws—the *Shari'ah*."[18] Books began
to appear which aimed at revealing "the crimes perpetrated against
the people by the Moslem priesthood" and the counterrevolutionary activities of these "enemies of the Soviet regime."[19] In 1923–24
a number of pamphlets and articles were published, particularly in
Revoliutsiia i tserkov (The revolution and the church), which "explained the reactionary character of individual precepts of Moslem
law."[20] Similar material appeared in the native languages. For instance, a journal in Tatar entitled "Science and Religion" came out
in Moscow in 1925, its object being "to reveal the harm done to the
workers by religious rites and the teaching of the Moslem priesthood."[21]

All of this activity was in line with the resolution of the Twelfth

14. Kolarz, *Russia and Her Colonies*, pp. 198–99.
15. Ibid.
16. *Bolshaia sovetskaia entsiklopediia* [Great Soviet encyclopedia] (hereafter *BSE*), 1st
ed. (Moscow, 1926–47), 61 : 855.
17. Smirnov, *Ocherki*, p. 142.
18. Ibid., p. 138.
19. Ibid., p. 149.
20. Ibid., p. 150.
21. Ibid., p. 162.

Party Congress (April, 1923) "On the State of Antireligious Agitation and Propaganda": "Inasmuch as the thirty million Moslems [an inexplicably exaggerated figure] of the Union of Republics has preserved almost untouched to this day numerous medieval prejudices, linked with religion and used for counterrevolutionary purposes, it is essential to work out forms and methods of liquidating these prejudices, taking into account the peculiarities of the different nationalities."[22]

But as the last words of this citation imply, caution was still the watchword of the party's campaign against Islam. The Thirteenth Congress (May, 1924) repeated this theme with a warning that "a careful attitude is particularly necessary in the Eastern republics and oblasts"[23] because, as a modern Soviet commentator explains, in those areas "Moslem traditions and religious survivals of all sorts still represented a serious force and the Moslem priesthood still enjoyed great authority and influence."[24]

1928–1938

At the end of the 1920s "the laws and traditions of Islam . . . continued to play a very great role in the private life of the people."[25] Since these traditions were incompatible with the policies embodied in the First Five-Year Plan, a radical revision of the regime's attitude towards Islam took place, as part of a general antireligious campaign, with methods common to all other areas. Between 1928 and 1933, seven thousand mosques were closed in the Tatar and Bashkir republics and five hundred in the northern Caucasus.[26]

By 1930, the antireligious propagandist, Iaroslavsky, was claiming that "even among such a backward mass as the Moslems a wide breach has been forged in the religious world-outlook of the masses."[27] Addressing the central council of the League of the Militant Godless on July 6, 1931, he was somewhat less optimistic: "The Moslem priesthood still plays a large role in the Soviet East. [It is] . . .

---

22. *KPSS v rezoliutsiakh i resheniiakh sezdov, konferentsy i plenumov Tsk.* [Resolutions and decisions of the congresses, conferences and plenums of the Central Committee of the CPSU] 7th ed. (Moscow, 1954), 1: 744.
23. Ibid. 2:53.
24. Smirnov, *Ocherki*, p. 145.
25. Ibid., p. 158.
26. Monteil, "Essai sur l'Islam en URSS," p. 65.
27. *Pravda*, 15 October 1930.

an open and irreconcilable opponent of all measures of the party and Soviet power, especially collectivization. . . . No prayers to Allah or any other nonexistent god will succeed in turning the enormous million-fold masses of the Soviet East from the socialist path."[28]

Indeed, these early attempts to suppress Islam were not completely successful. In 1930 it was admitted that three-quarters of the Communists in certain districts of Daghestan still took part in religious rites.[29] In 1931 in Chechenia (liquidated in 1946) there were still 2,675 mosques, 1,250 mullahs, 34 sheiks, and 250 religious elders.[30] In Ingushetia (likewise liquidated in 1946) children refused to learn from books which they thought were antireligious; teachers were even discharged for criticizing Islam; party and Komsomol members, instead of working against Islam, themselves frequented the mosques.[31]

A concomitant development of the 1930s was the effort to establish a recognized party "line" on Islam, beyond a general condemnation of it as reactionary. One theory about the origin of the Moslem faith put forward in the early 1930s suggested that it had begun as "an ideology of the poor, the expression of the interests of the impoverished section of the people." This view was soon condemned as "vicious" and as "going against the basic premises of Marxist teaching on the essence of religion in class society."[32]

Likewise, Soviet Islamic scholars travelled a long and difficult road to "overcome the bourgeois-idealistic conception of merchant capitalism as the guiding force in the creation of Islam."[33] The "triumph" of the opposing point of view, "which regards Islam as the ideology of a developing feudal system," was consolidated in 1935 when the article on Islam appeared in the *Bolshaia sovetskaia entsiklopediia*.[34] This article described Islam as "a fantastic reflection of social life" which "changed in accordance with the changes taking place in social relations"; currently efforts were being made "to adapt the feudal ideology and organization of Islam to the new

28. Smirnov, *Ocherki*, p. 161.
29. *Revoliutsiia i natsionalnosti* [The Revolution and the nationalities] (organ of the Council of Nationalities of the Central Executive Committee of the USSR), 1930, no. 2, p. 38.
30. Kolarz, *Russia and Her Colonies*, p. 187.
31. *Antireligioznik* [The antireligious worker], 1931, no. 11, p. 72.
32. Smirnov, *Ocherki*, p. 195.
33. Ibid., p. 190.
34. Ibid., p. 241.

capitalist conditions."[35] Within the USSR, the article continued, Islam had been used "for the struggle against the Soviet regime."[36] After the civil war "Islam and its organizations continued to serve as rallying points for counterrevolution,"[37] whereas at present "counterrevolutionary elements, making use of the Koran, are trying to play on the religious feelings of believers, to hinder socialist construction and to enkindle national and religious hatred in order to break the united front of the workers of the Soviet Union."[38]

Soviet Moslems suffered severely during the purges of the late 1930s. Atheistic propagandists were extremely vituperative in their charges. For example: "The Moslem religious organizations and mosques . . . are centers of the activity of anti-Soviet, nationalist elements. The enemies of the people carry on their treacherous work under the flag of the defense of religion.[39] "The activity of the counterrevolutionary Moslem priesthood in the USSR is directed by the Japanese secret service."[40]

Pravda had elaborated this theme in the summer of 1937:

A special place in the system of the Japanese secret service is occupied by the exploitation of counterrevolutionary bourgeois-nationalist Moslem elements. Aiming at organizing mass diversions in the deep rear of the USSR (Central Asia, the Urals, Tataria) . . . the Japanese openly support the leaders of the counterrevolutionary Moslem emigration. In Japan the chief organizer of espionage and diversionary work "on the Moslem line" is the mullah Kurbangaliev, who long ago entered the service of Japanese intelligence.[41]

Akmal Ikramov, first secretary of the Uzbek Communist party for many years until he was purged as a "spy" and shot in March, 1938, was brought to confess that he had "helped the Moslem priesthood to organize sabotage and diversion."[42] Similarly, the chairman of the Turkmen Supreme Soviet, Nederby Aytakov, executed at about the same time as a "traitor," was accused of protecting religious leaders.[43] Many mullahs were imprisoned for practicing ritual

35. *BSE*, 1st ed., 29: 371–72.
36. Ibid., p. 393.
37. Ibid., p. 394.
38. Ibid., p. 396.
39. F. Oleshchuk, *Borba tserkvi protiv naroda* [The church's fight against the people] (Moscow, 1939), p. 50.
40. Ibid., p. 87.
41. *Pravda*, 9 July 1937.
42. Oleshchuk, *Borba tserkvi*, p. 88.
43. Ibid., p. 89.

circumcision, which was equated with criminal mutilation. But late in 1938, when antireligious violence abated somewhat in view of the imminence of war, they were released on the ground that circumcision had never been forbidden by law.[44]

1939–1947

When war broke out Soviet Islam was in a much weakened state. As early as 1933 the *Shari'ah* had been denounced as a "tool of the enemies of socialist construction," which, as a result of "decisive struggle" by the Soviet government, "has now ceased to exist in the Soviet Union."[45] The *medresseh*, the Islamic academies, had all been "liquidated" by 1938.[46] In the whole of the USSR in 1941 there were only 1,312 mosques served by 8,052 mullahs.[47]

Despite all these measures, during the war the Moslems "did much to promote the drive for funds and the collection of gifts for the Soviet army."[48] On July 18, 1941, the Central Moslem Religious Board in Ufa, the governing body of Soviet Islam, summoned the faithful "to rise up in defense of their native land, to pray in the mosques for the victory of the Red Army and to give their blessing to their sons, fighting for a just cause."[49] On September 2, Mufti Abdurakhman Rassulev, the head of the board, again called on Soviet Moslems "to defend our country in the name of religion and to appeal to all our brother Moslems to do the same," and concluded: "In mosques and in private pray to Allah to help defeat the enemy of the Red Army."[50] One month earlier, on August 7, the Soviet Moslem leaders had appealed to Moslems throughout the world. Declaring that the Islamic peoples of the Soviet Union "have risen as one man to resist the German fascist invaders," they warned that "Islamic civilization . . . all the world over is today menaced with destruction by the German fascist bands unless the Moslems of the world stand up to it and fight!"[51]

44. *Sovetskaia iustitsiia* [Soviet justice], 1938, nos. 23–24.

45. *BSE*, 1st ed., 61: 855.

46. Ibid., 38: 634.

47. *Religious Communities in the Soviet Union* (London, Press Department of the Soviet Embassy), August 1941, p. 3.

48. G. Spasov, *Freedom of Religion in the USSR* (published by *Soviet News*, organ of the Soviet Embassy, London, 1951), p. 19.

49. Stanley Evans, *The Churches in the USSR* (London, 1943), p. 158.

50. Ibid., pp. 158–59.

51. Ibid.

Protestations of loyalty to Stalin followed. In November, 1942, Mufti Abdurakhman Rassulev sent "hearty greetings in the name of the Moslems of the USSR to you . . . champion of the liberation of oppressed peoples and a man ever attentive to the needs of the peoples." He concluded: "May Allah help you to bring your work to a victorious end."[52]

This support did not go unrewarded. Representative heads of Soviet Islam were permitted to meet at Ufa in May, 1942. Subsequently a Central Asian Moslem conference was held at Tashkent in October, 1943, and another, of Transcaucasian Moslem leaders, at Baku in May, 1944. Important changes in the Moslem ecclesiastical organization were sanctioned. The former Central Board at Ufa was replaced by four regional boards: Central Asia and Kazakhstan (in Tashkent), under the aged Mufti Ishan Babakhan Abdumedzhidkan; the European part of the USSR and Siberia (in Ufa), under Mufti Abdurakhman Rassulev; the northern Caucasus (in Buynaksk) under Mufti Khizri-Kady Gebekov; and the Transcaucasus (in Baku) under Sheikh-ul-Islam Ali-Zade Akhund-Aga.[53]

Working in coordination with the new governmental Council for the Affairs of Religious Cults, these boards were responsible for the opening of new mosques "where the need for them exists," the appointment of mullahs and muezzins, and the training of religious leaders.[54] Writing in 1954, Mufti Ishan Babakhan reported that his board was composed of eleven members elected at a congress of representatives of the Moslem congregations and priesthood, its "main mission" being "to see that all the activities of the religious communities and priesthood conform strictly to the teachings of Islam."[55]

The rapprochement between the government and Soviet Islam was apparently not affected by the abolition of the Crimean and Chechen-Ingush political units and the deportation of their Moslem inhabitants, along with other Caucasian Moslem peoples, for alleged treachery during the war. Certainly the reopening of a number of mosques was permitted. In December, 1944, the Mufti of Ufa said that ten mosques had been opened in Gorky, Omsk, Novosibirsk and

52. *Pravda*, 12 November 1942.
53. *BSE*, 1st ed., vol. on the USSR, p. 1789.
54. Spasov, *Freedom of Religion in USSR*, p. 27.
55. *USSR Information Bulletin* (Rangoon), 7 May 1954, p. 4.

other towns, while others were to be opened shortly in Chkalov, Cheliabinsk, and elsewhere.[56] In October, 1947, I. V. Poliansky, chairman of the Council for the Affairs of Religious Cults, said there were three thousand mosques in the Soviet Union.[57]

Moreover, once again the *Hajj* (the pilgrimage to Mecca which is the canonical obligation of every believer once in his lifetime, if he has the material means) became a possibility for some Soviet Moslems. In 1945 a group was permitted to travel to Mecca, with all its facilities, including aircraft, provided by the Soviet government.[58] According to its leader, Mufti Ishan Babakhan of Tashkent, the group numbered two hundred pilgrims drawn from all the Moslem areas of the USSR. Pro-Soviet propaganda was clearly a primary aim of the pilgrimage, which was to disprove, in the words of the Mufti, "the many enormities uttered concerning us."[59] According to the 1950 account of Mufti Babakhan to the visiting French General Tubert, a further *Hajj* was planned for 1946 but never materialized. He had received two hundred applications from the faithful of Central Asia and Kazakhstan, but since most of the applicants were too old and destitute he had forwarded only seventeen applications to the Council for the Affairs of Religious Cults, which though approving them "was unable to obtain visas from the governments concerned," namely, Iran and the Hedjaz.[60] Mufti Babakhan tells a similar story of 1947, when he forwarded forty applications, which were approved by the council. Again, according to the Mufti, "two governments which call themselves Moslem, those of Turkey and Iran, refused us transit visas,"[61] although the official reason given for the abandonment of the 1947 *Hajj* was the cholera epidemic then in the Middle East.[62]

1948–1954

In 1948 there came another shift in the regime's attitude to Soviet Islam, although this was felt more at the level of propaganda and indoctrination than in administrative attack.

In fact, at first the number of mosques increased slightly. In 1950

56. Moscow Radio, 16 December 1944.
57. *Alger Républicain*, 7 October 1947.
58. *USSR Information Bulletin* (Rangoon), 7 May 1954, p. 5.
59. *Alger Républicain*, 20 December 1950.
60. General Tubert, *L'Ouzbekistan, Republique Sovietique* (Paris, 1951), pp. 127–28.
61. *Alger Républicain*, 20 December 1950.
62. *Izvestiia*, 17 October 1947.

Mufti Ishan Babakhan spoke of "more than" three thousand in the USSR,[63] of which six hundred were in Uzbekistan, including fifty local mosques and seventeen great mosques in the city of Tashkent, each regularly attended by more than three thousand faithful.[64] Congregations seem to have been large and fervent. In June, 1952, a congregation of five thousand in the Tillya-Sheikh mosque in Tashkent was reported.[65] In September of the same year a Syrian visitor was told by the Imam of the Moscow mosque that he was "living happily and in security, whereas in the past he had been subjected to oppression." The visitor joined "some hundreds of worshippers" at prayer and noted their "strong attachment to their religion."[66] For the festival of Kurban-Bairam in June, 1954, there was a congregation of over ten thousand in the central mosque in Tashkent, while twenty thousand of the faithful gathered before the Shah-i-Zind mausoleum in Samarkand,[67] and there was a congregation of some three thousand in the main mosque of Ufa.[68]

Moreover, in 1948 the resumption of Islamic theological training was permitted on a small scale. In December the Board of Central Asia and Kazakhstan held a conference in Tashkent which discussed opening *medresseh* and training religious leaders.[69] By 1950, according to Mufti Ishan Babakhan, there were two *medresseh*, one in Tashkent and the other in Bukhara, each with a hundred pupils.[70] His claim is similar to, but does not exactly coincide with, the 1953 report of General Tubert that "a *medresseh* is functioning in Bukhara (another under construction in Tashkent) with about a hundred pupils who could not be admitted until they had completed the seven years of public [that is, Marxist] schooling obligatory throughout the Union."[71] Finally, in 1954, Mufti Ishan Babakhan wrote that his board "maintains a *medresseh* in Bukhara in the Mir-i-Arab building." (It is worth noting that in Bukhara alone, in 1902, there were 103 *medresseh*.)[72] The program and methods of teaching were, he said,

63. *Alger Républicain*, 20 December 1950.
64. Tubert, *L'Ouzbekistan*, pp. 85, 127.
65. Tass, for abroad, 19 June 1952.
66. Moscow Radio, in Arabic, 30 September 1952.
67. Tass, in English, for abroad, 3 June 1954.
68. Tass, in Russian, for abroad, 2 June 1954.
69. Monteil, "Essai sur l'Islam en URSS," p. 63.
70. *Alger Républicain*, 20 December 1950
71. Tubert, *L'Ouzbekistan*, p. 127. (The Barak Khan *medresseh* in Tashkent finally opened in 1956.)
72. V. Monteil, "Essai sur l'Islam en USSR," p. 16.

"decided by the pedagogical council of the *medresseh*." The curriculum included "*Tafsir* [interpretation of the Koran], *Mashqat* [study of the prophets], history of Islamic law, the Arabic and Persian languages, the national language of the student, and some general school subjects."[73]

In the summer of the same year the Italian scholar Alessandro Bausani gave an account of this curriculum.[74] He described a five-year course, a large proportion of which (4,392 hours out of 12,081) was devoted to the study of Arabic; Persian was taught on a lesser scale. During the first year, instruction in the Soviet constitution occupied two hours per week while study of Russian continued throughout the course. In the first two years, four hours per week were devoted to the study of "the origins of religion," though he did not say from what point of view. Apart from ninety-six periods for reading and recitation of the Koran, no other specifically religious instruction was given until the third year. The two periods a week given to history in the first three years did not include Islamic history, which was dealt with in seventy-two hours of instruction in the last year. From the third year a certain amount of religious instruction was given. *Tafsir* in fact took up only seventy-two hours out of a the total of 12,081. The *Hadith* (the complex of local and tribal laws, traditions, and customs in use among a given Moslem population) was taught for three periods per week in the last three years.

In November, 1954, the director of the *medresseh* reported that the term of studies had been extended to nine years, but whether this has allowed a more thorough and extended religious instruction of the students than under the earlier program is unknown. According to an Arabic broadcast of Moscow radio, tuition is free and students receive maintenance grants.[75]

It is clear that this resumption of Islamic theological training has been on a very small scale.[76] As stated, the Mir-i-Arab *medresseh*, with fifty *hujra* (cells), had one hundred students in 1953–54, and

73. *USSR Information Bulletin* (Rangoon), 7 May 1954, p. 5.
74. *Oriente Moderno*, August–September 1954.
75. Moscow Radio, in Arabic, 14 September 1953.
76. Perhaps in partial compensation, in 1955 three graduates from the Mir-i-Arab *medresseh* were admitted to the Moslem university of El Azhar in Cairo and others have followed since (*Akher Sa'a* [Cairo newspaper], 26 March 1955).

reached its maximum in 1956 when it had a complement of 105.[77]

The same sort of limitations characterize the publication of Moslem literature. In 1948, for the first time since the October Revolution, permission was given to publish an edition of the Koran,[78] and since then other small editions have appeared, Otherwise, Moslem publications seem to have been confined to a few books and religious calendars.[79]

No visits to Mecca were permitted from 1948 until after the death of Stalin, at which time a few Soviet Moslems were once again enabled to perform the *Hajj*. The pilgrimages of 1953 and 1954, however, were less a concession than part of the "peace" activities of official Soviet Islam to which, in view of the vast potential audience in the Middle East, a role was allotted which soon rivalled that of the Russian Orthodox church.

By 1950 Moslem leaders had been fully enrolled in this campaign. In August the head of the Transcaucasian board appealed to Moslems in Iran and Iraq "to join the great movement of peace supporters, and to give their signature to the Stockholm Appeal."[80] Mufti Ishan Babakhan called on the heads of world Islam to join in agitating "for the cessation of the aggressive war started by the Americans in Korea."[81] In October he was elected to the Soviet Peace Committee by the Second All-Union Peace Conference in Moscow,[82] at which Soviet Moslems were represented by Sheikh-ul-Islam Ali-Zade from Transcaucasia and Mullah Shakir Khiialetdinov from Central Asia.[83] In April, 1951, the latter, on becoming mufti of the European part of the USSR and Siberia, succeeding the deceased Mufti Abdurakhman Rassulev, declared: "The world is divided into two

77. *L'Afrique et l'Asie*, 1960, no. 4. Since then its numbers appear to have declined considerably. In 1962 it had less than fifty students. The numbers at the Barak Khan *medresseh* are reputedly even lower.

78. *L'Afrique et l'Asie*, 1960, no. 4.

79. In 1957 *Knizhnaia letopis* [The book chronicle], a journal in which the books and brochures published in the USSR in all languages and in all branches of knowledge are registered, mentioned a book called *Islam i musilmanskoe bogosluzhenie* [Islam and Moslem worship]. Its author was head of the Spiritual Board for European Russia and Siberia, and it included sixty-nine pages of text in Kazan Tatar in Arabic characters (*Knizhnaia Letopis*, 1957, no. 39, p. 90.) In 1958 the same source said that the Board for Central Asia and Kazakhstan had put out a twelve-page calendar written in Uzbek in Arabic letters, in an edition of ten thousand copies. (Ibid., 1958, no. 2, p. 105.)

80. *Soviet Monitor*, no. 11,792, 16 August 1950. Issued by Tass, London.

81. Ibid., no 11,795, 17 August 1950.

82. *Izvestiia*, 19 October 1950.

83. *Soviet Monitor*, no. 11,957, 12 October 1950.

camps, the camp of peace, headed by J. V. Stalin, and the camp of war, headed by the Anglo-American imperialists. . . . If all the peoples unite in their struggle for peace, the imperialists will be unable to unleash war."[84]

These appeals were often coupled with calls for loyal support of the Soviet government. The Imam of the Moscow mosque, preaching in July, 1952, exhorted the faithful to "work for their native land and love their Motherland for all the benefits which all the peoples of the Soviet Union enjoy with equal right." They prayed, he said, "wholeheartedly for success for those who are struggling for peace throughout the world."[85] Sheikh-ul-Islam Ali-Zade also "expressed sincere gratitude on behalf of Islam to the Soviet government for its solicitude for the development of the well-being and culture of the Moslem peoples of the USSR, and for the complete freedom in practising the Moslem religion ensured to all of us."[86]

The Third All-Union Peace Conference in Moscow (November, 1951) was attended by the heads of the boards of the European part of the USSR and Siberia, Central Asia and Kazakhstan, and Transcaucasia.[87] Mufti Shakir Khiialetdinov, speaking also on behalf of Mufti Ishan Babakhan, appealed to "Moslems of the whole world, and primarily to the Moslems of Turkey, Egypt, Iran, Syria, and other Moslem lands, to struggle against the efforts of the Anglo-American imperialists to drag the peoples of these countries into a new war."[88] Sheikh-ul-Islam Ali-Zade observed that "the monsters of humanity, the imperialists of the USA, insolently trampling on the laws of God and man, are preparing to plunge the whole world into the bloody abyss of a new war." He acclaimed Stalin as "the wisest man on earth, the luminary of peace."[89]

In May, 1952, the Zagorsk religious peace conference was attended by delegations from each board, headed by Mufti Shakir Khiialetdinov, Sheikh-ul-Islam Ali-Zade, Mufti Mohammed-Gadji Kurbanov, acting head of the North Caucasus board in succession to Khizri-Kady Gebekov, and Ziiautdin Babakhan, son and deputy of Mufti

84. Ibid., no. 12,443, 13 April 1951.
85. *Soviet News*, 9 July 1951.
86. *Soviet Monitor*, no. 12,679, 10 July 1951.
87. *Tretiaia vsesoiuznaia konferentsiia storonnikov mira*, [The third All-Union conference of the supporters of peace] (Moscow, 1952), pp. 152, 195.
88. Ibid., pp. 152–54.
89. Ibid., pp. 195–96.

Ishan Babakhan. All took part in the debates and supported the resolutions adopted.[90] A few days later Mufti Shakir Khiialetdinov declared:

I appeal to Moslems in Turkey, Egypt, Arabia, Pakistan, Afghanistan, and other countries to heed the commandments of Almighty Allah to join the peace movement and combat the aggressive plans of the US incendiaries of a new world war. All faithful Moslems, guided by the commandments of Almighty Allah, should follow the peace-loving nations, for only then can we live in peace and happiness. I invoke Almighty Allah to help us destroy all the plans of the warmongers. Amen.[91]

In November an appeal by Mufti Ishan Babakhan to Moslems of the Middle East was broadcast by his son:

As a Moslem I call on you to support the resolutions [of the World Peace Council] on the need for the unification of Germany . . . and those backing the Japanese people in their struggle against the San Francisco Treaty imposed on them by the USA. I fully endorse the resolutions of the Peking peace conference in Korea where the American aggressors under the banner of the UN are exterminating towns, villages, and peoples by the use of gas and germ bombs. . . . If the peoples do not take up the cause of peace today, what is happening in Korea will happen in their countries also. I call upon the people of the East to prepare for the Vienna Peace Congress.[92]

The pilgrimage of Soviet Moslems in 1953 was to some extent a reward for, but even more an extension of, these "peace" efforts. In mid-August two small groups, totalling eighteen persons,[93] left Moscow in an aircraft provided by the government to visit Mecca, Medina, and other holy places. The first group, led by Mufti Shakir Khiialetdinov, included Moslems from the Bashkir and Tatar ASSRs and the Penza and other oblasts. The second, led by Ziiautdin Babakhan, consisted of theologians, mullahs, and students of the Mir-i-Arab *medresseh*.[94] The pilgrims subsequently visited Cairo and were received by the grand mufti of Egypt.

Statements made by them on their return revealed what at least publicly was the predominantly propagandist nature of the expedi-

90. *Izvestiia*, 10, 13 May 1952; *Zhurnal moskovskoi patriarkhii* (Journal of the Moscow patriarchate), 1952, no. 5, pp. 14–17.
91. Moscow Radio, in English, for Southeast Asia, May 16, 1952.
92. Moscow Radio, in Arabic, 29 November 1952.
93. Arab News Agency, 19 August 1953.
94. Tass, in Russian, for abroad, 14 August 1953; *Izvestiia*, 15 August 1953.

tion. Mufti Shakir Khiialetdinov was quoted as saying: "The help given to the pilgrims is evidence of the profound respect felt by the Soviet government for the customs and religious beliefs of the people." Ziiautdin Babakhan spoke of the impression they had made: "During our talks we spoke about the condition of religious life in the Soviet land, and about the complete freedom of all faiths, including Islam. Our talks made a deep impression on our listeners because, as a result of the slanderous propaganda spread by the enemies of peace, the majority of them did not have a true idea of the life of Soviet Moslems."[95]

A congress of Moslem dignitaries which met in Ufa in June, 1954, reportedly received messages from many Soviet Moslem communities "expressing profound gratitude to the Soviet government for ensuring complete freedom of worship and free discussion of religious problems."[96] The conference seems to have been convened primarily for "peace" purposes. Mufti Ishan Babakhan, who attended as a guest, declared: "As a member of the Soviet Peace Committee, I would like to point out that the congress not only examined religious and theological questions, but also paid great attention to . . . the defense of peace."[97] At its final session the congress issued an appeal to the Moslems of the world: "Those taking part in the Moslem congress . . . declare their support for the World Peace Council's appeal for a struggle to conclude an international agreement prohibiting the use of atomic and hydrogen weapons, and for the peaceful settlement of the disputes in Korea and Indo-China."[98]

In August of the same year Sheikh-ul-Islam Ali-Zade, declaring that "the final outcome of the battle between the forces of good and evil depends in large measure on the Moslems of the world," demanded of Moslems in Turkey, Pakistan, Egypt, Iran, Afghanistan, Iraq, Syria, Lebanon, and Saudi-Arabia whether they "who ought to remember the precepts of Allah, have forgotten them." He added: "I follow the political courses of those countries and fail to understand them. Why seek friendship with the enemies of peace?" His words were repeatedly relayed by the Soviet radio to the Moslem world.[99]

95. Tass, in Russian, for abroad, 15 September 1953.
96. Tass, in English, for abroad, 14 June 1954.
97. Tass, in Russian, for abroad, 23 June 1954.
98. Moscow Radio, in Arabic, 15 June 1954.
99. Moscow Radio, in English, for Southeast Asia and in Arabic, 4 August, 1954; in Arabic, 12 August 1954.

This address appears to have anticipated the "pilgrimage" of two groups, from the same Moslem areas as before, totalling twenty-one persons,[100] who in August visited Mecca and Medina, via Turkey, Syria, Lebanon and Egypt. They, too, told Moslems abroad "about the happy life of people in our country."[101] Subsequently they figured in a program broadcast by Radio Moscow to Middle Eastern audiences; the muezzin of the Moscow Mosque, who had taken part, reported: "We said that all peoples of the Soviet Union, the Moslem peoples included, live together in friendship and harmony, and that every creed practices its religion in complete freedom. . . . We noticed that the enemies of peace and friendship between peoples had spread among our Moslem brothers abroad propaganda based on lies and falsehood concerning the conditions of Moslems in the Soviet Union."[102]

In these same postwar years, when the number of open mosques increased slightly, when religious education was permitted partial resumption, when religious publications began on a restricted scale, and when Soviet Moslem leaders were ambitiously enrolled in the government's "peace offensive" at home and abroad, a renewed antireligious campaign directed at Islam was undertaken, perhaps to offset these "concessions."

At first this campaign was confined to the Moslem areas in Central Asia. Thus in Kirghizia in July, 1948, the party complained: "In a number of places, the activities of religious communities and mullahs have increased. In the town of Osh, for example, many of the local inhabitants attend services organized by the mullahs. . . . The backward part of the population still turns to the mullahs for the solution of everyday problems.[103]

Many Communists and Komsomols were not only not fighting against "religious prejudices" but themselves took part in religious ceremonies. Not only was Islam "antiscientific," but its rites and festivals lowered collective-farm output and undermined labor discipline. This theme was repeated in a lecture to the intelligentsia of Frunze in September.[104]

100. Arab News Agency, 27 July 1954.
101. Moscow Radio, in English, for Southeast Asia, 1 September 1954.
102. Moscow Radio, in Arabic, 27 November 1954; also in Turkish, 28 November 1954.
103. *Sovetskaia Kirgiziia* [Soviet Kirghizia], 23 July 1948.
104. Ibid., 11 September 1948.

In 1949 more energetic anti-Islamic steps were taken. In Tashkent an antireligious museum was opened.[105] On August 6 the presidium of the Tadzhik Supreme Court decreed: "The weekly day of rest throughout the whole territory of the Tadzhik SSR is transferred from Friday to Sunday."[106] In November the central propaganda apparatus went into action. Moscow Radio declared: "The Koran justifies the exploitation of man by man. The Moslem religion, moreover, advocates hatred towards all non-Moslems and so opposes international working-class solidarity."[107] Societies for the dissemination of political and scientific knowledge, already established in all the Moslem republics, began to flourish. The Kazakh society, for example, soon had fifteen oblast and 209 town and *raion* branches and 815 propaganda bureaus.[108]

The campaign was markedly intensified in 1950, particularly in the Caucasus. On July 14, Bagirov told a congress of intellectuals in Baku that Islam, founded by "a representative of the feudal merchant nobility," was "widely employed by them for their wars of conquest, and for the subjugation and enslavement of many peoples." He added that "often the servants of the Moslem religion have been and are employed as spies and saboteurs."[109] In that same summer a dark reassessment of the nineteenth-century Caucasian hero, Imam Shamil, and his regime began. Whereas the *Bolshaia sovetskaia entsiklopediia* had described him earlier as the "leader of the national-liberation movement of the mountain peoples of the Caucasus against the colonial policy of czarist Russia" who, in Marx's words, was "a great democrat,"[110] he was now unmasked as a "tool in the hands of foreign states" while "in the movement he led there was not and could not be anything progressive or democratic."[111]

Shamil's regime, formerly interpreted as fundamentally religious and based on the *Shari'ah*, was now, in the new work of A. Daniialov, *On Distortions in the Elucidation of Muridism and the Movement of Shamil*, described politically: "The *Shari'ah* and Muridism, imposed by violence, were alien not only to the ordinary mountaineers. . . .

105. *Pravda vostoka* [*Pravda* of the East], 5 October 1949.
106. *Kommunist Tadzhikistana* [Communist of Tadzikistan], 9 August 1949.
107. Moscow Radio, 15 November 1949.
108. *Kazakhstanskaia Pravda* [Kazakhstan *Pravda*], 1 March 1952.
109. *Bakinsky rabochy* [The Baku worker], 18 July 1950.
110. *BSE*, 1st ed., 61: 804–6
111. Smirnov, *Ocherki*, p. 253.

Often village elders and members of the clergy, opposed to the *Shari'ah*, turned for protection to the Russian authorities.[112]

"The regime of the *Shari'ah* established by Shamil," he continued, "weighed extraordinarily heavily on the population of Daghestan." The *Shari'ah* became "a very great brake on the progress of the Daghestan peoples."[113] As long as a Moslem leader who stood for the *Shari'ah* was officially recognized as a national hero, the Moslems of Daghestan, and the whole USSR, might feel entitled to respect for their faith. Therefore *Shari'ah* was now abused as "a collection of the most unjust, the most infamous 'laws'."[114]

In Uzbekistan any lingering illusions about the regime's attitude to Islam were dispelled by the local party newspaper which exulted: "The revolutionary storm of the popular masses will sweep away the decayed Moslem religion from the face of the earth."[115]

Extensive anti-Islamic activity was reported from the "scientific centers" in Moslem areas, particularly Kazakhstan. Works published by the Kazakh Academy of Sciences in 1950 singled out the *medresseh* as "channels through which flowed all sorts of reactionary currents, as, for instance, pan-Islamism and pan-Turkism, which were the political ideology of the exploiting upper classes (khans, mullahs, landowners, merchants) and strove to unite into one whole all the peoples professing Islam, and which now serve the interests of the American and English imperialists."[116]

Throughout 1951 the propaganda campaign against Islam continued, with such themes as "The Origin and Reactionary Essence of Islam," "The Reactionary Essence of the *Uraza* [the fasting practiced during the season of Ramadan]," and others.[117] In 1952 the themes of anti-Islamic propaganda became even more strident: "The Anti-Popular Nature of the Religious Ideology of Islam," "The Harmful Character of Religious Rites and Prejudices,"[118] "The Danger to Health from Fasting," "The *Uraza*, Pernicious Survival of the Past,"[119] and more.

112. *BSE*, 1st ed., 61 : 805.
113. *Voprosy istorii* [Problems of history], 1950, no. 9, pp. 9, 11–12.
114. *Kommunist Tadzhikistana*, 12 July 1951.
115. *Pravda vostoka*, 15 October 1950.
116. Smirnov, *Ocherki*, p. 259.
117. *Pravda vostoka*, 28 June 1951.
118. Ibid., 15 May 1952.
119. *Kommunist Tadzhikistana*, 28 May 1952.

In August the festival of Kurban-Bairam was violently attacked by the veteran L. Klimovich, who wrote that Soviet citizens must get rid of "survivals of capitalism, blemishes from the time when the people languished in poverty and backwardness," such as "Islam with its rites, feasts, and fasts, alien and harmful to the people." Kurban-Bairam, "one such survival," originally "imposed by violence on the people" of Central Asia "just like Islam itself," with its "fairy tale about sacrifices being rewarded in heaven," was "not only anti-scientific but also profoundly hostile to the optimistic world-outlook of the Soviet people"; it was "directed to the deception of man." As for the *Hajj*, it was "a source of income for the merchants and feudalists of Arabia" and an opportunity "widely used by the imperialists for recruiting spies and diversionists." Mecca had "long been in the hands of a henchman of English imperialism"; now "The American imperialists also hold sway there." Klimovich concluded: "Thus Kurban-Bairam is a survival alien and hostile to the people. In it there is nothing which could justify its existence today. Both in the past and in the present it has served, and serves, to harm the workers. It ill befits Soviet people . . . to turn to reactionary rites and customs."[120]

The year 1953 opened with a broadside against Islam in the form of an authoritative article in the second edition of the *Bolshaia sovetskaia entsiklopediia*, which declared: "Islam has always played a reactionary role and been a weapon in the hands of the exploiting classes for the spiritual oppression of the toilers, and has been used by foreign colonizers to enslave the peoples of the East. . . . In the USSR Islam exists only as a survival of one of the ideolgical forms of exploiter society."[121]

During and after the Revolution, it was charged, Islam had been "used by internal counterrevolutionaries and foreign imperialists for the struggle against the Soviet state." For example: the establishment in the northern Caucasus in 1919, "on the initiative of the English imperialists," of "an 'emirate' headed by a sheikh whose declared intention was to rule according to the precepts of the *Shari'ah*," and the demand of Moslem religious leaders of Turkestan, "agents of the foreign imperialists," that "the country be administered according

120. *Pravda vostoka*, 28 August 1952.
121. *BSE*, 2nd ed. (1949–58), 18: 516, 519.

to the *Shari'ah*." Thereafter the "remnants of the exploiter classes" had "used Islam for the struggle against socialism." Moslem religious leaders had "committed terrorist acts." The Koran and the *Shari'ah* had been "used particularly actively for the struggle against industrialization and collectivization." This identification of Islam with past acts of treason, anticommunism, and the like, has been continued to the present by such allegations as: "The Anglo-American imperialists are using Islam for the struggle against revolutionary and national-liberation movements and against the movement of peace partisans."[122]

A lull in the campaign followed the death of Stalin in 1953, but it did not last. In the spring of 1954 in Tadzhikstan the local party paper said that "Islam and its rites play a reactionary role since they hold back the development of the national and class consciousness of workers and peasants." *Ramadan* was singled out for particular condemnation since "the observance of the *uraza* distracts believers to a significant degree from engaging in everyday, urgent work." In 1953 this festival had coincided with spring and summer field work and "the productivity of labor was reduced and cases of absenteeism became more frequent in individual collective farms." For this, "insufficiently extensive antireligious propaganda was to blame."[123]

Similar complaints by the party that anti-Islamic propaganda was not being given "the necessary attention" came from Uzbekistan. In some areas of the republic atheist propaganda was said to have been "completely discontinued," while some young people had come under the influence of religion. In 1953 in the Tashkent rural *raion* of the Tashkent oblast, only 120 lectures on "scientific-atheist" themes had been given, ninety-six of them on the days of *uraza* and *Kurban-Bairam*—which showed "the absence of systematic daily scientific-atheistic propaganda." In the first quarter of 1954 in the republic as a whole, "only 644" atheist lectures had been given. The Uzbek Society for the Dissemination of Political and Scientific Knowledge, the Komsomol, and the republic's press and publishing houses were severely taken to task for these failures.[124]

To reinforce the campaign, which had lagged briefly, the Institute of History of the Academy of Sciences of the USSR issued, in an

122. Ibid.
123. *Kommunist Tadzhikistana*, 25 April 1954.
124. *Pravda vostoka*, 18 June 1954.

edition of four thousand copies, a 275-page volume entitled *Outlines of the History of the Study of Islam in the USSR*. The first part of the book, dealing with Islamic studies in prerevolutionary Russia, was designed to "select the most valuable" of these studies "for the elucidation of the social function of Islam in the history of the Eastern peoples, and equally for the struggle against its survival in our country."[125] The second part, covering Soviet Islamic studies, 1918–50, was intended to "determine the degree to which the works of Soviet authors answer the chief demand made upon them: to serve as an ideological weapon in the hands of the party for the communist education of the workers, and for the struggle against harmful survivals in people's consciousness of an ideology alien to us."[126]

Soviet Islamic scholars were instructed by the author of this book to "pay much more attention to unmasking the contemporary role of Islam in support of the exploiting classes and the colonial regime, and to revealing the reactionary, antipopular essence of the ideology of pan-Islamism and pan-Turkism, which is exploited primarily by American imperialism for the enslavement of the peoples of the East." Their works should also "arm our propagandists with knowledge to assist them to struggle against religious survivals" and to "educate the workers in the spirit of Soviet patriotism."[127] The line which they should follow was made absolutely clear: "Islam and the Koran defend, preserve, and justify the rule of the possessor classes, and the whole teaching of Islam is so constructed as to gloss over class contradictions, to distract the attention of the workers from the class struggle."[128]

In August, 1954, at the very time when the few privileged Soviet Moslems were making their *Hajj*, Ashkhabad Radio broadcast a bitter attack on Islam, "the ideology of the feudal Arabs." The Moslem clergy were accused of having "conspired with counterrevolutionaries and White Guards against the Soviet government" during the Revolution and the Civil War. They had thereafter opposed the abandonment of the old Arabic script in order "to keep the people illiterate." Now the "reactionary clergy" (whether in Turkmenia or

125. Smirnov, *Ocherki*, p. 4.
126. Ibid., p. 6.
127. Ibid., pp. 270–71.
128. Ibid., p. 187.

abroad was not made clear) "engage in propaganda for pan-Islamism . . . and seek to separate Soviet Turkmenia from the family of the USSR and from the great Russian elder brother." The clergy were said to have "gone into service with their new masters, the Anglo-American imperialists, who use them against the USSR and the people's democracies." Moslem fasts and festivals were denounced as "capitalist remnants"; religious leaders, in order "to preserve the poison of religion in the minds of backward people, call upon the faithful to carry out burial customs and prayers." The republic's Ministry of Culture, radio-information, film administration, and the Society for the Dissemination of Political and Scientific Knowledge were castigated for having "failed to take the opportunity to intensify antireligious propaganda."[129]

That fall the organ of the Kazakh Communist party denounced Islam as "an ideological tool of the exploiters in their struggle against the workers" and a means for their "spiritual oppression." Islam "in the name of Allah preaches the inviolability of private property, defines and justifies class inequality, the exploitation of man by man, and national divisions." There had been "many predatory and reactionary wars waged under the banner of Islam's 'holy war'," in particular national risings against czarism in the Caucasus and Kazakhstan which were "directed towards . . . separating [our peoples] from their elder brother and friend—the great Russian people." Islam "proclaims a Moslem cosmopolitanism—the ideology of pan-Islamism which . . . the exploiter classes of the countries of the East are striving today to use . . . for carrying out their predatory plans." Pan-Islamism also "serves American imperialism . . . in the cause of preparing a new war." The October Revolution had "dealt a crushing blow to the reactionary priesthood and religious superstitions" and the "Kazakh people" had been "liberated . . . from the corrupting influence of the Islamic religion." Nevertheless, religious "survivals" still "poison the minds" of some. Islam had "had a revival" in parts of the republic "as a result of the slackening of antireligious and scientific-atheist propaganda." Therefore, "it is necessary to carry on a constant and unrelenting struggle," because Islam, "like every other religion," tried to "keep believers in darkness and ignorance." No man could be "an active builder of communism, a

129. Ashkhabad Radio, in Turkmenian, 12 August 1954.

cultured and educated person," if he had not "entirely banished the survivals of religious ideology."[130]

A month later the anti-Islamic campaign flared up anew in Transcaucasia. An attack on the "Origin and Reactionary Essence of Islam," by Klimovich, appeared in the Georgian Communist party's newpaper. Islam, he said, "is incompatible with the fundamental interests of the Soviet peoples." Having "nothing 'miraculous'" in its origin, it arose from "changes in the economic and social life" of the Arabs; Islam was then spread "by violence" to the Caucasus and Central Asia whose inhabitants sought to "put up a persistent and heroic resistance." To depict the early conquests of the caliphs as "a kind of good deed and 'illumination' of unbelievers with the 'light of Islam'" was "historically incorrect and harmful." Moreover, the caliphs later became "puppets of the imperialists." The Koran and the *Shari'ah* were compiled "to please the caliphs, feudal lords and merchants." The Koran contained "reactionary principles, myths and legends" and its teachings were "primitive and antiscientific . . . the fruit of the most ignorant ideas of ancient man about nature." It taught that "people must patiently suffer any adversity and torture, and the most terrible oppression," its ideals "having nothing in common with a genuine love for mankind." The customs and rites of Islam "aim at duping man and depriving him of his personality." Its festivals, "survivals of the distant past when man was helpless," had "never had anything in common with popular and national customs."

Today, Klimovich continued, these festivals "bring only harm to the workers of our country, distracting them from their work, injuring their health and prejudicing the national economy." The "thousands of people" in the USSR who still adhere to Islam "undermine labor discipline and harm themselves and their comrades in production by taking part in organized holy pilgrimages." Conspiracy by foreign Moslems against the Communists was alleged:

Highly illuminating . . . are the plans for united action by Islam and Catholicism with which the pope and the sheikhs of the Higher Moslem School of Al-azhar in Cairo have come out. These plans of the Vatican and the reactionary priesthood are directed against the defenders of progress and democracy. Islam is necessary to the imperialists and 'its own' exploiting

130. *Kazakhstanskaia Pravda*, 17 September 1954.

classes only as an instrument of their supremacy, a means of poisoning the consciousness of the masses and helping to oppress and exploit the workers.

The article concluded that in the Soviet Union "Islam is a tenacious survival" which "does not die without a struggle."[131]

The November, 1954, decree of the party's Central Committee condemning antireligious excesses brought Soviet Islam a respite. Moslem leaders redoubled their efforts in support of the regime's policies, evidently in the hope of prolonging this respite. Mufti Ishan Babakhan told Tass: "The Imams . . . are constantly explaining to believers that the struggle for peace conforms to the teachings of the Koran and that it is the duty of every Moslem to come out resolutely against all the machinations of the warmongers."

Behind "provocative rumors" presenting the position of Soviet Islam "in a false light," he descried "the hand of the enemies of peace who are trying to slander the great country of freedom and peace." He appealed "on behalf of the Moslems of the Soviet East" to Moslems abroad to "redouble their efforts" in the "peace campaign.[132]

At the New Year the mufti and other senior Moslem leaders of the European part of the USSR and of Siberia issued a statement "on questions of defending peace." Recently, they declared, the Western powers "flagrantly violating international treaties under pressure from the American aggressors, concluded a shameful deal to revive German militarism in West Germany, to set up German armed forces and draw German militarism in West Germany into a military group directed against the Soviet Union and the peace-loving democratic countries of Europe." This "shameful deal under the banner of the London and Paris agreements" was a "direct threat to peace and to the lives of all of us." The Moscow Security Conference, on the other hand, had been "an expression of the will . . . of all progressive mankind and points out the direct road to peace." The signatories of the statement and their followers "resolutely condemn the policy of reestablishing German militarism and fervently support the Moscow Declaration." They "call upon Moslem religious leaders of other countries to apply all their energy, to

131. *Zaria vostoka* [Dawn of the East], 10 October 1954.
132. Tass, in English, for abroad, 17 November 1954.

utilize every opportunity for the preservation of peace . . . and in this
way to put an end to the actions of the warmongers."[133]

Post-1954

Whatever the reason for the November, 1954, decree—whether as a
step away from Stalin's anticosmopolitanism and his policy of russification, or as a maneuver for power by Khrushchev against Malenkov, or simply as a move to put the regime's antireligious work on a
sounder basis—the result for Soviet Islam was an abatement of the
ideological pressure it had been subjected to since 1948. This pressure was not to be seriously reapplied until 1959, with the massive,
generalized antireligious campaign launched under Khrushchev's
leadership. By that year, according to Moscow Radio, there were
some 30 million Moslems in the Soviet Union, although this figure
is obviously based on nationality rather than active religious affiliation.[134] (This can be compared with the 16.25 million Moslems
residing in the Russian Empire as of January 1, 1912.)[135] There are
no available figures for the overall number of functioning mosques,
although one report of 1969 gave some two hundred central and one
thousand district mosques in Soviet Central Asia,[136] which includes
what in czarist times were the province of Turkestan and the vassal
states of Khiva and Bokhara. Pre-1917 figures for active mosques
are twelve thousand in Turkestan, three thousand in Khiva, and 360
in the city of Bokhara alone. [137] If the figures given for this area of
Moslem population are characteristic of other areas of the Soviet
Union, then a rough indication is available of the decrease in Moslem
religious sanctuaries during the first forty years of Soviet rule.

What further losses have been suffered in the last decade, either
because of the 1959–64 campaign or through the educational and

133. *Izvestiia*, 5 January 1955.
134. Moscow Radio, in Arabic, 5 July 1959.
135. This figure includes 4,635,000 in European Russia, 7,955,000 in Central Asia,
3,335,000 in the Caucasus, and 120,000 in Siberia. There were then 24,321 Moslem
communities and 26,279 mosques (*Mir Islama* [The world of Islam], publication of the
Imperial Society of Oriental Studies, 1913, no. 11, pp. 269–71). By January 1, 1914, the
number of communities had risen to 24,582, including 2,125 in the region of Ufa and
1,010 among the Tatars of Kazan, 13,005 in Central Asia, and 1,856 in Daghestan
(*Statistichesky ezhegodnik Rossii* [Statistical yearbook of Russia] [Moscow, 1914], pp. 85–
86).
136. Tashkent Radio, 19 January 1959.
137. A. A. Gordienko, *Sozdanie sovetskoi natsionalnoi gosudarstvennosti v srednei Azii*
[The creation of Soviet national statehood in Central Asia] (Moscow, 1959), p. 26.

propagandistic pressures that have survived the fall of Khrushchev, is presently unclear. Articles in *Nauka i religiia*, the official journal of Soviet atheism, while claiming that the number of practicing Moslems in the Soviet Central Asian republics has declined sharply in recent years, deplore the way local nationalities cling to ceremonies derived from the Koran, and the "tenacious survival" of the Moslem religion generally.[138] Two considerations have emerged or sharpened in the last decade which may, in the future, redound to the benefit of Moslem believers in the Soviet Union. The first, as suggested above, is the Soviet government's bid for influence in the Arab world. As early as 1957, M. B. Mitin, writing in *Voprosy filosofii* (Problems of philosophy), testified to the difficulties inherent in the contradiction between domestic and foreign policy in this area.

In demonstrating the antiscientific character of Islam, we must at the same time take into consideration the part it is playing under present-day conditions, when under its banner there are a number of movements of great progressive importance—in particular, the fight of the Arab people, led by Egypt, for their independence. In the eastern countries there is still a large number of people whose religious sentiments fuse with their national sentiments. At the same time . . . it is essential to keep in mind that the imperialists try to use Islam for their own purposes in order to stir up enmity between the peoples, in order to weaken their forces in the fight for independence. . . . From this it follows that our lectures must have great political insight, and a profound grasp of the contemporary process, in order to carry on a proper fight against Islam.[139]

The second consideration, of more recent origin, is the current struggle for influence in Central Asia between China and the Soviet Union. The Chinese Communist regime has treated its Islamic minority in much the same way as the Soviets have. Their religious and national practices and attitudes have run afoul of the Communist ideology and have therefore been systematically suppressed. In 1958 Moslems in China, resentful at the treatment meted out by the Chinese government, flared into open rebellion in a number of areas. These outbreaks were put down severely.

Little information is yet available on the Soviet reaction to these events in China. It seems likely, however, that the Soviet government is aware of the possibilities if such a situation should be repeated. Efforts to win the allegiance of Chinese Moslems would become

138. *Nauka i Religiia*, May 1965, February 1966.
139. *Voprosy Filosofii*, no. 5, 1957, p. 224.

probable. Given the fact that the borders of the predominantly Moslem republics of the Soviet Union are contiguous with the Chinese border, it may become increasingly necessary for "tact" in the treatment of Soviet Moslems if such efforts are to meet with any success.

In addition to these considerations of foreign policy, the future of Soviet Islam will be affected by the stand, still unclear, that the post-Khrushchev government will take towards religion and religious institutions. If the antireligious program is limited to "atheistic education," with a higher degree of legality and the abandonment of the harsh administrative measures of other periods, it is possible that the exigencies of foreign policy may earn Soviet Moslems and their leaders a respite. Antireligion itself, because of the tendency of Communists, principally in the West, to reexamine the position of atheism in Marxism, may in time undergo alteration in the Soviet Union, that is, to the extent that Soviet society becomes a more open society.

On the other hand, Islam in the Soviet Union has suffered substantial setbacks over the past fifty years, not only from Communist ideology and practice but also from the impact of the rise of an urban, technological society.[140] That this trend will continue seems extremely likely. Nonetheless, both the religious and national aspects of Islam have proved to be remarkably tenacious against all pressures. And this, too, is a factor to be reckoned with in any prediction of its future.

140. See Bohdan R. Bociurkiw, "Religion and Atheism in Soviet Society," chapter 4 above.

13

MENNONITES
IN THE SOVIET UNION

About 110,000 Mennonites, including unbaptized children and young people, resided in Russia at the time of the Bolshevik Revolution in 1917. Scattered from the Ukraine to Siberia in over fifty major agricultural settlements, they occupied some 365 villages, with nearly as many churches, and owned about four million acres of land. They also possessed a monopoly on the flour-milling industry, and their factories produced 6 percent of the total output of all agricultural machinery and implements in Russia.[1]

The Russian Mennonites matched or surpassed their coreligionists in western Europe and North America not only in wealth, but in their level of education as well. By 1917 the Mennonites in Russia had established four hundred elementary schools, thirteen high or central schools, four girls' schools, two teachers colleges, two four-year trade schools, one eight-year business college, one school for the deaf and dumb, one nursing school, one Bible school, and several hospitals, including one for the mentally ill. About 250 students were

---

1. Cornelius Krahn, "Russia," in *Mennonite Encyclopedia* (Scottdale, Pa., 1959), 4: 392. This article gives a concise summary of Russian Mennonite settlement and development. Cross-references, maps, and charts of the mother and daughter settlements, plus a bibliography, make this a valuable reference on Russian Mennonite history.

Frank H. Epp

attending Russian institutions of higher education and fifty were in seminaries and universities abroad.[2]

In 1883 the local Mennonite churches, which previously had been quite isolated from one another, organized the General Conference of Mennonite Congregations in Russia. Within this conference there were two major groups. Members of the larger group were known as *kirchliche* or "church" Mennonites. The *Brueder* group, also known as the Mennonite Brethren, was an offshoot of the parent *kirchliche* group and had been formally founded in 1860. The Brethren were distinguished by the fundamentalist nature of their piety, as well as by differences in ritual observance, for example, the practice of baptism by immersion, not by sprinkling or pouring. While missionary activity of both groups was officially frowned upon in Russia, in 1917 the *kirchliche* group, working through the Dutch Mennonite community, was supporting fourteen workers in Sumatra and Java, while the Brethren had several missionaries working with the Baptists in India.

The historical importance for Mennonites of the right of exemption from conscription will be examined below. Here it will suffice to say that prior to the Revolution this right had been respected through a program of alternative service. In World War I some six thousand Mennonites were sent to the hospital and ambulance corps, with an additional six thousand serving in the forestry corps. The Mennonite community itself financed this program, which in 1917 alone cost three million rubles. No Mennonite young men were conscripted and only a few volunteered for military service.

Sociologically and geographically isolated, the Mennonites were left in control of much of the civil administration of their communities. Thus, in many ways Russia had proved to be a most desirable place in which to settle. The freedom of Mennonites to preserve their religious and cultural traditions, to regulate their own lives with a high degree of autonomy, and to pursue their livelihood without interference led one historian to refer to this pattern of life as "The Mennonite Commonwealth of Russia."[3]

2 Frank H. Epp, *Mennonite Exodus: The Rescue and Resettlement of the Russian Mennonites Since the Communist Revolution* (Altona, Manitoba, 1962), p. 571. With its 15 maps, 132 illustrations, and 39 tables this book tells in greater detail than Krahn's work the story of the conflict between the Soviet state and the Mennonites. Exhaustive bibliography.

3. E. K. Francis, *In Search of Utopia: The Mennonites of Manitoba* (Altona, Manitoba, 1955), p. 294. Contains a sociologist's flashback to the Mennonites in Russia.

In the light of earlier Mennonite history it is easy to see why this Russian experience seemed like a veritable paradise. The movement had first taken shape in the sixteenth century in both northern (Holland) and southern (Switzerland) Europe. The Mennonites who eventually settled in Russia were primarily descendants of the Dutch group. Their leader, Menno Simons (c.1496–1561), a former Catholic, had renounced his priesthood in 1536 to devote himself to preaching the doctrine of nonresistance, the priesthood of all believers, separation of church and state, and the absolute authority of the Bible.[4]

The rejection by Simons and his followers of the norms and practices of both the Catholic and the newer Protestant state churches resulted in severe persecution by both. As nonresistant Christians they refused to fight back, choosing rather to flee where this was possible and to suffer where this became necessary. Several thousand of these Anabaptists, as they were also called, were martyred.

Many of those who fled settled in what was later called Prussia and Poland where, as Dutchmen experienced in diking operations, they successfully reclaimed and developed the rich lands of the Vistula delta, while enjoying full religious freedom, including the all-important right of exemption from military service. Over the years these Dutch refugees gradually came to use the German language. Despite considerable cultural evolution, there were no changes in the central tenets of their religious faith—opposition to political absolutism and to military service. When economic and religious restrictions caught up with them two hundred years later, they began to look for a new place to settle.

It was precisely at this time that Catherine II (1729–96) issued a general invitation to western Europeans to colonize lands recently secured from the Turks. Beginning in 1789, about ten thousand Prussian Mennonites accepted this invitation. Two large colonies in the Ukraine, Chortitsa and Molotshchna, roughly a hundred miles apart, were founded between 1790 and 1810. In the 1850s two smaller colonies were also established along the middle Volga. After the first difficult years of pioneering, the colonies grew and expanded

---

4. C. Henry Smith, *The Story of the Mennonites*, 3d ed. (Newton, Kansas, 1950), p. 833. C. J. Dyck, ed., *An Introduction to Mennonite History* (Scottdale, Pa., 1967), p. 324. These two books represent the best overall surveys of world Mennonite history.

rapidly, eventually establishing fifty "daughter" colonies.[5]

These self-contained religious settlements were one cornerstone of the Russian Mennonite "Commonwealth." In addition to the economic assistance which had made colonization possible, the first settlers also obtained perpetual exemption from military service, tax exemptions for a specified number of years, complete religious freedom and the right to maintain their own churches and schools, wide latitude in matters of local government, and the right to own serfs.

These combined privileges helped the Mennonites to develop at will their religious and educational institutions, a strong and independent economy, and a closed sociological and cultural community, all of which were factors in the disastrous collision with the Communist government after 1917. It would be wrong, however, to assume that relations between the Mennonites and the central government had proceeded smoothly at all times prior to 1917.

On the contrary, at least three major developments before 1917 gave strong hints that serious friction between the Mennonites and the Russian society and its government was inevitable. The first trouble came in the 1860s as a result of the programs of reform, nationalization, and russification inaugurated at that time. While these programs freed the serfs and generally represented progress for the nation, they threatened the privileged status of the Mennonites. Not surprisingly the Mennonite community had been largely ignorant of and indifferent to conditions elsewhere in Russia, with a few notable exceptions. (For example, their medical facilities were always available to Russians. Also, an outstanding agricultural leader, Johann Coruies—1789–1848—introduced vocational training to some Russian villages.)

The passage of the universal military training law in 1874 was the second development which shook the "Commonwealth," this time sufficiently to cause the migration of eighteen thousand Mennonites to Canada and the United States. Those who remained in Russia were eventually able to work out a compromise on this matter. This was the program of alternative service mentioned above.

---

5. David G. Rempel, "The Mennonite Colonies in New Russia. . . ." (Ph.D. diss., Stanford University, 1933, available in microfilm at Bethel College Historical Library, North Newton, Kansas); "The Mennonite Migration to New Russia, 1787–1870," *Mennonite Quarterly Review* 9 (April 1935): 71. Dr. Rempel, who recently visited archives in Leningrad and Moscow, is now preparing a two-volume history of the Russian Mennonites.

A bargain was also struck in the matter of the russified school curriculum. By the terms of this agreement religion and the German language could be taught in German. The resultant identification of German and religion became so pronounced that the two seemed inseparable to Russians and Mennonites alike.

After these adjustments had been worked out, relative peace returned to the Mennonite settlements. Some of the leaders, however, whose contacts went beyond the local community, realized that all was not well with Russian society after the disturbances of 1904–05. They saw that in all probability the trouble was far from over. To them it was obvious that the Mennonite island could not remain secure in a turbulent sea forever. In 1909, for instance, Elder Isaac Dyck of Chortitsa confided to an American visitor that he saw the inevitable clash, but could not say so publicly because the Mennonite people just would not accept a pessimistic appraisal of their utopian situation.[6]

Then came World War I with Germany, and predictable governmental pressure on the German-speaking peoples within the country, which included not only Mennonites but also Lutherans and Catholics. Decrees were issued forbidding the public use of the German language. Furthermore, there was strong sentiment for the expropriation of all property owned by German-speaking citizens. Mennonite leaders were at pains to persuade St. Petersburg of the Dutch origins of their people. Efforts to obtain freedom from these measures came to be known as the *Hollaenderei* of the Russian Mennonites.[7]

It appears that the position of the Mennonites improved somewhat as the war continued, but it is uncertain whether this was due to positive action by the government, or simply to the confusion and disruption of communication which resulted from the prolonged conflict. In any case, the relief was only temporary. With the Communist revolution forces were set in motion which eventually destroyed most of the Mennonite settlements in Russia.

The first difficulties after the Revolution were not in themselves a result of Bolshevik attitudes towards religion. Rather they accrued from the general anarchy which followed the collapse of govern-

6. Epp, *Mennonite Exodus*, p. 3.
7. Ibid., p. 30.

mental and social life, the chaos of civil war (1918–20), the raids of roving bands of lawless brigands, and the plague and famine which were widespread during this entire period. For a time the civil war between the Red and White Russian armies centered in the Ukraine, with the battlefront moving back and forth over some Mennonite areas as many as twenty-three times. In addition to the havoc caused by this warfare, conditions were made much worse by outlaw bands. Nestor Makhno, a former political prisoner and a man of uncertain political allegiance, was one such outlaw. Makhno knew the Mennonites well, having worked for them as a young man; he even spoke the Low German language. He felt that he had been exploited by the Mennonites during his term of service with them and he played upon similar dissatisfaction among the local Ukrainian peasantry to take revenge. As a result of this reign of terror, hundreds of Mennonites were killed (in November, 1919, 240 in Zagradovka alone), and dozens of villages were completely destroyed.[8]

It is to their credit that most Mennonites, following the example and exhortation of their leaders, endeavored to preserve their principle of nonresistance, as well as the Gospel injunction to love their enemies. For a minority of young men, however, this was too difficult to accept in the face of murder, rape, and wholesale plunder. They organized what was known as the *Selbstschutz* or "self-defense," and were partly supplied with equipment by the German occupation forces. During the winter of 1918–19, they offered successful resistance to Makhno. Mennonite church conferences later condemned the *Selbstschutz* as a tactical blunder, because it violated the principle of nonresistance, and because it later resulted in heightened suffering for both the collaborators and the community at large. Several dozen men also fought with the White armies and were forced to retreat with them and escape via Constantinople.

Between 1921 and 1923 Russia experienced a severe famine, and thousands of people throughout the country succumbed to it. In desperation the Mennonites sent four of their best men to North America to plead for help from the local Mennonite churches. The Mennonite Central Committee, which was organized there in 1920 in response to this request, sent immediate help and averted heavy

---

8. Adolf Ehrt, *Das Mennonitentum in Russland: Von seinen Einwanderung bis zur Gegenwart* (Langensalza, Berlin, and Leipzig, 1932), p. 175. Statistics on the Russian Mennonite experience in the Civil War are given.

casualties among the Mennonites as well as aiding non-Mennonites wherever possible.

It is estimated that no less than twenty-two-hundred Mennonites perished in Russia during these years as a result of war, famine, and the typhus epidemic which ensued. The four men who had been sent for help had, in the meantime, explored settlement possibilities in Canada, and by 1923 a steady flow of immigrants was swelling the ranks of those who had settled there in the 1870s. Before the decade ended twenty thousand succeeded in migrating to Canada, the dispossessed landowners being among the first to go.

Those remaining in Russia began the difficult task of rebuilding their communities. Their work was somewhat facilitated by the advent of the New Economic Policy and the attendant postponement of several Bolshevik programs which would have prevented Mennonite reconstruction. Two agricultural associations were formed to coordinate this work and to speak for the Mennonites in their contacts with the central government. Their offices in Kharkov and Moscow also became clearing houses for emigration, which not unjustifiably made them suspect in the eyes of the authorities.

The Moscow office also provided liaison with the government in matters of conscientious objection, which now had to be arranged on a strictly individual basis. Of 131 Mennonites seeking exemption in 1925, 64 were recognized, 47 were imprisoned, and 20 were forcibly drafted. In other years at other places men were executed. Finally, in 1925 the Moscow office began publishing *Der Praktische Landwirt* (The practical farmer) to encourage the Mennonites, and to keep them in touch with each other. Another publication, *Unser Blatt*, was begun the same year to speak to spiritual needs and issues.

Unser Blatt was actually an outgrowth of the last session of the General Conference of Mennonite Congregations in Russia, which met in Moscow, January 13–18, 1925. In a singularly uncompromising way, the delegates stipulated guarantees of religious freedom as a basic need for survival. The conference submitted eight points to the central executive committee as "the minimum prerequisite for the continued existence of the Mennonites as a religious fellowship," including: (1) undisturbed religious meetings and discussions in churches and private homes for adults and children; (2) unrestricted religious societies, choirs, and 'instruction in religion (especially for children and young people); (3) unrestricted erection of new church buildings and the exemption of churches and ministers from special taxes; (4) unrestricted creation of orphanages offering a Christian training; (5) undisturbed acquisition of Bibles and other Christian literature, including periodicals for the congregations; (6) undisturbed Bible courses conducted for the training and the further education of ministers; (7) recognition of the schools as neutral territory where neither religious nor antireligious propaganda is disseminated; (8) exemption from military service and basic military preparation and the granting of a useful alternative service. There is little evidence that the petition received the desired hearing.[9]

The NEP period came to an end with the promulgation of the First Five-Year Plan in October, 1928. Among other things, this plan called for the forced collectivization of all farms. When word of this reached the Mennonite communities, many who had earlier elected to remain in Russia reconsidered their decision. In a desperate attempt to escape, some thirteen thousand Mennonites made their way to Moscow in the fall and winter of 1929–30, but only 5,677 managed to get to Germany, where they were sent on to Canada and South America. More might have received permits to emigrate if Germany and Canada had been quicker to grant visas, but these nations were experiencing widespread unemployment and other problems of their own as a result of the depression. A few additional Mennonites left in 1930, before all further emigration was prohibited. This brought the number of those who had moved to Canada since 1923 to 20,201. Approximately six hundred made their escape eastward across the Amur River into China. Others left through the Caucasus and Central Asiatic Russia.[10]

Of the eight thousand Mennonites who were denied permission to emigrate, many ended up in prison or in the labor camps of the far north and were never heard of again. They were followed by scores of kulaks and business people, as well as community leaders, who were considered obstacles to Soviet plans for collectivization. Many of these exiles also disappeared without a trace.

The experience of Jakob A. Rempel, an outstanding leader of the Russian Mennonites, was not untypical—he was refused an exit visa

9. "Protokoll der Bundes-Konferenz der Mennoniten-Gemeinden in Russland vom 13–18 Januar 1925, in Moscow," *Mennonitische Rundschau* 49 (1 April 1925): 5–8. See also succeeeding issues.

10. Epp, *Mennonite Exodus*, pp. 221–77.

and imprisoned. Educated in Basel, Switzerland, before World War I, he was an elder of the Mennonite church in the Neu-Chortitsa settlement. He elected not to emigrate in 1923 when five hundred others from his settlement went abroad. He felt obligated to serve those who remained. In 1925 he was the Russian delegate to the First Mennonite World Conference in Switzerland. Once again he considered emigration. He wrote: "I think I could forget everything and begin a new life, but what about the needy back home, the many large churches? My wife and children I could take with me but not the church." So he returned to the USSR.[11]

As a religious leader, he was subjected to a four-week imprisonment in September, 1929, after which he and his family joined the flight to Moscow. Along with many others refused an exit visa, Rempel was sentenced to the notorious Butyrka prison where he remained for eight months. From there he was sent to the Solovki Islands in the White Sea which the Soviets had made into a political prison and to which many clergymen were sent. After several unsuccessful escape attempts, Rempel succeeded in making his way to Turkestan, where he spent the winter of 1934–35 with some fellow Mennonites near Khiva. In the spring he was able to visit his family, who had been living in extreme poverty in the Ukraine. In 1936 he was exiled again, together with his eldest son, Alexander. The latter was sent to the Solovki Islands, whereas the father was banished to Orel, where he is believed to have been shot by the Soviets when German troops entered the city in 1941.

Meanwhile the terrors of collectivization were followed by another famine in 1932–33, in which from five to eight million people died, including over a hundred thousand German-speaking people. The world Mennonite community was again able to send some help to the Mennonites in Russia.

The manifold sufferings of the twenties and early thirties, together with the massive disruption of traditional modes of existence, gave rise to an unprecedented moral and spiritual decline among Russian Mennonites. Many mothers whose husbands had been deported had all they could do to provide for their children, who grew up without proper parental attention and without Christian training.

11. P. A. Rempel, "Aelt. J. A. Rempels Lebens—und Leidensgeschichte," in A. A. Toews, *Mennonitische Maertyrer*, 2 vols. (Winnipeg, 1949, 1954), 1: 30–46. This study gives many reports on Mennonite ministers in exile.

By 1935 a majority of the churches were being used as clubhouses, stables, theaters, or granaries. Membership in the congregations had declined rapidly because of antireligious propaganda and other harassments. Many of the strongest leaders had escaped to Canada and most of those who remained behind were soon sent into exile. Non-Mennonites settling in Mennonite villages contributed further to the cultural disintegration of the communities. Some potential new leaders chose to throw in their lot with the Revolution. Finally, the purges of 1937–38, which affected over seven million people, also hit the Mennonites. Many of the leaders and ministers who were still at liberty were sent into exile. While the exact number of all who were purged is not known, in two years the Chortitza settlement alone lost eight hundred men. The stories of many of these have been told in the two-volume *Mennonitische Maertyrer.*[12]

Thus, with the exception of the brief NEP period, the first two decades of Soviet rule were difficult ones for the Mennonites, and new tribulations came with the German invasion in 1941. To begin with, the war resulted in the dissolution of most of the Mennonite communities, with their dispersion in both easterly and westerly directions. Forced evacuation to the eastern territories began in 1941 because the Soviets feared that the 1.5 million German-speaking citizens of the USSR, among them the Mennonites, might collaborate with the occupation forces.

At the time of the forced resettlement in the east of the five hundred thousand Germans in the Volga-German autonomous region, the Mennonite colonies in the middle Volga area were also dissolved. Deportation also proceeded from the Crimea, Caucasus, and Ukraine, but before the large Molotshchna colony was half emptied of its women and children, the rapidly advancing German front brought a halt to the evacuation. The men, of course, had been recruited for military duty (if not for actual combat, then for the digging of trenches).

For those remaining in their native villages in the Chortitsa colony and elsewhere, the German occupation brought a brief period of relative freedom. While Russians, Jews in particular, suffered extensively at the hands of the Nazis, the German-speaking peoples enjoyed numerous privileges. Their churches were reopened and reli-

12. Ibid.

gious instruction was once again introduced into the schools. New ministers were elected, choirs were organized, and massive baptismal services were conducted. Mennonites were even appointed to administrative posts with the occupation government.

But the relief the Mennonites hoped for never fully materialized. The occupation forces soon began a systematic exploitation of the human and natural resources of the Ukraine, with increased urgency as their campaign faltered. In general the occupation became increasingly oppressive. As the Wehrmacht retreated, the thirty-five thousand Mennonites then remaining in the Ukraine were taken along. While the majority reached east German areas, over twenty-thousand were later brought back by Soviet repatriation teams. Among those returning were scores of men who had been drafted into the Wehrmacht and captured by the Soviet armies. Those thus repatriated were scattered throughout the Soviet Union. Many were sent to labor camps. Very few returned to their former homes.

If the Mennonites in various parts of the country knew very little about one another, even less information about the fate of the communities was available in the West. Mennonites abroad made efforts to establish contact with their Soviet coreligionists, particularly after the death of Stalin in 1953. The *Suchdienst* (Information Service) established in Frankfurt in 1953 by the Mennonite Central Committee had as its primary purpose the collection of data which could lead to the reunion of families, members of which were still in the Soviet Union. This information was supplemented by the Russian Baptists who visited North American Mennonites in 1956 and 1964 and by Mennonites visiting Russian Baptists and Mennonites in the USSR in 1956, 1959, 1960, 1966, and 1967.[13] Another important source of information was the letters which were received in the West, excerpts from which were regularly published in the Canadian Mennonite weeklies, *Der Bote* and *Die Mennonitische Rundschau*.[14]

The general amnesties granted in 1953, 1955, and 1957 to inmates of the labor camps, and the internal relaxation accompanying the de-Stalinization of the 1950s, gave rise to a certain religious renewal and social consolidation. While the Mennonites were not permitted to

13. Reports of these delegations are filed in the archives of the Mennonite Central Committee, Akron, Pennsylvania, and are available for research at that address.

14. *Der Bote*, weekly, published since 1924 at Rosthern, Sasakatchewan, and *Die Mennonitische Rundschau*, weekly, published since 1923 at 159 Henderson Highway, Winnipeg, Manitoba, in four decades have published hundreds of "Briefe von Russland."

return to their former homes in the middle Volga and the Ukraine, many found new homes in the Kazakh SSR in Central Asiatic Russia. Some joined the Siberian Mennonite settlements near Barnaul, Omsk, and Tomsk which had never been dissolved. Others found their way to the Orenburg settlement near the Urals in European Russia, also left intact except for collectivization and social integration.

Wherever they settled, in agricultural collectives or industrial centers, religious and social renewal seems to have been a general phenomenon. In the coal-mining city of Karaganda four hundred Mennonites were baptized in 1958. The church in Kant grew from two hundred to seven hundred in a few years' time. In Novosibirsk 150 persons were baptized at one time. And in Orenburg, too, as many as ninety were baptized in a single year.[15]

Their German language and cultural orientation continued to be a problem for the Mennonites and resulted in numerous restrictions being placed on them. More often than not their greatest religious freedom was achieved when they associated with the Russian Baptists who were registered with the Soviet government through the All-Union Council of Evangelical Christians-Baptists. Since Mennonites were weak and had little hope of registering their own congregations, Western leaders encouraged this close association with the Baptists.

This was easier for the Brethren than for the "church" Mennonites, the former having baptismal form and other matters in common with the Baptists. In October, 1966, sixteen thousand of the twenty thousand Brethren joined the Baptist Union through their congregations. Their delegates attended the annual Union Conference in Moscow. At almost the same time one of the "church" congregations at Tokmak independently completed its registration with the government and three others made application to do the same.[16] The "church" Mennonites have an estimated baptized (that is, adult) membership of twenty thousand.

So, after years of great tribulation, at the beginning of 1967, the situation appeared to be improving. A new generation of leaders,

15. Peter J. Dyck, "Report No. 1, Mennonite Central Committee East–West Office" (October 1959), Mennonite Central Committee, Akron, Pa. (A mimeographed report.)

16. D. P. Neufeld, "Report of the Visit to the Soviet Union, October 26–November 14, 1966," Mennonite Central Committee, Akron, Pa. (A mimeographed report.)

who felt strongly that their mission lay in the USSR, was beginning to emerge. These men spoke with considerable optimism of both their church and the Soviet state, though all were keenly aware of restrictions placed upon them. Attempts were being made to build bridges not only to the Baptists but also between the two Mennonite groups. Ministers from the two groups served the pulpits of both, and choirs also served jointly. Some hitherto closed Brethren congregations practiced open communion.[17]

There was, however, a great shortage of Bibles, hymnals, and theology books. Ministers had little education and served at great personal sacrifice, although financial support increased as the material well-being of the Mennonites improved. Preachers placed much emphasis upon personal salvation, faith, and eschatology. Funerals were usually very important and impressive events, with as many as four Mennonite and six Baptist ministers speaking at one service in Karaganda.[18]

While some members of the older generation were anxious to emigrate in order to be reunited with their relatives and friends in the Western Hemisphere, the majority had come to believe that their future lay in the Soviet Union. Many Mennonites, of course, were losing not only their German culture but also their religious convictions, and some had even become members of the Communist party.[19] Scores of young people were attending the universities, later to receive appointments as engineers, teachers, and doctors, and the younger men were responding to the draft.

Despite strong influences toward acculturation, however, fifty years after the Revolution it appears that the Mennonites may well be regaining some of their traditional religious vitality. Many American visitors to the USSR have felt that the Russian Mennonite sincerity, the emphasis on the simple life, the sense of community and love for the brethren surpassed the religious expressions of the North American Mennonites, whose economic wealth and cultural sophistication have made inroads on the faith inherited from their fathers. And Russian Mennonites who have migrated to Canada or

---

17. Frank C. Peters, "Meeting in Moscow with Eight Mennonite Leaders," *The Canadian Mennonite* 14 (13 December 1966): 1–2.

18. "Briefe aus Russland," *Mennonitische Rundschau* 91 (5 December 1962): 1–2.

19. Peter J. Dyck, "Supplement to Report II, East–West Office," January 1960 (excerpts from *Neues Leben* published by *Pravda*), Mennonite Central Committee, Akron, Pa. (A mimeographed report.)

come for short visits have frequently expressed dismay at the material wealth and luxuries enjoyed by their brother Christians. Some of them, to the consternation of Western Mennonites, have even spoken of the superiority of religious life in the USSR.

A comprehensive report about Soviet Mennonites came from a meeting of three North American Mennonite leaders with nine Soviet counterparts in Moscow in November, 1966. The Western delegation made an extensive report of their interview.[20] To begin with, they were told that mutual aid is once again a common policy within the communities; whatever is left over after living expenses are paid is shared with the community or used for the support of the leaders of the church, thus allowing them to visit the members of their congregation who live away from the main group. Each local church has several deacons who, in addition to conducting house meetings, spread the word about those in need. (This mutual aid is not channelled through a central treasury, but is on a "word-of-mouth," direct contribution basis.) The Soviet Mennonites said that this sense of community was based upon the Scriptures, but that the overall social conditions of life in the country also foster this development. Even though personal savings can be accumulated in the Soviet Union, Mennonite leaders preach against this for their followers.

In the matter of military service, the leaders have thus far been unable to negotiate any program of alternate service or exemption. Until 1960 they were generally not taken into the army; the government had in fact used them in a sort of alternate service, namely, the construction of housing units. The period for this work has generally been three years, and discharge papers attest that these services were regarded as time spent in the military service. Since the early sixties, however, some Mennonites have been called to serve in the military.

The communities appear to be quite dynamic spiritually, with a high percentage of children entering the church. Their piety is austere and humorless, but family ties are strong and family prayer around the house altar is common. Each church has a number of preachers, though these are not necessarily ordained; the theology of the ministry tends to see this position in terms of function rather than as a recognized office or dignity. Each minister must register with the local authorities before he can be ordained. In general those churches

20. Frank C. Peters, "Churches in USSR Preach Against Accumulation of Wealth," *The Canadian Mennonite* 14 (27 December 1966): 3.

which are registered abide by the law and do not attempt any unauthorized expansion. Occasionally individuals are taken in for questioning, and as a matter of course all church activities must be reported to governmental authorities.

As to the future of Soviet Mennonites, speculation is very dangerous. At the height of the Khrushchev campaign in the early sixties, Western Mennonite visitors in the Soviet Union felt that the end of Mennonitism in Russia was just over the horizon. Events of the last three or four years have tended to alter this picture, as just noted. That there is a new note of optimism among the communities today is undeniable. Whether this confidence in the future will be vindicated remains to be seen.

14

PROTESTANT SECTARIANS IN THE FIRST YEAR OF SOVIET RULE

The Bolsheviks who took power in Russia in 1917 were heirs of a long and tortured revolutionary tradition. Perhaps the most notable constant in this tradition was the vision of a new society the precise features of which had never been described because the revolutionaries had to expend their theoretical energies on more immediate concerns. Who would build the new world? What tools would they require? When would the actual construction work begin? The victorious Bolsheviks declared that they were the architects, the proletariat was the essential builder, state power was the necessary tool, and the present was the propitious moment to start the construction of this new order.

Like other revolutionary factions, the Bolsheviks had only the most rudimentary blueprint for their proposed society. They recognized that religion had been an integral part of the preceding order, and therefore believed that it could have no place in the order which was coming into being. Once in control of state power, they expected to preside over the demise of religion in Russia and to witness a similar process in other lands directed by ideological comrades. Local conditions would create minor differences, but all areas would experience two major phases in common. The first one, to be completed as quickly as possible, consisted of a restriction of the role of religion in society by legally separating the church from the state and

Andrew Q. Blane

the school from the church. The second phase, to be realized in the indefinite future, involved twin developments: (1) the creation of a socialist order in which religion would be an anachronism (by means of appropriate economic and social measures), and (2) the enlightenment of the pious masses in regard to the harmful nature of religion (by means of proper educational and cultural policies).[1]

What role the various religious groups were to play in this grand prospectus was never stated. During czarist days the Bolsheviks had displayed a certain amount of sympathy and concern for the welfare of the Protestant sectarians.[2] This attitude sprang partly from a natural sympathy for fellow sufferers at the hands of the czarist police, but mostly from a doctrinal heritage which conceived of the sectarians as potential allies in the future overthrow of the autocracy.[3] But how the sects were to be regarded once the Bolshevik party assumed political power had never been clarified. Consequently, the coup d'etat of November 7, 1917, confronted the sectarians with a serious dilemma.[4]

To the extent environmental conditions permitted, the responses of the various sectarian bodies to the October Revolution were governed by their respective ideological objectives. Like the Bolsheviks, the Protestant sectarians envisioned a utopian society; unlike the Bolsheviks, they regarded mass individual conversions along religio-ethical lines, leading to a national conversion of the same nature, as the sine qua non for realizing this society. Under czarist rule the sects argued that the first requirement for the conver-

1. The most complete collection of Lenin's writings on religion, hence of the Bolshevik view of religion, is V. I. Lenin, *Religiia, tserkov i partiia* [Religion, the church and the party] (Moscow, 1930). A useful selection in English translation was put out in New York in 1933 by International Publishers. The most extensive and best documented study of the problem published by a Soviet is M. I. Shakhnovich, *Lenin i Problemy Ateizma* [Lenin and problems of atheism] (Moscow, 1961). An excellent brief analysis by Bohdan R. Bociurkiw entitled "Lenin and Religion" is in Leonard Schapiro and Peter Reddaway, *Lenin: The Man, The Theorist, The Leader: A Reappraisal* (London, 1967).

2. The term "Russian Protestant sects" used in this paper refers to two religious bodies, known separately in 1918 as the Baptists and the Evangelical Christians. Their nineteenth century ancestors bore a great variety of names, the most common being Stundists, Baptists, and Pashkovites; their present-day descendants, having merged their forces in 1944, officially go by the hyphenated name Evangelical Christians-Baptists, but in popular parlance simply by the Baptists.

3. No satisfactory study of this important problem exists. A brief, preliminary analysis is to be found in the present author's doctoral thesis, "The Relations Between the Russian Protestant Sects and the State" (Duke University, N.C., 1964), pp. 98–129. For another summary see Bociurkiw, "Lenin and Religion," pp. 111–16.

4. The dates used throughout accord with the Gregorian, or new, calendar.

sion of Russia was the purification of existing religious life by the emancipation of religion from political control, that is, by the separation of church and state. In 1917 a new priority emerged. Before a genuine separation could be accomplished, a government stable enough to restore order to the strife-torn land had to be constituted.[5] Therefore, the Bolshevik coup raised for the Protestant sectarians the critical questions of (1) whether the new rulers would advance or hinder the establishment of a strong social order, and (2) whether they would promote or inhibit an authentic separation of church and state.

The only clue as to how these questions might be answered was contained in the Bolshevik program. What the rank-and-file sectarians knew about this program was approximately the equivalent of what the average Russian knew. A scholarly member of the Russian intelligentsia living in Petrograd at the time of the October Revolution succinctly states this as: (1) peace—the immediate cessation of a war whose ends were never sufficiently understood by the masses; (2) land—the immediate gratification of the peasants' longing to have the landlords' estates confiscated and divided among them; (3) bread—the immediate alleviation of the food crisis in the major cities; and (4) "all power to the Soviets"—the abolition of bureaucracy, direct rule by the masses, and the likelihood of the cessation of taxation and compulsory military service.[6] With this conception of Bolshevism, it is clear that the average sectarian saw in the seizure of power by Lenin and his lieutenants little threat to his material and spiritual yearnings; he might even have seen some hope for their realization.

But this was not the response of the leaders of the Protestant sectarians. Their understanding of the Bolshevik program went beyond the slogans of peace, land, bread, and "all power to the Soviets." In the broader Bolshevik platform they perceived a number of serious ambiguities. On the one hand, the class war which the Bolsheviks promoted could only lead to the further dissolution of social order in Russia, not to its healing. On the other hand, the Bolsheviks stood

5. A useful summary of these views was presented in the statement of the All-Russian Union of Evangelical Christians at the Moscow State Congress in August, 1917, whose proceedings were published in *Gosudarstvennoe Soveshchanie* [State assembly] (Moscow, 1930), pp. 70–73.

6. N. S. Timasheff, *Religion in Soviet Russia, 1917–1942* (New York, 1942), pp. 16–17.

at the forefront of those political parties which advocated the immediate withdrawal of Russia from the World War and the conclusion of a peace treaty, a plank dear to the hearts of rank-and-file sectarians and their leaders alike. On a more directly religious level, the Bolsheviks openly proclaimed their militant opposition to all religion, yet for more than a decade they had championed the separation of church and state and the introduction of full freedom of conscience. Moreover, there were more than a few Bolsheviks who had given sympathy and succor to the sectarians when they suffered trials and tribulations under the czars.

Now that the Bolsheviks had come to power, would they end the tragic war and bring peace? Would they establish order in Russia, or would they spread fresh chaos and bloodshed by promoting class antagonisms? Would they institute genuine freedom and equality of religion, or would they take measures against religion and those who believed in God?[7] Troubled by these uncertainties, the initial attitude of the Protestant sectarian leaders to the Bolshevik seizure of power is best described by the phrase "wait and see." The principal reason for adopting this position was the pervasive doubt as to whether the Bolsheviks could hold power; the necessity of this posture was dictated by the powerlessness of the sectarians to act otherwise with effect. As it turned out, their wait was brief. The direction Russia would take soon became apparent.

---

7. The deep doubt which some of the sectarian leaders had as to whether they shared common dreams with the revolutionaries is expressed in an article printed in the August, 1917, number of the Baptist journal, *Slovo istiny* [The word of truth]: "If by not having thought the matter through, if by not knowing the teachings of Christ, the socialists consider Him to be a revolutionary, an anarchist, a fighter for freedom, equality, and brotherhood in the sense in which they understand these terms, then believers in Christ as the Son of God, as personal Saviour, must know how to evaluate this so that 'tempting words' and 'flattering sounds' do not deceive their hearts. . . . Is our freedom from sin, that freedom of the internally whole man, that freedom of the soul, really the same freedom which the revolutionaries summon us to—civil freedom, freedom of the external man, the slave of sin? Is our equality . . . based on love and reconciliation really similar to that external equality based on rights and responsibilities recorded in civil laws, to that legal equality of every citizen? Is that 'brotherhood' flying on the banners of the revolutionaries, that brotherhood without love, brotherhood without a father, brotherhood simply conjured up, really identical to our brotherhood in Christ? We are brothers because we have a Father, but where and who is their father? Can we really be brothers without a father?" (F. Putintsev, *Politicheskaia rol i taktika sekt* [The political role and tactics of the sects] [Moscow, 1935], pp. 291–92.)

I

On the afternoon of November 7, 1917, V. I. Lenin stepped to the platform at the Smolny Institute and triumphantly announced to the Petrograd Soviet: "We shall now occupy ourselves with building up in Russia a proletarian socialist state."[8] On the religious front this meant first and foremost the creation of a secular state by the severance of existing ties between government and religion. With this end in mind, the Soviet leaders enacted a series of laws, decrees, and instructions in the first year of their rule, the most important of which were:

1. A decree of November 8, 1917, which nationalized all land, including that owned by the churches and the monasteries.
2. A decree of December 24, 1917, which nationalized all schools, including the secondary schools and the theological seminaries and academies that belonged to the Orthodox church.
3. A decree of December 29, 1917, which limited legal recognition of divorce to civil divorce.
4. A decree of December 31, 1917, which limited legal recognition of marriage to civil marriage and which ordered all of the records of births, marriages, and deaths kept by ecclesiastics to be turned over to government officials.
5. A decree of February 2, 1918, which established the principle of a secular state by declaring the separation of the church from the state and the school from the church.
6. A decree of February 6, 1918, which (as of February 14) replaced the Julian calendar with the Gregorian calendar.
7. A decree of April 12, 1918, which ordered the removal of plaques and insignias representing the old order from hospitals, schools, and other public premises, including ikons, crosses, and all other religious symbols.
8. The Constitution of the Russian Socialist Federated Soviet Republic (RSFSR) of July 10, 1918, which affirmed the principle of the separation of church and state.
9. The Instruction of the People's Commissariat of Justice (NKIu) of August 24, 1918, which gave directions for the implementation of the decree of separation of church and state.

8. *Izvestiia*, 8 November 1917.

10. A decree of December 7, 1918, which nationalized all burial grounds and established a civil order of burial.[9]

Three of these enactments (5, 8, and 9) contain the basic elements of all the rest. They deserve detailed examination, especially in their effect upon the life and welfare of the Protestant sectarians.

One month after the Bolsheviks seized power, on December 11, 1917, the question of a decree to separate the church from the state came up at a meeting of the Council of People's Commissars. After some discussion, a commission was appointed to draft a text. Its members were A. V. Lunacharsky, P. I. Stuchka, P. A. Krasikov, M. A. Reisner, and an unnamed priest. Six weeks later the commission made its report. Lenin introduced several amendments to the draft, and in short order the "Decree on the Separation of Church from State and School from Church" was adopted. One of Lenin's amendments, the only one of any consequence, reflected the militant role which the new rulers were prepared to play in establishing their conception of a secular state. Whereas article 1 of the draft version stated that "religion is the private affair of every citizen of the Russian Republic," the final version replaced this with a blunt "the church is separated from the state." Lenin would have no part of the first phrasing, for it parroted a formula current in European socialist circles since the 1870s against which Lenin had long struggled on the grounds that it obscured the reactionary nature of religion.[10]

In addition to declaring that the church was separated from the state, the new decree guaranteed to every citizen the right to profess any or no religion and affirmed that all religions were equal under the law. Free performance of religious rites was assured to all persons, so long as they did not disturb public order or the rights of the citizens of the Soviet Republic. No citizen might refuse to partake of civil

9. For items 1–6, see *Dekrety sovetskoi vlasti* [Decrees of the Soviet state], vol. 1 (Moscow, 1957), pp. 17–20, 210–11, 237–39, 247–49, 271–74, 404–6; for items 7–8, see ibid, vol. 2 (Moscow, 1959), pp. 95–96, 550–66; for items 9–10 see P. V. Gidulianov, ed., *Otdelenie tserkvi ot Gosudarstva v SSSR Polny sbornik dekretov, vedomstvennikh rasporiazhenii i opredelenii verkhsuda RSFSR i drugikh sovetskikh sotsialisticheskikh respublik: USSR, BSSR, ESFSR, Uskbekskoi i Turkmenskoi* [The separation of church from state in the USSR. Complete collection of decrees, official circulars and decisions of the supreme court of the RSFSR and other Soviet republics; UKSSR, BSSR, ESFSR, Uzbek and Turkmen], 3d ed. (Moscow, 1926), pp. 622–32, 452.

10. *Kommunisticheskaia partiia i sovetskoe pravitelstvo o religii i tserkvi* [The Communist party and the Soviet government on religion and the church], (Moscow, 1959), pp. 39–43, 113–14. See Joshua Rothenberg, "The Legal Status of Religion in the Soviet Union," chapter 5, n. 7, above.

duties on the grounds of religious conviction, although individual exceptions could be granted by the people's courts through the exchange of one civic duty for another. Whereas citizens could privately give or receive religious instruction, the teaching of religion was prohibited in all state, public, and private institutions of general education. Henceforth churches and religious societies were to be deprived of the right of juridical person and of owning property. All church properties were declared nationalized; buildings and objects used for divine worship were to be given over to the churches for their use free of charge according to special agreements to be concluded with the local or central authorities.[11]

This decree was published on February 2, 1918. Even before its appearance severe clashes between representatives of the new government and zealous members of the Orthodox church had taken place. With the formal declaration of the separation of church and state, as one scholar has observed, "it is not surprising that the *Sobor* and the Patriarch, already bitterly opposed to the Soviet regime, displayed still more hostility . . . declared open war on the Soviet regime and called on the faithful to fight it."[12] Fresh and bitter conflicts broke out in the capital and quickly spread to the provinces. A number of encounters resulted in a loss of life. Nevertheless, the struggle was not as severe as it might have been. The masses failed to respond to the call of the *Sobor* for a crusade against the regime, partly because difficulties of communication kept many of them from hearing the call, but mostly because their local parishes continued to function, their priests remained unharmed, and their sacred articles untouched.

Moreover, the government lacked the desire or the machinery to implement the new decree fully. At one stage, in March, 1918, it even became possible for the members of the *Sobor* and representatives of the government to meet in the Kremlin and to show a willingness to compromise. This spirit, however, did not prevail. Bitter civil war had already broken out in the country, and on both sides militant elements came quickly to the fore. Seeing in the antireligious bias of the new regime a mortal threat to the very soul of Russia, Orthodox church leaders renewed their calls for a crusade against the Bolsheviks. In its turn, confronted by the rise of counterrevolutionary

11. *Dekrety sovetskoi vlasti*, 1 : 371–74.
12. J. S. Curtiss, *The Russian Church and the Soviet State* (Boston, 1953), pp. 47, 54.

armies and Allied intervention that threatened its very life, the infant Soviet State adopted more drastic measures, "both in respect to the church and regarding hostile secular organizations."[13]

This new bitterness is to some degree reflected in the Constitution of the Russian Soviet Federated Socialist Republic adopted by the Fifth Congress of Soviets on July 18, 1918. Once again Lenin rejected the phrase, "religion is a private affair of each citizen," which had been recommended for article 13 by the constitution committee. The version which was accepted read: "To secure for the toilers real freedom of conscience, the church is separated from the state, and the school from the church, and freedom of religious and anti-religious propaganda is recognized as the right of every citizen."[14] A new stringency, however, appeared in article 65, which created a second-class citizenry by withholding the right to vote and to hold elective office from capitalists, merchants, members of the czarist police, criminals, and imbeciles, as well as "monks and clerical servants of churches and religious cults."[15] Although not stated in the constitution, this loss of franchise in practice resulted in severe limitations in rations, housing, and the like.

The new militancy and intolerance of the Bolshevik government was even more clearly mirrored in the instructions of the People's Commissariat of Justice of August 24, 1918, "On the Procedure for the Implementation of the Decree on the Separation of Church from State and School from Church."[16]

II

It is clear that for the Russian Orthodox church the religious measures introduced by the Soviet government in 1918 seemed incredibly harsh. Even from the perspective of nations in which for a century or more the separation of church and state had been a matter of course, several of the Soviet regulations could be judged as severe, notably the deprivation of the churches' juridical rights, the confiscation of their property, and the relegation of their clergy to second-class status as citizens. The Protestant sectarians' estimate of

13. Ibid., p. 161.
14. G. S. Gurvich, *Istoriia sovetskoi konstitutsii* [History of the Soviet constitution], (Moscow, 1923) pp. 79–80.
15. *Dekrety sovetskoi vlasti*, 2: 553, 561–62.
16. For fuller details of all of these earlier pronouncements see Rothenberg, chapter 5 above, pp. 65–67.

this legislation was quite different. In the first place, the nationalization of church property did not strike them with anything like the force with which it struck the Orthodox church. As one sectarian observed about his people: "they had no magnificent cathedrals and churches, nor any property to be taken away—their treasures were not earthly ones";[17] or, in the felicitous phrase of one American churchman, "they had nothing to lose but their chains."[18] Of course these expressions are exaggerations; for example, the Evangelical Christian Union lost two buildings and a bank account of thirty thousand rubles in Petrograd alone.[19] Nevertheless, the just-quoted remarks point to the general truth that the Protestant sects suffered relatively little loss when the Soviets nationalized religious properties.

More serious than the loss of land and capital by the Protestant unions was the loss sustained by a number of their wealthy members and benefactors. The socialist revolution stripped away the riches of sectarian leaders like Count Bobrinsky, Count Shuvalov, Princess Levin, Princess Gagarina, Princess Chernisheva, Prince Bariatinsky, General Chertkov, and the Mazaev brothers.[20] Although certainly a blow to the sects, the loss of income resulting from the impoverishment of such wealthy patrons must not be overestimated. Only a handful of the Protestant sectarians were among the propertied and the rich. The sects' adherents were predominantly artisans and tradesmen from the lower middle-class, and workers and peasants from the lowest class. Although hard evidence is lacking in the sources available, surely some sectarian peasants benefited from the dissolution of the landed estates.[21]

17. N. I. Salov-Ashtakov, *Christianity in Russia* (New York, 1941), p. 113.

18. Matthew Spinka, *The Church and the Russian Revolution* (New York, 1927), p. 318.

19. A. V. Lunacharsky, ed., *Antireligiozny uchebnik* [Antireligious textbook] (Moscow, 1933), pp. 298ff.

20. P. A. Efimov, "O preodolenii baptisma v SSSR v 1923–1929 gg." [On Overcoming the Baptists in the USSR in 1923–29], *Ezhegodnik muzeia istorii religii i ateizma* [Yearbook of the Museum of the History of Religion and Atheism] 6 (Moscow, 1962): 165; also Putintsev, *Politicheskaia rol*, pp. 183–84.

21. The usual procedure in the first years after the Revolution was for the peasant to possess the land on which he lived and worked. A number of the landed gentry of Protestant sectarian persuasion created sectarian communities on their estates by evangelizing their Orthodox peasants and by populating these estates with sectarian peasants who had become impoverished in other locales. See Efimov, "O preodolenii," p. 165; *Bratsky vestnik* [The brotherly herald], 1947, no. 5, pp. 39–44. It would have been natural if those peasants to some extent benefited from the property losses inflicted on the sectarian gentry.

Finally, several of the sectarians who lost their worldly goods found themselves freed from such cares and able to give themselves in new and more effective ways to their religious communities. According to one authority, after G. I. Mazaev was divested of his riches he became a full-time evangelist who converted thousands to the Baptist cause.[22] A similar transformation took place in the life of the wealthy book publisher, I. D. Sytin, who, although not formally linked to either the Baptist or the Evangelical Christians, was of an evangelical persuasion.[23]

Nationalization, then, did not significantly affect the Protestant sectarians. Neither did the disenfranchisement of the clergy. Until 1922–23 the theory behind the law which deprived the clergy of the right to vote was that religious work was not useful employment. This outlook is clearly disclosed in a decree of the fifth division of the Commissariat of Justice of July 20, 1920. According to this ruling, if "servants of the cult" refused compensation for their religious services and entered into socially useful labor they could be considered working members of the society and granted full civil rights.[24]

Such an interpretation was of great benefit to the Protestant sectarians, who by tradition and theology were essentially a lay movement whose ordained ministers worked in secular occupations to gain a livelihood. It is true that czarist conditions permitted them scarcely any other choice; nevertheless this pattern arose as much from religious belief as from political circumstance. Indeed, one of the doctrinal disagreements which early developed among the Protestant sectarians and hindered their efforts to unite their forces concerned a paid ministry.[25] The president of the Evangelical Christian Union, I. S. Prokhanov, worked as a mechanical engineer with the Westinghouse Brake Company in Petrograd.[26] The president of the Baptist Union, D. I. Mazaev, managed a vast lumber and sheep-raising

22. W. Gutsche, *Religion and Evangelium in Sowjetrussland* (Kassel, 1959), p. 36; G. I. Mazaev, *Obrashenie na istinny put i vospominaniia baptista G.I.M.* [Conversion to the path of truth and reminiscences of the Baptist G.I.M.] (Omsk, 1919), cited in Putintsev, *Politicheskaia rol*, p. 183.

23. V. Martsinkovsky, *Zapiski veruiushchego. Iz istorii religioznogo dvizheniia v sovetskoi Rossii, (1917–1923)* [Notes of a believer. From the history of the religious movement in Soviet Russia (1917–1923)] (Prague, 1929) pp. 122–23.

24. Gidulianov, *Otdelenie*, p. 292.

25. Pavlov, "The Baptist Body in Russia," p. 159.

26. I. S. Prokhanov, *In the Cauldron of Russia* (New York, 1933), p. 120.

enterprise in Siberia.[27] The same was true of lesser leaders, as is evidenced by fragmentary biographical accounts.[28]

Actually, it was not until after the October Revolution that individual Protestant sectarians began to abandon their secular occupations in order to devote themselves more fully to evangelical pursuits. By the end of 1928, Prokhanov's Preachers' School in Leningrad (1923–28) and the Baptist Bible College in Moscow (1927–28) had trained and sent out more than four hundred professional religious workers.[29] Nevertheless, in the sense that most leaders were gainfully employed in secular occupations, the Protestant sects continued to be a lay movement. According to Salov-Ashtakov:

approximately 14,000 ministers and deacons were occupied with the preaching of the Gospel until [1929, when] the last great wave of persecution swept over the country; these all had some employment or vocation, and they earned a living for themselves and their families. In the villages they worked their farms like the other farmers. In the cities they either had their own businesses, or worked in offices, factories, and other places. Their evenings, Sundays, and holidays, were devoted to the preaching of the Gospel, the visiting of homes and the sick, as well as taking care of other work connected with the Church. . . . Only the leading workers of large districts, a few pastors of some of the large cities, and the travelling Bible teachers and evangelists who were set apart by the church to visit the local churches, received financial support from the main office of their respective denominations but not from the local churches.[30]

The single provision of the Soviet legislation of 1918 through which the sects incurred real limitations was the denial of the rights of a juridical person to their congregations. But even this must be qualified. In the Ukraine, where more than half of the Protestant sectarians resided,[31] this stricture was not leveled against them until August 3, 1920, when orders came to harmonize the law on the separation of church and state in the Ukrainian Republic with that in the RSFSR.[32] Moreover, even in the RSFSR in 1918, this restriction was more precept than practice. Finally, the negative psychological effect of this ruling was certainly mitigated by the strong memory which the Pro-

27. *Bratsky vestnik*, 1953, nos. 2/3, pp. 96–97.

28. Ibid., 1945, no. 2, pp. 33–39; 1947, no. 1, pp. 61–62; 1947, no. 3, pp. 20–22; 1954, no 2, pp. 63–64; 1955, no. 1, pp. 57–60; 1947, no. 5, pp. 16–25, 66–69; 1949, no. 1, pp. 52 ff.; 1961, no. 3, pp. 64 ff.

29. Ibid., 1957, no. 4, p. 20.

30. Salov–Ashtakov, *Christianity in Russia*, pp. 113–14.

31. *Bratsky vestnik*, 1958, no. 1, pp. 22–32.

32. Gidulianov, *Otdelenie*, p. 4.

testant sectarians retained of the minimal advantages which the right of juridical person brought them under the czars. Besides, this loss was small indeed when seen in the context of the host of legal advantages which Soviet legislation had brought them.

The extent of legal advances which the Protestant sectarians made in 1918 can best be shown by juxtaposing their prerevolutionary legal status with their new status. As concerns worship services, czarist law had permitted the organization of religious meetings in licensed houses of prayer, provided the police were notified in advance of the time of each meeting. The sectarians had not been allowed to advertise these meetings among nonmembers, nor could they arrange special services for the young. They were strictly forbidden to have any Orthodox children present at their gatherings, and warned not to make any derogatory comments about the Orthodox church or to call for the renunciation of this church whenever Orthodox adults were in attendance. Violators were to be criminally prosecuted. The likelihood that violations would come to light was to be assured by police surveillance at all sectarian meetings.[33]

Except for the stipulation that licensed church houses be used strictly for religious purposes, Soviet law wiped away all of these restrictions. In addition, the phrase "religious purposes" was now given a broader interpretation. Czarist law defined any gathering for conversation, discussion, or reading, regardless of the subject matter, as a nonreligious meeting and prohibited in the sectarian prayer houses.[34] In contrast, the Soviet rulers prohibited inside the church houses only political activity which opposed the existing regime. This is clear from the model agreement employed by local officials in turning over church properties to groups of twenty believers or more:

1. We, the undersigned citizens, pledge to take care of the national property passed over to us and to use it only in accordance with its designation, and we take upon ourselves the whole responsibility for preserving and safekeeping the property handed over to us, and also for fulfilling the other obligations placed upon us by this agreement.
2. We pledge to use, and to allow all persons of our faith to use, the church houses and all religious objects found therein exclusively for the satisfaction of religious needs.

33. *Missionerskoe obozrenie* [Missionary Review], (June, 1910), pp. 899–902.
34. *Tserkovniia vedomosti* [Church bulletin] (26 February 1911), official part, pp. 43–44.

3. We pledge to take all measures to insure that the property entrusted to us is not utilized for purposes not corresponding to Articles 1 and 2 of this agreement. In particular we pledge not to allow in the religious buildings whose management we have accepted:

a) political gatherings inimical to the Soviet government;

b) the distribution or sale of books, brochures, leaflets, and messages directed against the Soviet government or its representatives;

c) the delivery of sermons or speeches inimical to the Soviet government or to its individual representatives; and,

d) the sounding of the tocsin to summon the population with the aim of arousing it against the Soviet government, in view of which we pledge to submit to all the decrees of the local Soviet of Workers' and Peasants' Deputies concerning the use of church bells.[35]

A further advantage of the new law from the point of view of the sectarians was the decrease from fifty to twenty in the minimum number of persons required to form a congregation.[36]

In like manner the new regulations for organizing divine services outside of the registered prayer houses, including baptism under the open skies, markedly improved the legal positions of the sectarians. Czarist law allowed such services only with special permission for each occasion from the Ministry of Internal Affairs;[37] after 1910, it became exceedingly difficult if not impossible to obtain this permission.[38] Soviet regulations similarly obliged the sects to obtain permission for all religious services which were to be held outside of the church buildings, but this permission was to be sought from local rather than central authorities. If nothing else, this was technically a simpler task.

There were, however, more substantial improvements. In considering such requests, the local authorities were instructed to adhere to article 5 of the decree of February 2, which simply stated that "free performance of religious rites is permissible so long as it does not disturb public order, or interfere with the rights of the citizens of the Soviet Republic."[39] In 1918 the sectarians were successful in organizing a considerable number of religious meetings in public places; whether they were able to do this because of a liberal spirit on the part of local authorities or because existing conditions made it impossible

35. Gidulianov, *Otdelenie*, p. 630.
36. Ibid.
37. See footnotes 33 and 34 above.
38. Blane, "Relations Between Russian Sects and State," pp. 83–85.
39. Gidulianov, *Otdelenie*, pp. 616, 629.

for the authorities to act stringently, is not clear. The Moscow community conducted religious services in a factory.[40] The Evangelical
Christians of Petrograd carried out a series of street missions, and in
this connection published in 1918 ten issues of a special journal,
Prizyv (The summons).[41] The Baptists in the province of Kozlovsky
(presently Michurinsky) formed a "Soldiers' Mission," equipped it
with a tent, which, when set up in the open fields, would seat 150
persons, and sent the mission from village to village to conduct evan-
gelistic meetings.[42] At the same time, according to one report,
sectarians everywhere performed open-air baptisms without hindrance.[43] In the spring of 1918, V. P. Martsinkovsky, an itinerant
lecturer for the Christian Student Circles, delivered religious addresses on public premises at Tula, Riazan, and Ivanovo-Voznesensk.
Later in the same year, before, during, and after Samara's brief
occupation by Czech troops, Martsinkovsky presented a series of
religious lectures in one of the public halls of the city.[44]

Indirectly (more exactly, by neglect), the Soviet decrees of 1918
also improved the conditions under which the sectarians could convene their congresses. In 1910, the czarist government promulgated
rigid rules to govern the organization of sectarian congresses.[45] After
1911, the Evangelical Christians failed in every attempt to obtain
permission for a congress, and the Baptists, although sporadically
successful, encountered mounting difficulties.[46] The Bolsheviks
abolished all of these laws, and until 1922 made no effort to replace
them.[47] In the intervening years, either out of unconcern, good will,
or impotence, the Soviet government seems to have placed no obstacles in the way of sectarian congresses. The Evangelical Christian
Union convoked its Fifth All-Russian Congress in Moscow in 1918.[48]

40. *Bratsky vestnik*, 1957, no. 1, p. 62.
41. Ibid., 1947, no. 5, p. 18.
42. E. Is. Bograd, "Opyt izucheniia sovremennogo sektantstva v Michurinskom
raione" [An experience in the study of contemporary sectarianism in the Michurinsk
region], *VIRA* 9 (Moscow, 1961): 122.
43. A. Iartsev, *Sekta evangelskikh khristian* [The evangelical Christian sect] (Moscow,
1928), p. 8.
44. Martsinkovsky, *Zapiski veruiushchego*, pp. 48–51, 57–72.
45. *Tserkovniia vedomosti*, 1 May 1910, official part, pp. 146–48.
46. See footnote 41.
47. Gidulianov, *Otdelenie*, pp. 117–18.
48. Accounts vary on the date of this congress. All agree on the last days of December
and the first days of January, but they disagree as to whether this was 1917–18 or 1918–19.
See *Bratsky vestnik*, 1947, no. 5, pp. 49, 67; ibid., 1957, no. 1, p. 62; ibid., 1957, no. 6,
p. 40. In either event the congress falls roughly within the first year of Soviet rule.

In the spring of the same year the Christian Student Circles held a conference in Samara.[49]

Of even greater significance for the future of the Protestant sectarians, because it unleashed their missionary zeal, was the change made by Soviet law concerning religious propaganda. Czarist law forbade, with the threat of severe reprisal, any attempts by the sectarians to proselytize among the Orthodox. This prohibition encompassed the vast majority of the population in the Russian Empire, partly because the czarist regime refused legally to recognize unbelief, but mostly because Orthodoxy was the traditional faith of the land.[50] In guaranteeing to every citizen "the freedom of religious and antireligious propaganda," the Constitution of the RSFSR opened up new possibilities for the sectarians to influence Russia's religious life.[51]

Assessed as a whole, then, the introduction of Soviet law in 1918 markedly increased the scope of religious freedom legally available to the Protestant sectarians. Nevertheless, the practical impact of this law on the life and outlook of these sectarians must not be exaggerated. Certain provisions of the new law, such as the denial of the rights of a juridical person to religious congregations, did fall short of sectarian aspirations. And in actual life the new legislation brought the sects no freedoms which they were not already enjoying, even if counter to the letter of the law.

The provisional government which briefly preceded the Bolsheviks in ruling Russia made no attempt to erase the vast majority of czarist laws which discriminated against the sects, but it also made no effort to enforce them.[52] As a consequence, throughout the eight months which separated the February and October Revolutions the sectarians enjoyed actual if not legal religious freedom. Paradoxical as it may seem, if the Bolsheviks had been able to implement their laws

49. Martsinkovsky, *Zapiski veruiushchego*, pp. 66–67.
50. *Tserkovniia vedomosti*, 26 February 1911, official part, pp. 43–44.
51. *Dekrety sovetskoi vlasti*, 2: 550–66.
52. On March 16, 1917, the provisional government decreed "the abolition of all social, religious, and national restrictions" and "an immediate general amnesty for all political and religious offenses" (*Izvestiia*, 16 March 1917). This government enacted only one other law that improved the status of non-Orthodox believers, such as the religious sectarians. A law of July 17, 1917, recognized freedom for all citizens to change religion or to profess no religion at all (*Sobranie ukaz* [Collection of laws] [Petrograd, 1917], vol. 1, pt. 2, no. 1099). Except for the unprecedented privilege of registering as an unbeliever, this law was little more than a reconfirmation of Nicholas II's Act of Toleration of April 30, 1905.

immediately and uniformly, the effect on the sectarians would have been an increase in their de jure freedom but a decrease in their de facto freedom. As it was, throughout 1918 the Soviet government was in no position to enforce its laws; consequently, the sectarians continued to enjoy the same practical religious freedom gained the preceding year in the wake of the February Revolution.

Where the new legislation brought most tangible benefit to the sectarians was in the realm of religious equality. In decreeing that all religions were equal under the law, the Soviet regime severed with a single stroke the manifold privileges granted by the state to the Russian Orthodox church, the most persistent and formidable antagonist of the Protestant sectarians. Before 1905 any member of the Orthodox church who chose to convert from this faith to another faith or to no faith at all subjected himself to the loss of personal and civil rights.[53] The revolution of that year considerably amended this regulation. Henceforth any Orthodox person who wished to leave or to change his faith need fear no reprisals, although the process for legal transfer was hedged with sufficient formalities to deter any but the most deeply convinced.

Nevertheless, to safeguard the loyalty of the Orthodox ranks the czarist state continued after 1905 to grant to the Orthodox church a virtual monopoly over the instruments of indoctrination and propaganda. Clerics of the church kept the official books in which the births, marriages, and deaths of all Orthodox citizens were recorded. In addition to control of its own network of educational institutions, which included theological seminaries and academies, parochial and secondary schools, the Orthodox church was entrusted with major (although not exclusive) responsibility for the required courses in religion offered by the public schools.

This formidable power of indoctrination was buttressed by the legal right conferred upon the church to censor all religious literature published and distributed in the Empire. Finally, whereas non-Orthodox communions were barred from proselytizing among Orthodox citizens (a regulation zealously defended by numerous local priests, who reported violations of it to the police), the Orthodox church received the right and often the encouragement of the Crown

---

53. *Sobranie uzakoneny i rasporiazheny pravitelstva* [Collection of laws and government decrees] (St. Petersburg and Petrograd, 1905) no. 526.

to propagandize its creed among all the citizens of the land.[54] In 1918 all of these rights and privileges were abolished by Bolshevik fiat, although for some time thereafter in various places and in different degrees they continued to be exercised, simply because the new rulers were unable to implement their will throughout the country.

A further blow against the Orthodox church was the nationalization of its vast holdings in landed estates, monasteries, schools, candle factories, printing plants, capital investments, cash reserves, and local church property. The effect of this policy on the parishes proved minimal, since most of the properties required for local religious usage were leased back to the believers without fee. The major damage was inflicted on the central administration of the church. Here the loss was enormous. Although this would bring the Orthodox hierarchy untold hardships before long, throughout most of 1918 these difficulties were somewhat mitigated by the slowness with which the Soviet regime was able to implement nationalization.[55]

According to W. Gutsche, who for a number of years worked in their midst, the Protestant sectarians showed little sympathy toward the Orthodox church during the period of these early collisions with Bolshevik state power. For some, the memory of long years of conflict with the czarist government, more often than not inspired by Orthodox clerics, remained all too fresh in the mind.[56] Others believed, as did certain reformist elements within Orthodoxy, that the separation of church and state could only work to the benefit of the Orthodox church. In Prokhanov's words, "the majority of the Greek Orthodox clergy were very discontented with the disestablishment, but the enlightened members of the clergy understood this reform and approved of it."[57]

The extent to which the Protestant sectarians gained from the efforts of the Bolsheviks in 1918 to reduce the status and power of

54. J. S. Curtiss, *Church and State in Russia: 1900–1917* (New York, 1940), pp. 37–38, 181–82, 231.

55. As concerns implementation of the decree of the separation of church and state, including the nationalization of church property, it was not until the Eighth Congress of Soviets in November, 1920, that "The Eighth Division of the People's Commissariat (of Justice) was able to report that this work was almost complete and had proceeded without real difficulty" (Curtiss, *The Russian Church and the Soviet State*, pp. 46–47, 73).

56. Gutsche, *Religion in Sowjetrussland*, p. 21.

57. Prokhanov, *In the Cauldron of Russia*, p. 176. In retrospect, Prokhanov said, only after disestablishment "did the priests of the church awake to their responsibility toward the members of their congregations" (p. 243). This opinion is not unlike that presently voiced by Russian churchmen in the USSR.

the Orthodox church is not possible to assess at this time. But they did register some gain. On at least two occasions the sects capitalized on the confusions created by nationalization. In December, 1917, as government officials prepared to destroy a reserve of Bibles stored in the recently expropriated printing house of the Holy Synod, a group of sectarians entered the building, "paid the Communists for the Bibles, and quickly distributed them among the people."[58] In similar fashion, Salov-Ashtakov "was able personally to rescue from the Communists a large store of religious literature stocked in a publishing house which had been confiscated, and . . . to distribute hundreds of thousands of fine religious books all over the country."[59] Besides these incidents, scattered evidence suggests that during 1918 a number of Orthodox believers switched their allegiance to the Protestant sects.[60] Even so, by and large, the masses remained loyal to the Orthodox church.[61]

This persistence in faith of the Orthodox masses in the face of the civil war that was raging in the country strongly influenced the tempo and style in which the Soviet government sought to realize its religious legislation. Until August 24, 1918, when the Commissariat of Justice sent out detailed instructions "On the Procedure for the Implementation of the Decree on the Separation of Church from State and School from Church" little had been achieved or attempted. From this date onwards, prodded and directed by the new guidelines, local political officials tackled the work of implementation with new seriousness. Even so, progress was slow.[62] Moreover, advance was frequently delayed or thwarted by the blunders of local authorities who strayed from the course set by the leaders at the center. The nature of these grass-roots errors and the character of the policy promoted by the central officials are well depicted in a circular published in December, 1918, by the Commissariat of Justice. "According to recent reports from local areas," began the circular, "it appears that not all of the local workers correctly under-

58. Salov-Ashtakov, *Christianity in Russia*, p. 104.
59. Ibid.
60. Timasheff, *Religion in Soviet Russia*, p. 60; Martsinkovsky, *Zapiski veruiushchego*, pp. 13–14; *Antireligioznik* [The antireligious worker], 1926, no. 6, pp. 10–11; A. Dolotov, *Tserkov i sektantstvo v Sibiri* [Church and sectarianism in Siberia] (Novosibirsk, 1930), p. 77.
61. Martsinkovsky, *Zapiski veruiushchego*, pp. 127–29; Timasheff, *Religion in Soviet Russia*, p. 60; Curtiss, *The Russian Church and the Soviet State*, pp. 103–5.
62. See footnote 55; also Curtiss, *The Russian Church and the Soviet State*, pp. 62–63.

stand the tasks of the Soviet government in the work of separating the church from the state." A detailed description of their mistakes then followed.[63]

The spirit which permeated this circular was aptly expressed in the assertion that: "It is necessary to remember that the struggle with religious prejudices and the darkness of popular superstitions should not be carried out with punishments and repressions but with the improvement of schools, with the propagation of communism, and with the organization of the economy on communist principles."[64] These words echo the words of Lenin in a speech delivered one month earlier at the First All-Russian Congress of Workers. "In order to struggle with religious prejudices," the Soviet leader warned his listeners, "extraordinary care is needed. Much harm is introduced by those who would bring into this struggle an offense to religious feelings. It is necessary to struggle by means of propaganda, by means of enlightenment."[65]

As the first year of their rule came to a close, the Bolsheviks turned their attention to curbing excesses and to promoting moderation in the administrative aspect of the task of secularization. On a more aggressive note they stepped up the appeals to their followers to wage a propaganda war against religious superstition, but circumstances in 1918 were such that little, if anything, was accomplished.[66] For this reason, too, but primarily because of the benefits which the new legislation bestowed on the sectarians, there is little wonder that, as regards early Soviet religious policy, I. S. Prokhanov, the most prominent sectarian leader of the time, was later (in 1933, in exile in the West) moved to declare:

At first they did not insist on their atheistic doctrines. . . . they declared opposition to the reactionary section of the Greek Orthodox church, but generally speaking in the beginning they showed a friendly spirit to the evangelical movement and various other religious organizations and sects originating among the people which were persecuted under the tsarist regime. . . . In their papers and speeches the leaders of the Bolsheviks sometimes recalled the fact that in the places of exile Stundists and Evangelical Christians found themselves together with the Social Democrats. . . . In the

63. For fuller details see Rothenberg, chapter 5 above.
64. *Kommunisticheskaia partiia i Sovetskoe pravitelstvo*, pp. 45–50.
65. V. I. Lenin, *Polnoe sobranie sochineny* [Complete collection of writings], 4th ed. (Moscow, 1941–51), 28: 161.
66. For the slow start of the antireligious propaganda campaign, see Joan Delaney, "The Origins of Soviet Antireligious Organizations," chapter 6 above.

general policy of the Bolsheviks toward the religious organizations they gave full freedom to all, with the exception of those groups and members of the clergy who were infected with political opposition to the new regime.[67]

III

Although the religious front was unquestionably the most important, it was not the only front about which the sectarians felt deeply. They were concerned also with other governmental policies, internal and external. But what transpired in 1918 was less encouraging. In the same month that the Bolsheviks cheered sectarian spirits by enacting a long-sought decree on the separation of church and state, they dampened their hopes for a democratically elected government by dissolving the constituent assembly with an armed guard. Two months later, in March, 1918, after a long and bitter dispute, Lenin succeeded in removing Russia from the war and signing a peace treaty with Germany. Some sectarians were disturbed by the truly fearful sacrifice forced upon Russia by the German peace terms, but most of their leaders, unlike the majority of the Orthodox hierarchy, and practically all of their rank-and-file members welcomed the peace with joy.[68] The regime quickly lost this gain in popular standing, for in the same month that saw the Brest Litovsk Treaty ratified, a bitter civil war erupted which to no small degree was perpetrated by the militant and dictatorial policies of the Bolsheviks. By the end of 1918 the entire country was torn with strife and filled with terror instigated by Reds and Whites alike.

These dark occurrences along with the rather bright happenings on the religious front formed the mottled context in which the Protestant sectarians slowly evolved an attitude and a response to the new rulers of Russia. As noted earlier, when the Bolsheviks seized power in November, 1917, the leaders of the Protestant sectarians responded to the new circumstances with a wait-and-see attitude. This decision was dictated primarily by the ambiguities of threat and promise which the Bolshevik program offered the sectarian movement. Only time, they felt, would disclose the direction the new regime would take, and conditions in the country at the end of 1917 were still sufficiently fluid to permit the luxury of fence-sitting. Twelve months

67. Prokhanov, *In the Caldron of Russia*, p. 175.
68. Putintsev, *Politicheskaia rol*, p. 111; *Revoliutsiia i tserkov* [Revolution and the church], 1919, nos. 3–5, p. 153.

later the sects had learned more, but very little more, about the type of rule which the Bolsheviks sought to impose on the country. Occupied in a life-or-death struggle to retain state power, the new rulers had found little opportunity to utilize that power to transform Russia into the socialist paradise they envisioned. The Civil War soon bathed the country with a dim and dismal light. In these conditions it was difficult to foresee what would become of those concerns dearest to the sectarians—the construction of a peaceful and viable social order, and the preservation of freedom and equality of religious belief.

Evidence to assess the whole political outlook of the Protestant sectarians at the end of the first year of Soviet rule is slim, and any evaluation at best must presently remain tentative. What appears from the testimony available is a strained effort on the part of the sectarian leaders to continue to wait-and-see.[69] But signs had become visible of a drift created by the pressure of events. This drift was neither toward nor against allegiance to the Bolsheviks. Rather it took the direction of quietism, toward a withdrawal from the world. Though traditionally associated with religious sectarianism, this attitude had been generally foreign to the history of the Russian Protestant sects.[70]

IV

It would be well to conclude this circumscribed exploration with some observations of a general nature which it suggests. For the experience of the Protestant sectarians in the first year of Soviet rule does have insights to offer to an understanding of the broader and more contemporary picture of Soviet religious life. As concerns the Russian Baptist church today, the selective praise which its leaders have from time to time bestowed on the Soviet state for the religious policy introduced with the Revolution cannot be explained away simply on the grounds of police intimidation or political opportunism, but must also be seen as a matter of historical record.[71] Indeed, the most severe critics of contemporary Russian Baptist leaders—the

69. Blane, "Relations between Russian Sects and State," pp. 144–57, 183–90, 251–61.

70. Illustrative of this growing quietist sentiment are extended statements in the Baptist journal, *Slovo istiny*, in the June 1918 and August 1918, issues, as quoted in Putintsev, *Politicheskaia rol*, pp. 298 and 117, respectively.

71. See, for example, *Bratsky vestnik*, 1967, no. 4, pp. 8–21 (esp. pp. 19–20); ibid., 1967, no 5, pp. 4–10 (esp. p. 4).

bold and radical *Initsiativniki,* or Baptist dissidents—seek a return to "Leninist legality" not so much from a romanticized view of the past as from a positive remembrance of actual historical experience.[72]

A second implication of the story told here is that the multi-faceted, tactical nature of Soviet religious policy characteristic of most of the postwar years finds its precedent in the earliest days of the Soviet state. Still another suggestion of this study—one which deserves examination in other dimensions of Soviet religious history—is that even those elements of Soviet religious policy that seem immutable and which are commonly applied to all religious groups can have distinct meanings to different communities because of the peculiarities of their prior historical experience.

72. See the petition of G. K. Kriuchkov and G. P. Vins, on behalf of the Organizing Committee of the Evangelical Christian-Baptist Church, sent on April 14, 1965, to L. I. Brezhnev, the president of the commission charged with drafting a new constitution; printed in English translation in Michael Bourdeaux, *Religious Ferment in Russia,* pp. 105–113.

15

THE COMMUNIST PARTY AND SOVIET JEWRY: THE EARLY YEARS

The Jewish community in the Russian Empire was at once an ethnic and a religious entity. Jewish culture has always been dominated by religious forms and concepts and has been aptly characterized as a "religious civilization." Indeed, it was only in the nineteenth century that some East European Jews began to claim Jewish identity for themselves while simultaneously rejecting Jewish religion. In 1917, however, the great majority of East European Jews still conceived of Jewish identity as composed of inseparable religious and ethnic dimensions. Thus, in line with their general policy of "militant atheism," the Soviet government and Communist party were confronted with the delicate problem of mounting a campaign against the Jewish *religion*, without having this interpreted by both Jews and Gentiles as an attack on the Jewish *nationality*. Obviously, the solution to this dilemma lay in creating a body of militant Jewish atheists who could present the attack on the Jewish religion as a form of internecine warfare rather than as an outside attack which could be labelled anti-Semitic. Happily for the Bolshevik regime, most of the Jewish socialist parties of the prerevolutionary era had adopted an antireligious posture, and had thereby driven a wedge into the relatively cohesive Jewish community. Moreover, the party had within it a Jewish Section, or *Evsektsiia*, many of whose leading activists had previously belonged to Jewish socialist parties. The

Zvi Gitelman

Evsektsiia could—and did—serve as the agency of antireligion "on the Jewish street."

In contrast to the antireligious campaigns of the post-1945 era, the atheistic activity directed against Judaism in the 1920s and 1930s was carried out by Jews, largely in the Yiddish language. This made for a conflict of a peculiar character. Even after the Bolshevik seizure of power the religious community remained a potent force. Because so many Soviet Jews (particularly of the older generation) had strong ties to the traditional Jewish milieu with all its religious customs and ceremonies, the antireligious campaign in the first two decades of Soviet power was a bitter struggle ranging Jew against Jew, father against son, and even husband against wife. In order to appreciate the intensity of feeling, the violence, and the bitterness which characterized the conflict between atheistic and religious Jews, one must examine the roots of internal Jewish differences which had already manifested themselves in the Russian Empire. In particular, it is necessary to understand the reasons for the hostility of Jewish socialists to Judaism.

I

While the Bund, the leading Jewish socialist party before 1917, was basically a-religious and anticlerical, the *Evsektsiia*, the Jewish Section of the Communist party, was both antireligious and anti-clerical. As a socialist party, the Bund had a materialist philosophy and vigorously opposed what it saw as clerical subservience to the oppressors of the working class; as a part of a totalitarian organization, the *Evsektsiia* had a fiercely exclusivist outlook which could not brook the existence of any competing, dissenting, or merely different ideologies. It would be erroneous to assume, as many have, that the persecution of religion by the *Evsektsiia* was merely the fulfillment of the old Bundist program, though there is no doubt that the *Evsektsiia* leaders of the antireligious campaign were the ex-Bundists and other ex-socialists. The Bund had rarely attacked faith or religious customs, and had concentrated its fire on the clergy. Believing, with Marx, that religion was a phenomenon of the capitalist order, Bundists were confident that under socialism religion would die a natural death and it was useless to expend energy on combating it in presocialist Russia. Furthermore, a campaign against religion would have served no purpose but to isolate the Bund from the Jewish community and alienate potentially sympathetic religious workers. Bundists were intellectually atheistic, but many of them were psychically and emotionally tied to the religious symbolism and culture of the Jewish *byt* or way of life. Bundists generally were not inclined to use the kind of coercive methods the *Evsektsiia* employed, and even the militant atheists in the Bund would not consider forcible seizure of synagogues or other religious institutions. Finally, the Bund may have refrained from attacking the Jewish religion because it was an oppressed religion, barely tolerated by the czarist government.[1]

The cleavages created in the Jewish community by the tragic episode of the "Cantonists" in the early part of the nineteenth century were widened by the refusal of Jewish factory-owners to hire Jewish labor and their vigorous opposition to the Jewish revolutionaries who wanted to undo the social and economic order. Since Jewish workers were often forced by economic necessity to work on Saturday, while Jewish merchants and entrepreneurs kept the Sabbath, the rabbis regarded the former as sinners and desecrators of the Sabbath and the latter as pillars of the community. In addition, it was the Jewish middle class which gave financial support to the *kehilla* (the local unit of Jewish self-government) and to the religious functionaries. Some rabbis were aware of the impossible situation of the workers, but others saw them only as dangerous sinners who threatened to disrupt the religious life of Russian-Polish Jewry. Rabbi Khaim Zak, the rabbi of Mezrich, founded a *Makhzikai HaDat* society (Upholders of the Faith) "to fight the Saturday morning socialist meetings of boys and girls . . . who preach deviations from the ways of the Torah and Judaism and who oppose the government, thereby persecuting the entire community of Israel and desecrating the name of God."[2] The rabbis, who certainly hated the czar and his government (the persecutors of the Jewish religion as well as of the Jewish people) as much as they hated the socialists, were afraid that Jewish revolutionary activity would only aggravate czarist persecution

1. The reasons for the Bund's reluctance to attack the Jewish religion were outlined by Professor Erich Goldhagen in a talk on "The Fight against the Jewish Religion in Russia in the 1920s and Its Implications Today," at the Thirty-Ninth Annual Conference of the YIVO Institute for Jewish Research, January 18, 1965. For the last point I am indebted to Mr. Hillel Kempinsky, archivist of the Jewish Labor Bund Library and Archives, New York.

2. Quoted in Abba Lev, *Religie un klaikoidesh in kamf kegn der idisher arbeter-bavegung* [Religion and religious functionaries in the struggle against the Jewish workers' movement] (Moscow, 1923), pp. 25–26.

and bring down the wrath of the authorities and the loyal population upon the heads of the entire Jewish community. Had the czarist government adopted a more tolerant attitude toward the Jewish religion and its institutions, it might have won some support among religious Jewry and have caused an even greater division within Jewish society.

The opposition of many rabbis to the socialist movement did not, however, prevent religious workers from associating themselves with it. Some of the more naïve workers saw it as a quasi-religious movement whose ideals of social justice were precisely those advocated by the Jewish religion. In fact, in the very town where Rabbi Zak was organizing against the socialists, there was a large number of religious workers who identified themselves with the socialist movement.

II

In 1917 religion became a live political issue because of the *kehilla* and questions of Jewish autonomy. The Bund opposed an official state religion and demanded religious freedom for all citizens. There was to be complete separation of church and state so that even the *kehilla* would have no religious functions, and nonreligious Jews would not have to provide financial support for religious institutions. The Bund carefully pointed out that "we do not at all wish to uproot the Jewish religion. Religion, in its pure form, is an intimate feeling . . . like love—and we do not oppose it. We fight only against religion having the social power to force someone into doing something."[3]

A more hostile and emotional attitude was displayed by David Zaslavsky in a famous pamphlet, *Farshvekhte rainigkeitn*. Zaslavsky was prompted to write his "answer to the rabbis" by an incident which had occurred in Kiev at a Jewish convention. A rabbi had asked all those "who honor the Holy Torah" to rise. A furor was created when the Bundists remained seated. Zaslavsky then wrote that he would honor the "bloodied and torn" scrolls which had been destroyed in the pogroms, but not those scrolls which had been presented by the Jews to the czar.

Why don't you bury *those* scrolls? . . . . Because they are witnesses to your shame. If only those scrolls could speak—"Away from here!" they would say . . . . You fine Jews and guardians of religion—you would bow to the

3. A. Zeldov (Nemanskii), *Di religie iz a privat zakh* [Religion is a private affair] (n.p., 1917), p. 13.

earthly god, to the idol of autocracy, and you would bring a sacrifice of your holy Torah scrolls . . . . For pogroms—a Torah to the Czar; for exiles—a Torah to the Czar; for the Beilis trial—a Torah to the Czar . . . . With hatred in your hearts and a hypocritical smile on your lips you presented your Torahs to the Czar . . . . you trembled like slaves, like beaten dogs, and thereby profaned your own holiness. . . . The people did not ask you to do this. The Jewish masses—they are no slaves. Simple Jewish workers and artisans did not go to prostrate themselves. . . . Slaves you were and slaves you have remained.[4]

Even Zaslavsky's attack was a purely political one. He resented the efforts of the religious community to "preserve your rule over the nation with your Torah." "But the Torah should be in the House of Study and only in the House of Study. . . . We respect sincere religious feelings . . . a private affair, a matter of conscience. With the greatest care we take the Torah out of your hands and carry it to its proper place—the House of Study. And now let us argue as good people do, and not involve God in our earthly affairs."[5]

The *Evsektsiia* inherited this righteous indignation but, like the party as a whole, refused to draw any distinction between religion and politics, and insisted upon giving the Jewish religion a class character. It is not surprising that the first large-scale and generally successful efforts of the *Evsektsiia* were in the direction of destroying the old Jewish order. For in the early 1920s the *Evsektsiia* was beginning to assume some of the characteristics of a mobilization agency of a modernizing party-state—that is, it was entrusted with the task of the social mobilization of Yiddish-speaking Jews, a "process in which major clusters of old social, economic and psychological commitments are eroded and broken and people become available for new patterns of socialization and behavior."[6] In this process of social mobilization the *Evsektsiia* acted as a "political entrepreneur" on behalf of the Communist party, organizing individuals for particular political purposes and roles in socialist society. The *Evsektsiia* saw its task as the clearing away of traditional authority-structures as a prerequisite to Bolshevizing the Jewish masses.

The abolition of the *kehillas*, decreed in 1918, was the first step in the campaign against the Jewish religion. Though the lack of a

4. *Farshvekhte rainigkeitn* (*An entfer di rabonim*) [Violated holy things (In reply to the Rabbis)] (n.p., 1917), p. 6.
5. Ibid.
6. Karl Deutsch, "Social Mobilization and Political Development," *American Political Science Review* 15, no. 3 (September, 1961): 494–95.

kehilla structure to some extent atomized the religious community, this community remained in a relatively strong position, partially because it was the chief recipient of American relief aid or at least often served as the channel through which organizations such as the Joint Distribution Committee distributed their funds. Its moral force was even stronger and pervaded even the sanctum sanctorum of the *Evsektsiia*, its central daily newspaper, *Emes*. To the great chagrin of the editor-in-chief, Litvakov, the typesetters refused to work on the High Holidays. This was the unkindest cut of all. Immediately following the holidays, however, they had to print Litvakov's sarcastic diatribe.

Do they really fear the sound of the Great Shofar so much? Pehaps not. But the ne'er-do-well inertia, slothful thought, weakening of revolutionary resolve is so pronounced among them that they want to observe all the little Judaistic [*idishlakhe*] laws and customs . . . . Unfortunately, this is almost a mass phenomenon. The Jewish worker remains mired in the old Judaistic refuse: he sends his children to *kheder*, observes the Sabbath and holidays and often trembles over the most minute religious detail.[7]

The antireligious campaign was the main concern of the *Evsektsiia* in 1921–22. Basically, three methods were used: agitation and propaganda; feigned accession to the "demands of the toiling masses"; naked force. This campaign was conducted almost exclusively by Jews against other Jews because, as noted before, the participation of non-Jews would have smacked of the earlier czarist oppression of the Jewish religion.[8] In fact, the *Evsektsiia* jealously guarded its monopoly over the persecution of the Jewish religion. When the local

---

7. M. Litvakov, "Habokhur hazetser" [Mr. Typesetter], *Emes* [Truth], 2 October 1921. In Vitebsk in 1919 the presidium of the trade union council recognized Rosh Hashanah as a nonworking holiday. *Der shtern* [The star], 2 September 1919.

8. Jewish Communists failed to display a similar tact. Maxim Gorky, a sincere and devoted friend of the Jewish people, pointed out that when the Russians, especially the peasants, saw young Jewish Communists wrecking the churches, anti-Semitic feelings were aroused. "Moreover: in the spread of Judophobia, the Jewish speculators play a significant role. . . . They are helped by the orthodox Jewish Communists with their hostile attitude to the teaching of Hebrew in the schools, to the magnificent products of Jewish talent such as the 'Habimah' theater and, in general, to the cultural activities of non-Communist Jews." Gorky said that the activity of the *Evseks* is "devoid of all tact." He added, however, that, "I know of cases where the Jewish Communists were purposely put in the ranks of those persecuting the Russian church and its priests in order that the Russian peasants should see with their own eyes that the Jews are desecrating their holy places. . . . It seems to me that the Bolsheviks did this partly out of fear and a clear intent to compromise the Jews" (Letter of May 9, 1922, in the Levitas Archive II-1, YIVO Archives, printed in *Novoe russkoe slovo* [New Russian word] [New York], 2 December 1954).

The *Evseks* were greatly embarrassed by Gorky's letter, and Esther Frumkin, a leading

revolutionary tribunal in Smolensk decided to seize the choir-synagogue and give it to the *Evsektsiia*, the latter poutingly refused to accept it as a meeting place because the tribunal had "usurped" its prerogative. The *Evsektsiia* activists sulkingly halted the antireligious campaign just to spite the tribunal.[9]

The agitprop and "mass participation" phases of the *Evsektsiia*'s war on religion included meetings and lectures in places of work, floods of articles in the Jewish press, public debates reminiscent of medieval disputations, and elaborate show trials of religious functionaries and even of customs and institutions. At a workers' meeting a resolution to close the local *kheders* (one-room elementary schools) would be presented by the *Evsektsiia* and, of course, approved. A special commission would then be formed to aid in this project. Only then would the local *ispolkom* decree the closing of the *kheder*, and after it was closed feeble efforts would be made to provide the children with another form of education.[10] The workers' meetings did not always go smoothly for the *Evsektsiia*. Gomel Rabbi Barishansky, one of the most courageous opponents of the *Evsektsiia*, defended the *kheder* vigorously and challenged the *Evsektsiia* to improve, rather than destroy it—the *Evsektsiia* having charged that the *kheder* was unsanitary and injurious to the health of the student.

The press was also mobilized for the fight against religion. Aside from a constant stream of articles, special newspapers and supplements were published, with eye-catching headlines and vicious cartoons which would have been branded anti-Semitic if it were not for the fact that they were published by Jews themselves. The *Evsektsiia*

figure in the antireligious campaign, complained that "it is known that even Maxim Gorky took part in the foreign hunt of the Jewish Communists for their self-sacrificing struggle against ignorance and fanaticism" (Maria [Esther] Frumkin *Doloi ravvinov* [Down with the rabbis] [Moscow, 1923], p. 40). Actually, had the Jewish Communists not played such an outstanding role in the antireligious campaign, they probably would have been accused of sponsoring it anyway. The Russian church, some of whose leaders believed that Russia "had fallen under the power of godless men—Jews and Chinese"(!)—was prone to blame the Jews for its troubles. "The opposition to the confiscation of church property is increasing and is causing anti-Jewish feeling, as the Jews are held responsible for the decree" (from a report of the U.S. Commissioner in Riga, 21 April, 1922, in Boleslaw Szczesniak, ed., *The Russian Revolution and Religion* [Notre Dame, 1959], p. 70.) The "theory" of "Chinese-Jewish" rule of Russia is expressed in an Epistle to Russian Refugees Abroad sent by the Metropolitan of Kiev, also quoted in Szczesniak, *Russian Revolution and Religion*, p. 60,

9. A. Merezhin, "Erger fun batlones" [Worse than stupidity], *Emes*, 2 October 1921.

10. See M. Levitan, "Kulturnye dostizheniia evreiskikh mass RSFSR" [Cultural achievements of the Jewish masses of the RSFSR], *Zhizn natsionalnostei* [The life of nationality groups] 1 (Moscow, 1923): 246.

was not above appealing to the prurient interests of the readers and sometimes printed lurid tales of rabbis who were sexual deviates, seducers of young girls, and the like. In the initial stages of its campaign, the *Evsektsiia* published more serious material, most of it in a mild, semischolarly tone.[11] Later on, the literature became more simplistic, more frankly polemical.[12]

The most bizarre aspect of the campaign was the show trials. On Rosh Hashanah, 1921, the *Evsektsiia* in Kiev "tried" the Jewish religion in the same auditorium, ironically, where the Beilis trial had been held. According to a non-Communist source, a weird cast of characters appeared before the "judges": a lady dressed in old-fashioned clothes explained that she sent her children to *kheder* because, she proclaimed haughtily, she was no "low-class tailor or cobbler" but of a "distinguished religious family." This was submitted as evidence that the Jewish religion was a creature of the bourgeoisie. A "rabbi" testified that he taught religion in order to keep the masses ignorant and servile. When someone in the audience accused him of being a "lying ignoramus," "stormy applause" broke out, according to the stenographic report. The culprit in the audience was immediately arrested. After further testimony by a corpulent "bourgeois," bedecked with glittering gold and diamond rings, the *Evsektsiia* "prosecutor" summarized the "case against the Jewish religion" and asked for a "sentence of death for the Jewish religion." Moshe Rozenblatt, a Kiev Hebrew teacher, rose to defend Judaism and the sympathies of the crowd were clearly with him. He was arrested immediately after completing his speech. The "judges" retired to their chambers and returned with a verdict of death to the Jewish religion.[13] A similar trial—this time of the *kheder*—took place

11. For example, the pamphlet *Yom Kippur* [Day of Atonement], by H. Lurie (Kharkov, 1923), used the writings of Edward Taylor, Herbert Spencer, Emile Durkheim, and George Simmel. Other pamphlets in this vein were Lurie's *Peisakh* [Passover] (Kharkov, 1924), *Toire* [Jewish law] (Kharkov, 1923), and *Shabes* [The Sabbath] (Odessa, 1922). Sometimes Yiddish translations of semischolarly Russian works were used. An example of this is Professor N. Nikolsky's *Yidishe yomtoivim: zeier ufkum un antviklung* [The Jewish festivals: their origin and development] (Minsk, 1925).

12. See, for example, I. Sudarsky, *Farvos kemfn mir kegn religie* [Why do we fight religion?] (Kharkov, 1931), and Y. Novakovsky, *Gots strapshes* [God's whips] (Kiev, 1930). Some of the literature was copied from antireligious tracts written by Jewish anarchists in the United States.

13. Y.D.K., "Der mishpet iber der yidisher religie" [Jewish religion on trial], in E. Tsherikover, ed., *In der tkufe fun revolutsie* [In the period of the revolution] (Berlin, 1923), pp. 385 ff.

in Vitebsk.[14] The *yeshiva* was tried in Rostov, and circumcision was "put on trial" in Kharkov as late as 1928.

Pageantry was used in yet another form. Realizing that "nature dislikes a vacuum" and that there was a need felt by Jews for ritual and ceremony, the *Evsektsiia* designed an elaborate antireligious ritual. It was suggested that greeting cards be sent on the anniversary of the October Revolution instead of on *Rosh Hashanah*, that the traditional *khalah* be baked in the shape of a hammer and sickle, and that the answer to the "four questions" on Passover be a recounting of the history of the October Revolution.[15] In Vitebsk in 1920 a *Evsektsiia* "Yom Kippurnik" consisted of a demonstration outside the main synagogue on the Day of Atonement. Using axes and saws, the demonstrators created such a fearful racket that services were disrupted. This custom spread to other cities, with torchlight parades, clowns, and free lunches as added embellishments.[16] In 1924 a "Red Haggadah" was read which substituted the deliverance from czarist rule for deliverance from pharaoh's oppression.[17] Following the example of the Living Church, the *Evsektsiia* tried to set up a "Living Synagogue" in 1924. "Communism is the Mosaic Torah translated by Lenin into the Bolshevik tongue," one of its founders declared.[18] Apparently, the Jews preferred to study the Torah in their own tongue because the "Living Synagogue" died a quick death.

14. For a detailed account of this, based on the stenographic notes of "Defense Attorney" Wolfson, see A. A. Gershuni, *Yahudut Berusiya Ha-Sovietit* [Judaism in Soviet Russia] (Jerusalem, 1961), pp. 26–36. The *Evsektsiia* version of this trial is L. Abram, Y. Khinchin, and Y. Kaplan, *Der mishpet ibern kheder* [The Kheder on trial] (Vitebsk, 1922).

15. A. R. Tsveig, "Der neier shtaiger un der yontev" [The new way of life and the Jewish festival], *Emes*, 13 October 1923.

16. On events in Borisov, Odessa, and Minsk, see *Emes*, 1 November 1922, and Gershuni, *Yahadut Berusiya*, pp. 82–85. These demonstrations sometimes got out of hand and led to miniature civil wars, especially in the smaller towns. M. Altshuler warned that demonstrations were fit for the larger cities, but that in the small towns they divided the community into "insistent believers and hesitant atheists," thus obscuring the class question (Altshuler, "Fragn fun taktik in kamf mitn klerikalizm" [Questions of tactics in the struggle against clericalism], *Der Komunist* [The Communist] [Kharkov], 25 November 1921).

17. "Slaves we were to capital until the October Revolution came and rescued us with a mighty hand from the land of slavery. And were it not for October, then surely we and our children and our children's children would have remained slaves to capital. . . . Today the revolution is only here, next year—world revolution" Gershuni, *Yahadut Berusiya*, pp. 84–85. For a complete description of a "Red Seder," see *Der veker* [The Awakener], 3 April 1923.

18. Poltava had a "living Synagogue" derisively referred to as the *Evsov-Promoldom*—the "Jewish Soviet Proletarian Prayer House." *Emes* satirized it in a hilarious article on 5 June 1924.

Propaganda and pageantry had almost no influence on the older generation, deeply rooted in the Jewish tradition and not seduced by "Red Haggadahs" or "Living Synagogues." In fact, even the most reliable social class, the workers, disappointed the *Evsektsiia.* "The less conscious . . . Jewish worker at first did not understand why we so bitterly fight the whole clerical coterie. . . . He absolutely failed to understand what the Jewish Communists want of the rabbi and the *kehilla,* of the *minyan* and House of Study. . . . The rabbi, it seemed to him, is an innocent creature. Unlike the priest, he was never to be found in the czarist regime."[19]

To the intense annoyance of the antireligious specialists, Jewish workers and, especially, their wives, continued observance of Jewish customs and some rituals long after they had renounced Jewish faith. Osherovich complained that "the backward woman thinks that with the help of customs and traditions which her husband maintains (weddings, *seders, kiddush*) she will be able to strengthen the familial bond between herself, her husband and her children."[20] The younger generation was more malleable and may have enjoyed the *Evsektsiia* celebrations and morality plays whose crude characterizations and simplistic black-and-white plots often resembled a children's puppet show. The younger generation was weaned away from religion by the economic necessity of working on the Sabbath and holidays, and by a variety of social and political pressures which relegated the Jewish worker or employee to second-class citizenship if he sent his children to *kheder,* had them circumcised, or himself attended the synagogue.[21]

---

19. Lev, *Religie un Klaikoidesh,* p. 3. Abba Lev was one of the earliest figures in the Jewish labor movement. He was very active in antireligious work in the 1920s and 1930s, but in 1945, when he was archivist of the Jewish Anti-Fascist Committee, he was in a Moscow synagogue on Rosh Hashanah where he came "in order to find some warmth," he said. Lev was completely crushed by the Nazi slaughter of the Jews. See Wolf-Hersch Ivan "A bezbozhnik a ba'al t'shuve" [An atheist who repented] *Dos yidishe vort* [The Jewish word] (Winnipeg), 24 September 1965.

20. *Der veker,* 8 April 1923. The issue of April 19 cites the case of a Communist, a leader in the antireligious campaign, who secretly observed Passover.

21. For instance, a worker who donated money toward the purchase of a Torah was tried publicly. *Komunistishe fon* [The Communist banner], 12 February 1924. Circumcision, the ceremony by which a male is initiated into the congregation of Israel, was one of the hardiest survivors among religious practices. Even sincere Jewish Communists would go to enormous lengths to have their children circumcised. Circumcision was outlawed as unhygienic, but Jews clung to it for nationalistic, as well as purely religious, reasons. The subterfuges used by secret policemen to have their children circumcised, and the tragi-comic results, are described in Gershuni, *Yahadut Berusiya,* pp. 77–79.

The propaganda campaign actually did not have much effect and sometimes even boomeranged, as at the show trials. But there was a grimmer aspect to the *Evsektsiia*'s antireligious drive. If Jewish Communists participated in the spoliation of Christian churches, they hurled themselves with such a frenzy into the battle against their own houses of worship that a non-Jewish Communist was moved to remark, "It would be nice to see the Russian Communists tear into the monasteries and holy days as the Jewish Communists do to Yom Kippur."[22]

The law was also made use of to constrain religious activity. All religious associations were required to register with the authorities and submit membership lists. Premises for any sort of religious activity had to be leased from municipal housing departments. Rabbis and other religious functionaries were deprived of the vote and of all political rights. Religious instruction for persons under eighteen was made illegal. In 1922–23 over one thousand *kheders* were closed. In Vitebsk alone, 39 *kheders* with 1,358 students and 49 teachers were shut down.[23] These closures took place despite the fact that even the local *Evseks* admitted that their students could not be provided with other schooling and protested against the forcible closing of the *kheders*.[24] "Comrade Fuks . . . comes to Dukor where he arranges a meeting in the House of Study. 'Sign the agreement,' he proposes, 'you have to accept the responsibility of maintaining a Yiddish Soviet school.' 'We don't need it, we don't want it,' the audience cries. 'Don't listen to them, the speculators!' shout the youth. . . . 'We'll sign on condition that the Bible and commentaries will be taught there.' 'That is unacceptable,' announces Comrade Fuks. The agreement is signed. (The audience wisecracks: 'by the time they ferret out a teacher, the *kheder* children will be adults.')"[25]

22. Quoted in Yaakov Lestschinsky, *Dos sovetishe identum* [Soviet Jewry] (New York, 1944), p. 313. Kalinin remarked that "As president of the Central Executive Committee, I have very often had to resist the demands of the Jewish youth who want to confiscate the synagogues and convert them into clubs." (M. I. Kalinin, "Evreisky vopros i pereselenie evreev v Krym" [The Jewish question and the resettlement of Jews in the Crimea], *Izvestiia*, 11 July 1926).

23. *Doloi ravvinov*, p. 29.

24. *Emes*, 23 June 1922.

25. *Der veker*, 14 February 1923. This incident highlights (1) the bogus nature of the "mass meetings" which "demanded" the closing of *kheders;* (2) the fact that the older generation in the small towns was religious; (3) the wedge that was being driven between generations; (4) the difficulties in obtaining Yiddish teachers who would teach in Soviet schools.

Finally, gold and silver ornaments in the synagogues were seized and sold, purportedly to aid the poor.[26]

The velvet glove of the law was frequently dispensed with. When the *Evsektsiia* attempted to seize a synagogue in Vitebsk, the religious community staged a demonstration, and when a detachment of fifteen men was sent to clear the synagogue they were beaten up and forced to retreat. Finally a cavalry detachment had to be dispatched to evict the assembled Jews.[27] When a forcible seizure of the Minsk synagogue was attempted, two Jews fought back and were killed, and in Odessa a rabbi met the same fate in another incident. Most rabbis, however, abhorred the use of force and counseled restraint.[28]

In contrast to what was happening in the Russian Orthodox church, there were only a few isolated attempts by Jewish religious leaders to reconcile themselves to the new regime, perhaps because the Communist party made no attempt to win over the Jewish religious establishment. The first rabbi to display a favorable attitude toward the Soviet regime was the rabbi of Slefianka who declared that "the present government tries to disseminate knowledge and work among the Jewish population, not the *luftmensh*-ism and swindles which existed under the bourgeois order."[29] The *Evsektsiia* gleefully proclaimed a "split in the ranks of the Jewish functionaries," but this was hardly the case.[30] Actually, of the one thousand rabbis in the USSR only six are known to have had pro-Communist sympathies; only two rabbis attacked religion itself.[31]

26. The decision to seize the ornaments was taken on February 9, 1922. See *Emes*, 12 February 1922.

27. Gershuni, *Yahadut Berusiya*, pp. 60–61.

28. Joint Foreign Committee of the Board of Deputies of the British Jews and the Anglo-Jewish Association, *Memorandum on the Correspondence with the Soviet Government Respecting the Persecution of Judaism in Russia* (London, 1924), p. 4.

29. *Emes*, 6 July 1923. This rabbi published an eight-page pamphlet, *Dos diment bletl* [The diamond leaf], which contended that "the diamond of communism" had once hung on Abraham's neck.

30. For other "pro-Communist" statements, such as "Moses was a Marxist," see Em. Iaroslavsky, *Tsiln un metodn fun antireligiezer propaganda* [Goals and methods of antireligious propaganda], trans. P. Shprakh (Moscow–Kharkov–Minsk, 1930), p. 46.

31. Gershuni, *Yahadut Berusiya*, pp. 109–10. An interesting, and apparently sincere, attempt to reconcile Judaism and Communism was made by Rabbi Samuel Alexandrov of Bobruisk. Alexandrov had corresponded with Rabbi A. I. Kook, Chief Rabbi of Palestine, Akhad HaAm, the ideologist of "cultural Zionism," and M. J. Berdichevsky, a noted Hebrew writer. He emphasized "the justification of God's historical acts." The Communists were brought into being by God "who has wrapped himself in a cloak of materialism and in so doing has brought life to the world." Materialist Marxism is a prologue to the revelation of faith in one God. "Behold there are days which are coming in which the

Mention should also be made of the resistance put up by the religious community, a chapter of Russian Jewish history which has not received the attention it deserves. Well into the late 1920s there existed in the Soviet Union a network of underground *kheders* and *yeshivas*. The leader of the religious resistance and the coordinator of much underground activity was Rabbi I. I. Schneerson, the "Lubavicher Rebbe." He was constantly hounded by the *Evsektsiia* and the secret police and was finally forced to leave the Soviet Union, but not before he had trained many teachers whose influence was to be felt in the USSR long after his departure.[32] The *Rebbe* failed in an attempt to raise large sums for the maintenance of illegal schools and an anti-*Evsektsiia* campaign.[33] Cantors, too, played an important part in keeping the Jewish religion alive, by traveling around and giving popular concerts.

Especially in the smaller towns, religion, and not communism, was the dominating force in Jewish life until the 1930s. As late as 1926 a conference of Soviet rabbis was held, and one publisher of religious books managed to print one hundred thousand such books in 1927–29. (The presses of some other religious publishing houses were also able to function to a certain extent at this time.) It is impossible to measure the degree of religious observance, both because it was carried on clandestinely and because religious observance is inherently difficult to quantify. For instance, in 1925, in Gomel, of 560 Jewish artisans investigated, 431 rested on Saturday, 86 on Sunday, and 41 put themselves down as "undetermined." One hundred fifty-nine called themselves "religious," 104 "half-religious," and 275 "nonreligious."[34]

eyes of man will be opened to see the Divine, moral kernel which lies hidden in dialectical materialism." Quoted in A. Shauli, "Jewish Theology in Soviet Russia," *Reconstructionist*, 4 October 1957. Alexandrov apparently attempted a neo-cabalistic metaphor in which God's truth was seen as covered by the *Klipah* [shell] of *diamat* [dialectical materialism]. For a discussion of Alexandrov and his book, *Mikhtavei Mekhkar Ubikoret* [Critical and scholarly letters], see Gershuni, *Yahadut Berusiya*, pp. 126–28.

32. See *Di yisurim fun libavitshn rebn in sovet-rusland* [The tribulations of the Lubbavitcher Rabbi in Soviet Russia] (Riga, 1930); *Di rabonim in dinst fun finants kapital* [Rabbis in the service of finance capital] (Moscow, 1930), an *Evsektsiia* pamphlet attacking the *Rebbe*; Gershuni, *Yahadut Berusiya*, pp. 156–208.

33. "Religious Instruction in Russia: Note by the Secretary," Joint Foreign Committee, 21 June 1928, Lucien Wolf Archive, box 17, packet 114, YIVO Archives.

34. I. Pulner, "Iz zhizni goroda Gomelia" [From the life of the town of Gomel] in B. G. Tan-Bogoraz, *Evreiskoe mestechko v revoliutsii* [The Jewish town in the revolution] (Moscow and Leningrad, 1925), p. 196. The *Evsektsiia* invariably overemphasized the

Some religious functionaries entered the Jewish agricultural colonies promoted by the *Evsektsiia*, and in a number of these colonies religious life was very strong. The *Evsektsiia* was well aware of this and tried to force the colonists to break with tradition by raising pigs. But in 1929 only 45 out of 235 Jewish collective farms were engaged in hog-breeding, and on some of these farms non-Jews were hired to tend the hogs. The *Evsektsiia* would frequently "unmask" rabbis and religious practices in these colonies, and a great hue and cry would be raised in the press.[35]

In 1929 the *Evsektsiia* discovered, to its horror, that some Moscow workers and university students, among them members of the Communist party, had joined a secret society, *Tiferes Bakhurim* (Glory of Youth). Founded by a Lubavicher *Hasid*, Rabbi Yaakov Landau, the society adopted as its slogan "Be a complete Jew in your own home, be a complete Jew when you go out into the world."[36] The society demanded full observance of Jewish law and daily study of the Bible, the Talmud, the Law, and Hasidism. The university students made no attempt to hide their religious beliefs and refused to take examinations on the Sabbath. The society had branches in Leningrad, Minsk, Smolensk, and Poltava. It ceased operations in 1930 but revived at a later date.[37]

The antireligious *jihad* was one of the wildest episodes in *Evsektsiia* history. It involved more people—on both sides of the fence—than any other Jewish Communist campaign heretofore. It ranged from clumsy buffoonery to riots and large-scale violence. And it is fair to say that it aroused both more support and more opposition than any other *Evsektsiia* activity. Local Jewish Sections, and especially their Komsomol adherents, often got so carried away that

extent of religious commitment, while other Communists, such as Tan-Bogoraz, minimized it. See, for instance, A. Kirzhnitz, *Di "hailike" shediker un undzer kulter-revolutsie* [The holy destroyers and our cultural revolution] (Moscow, 1929), pp. 10–26; and M. Kiper, *Dos yidishe shtetl in Ukraine* [The Jewish town in the Ukraine] (Kiev, 1929).

35. On religion in the colonies, see Kh. Szmeruk, "HaKibutz Hayehudi VeHahityashvut Hakhaklait Hayehudit BeByelorusia HaSovietit 1918–1932" [The Jewish community and the Jewish agricultural settlement in Soviet Belorussia, 1918–32], Ph.D. dissertation, Hebrew University (Jerusalem), 1961, p. 126.

36. This was undoubtedly a parody of the dictum of Y. L. Gordon, a Hebrew poet of the *Haskalah*, or Enlightenment. Gordon had written in 1863, "Be a human being [Ben Adam] when you go out in the world, and a Jew in your own home." Many interpreted this, perhaps erroneously, as an exhortation to assimilate and to relegate Judaism to the privacy of one's home.

37. Gershuni, *Yahadut Berusiya*, pp. 131–33.

the center had to rein them in. Criticizing the inactivity of the *Evsektsiia* in other fields, M. Altshuler pointed out that it came alive only at the time of antireligious campaigns. "We are not a party of Sabbath desecrators—we are a revolutionary Marxist party. . . . A plan for work is necessary—not from holiday to holiday but from day to day; not from campaign to campaign, but on a regular basis."[38]

While in 1921 the antireligious demonstrations were limited to the western provinces—Gomel, Minsk, and Vitebsk—by 1922 they had spread to the Ukraine. Esther Frumkin claimed that between twenty-five and thirty thousand Jewish workers were involved in the demonstrations of 1922.[39]

The war on religion continued to smolder in 1923–24. There were campaigns directed against three major holidays in eighty-one different localities, and thirty-nine campaigns to close *kheders*, abolish the day of rest on Saturday, and close Houses of Study. Of 303 *Evsektsiia* campaigns between January, 1923, and March, 1924, a total of 120 were antireligious in nature.[40] Nevertheless, the campaign had been toned down. "This year we did not fire any heavy artillery in our antireligious campaign [around the High Holidays]. . . . It is not for nothing that this year's antireligious campaign was called 'new way of life' and not 'struggle against clericalism'—the struggle is really almost over."[41]

The Thirteenth Congress of the party held in 1924 resolved that the antireligious campaign was to be carried out only by agitprop and using only educational methods.[42] In September, 1925, the *Evsektsiia* Central Bureau ordered the cessation of "carnivals, demonstrations, etc."[43] From now on the *Evsektsiia* campaign against religion was to be in the nature of sporadic skirmishes rather than full-scale battle.

38. *Komunistishe fon*, 19 May 1923.
39. *Doloi ravvinov*, p. 20.
40. The others were designed to increase the circulation of the *Evsektsiia* press, and to promote Jewish colonization. *A yor arbet fun der RKP in der idisher svive* [A year's work of the RKP in the Jewish environment] (Moscow, 1924), pp. 27–28.
41. *Der veker*, 21 September 1923.
42. *Izvestiia*, 3 June 1924.
43. *Emes*, 15 September 1925. Alfred A. Greenbaum suggests that "the militancy of this antireligious work grew and waned in the same cycles as the general antireligious campaigns" which were "curtailed or abandoned in response to considerations of foreign policy." In 1925 the Central Bureau was trying to get American funds for Jewish land settlement and it "informed the local branches not even to hold antireligious lectures on Jewish *holidays*, let alone the usual demonstrations during the hours of worship." "Soviet Jewry During the Lenin–Stalin period—I," *Soviet Studies* 16, no. 4, (April, 1965): 410.

Despite the ferocity of the attack upon it, the Jewish religion continued to be an important factor in Soviet Jewish life. Even the *kehillas* showed remarkable resilience, though they had been officially stripped of all their social welfare functions and remained only congregations of worshippers. In 1925 there were 418 *kehillas* registered in the RSFSR and in 1926 there were 1,003 *kehillas* registered in the Ukraine.[44]

But in 1929 a new and harsher antireligious campaign was launched. "A year ago it was possible for the committee to report that although the restraints on the Jewish religion, and more particularly on the religious education of the young, were extremely harsh, they were tempered by exemptions of which it was possible to make more or less effective use. This is no longer the case. . . . In the same way as the former exemptions from collectivization have been swept away, the exemptions from the more rigorous applications of the antireligious laws have also been abolished. . . . The obstacles placed in the way of the faithful have become well-nigh insuperable."[45]

The children of religious functionaries could find no jobs and they sometimes changed their names and moved to other towns in order to find work.[46] Yet small, isolated pockets of religious life still remained. In the *shtetl* (Jewish hamlet) of Peresfe in 1929 there were eight Houses of Study, a *yeshiva*, a *kheder*, and a branch of the *Tiferes Bakhurim* with twenty-four members, some of whom belonged to trade unions, among them a bookkeeper for the militia.[47] In many small towns the religious community was still the main welfare agency.[48] There were still about five hundred synagogues and Houses of Study in Belorussia.[49] In the Ukraine the number of synagogues had declined only from 1,034 in 1917 to 934 in 1929–30. The number of rabbis in the Ukraine had fallen from 1,049 in 1914 to 830 in 1929–30. In all, 646 synagogues had been seized since the Revolution.[50]

---

44. Each had a minimum membership of twenty and was registered with the local soviet. The Ukrainian *kehillas* included 137,000 members.

45. Joint Foreign Committee, "Report of the Situation in Russia," 5 March 1930, Lucien Wolf Archive, box 10, packet 73, item 8730, YIVO Archives.

46. Ibid., packet 74, item 9747 (report of a Viennese traveler).

47. *Oktiabr* [October], 8 February 1929.

48. See the editorial in *Oktiabr*, 1 November 1929.

49. *Oktiabr*, 1 February 1929.

50. *American Jewish Yearbook 5690*, pp. 68–69; *AJYB 5961*, p. 118.

III

More serious for Jewish religious life than the new antireligious campaign, though not fully separable from it, was the "second revolution" of the 1930s, which transformed Russia into a modern industrial society. This produced the same effects upon religion as had been observed in America and Western Europe.[51] As the Jew was drawn into the social and economic mainstream of society he was assimilated linguistically, culturally, and religiously. In an officially atheistic society the decline in religious affiliation was, of course, accelerated, and a synthesis of socio-economic integration and religious identification was not possible. Powerful social forces that were introduced in this second decade of Soviet rule, such as urbanization and industrialization, broke up the *shtetl*, the stronghold of Jewish tradition and religion. As the unemployed youth of the *shtetl* rushed into the large cities and the new industrial centers emerging under the impetus of the five-year plans, they often left their religious and even ethnic affiliations behind them. In the 1930s the rate of intermarriage among Soviet Jews was very high, probably reaching 30 percent in the Russian Republic.

Aside from secular trends in the economy and in social life, the 1930s witnessed another phenomenon which had been largely unknown in the previous decade—mass terror. The atmosphere of fear and suspicion that characterized the period of the purges had a profound effect on Jewish religious and cultural life. Many Jewish political leaders, including former *Evsektsiia* officials, fell victim to the purges. Yiddish cultural institutions—schools and newspapers in particular—were closed down. Religious practices and institutions were now considered not only ideologically reprehensible but even politically traitorous. Some leading rabbis became victims of the purges and a mixed bag of unsavory informers appeared in the synagogues. Intensified ideological indoctrination pitted fathers against sons and former friends against each other. The twin hammers of forced-draft industrialization and extremely rapid modernization, on the one hand, and the pervasive terror, on the other, combined to exert enormously powerful pressures on the remnants of religious Jewry in the USSR. The Jewish religion fought a rearguard action

51. See Bohdan R. Bociurkiw, "Religion and Atheism in Soviet Society," chapter 4 above. The author discusses the impact of industrialization on all religions in Russia, especially Russian Orthodoxy.

against the forces which would destroy it; but fresh reserves were not forthcoming and the army of the faithful dwindled into an aging and exhausted band of believers.

It is interesting that the Islamic religion was not attacked by the same methods in the very early years, though it resembled the Jewish religion in regulating the entire life of its adherents and making great demands upon them. The Jewish *Halakha* is closely paralleled by the Islamic *Shari'ah* in its detailed prescriptions of daily conduct. Both the Moslems and the Jews were persecuted under the czarist regime and both were economically backward, though the Jews were less so. But the antireligious campaign among the Moslems was *at first* much subtler and milder than the *Evsektsiia*'s battle with the Jewish religion. Undoubtedly, this was due to the stronger hold of Islam on the Moslems, the lack of Communist Moslem cadres, and the fear of alienating such a large and powerful group. M. Sultan-Galiev, a prominent Bolshevik Moslem, acknowledged that "there are a number of reasons for adopting methods absolutely different from those used among other peoples." He cited the comparatively recent origin of Islam, and hence its vigor and strength as a religion, as well as the "political, social and economic enslavement of almost the entire Moslem world" and the Moslem identification of attacks on Islam with political oppression of Moslems. Therefore, Sultan-Galiev urged "a very careful and dexterous approach."[52]

In contrast to the Moslems, the Jews had shown an eagerness to assimilate into European culture and had provided their own anti-religious cadres. Lacking their own territory and having proved adept at being absorbed into European society and making outstanding contributions to it, they were the natural vanguard of the movement toward a Luxemburgist cosmopolitanism or, at least, a Leninist internationalism. In 1948, of course, they were attacked for this cosmopolitanism, which was described as "rootless," implying non-allegiance to the Soviet state.[53] Perhaps the idea that the Jew is so assimilable contributes to the Soviet authorities' irritation with that part of Soviet Jewry, most visibly the small religious community, which continued and continues to insist on a distinct identity.

52. M. Sultan-Galiev, *Metody anti-religioznoi propagandy, sredi musulman* [Methods of antireligious propaganda among the Muslims] (Moscow, 1922); translated in Xenia J. Eudin and Harold H. Fisher, *Soviet Russia and the East 1920–1927* (Stanford, 1957), pp. 46–47.

53. See Bernhard Wilhelm, "Moslems in the Soviet Union, 1948–1954," chapter 12 above. Mr. Wilhelm argues that in 1948 the Moslems suffered a similar attack.

16

THE JEWISH RELIGION IN THE SOVIET UNION SINCE WORLD WAR II

Soviet Jewry emerged from the war broken in body and spirit. One and a half million Jews were murdered by the Nazi invaders; many more died as a result of the ravages of war. Large numbers of Jews managed to escape from the occupied territories, where roughly three-quarters of the Jewish population of the Soviet Union had lived; they spent the war years as refugees, uprooted from areas in which, over the course of centuries, they had created a social environment and a culture of their own.

The Mid-Forties to the Mid-Fifties

In the postwar period Soviet Jewry represented a disoriented mass of people in search of spiritual and physical rehabilitation.[1] This search

In addition to the books and publications specifically noted in the references, many facts and findings in this study were culled from articles in the Soviet press dealing with Jews and Jewish topics, reprinted in the publication *Evrei i evreisky narod, sbornik materialov iz Sovetskoi pechati* [Jews and the Jewish people, collection of materials from the Soviet press], Contemporary Jewish Library, London. The first volume of the collection was published in 1960, the last volume used for this study, no. 22, appeared at the beginning of 1966.

Also, several findings and observations are based on material printed in *Jews in Eastern Europe, a Periodical Survey of Events*, edited by Emanuel Litvinoff and published in London.

1. Ben-Zion Goldberg, a Yiddish journalist who, at the time of his visit to the Soviet Union in 1956, was strongly pro-Soviet, described the state of Soviet Jewry in the following words: "I found an emaciated, crumbled Jewry, almost no longer a people, just stray in-

Joshua Rothenberg

for roots combined with the experience of Nazi genocide and the unexpected growth of Russian chauvinism and anti-Semitism to bring
about a parallel increase of Jewish nationalist feelings and Jewish
cohesiveness. As Jews returned to their old places of residence,
attempts were made to revive Jewish culture. Soviet authorities,
however, were very slow in lending assistance.[2] In spite of steadily increasing obstacles Yiddish books were published and sold very well.[3]
The Yiddish Art Theatre reopened in Moscow and several artistic
groups became active.

On the whole, the Jewish religion, like all other religious cults in
the Soviet Union, enjoyed a relatively greater measure of tolerance
during, and immediately after, the war. Yet Jewish religious leaders
were not able to take full advantage of this situation. Several factors
can be isolated here. Most Jews were at that time refugees, living in
temporary residences. Furthermore, the Jewish religion lacked a
central organization capable of making demands of the regime and
of giving any organizational form to the concessions granted. Also,
unlike the Russian Orthodox and the Moslem religious bodies, the
organized Jewish religious cult had had very little political assistance
to offer the Soviet government. During the war, Soviet leaders considered it more expedient to solicit Jewish support abroad through
secular rather than religious Jews.[4] And after the war representatives
of the Jewish religious community were not always invited to join
with other religious leaders in undertakings organized by the Soviet

dividuals, harried and gloomy, haunted by shadows of death, and hate, and abuse" (*The
Jewish Problem in the Soviet Union, Analysis and Solution* [New York, 1961], pp. 49–50).

2. Ibid., p. 84. Ben-Zion Goldberg remarked: "All doors opened automatically for the
general cultural effort, [but] the hinges on the gate to Yiddish culture were rusty, and the
gate opened reluctantly and only slightly."

3. In 1946, 1947, and 1948, 114 Yiddish books were published. In 1939 alone, 339
Yiddish books had been published, in spite of the progressive curtailment of Yiddish
culture and education that had started in the mid-thirties. In the same year two Yiddish
dailies, several periodicals, and a dozen professional theatrical companies were still in
existence. The number of Yiddish cultural institutions decreased between 1938 and 1941 in
spite of the growth of the Jewish population by two million, primarily from the newly
acquired territories. See Kh. Shmeruk, ed., *Pirsumim Yehudim Be-Brith Hamoatzot*
[Jewish Publications in the Soviet Union] (Jerusalem, 1961), preface, pp. 88–89, 101.

4. The Soviet government handpicked for participation in the wartime Jewish Anti-
Fascist Committee individuals active in the field of Yiddish letters and art, and other
prominent persons of Jewish descent. The delegation sent to the United States in 1943 to
solicit the support of American Jewry for the war effort consisted of the Yiddish poet Itzik
Feffer and Solomon Mikhoels, an actor and director of the Moscow Yiddish theatre (Sals
W. Baron, *The Russian Jews under Tsars and Soviets* [New York, 1965], p. 305).

government; for instance, they were not invited to join the Committee for the Defense of Peace in 1951.[5]

Government policy towards the Jewish religion has not always been identical with its policy towards other religions, and the accepted division of Soviet religious policy into defined periods does not necessarily apply to the Jewish religion, as pointed out by Nikita Struve and Walter Kolarz.[6] This is particularly true for the postwar period.

The changing attitude towards Jews as a Soviet nationality in the late forties, and the policy of the Soviet Union towards the state of Israel since its establishment in 1948 have, no doubt, had an influence upon Soviet policy towards the Jewish religion, but the extent and relationship of the two factors remain uncertain.[7] In November, 1948, the only remaining Jewish organization, the Jewish Anti-Fascist Committee, and the sole remaining Yiddish periodical *Ainikeit* (Unity), were closed, most of the leaders of Jewish cultural life (including most Yiddish writers) were arrested, and the publication of all Yiddish books ceased.

These developments came as a shock to Soviet Jews. Secular and religious Jews alike feared that the sudden liquidation of all Jewish cultural institutions and activities would usher in the liquidation of

5. In other joint religious undertakings, where Jewish representatives *were* included, such as the Zagorsk conference in May 1952, only two individual synagogues (those of Moscow and Kiev) were chosen to participate (Walter Kolarz, *Religion in the Soviet Union* [London, 1961], p. 35). The Jewish religious establishment seems to have been viewed by the authorities with a measure of indifference, probably because it could not be of much help to the government. Jewish religious leaders, sensing the indifference, were not as bold in their demands as leaders of other religious cults, or perhaps they concluded that their efforts were of no avail anyway.

6. Nikita Struve, in his book *Les Chrétiennes en l'URSS* (Paris, 1963), distinguishes three periods: (1) persecution—until 1941; (2) tolerance—from 1941 to 1948; (3) persecution again, dating from 1959. Yet the author adds that "Judaism under Soviet rule is a subject to itself." Similarly, Walter Kolarz maintains that Judaism was singled out by the regime for special treatment: "Stalin anticipated that religious Judaism would disappear much more quickly than other religions which had preserved their sociological roots, and he was determined to hasten this natural process as effectively as possible. It became clear that Stalin would not extend to the Jews the concessions he was prepared to grant to other religious communities" (*Religion in the Soviet Union*, p. 388).

7. The emergence of a Jewish state aroused the interest and pride of many Soviet Jews. The initial positive attitude of the Soviet government towards the state of Israel encouraged many of these Jews to express their feelings openly, particularly during the visit to the Moscow synagogue of the first Israeli envoy to the Soviet Union, Golda Meir (Ben Ami, *Bein Hapatish ve-hamagal* [Between the Hammer and the Sickle], [Tel Aviv, 1965], pp. 29–32; Kolarz, *Religion in the Soviet Union*, p. 388).

Soviet Jewry as a distinctive cultural, ethnic, and religious group.[8]

The climax of this renewed pressure against Jewish culture came on January 13, 1953, when the so-called "Doctor's Plot" was disclosed; nine physicians were arrested on the fantastic charge of organizing a plot to poison the leaders of the Soviet Union. They were accused of having been "connected with the international Jewish-nationalist organization [The Joint Distribution Committee of America, a philanthropic organization], established by American Intelligence."[9] As a result, anti-Semitism erupted into the open as never before.[10]

The "black years" of 1948–53 have had a profound effect upon Soviet Jews. No present action, or *inaction,* in either the secular or the religious sectors of Jewish life can be understood or explained without considering the traumatic experiences of this period. Perhaps paradoxically, the mass liquidation of Yiddish cultural institutions and of Yiddish writers in 1948–53[11] was *not* accompanied by a comparable liquidation of synagogues and of Jewish clergymen. Although several rabbis were arrested during these years, most of them were soon released, while those Yiddish writers who escaped the execution squads remained in prison.

The less stringent policy toward organized Jewish religion seems to have been dictated by the Soviet government's belief that stern measures were unnecessary, as Jewish religion was on the verge of extinction anyway. "Jewish nationalism" on the other hand, began to be viewed in the postwar era as a regenerated force that con-

---

8. An article by Ilya Ehrenburg in *Pravda,* 21 September 1948, contended that the Jews were not a people, and that Jews the world over had no common link, except persecution. Writers and intellectuals of Jewish descent soon came under attack as cosmopolitans without any attachment to a homeland. In August, 1952, twenty-four leading figures of Yiddish arts and letters were executed (B. Z. Goldberg, *Jewish Problem,* pp. 101–114).

9. *Pravda,* 13 January 1953.

10. S. Shwartz, *Evrei v sovetskom soiuze s nachala vtoroi mirovoi voiny (1939–1965)*[Jews in the Soviet Union since the beginning of the Second World War, 1939–1945] (New York, 1966), pp. 220 ff. Rumors spread that Jewish physicians and pharmacists were poisoning non-Jewish patients (an accusation reminiscent of the medieval charge that Jews poisoned Christian wells), and an impending mass deportation of the Jewish population was expected. Soviet Jews were now ostracized as "security risks" who were not to be trusted in sensitive positions, and although after Stalin's death the "Doctor's Plot" was declared to have been a fraud, the atmosphere has never been fully cleared. (See also, B. Z. Goldberg, *Jewish Problem,* pp. 101–7.)

11. S. Schwartz, *Evrei v sovetskom soiuze,* pp. 201 ff.; B. Z. Goldberg, *Jewish Problem,* pp. 101 ff.

stituted a potential and growing danger to the Communist ideology and to the Soviet regime.

The wartime Jewish Anti-Fascist Committee and the Jewish writers who gathered around it fell under the suspicion of fostering Jewish nationalism and thereby of subverting the Soviet order. This group included: S. A. Lozovsky, the former chief of the Profintern, the international organization of trade unions friendly to communism; S. Mikhoels, the actor and director of the Moscow Yiddish theatre, famous throughout the Soviet Union; and P. Markish, a poet whose long ode to Stalin in 1939 had filled a good part of one issue of *Pravda* and had earned him the order of Lenin. Next to these prominent cultural figures the religious leaders of the Jewish congregations in the Soviet Union appeared totally insignificant. The religious leaders, if men of such limited authority may be called leaders, were obscure men, scarcely known beyond the circle of the synagogue; some among them were so unworldly that they were completely ignorant of the Russian language. It is not surprising that they were incapable of exciting the suspicion of the Soviet authorities who were then generally susceptible to tales of Jewish faithlessness, subversion, and treason. Nor were these rabbis suited to play parts in some imaginary plot framed by the secret police, and to be displayed at a public trial. They were too removed from the mainstream of Soviet life to give even faint plausibility to the charge of subversion that might be brought against them. And so the anti-Semitic wave which was then sweeping over Russia, spreading terror and destroying nearly all the Jewish cultural establishments, practically bypassed the synagogues. They continued to function, protected by their weakness and insignificance.

In comparison to the regime's policy of total liquidation regarding Jewish secular culture, the attitude towards Jewish religion seemed almost benevolent. In fact, Jewish religion continued to remain under heavy pressure; the earlier ban in the fields of religious training, publishing, provisions of articles of cult, and the like—rights that were at that time granted to most other religious cults—remained in force.[12] Antireligious propaganda, which had largely been suspended

12. Concerning the privileges granted the Russian Orthodox church see A. A. Bogolepov, "The Legal Position of the Russian Orthodox Church in the Soviet Union," chapter 9 above. For the difficulties encountered by the Moslems see Bernhard Wilhelm, "Moslems in the Soviet Union, 1948–54," chapter 12 above.

at the outbreak of the war and relegated to the schools after 1945, was resumed on a large scale in the early fifties. The force of this activity was further intensified by an edict of the party in 1954.[13]

The Mid-Fifties to the Mid-Sixties

In 1957 the regime allowed the publication of a new prayer book in five thousand copies and permitted a *yeshiva* for the training of religious personnel to be established.[14] Some may have thought that a new tolerance was emerging, but it seems more likely that these concessions were to counter protests from abroad at the renewed antireligious campaign which began slowly in 1956 and accelerated rapidly after 1959. Large numbers of synagogues were closed in this new campaign.[15]

In the early 1960s Jewish antireligious propaganda became even more intensive. In addition to the well-known Marxist arguments against religion in general, the following distinctively Jewish points were emphasized: the Jewish religion propagates the idea of "a chosen people," which leads to hatred of other peoples; the Jewish religion propagates allegiance to another state, Israel, and to a reactionary, proimperialist and anti-Soviet movement, the Zionist movement; the Jewish religion is immoral, since money is its God; the Jewish religion is in its essentials the most pernicious of religions.

It is not surprising that two Jewish observances were attacked with particular vehemence: the rite of circumcision, allegedly symbolizing the concept of the "chosen people"; and the observance of Passover with its national overtones, for example, the phrase "next year in

---

13. *O krupnykh nedostatkakh v nauchno-ateisticheskoi propagande i merakh ee uluch-shenii* [On the great shortcomings in scientific-atheistic propaganda and measures for its improvement], Postanovlenie TSK KPSS [Ordinance of the Central Committee of the CP of the Soviet Union], 7 July 1954, in *O religii i tserkvi, sbornik dokumentov* [On religion and church, a collection of documents] (Moscow, 1965), pp. 71–77. The omission of any mention of the Jewish religion in this ordinance (in spite of the fact that synagogues still existed in the country) can hardly be explained away as an oversight. The policy of the regime at the time seems to have been to delete references to Jews whenever possible, in order to relegate the Soviet Jews to the status of a "nonpeople." An indication of this policy is evident, in both the *Soviet Encyclopedia* and in textbooks published in that period, by the omission, for the first time, of the Jewish group from the list of "Heroes of the Soviet Union." See also S. Golikov, *Vydaiushchiesia pobedy Sovetskoi armii v Velikoi Otechestvennoi Voine* [Outstanding victories of the Soviet Army in the Great Fatherland War] (Moscow, 1956).

14. Joseph B. Schechtman, *Star in Eclipse, Russian Jewry Revisited* (New York and London 1961), pp. 122–24, 127.

15. Ibid., pp. 140 ff.

Jerusalem" with which the Seder, the traditional Passover ceremony, ends. Information on the medical value of circumcision available in the West has not been discussed, even in Soviet medical journals. The baking of matzos, not prohibited even in Stalinist times, has been made very difficult and for the last two years has been virtually prohibited.[16]

Propaganda against the Jewish religion, conducted before the war almost exclusively in Yiddish, now appeared in the languages of other nationalities, particularly in Ukrainian and in Moldavian, although these are the "native tongues" of only a small number of Jews.[17]

The book, *Iudaizm bez prikras* [Judaism without embellishment] by Trofim Kichko, included many of the perennial crude clichés of anti-Semitism. It was published, however, under the auspices of the Soviet Academy of Sciences. Perhaps it was this endorsement which impelled several prominent Western Communists to protest its publication. Eventually the Ideological Commission of the Party, while not repudiating the book as a whole, did criticize several passages and caricatures that "might be interpreted as abusive." The book was apparently withdrawn from circulation.[18]

In the early sixties several of the remaining large synagogues were closed, following a discernible three-stage pattern. First, articles and letters were published in local newspapers charging that illegal activities and/or pro-Israeli propaganda were conducted in the synagogue. Second, there followed a barrage of letters by readers, including "believers," requesting the closing of the synagogue.

16. Ibid., pp. 128–31.
17. According to the census of 1959 only a tiny minority of the Jewish population has declared Ukrainian, Belorussian, or Moldavian as its native tongue—3 percent in the Ukraine, 2 percent in the Belorussian SSR, and 1 percent in the Moldavian SSR (*Itogi vsesoiuznoi perepisi naseleniia 1959 goda* [Results of the all-union census of 1959] [Moscow: Central Statistical Bureau, 1962], table 53, "Raspredelenie naseleniia po natsionalnosti i rodnomu iazyku" [Distribution of the population by nationality and native language]). The same information appears in Table 53 for each of the volumes for the individual republics. See footnote 24 below for dates of individual volumes. Propaganda conducted in other than Russian and Yiddish, therefore, clearly could not be destined for Jewish consumption. Characteristically, the few antireligious articles that have appeared in the Yiddish *Birobidzhaner Shtern* and *Sovetish Heimland* are devoid of the "specific" charges meted out to Jewish religion in the non-Yiddish media. (For examples see *Sovetish Heimland*, 1963, no. 1, pp. 88–92; 1963, no. 2, pp. 20, 22.)
18. The book was also belatedly criticized in *Radianska Kultura* [Soviet culture] (Kiev), 26 March 1964. There is an English translation of this article in *Jews in Eastern Europe* (London), July 1964.

Third, there was a decision by the local authorities, "in compliance with the request of the community," to dissolve the "religious society" and to close the house of prayer. The large synagogues of Lvov and Chernovtsy (Ukrainian SSR) were closed in this manner.[19]

Simultaneous with these events, the situation of Jews throughout the country was influenced by two campaigns concurrently conducted by the regime: the campaign against the state of Israel, in which Israel was depicted as a puppet of Anglo-American imperialism in the Near East; and the campaign against black marketeering that publicized and underscored the cases in which Jews were involved. It was inevitable that widespread anti-Jewish sentiment would be stirred up by the two campaigns.

But again, paradoxically, as the pressures against Jewish religion began to increase, the regime somewhat relaxed its ban on Jewish culture. Starting in 1957 small artistic ensembles were permitted to perform; the first Yiddish book, after an interval of eleven years, was published in 1959, and, in 1961 a literary bimonthly, *Sovetish Heimland*, began to appear.[20]

The Present Situation
JEWISH POPULATION

According to the census of January, 1959 (conducted at a time when pressures against the Jews were particularly heavy, and when publications in Yiddish were still prohibited), 2,268,000 persons declared themselves to be of Jewish nationality, making the Jews the eleventh largest national group in the country.[21] The author estimates that the actual number of Jews in the Soviet Union is closer to 3 million.[22] Of the 2,268,000 persons of Jewish nationality,

---

19. Ben Ami, *Bein Hepatish ve-hamagal*, pp. 48–52. See also *Radianska Bukovina* (Chernovtsy), 19 January 1962.

20. Baron, *Russian Jews*, pp. 342–43.

21. *Itogi vsesoiuznoi perepisi*, p. 184.

22. According to the previous census (1939), the Jewish population numbered 3,020,000 in that year (L. Zinger, *Dos Banaite Folk* [The renewed people] [Moscow, 1941], app. 2). After the territories of Poland, Rumania, Czechoslovakia, and the Baltic states had been incorporated into the Soviet Union, the Jewish population was estimated at close to five million (S. Schwartz, *Evrei v sovetskom soiuze*, p. 44). Of these, about two million were killed by the Nazis and after the war, between 150,000 and 200,000 left the Soviet territories (including former Polish citizens who were repatriated). Accordingly, the present number of Jews in the Soviet Union, allowing for a slight natural increase, is probably close to three million.

2,027,000 or close to 90 percent resided in the Russian Federal Republic and in the other European republics of the Soviet Union.[23] With the exception of a small number in the Caucasian area of the Russian Republic these are western "Ashkenazic" Jews, for whom the official national language is "Evreisky Iazik," that is, Yiddish. The remaining 241,000 Jews live in the three republics of the Caucasus and in the five republics of Central Asia. Approximately half of these 241,000 are "western" Jews and half are "oriental" Jews, members of ancient Jewish communities, some of which were established in this region before the Roman conquest of the land of Israel in A.D. 70.[24]

The census of 1959 recognizes as the language of the "Jewish nationality," besides Yiddish, the four other languages of the "Oriental" Jews. These are: Tat, the language of the "Mountain Jews" in the Caucasus; Tadzhik, or the Bukharan-Jewish language, of the "Bukharan Jews" of Central Asia; the Crimean-Tatar language of the Crimean Jews; and the Georgian language of the Georgian Jews. Georgian is the only language of a majority nation in a Soviet Republic recognized as a "Jewish national language."[25]

Approximately 487,000 persons, or over 21 percent of all Jews, have declared Yiddish or one of these four languages as their native tongue. Of these, 405,936, or 17.9 percent of all Jews and 18.8 percent of all "Western Jews" have declared Yiddish as their national language; 25,225 claim the Tat language, 20,763 the Bukharan-Jewish (Tadzhik) language, 35,673 the Georgian language, and 189 the Crimean-Tatar language as their native tongue.[26]

National literatures existed in all of these five languages. Publications in the Tat language were halted when publications in Yiddish

23. In this census, 875,000 persons registered as being of Jewish nationality in the Russian Federal Republic, 840,000 in the Ukraine, 150,000 in Belorussia, 95,000 in Moldavia and 67,000 in the three Baltic republics (*Itogi vsesoiuznoi perepisi*, p. 300).

24. Ibid. The total for the Jewish population in the eight republics was compiled from the data in the respective census volumes for these republics. The individual volumes were published in 1962 and 1963, as follows: the Belorussian SSR (1963); the Ukrainian SSR (1963); the Georgian SSR (1963); the Uzbek SSR (1962); the Kazakh SSR (1962); the Azerbaidzhan SSR (1963); the Kirghiz SSR (1963); the RSFSR (1963); the Tadzhik SSR (1963); the Turkmen SSR (1963); the Armenian SSR (1963); The Estonian SSR (1962); the Latvian SSR (1962); the Lithuanian SSR (1963); the Moldavian SSR (1962). The information cited here is in Table 53 of each of these volumes.

25. Ibid., pp. 134 ff. Census report for the Georgian SSR.

26. Almost all Crimean-Tatar-speaking Jews, or, as they are called, "Krimchaks"— five thousand in number—were killed by the invading German forces. A few "Krimchaks" managed to leave the Crimea before the occupation.

were suspended, and then were permitted to appear again when Yiddish publications recommenced in 1960. The parallelism in regard to diverse Jewish cultural groups suggests not only the existence of common guidelines in the regime's policy toward the Jewish minority, but also that these guidelines have been based primarily on ethnic, rather than cultural, linguistic, or religious considerations. A partial and somewhat puzzling exception is evident in the relative indulgence shown Georgian Jews.

The linguistic assimilation of the European Jews increases from west to east, in approximate proportion to the distance from the areas of former compact Jewish concentrations in the western part of the Soviet Union.[27] A comparison of the 1939 and 1959 censuses indicates that although linguistic assimilation has advanced markedly in the last twenty years (about 70 percent of the oriental Jews have declared one of the national languages as their native tongue),[28] relatively large "islands" of Yiddish-speaking people still exist in the "old areas" of the Soviet Union.

Birobidzhan, the so-called "Jewish autonomous region," is a clear misnomer, for its Jewish characteristics are only vestigial. The project is now an admitted failure. In 1959 the Jewish population of the region numbered 14,269 persons, or a mere 9 percent of the total population. The "Jewishness" of Birobidzhan is best illustrated by the fact that not one Jewish school exists in the region; the only Jewish institutions are a little synagogue located in a shack and a local Yiddish newspaper published three times a week in one thousand copies.[29]

The Karaites, a sect which accepts the law of Moses but rejects the

27. While Yiddish was declared as the native tongue of 8.5 percent of the Jews in Moscow and 8.7 percent of those in Leningrad, the percentage vacillates around 10 percent in the interior parts of the Russian and Ukrainian republics. The western areas show a much higher percentage: The Kiev oblast (district), 32 percent; Vinnitsa oblast, 38 percent; the Zakarpatsky and Chernovtsy oblasts, 49 percent and 50 percent respectively; the Latvian Republic, 48 percent; the Lithuanian Republic, 69 percent. (See the census volumes of the respective republics.)

28. It is impossible to ascertain the exact number, or percentage, of the respective groups, as all Jews, "oriental" and "western" alike, are included in the same "Jewish nationality" rubric. How many "oriental" and how many "western" Jews have declared Russian as their native language is not indicated in the census, and the exact magnitude of the linguistic assimilation process in each group cannot be determined.

29. Baron, *Russian Jews*, p. 343, Ben Ami, *Bein Hapatish ve-hamagal*, pp. 182-94. From 1948 until the publication of *Sovetish Heimland* in 1961 the regional newspaper *Birobidzhaner shtern* was the only existing Jewish periodical in the Soviet Union.

Talmud, and according to the 1959 census numbers six thousand, are not considered by the census as a Jewish group.[30]

JEWISH RELIGIOUS LIFE

Jewish religious life in the Soviet Union manifests itself in two ways: in services and observances in synagogues and prayer houses, and in rites and observances not necessarily connected with a synagogue.

Soviet law recognizes two types of religious associations: "religious societies" administered by *dvadtsatka*'s (groups of twenty) and "groups of believers," formed when believers in a given area are not numerous enough to organize a "religious society."[31]

Jewish prayer houses belonging to the first category are commonly called "synagogues"; prayer houses of the second category are called "legal *minianim*." But there is a third category: unregistered prayer groups, that may in turn be divided into several kinds: groups that meet regularly; groups that are formed during the High Holidays and dissolve at the close of the holiday season; and small groups that are organized temporarily in private quarters, primarily with the purpose of enabling a mourner to say the "Kaddish" prayer. All of these latter groups are considered illegal, although Soviet law provides for

---

30. *Itogi vsesoiuznoi perepisi*, Table 53. It is interesting to note that although Soviet authorities admittedly do not recognize and are not interested in the religious beliefs of individuals, members of the Subbotnik sect were sent by the authorities to settle in new Jewish agricultural settlements, although culturally and linguistically these Russian peasants had nothing in common with the Yiddish-speaking Jewish settlers. Indeed, the only link between them was a similarity in religion. (See Goldberg, *Jewish Problem*, pp. 36-40.)

31. The "Law on Religious Associations" of 1929 and the administrative "Instruction" to the law were published in *Sobranie uzakoneny i razporazheny rabotche-krestianskogo pravitelstva RSFSR*, no. 35 (1929), text no. 353; amendments in ibid., no. 8 (1932), text no. 41, II, 6. Texts also in N. Orleansky, *Zakon o religioznikh obedineniiakh* (Moscow, 1930). For an English translation of the text see the Appendix, sec. 2B, C below. Paragraph 22 of the Instruction of the People's Commissariat of the Interior of 1929 allows "the holding of prayer meetings in premises which are not especially adapted" for religious purposes and states: "*believers who have not formed a religious society or a group of believers* must notify authorities regarding each such prayer meeting separately." (Italics added). For a fuller discussion of the relevant laws see Rothenberg, "The Legal Status of Religion in the Soviet Union," chapter 5 above.

A vivid description of Yom Kippur services held without the permission of the authorities may be found in the account of an anonymous Soviet Jew smuggled out of the country and published in the form of a book, *El Akhai Be'mdinat Israel* [To my brethren in Israel] (Jerusalem, 1957), pp. 122–26; the services were held in quarters rented from a sympathetic non-Jew. The local police interrupted the services, wrote down the names of those present, and impounded all prayer books. Yom Kippur services held in spite of an explicit denial of permission are also related in the book by Mikhael Shashar, *Israeli B'Moskva* [An Israeli in Moscow] (Jerusalem, 1961), pp. 117–24.

the legal existence of small, ad hoc organized religious groups that hold services.

Information about these illegal groups is, of course, scarce. Not much more information is available about the "groups of believers." The existing law states that when a "religious society" is short of twenty members it may be converted into a "group of believers." Yet one of the methods frequently utilized by the Soviet authorities to close a synagogue (or "religious society") is to take advantage of every situation where the number of "religious activists" falls below twenty—or in some cases, even to create such a situation. Legally and technically, the *dvadtsatka* could then be converted into a "group of believers" whose house of prayer could continue to exist, either in the same place or in privately rented quarters. As far as we know, such a case has never occurred in regard to a Jewish "religious society." Indeed, this kind of transformation has been extremely rare for any of the denominations.

Information about synagogues or legal Jewish "religious societies" has been more readily available. Statistics on the number of functioning synagogues, however, as stated from time to time by the Soviet authorities, are contradictory and usually seem inflated. According to the best available information, sixty-two officially recognized synagogues were functioning in 1965 in the Soviet Union. The geographical distribution of the sixty-two is very revealing. Thirteen of them are located in Georgia. Thus 20 percent of all synagogues in the country are located in a Jewish community that constitutes not more than 2.5 percent of the Jewish population of the USSR. An additional seventeen synagogues are located in the Azerbaidzhan SSR, in the Caucasian area of the RSFSR, and in four Central Asian republics. (There is no synagogue in the Turkmen SSR.) Thus, roughly one-half of all the recognized Jewish congregations (thirty) are located in an area inhabited by less than 10 percent of all Soviet Jews, in the non-European part of the country.[32]

The large number of synagogues—and the greater measure of religious liberty—granted to "oriental Jews," is probably due to two principal factors: the greater tolerance of religious observances in

32. See Joshua Rothenberg, *Synagogues in the Soviet Union* (Waltham, Mass.: Brandeis University, 1966). There are nineteen synagogues in the Russian Federal Republic (including the Caucasian areas and Siberia), eight in the Ukrainian SSR, only one synagogue in all of Belorussia, five in the Baltic republics, and one in the Moldavian SSR.

the non-European areas, which are considered to be more backward and therefore deserving of a more patient attitude; the weaker consciousness of national identity as distinguished from religious identity among "oriental Jews,"[33] and the apparent recognition by the Soviet government that the "oriental" Jewish communities constitute a lesser *nationalistic* danger. (This emphasizes that Jewish religion in the Soviet Union is being fought not only as a religion but also, or perhaps even more, as a nurturing element of Jewish nationalism.)[34] In non-Moslem Georgia a factor contributing to the milder treatment is the attitude of the Georgians toward the Jewish minority, whom they consider to be a part of the native population, perhaps because the Jews claim Georgian as their national language.

Soviet Jewish religious life does not have a central organization or representative body, as do many other religious cults (and as Judaism has in the countries of the "socialist bloc"). Each synagogue is a separate unit ruled by its own board or *dvadtsatka*, and its executive body of three. The large Moscow synagogue, by virtue of its location in the capital, assumes, on occasion, the de facto status of representing the Jewish religious community in the Soviet Union.

With the exception of the small edition of a prayerbook in 1957, as noted above, and of crudely made Jewish calendars published occasionally by synagogues, no religious literature, pamphlet, or bulletin has been published since 1928. Promises of permission to publish a new edition of a prayerbook have yet to be kept. Formal religious education of children is not tolerated except, to some degree, in the "oriental" communities. The only Jewish religious educational institution for adults was the *yeshiva* established at the Moscow synagogue in 1957. Since 1965, this *yeshiva* has existed in name only.[35]

Religious observances and attendance of synagogue prayers follow, in the main, old, established patterns. Synagogue attendance, as in

33. This is clear from the language assimilation pattern considered earlier in this paper.

34. There are many indications that the fight against Jewish religion is primarily dictated by considerations of its "Jewish-nationalistic danger." An example is the conversation held by Joseph Schechtman with an "old Bolshevik" in the editorial offices of *Pravda*. He was told: "Synagogues are in themselves of no consequence. But they serve as the last assembly for our Jews, often for those who are no longer religious. They help to maintain cohesion, to nurture the feeling of belonging to a distinctive Jewish entity. And this is exactly what we are trying to prevent" (Schechtman, *Star in Eclipse*, p. 146).

35. Among the manifold difficulties encountered by the *yeshiva*, the most notable was the refusal of authorities to grant permission to out-of-town students to take up residence in Moscow. See the most recent eyewitness report in Elie Wiesel, *Jews of Silence* (New York, 1967).

other countries, is much larger on the days when the *Yizkor*, the prayer for the dead, is said. Reportedly, many persons, including nonbelievers, attend these services with the sole purpose of remembering their departed relatives, which they prefer to do in the traditional Jewish manner. Some practices, however, are peculiar to the Soviet Union, for example, the manner of celebrating Simkhat-Torah. It has become customary for thousands of people, particularly young people, to assemble in the larger cities near the synagogue to sing Jewish songs, dance, and mix with the worshippers. This type of celebration, and the presence of many young people who declare that they are not religious, indicate that such assemblies compensate for the void created by depriving Soviet Jews of other avenues of expression of their Jewish identity.[36]

Synagogue attendance is highest on the holidays of Simkhat Torah, Yom Kippur, and Rosh Hashanah, when as a rule prayer houses cannot accommodate all the worshippers, and the crowds often overflow into adjacent streets. These holidays are an occasion for Soviet Jews, nonreligious ones among them, to identify with the Jewish people. Also, on the High Holidays many religious Jews, otherwise meek and law-abiding citizens, boldly take their chances in defying Soviet law and assemble "illegally" for community prayer, wherever permission for holding religious services is not accorded them.

The exact number of practicing rabbis is not known but it is believed to be between thirty-five and forty. In at least half of the existing synagogues the religious functions are fulfilled by various lay members of the congregations. The average age of the rabbis and of other practicing clergymen is over seventy. The present possibilities for the training of rabbis and other religious personnel will not permit the replacement of losses from even the presently small number of Jewish clergymen. Several of the larger synagogues employ permanent cantors and have a choir.[37]

A small number of Jewish communities in the European part of the country, and most religious communities in the "oriental" areas, have slaughterers of kosher meat (*shokhtim*). Kosher slaughtering of

36. In 1966, for the first time, large numbers of young people also attended the Passover services held in the Moscow synagogue (*The Day-Morning Journal* [New York], 26 April 1967).

37. Cantors command relatively high salaries. Some larger synagogues employ very talented professional singers as cantors.

cattle is, as a rule, impossible. Kosher slaughtering of fowl exists in the few places where ritual slaughterers are available.

Certain Jewish holidays assume their special significance by celebration at home. Foremost among them is Passover. Judging from reports by visitors, and by the vehemence with which the holiday and the use of matzos on the holiday is attacked in the Soviet press, the observance of Passover is still fairly widespread among Soviet Jews, although often in a rudimentary form and under various disguises. The baking of matzos (or receiving them from abroad) has been made progressively difficult, and it was practically banned in 1962 (except, again, in the oriental Jewish communities).

The holiday of Chanukah, the Festival of Lights, is rarely celebrated by Soviet Jews. Also, the holiday of Purim, which has the least religious connotation of all Jewish holidays, and which, in the countries of the Jewish diaspora, had assumed the character of a joyful folk celebration, has almost been forgotten in the Soviet Union. Surprisingly, Simkhat Torah, connected with the Torah, and not the irreverent folk feast Purim, has become the gay holiday of Jewish young people in the Soviet Union.[38]

Objects of Jewish ritual, like prayer shawls (*taleisim*), or phylacteries (*tfilin*) are not permitted to be manufactured or imported. The black market in Jewish religious articles which exists in the Soviet Union is a frequent object of attacks in the Soviet press and is a clear admission by the Soviet authorities of both the need for, and the failure to provide, Jewish religious objects.

Although circumcision is not prohibited by law, and is practiced by the majority of Moslems, when performed by "western Jews" this practice comes under heavy fire and harassment. The circumciser is always in danger of punishment. He tries to be as inconspicuous as possible, and only a few perform their services openly.

Jewish religious leaders, to date, have not traveled abroad,[39] and contact with rabbis and religious institutions in other countries is

38. Urbanization is not conducive, either in the Soviet Union or in other countries, to the celebration of holidays requiring the outdoor display of religious symbols (for example, the holiday of Sukkot or Tabernacles, requiring the building of huts). In the Soviet Union "sukkot" (huts) can only be found near synagogues.

39. In June, 1968, Rabbi Yehuda Leib Levin of the Moscow Choral Synagogue and Cantor David Stisken of the Leningrad synagogue made a visit to the Jewish community on the eastern seaboard of the United States. In October, 1969, Rabbi Levin and the chairman of the Moscow Choral Synagogue *dvadtsatka* visited the Jewish Community in Hungary.

limited to the exchange of New Year greetings with the chief rabbi of Israel. No Jewish religious student has to date been sent abroad for study.[40]

JEWISH CULTURE

A slight relaxation was observable in the years 1965–66 in the field of Jewish culture and literature. The literary bimonthly *Sovietish Heimland* was converted into a monthly and increased in size (to 160 pages), and has acquired a literary quality of a high order. In the first five years since the publication of books in Yiddish was again allowed, however, less than ten books were actually published. In 1965 and in the first months of 1966 six Yiddish books appeared, among them, for the first time, books by *living* authors who wrote in Yiddish but whose works had previously only appeared in translation into other languages. Stage appearances in Yiddish are slightly more frequent; a noticeable change in attitude towards the Hebrew language, previously considered to be of an inherently reactionary character, can be detected.[41] Several Yiddish art and state groups are known to exist. Three books in the Tat language are known to have been published since 1960, but no books have been published since World War II in the Jewish-Bukharan or Crimean-Tatar languages. Finally, not one Yiddish or Hebrew school presently exists in the Soviet Union, and no Yiddish or Hebrew textbooks and alphabets are being printed or are available.

Conclusions

1. An effort has indeed been made by the Soviet regime, especially since 1948, to dissolve the Jewish group as a separate entity, both in the religious and national sense. The government sought to achieve this goal by liquidating all Jewish cultural institutions, by closing all

40. By 1967, as far as is known in the West, the following religious groups in the Soviet Union were permitted to send students for theological training abroad: Russian Orthodox (two), Armenian Church (one), Baptists (six), Moslems (at least three), Lutherans (two). On March 24, 1969, *The New York Times* reported that a Jewish student from Georgia would soon be permitted to go to Hungary to study for the rabbinate. As of December, 1969, no further developments on this visit have been reported.

41. A Hebrew song was allowed to be included in the repertoire of a Yiddish singer. Certain translations of works by Hebrew Communist writers in Israel were published, as well as translations of medieval Hebrew poets in the Yiddish *Sovetish Heimland*. Also, announcements of the availability of Hebrew dictionaries in the Leningrad Public Library and of an exhibit, "How to Study Hebrew Privately," were printed in the 1966 issues of *Sovetish Heimland*.

avenues of national expression, and by speeding up the withering away of the remaining religious institutions. It is difficult to say whether the slight improvement in the recent situation of Jewish culture, still far short of restoring the state of affairs before 1941, is the result of pressures from abroad, or whether it has been caused in some measure by the reverse effects of the suppressive policy that has made the synagogue the only focal point of Jewish identity, and thus has inadvertently contributed to the synagogue's gain in prestige.

2. A slight change has been observed since 1965 in the tone of antireligious propaganda, which has become somewhat less offensive; recent closings of synagogues have not been executed with the customary fanfare, as had been the practice in previous years.

3. Discrimination against Jews in certain occupations, although difficult to specify and to measure, does exist. The proportion of Jews in responsible positions among the leading cadres of the government and the party, in the diplomatic service and in the armed forces has drastically changed from that which prevailed before 1948. Such a drastic change could not have been accomplished without substantial discrimination. National quotas, working against Jews, whether religious or nonreligious, exist in the more desirable fields of education and in the more attractive institutions of higher learning.

4. Although the Soviet government has consistently denied the existence of a "Jewish question" in the Soviet Union, both in the religious and the secular meaning of the phrase, Communist parties abroad and liberal elements of Soviet society acknowledge the problem, as witnessed by various pronouncements of both foreign Communists and literary figures in the Soviet Union. Attempting to achieve two goals simultaneously (the disintegration of the Jewish group and its assimilation into the majority nations, and the reduction of the proportion of Jews in important fields of endeavor), the Soviet leadership has created a situation full of inner contradictions which to some extent has been self-defeating. Instead of a decrease of Jewish consciousness there has been the opposite; even among the young Jewish generation there has been an increase in pro-Israel sentiments, and an activation of nationalist manifestations sublimated into religious symbols.

5. The fact that the Jewish group constitutes both an officially recog-

nized nationality in the multinational Soviet Union, and also a legal religious faith, and that membership in both groups is not clearly definable, creates a situation whereby the government's policy concerning either aspect affects the other. This is compounded by the fact that national and religious elements and customs cannot always be clearly distinguished in a culture where for many centuries they were inseparable.

6. The theoretical foundation of Jewish national status in the Soviet Union has always been hazy and full of inconsistencies, and this includes the pronouncements of Lenin and Stalin on the subject. Jewish nationality has been given only an uncertain de facto and not a de jure recognition. As a result, Jewish religion was bound to assume an increased Jewish-national significance. The Soviet leadership grapples constantly with this problem but does not seem to be able to solve it. At present the principal demands on the Soviet government of the Jewish people the world over, as well as of many non-Jews, are to grant to the Jewish religion in the Soviet Union at least all of the rights that other recognized religions have, to grant to the Jewish nationality the rights that other nationalities enjoy, and to accord the Jewish population at large full equality in all areas of life. Clearly, the ultimate fate of the religious and national heritage of Soviet Jewry is uncertain. The curious and unexpected coalescence of its religious and national currents in recent years, however, does give reason for a measured optimism that would not have been warranted a decade ago.

17

CATHOLICS IN THE SOVIET UNION

Before attempting to describe the situation of the Catholics in the Soviet Union, it will be useful to recall three points which help to explain some peculiarities of their situation.

1. Catholics have always been much more numerous in the south-western districts of the Soviet Union than in the rest of the country.[1] Inasmuch as the western borders of the Soviet Union have changed several times since 1917, distinctions will have to be introduced appropriate to these different periods.

2. When compared with certain religious groups, the needs of the Catholics in the matter of freedom of worship may seem rather high. Some tenets of the Roman Catholic faith involve consequences of a peculiar kind which may not exist for members of other religious persuasions. Catholics believe that God entered into human history for the illumination and salvation of the human race and that he remains present in the world in a visible society which they call the church. That church exists transcending many human contingencies, such as political borders, and lives in union with the bishop of Rome who, they firmly believe, has received from God the special mission of maintaining the unity and the independence of the church and

---

1. Walter Kolarz, *Religion in the Soviet Union* (London: St. Martin's Press, 1961), pp. 179–81. Also Stanley Evans, *The Churches in the USSR* (London: Cobbett Publishing Co., 1943), p. 32.

Paul Mailleux, S. J.

the purity of the faith. Therefore, any human power which would not allow them to maintain free relations with the bishop of Rome would prevent them from acting according to their conscience.

3. The Catholics living within the present boundaries of Soviet Russia belong to different ethnic groups. They also follow various traditions which find expression in their entire style of life, in their liturgy, their discipline, and to some extent in their theological systems. These different styles of life are what are called the "rites" of the Roman Catholic church. Each rite will be considered separately. One Soviet republic has a population which is in the great majority Catholic: the Lithuanian SSR. That republic is the object of a special study in this volume.[2] We shall consider in two separate sections Catholics of the Roman rite and Catholics of the various Eastern rites.

The Catholics of the Roman Rite

Here again, a distinction must be made between two periods: 1917–45 and 1945 to the present.

1917–45

With few exceptions, the Catholics of the Roman rite who lived in the former Russian Empire before 1917, that is, excluding the Kingdom of Poland, were of foreign origin. In the latter part of the nineteenth century, before the Edict of Toleration, published on April 17, 1905, no Russian was permitted to join the Catholic church because proselytizing was considered to be the monopoly of the established Orthodox church. Catholicism was tolerated, however, and after 1905, during the years immediately before the Revolution, Catholics enjoyed liberty of worship and could engage in corporate social activities.[3] There was a Catholic Ecclesiastical Academy in St. Petersburg, there were diocesan seminaries, and, in the Catholic schools, children could receive religious instruction. Some monastic or religious congregations were tolerated, and with some restrictions the Catholic church could own property. The imperial government maintained a permanent Legation to the Holy See in Rome.[4]

---

2. V. Stanley Vardys, "Catholicism in Lithuania," chapter 18 below.

3. Evans, *Churches in USSR*, pp. 27, 33.

4. Cf. Nicholas Bock, S.J., *Rossiia i Vatikan nakanune revoliutsii: vospominaniia diplomata* [Russia and the Vatican on the eve of the revolution: Reminiscences of a diplomat] (New York: Russian Center, Fordham University, 1962).

Unfortunately, all correspondence about religious matters with the See of Rome still had to pass through the censorship of the Ministry of the Interior and no document coming from Rome could be published without the permission of the emperor. It was only in 1917 that the provisional government began to remove these restrictions.

On October 26, 1917, the day following the October Revolution, the Bolsheviks published a decree abolishing private ownership of landed estates by churches or monasteries and transferring their provisional administration to district soviets of peasants. Together with the other churches the Catholic church lost all its properties, which were nationalized without compensation.

A decree signed by Lenin and Lunacharsky (published in *Pravda* on December 22, 1917) gave the most radical interpretation to the decree for the separation of school and church.[5] The Catholic Ecclesiastical Academy with its unique library founded in the sixteenth century, the diocesan seminaries, and all parochial schools were closed, and their property was confiscated. The teaching of religion in public schools was suppressed.

The instruction on separation of church and state promulgated on August 30, 1918, deprived all religious organizations of their status as legal entities.[6] To obtain the use of church buildings a request had to be signed by at least twenty parishioners. The buildings remained the property of the people, represented by the government.

Catholics in Petrograd and other cities had started to create these committees, when, on April 19, 1919, Archbishop Ropp, head of the Catholic church in Russia, was arrested. He was eventually sent to Poland in exchange for the Communist Karl Radek.

The successor of Archbishop Ropp, Archbishop Cieplak, issued a circular letter on September 12, 1919, in which he expressed his views about the alienation of church properties.[7] He declared that they had been given by donors for the service of the church and that several of them had been consecrated for worship. Therefore, it would be unlawful and, in some cases, sacreligious to hand these properties over without the explicit agreement of the church author-

5. See Appendix, sec. 2A, below. For a somewhat different interpretation see Andrew Blane, "Protestant Sectarians in the First Year of Soviet Rule," chapter 14 above.

6. See Appendix, sec. 2A, below.

7. Joseph Ledit, S.J., *Archbishop John Baptist Cieplak* (Montreal: Palm Publishers, 1963), pp. 60ff. See also Paul B. Anderson, *People, Church, and State in Modern Russia* (New York: Macmillan Co., 1944), p. 58.

ities. Patriarch Tikhon of the Orthodox church made a similar declaration, and Orthodox and Catholics together protested to the government against the seizure of church property. In Petrograd clerical conferences studied the teaching of the Communists and finally declared that no Catholic could in good conscience become affiliated with the Communist party.

The situation of the Roman Catholics soon became even more precarious due to the fact that the great majority of them were of Polish origin. Many were descendants of Catholics who had been deported to the different parts of European and Asiatic Russia after the two uprisings which took place in Poland in 1830 and 1863. In the western provinces of the Soviet Union many of them lived mixed with a White Russian and Jewish population. Against this background these Catholics did not hide their pro-Polish feeling. Many therefore suffered when the Russian armies plundered their homes, first after the military retreat before the Germans and even more during the Soviet-Polish war, which lasted from the spring of 1919 until the Treaty of Riga was signed on March 18, 1921.

On February 26, 1919, a protest against the government's anti-religious policy was signed simultaneously by the Orthodox metropolitan of Petrograd, Benjamin, by Archbishop Ropp, head of the Latin rite Catholics, and by Exarch Leonid Feodorov, head of the Byzantine rite Catholics, and was sent to Moscow. This is the period when, through diplomatic action at the Conference of Genoa, the Vatican was trying to obtain guarantees of: (1) full liberty of conscience for all Russian citizens or foreigners in Russia; (2) respect for the public and private exercise of religion; and (3) the return of and respect for property belonging to any and all religions. These efforts failed.

In 1921 further suffering came from the severe famine. Along with the American Relief Administration, Pope Benedict XV organized a relief expedition. These two agencies saved the lives of thousands of Russian citizens stricken by famine, both Catholic and non-Catholic alike. When in connection with the famine the Soviets began the seizure of the sacred vessels in the Catholic churches,[8] the Pope, on May 14, 1922, sent a telegram to Chicherin expressing his willingness "to buy these sacred vessels . . . the price agreed on will be immediate-

8. See Joan Delaney, "The Origins of Soviet Anti-Religious Organizations," chapter 6 above.

ly paid to any . . . whom the government may nominate." Meanwhile the Catholic clergy refused to hand them over. On December 5, 1922, all the Catholic churches in Petrograd were closed and sealed. On the night of March 2–3, 1923, Archbishop Cieplak, fourteen Catholic priests, and one Catholic layman were ordered to go to Moscow to appear before the Revolutionary High Court. The famous Moscow trial of March, 1923, took place.[9] Archbishop Cieplak and Father Constantine Budkiewicz were condemned to death; the other priests were given sentences ranging from three to ten years' imprisonment. Only Father Budkiewicz was executed. Archbishop Cieplak and the other priests were later exchanged for Communists arrested in Poland.

Very soon the remaining Catholic bishops were arrested. Bishop Zygmunt Lozynski of Minsk was arrested and exiled in 1922. Bishop Ignatius Dubowski of Zhitomir was arrested in June, 1923, and exiled in 1925. Bishop Peter Mankowski of Kamieniec was exiled in 1923. This was also the fate of Msgr. Adrian Smets, administrator of the diocese of Tiraspol, and of the Siberian church leaders, Bishop Charles Sliwowski of Vladivostok and the vicar apostolic of Siberia.

On March 19, 1926, when there was no Catholic bishop left in the USSR, the apostolic delegate to Berlin, Archbishop Eugenio Pacelli, consecrated a French Jesuit, Father Michael d'Herbigny.[10] He was sent to Russia three times by the Holy See to try to reestablish the hierarchy in that country. On his second visit he secretly consecrated three bishops in Moscow: a French Assumptionist, Bishop Eugene Neveu, for Moscow; Bishop Alexander Frizon for Odessa; Bishop Boleslav Sloskans for Mogilev and Minsk. Bishop Sloskans was soon arrested, sent first to Siberia, then to Solovki, and finally was exiled in 1933. (He is now living in Rome.) Bishop Frizon was arrested four times and finally shot in August, 1937. Bishop Neveu, however, enjoyed relative immunity because of his French citizenship. In 1936, he went to Paris for medical treatment. Although he had received the promise of a reentry visa, he waited years without receiving it. The visa was granted a few hours after his death in Paris in 1946.[11]

9. Francis McCullagh, *The Bolshevik Persecution of Christianity* (New York: E. P. Dutton and Co.), pp. 99–281.

10. Cyrille Korolevskij, *Metropolite André Szeptyckyj: 1865–1944* (Rome: Societas Scientifica Ucrainorum, 1964), pp. 208–11.

11. Albert Galter, *The Red Book of the Persecuted Church* (Westminster, Md.: Newman Press, 1957), p. 45.

In the Russian Catholic dioceses, statistics were generally published with the liturgical calendars printed every year. It is, therefore, not too difficult to give an estimate of the number of Catholics of the Latin rite who were in the country in 1918. There were at that time about 1,600,000 Catholics, with 896 priests, 614 churches and 581 secondary chapels. No one knows how many were still in the country twenty years later, on the eve of World War II. Of the 1,195 churches and chapels, all had been closed except the Church of St. Louis des Français in Moscow and that of Notre Dame de France in Leningrad. And even these two churches have been closed at various periods.

In 1933, as a result of the Litvinov-Roosevelt agreement, an American priest, the Reverend Leopold Braun, was able to go to Moscow as Catholic chaplain of the foreign colony. He lived for several years with Bishop Neveu and celebrated services with him at St. Louis des Français. When Bishop Neveu went to Paris in 1936 Father Braun remained alone in Moscow. He was there throughout the war, during which period he was permitted to minister to Soviet citizens.

A French Dominican, Father John Baptist Amoudru, who had been able to remain in Leningrad, was secretly consecrated a bishop in 1935, probably by Bishop Neveu, but he was soon expelled from the country.

Besides the priests of Moscow and Leningrad, there were certainly a few Catholic priests working in the underground. But there were very few; nearly all of the 896 priests who were still in the Soviet Union in 1923 had been sent to concentration camps, had been exiled, or had died.

During the wartime Rumanian occupation of Odessa, the Catholic parish there was reorganized with two priests who had come from Italy, Father Jean Nicolas, a French Assumptionist, and Father Peter Leoni, an Italian Jesuit. Both remained in Odessa when the Soviets reconquered the city. One year later they were arrested, sent to Vorkuta, and a few years later expelled from the Soviet Union.

After 1945

After the Second World War, new territories with a large number of Catholics found themselves within the expanded borders of the Soviet Union: Lithuania, Estonia, Latvia, Belorussia, the Western

Ukraine, Carpatho-Russia and Bessarabia. The Western Ukraine and Carpatho-Russia will be taken up when the fate of the Catholics of the Byzantine rite is dealt with.

The Catholics in Latvia represent only a minority, about one-fourth of the population or 476,000 people. While the country was independent, from 1918 to June, 1940, Catholics enjoyed complete freedom, as did the Orthodox and the Lutheran majority. After the Soviets entered the country, they immediately nationalized all church property. Heavy taxes were imposed upon the churches. Monasteries, religious houses, and all Catholic schools were closed and confiscated by the state. Atheism was introduced in all schools as a compulsory subject. Many priests were arrested; some were tortured. During the Nazi occupation, from July, 1941, to October, 1944, the nationalization of property remained in force and Catholic publications continued to be forbidden.

The Red Army seized Riga a second time on October 13, 1944. At the time, the Catholic bishop of Riga was Archbishop Antony Springovics. Earlier, Bishop Anthony Urbs of Liepaja, Bishop Joseph Rancans, auxiliary of Riga, and Bishop Boleslav Sloskans, spiritual director of the seminary of Riga, had been deported to Germany by the Nazis. Archbishop Springovics was expelled from his residence, and forced to take refuge in a convent in Aglona. In 1947, Father Kazimiris Dulbinskis was consecrated auxiliary to Archbishop Springovics. He was twice arrested, and then deported to Siberia. After his release from exile, Bishop Dulbinskis was obliged to work in a kholkoz bakery in Belorussia. Recently he returned to Latvia. He now lives in the rectory of a country church but is not allowed to celebrate church services in public. In 1947, Archbishop Springovics (who died in 1961) consecrated a second bishop, Peter Strods, who succeeded him as archbishop of Riga. The chancellor of the diocese of Liepaja, Father Julian Vaivods, was allowed to attend the third session of the Second Vatican Council. In November 1964, while in Rome, he was consecrated a bishop. The Soviet government presumably granted permission for his consecration, although nothing was officially said about this. After the third session, Bishop Vaivods returned to the USSR and was later allowed to go to Rome for the fourth session with another Latvian priest, Father John Userovskis.

At present most of the Catholic churches of Latvia are open and the faithful attend services regularly. In Riga a seminary trains a small number of men for the priesthood with an average of two or three new priests ordained every year. Communication with the Vatican has again become possible. Nevertheless, the church still suffers from many restrictions, mostly in the field of publications. From the beginning of Soviet occupation until 1967, no periodicals, books, or pamphlets were printed by the Catholics in Latvia. In 1967 a small missal and prayerbook was published. When Archbishop Anthony Springovics died, no public announcement of his death was permitted. No books containing any information of a religious nature—even liturgical calendars—can be received from abroad. As everywhere else in the Soviet Union, atheistic propaganda is intense, especially among the younger people. Heavy moral pressure is used to try to discourage the few young men who want to study in the seminary.

In Estonia the number of Catholics was always very small. In 1940 there were six Catholic parishes in that country and fourteen Catholic clergymen. Not one of these priests is still there and their head, Bishop Profittlich, has been missing since 1941. Two of the six churches are open at present; they are ministered to by two priests sent by Bishop Vaivods of Latvia.

In the former Polish territories annexed in 1939 to the Belorussian republic, there were over two hundred Catholic churches of the Roman rite and 246 priests. About sixty-five priests are presently ministering in that region with about the same number of churches open. So far, the desires of the Catholics of that region to have their own bishop and to send candidates for the priesthood either to Lithuania or Latvia for their studies have not been fulfilled.

In the former territory of Carpatho-Russia, south of the Carpathian Mountains, there are at present about eighty thousand Catholics of the Roman rite, with twenty-six churches open for worship and twenty-two priests ministering in them. Besides the churches in Estonia, Latvia, Lithuania, Belorussia and Transcarpathia, we know of eight Catholic churches open in other parts of the Soviet Union, one each in Moscow, Leningrad, Tbilisi, Odessa, Kishinev, and two in Lvov. There is also a Catholic chapel in a suburb of Kiev but it has no resident priest.

Father Michael Tarvidis, the priest of the church in Moscow, was urged by the Soviet authorities to accept an invitation of Pope Paul VI to come to Rome to attend the end of the Second Vatican Council. Since 1950, the American Catholic priest residing in Moscow has not been allowed to minister to Soviet citizens; he celebrates services in a small private chapel in an apartment rented by the French Embassy.[12]

There are certainly thousands of Catholics spread all over the European USSR and Siberia but, besides those mentioned above, no priest is officially allowed to minister to them. A priest who spent some time in Krasnoiarsk, Siberia, estimates that there are from five to seven thousand Catholics in that region; although they remain faithful to the church they have no priests to preside at their prayers. On October 19, 1958, the paper *Sovetskaia Rossia* denounced with indignation a sixty-year-old Lithuanian Jesuit, Father Jonas Paukstis, who had been deported to Siberia and was ministering to Catholics in four different places in the region of Iakutsk.[13] He was arrested once more after this denunciation and died soon afterwards. Father Paukstis was only one of the many Catholic priests unrecognized by the government who have tried to help believers by working in the underground in the concentration camps where, during Stalin's reign, they all spent a number of years of their lives.[14]

Since 1917 Catholics in the Soviet Union have only a small prayerbook, published in Latvia, and the first part of a new ritual, published in Lithuania in 1966, designed to familiarize the faithful with the liturgical reforms introduced by the Second Vatican Council. This new volume is nicely printed with the texts of some prayers given in Latin, Lithuanian, Latvian and Polish. It remains to be seen whether this recent publication means that the Soviet administration has agreed to be less intolerant toward Catholics. From the point of view of publications the Catholics have been in a worse position than the members of the other faiths (excepting the Jewish community).[15]

The Catholics of the Eastern Rites

Besides the believers who follow the Roman rite (mostly Lithuanians, some Latvians, and some people of Polish and German extraction)

12. Since the Litvinov-Roosevelt Agreement of 1933, the chaplain to the diplomatic community has held the office of Apostolic Administrator of the USSR.

13. *Sovetskaia Rossiia* [Soviet Russia], 19 October 1958.

14. Some of them have been able to publish a description of their activity. For example, Walter J. Ciszek, S.J., *With God in Russia* (New York: McGraw-Hill, 1964).

15. For further information on the situation of the Jewish community in the Soviet Union, see *Jews in Eastern Europe*, a periodical published by European Jewish Publications, London. See also Joshua Rothenberg, "The Jewish Religion in the Soviet Union since World War II," chapter 16 above.

there have also been in the Soviet Union small Catholic communities of the Armenian rite and larger communities of the Byzantine rite, although the majority have been annihilated, driven underground, or forcibly separated from communion with Rome.

Byzantine rite Catholics are Christians who in their manner of worship, their canonical discipline, and their theological and ascetical orientation follow the traditions which originated in the eastern capital of the ancient Roman Empire, Byzantium, while at the same time believing that in conscience they must accept the pastoral leadership of the bishop of Rome and be in communion with him. They are often called "Greek Catholics" or "Uniates."

In the Soviet Union we can distinguish three groups of Byzantine rite Catholics.

First, there was a small but active group of Russians who, for the most part, joined the Catholic church after the publication of the edict of religious toleration by Czar Nicholas II, in 1905, under the influence of the philosopher Vladimir Soloviev and of his friend Princess Elizabeth Volkonsky. Even after 1905 Catholic churches of the Byzantine rite were not permitted, so these Russians had to wait until the beginning of 1917 to open chapels legally in Petrograd and Moscow. On May 29, 1917, Father Leonid Feodorov was named Exarch of Russia.[16] On March 1, 1921, Pope Benedict XV issued a brief, *Ex amplissimo*, confirming Father Leonid "Exarcham pro catholicis ritus slavonici" in Russia.

By the end of 1922, there were in the USSR ten priests of this rite. Their leader, Exarch Leonid Feodorov, was condemned to ten years imprisonment together with fourteen Latin rite priests, at their trial in Moscow in 1923. He spent several years in Solovki and other prisons and died exiled in Vyatka in 1935. Another priest of that group, Father Vladimir Abrikosov,[17] was expelled from his country in September, 1922, together with about thirty well-known Orthodox intellectuals—Father Sergei Bulgakov, Nicholas Berdyaev, and others.[18] Two priests of this group of Byzantine rite Catholics left

16. Donald Attwater, *Leonid Feodorov and the Catholic Russians* (New York: Russian Center, Fordham University, 1954). See also Paul Mailleux, S.J., *Exarch Leonid Feodorov: Bridgebuilder between Rome and Moscow* (New York: P. J. Kenedy, 1964).

17. Korolevskij, *Metropolite André Szeptyckyj*, pp. 238–45, 248. The author gives a summary of the remarkable story of Mother Catherine and Father Vladimir Abrikosov.

18. See Paul B. Anderson, "Reflections on Religion in Russia, 1917–67," chapter 3 above.

Russia on their own. The six others were sent to concentration camps in the course of 1923, and since then have died. The two chapels of Moscow and Petrograd were closed in 1922. They never were reopened. In Moscow a community of some twenty Dominican nuns following the Byzantine rite had been started by Mother Catherine Abrikosov. She was arrested in November, 1923, with most of her nuns and died in prison on June 23, 1936.

A second, much more numerous group of Byzantine rite Catholics who presently find themselves in the boundaries of the Soviet Union are the Western Ukrainians. They were for several centuries under Polish rule, and since 1772 had constituted a province of the Austro-Hungarian Empire called Galicia. In the thirty years from 1914 to 1944 they found themselves under eight different political masters, most of them hostile, who took cruel reprisals against those who did not welcome their arrival.

On the eve of the Second World War, this group numbered about 3.5 million faithful. They had 2,275 priests in the three dioceses of Stanislavov, Peremysl, and Lvov. This last city was the see of the archbishop and metropolitan. Each diocese had its own seminary and, in addition, there was an Ecclesiastical Academy in Lvov, three religious congregations of men, and eight congregations of nuns.

Since 1901, the metropolitan of Lvov had been the Archbishop Andrew Szeptitsky. When, after World War I, Lvov and the surrounding territory became incorporated into the new Poland, the metropolitan spared no effort to raise the spiritual and cultural level of his people. In 1938 the Polish government brutally seized and often destroyed certain Orthodox churches and properties in the eastern regions of Poland. Metropolitan Szeptitsky wrote a letter to his flock expressing his sorrow and protest, but the letter was seized by the Polish government. During the Nazi occupation which followed, he protested in the same way against the persecution of the Jews. After forty years of this kind of pastoral leadership in such difficult circumstances, he was held in exceptional veneration by his people. Probably for this reason, when the Soviets occupied Galicia for the second time in 1944, they initially avoided antagonizing the Catholic population. They at least permitted freedom of worship; the seminaries continued to exist and the teaching of religion to children (in the churches, not in the schools) was allowed.

Metropolitan Szeptitsky died on November 1, 1944. His funeral was very solemn; many delegations came to express their homage. Among those who attended was Nikita Sergeevich Khrushchev. He was at that time secretary of the Communist party in the Ukraine. The inauguration of the new metropolitan, Archbishop Joseph Slipyi, took place without incident.

During the winter which followed, the Catholic clergy were obliged to attend conferences of reeducation. In those conferences, party speakers treated questions of sociology and history but seized every opportunity to attack the Catholic church. Then on April 8, 1945, a violent article against the late Metropolitan Szeptitsky was published in the newspaper *Volna Ukraina* and afterwards disseminated among the people in pamphlet form.

Three days later, the new metropolitan was arrested. On the same day the bishop of Stanislovov, Gregory Khomyshyn, and his co-adjutor, Bishop John Latyshevsky, were put in jail with two other Ukrainian bishops who were in the country at that time, Nicholas Charnetsky, apostolic visitator of Volynia, and Nikita Budka, who had been exarch for the Ukrainians in Canada. The bishop of Peremysl, Josephat Kozilovsky, together with his auxiliary, Bishop Gregory Lakota, were then on Polish territory. Their extradition was soon obtained and they were sent to prison with the others.

These bishops were later brought before a secret tribunal in Kiev and given sentences of from five to ten years at forced labor. The indictment was published at the beginning of March, 1946, by the public prosecutor of the Ukrainian Soviet Socialist Republic. It gave as the motive for the condemnation "treason and collaboration with the German occupation forces."[19]

In fact, only one of the eight condemned bishops was at the head of a diocese at the time that they were accused of having collaborated with the Germans. One of them, Bishop Nicholas Charnetsky, had been kept out of the territory of his jurisdiction by the Germans. Strangely enough, M. M. Sheinman, the Soviet writer who has made himself a specialist in studies about the Catholic church and who has published several books about the activities of the Vatican in editions published by the Academy of Sciences of the USSR, does not mention in his work *The Vatican During the Second World War* any act of collaboration by these bishops with the Germans. If there had

19. *First Victims of Communism* (Rome: Analecta OSBM, 1953), p. 34.

been any such activity, he would certainly not have kept silent about it.

During the same period, the superiors of the two seminaries and the members of the diocesan curias were arrested. Simultaneously, the Soviet authorities issued new regulations for the clergy. Priests who wanted to exercise their ministry had to register at special state offices. To keep a church open, a request had to be sent to the same office signed by at least twenty citizens. These citizens would be responsible for the administration of church property and could request a minister of worship chosen from among the "authorized."

Shortly after this, three former Catholic priests, Fathers Gabriel Kostelnik, John Melnik, and Antony Pelvetsky, each representing one of the three dioceses, announced that they were constituting an "Initiative Group for the Reunion of the Greek Catholic Church with the Russian Orthodox Church." On May 28, 1945, that committee sent an appeal to the Soviet of the Commissars of the Ukrainian Soviet Socialist Republic to ask for its support. On June 18, Citizen Khodchynko, in the name of the Supreme Soviet of the USSR, answered favorably but also committed to the committee a special obligation: "As the registration of Greek Catholic deaneries, parishes, and religious houses proceeds, the Initiative Group will send to the representative of the Council of Peoples' Commissars of the Ukrainian SSR for the Affairs of the Russian Orthodox Church the list of deans, priests, and superiors of religious houses who refuse to submit to the jurisdiction of the Initiative Group for the reunion of the Greek Catholic Church with the Russian Orthodox church."[20]

On July 1, 1945, the eight priests who were still free in Lvov decided to send a letter to Molotov. The letter was signed by three hundred other priests. In that letter they declared that it was against their consciences to submit to the Initiative Group and they tried to explain that the action of the group was harmful to church and state. No answer was received. Instead, a synod to proclaim the union of the Greek Catholics with the Russian Orthodox church was convoked for March 8–10, 1946. Of 2,270 priests, 216 attended the convocation. Bishop Makarius was sent by the patriarch of Moscow to occupy the see of Lvov. In the official bulletin of his diocese, he stated that 1,111 priests had accepted his jurisdiction.

20. *Diannia soboru hreko-katolytskoi tserkvy, 8–10 bereznia 1946 r. u Lvovi* [Proceedings of the council of the Greek-Catholic church in Lvov, 8–10 March 1946] (Lvov, 1946), p. 125.

All the Catholic bishops mentioned above have died in prison except Metropolitan Slipyi, who was allowed to leave Soviet Russia in February, 1963.[21] When the metropolitan was released, his liberation was attributed to a personal request of Cardinal Bea to the Soviet government through the observers from the Moscow patriarchate to the Second Vatican Council. But on November 7, 1964, Norman Cousins, editor of the *Saturday Review*, explained in a lead article in that periodical how he had two long meetings with Nikita S. Khrushchev in 1962 and 1963, and had requested and finally obtained the liberation of the metropolitan. The only condition expressed, at least implicitly, for his release was that the Vatican not take the opportunity "to publish big headlines that the bishop was tortured by the Reds." And without giving details, Khrushchev said simply "that the bishop had been imprisoned for good and sufficient reasons."

At the same time, the seminaries were closed and most of the seminarians were drafted into the army. All the religious schools and orphanages, the convents, religious associations, and religious periodicals were also suppressed. The majority of the churches have been closed. About three hundred priests have succeeded in fleeing abroad; several hundred were arrested and have spent long periods of time in concentration camps. The exact fate of nearly all of the rest of the priests is unknown.

Father Kostelnik was tragically and mysteriously murdered on a street in Lvov on September 21, 1948. The second member of the "Initiative Group," Father John Melnik, who had been consecrated a bishop, died in mysterious circumstances in Kiev on October 9, 1955. The third member, Father Antony Pelvetsky, who also had become a bishop, died in February, 1957.

Since 1946, not a single Catholic church of the Byzantine rite has remained open in the Western Ukraine and no Catholic priest of that rite may celebrate services publicly. It seems, however, that some do so secretly. Also, tourists who have been in Lvov have seen in the Latin rite Catholic churches which are still open in the city a good number of people who make the sign of the Cross in the Eastern

---

21. Metropolitan Slipyi was named to the rank of cardinal by Pope John XXIII on February 22, 1965. On his unique status in the Roman Catholic church, see Victor J. Pospishil, "The Ukrainian Major Archiepiscopate," *Diakonia* 3, no. 1, (1968): 5–22.

manner, that is, from the right to the left shoulder. They are obviously Byzantine rite Catholics who attend the Latin rite churches.

A third group of Catholics of the Byzantine rite is found in the eparchy of Mukacevo. Before 1917, that region was under Hungarian rule. Towards the end of the Hungarian regime, in 1913, reacting against the policy of that government, some Catholics left the church to start an Orthodox community in the country. This movement increased as the Hungarian government became more oppressive. After World War I, the eparchy of Mukacevo covered the region called Sub-Carpathian Russia, now one of the three main divisions of Czechoslovakia. Presently part of the Soviet Union, it is called *Zarkarpatskaia oblast*, or the Transcarpathian region.

The official statistics published by the Czech government in 1930 clearly describe the religious situation of that region before World War II. The total population was then 725,357. Of this number, 359,166 (roughly 50 percent) were Byzantine rite Catholics, 69,262 were Latin rite Catholics, 112,034 were Orthodox, 102,512 were Jews, and 70,833 were Protestants. In 1944, the same diocese numbered 461,555 Catholics of the Byzantine rite with 281 parishes, 459 churches and chapels, 354 diocesan priests, 5 monasteries with 35 members and 3 convents with 50 nuns. There were 84 seminarians in the single seminary.

The Soviet army occupied the region in 1944, and the Soviet government immediately took advantage of the opposition which existed between Orthodox and Catholics to eliminate the Catholic clergy. By the end of November, 1944, fifteen Byzantine rite Catholic churches had been seized and their priests expelled. Bishop Theodore Romza, the young bishop of Mukacevo, protested strongly to both the civilian and military authorities, but the churches were not returned.

On December 7, 1944, a delegation led by the Orthodox Abbot Theophane Sabov flew to Moscow to petition the church of Moscow to receive the Orthodox church of Sub-Carpathia under its jurisdiction. Until then, this church had been under the jurisdiction of the Serbian church. The church of Moscow agreed.

Pressure on the Catholic church was now intensified. Church schools and charitable institutions were confiscated, and any religious instruction to those under eighteen years of age was forbidden. The bishop of Mukacevo, Bishop Romza, was deprived of his printing press. To remain in touch with his clergy he started visiting all his parishes in his usual horse-drawn wagon. On October 25, 1947, he was run over by a heavy Soviet army truck and died a week later, November 1, 1947.[22]

On February 22, 1948, his cathedral was seized and given to a bishop sent from Moscow. On August 28 of that same year the Greek Catholic church was proclaimed "liquidated." Priests who refused to submit to the patriarch of Moscow were arrested. The seminary was transformed into a museum and the former episcopal residence into a state library. Not a single church remained open for the Byzantine rite Catholics, and a good number of the churches which were turned over to the Orthodox have subsequently been closed.

Although Exarch Leonid Feodorov had apparently taken steps to establish an exarchate for Belorussia as early as 1917, no one was named to that office until May 1940 when Metropolitan Andrew Szeptitsky appointed Father Anthony Niemantsevich, S.J.[23] His appointment was confirmed by Pope Pius XII on November 22, 1941. When the Nazis occupied Belorussia, the exarch was arrested. In August, 1942, together with nine Belorussian Catholic priests, he was shot.

On the other side of the Soviet border, in Slovakia, there was another small Catholic diocese of the Byzantine rite in Preshov with 325 priests for about 305,000 faithful. The same methods were used to separate it from communion with Rome.

In 1950 Bishop Goydich of Preshov and his auxiliary, Bishop Basil Hopko, were thrown into jail and on April 28 of that year the union with Rome was officially declared to be suppressed.

In recent years there have been some references to the continued existence of groups of Byzantine rite Catholics. In 1963 it was reported that a Ukrainian woman returning from abroad was arrested by customs officials because she was trying to smuggle crosses and medals into the Soviet Union hidden in little loaves of

---

22. Galter, *Red Book of the Church*, pp. 107–8.

23. Employing special faculties granted him by the Holy See, Metropolitan Andrew constituted four exarchates on October 9, 1939: (1) Volynia, Podlachia, and Kholm-shchina (Exarch Nicholas Charnetsky); (2) Belorussia (Exarch Anthony Niemantsevich); (3) Great Russia (Exarch Clement Szeptitsky); (4) Great Ukraine (Exarch Joseph Slipyi). When Pope Pius XII ratified these nominations, their jurisdictions became apostolic exarchates. For further details see Korolevskij, *Metropolite André Szeptycki*, pp. 364–65.

bread.[24] Careful inspection of the writings she had on her person led to the discovery of a community of ten Byzantine rite Catholic nuns who lived together at number 43, Muchnaia Ulitsa, in Lvov. During the day, they served as nurses in a hospital. They had a chapel in their house where several Catholic priests had celebrated services as their chaplains, but these men had all been arrested one after the other.

A Ukrainian periodical reported in 1964 that the police had discovered in the apartment of Father Michael Vinnitsky, a Redemptorist priest of the Byzantine rite, enough material to manufacture fifty thousand small icons and crosses.[25]

In 1965 the leading "scientific atheistic" journal published an article on church attendance in the Ukraine.[26] The author wrote: "In the region of Lvov, by the vagaries of history, many religious confessions are intermixed. And their adherents are still rather numerous." He pointed out that in some places big factories had been built—in Stebnik, for example—but, nevertheless, the majority of the population still goes to church on Sundays. "They go to church by tradition and because they fear they will be blamed by others if they do not go." Marianov then asked the question: "In the antireligious lectures given in factories and in the schools, should we still attack the *Uniia*? Some answer that we should not; the *Uniia* practically speaking, they say, is a question of the past. To speak about it only rekindles an unhealthy interest in it. . . ." The author did not share that opinion and called such an attitude oversimplified dogmatism.

Whether the Christians of the Western Ukraine would choose to be united again with the Roman Catholic church, if they were allowed to do so, is impossible to say as long as real religious liberty does not exist in that country. Presently, no Christian of the Byzantine rite in favor of the union with Rome in those regions will express his mind openly, and if these former "Uniates" have been able to maintain any activity it can only be clandestine. In Transcarpathia and in the Western Ukraine, priests and laymen who have remained loyal to Rome have descended into the catacombs.

The sparse information available to the West makes us aware that

24. "S dvoynim dnom" [With a false bottom], *Ogonek* [Little flame], no. 46, November 1963.
25. *Molod Ukraini* [Ukrainian youth], May 1964.
26. B. Marianov, "Reflections on the Region of Lvov," *Nauka i religiia* [Science and religion], June 1965.

at the present time, while there exists a fidelity which is sometimes heroic, there is also a certain confusion in the consciences of the people. Since the Second Vatican Council more cordial relations have been established between the church of Rome and the patriarchate of Moscow. Both the council and the Secretariat for Promoting Christian Unity, founded by Pope John XXIII, have adopted a most positive attitude toward Christians who are not united with Rome. Certain Ukrainian priests who were formerly Catholic and who have been within the jurisdiction of the church of Moscow since the events of 1945, have pointed to the change in the Roman attitude to demonstrate to Ukrainians and Carpatho-Russians who remain faithful to the Holy See that they are wrong in persisting in their loyalty. For those groups which have remained secretly united with Rome, these events have caused no small amount of surprise and confusion.

During 1966, the *Zhurnal moskovskoi patriarkhii* (Journal of the Moscow patriarchate) published a dozen articles to commemorate what it called "the twentieth anniversary of the return of the Uniates to the church of Moscow."[27] Unquestionably one should see in the unusual number of articles on the same subject, in a periodical which has a strictly limited number of pages, an indirect hint to the Roman Catholic church of how greatly the church of Moscow desires that the question of the Uniates not be raised again between the two communions. *L'Osservatore Romano*, the semiofficial organ of the Holy See, replied to these articles on November 13, 1966. In a tone both serene and irenic, this article in effect emphasized that so grave a question, one which causes deep distress to consciences, cannot be settled in a unilateral fashion. All those who have a thorough awareness of the human and theological problems which divide the churches of Rome and Moscow are persuaded that the particularly delicate question of the Uniates will find adequate solution only in the reestablishment of communion and of visible and juridical unity between the two churches.

In 1920, about fifty thousand Catholics of the Armenian rite were established in the southern regions of Soviet Russia. They had forty-

27. An indication of the role which the "return of the Uniates" is playing in official Orthodox historiography is the fact that the exarch of the Ukraine, Archbishop (now Metropolitan) Filaret, devoted two out of thirteen paragraphs to this subject in his encyclical letter on the occasion of the fiftieth anniversary of the Ukrainian Soviet Socialist Republic. See *Zhurnal moskovskoi patriarkhii* [Journal of the Moscow patriarchate] 1968, no. 1, pp. 7–9.

seven priests with sixty churches or chapels. Their apostolic administrator, Father James Begaratian, had his residence in Tiflis. He died
in the penal camp of Solovki in 1936. By 1940 all their churches were
closed and all their clergy had died or been deported to concentration
camps. In Lvov, in the Ukraine, there was also an Armenian colony
which was in communion with Rome. The Armenian rite archdiocese
in Lvov dated from 1630. Its last incumbent, Joseph Theodorowicz,
was elected on December 16, 1901, and was still serving at the time
of the October Revolution. In 1946 the priest in that group was
arrested and sent to Siberia.

On May 18, 1965, the Armenian catholicos of Etchmiadzin,
Vazgen I, head of the Gregorian Armenians, invited the head of the
Armenian rite Catholics in the diaspora, Patriarch Ignatius XVI
(Batanian), to come to Soviet Armenia for the celebration of the
tenth anniversary of Vazgen's election and at the same time to commemorate the fiftieth anniversary of the terrible massacres of Armenians in Turkey in 1915.[28] The patriarch accepted the invitation,
and on October 28 of the same year visited Soviet Armenia with two
of his priests. The reception was as cordial as it could be. This trip
also gave the patriarch the opportunity of renewing contact with his
fold.

The number of Armenian Catholics established in Armenia and
Georgia is presently well over one hundred thousand. Only two of the
forty-seven priests who were ministering to these Catholics in 1920
are still alive; both are over eighty years old and have spent several
years in concentration camps. They are not allowed to celebrate
church services. Of the sixty churches, only three are still kept for
religious services; the others have been demolished or are used for
secular purposes. Patriarch Ignatius petitioned Andon Kochinian,
president of the Council of Ministers of the Armenian SSR in Erevan,
and Vassil Palavandishiuli, president of the Committee for Religious
Affairs of the Georgian SSR in Tbilisi, to be allowed to send a priest
to the region of Akhaltzikhe where Armenian Catholics are particularly numerous. So far, his petition has not received a favorable answer.

Catholics in Russia never received the support of the state; they
were always a minority. Therefore they were better prepared than
the members of the Russian Orthodox church to meet the trials of

28. See Mesrob K. Krikorian, "The Armenian Church in the Soviet Union, 1917–67,"
chapter 11 above.

these last fifty years. In general, they have remained faithful to their church even when isolated and without priests. Catholic fathers and mothers do their best to give their children a Christian education. Atheism and antireligious propaganda remain more than ever an integral element of Soviet education, however, and parents often feel powerless against these efforts.

In the course of the last five years, the tension between the Soviet government and the Catholic church has diminished somewhat. The efforts of the last two popes for justice and peace in the world have been acknowledged and praised by the Soviet press. Observers from the patriarchate of Moscow were allowed to attend the four sessions of the Second Vatican Council. On April 27, 1966, Andrei Gromyko, minister of foreign affairs for the USSR, was received by the pope, and on January 30, 1967, N. Podgorny, chairman of the Presidium of the Supreme Soviet of the USSR, was solemnly received at the Vatican. Some repercussions of these events have been felt in the Catholic communities of the Soviet Union, in that administrative decisions about them reflect more benevolence. For example, in March, 1967, Bishop Matulaitis, apostolic administrator of Kaunas, Lithuania, and Bishop Vaivods of Riga were allowed to go to Rome to attend a meeting of canonists for the reform of Catholic canon !aw. Unfortunately, however, the basic restrictions on religious liberty have not been removed. More time will be needed to determine the real meaning of improvements in external relations.

18

CATHOLICISM
IN LITHUANIA

The largest concentration of Roman rite Catholics in the Soviet Union is found in Lithuania, where Catholicism through the centuries has been strong and influential. After the fall of Poland in 1939, Pope Pius XII referred to Lithuania as the "northernmost outpost of Catholicism in Europe."[1] Independent Lithuania, however, did not long survive the outbreak of hostilities. On June 15, 1940, at the time Paris fell to the Germans, the country was occupied by the Red Army and soon afterwards incorporated into the Soviet Union. Since that time, Lithuanian Catholicism has been subjected to the same strictures as the other religious communities in the USSR.

Legal Position of the Church

The regulation of religious life in Lithuania is based on the revolutionary decree of January 21, 1918, which separated church from state and school from church in Russia.[2] Since that time, of course, a number of additional regulations have been added to supplement this decree. In Lithuania, these regulations differ only slightly from the rules that apply in the other republics.[3]

1. For information on the position of the Church in independent Lithuania, see V. Stanley Vardys, ed., *Lithuania Under the Soviets: Portrait of a Nation* (New York, 1965), pp. 28ff., 215–16.

2. For English text of the decree see Appendix, section 2A, below.

3. See Joshua Rothenberg, "The Legal Status of Religion in the Soviet Union," chapter 5 above.

V. Stanley Vardys

Soviet law deals with the subject of religion in a rather euphemistic manner, and statutes concerning church activity are not readily available for the average citizen. The civil and criminal codes of the Lithuanian SSR and the six-volume collection of decrees passed by the republic's Supreme Soviet and the council of ministers between 1941–59 contain only three items directly concerning religion. Article 143 of the criminal code specifies that the violation of the laws on the separation of the church from the state and the school is punishable by deprivation of freedom or "corrective labor" of up to one year and a fine of up to one hundred rubles. Article 227 prohibits the organizing of groups which, under cover of the propagation of faith or religious exercises, "inflict damage on citizens' health, attempt to deny them their rights as citizens, or discourage them from participating in public activities or from fulfilling civic obligations."[4]

Leaders of such groups may be punished by exile or deprivation of freedom for up to five years and by confiscation of property. Participation in such groups is punishable by a maximum three-year deprivation of freedom or up to one year of corrective labor. If the violators are not considered "very dangerous" to society, they may avoid prison but then would be dealt with by means of "social pressure." A third article (article 145) provides punishment of up to one year for "preventing the performance of religious rites insofar as these rights do not disturb public order and are not connected with attempts to deprive citizens of their rights."[5] All of these provisions are almost verbatim translations from the criminal code of the Russian Soviet Federated Socialist Republic.

These three provisions are applied very broadly and are used to ban a number of practices considered to be illegal and presumably listed as such in some collection of statutes.[6] Priests may preach in church, for example, but cannot criticize either the government or atheistic propaganda or instruct their congregations not tŏ support atheistic activity. Furthermore, they cannot organize any groups for church or social activity, whether these are merely sports activities or

---

4. *Lietuvos Tarybu Socialistines Respublikos Baudziamasis Kodeksas* [The criminal code of the Lithuanian SSR] (Vilnius, 1962), pp. 81–82. This is the criminal code of the Lithuanian SSR.

5. Ibid.

6. Based on A. Veščikovas, *Tarybiniai Istatymai apie Religinius Kultus* [Soviet law on religious cults] (Vilnius, 1963). This is a brochure summarizing Soviet laws on church activity.

religious instruction, acolyte societies, participation in the church choir, or groups to prepare children for first communion. Another regulation prohibits the church burial of atheists or Communists and the celebration of requiem Mass for enemies of the state. Priests are also not allowed to organize or engage in charitable work, nor may they administer the sacraments—even extreme unction upon request —in any public buildings, for example, hospitals. Religious processions are confined to church yards. Church collections are permitted only in church buildings and must be voluntary. This means that priests cannot solicit contributions or exact fees for services. All collections must be taken up by parishioners. The clergy, finally, cannot issue to the faithful any binding regulations.

Conceivably, this list of restrictions, all reducible to articles 143, 144, and 145 of the criminal code, is incomplete. Many other restraints no doubt exist but are not available in writing because the republic's representative on the Council for Religious Affairs of the USSR, the person who controls church activities, issues his orders mostly by phone and eschews written communication.

The church, it logically follows, is denied the rights of a legal person. Congregations cannot protect themselves in court and cannot own property. All houses of worship—the only type of building where collective worship is allowed— belong to the state. Churchmen and churches are controlled by the republic's council of ministers and by the above-mentioned representative of the Moscow Council for Religious Affairs. (In Lithuania, this position has been occupied for many years by Justas Rugienis, a person who is reported to have a background of experience in police administration.)

This representative of the Council for Religious Affairs actually regulates the life of the Catholic church in Lithuania and, since the recent reorganization in Moscow, apparently controls the Orthodox church there as well.[7] All congregations and priests must be registered with him. He can grant permits to build new churches or order the closing of old ones. He sets the amount congregations have to pay for the use of houses of worship and thus collects for the government a considerable sum of money. For example, the cathedral of Kaunas has to pay six thousand rubles a year. Presumably, in case of failure to pay, the congregation can be evicted, but in Lithuania there has been no reported case of such action. The regime's intention seems to

7. *Tiesa*, 8 March 1966.

be to apply financial pressure to the limit, without taxing the churches out of existence.

The representative of the Council for Religious Affairs also controls the clergy and their work. All priests must register with him and are issued working permits that make them eligible for parish appointments. These working permits are frequently withdrawn, if the priest commits any infraction of the regulations. In such a case, if he is not arrested, the priest is fired or may be ordered to work in some industrial enterprise. Theoretically, a priest can own or inherit property, can vote, and enjoy the protection of all other constitutional guarantees, but it is futile for him to complain of discrimination at work or from the tax assessors or local government bodies—the ad hoc directives of the officials concerned take precedence over these guarantees.

This government representative also controls church appointments and issues regulations concerning church work. Although formally the structure of church government which obtained in independent Lithuania remains, only two of the six dioceses are actually administered by bishops. The bishop of Kaunas, in addition to his own, administers the diocese of Vilkaviškis, while Msgr. P. Bakšys who administers the diocese of Kaišiadorys is also supposed to supervise the diocese of Panevėžys. Bishops or administrators are helped by canons of the cathedral chapter, or where these no longer exist, by three counsellors the appointment of whom has recently been allowed by the government representative. Diocesan administrators must clear all appointments and all regulations with this representative. This actually puts ultimate control of the church in the hands of the government. The republic's council of ministers and the representative of the Council for Religious Affairs can even specify the length of time for the ringing of church bells, when they are allowed to be rung at all.[8]

The differences between the legal position of the Catholic church in Lithuania and non-Catholic churches in other parts of the Soviet Union are minimal and largely the result of Lithuania's shorter experience as a Soviet republic.[9] Thus, in Lithuania, cemetery management was taken away from the clergy as recently as March 8, 1958, and only since 1963 have priests been forbidden to make their traditional

8. Veščikovas, *Tarybiniai Istatymai*, p. 37.
9. Paul Mailleux, S.J., "Catholics in the Soviet Union," chapter 17 above.

annual visits to the parishes' families (*calenda*). In Lithuania, registration with the civil authorities for the baptism of a child is still not required.[10] Lithuanian priests do not keep lists of any sort and parish committees have not yet been completely put under governmental control. Threats to do so, however, have been made repeatedly. The effect of such action would be to make the priest a mere employee of the church committee and to subordinate him to a group dominated by government appointees.

Clearly Soviet law is, at best, heavily slanted against the church. Religious worship is merely tolerated, and much religious activity as it is generally understood in the West, is outlawed. Since the enforcement of government policies depends largely on local administrators, it is understandable how the Lithuanian government and party managers become important in the daily affairs of the church. The nature of this enforcement constitutes a further difference in the treatment of churches in different Soviet republics.

Soviet policy toward the Catholic church in postwar Lithuania can be broken down into four separate periods: (1) the Stalinist stage of direct assault and terror (1944–53); (2) the years of the thaw (1954–57); (3) the period of concentrated atheistic attack (1958–64); and (4) the post-Khrushchev years, a period which it is still difficult to characterize except to say that while the tempo of the 1959–64 campaign has abated considerably, it is only in comparison to it that one may speak of a relaxation of pressure today. With this periodization in mind, it is possible to proceed to a detailed analysis of Soviet policy of the past twenty-five years.

The Stalinist Period (1944–1953)

After reconquering the Lithuanian territory and reestablishing a civilian regime, in 1944–45 the Soviets reinstituted all antichurch measures that had been adopted during the first occupation, in 1940–41. This could be done very easily because the Nazis retained most of the Soviet regulations, especially those concerning church property, schools, organizations, and the press. Some German concessions (for example, allowing religious instruction in schools) were eliminated. Generally, during this period the regime, after unsuccessfully attempting to use the church hierarchy for its own purposes, directed its energies

10. For the situation in the RSFSR see Donald A. Lowrie and William C. Fletcher, "Khrushchev's Religious Policy," chapter 7 above.

toward the destruction of the church leadership and organization. The situation was aggravated by the extensive activities of the anti-Soviet guerilla movement which operated between 1944 and 1948 (and, to a lesser extent, as late as 1952).[11] This movement, as the government correctly suspected, was supported by many clergymen, although the church did not officially sanction it. Many priests organized guerilla groups and participated in certain aspects of their work. This activity led to numerous arrests among the clergy. Knowing the church's influence in the country, the Soviets put pressure on priests and bishops to help the government by inducing the guerillas to lay down their arms. In most cases, the clergy refused and this noncooperation led to heightened repressive measures on the church.

Early in 1946, the government asked the bishops to issue a collective appeal to the guerillas and the population at large calling for the cessation of armed resistance. To intimidate the hierarchy into compliance, in February of that year Bishop Vincentas Borisevičius of Telšiai was arrested. Later that same year, the Soviets imprisoned Pranas Ramanauskas, the auxiliary of the same diocese. In 1947, Borisevičius was sentenced to life imprisonment while his colleague was given a term of twenty-five years. Next Bishop Teofilius Matulionis, who had already spent several years in Soviet prisons, was arrested, as was Archbishop Mečislovas Reinys of Vilnius (Vilna). The precise charges against these bishops are not known. It seems, however, that in the case of Borisevičius and Ramanauskas the charges included that of having rendered support to anti-Soviet "bandits." Archbishop Reinys was arrested after declaring in his cathedral that he did not write the statement supporting Soviet foreign policy that was published under his name in *Pravda*. Thus, in 1947, only one bishop, Kazimieras Paltarokas of Panevėžys, was still at liberty. Significantly, he was the only one of the bishops who issued the requested appeal to the guerillas.

The list of measures designed to destroy church organization included the deportation of clergy, attempts to cut off the supply of future priests, endeavors to separate the church from Rome, and efforts to undermine mutual confidence among the priests. Some of these methods were tried in 1940–41 and did not work. Now, how-

11. V. Stanley Vardys, "The Partisan Movement in Postwar Lithuania," *Slavic Review* 22, no. 3 (September 1963): 499–522

ever, the Soviets were faced with considerable resistance to the sovietization of the country, and for this reason all restraints were abandoned. In the waves of deportations which followed, about three hundred thousand people were banished to camps and settlements in northern Russia and Siberia. Among these were an estimated 180 priests of the total of about one thousand. Almost all priests in positions of leadership were either deported, arrested, or harassed in some manner. From 1944 to 1956, for example, four rectors of the one surviving theological seminary in Kaunas were deported.[12] The seminary was at first allowed to register 150 students (the number in 1940 for all seminaries was in excess of four hundred), but this number was quickly cut in half and then reduced to sixty. Thus, the clergy was denied the possibility of replenishing its depleted ranks, and since that time the number of priests in Lithuania has continued to shrink. To disorganize the remaining priests and to convert the church into an instrument of the regime, the Communists now attempted to infiltrate it by enrolling secret police agents in the seminary. They also promoted desertion from the ranks of the clergy and attempted to recruit priests as police informers. These efforts were topped by an ambitious but unsuccessful plan for the creation of a "national" Catholic church. Church authorities were summoned by party, government, and KGB officials to discuss such a plan, but to no avail. No prominent clergyman could be found who would engage in such a scheme, and the plan was quietly dropped.

Early in this period the church was placed under a Commissar for Religious Affairs, a man named Pušinis. His office, periodically reorganized according to directions from Moscow, acquired more and more authority as time went by.

The regime's preoccupation with the destruction of the church organization and the brutality with which this policy was carried out during the Stalinist period did not mean that so-called "methods of persuasion," that is, antireligious propaganda, were abandoned. The government simply did not have enough time for propaganda during the years of armed resistance, and it took four or five years before the Society for the Dissemination of Political and Scientific Knowledge, first established in 1947, was effectively organized in Lithuania.

---

12. "La Chiesa in Lituania." A statement (pro-memoria) submitted by Bishop Vincentas Brižgys (auxiliary bishop of Kaunas, now in exile in the United States) to the Second Vatican Council, p. 7.

The main attack was directed against the clergy—the priests and bishops—picturing them as nationalist "murderers," Hitlerites, agents of the Vatican and of Western imperialists, criminals, and morally corrupt enemies of the Lithuanian people and of the Soviet government.

The Years of the Thaw (1954–1957)

The general thaw that followed Stalin's death and the overall relaxation of social relations in the Soviet Union brought relief to Lithuania as well. Here the thaw was especially felt in the area of national culture and traditions, and in that of religion. There was a certain relaxation of the program of russification and a brief renaissance of Lithuanian language, literature, and the arts. At the same time there were attempts to eliminate at least some of the tensions between the government and the church and to find new approaches to dealing with religion. The regime apparently felt that the population had been alienated by the arbitrary terror of the Stalin period and that a rapprochement was needed for the good of Communist rule and for economic progress. The Communist party's Central Committee, in a declaration published November 10, 1954, called for the elimination of brutality, arbitrariness, and the use of force in the antireligious campaigns.[13] In Lithuania the regime now sought to build bridges to the faithful. Thus, while continuing their commitment to antireligious activity, the authorities were anxious to emphasize that this activity called for "an ideological duel" between the religious and materialist ideologies and was not a war against believers as people. The party organ Tiesa emphasized that, according to party teaching, many religious people were good workers and dutiful citizens, and should not be politically suspect merely because they were believers.[14] To clarify this distinction and to demonstrate that the regime was the enemy of religion only, and not of the law-abiding faithful, Tiesa allowed public discussion of the relative merits of religion and materialism and of the conflict between the two.

The seriousness of the government's purpose was demonstrated by concessions to the clergy and the faithful. Thus, the government

13. For details of this declaration see Rothenberg, "Legal Status of Religion," pp. 61–102 above.
14. Tiesa, 10 August 1955.

allowed most of the deported priests to return. Some 130 priests who survived the labor camps and did not remain in Russia for missionary work returned home together with thousands of other exiles. In 1956, two bishops, Ramanauskas and Matulionis, were also released from prisons in Russia. They were not restored to their bishoprics but confined to provincial domiciles. Ramanauskas died on October 15, 1959, without regaining his rights of office. Bishop Matulionis, elevated to the rank of archbishop by the pope, died on August 20, 1963, without having been reinstated.

Furthermore, during this period of relaxation, the regime allowed the church to fill at least some of the sees vacant since 1946. In 1955 Moscow quietly agreed to the consecration of Msgr. Petras Maželis, whom the pope appointed to administer the diocese of Telšiai, and of Msgr. Julijonas Steponavičius, who became the apostolic administrator of the dioceses of Vilnius and Panevėžys. Two years later, in 1957, Bishop Matulionis, with the approval of the Vatican, consecrated still another bishop, Msgr. Vincentas Sladkevičius. Matulionis apparently hoped that the new bishop could take over the administration of his diocese, but the government suspended Sladkevičius almost immediately after his consecration. This suggested that the political climate was beginning to change again.

The period of the thaw was remarkable in at least three other ways. First, for the first time in the postwar period the regime allowed publication of a prayerbook and a religious calendar. Second, also for the first time since the war, bishops were allowed to visit parishes and to administer the sacrament of confirmation to thousands of young people. Even more spectacular was the permission, quietly given, to construct a church in the port city of Klaipeda. This era of "good feeling" was used by the faithful to repair many church buildings that had been in disrepair for more than a decade.[15]

All of these concessions, however, proved to be temporary. As early as 1957, as previously indicated, elements of the earlier policy began to reemerge. The thaw had served its purpose; the regime in Moscow had become stable. In June of that year, Khrushchev won out over his competitors in the party and began to consolidate his position. He now resumed the drive for integration and control that had been temporarily suspended to meet the post-Stalin exigencies.

15. *La Chiesa in Lituania*, pp. 10–11.

The result was a reorganized attack on religion which in its psycho-logical intensity surpassed even that of Stalinist times.

The Period of Atheistic Attack (1958–1964)

From December, 1957, a number of Central Committee plenums in Moscow and in Vilnius decreed measures aimed at strengthening ideological work, especially among the youth. The target was to be the school. The main objective was to advance atheist indoctrination. Atheist work, always considered "an integral part of Communist education," was now given particular attention and elevated to new prominence.[16] The reasons for this preoccupation with educational means are not difficult to find. Khrushchev hoped to substitute ideology for the use of the arbitrary force which Stalin had em-ployed. Campaigns of ideological indoctrination were expected to rejuvenate people's loyalties to the government. The undertaking could not be interpreted as a sign of the regime's strength; it was a measure taken to restore sagging popular support, to help Khrush-chev, and to win a new lease on life for the regime.

In Lithuania, special significance was attached to atheist indoctri-nation for two other crucially important reasons. First, atheism was considered a tool for combating nationalism, and second, it was re-garded as a protection against Western influence. Although early Lithuanian Catholicism had served the efforts of polonization, since the beginning of the twentieth century it had been closely linked to Lithuanian nationalism. Since this link was of recent origin, it never became as intense as in Poland, but nevertheless was a fact widely recognized by Communists and anti-Communists alike. Even in the sixties, a good number of Lithuanians still believe that "a real Lithuanian" cannot be an atheist and that atheism, contrary to Catholicism, was imposed by the Russians. It is understandable, then, why V. Niunka, a secretary of the Lithuanian Communist party's Central Committee, and the person in charge of the ideological struggle against Lithuanian Catholicism, bluntly declared that to fight against the church meant to fight against "bourgeois nationalism."[17]

---

16. J. Baužys, "Religiniu Prietaru Egzistavimo Kolukieciu Samoneje Priezasciu Klausimu" [On the causes of the existence of religious superstitions in the subconscious of collective-farm workers], *Lietuvos TSR Mokslu Akademijos Darbai* [The works of the Lithuanian Academy of Sciences], 1965, Series A, no. 2, pp. 259, 265; similarly, J. Minkevičius in *Komunistas* [The Communist], 1960, no. 9, pp. 16ff.

17. *Komunistas*, 1961, no, 10, p. 2.

The practical connection between nationalism and the church was similarly recognized by the Lithuanian minister of education, M. Gedvilas, who specified two educational objectives of indoctrination: "internationalism" (the opposite of nationalism) and, hand in hand with it, "atheism" (in Lithuanian circumstances, the opposite of the Catholic church).[18] Furthermore, this atheistic education was considered important since many Lithuanians apparently supported the church not for any religious reason but because it was a "Western" church that allowed a fragile, but real and refreshing, tie with Western culture. Atheism, the regime believed, would also help to separate Lithuanian Catholics from the Vatican, the "world center of obscurantism and reaction."[19]

Atheistic work was to be conducted in a new manner. A. Barkauskas, a secretary of the Lithuanian Communist party's Central Committee, praised the party's condemnation of harsh Stalinist methods which were now seen to be particularly harmful. On November 10, 1954, the Central Committee had forbidden outbursts against the clergy and the faithful; Barkauskas prohibited the arbitrary interference with the activities of religious communities.[20] "It is important to remember," the committee's decree read, "that insulting activities directed against the church, the clergy, and the faithful are incompatible with the policy of scientific-atheistic propaganda, as directed by the party and the government, and are contrary to the constitution of the USSR which guarantees Soviet citizens freedom of conscience."[21] Simultaneously, however, the committee ordered the intensification of atheistic work and urged that it be "ideologically" oriented. In general this meant that authorities should refrain from using "administrative" methods and concentrate on "persuasion." Persuasion was understood in Pavlovian terms, that is, as the creation of economic, social, and legal conditions which would cause atheistic reflexes in youth. Atheistic workers were advised that in addition to religious ideology one ought to study religious psychology.[22] The introduction of the socialist system, according to atheistic

18. Speech to a teachers' convention; text in *Tarybinis Mokytojas* [The Soviet teacher], 1 January 1961, p. 4.
19. *Komunistas*, 1961, no. 10, p. 14.
20. A. Barkauskas, "Ateistine Propaganda—Sudetine Komunistinio Auklejimo Dalis" [Atheistic propaganda—an integral part of Communist education], *Komunistas*, 1954, no. 11, p. 6.
21. Ibid.
22. A. Čedavičius, *Komunistas*, 1963, no. 5, p. 30.

theoreticians in Lithuania, destroyed the reasons for the rise of religious views, and religious emotions. Remnants of these things were still there, and the youth thus had to be indoctrinated with "scientific materialism" and reconditioned in such a way that they would "spontaneously" feel antagonism toward religion.

After 1958, the first part of the decree of 1954 was completely forgotten, and only exhortations to a broadly understood atheistic indoctrination were followed and enforced. The point is that, despite Barkauskas' assertion to the contrary, the Central Committee's warning against the use of arbitrary "administrative" measures had already served its purpose. Furthermore, purely "ideological" persuasion during the thaw period held no promise for the future, and consequently "administrative" arbitrariness was reintroduced under a number of disguises.

The regime again hit church leadership, and in 1957, as noted above, forbade the newly consecrated Bishop Vincentas Sladkevičius of Kaišiadorys to exercise his administrative duties. The bishop was exiled to Radviliškio Nemunėlis, a small town near the Latvian border. Bishop Julijonas Steponavičius, the apostolic administrator of the dioceses of Vilnius and Panevėžys, was deposed in 1961 and confined to Žagarė, another small town far away from the centers of his bishopric. Some monsignors who were appointed on a temporary basis to administer the dioceses of Kaišiadorys and Panevėžys (Meidus and Šidlavskas, respectively) were removed. The administrator of the Kaišiadorys and Panevėžys dioceses, Msgr. P. Bakšys, was not allowed to travel in the latter diocese. Bishops, generally, could not travel to confer the sacrament of confirmation, even within the confines of their own dioceses. The quota of students at the only seminary in Kaunas was reduced to forty, and then to twenty-five. Only one student from each diocese was permitted to enter the seminary in a given year.

The newly-built church of Our Lady of Peace in Klaipeda was expropriated before the festivities announced for its consecration could take place, and its priests, in a protracted trial in 1962, were given prison terms for "economic speculation." The regime claimed that the church had been built illegally. The frequency of church closures generally increased. In 1958 all Catholic cemeteries were withdrawn from parish control, and apparently in the early sixties (the exact date is not clear) the clergy were forbidden to make the traditional annual visitation of parishioners. These visitations had served a dual purpose: as a contact with parish families and an opportunity to collect church dues and gifts for church maintenance. Prohibition of these visitations was obviously intended to undercut the church's financial support.

Again, contrary to the warning of 1954 not to insult the religious feelings of the faithful, personal attacks on particular individuals were intensified. In 1961, party secretary Barkauskas wrote that previously "the main direction antireligious activities took was the unmasking of the church and of the servants of the cult." "Now," he continued, "we have come to criticize religious ideology and to discuss positively the assertions of a scientific weltanschauung, and we firmly oppose any administrative measures."[23] In effect, the newspapers, in stories about the personal behavior of the clergy, denounced them as drunkards, men of corrupt morals, speculators, embezzlers, and the like. According to this literature, priests were "drunkards" if liquor was served at rectory dinners on religious feast days; priests were "immoral" if they asked young boys to serve mass or young girls to sing in the church choirs; they were speculators if they distributed homemade religious articles; embezzlers if they built a parish rectory and registered it in their own name (this cannot be done in the name of the congregation because the latter has no legal rights). The priests, furthermore, had to pay heavy income taxes and were fined for disputing the assessment.

The purpose of such propaganda and pressure was to discredit and to isolate the clergy because their influence disturbed the laboratory-like conditions needed for the atheistic reconditioning of the people, especially the young. The priests, according to the Soviet Lithuanian press, "know that the church is doomed if the clergy do not succeed in establishing their influence over the younger generation. Therefore, they organize youth choirs, youth groups, excursions, arrange church services for the young, and preach especially to them."[24] All of this was, however, no longer legal. The direct teaching of religion, of course, had been illegal for years, although it is not clear exactly when religious instruction became a crime. Apparently, in the last decade, it became a crime even for parents to teach religion to their own children or to request them to attend church against their will. According to recent reports, it is illegal for young people themselves

23. *Komunistas*, 1961, no. 11, p. 7.
24. Veščikovas, *Tarybiniai Istatymai*, p. 6.

to receive religious instruction until they reach the age of eighteen.[25]

These restrictions, of course, constituted only one side of the "ideological" antireligious activity. The other side covers the "positive" atheist indoctrination. This was developed much more broadly than in Stalinist times and employed not only the old tools of the printing press and the radio, but also the recently created local film industry and television.[26] A number of antireligious "documentaries" and full length films have been produced by the Lithuanian Film Studios. According to Soviet data, in 1965 there were 184,000 television sets and 484,000 radios in Lithuania.[27] Both radio and television carried daily programs of an atheistic content. No field, apparently, escaped atheistic indoctrination, since programs like "Science and the World," "The Universe, the Atom, and Life," "Culture and Society," "Radio Club of Youth," and "The Trumpet of the Pioneers" were listed as serving "atheist thought," in addition to the regular programs for atheists like "The Atheist Radio Club."[28]

Atheist coverage by the press was greatly expanded simply because of the general growth of circulation. From 1950 to 1965 single-edition newspaper circulation increased from 577,000 to 1,328,000 copies.[29] Publication of specifically atheistic literature was similarly increased. Between 1954 and 1964, the republic's publishing houses published 229 titles of antireligious propaganda and scientific popularizations which attacked religion.[30] The comparative volume of the current purely antireligious publications can be gauged from the fact that in 1966 the State Publishing House for Scientific-Political Literature planned to publish seven atheistic books and a series of brochures while, in the same period, it planned to publish only eleven books in the field of history.[31]

Another aspect of this new program was a scheme to supplant religious rites and traditions with secular or Communist traditions.[32]

25. See Lowrie and Fletcher, "Khrushchev's Religious Policy," pp. 143–44.

26. Ibid., pp. 137–138.

27. *Narodnoe khoziaistvo SSSR v 1965* [The national economy of the USSR in 1965] (Moscow, 1966), pp. 517–18.

28. Barkauskas, "Ateistine Propaganda," p. 7.

29. *Narodnoe khoziaistvo*, p. 739.

30. Barkauskas, "Ateistine Propaganda," p. 7.

31. See *Knigi na litovskom iazyke iz SSSR* [Books in the Lithuanian language from the USSR], no. 5 (Moscow, 1966), pp. 6–13.

32. Ibid., pp. 10–12; also, Alexander Veinbergs, "Lutheranism and other Denominations in the Baltic Republics," chapter 19 below.

Saint Nicholas has become Father Frost; Christmas has been supplanted by the New Year celebration; Easter is Spring Holiday. The regime has encouraged the celebration of birthdays instead of the traditional Christian name days. In 1963, a special group was established in Vilnius to search for substitutes for the many traditional religious customs. One of the proposals was a ritual for naming infants, intended to replace baptism and the christening party that usually follows in homes. Stress was laid on a civil marriage ceremony. Larger and more comfortable quarters were sought for marriage bureaus and more ritual was introduced into the wedding ceremony. The state was to pay for the ceremony and give gifts. Collective-farm administrators were encouraged to provide free means of transportation and a wedding party for those willing to marry, not in church, but only at the marriage bureau. Similarly, rituals were sought for secular or Communist funerals, but even Communists were frequently buried with a priest officiating.

Finally, *Žinija*, the government-sponsored association for atheistic work, mobilized scientists to help in atheistic propaganda.[33] Soviet newspapers indicate that some of these scientists participated only very reluctantly or tried to avoid the involvement altogether. Their cooperation, however, was considered important because their authority added strength to the propagandist claim that religion is the enemy of science.

The methods and the content of this immense program of ideological indoctrination actually deserve to be treated in a separate study. Many nationally staged advertising campaigns in a country like the United States are pale by comparison.

The Post-Khrushchev Period

In the mid-sixties subtle changes began to take place which contributed to the easing of tension. In the early 1960s, a small number of church administrators were allowed to attend Vatican Council II in Rome, and afterwards some clergymen were permitted visits to the Vatican to attend meetings of commissions to which they were appointed. In December, 1965, one of them, the seventy-year-old Msgr. J. Labukas-Matulaitis, was consecrated bishop of the diocese

33. Order of the Presidium of the Supreme Soviet of the Lithuanian SSR, no. 96–98, *LTSR Aukiščausios Tarybos ir Vyriausybės Žinios* [Bulletin of the Supreme Soviet and of the government of the Lithuanian SSR] (Vilnius), no. 14, May 1966.

of Kaunus. The consecration took place in Rome, but the new bishop was permitted to return to Lithuania. He was appointed to administer the dioceses of Kaunas and Vilkaviškis.

Then in 1968, Moscow allowed the consecration of another bishop, Msgr. J. Pletkus of the diocese of Telšiai, who replaced the recently-deceased Bishop P. Maželis of the same diocese. This consecration took place at the bishop's cathedral and was reported, together with the death of Bishop Maželis, by *Tiesa*, the main party daily in Lithuania.

Some religious publications were also permitted during this period. In 1966, two parts of *Apeigynas*, a Vatican-approved collection of Lithuanian texts for the administration of church sacraments, together with a hymnal, were printed in Vilnius.[34] Similarly, a Lithuanian missal with texts for all parts of the Mass, including the canon, has been approved by the Vatican and published in Lithuania. Finally, it is also reported that a Lithuanian translation of the constitutions and decrees of Vatican Council II is ready and will be published in Vilnius. It is to be hoped that the faithful in Lithuania will have access to these publications. The Vatican also granted permission for the use of the vernacular in the Mass. It is not expected that the regime will allow the publication of any cathechetical-educational material.

As a result of a recent decree by Moscow and by the republic's Supreme Soviet, atheistic propagandists were forbidden to threaten believers with the loss of their jobs.[35] This same decree, however, broadened the range of prohibitions on the clergy's pastoral work and provided stricter sentences (three years instead of two) for the violation of article 143 of the republic's criminal code that lists activities forbidden to religionists. These "reforms," as is clear from their announcement in *Tiesa* (August 17, 1966), were introduced in Lithuania later than in the Russian Republic.

In 1968 the quota of students at the theological seminary in Kaunus was reduced from twenty-five to twenty, and only seventeen could actually attend.

In sum, the post-Khrushchev period has seen some liberalization, allowing some clerical contact with the outside world and the publi-

---

34. It is interesting to note that the Lithuanian liturgical texts are binding not only for Lithuania, but for all Lithuanian emigrants as well.
35. The English text of this decree is in the Appendix, section 3A, below.

cation of a certain amount of religious literature, and it has also seen some further repression, particularly pressures on the clergy.

The Effects of Soviet Efforts

The question of Soviet effectiveness in the struggle against religion is, needless to say, crucially important for the regime as well as for the church. The success or failure in alienating youth from religion has a direct bearing on the future of Communist power. For the church it is a question of survival. What, then, have been the results of the atheistic campaign in Lithuania over the past twenty-five years?

CHURCH BUILDINGS

There is no doubt that the church has suffered great losses under Soviet rule.[36] Although its organization and its union with Rome have survived, it has lost in almost every other respect. First, some 15 percent of the houses of regular worship and all of the occasional or institutional chapels have been closed. Thus, the number of church buildings has been reduced from 708 in 1940 to 606 in 1965, while of the 314 chapels used for seasonal services (for example, in hospitals, convents, or prisons) in 1940, all but four were closed by 1965. The churches were either completely shut or adapted for such secular uses as warehouses (the fourteenth-century church of St. John the Baptist and St. John the Apostle in Vilnius), atheist museums (the church of St. Casimir in Vilnius, which houses, according to Communist information, an atheistic museum second in importance only to the central museum of atheism in Leningrad), art galleries or concert halls (the famous Vilnius cathedral), dance halls (the seventeenth-century Holy Trinity Church in Kaunas), factories (the church of the Resurrection in Kaunas), or museums (the church of the Pazaislis monastery). Others have been simply razed (the church of the Exaltation of the Holy Cross in Kaunas). Most churches have

---

36. The data given here on churches and the clergy is the most complete and reliable information obtainable. It was obtained from *Lithuanian Religious Information* in Rome. The figures differ somewhat from those given by Bishop Brižgys in *La Chiesa in Lituania* and those used by Dr. J. Savasis, *The War Against God in Lithuania* (New York, 1966). These latter sources present somewhat less complete figures because the sources are based on earlier information. (Savisis' book, however, is especially useful for illustrations of particular aspects of religious persecution.) At the end of 1967 and early in 1968, authentic figures for clergy in Lithuania were published by the Italian Communist paper *Unità* and the French Communist paper *L'Humanité*. These figures are essentially the same as those presented here except that neither source published the breakdown of the clergy by age.

been closed in urban areas where the concentration of population is the largest. Vilnius, formerly a city of about thirty-six Catholic churches, has only eight left open for services. On the other hand, the construction of new churches, with the exception of two, was not allowed, and one, newly constructed in 1962, has recently been converted into a concert hall.

THE CLERGY

Losses of clergymen, which for Roman Catholic religious continuity is more important than the number of churches, were even larger. Of about one thousand priests at the start of the second Soviet occupation in 1944–46, by 1967 only 848 were left, despite the fact that some 300 new priests were ordained between 1944 and 1967. These 848 priests have to service an area equal to and a population larger than that served in 1940 by 1,451 priests. As a result, priests in rural areas frequently have to travel to several churches or else deny religious rites to rural Catholics and risk the closing of churches on grounds that they are not used.

Of special significance for the survival of the church is the composition of the Lithuanian clergy in terms of age. Of the 848 priests functioning in 1967, 286 were very old men, between sixty and ninety years of age. This group, educated from grade school to the seminary during the time of Lithuania's independence, or even earlier, is the strongest of the clergy in theological conviction and national consciousness, but weakest physically and with the shortest life-expectancy. Moreover, they are not the largest group. The most sizeable and vigorous group of the present clergy, numbering 449, is found in the age bracket of forty to fifty-nine. These priests, too, received either all or at least most of their high school education before World War II and were ordained either in independent Lithuania or at a time when Soviet control over the church and the clergy was not yet complete. They are, quite obviously, the group on whom the church will have to rely in the immediate future, but their life expectancy, at best, averages only about twenty years. The third, and smallest group of clergymen (105) belong in the age bracket of thirty to thirty-nine years. These priests received only their primary education before Soviet occupation and were ordained either during Stalin's lifetime or in the thaw period. The number of priests between twenty-four and twenty-nine is negligible. In 1967 there were only eight of them, and they have no direct experience of the period of national independence or religious freedom. These two latter groups have a life expectancy of some forty years, but twenty years from now, when the middle group will be gone, there could be less than the present 113. It is to be remembered that the population of the country has grown steadily and in 1966 reached 3 million. There are no prospects that the number of theology students, and thus of young priests, will substantially increase. In 1965, for example, the regime did not allow registration of the full contingent of twenty-five theology students; the seminary opened with only twenty-four seminarians. In 1968 the *numerus clausus* was reduced to twenty, and only seventeen seminarians were admitted for study.

To this bleak estimate one must add still another difficulty which many see as a real danger. This is the direct infiltration of the clergy by Soviet agents, widespread submission of the clergy to the government, or the ordination to the priesthood, at the behest of the regime, of persons lacking in personal and moral integrity. Actually, to date, the number of priests who have abandoned the priesthood in Lithuania is very small; it does not exceed two dozen. But such cases are becoming more frequent. More frequent also is the infiltration of the seminary. For example, one of the reasons that allegedly caused the Soviets to remove and intern Bishop Julijonas Steponavičius was his refusal to ordain to the priesthood three candidates who were reliably reported to be government agents.[37] The danger of such destruction from within is very real and with time might become more and more difficult to combat.

THE FAITHFUL

The situation among the faithful, interestingly enough, is discouraging but relatively not as bad. It is extremely difficult, of course, to evaluate the attitudes of Soviet citizens, especially on matters toward which the regime assumes a critical attitude. In 1965, however, the Soviets themselves published data that can be used to assess this situation. According to Moscow's *Nauka i religiia*, the extent of religious belief in Lithuania is higher than in the other republics, and, furthermore, it is higher among Lithuania's Catholics than among the other religious groups in the republic.[38] Reception of the

37. Savasis, *War Against God*, pp. 83–84.
38. V. Pomerantsev, "Vchera i segodnia" [Yesterday and today], *Nauki i religiia* [Science and Religion], no. 4 (April 1966), pp. 5ff.

sacraments and attendance at services are reported to have declined among all groups, but in 1964 were still considerable: 58 percent of all newborn babies were baptized, 38 percent of all marriages were celebrated in churches, and 60 percent of all burials were performed by the clergy. This represented a drop from, respectively, 81 percent, 64 percent, and 79 percent in 1958. These figures, like any others of similar nature, are not to be taken at face value. No records are kept by the churches of those rites that are performed secretly, and the Soviets must be merely estimating the percentages or reporting only what is publicly known.

It is clear, however, that the church has lost adherents and, furthermore, that these losses have occurred primarily in the cities, which in 1965 contained 43 percent of the republic's population. The same journal reported that in 1964 in Kaunas, the second largest and ethnically most Lithuanian city (with a population of 269,000), only 13 percent of all marriages were performed in church, only 58 percent of all newborn babies were baptized, and 50 percent of all funerals were held with church services.

In the villages church attendance is still very high, reception of communion is frequent, and religious loyalties are still strong. This is largely because the government control-apparatus in the villages does not work as efficiently and because kolkhoz workers are relatively less afraid of economic and other pressures. In the cities, better control and greater fear of reprisals work against the faithful. In the cities, exposure to atheistic indoctrination is more intense, and the church there has suffered much greater losses.

Samples recently provided by separate Communist sociologists who work with atheist indoctrination make it possible to compare the urban and rural situations more systematically. This work may be slanted, but it is potentially very revealing. In 1964–65, students of the Pedagogical Institute at Šiauliai, a city of seventy-five thousand, conducted a sociological inquiry into the family environment of children at one of the city's primary schools.[39] The students surveyed attitudes of 312 families and found that 96 of them were atheistic and consequently supported the school's atheistic education. Seventy-four families observed religious traditions. These people, according to the investigators, were religious because they did not want to differ from their religious neighbors and were supported in

39. See *Tarybinis Mokytojas*, 28 January 1965, p. 1.

their attitudes by "religious grandmothers." In six other families the students found "ideological struggle" among members of the family. Parents were nonbelievers, while grandmothers frequented the church and "forced" children to do the same. The largest group of families (eighty-nine) consisted of "wavering" people. They did not oppose the atheistic education of their children at school (they attended atheistic programs), but at the same time they occasionally attended church secretly and did not restrain grandmothers from teaching religion to their children. The other forty-seven families were "fanatically religious." They opposed atheist instruction at school and at home sought to undo the work of the teachers. The school, the researchers concluded, could only rely for support of its atheist education on the actually atheist parents, that is, only on some 30 percent of all the parents of the school. Translating this idiom, we would say that 70 percent of all parents in that part of the city of Šiauliai were churchgoers, performing their religious obligations on a selective basis and more or less frequently. It is not clear to what degree these city faithful receive the sacraments, though it apparently can be assumed that most of them participate in religious weddings and other rites.

At present, there is no comparable data on ideological orientation in the villages. J. Baužys, a Soviet Lithuanian and author of a recently published study of the attitudes of village faithful based on data collected in the Kartena area near the city of Klaipeda, insists that "religion in the Lithuanian village is in deep crisis."[40] The grounds for this conclusion is his impression that only 10 to 20 percent of those classifying themselves as faithful really are such.

Baužys groups the faithful found in the villages of Dauginciai and Cigoneliai into three categories: "active," "doubting," and "wavering." The first group consists of older people, over fifty years of age. These people attend church services, support the church, and participate in parish committees that help the priests with parish administration. They teach religion not only to their own children but to those of their relatives and friends, and frequently do so under direct clerical supervision. Their faith is to some extent connected with nationalism, although, the author remarks, most people of this group are loyal to the Soviet regime and actively participate in the work of the collective farms. The second, the "doubting" group, are

40. Baužys, "Religiniu Prietaru," p. 253.

religious themselves but do not proselytize. They are patient with atheism, they believe in freedom of conscience, but they teach religion to their children. Their faith, according to the author, rests not so much on theological arguments as on tradition, on the authority of parents and grandparents and on that of the faithful majority. Some of these people, however, attend church only rarely.

The third group, the "wavering" believers, accounts for between 80 to 90 percent of all believers, in the author's view, and is the product of atheist propaganda conducted among the "doubting" Catholics of the second group. Finally, the author finds that a part of the deeply religious faithful seek to reconcile their faith with communism while others regard these two as permanently antagonistic. On the other hand, Baužys speaks of people who do not believe in God but go to church and defend religion because they oppose Soviet rule.

In the view of this Communist researcher, then, while religious traditions in the villages (for example, family evening prayers) are disappearing, the church has a firm grip over christening, marriage, and funeral rites, even though church attendance is shrinking. Similarly popular in the villages are the celebrations of Christmas and Easter, often celebrated by nonbelievers as well. It may be added that the number of atheists in the villages is still very small. This last condition seems to be the greatest difference between the city and rural populations, in addition to the greater ease with which religion is practiced in the villages.

Communist data is even more scarce concerning their success with the main target of the recent atheistic campaign, namely, the youth. A survey conducted by teachers in the number 2 secondary school of Tauragė, a town of thirteen thousand, showed, for example, that in senior classes only certain students continue to attend church and that the school has more than one hundred pupils in its atheist group. More than four hundred students, however, are classified as "inactive nonbelievers," and a correspondent reporting on this data regards this as a warning to the teachers "that a number of students are indifferent and apathetic to the duel between the two diametrically opposed ideologies, and that in the future this might lead to concessions to church supporters."[41] Some teachers regard such data as only 80 to 90 percent reliable, which should be interpreted as further

41. *Tarybinis Mokytojas*, 28 March 1965, p. 3.

undermining the claim of the Tauragė teachers that only rare individual pupils continue to practice religion.[42]

Three points must be stressed in appraising the effect of atheistic
propaganda on the youth. First, progress has been made, and the
number of atheist clubs and members is growing, though it is difficult
to determine their percentage in the total school enrollment. Second,
some young people whom the Soviets regard as either atheistic or indifferent are actually believers and privately receive religious instruction from itinerant teachers—the "bees," as *Tiesa* recently called
them.[43] There is little doubt that from their early days, Soviet pupils
are taught duplicity in religious matters. In one primary school, a
raion school inspector, after looking over a display, "heaven and
earth," that apparently was to serve atheistic purposes, asked pupils
where God lived, and received answers such as "in heaven" or "in
church." There was only one pupil who said that God did not exist.[44]
Similarly, innumerable newspaper stories tell about Komsomols who
attend church and marry in church, who distribute homemade
religious articles, and who arrange Bible discussion sessions in the
local "clubs of culture." There is also the internationally known
testimony of the faith of the young Lithuanian girls deported to
Siberia. They wrote a prayerbook which was smuggled out of the
Soviet Union and published in six languages, among them English,
with a total circulation of more than a million copies. There is also
the moving confession of faith of a twenty-year-old girl that *Tiesa*
published on December 22, 1960. Her faith, she said, was the most
precious of all her values and she would rather lose her life than
her faith.[45]

There is, however, a third group of young people, probably the
largest, which seems to grow ever larger, namely, the group of the indifferent. The propagandist saturation of everyday life has apparently
produced skepticism and indifference rather than hostility to the
church, tolerance rather than the active atheism that the regime
seeks to inculcate. The fashionable view among students of higher institutions of learning and among the young intelligentsia is that
"religion is a private affair" over which the state should have no

42. Ibid., 18 February 1965, p. 2.
43. *Tiesa*, 15 November 1968.
44. *Tarybinis Mokytojas*, 9 June 1963, p. 2.
45. For concrete examples of religious resistance see Savasis, *War Against God*, pp.
117–34.

control.[46] A segment of this religiously indifferent youth has become skeptical concerning ideological thought altogether.[47]

Conclusions

There would seem to be no reason to be overly optimistic about the situation of the Church in Lithuania. Many optimists maintain that the church will survive because man is religious by nature. Furthermore, they feel that it is not in the interest of the Lithuanian Communists to destroy it completely. These Communists are said to see the church as a valuable prop of Lithuanian nationalism which they themselves are thought to want to preserve. On the other hand, it is equally difficult to agree with the pessimists, who believe that the church in Lithuania will be completely liquidated in less than a generation.

The church's future in Lithuania is doubtless very dark. In twenty years, if things continue as they are, there will not be enough priests left to say Mass even in a quarter of the churches open today, not to speak of the physical impossibility of administering the sacraments to more than a fraction of the total Catholic population. Also, the quality of the clergy and their theological reliability seems destined to decline. On the other hand, the atheistic campaign has not made sufficient headway to permit one to speak of an early and complete de-Christianization of the republic. What probably lies ahead is the prospect of a church considerably reduced in size and largely serviced and managed by laymen, most probably in actual underground conditions.

There is, however, a factor of utmost importance that needs to be taken into consideration, namely, pressures within the Soviet Union, many of them arising from Soviet self-interest, which would like to see the government seek greater communication with the West. This is happening not only in the field of politics but also in the field of religion. As noted above, a number of Lithuanian priests and church administrators were allowed to attend the Second Vatican Council in Rome. In December, 1965, as a result of a tacit understanding between Moscow and the Vatican, a new bishop for the diocese of Kaunas was consecrated in Rome and allowed to return to Lithuania.

46. See my "Soviet Social Engineering in Lithuania: An Appraisal," in Vardys, *Lithuania Under the Soviets*, pp. 255ff.
47. See Bohdan R. Bociurkiw, "Religion and Atheism in Soviet Society," chapter 4 above.

These contacts may lead nowhere, but in view of the continuously and unpredictably changing domestic Soviet situation, these contacts and small concessions might sustain the life of the church in Lithuania until there is a turning point in the total development of Soviet society. This might save religion and allow the church's reemergence from its present semiunderground conditions, especially since the strength of religious convictions among the committed Catholics reportedly is very strong. If, however, the Soviet Union does not pursue the opening toward the West with accompanying fundamental political changes at home, within a generation the church's situation will have become immeasurably worse than it is at present.

19

LUTHERANISM
AND OTHER DENOMINATIONS
IN THE BALTIC REPUBLICS

Although from the point of view of religion the three Baltic republics of the USSR—Latvia, Estonia, and Lithuania—are not homogeneous, the fact of their simultaneous annexation and the similarity of the antireligious program which has been carried out in each of them provide sufficient justification for considering them together here. Naturally, there have been and continue to be significant differences from region to region and from republic to republic, but these differences can be adequately treated within the general framework of common experience. In the past, information concerning particular churches in the Baltic area has frequently been very difficult to obtain. Furthermore, whatever news was received usually did not find wide distribution. It is precisely this situation which occasioned the present study and its method.

Historical Background

On three occasions the Baltic countries have come under Soviet occupation. Since only the last of these has been extensive, most attention will be given to it. The first, brief period of Soviet occupation of the Baltic countries came shortly after the October Revolution, in 1918–19. After the collapse of the German occupation in 1918, all three countries proclaimed their independence, but in a few months they found most of their territory occupied by the Red Army. During

Alexander Veinbergs

the German occupation even those Latvian and Estonian pastors who had not signed the "Declaration of Submissiveness" telegram sent to the Kaiser were not harassed. This was not true of this first period of Soviet rule. In Latvia 56 percent of the population belonged to the Evangelical Lutheran church. Of its 196 ministers, twenty-six were shot or died in prison and forty others fled the country, many because they were German nationals.[1] In the province of Kurzeme, which had proportionately more German nationals than the country at large, half the Lutheran congregations were left without pastors. By contrast the Catholic church (which claimed 25 percent of the population in Latvia) and the Orthodox church did not experience comparable persecution. As noted, the difference in treatment can probably be traced to the German connections of the Lutheran church. The Estonian Lutheran church suffered less, largely because the occupation did not last as long there.

The second period of Soviet occupation began after August 23, 1939, the date on which the Soviet-German nonaggression pact was signed. This agreement was followed by a series of Soviet ultimatums concerning the establishment of Soviet military bases in the Baltic countries. Formal occupation took place between June 16 and 18, 1940, at a time when the German forces were preoccupied with events in Western Europe. (According to the terms of the Molotov-Ribbentrop Pact, Lithuania was to have come under German influence.)

During the night of June 13–14, 1941, 34,000 Latvians, 10,205 Estonians, and 65,000 Lithuanians were deported to the Soviet Union, among them many priests and ministers. (In Estonia the entire Catholic church, with its six congregations and fifteen priests, simply ceased to exist, primarily because of these arrests.)[2] After the war some of the members of those families who had been arrested returned, but none of the clergymen did. Estonia lost four bishops (Lutheran, Catholic, and Orthodox), six district deans, twenty-six pastors and priests, and 163 church board members.[3] In Latvia eleven Catholic priests were arrested and six of them were

---

1. Hans Wenschkewitz, "Die Christlichen Kirchen in Lettland," in R. Wittram, ed., *Baltische Kirchengeschicte* (Göttingen, 1956), pp. 267–68.
2. See Paul Mailleux, "Catholics in the Soviet Union," chapter 16 above.
3. Jakob Aunver, "Estlands Christliche Kirche der Gegenwart," in *Acta Baltica I* (Institutum Balticum in Königstein im Taunus, 1962), pp. 82, 84.

shot;[4] thirteen Lutheran ministers were also arrested, and these were ethnic Latvians, not of German origin as had been the case of many of those arrested in 1919.

With the German invasion of the Soviet Union in 1941, Soviet rule in the Baltic territories was again interrupted, only to be re-established towards the end of the war. Information about events of the immediate postwar period was generally not available until after Stalin's death in 1953. The sources are varied: (1) the local communications media, especially the press and radio; (2) a few church publications which, though scanty in their coverage, provide useful information;[5] (3) visits of individuals back and forth that have been extremely illuminating, especially in the last ten years; (4) personal correspondence of impressive proportions in recent years, which has become progressively more explicit in matters of religion. Clearly, the failure to integrate information from all these sources would tend to give an unrealistic and one-sided picture. For example, official publications have been silent on the mass deportations of 1949, whereas letters indicate that this roundup was even larger than the arrests of 1941, and in Estonia reduced the number of Lutheran clergy from eighty to fifty.[6]

In summarizing the years 1945 to the present, several distinct periods can be discerned. The first period, from 1945 to 1948, was not as difficult as might be expected. One reason for this was the continuation of the wartime modus vivendi worked out between the churches and the Soviet government; another is the fact that the area was not

4. Karlis Rukis, "Die Verfolgung der Katholischen Kirche in Sowjetlettland," in ibid., pp. 95, 96.

5. The Lutheran Church Yearbook in Latvia has appeared annually since 1947, ranging in size from 32 pages in 1951 to 116 pages in 1967. A very simple Estonian Yearbook was published for the first time in 1956. The number of copies printed is not given, but reliable estimates put the number at approximately five thousand per year. These publications are referred to as "church calendars," but often appear quite late in the year for which they are intended, rendering them less than fully useful for pastoral purposes. The price per copy is relatively high. Church officials explain that the sale of the calendars is one of the principal sources of income for the Lutheran church's Supreme Board of Administration in Latvia and for the church consistory in Estonia. Monies so acquired are frequently used to defray the expenses of church representatives to foreign conferences. Though lacking statistics, including consistent lists of pastors and their addresses, these calendars do offer direct information relating to ecclesiastical events of the preceding year, as well as much indirect information on the whereabouts of bishops and pastors.

6. *The Evangelical Lutheran Church of Estonia in Exile* (Stockholm: Committee of the Estonian Church, 1957), p. 9. Peteris Egle, elected head of the Latvian Baptists in 1966, and Julians Vaivods, a Catholic priest (consecrated bishop in Rome in 1964), were both deported in 1949 and later released.

yet fully pacified. Although in 1947 a general amnesty was declared for those who gave up armed resistance and came out of hiding, this resistance continued until at least 1950. Also in 1947 the Soviets encouraged the Lutheran churches of Latvia and Estonia to hold synods to elect new leaders to replace those who had fled or been evacuated by the Germans as they withdrew. This was apparently motivated by the desire to bring religious leaders to the fore who would lend their support to Soviet pacification efforts.

The years 1949 to 1953 saw a return to harsh and repressive antireligious measures. The wave of arrests which began this period has already been cited. After the death of Stalin another period of relative calm ensued, which lasted from 1953 to 1959, with a gradual deterioration setting in about 1956, at the time of the Hungarian revolution. A second period of severe persecution began in 1959 and lasted until Khrushchev's removal from power in 1964.[7] A fourth period, one of relative calm, apparently began in 1965–66, although as yet it is somewhat difficult to speak too boldly or to be too precise about this period.

The periods of greatest difficulty, then, were 1949–53 and 1959–64. In these years the churches suffered greatly. One may ask what prompted the amelioration of conditions in the intervening years noted above—1945–48, 1953–59, and 1964 to the present. For the immediate postwar period the continuation of wartime agreements and the need to deprive the partisans of a distinct advantage were doubtless the motivation, as noted. In the first years following Stalin's death we may cite the confusion attendant upon the succession crisis, and the fact that local Communist leaders enjoyed a greater degree of independence. Though these leaders are undoubtedly doctrinaire Marxists in matters of religion, they seem to have felt that religion was in some way connected with the nationalism that they espoused, and this contributed to a mitigation of the more repressive antireligious measures. To the extent that the last few years have seen less repression, one may speculate that this is the result of either another succession crisis or the pressures attendant upon the Sino-Soviet split and the regime's need to adjust to the outspoken disapproval of Soviet religious policy on the part of certain foreign Communists.[8]

7. See Donald A. Lowrie and William C. Fletcher, "Khrushchev's Religious Policy, 1959–64," chapter 7 above.

8. See Bernhard Wilhelm, "Moslems in the Soviet Union, 1948–54," chapter 12 above.

In short, until the present at least, official relaxation of anti-religious measures appears to have been merely a tactical shift. Even in the calmer periods, party ideologues have never ceased to proclaim the need for the complete elimination of all vestiges of religion. Whether or not there are influential men in the party today who question the necessity of such a position and who will consequently tend to inaugurate new policies accordingly, remains to be seen. To date there is no evidence that the embryonic dialogue between Christians and Marxists in the West (and to a lesser degree in eastern Europe) has found any supporters within the Soviet Union.

Antireligious Tactics

The patterns of antireligious activity carried on by the regime against the Lutheran church and the other denominations are worth noting in some detail. One of the primary objects of this activity has been the alienation of young people from religion.[9] That the campaign has been effective is illustrated by a report in *Padomju Jaunatne* (Soviet youth) for August 9, 1965, in which it was stated that only one of sixty-four students at a secondary school in Skriveri could recognize the first words of the Our Father. Various means to reach the youth have been employed. On November 10, 1964, Riga Radio reported that all school children in the country had been asked to fill out a questionnaire directed toward learning their own and their parents' attitudes toward religion. (The questionnaire, while encouraging for churchmen in some of its results, shows how thorough this effort has become.) Students are employed in discovering who attends church services and they report to their school or club superiors. On January 4, 1966, Rita Krajevska, the vice-president of the Militant Atheists' Club of Vecumnieku High School, said in a broadcast over Riga Radio: "While even one believer remains within the territory of our club, the members will work to find him out, although we leave their individual reeducation to the professional atheists of the village council."

In a similar broadcast on April 12, 1966, Lucija Cigane, a teacher from Vilaka, said:

I have worked as a teacher in Vilaka for twelve years. When I first came here the first thing I noticed was how well-attended the church services were. It was August 15, a Catholic feast day. It occurred to me that it would not

9. See Lowrie and Fletcher, "Khrushchev's Religious Policy," pp. 135–37.

be easy to work in such a place. I was right. The greatest difficulties are created by parents who are faithful and who not only attend church themselves, but also drag their small children along. Now in comparison with the past, the number of believers is becoming smaller and smaller, especially among the young people. I can confidently predict that among the high school graduates of this and next year there will be no believers.

Ridicule has been widely employed, but with particular virulence where children are concerned. They are often named in the newspapers and pointed out in class when they have been observed attending church. In one case a girl by the name of Gunta Rieksts, whose address was even printed, was caricatured as having fallen to her knees, clutching the garments of a minister.[10]

A leading figure in this campaign is Dr. Dzidra Meiksane, a former teacher and head of the Pedagogical Research Institute. In addition to her numerous articles in the press and hundreds of lectures, she has written a manual entitled "The antireligious education of children" (1963) which chronicles the uneven struggle between the atheistic school and the religious home. Dr. Meiksane defends, at least by implication, several practices which are aimed at weaning young people away from the church. In addition to ridicule, students are given poorer marks than their work merits and ranked low in conduct. They are frequently denied certain privileges, such as school outings, which, incidentally, are often scheduled on Sunday mornings. Finally, young people have been refused entrance to the university and denied job placement if it is learned that they attend church. (As noted, Komsomol members and members of atheist clubs commonly come to church services to note which of their schoolmates are there.)

School district officials are, of course, particularly keen to discover believers among their staff. When they do, they publicize the case and the attendant disciplinary measures that are invoked serve as an example to others. Such was the case of a young Estonian Lutheran, Alli Lokk, who was removed from her position as a result of having been confirmed and married in church. The Estonian teachers' magazine attacked her viciously and implied similar sanctions for any who imitated her example.[11]

It is impossible to give an accurate assessment of the effectiveness

10. *Cina* [The fight], in Latvian, July 1961; cf. "An Atheist with a Bible," *Padomju Jaunatne* [Soviet youth], in Latvian, 4 December 1965.

11. *Naukoje Opetaja* [The Soviet teacher], in Estonian, as quoted in Leonard Vahter, "Aspects of Life in Estonia," in *Baltic Review*, no. 28, p. 53.

of such efforts, and perhaps Communist estimates of the situation are not wholly trustworthy. Nonetheless, there would seem to be much accuracy to the remarks which follow, made by a teacher in charge of such a program in Latvia: "Lately more and more young people have been participating in mass cultural projects, in the true Communist spirit, and many of these come from formerly religious families. . . . As yet not all young people have been taken up in these programs; those of Adventist and Baptist families in particular resist our efforts.[12]

Padomju Jaunatne claimed in 1966 that well over half of the young people of Latvia were fully behind Communist principles and had completely abandoned all religious ideology and observance.

Uldis Krišjanis, vice-president of the Jelgava Bureau of Scientific Atheism, outlined the program of his organization in a radio broadcast of November 10, 1964. Following the directives of the Ideological Commission in Moscow, he reported that his bureau had organized atheist clubs in factories, schools, and universities. "Atheist mornings" to replace church services had been organized on a wide scale. Also, secular ceremonies to replace religious ceremonies had been vigorously promoted with considerable success.

Name-giving ceremonies to replace Christian baptism and coming-of-age ceremonies to replace confirmation were quite successful at first. This was especially true of the latter; in many areas church confirmations dropped off almost completely. In recent months, however, it seems that the novelty of these rites has begun to wear off and Communist writers are asking what can be done to give them the same color and appeal of their religious counterparts.

On October 23, 1965, Riga Radio announced that, to date in that year, there had been over seventeen hundred atheistic lectures by 450 speakers. Earlier that year, in March, a three-day student conference was held in Riga to search for better methods of atheistic propaganda. The student participants were primarily medical students from all over the Soviet Union. In December, 1966, Latvian officials announced an interuniversity competition on the theme "scientific criticism of the Bible." Winners in each university were to form a team for their school, with a competition for the entire country scheduled for Easter, 1967. (It should be noted that in all the universities of the Soviet Union there are supposed to be departments of

12. Riga Radio, in Latvian, 7 September 1965.

scientific atheism, whose instructors not only teach at the university level, but also contribute their efforts to night-school courses and other antireligious efforts in their area.)

The antireligious press, including newspapers, magazines, and books, has produced an enormous volume of materials in the Baltic republics.[13] The quality and character of these materials range from scurrilous and subjective invective to learned and thought-provoking exegesis. An example of the former would be the spate of articles scorning Catholic pilgrimages that usually coincide with the harvest. On the other hand, textbooks used at the university level increasingly make use of relevant foreign publications and research, historical and contemporary, to permeate all academic subjects with atheistic ideology. Such publishing activity is most extensive in areas where the atheistic program encounters most difficulty. Accordingly, in Latgale, which has a high concentration of Catholics and Orthodox, a major center of atheistic propaganda was established in Daugavpils in 1959 under the auspices of the Daugavpils Teachers' Institute. In 1960 the first major work of the center appeared in the form of a detailed handbook on how to organize atheistic clubs.

A common feature of atheistic literature is the exploitation of clerics who renounce their religion. In each case the press and the radio are saturated with interviews and autobiographical sketches, devoted to contrasting religious superstition and practice with the relative sanity and selflessness of communism. The superintendent of the Lithuanian Reformed church, Adom Šernas, renounced his faith shortly before his death. His statement was first published by *Nauka i religiia* (Science and religion) and then in all the principal Lithuanian and Latvian newspapers.[14] Z. Springovičs, the nephew of the late Catholic archbishop of Latvia, published a pamphlet shortly after his renunciation of religion in 1961 entitled *Latgale un Katolu Baznica* (Latgale and the Catholic church) which chronicled his own path to atheism, together with frequent interpolations from atheistic handbooks and propaganda materials. Actually there have been fewer than twenty such defections from all the denominations in Latvia (none have been reported in Estonia), but they are carefully exploited when they do occur. A principal aim of these writings seems to be to persuade ministers and priests that there is no future for

13. See Lowrie and Fletcher, "Khrushchev's Religious Policy," pp. 135, 137.
14. *Cina*, 26 December 1964.

them and to encourage them to give up their "childish and foolish activities" in favor of real service and contribution.

Other themes of antireligious literature include the moral turpitude and selfishness of the clergy, the contradictions between space-age science and religion, the historical role of religion as the guarantor of the status quo and the ally of the exploiters, and religion as a psychological malady and a form of alienation.

Religious Statistics

The success of these and even harsher antireligious methods in eradicating religious belief is not simple or, finally, even possible to assess. Even to tabulate external signs of religious expression, difficult as this is, can be especially misleading in the Soviet Union. To begin with, most of the activities customarily associated with church life in the West, with the exception of worship as such, are forbidden. This includes a range of activities from religious instruction to charitable works. This fact is of utmost significance, and the reduction of the former breadth of religious life to worship or cult alone, even if full freedom of worship were permitted in practice, is a tremendous restriction on believers.

Nor do church attendance figures always provide accurate information on the nature and quality of religious life. Though not a state religion since the days of Swedish rule, Lutheranism in the Baltic countries came close to this status. Religion was taught in all schools and there were prescribed religious services in the armed forces. Understandably, then, the figures for church attendance before the war include many nominal believers who found church attendance desirable for nonreligious reasons. It would be equally understandable if, since the war, believers found the avoidance of regular church attendance to be not only desirable but necessary in the face of Soviet pressure. Nonetheless, church attendance figures do give some indication of the number of people whose religious sensibilities remain in the face of a materialist program of education, and who might provide the impetus for religious revival in the event of a change of official policy on religion.

The figures on church attendance which are available are not completely trustworthy, but a critical comparison of statistics from various sources can yield some conclusions. The World Council of Churches and the Lutheran World Federation have both published studies with statistics; these differ significantly in the different republics for the different denominations. Subsequent to the earliest compilations, Baltic church delegates have been permitted to travel in the West, and the information they have provided has improved the situation somewhat, although in some cases the information even these men had available was dishearteningly scanty. Finally, in the past few years Soviet sociologists have conducted surveys and made studies of the extent of religious survivals and the frequency of church attendance. Again, these statistics are not wholly reliable, given the reluctance of some of those questioned to tell the truth, but they provide one more estimate to consider.

Since 1944 attendance figures have fluctuated considerably, often for external reasons. The confusion of the war years and the patriotic sentiments of the mid-forties prompted increased attendance. However, at other times, for instance in the late forties and early fifties and during the Khrushchev campaign, there was a decline, if only because those who might ordinarily have gone to church, even occasionally, found it distinctly disadvantageous to do so.

In recent years reports of foreign churchmen and journalists on their visits to churches in the Baltic republics have been very helpful in a determination of church attendance. Perhaps their presence in a church (especially foreign church dignitaries), which was until recently a relatively infrequent occurrence, attracted more people to services that might otherwise have been there, but this does not discount the usefulness of their observations. The report of J. Flodman, a correspondent for the Swedish daily *Svenska Dagbladet*, is typical. In May, 1966, he attended services at several churches in Riga. He reported that in the Lutheran churches there are often two Sunday morning services at which the combined congregations of several former churches are present. Likewise, there are two or more weekday services which are only sparsely attended. He also noted that the influx of people from Latgale, a predominantly Catholic province, has resulted in Catholic services being better attended than either the Lutheran or Orthodox churches.[15]

The Latvian Lutheran church calendar for 1966 tells of a service for some visiting Finnish tourists that was attended by over fifteen hundred people. The same article tells of three thousand attending a cemetery memorial service at which Bishop Lauha of Helsinki

15. "Sightseeing in Riga," *Svenska Dagbladet*, 24 May 1966, p. 12.

preached. Other reports tell of numerous well-attended Methodist revival meetings. In 1965 there were more than 370 services in the Tallin Methodist church in Estonia with an average attendance of about five hundred people per service.[16]

There are indications that the number of believers exceeds that indicated either by church attendance or Soviet polls. One might cite the huge numbers who attend Christmas and Easter services, especially in the larger cities where anonymity can be preserved. Many of those who attend at such times are from the villages. They often come to the cities to have their children baptized or confirmed without being noticed. Another indicator, though more colored by the problem of patriotic attachment to a church, is the annual pilgrimage to the National Cemetery and memorial services for the nation's dead held in neighboring Forest Park Cemetery in Riga on the last Sunday of the Lutheran church year. This service, which is primarily religious, is well attended and most of those present join in the recital of the prayers. This, moreover, seems to be a phenomenon of recent development. Because it has been a thorn in the side of the authorities, there has been an effort to replace it by a secular service complete with orchestra and public oratory.

It must be noted that a somewhat puzzling picture of church attendance confronts the researcher. In some areas the few remaining churches are empty, or virtually so, Sunday after Sunday. In other regions, the churches are full and things seem to be quite normal. (This is true primarily of the Lutheran churches. In most places the remaining Catholic churches are consistently full for Sunday services.) Also, observers have noted the contrast, again for the Lutheran churches, between large attendance on important feast days and when visitors are present, and almost no attendance on normal Sundays, when the churches are empty. Finally, radio reports differ in their statistics, depending on whether or not they are beamed abroad or only for domestic consumption. On June 14, 1965, in a Swedish language broadcast, Riga Radio announced that one thousand "listeners" attended a special service on the seventy-fifth birthday of Archbishop G. Turs. This item was not carried on domestic news broadcasts. Another factor which clearly affects church

16. *Evangelischer Nachrichtendienst* (East Berlin), 30 March 1966, as quoted in *Religion in Communist-Dominated Areas*, 15–31 August 1966.

attendance from month to month is the political climate of the moment.

One indicator of active membership in the Lutheran church is the number of people who receive the sacrament of communion regularly. The reports of the World Council of Churches and the Lutheran World Federation state that from one-third to two-thirds of the former members of most congregations are still churchgoers. This may indeed be true, but the number of regular communicants is something under 10 percent.

The information concerning the clergy provides a rather gloomy picture. The general shortage of pastors is so acute that many of those currently serving a congregation are quite elderly. One such pastor, Martinš Kartinš, a Lutheran, died at the age of 102 in 1967. By 1966 regular Lutheran Sunday church services in the Baltic countries were held only in the city churches where the pastor lived nearby. For country parishes pastors are so scarce that it is impossible for one minister to serve the several congregations assigned to him. The greatest known number of congregations to be served by any one Latvian Lutheran pastor is eight, and these churches are all about ten miles apart.

One reason for this situation is the fact that the training of Lutheran pastors is very sporadic. (By contrast, Latvian Catholics have retained their seminary which, even though small, still provides regular courses. It is housed in the residence of the archbishop of Riga and supplies priests to Estonia and other parts of the USSR.) The Latvian Lutheran church calendar shows that between 1955 and 1966 there were only ten graduates of the theological course. Understandably, the number of pastors in active service is diminishing at an alarming rate. In the same period there were twenty-three deaths listed. Because of the difficult conditions under which the training must be given, the quality of this education has deteriorated too. Recently one Latvian and one Estonian, both Lutheran, managed to obtain permission to study in England, at Oxford, but this permission was denied to other applicants.

During the Khrushchev antireligious campaign one of the main themes of the propaganda attacks on Lutheran clergymen was that that they were promoting "bourgeois nationalism." Studies were published that demonstrated historically how the clergy had been at the service of the state in prewar years. Several arrests were made and the men concerned were charged with anti-Communist and counter-revolutionary nationalistic activities. Others had their licenses revoked for alleged immoral actions, such as drunkenness, creating a public disturbance, and theft.

Other religious statistics are no less difficult to obtain or to assess with confidence. One report of interest is the June 1, 1965, Riga Radio broadcast on the results of a Soviet sociological survey conducted in the Valmiera district of Latvia, near the Estonian border. In 1944 there had been sixteen large Lutheran parishes in the district with more than twenty churches. More than half of these had been closed in the intervening twenty years. Also, the number of children baptized dropped from 189 in 1960 to 45 in 1964; the comparable decrease in weddings was from 107 to 12, and in confirmations from 66 to 2. Funerals, on the other hand, did not show a similar decrease, with the number for 1964 still roughly the same as it had been four years earlier at 119. (In 1933, however, during independence, the number of church funerals in the same district had been 1,157.) The highest ratio of professed believers in any village in the district was roughly 11 percent, and the lowest was 6.5 percent. This is a considerable drop when one recalls that before the war the Valmiera district had been staunchly Lutheran.

Although most of the Orthodox churches built in the Baltic area in the nineteenth century have been closed or are on the verge of collapse, six are still open in Riga and they seem to have large numbers of people, mainly Russians, in attendance at their services. Some Old Believer congregations still exist in the province of Latgale, and there is one in Riga, too. In Estonia the Orthodox church has had five bishops since 1944. In 1961 Aleksei Rudiger was appointed archbishop. Since 1964 he has been very prominent in the affairs of the Moscow patriarchate.[17] Both churches lost their autocephalous status immediately after the Soviet invasion and subsequently exchanged their ecclesiastical subordination under the patriarch of Constantinople to full subjugation to the Moscow patriarch.

Concerning the Lithuanian Protestants, some information has been obtained through Lutherans who were allowed to leave Klaipeda (Memel). They report that the Reformed and Lutheran

17. Evalds Dubnaitis, "Der Kampf gegen Religion und Geistlichkeit," *Acta Baltica* 5 (1966): 38.

churches there cannot claim more than 10 percent of their former membership. In 1940 there were 235,000 Protestants in the country; they formed 10 percent of the population, with 9.3 percent Lutherans and 0.7 percent Reformed church. The principal cause of their numerical reduction has been emigration.

The sectarians in the Baltic republics do not seem to have sustained comparable losses, and in some cases they have even shown a growth of membership. This is primarily true of the Baptists. In Estonia the Methodists, a small group of less than two thousand members, have also shown some growth in recent years. (In Latvia both the Methodists and the Moravian Brethren joined the Lutheran church.) However, the Salvation Army has ceased to function everywhere, and the Jehovah's Witnesses are universally prohibited. As for the Jews, in Riga and Daugavpils there are two synagogues open, and recent reports speak of others in Lithuania and possibly in Estonia as well.

Conclusion

Although it is an impossible task to give a totally comprehensive assessment of the result of the atheistic campaign in the Baltic republics, it is clear enough that the number of believers and the number of churches open is still proportionately much higher than in the areas of the Soviet Union which have been subjected to such campaigns since 1917.[18] Lacking any thorough statistical analysis, we are left to make estimates on the basis of observed data, such as church attendance. That even these determinations are not fully reliable is understood by the atheistic propagandists themselves, as witness the remarks broadcast over Riga Radio: "In order to know how to conduct atheistic work, one must understand the opposition. To this end we toured the neighboring churches and attended prayer ceremonies. We reached the conclusion that not many young people attend church, as if they were ashamed to be seen there. However, we realize that staying away from church for this reason does not mean that they have all freed themselves from the teachings of the churches by any means."[19]

In summary it may be said that the combined influence of the

18. The same would apply to the western Ukraine and the formerly Polish parts of Belorussia, which were not part of the Soviet Union until nearly thirty years after the Revolution.

19. Riga Radio, in Latvian, 4 October 1966.

atheistic campaign, the secularization of society, the end of the charade of religious observance by those who had been merely going through the motions, and the complexities of life in the nuclear age have combined to reduce the numbers of believers and of working churches. Also, the structures of the churches have undergone considerable change, both in their activities and their organization. Personal observation attests, however, to the continued existence of religion, and in many cases to a very vital religion indeed. Perhaps the most significant factor for the immediate future will be the policy, subtly influenced by a score of domestic and international factors, which is adopted by the present, post-Khrushchev government. At the moment there are signs that it may prove to be relatively benign. On the other hand, if this is simply a transitional period, a time of hesitation, this calm may not continue. The experience of the next two or three years is, in this context, of the utmost importance and bears careful observation.[20]

20. Before this volume went to press Dr. Veinbergs supplied the editor with valuable information of recent origin concerning the Lutheran church in the Baltic republics. Since this data refers primarily to circumstances in 1968 (that is, beyond the chronological frame of this book), it is appended here.

Citing bad health as the reason, Archbishop Jaan Kiivit of Estonia recently resigned. Made acting archbishop in 1948 when Archbishop A. Pähn was arrested for noncooperation with the authorities, Kiivit became archbishop in 1951. A man of charming personality, he acquired during his days as archbishop a certain prominence in international church organizations and the Communist peace conferences. Kiivit received honorary degrees from three European universities. Private sources, however, indicate that his popularity inside Estonia was significantly less than abroad and that unrest and dissatisfaction with him had been on the rise among the Estonian clergy. Kiivit has now been replaced by Alfred Tooming, a man slightly younger, although also in his sixties.

The Latvian church has likewise undergone a recent change in leadership. Dissatisfaction with Archbishop G. Turs, in office since 1945/1948, steadily increased over many years. The synod, which called for elections in March, 1968, found itself with only one possible candidate—the first vice president of the consistory, P. Kleperis. He could boast of even better relations with the government than Turs, who had been awarded a silver medal by the USSR peace committee. The writings of P. Kleperis in the church calendar made it clear that he was probably the most radically pro-Soviet and politically oriented of the Latvian clergy. Whatever the case, within a month of his installation as archbishop, while en route to a conference in Budapest, Kleperis died. His successor, A. Freijs, was a former professor of dogmatic theology at the University of Latvia. Widely respected in the nation as well as among the clergy—no doubt his eight years in prison during the Stalin era played a part—in November 1968, he too, regrettably, died. The Latvian church also lost five pastors in 1968 from an already small number of clergy, and not a single replacement was ordained in that year.

20

THE SIBERIAN TRIBES, THE SOVIET REGIME, AND RELIGION

The Russian Far East is a veritable museum of several tribes, some of them living in a most primitive state. This is why the area holds special interest for an ethnologist; one may find here forms of organization and culture which have not survived elsewhere. These tribes differ in language, anthropological type, and culture. They are conveniently classified into two groups: The Tungus-Manchu and the paleo-Asiatic (the most ancient inhabitants of Asia). To these, two larger groups must be added: the Buriats, of Mongol origin, and the Iakuts, the descendants of a Turkic people. Except for the last two, all of the tribes are numerically insignificant. Here are the figures for this population, according to the last Soviet census (1959).

Tribes	Numbers	Location
Evenki	24,000	East Siberia, Transbaikalia
Chukchi	12,000	Chutkotsk Peninsula
Eveny	9,000	Okhotsk Coast
Nanai	8,000	Lower Amur, Manchuria
Koryaks	6,300	Northern Kamchatka
Nivkhi	4,000	Lower Amur, Sakhalin
Kamchadals (russianized)	4,000	Kamchatka Peninsula
Ulchi	2,000	Maritime Territory
Buriats	253,000	Irkutsk Province, Transbaikalia
Iakuts	236,000	Lena River

J. J. Gapanovich

The aborigines played the major role in the economic life of the Far East so long as the area was not densely peopled by the Russians. This was the situation prior to the Revolution of 1917. Since then the Russian population has greatly increased through the government's explicit policy in this direction. The population of the area increased from 1,300,000 in 1926, to 2,350,000 in 1935 and 4,300,000 in 1959, without any appreciable increase in the native population. In the Buriat Autonomous Republic the comparative figures were 389,000 Russians and 166,000 Buriats in 1926, but 752,000 and 150,000 respectively in 1964. In the Iakut Autonomous Republic the figures were 287,000 Russians and 212,000 Iakuts in 1926 and 597,000 and 250,000 in 1964. Even the far north, which before 1917 had been almost devoid of Russian inhabitants, now has a total of 52,000 in the Chukotsk district and 36,000 in the Koriak region, while the aboriginal population has remained insignificant.[1] These figures are indicative of the extent of interethnic pressure in the area, in this case quite unfavorable to the aborigines.

Even without the government's program of russification, the tribes are losing their ethnic characteristics, in the first instance, their language. For example, among the Itelmen in Kamchatka 63 percent consider Russian their mother tongue; for the southern Tungus tribes, the figure is 22 percent. Only in the far north, despite the predominance of Russians, are there many aboriginal speakers who have not mastered Russian.

The negative aspects of nineteenth-century colonization are rightly criticized by Soviet writers, who in turn extol the "socialist transformation of native life" in Siberia. But these critics cannot deny at least one merit of the first Russian colonists—they did not recognize or practice racism. Faced with a shortage of women in the north, they did not shun intermarriage with native girls, thus contributing to the formation of a mixed ethnic type. (To be sure, there were unions outside of marriage as well. However, no stigma was attached to the offspring of such unions.) In the eyes of the Russian colonists the social status of a Siberian native was determined by his upbringing; there were many Buriats and Iakuts who received a Russian education, and they were treated on an equal footing with

1. I. Mironenko, "The Population," in a symposium on Siberia and the Far East, *Studies on the Soviet Union* 5, no. 1 (Munich, 1965): 49–51. There is a discrepancy between these figures and those given in the table, as fairly substantial numbers of Buriats live outside their republic.

the Russians in public service and social life. The aborigines were exempted from taxation and military service, and were given some special protection in civil law.

This humane approach to the aborigines was also reflected in the government's policy of religious toleration in Siberia. During the seventeenth century the Russian government did not interfere with native religion at all. In the eighteenth century, emulating Protestant missionary activity, the propagation of Orthodoxy began among the aborigines, but without any recourse to violence, as Empress Catherine II in particular insisted. This tradition was maintained throughout the nineteenth century, when missionary work was substantially expanded.

The results were apparently significant. The Iakuts were completely converted. Churches were built, a native clergy established, and the ritual adapted. Of course, as always happens in the case of mass conversion, some simplification of Christian doctrine was inevitable, but the foundations of Christian life were laid. The situation with the Tungus-Manchu tribes was somewhat different, with a more formalistic acceptance of Christianity which permitted the continued existence of native beliefs. Among the Evenki, the Koriaks, and the Chukchi the success of Christian teaching was slight, because of the competition of shamanism.[2]

The Buriats were on a higher level of culture than the primitive northern tribes, and Christianity might have met with a greater response here. However, a competitor in the form of Lamaism—Buddhism of the Yellow Hat sect— had penetrated to Buriatia early in the seventeenth century. The Russian government did not hinder its spread, and the cult was legalized by Catherine II in 1764, when its teaching by lamas was permitted, Buddhist *datsans* (monasteries) were recognized, and a center of Buddhism was solemnly established in Transbaikalia. The *datsans* engaged in serious Buddhist studies and thereby raised the prestige of the cult among the Buriats. It spread rapidly and by 1842 there were 5,545 lamas living in forty-two *datsans*. By 1917 the number of lamas was 14,000. It is interesting to note how Soviet writers explain the historical success of Buddhism. They maintain that it was encouraged by the Czarist government in an

2. Potapov's article in M. G. Levin and T. P. Potapov, *The Peoples of Siberia* (Chicago, 1964), esp. pp. 119–26. Translated from the Russian edition, *Narody Sibiri* (Moscow, 1956).

attempt to win over the feudal rulers of Buriatia. The work of the Orthodox church among the Iakuts is similarly explained.

In both areas, however, the fundamental beliefs of the aborigines still survived, and this was even truer of the other tribes of the Far East. The dominant religion was animism, which views the world as filled with numerous spirits, benevolent and menacing, which must be propitiated by means of sacrifices offered to them. This is not a religion as such, but rather the native view of the world of which the aborigine is a part. His life, and that of the tribe, depends on proper order in nature; when something is disturbed, the results can be disastrous. Shamanism was the aborigine's attempt to regulate nature.

After the Revolution, the Soviet authorities at first did not interfere with native life in Siberia, and Soviet experts such as V. G. Bogoraz, who had an extensive knowledge of the northern tribes (especially the Chukchi) suggested a policy of protecting the aborigines. For this purpose the Northern Committee was established, with its headquarters in the Far East (1924). The native administration was organized on the simplest possible lines: a system of tribal assemblies and executive committees. This system did not last long as "class enemies" were soon detected in the tribal committees. The new organization of autonomous republics and regions, national districts and *raions*, in which the Russian element finally prevailed, was introduced in 1930. A series of economic and cultural measures, some of them beneficial for the tribes, was inaugurated in the Far East. These measures aimed at nothing less than "the socialist transformation of native life." They were carried out hastily and violently, and often imposed great hardships on the aborigines.

Here we will consider only those measures which had a deep impact on tribal mentality. Simultaneously with collectivization in Russia, an attempt was made to drive the aborigines into communes with the wholesale socialization of their meager belongings. In native life there were some survivals of a primitive communalism, such as feeding the poor, sharing the day's catch of fish, and care of the aged and sick. But reckless collectivization imposed from outside was not congenial to the tribesmen, who tried to escape by flight or met it with fierce resistance. Total collectivization was not a success and was finally superseded by a lower form, that of "productive association," even though it was asserted that 75 percent of local holdings were collectivized (1943).

A more ambitious project was set up to abolish nomadism and to turn the aborigines into a sedentary people, They did not understand the benefits of this change and felt uncomfortable in wooden dwellings. The process was protracted and as late as 1950 had not been completed. M. A. Sergeev, an expert on the far north, admits there were shortcomings in this operation, and it was often traumatic to the native mentality.[3]

Progress in the cultural field, particularly in the area of education, came more easily, the background having been prepared under the czarist regime. A network of schools already existed, and there were competent native teachers. For the first time a native alphabet was created, and textbooks and pamphlets were published in native languages; at first the Latin script was used (1925), but later Russian script was adopted. So-called "cultural bases" were established in the far north, having been tested elsewhere in the Soviet Union. These complex institutions combine schools, nurseries, medical centers, cinemas, and museums. With useful training and general education they provide for political indoctrination too. Parents were not always enthusiastic about the nonpractical instruction given their children at such bases, and were antagonistic toward the Communist ideology which their children learned, both at school and in such organizations as the Pioneers. The "Red Tent" was a mobile unit for political propaganda among adults. How efficient this mass indoctrination of "backward peoples" was can be judged by the fact that, after the promulgation of the Constitution of 1936, there were instances of entire tribal assemblies joining the Communist party—reminiscent of earlier mass conversions to Christianity.

Native teachers were prepared at four colleges and an institute in Khabarovsk. With their extensive training in the principles of Marxism-Leninism, such people proved useful agents in the denunciation of the shamans in the first stages of the struggle for the socialist transformation of tribal life.

To understand why the shamans were subjected to persecution by the Communists, the nature of shamanism must be briefly explained. The very word "shaman" may be derived from the Sanskrit *sramana* or the Mongolian *qam*. As to its substance, it is closely connected

3. Walter Kolarz, *The Peoples of the Soviet Far East* (London, 1954), pp. 71–74. Sergeev's article in Levin and Potapov, *Peoples of Siberia*, pp. 503–8. For details, see M. A. Sergeev, *Nekapitalistichesky put razvitiia malykh narodov severa* [The Non-capitalistic development of the minor nationalities of the north] (Moscow, 1955).

with the animistic beliefs of the aborigines. In case of a spiritual crisis or a physical ailment, mediation between the man and the spirits, especially evil spirits, is necessary. Here the shaman, who knows how to master spirits, helps. This he does by means of incantations, ceremonial dancing, and special accoutrements. His performance, with its frenzied gestures and drum-beating, usually at night, is quite impressive.

To treat the shamans as imposters, as in the official Soviet view, is too simplified an approach. They sincerely believe in their powers over the spirits. They pass a period of very difficult training and receive little or no material compensation from their activities. Knowledge mastered by a shaman remains his secret and may be transmitted to his disciples as he sees fit. He is always respected by his tribesmen; in some cases they even fear him, as in the case of the black shamans of the Buriats who deal with harmful spirits. The shamans tend to professionalism and occasionally receive some remuneration for their services, usually a portion of sacrificial food, but generally they lead a dismal life. There are also female shamans, who are considered especially powerful. In the far north any member of the tribe can shamanize, but those who do fail to inspire much respect.[4]

Shamanism presupposes the neurotic condition of a group or an individual; the shaman has no mastery of spirits, but possesses the power of suggestion and is able to transmit his experience to the audience telepathically. His role as a medicine man and a psychoanalyst of sorts is impossible to deny—similar healing methods may be found elsewhere. All in all, the shaman's powers are inherent in the native mentality, and when he sees that the whole psychomental complex of his tribe is threatened with extinction, he understandably feels an urge to defend it. It would be incorrect, however, to reduce the whole of shamanism to psychopathology alone. One opinion put forth is that the conditions of life in the Arctic dispose people toward nervous diseases, namely *hysteria Arctica*, and that the shamans stand out of their milieu by reason of their hysteric or epileptic character. The shamans may be sick people, but they are respected just because they are able to overcome their sickness. When undergoing shamanist training, they master some theory of their craft; they

4. S. Shirokogoroff, *Psychomental Complex of the Tungus* (London, 1935), especially chaps. 22 and 23, where the substance and history of shamanism are presented.

have excellent memories, learning thousands of verses of popular literature by heart.

Shamanism among the tribes has been carefully studied by two outstanding scholars in this field, S. Shirokogoroff and Mircea Eliade. The emigré Russian ethnologist, relying on the vast material found among the Tungus, concluded that in shamanism primordial Siberian elements are combined with others which can be traced to Buddhism coming through Mongolia. This was, according to him, rather a recent phenomenon; it appeared in Manchuria in the twelfth century and in Mongolia before the fourteenth century. Professor Eliade, accepting Shirokogoroff's formula, "shamanism stimulated by Buddhism," chose to elaborate it further. As he says, mastery of spirits is one aspect of the shaman's work: its other aspect is a trance which produces the ascension to heaven. The Buddhist influences affected only the technique of the shaman's performance, while the accompanying religious ecstasy must be seen as a more archaic phenomenon, related to a mythical time when communication with the supreme being—whose presence is well-attested in all religions of north Asia—was open to every man. When this communication was disrupted and other cults appeared, those of minor gods and ancestors, the symbolism of the ascension to heaven could be realized only by a shaman who was able to survive the state of ecstasy. Later on, other innovations followed, such as his familiarity with the spirits and the descent to hell, and even the use of magic at the performance. In spite of all these accretions, Eliade concludes, we can find examples among the shamans of authentic mystical experience in the form of "spiritual" ascent to heaven comparable to the religious experience of great mystics elsewhere. Shamanism in the north thus has broader connotations and is not so primitive as might be expected.[5]

Official Soviet policy towards shamanism is simple: the shamans are harmful persons exploiting the superstition of backward people; prohibitions which they impose on hunting and fishing do damage to the economy of the north; generally, they disseminate reactionary propaganda against the Soviet regime, with all its innovations, especially in the field of culture.

5. Mircea Eliade, *Le chamanisme et les techniques archaiques de l'extase* (Paris, 1951), pp. 334–38. There is an English translation of this book: *Shamanism: Archaic Techniques of Ecstasy*, Willard R. Trask, tr., revised and enlarged edition (New York, 1964).

At first, when the tribes remained "outside of the Constitution of 1917," and for a brief period after 1924 when there was no interference with native life, the shamans were not hindered, as they were influential people in their tribes; they also caused discomfiture to the Russian church.[6] Even in Kamchatka, wholly converted to Christianity, the shamans still remained in the background, secretly competing with the Orthodox priests. Now they came out into the open and were directly used by the new Soviet regime to the disadvantage of the church. This unnatural symbiosis between the regime and the shamans did not last long. With the progress of collectivization, the shaman came to be seen as a "wrecker," opposed to communization.

The subsequent battle against the shaman was not primarily conducted on the ideological plane, since the propagandists were not sufficiently acquainted with the native mentality; instead, accusations of a more practical nature were brought. The shamans were attacked as "kulaks," that is, exploiters of their people, though most of the shamans were quite poor. They were suspected of being foreign spies, though on the whole foreign influence, namely American, could be found only in Chukotka. Unable to defeat the shamans on this ground, the authorities simply arrested them, hoping to prove to the people in this way that the shamans were indeed powerless.

The principal accusation was always that the shamans participated in the resistance movement against collectivization and resettlement. In fact, even without the shaman's interference, this process was slow and uneven, often because of mistakes committed by the administration itself. Sometimes the shamans were simply scapegoats for such failures and not the leaders of resistance, which was quite spontaneous. Nor were they responsible for the respect which the aborigines still had for them. They were influential in the tribal assemblies and even could be elected to executive committees—a situation unacceptable, of course, to the Soviet authorities. The chief target of the shaman's attacks were schools, cultural bases, and health stations; they had no confidence in them and were afraid of traps set by the Russians in order to destroy the aborigines. They were understandably hostile to the teachers, whose task it was to undermine their influence. Whether guilty of all the crimes ascribed to them, the shamans

6. For a somewhat similar treatment (of the sectarians), see Andrew Blane, "Protestant Sectarians in the First Year of Soviet Rule," chapter 14 above.

were consciously and unconsciously an obstacle to the regime's plans.

The development of antireligious propaganda was more difficult among the Iakuts and the Buriats. The educated Iakuts had developed strong feelings of nationalism under the czarist regime, and this attitude of distrust toward the Russians had been communicated to the common people in Iakutia as well. As there were native priests here, they, as educated persons, became the spokesmen of nascent nationalism. For the Soviet authorities, both the nationalism and the Christianity of these priests made them suspect. The church as such was less persecuted, however, than were extreme nationalists; it was tolerated as an agency of Russian influence, and churches are still found in the capital of Iakutia. Iakut nationalism, on the other hand, took on an anti-Russian character and appealed to the old tribal traditions, as in the case of the poet Kulakovsky. In his work, *The Dream of a Shaman*, he covertly treated the Russians as enemies and preached enlightenment for the preservation of Iakut identity. Many people, even among native Communists, were infected with this counterpropaganda, and it was forcibly liquidated in the thirties.[7]

Education was highly valued by the Iakuts; accordingly, the struggle between the old and the new was fought primarily in the schools. The number of schools was greatly increased—from 173 with 4,660 pupils in 1917 to 532 with 46,000 pupils in 1932; in addition, a small university was founded. For the political indoctrination of adults, Red Tents and 534 public libraries were organized. This approach was quite successful and even shamanism was affected by the propaganda, as shown by the writer Oiunsky's work, *The Red Shaman*.

The struggle between Buddhism and communism was fought on a religious plane, but not without political undertones. The Soviet administration found in Buriatia an established church, with its doctrine, monasteries, and lamas, and, at first, did not know how to deal with it. An attempt was made to adapt Buddhism and to create a Soviet Buddhist center in Buriatia. Buriat intellectuals, following the example of the Living Church in Russia, tried to revitalize Buddhism by interpreting it as a sort of materialism and adapting it to Marxism-Leninism. The leader of this movement was the learned Mongolist, Professor Zhamtsarano.

7. J. M. Suslov, *Shamanizm i borba protiv nego* [Shamanism and the fight against it] (Moscow, 1931). Kolarz, *Peoples of the Soviet Far East*, pp. 75–78.

Through this synthesis Buddhism in Buriatia managed to survive almost intact until 1937. In the violent antireligious campaign of the late thirties, however, the monasteries were closed and the lamas subjected to persecution. The chief lama, Dordzhiev, was arrested and died in prison in 1938. Altogether eighteen monasteries were closed, some by the authorities and some by the lamas themselves, whose numbers dropped rapidly. Buddhism itself, however, was far from extinct; even without its monasteries and lamas, it continued as a family cult and was widely practised on the region's collective farms. The Soviet government had to continue to reckon with it as a vital force and therefore attempted to harness its influence for political purposes. A central Buddhist council was created which operated under the guidance of the party. The twenty-five hundredth anniversary of Buddha's death was officially celebrated in 1956, and Buddhist leaders were introduced to important foreign visitors in the Kremlin; they were prominent in the peace movement when it was organized and took part in delegations sent abroad. Pilgrimages to famous *datsans*, which are still popular, are a chief object of antireligious propaganda. The strength of Buddhism was in its connection with education and medicine; the former has been weakened, but the latter is still influential, and even teachers occasionally consult the Tibetan doctors.[8]

It is very difficult to make the transition from primitive thought to modern socialism; many concepts in the new outlook simply cannot be translated into native languages. Accordingly, we find some unusual combinations of the old and the new. In some quarters there is veneration of the sun-gods, Lenin and Stalin, who live far away, but are all-powerful and benevolent toward the aborigines. Such tales are found in native folklore, allegedly created by the people, but really by local propagandists. More successful was the adaptation of sacrificial festivals to the practical needs of the regime; they were turned into popular gatherings which now celebrated the fulfillment of production norms and were connected as before with reindeer races, dances, and music.

The campaign against shamanism was waged most actively in the thirties and forties, with a short interval during World War II when religious toleration was widespread and was reflected in the activities of Soviet administrators in the north, too. In scientific and literary

8. Walter Kolarz, *Religion in the Soviet Union* (London, 1961), pp. 456–58, 461.

works published after 1950 there is no mention of the renewal of this struggle, except for occasional vague hints that the reactionary propaganda of the shamans has not yet been completely stamped out. But the pressure on both shamanism and Buddhism continues, both indirectly through measures of social transformation and directly through antireligious propaganda. Present indications are that this combination will eventually enable the Soviet regime to achieve its desired goal to a considerable degree.

APPENDIX
Soviet Religious Law
as of January 1, 1968

COMPILED BY

THOMAS E. BIRD AND ANDREW Q. BLANE

INTRODUCTION

This appendix contains materials which give a representative picture of the legal status of religion in the USSR as of the beginning of 1968. It does not purport to be a comprehensive historical survey. One omission consists of the variations of the law codes of the several republics; the data reproduced here refer first and foremost to the RSFSR. This omission is minor, partly because the RSFSR is the most populous republic, but primarily because the differences in the law codes of the respective republics are few and minor.[1] A somewhat more serious exclusion—required by considerations of space—involves laws and edicts not directly related to religious believers but which in an indirect fashion affect the character and quality of religious life. These include regulations on property rental, insurance, and taxation, as well as directives pertaining to housing, schooling, jobs, and pensions.

A potentially more serious omission is that of legal and administrative measures issued by the state, the party, or the police, whether by central or local organs, which for one reason or another are not available or are not known to the editors. These fall into three categories: (1) laws and decrees enacted prior to the adoption of the latest codes, but which are still in force; (2) laws and decrees enacted and published since the adoption of the latest codes, but which do not appear in legal publications distributed abroad; (3) laws and decrees enacted, but never published.[2] Evidence in documents smuggled out of the Soviet Union suggests that these last are the most important. One such document is the letter of December, 1965, from two Orthodox priests, N. I. Eshliman and G. P. Iakunin, to the head of the Russian Orthodox church, Patriarch Aleksy. The burden of this letter is an angry and powerful critique of existing church-state relations in the USSR. The letter accuses the church administration of being guilty of several errors, in particular:

... its obeying the unofficial oral instructions of the Council for the Affairs of the Russian Orthodox Church, which, in violation of the clearly stated Soviet law, were used as a means of systematic and destructive intervention in ecclesiastical life. Instructions by telephone, oral demands, undocumented and unofficial agreements —such is the unhealthy, mysterious atmosphere which has enveloped as in a heavy

1. See V. Stanley Vardys, "Catholicism in Lithuania," chapter 18 above.
2. See section 5 of this Appendix.

mist, the relations between the Moscow Patriarchate and the Council for the Affairs of the Russian Orthodox Church.[3]

The two priests simultaneously addressed a letter to N. V. Podgorny, chairman of the Presidium of the Supreme Soviet of the USSR. In it they itemized and illustrated eight violations of the Decree on the Separation of Church and State, article 124 of the Constitution of the USSR, and the Decree on Religious Associations of the All-Russian Central Executive Committee and the Soviet People's Commissars, a decree which had been perpetrated by state officials during the latter years of Khrushchev's power.

It is not surprising that, in order to implement their illegal activities, the representatives of the Council selected a method of unofficial oral dictates in contradiction to the law on secret instructions. In this way they tried to cover their illegal acts and to avoid accountability. The leaders of the Council for the Affairs of the Russian Orthodox Church have gone so far as to make an attempt to keep out of the public eye, which is characteristic of every illegal group: the building occupied by the Council does not have a distinctive sign. An insignificant detail, but very characteristic.[4]

The legal picture presented in this appendix cannot be called fully comprehensive for still another reason, namely, the lack of historical perspective. For example, there is no evidence here that in 1929–32 Soviet religious law became harsher, or that in 1943–45 some of the harsher restrictions were lifted (in practice if not in principle), or that in the post-1960 period conditions once again hardened—to name only the major shifts of the Soviet era.[5] The obvious reason for omitting this historical aspect is that the necessary materials would fill a large volume.[6]

Although not fully comprehensive, the picture of law and religion in the USSR given here is certainly representative.[7] The legislation reproduced below consists of all basic state law pertaining to religion in force as of January 1, 1968, as well as an official directive of similar bent.[8] The docu-

3. As translated in *St. Vladimir's Seminary Quarterly*, nos. 1–2 (1966), p. 80. See also Alexander Bogolepov, "The Legal Status of the Russian Orthodox Church in the Soviet Union," chapter 9 above.

4. *St. Vladimir's Seminary Quarterly*, nos. 1–2 (1966), p. 75.

5. For a fuller description, see Joshua Rothenberg, "The Legal Status of Religion in the Soviet Union," chapter 5 above.

6. Cf. P. V. Gidulianov, ed., *Otdelenie tserkvi ot gosudarstva: polny sbornik dekretov RSFSR i SSSR: instruksy, tsirkuliarov, i t.d.* [The separation of church from state; complete collection of the decrees of the RSFSR and USSR; instructions, circulars, etc.], 2d ed. (Moscow, 1924); N. Orleansky, comp., *Zakon o religioznykh obedineniiakh RSFSR i deistvuiushchie zakony, instrukstii, s otdelnymi kommentariiami* [The law on religious associations of the RSFSR and laws and instructions in force, with individual commentaries] (Moscow, 1930).

7. For a discussion of the relation of law to Soviet political, economic, and social history, see Harold J. Berman, *Justice in the USSR: an Interpretation of Soviet Law*, rev. ed. (Cambridge, Mass.: Harvard University Press, 1963).

8. In a sense, as Alexander Bogolepov makes plain in chapter 9 of this volume, the statutes or regulations of the religious associations themselves are also state law since they are promulgated only with the consent or by the direct order of the state itself. For the postwar statutes of the Russian Orthodox church see William B. Stroyen, *Communist Russia and the Russian Orthodox Church, 1943–1962* (Washington, D.C.: Catholic University of America Press, 1967), pp. 136–43; for those of the Baptist church see Michael Bourdeaux, *Religious Ferment in Russia* (New York: St. Martin's Press, 1968), pp. 190–210.

ments are divided into five categories: (1) pertinent articles of the Constitution of the USSR; (2) fundamental laws and decrees on religious practice in the USSR; (3) edicts from the codes of criminal law and procedure of the RSFSR clearly related to religion or which have been cited against citizens whose offenses against the state were essentially religious in character; (4) the RSFSR ruling against "social parasites," which has been similarly cited; (5) a secret directive from the (state) Council for the Affairs of the Russian Orthodox Church which, though contrary to published law (e.g., article 143 of the criminal code of the RSFSR), has carried the force of law.

1. CONSTITUTION OF THE USSR
of December 5, 1936[9]

Article 124. In order to ensure to citizens freedom of conscience, the church in the USSR is separated from the state, and the school from the church. Freedom of religious worship and freedom of antireligious propaganda are recognized for all citizens.

Article 135. Elections of deputies are universal: all citizens of the USSR who have reached the age of eighteen, irrespective of race or nationality, sex, religion, education, domicile, social origin, property status, or past activities, have the right to vote in the election of deputies, with the exception of insane persons and persons who have been convicted by a court of law and whose sentence includes deprivation of electoral rights.

Every citizen of the USSR who has reached the age of twenty-three is eligible for election to the Supreme Soviet of the USSR, irrespective of race or nationality, sex, religion, education, domicile, social origin, property status, or past activities.

2. LEGISLATION ON RELIGIOUS CULTS

A. Decree on the Separation of Church and State of January 23, 1918[10]

1. The Church is separate from the State.
2. It is prohibited to enact on the territory of the Republic local laws or regulations which would put any restraint upon, or limit freedom of conscience or establish any advantages or privileges on the grounds of the religion of citizens.
3. Each citizen may confess any religion or no religion at all. Loss of any rights as the result of the confession of a religion or the absence of a religion shall be revoked.
   The mention in official papers of the religion of a citizen is not allowed.

9. Originally published in *Konstitutsiia (osnovnoi zakon) soiuza sovetskikh sotsialisticheskikh respublik* [Constitution (basic law) of the USSR] (Moscow, 1938).

10. Originally published in *Sobranie uzakoneny i rasporiazheny raboche-krestianskogo pravitelstva RSFSR* [Collection of laws and decrees of the government of workers and peasants of the RSFSR], no. 18 (1918), text no. 263. This translation taken from U.S. Senate, Committee on the Judiciary, *The Church and State Under Communism*, 88th Cong., 2nd sess., 1964, vol. 1, pt. I, *The USSR*, app. 1, p. 11.

4. The actions of the Government or other organizations of public law may not
   be accompanied by any religious rites or ceremonies.
5. The free performance of religious rites shall be granted so long as it does not
   disturb the public order and infringe upon the rights of the citizens of the
   Soviet Republic. In such cases, the local agencies are entitled to take the
   necessary measures to secure public order and safety.
6. No person may evade his citizen's duties on the grounds of his religion.
   Exceptions to this provision, and only under the condition that a certain
   duty of a citizen shall be substituted by another, may be permitted by the
   decision of the people's courts.
7. Religious oaths shall be abolished.
   In cases where it is necessary only a solemn vow may be given.
8. The acts of civil status shall be kept solely by civil [status] agencies.
9. The school shall be separate from the Church.
   The teaching of religion is prohibited in all state, municipal or private
   educational institutions where a general education is given.
   Citizens may give and receive religious instruction privately.
10. All ecclesiastical and religious associations are subject to regulations pertaining
    to private societies and unions, and shall not enjoy any advantages or receive
    any subsidies either from the State or from local self-governing institutions.
11. The compulsory exaction of fees or impositions to benefit ecclesiastical and
    religious associations as well as any kind of coercion or infliction of punish-
    ment by these associations upon their members is prohibited.
12. No ecclesiastical or religious associations shall have the right to own property.
    Such associations shall not enjoy the rights of a legal entity.
13. All property belonging to churches and religious associations existing in
    Russia shall become public property.
    Buildings and objects intended especially for religious worship shall be
    handed over by special decision of local or central authorities, free of charge,
    for use by the religious associations concerned.

B. Law on Religious Associations of April 8, 1929 (as amended January 1, 1932)[11]

1. Churches, religious groups, sects, religious movements, and other associations
   for any cult or any denomination come under the Decree of January 23, 1918,
   on the separation of the Church from the State and the School from the Church
   (Collection of Laws No. 18, 1918, text No. 203).
2. Religious associations of believers of all denominations shall be registered as
   religious societies or groups of believers.
   A citizen may be a member of only one religious association (society or
   group).
3. A religious society is a local association of not less than 20 believers who are
   18 years of age or over and belong to the same cult, faith or sect, united for the
   common satisfaction of their religious needs. Believers who are not numerous
   enough to organize a religious society may form a group of believers.

11. Originally published in *Sobranie uzakoneny i rasporiazheny*, no. 35 (1929), text no.
353; amendments from ibid., no. 8 (1932), text no. 41, II, 6. This translation taken from
U.S. Senate, Committee on the Judiciary, *The Church and State Under Communism*, pp.
12–17.

Religious societies and groups do not enjoy the rights of a legal entity.

4. A religious society or group of believers may start its activities only after the registration of the society or group by the committee for religious matters at the proper city or district (raion) soviet.

5. In order to register a religious society at least 20 initiators must submit to the agencies mentioned in the previous Article an application in accordance with the form determined by the Permanent Committee for Religious Matters at the [Council of Ministers].

6. In order to register a group of believers, the representative of the group (Art. 13) must submit an application to the agencies mentioned in Article 4 of the city or district where the group is located in accordance with the form determined by the Permanent Committee for Religious Matters at the [Council of Ministers].

7. The registration agencies shall register the society or group within one month, or inform the initiators of the denial of the registration.

8. The registration agencies shall be informed on the composition of the society, as well as on their executive and accounting bodies and on the clergy, within the period and in accordance with the forms determined by the Permanent Committee for Religious Matters at the [Council of Ministers].

9. In the list of members of religious societies or groups of believers only believers who expressed consent thereto may be included.

10. For the satisfaction of their religious needs, the believers who have formed a religious society may receive from the district or city soviet, under a contract, free of charge, special prayer buildings and objects intended exclusively for the cult.

    Besides that, the believers who have formed a religious society or group of believers may use for prayer meetings other premises left to them by private persons or local soviets on lease. Such premises shall be subject to all regulations provided for in the present Law relating to prayer buildings; the contracts for the use of such premises shall be concluded by individual believers on their personal responsibility. Such premises shall be subject to technical and sanitary regulations.

    A religious society or group of believers may use only one prayer building or [complex of] premises.

11. Transactions for the management and use of religious property, such as the hiring of watchmen, buying of fuel, repairing of the building and objects destined for the rite, purchasing of products or property necessary for a religious rite or ceremony, and other transactions closely and directly connected with the doctrine and ritual of the cult, as well as for the renting of premises for prayer meetings, may be made by individual citizens who are members of the executive body of religious societies or are representatives of groups of believers.

    No contract embodying such arrangements may contain in its text any reference to commercial or industrial transactions, even if these acts are of a kind directly connected with the affairs of the cult, such as the renting of a candle factory or a printing establishment for the printing of religious books, etc.

12. For each general assembly of a religious society or group of believers, permission shall be obtained: in cities from committees for religious matters of the city soviets, and in rural areas from the executive committees of the district.

13. For the accomplishment of functions connected with the management and use of the religious property (Art. 11), and for outside representation, the religious associations elect at their general assemblies executive bodies from among their members by open ballot—a religious society, an executive body of three members, and a group of believers with one representative.

14. The registration agencies are entitled to remove individual members from the executive body of a religious society or the representative elected by a group of believers.

15. The general assembly may elect an auditing committee of no more than three members for the examination of religious property and money collected by religious associations from their members as donations or voluntary offerings.

16. No permission of the government authorities is necessary for the meetings of the executive and auditing organs.

17. Religious associations may not: (a) create mutual credit societies, cooperative or commercial undertakings, or in general, use property at their disposal for other than religious purposes; (b) give material help to their members; (c) organize for children, young people, and women special prayer or other meetings, circles, groups, departments for Biblical or literary study, sewing, working or the teaching of religion, etc., excursions, children's playgrounds, libraries, reading rooms, sanatoria, or medical care.
    Only books necessary for the purpose of the cult may be kept in the prayer buildings and premises.

18. Teaching of any kind of the religious cult in schools, boarding schools, or preschool establishments maintained by the State, public institutions or private persons is prohibited. Such teaching may be given exclusively in religious courses created by the citizens of the USSR with the special permission of the Permanent Committee for Religious Matters at the [Council of Ministers].

19. The activities of the clergymen, preachers, preceptors and the like shall be restricted to the area in which the members of the religious association reside and in the area where the prayer building or premises are situated.
    The activities of clergymen, preachers and preceptors who permanently serve two or more religious associations shall be restricted to the area of residence of the believers who are members of such religious associations.

20. The religious societies and groups of believers may organize local, All-Russian or All-Union religious conventions or conferences by special permission issued separately for each case by
    a. the Permanent Committee for Religious Matters at the [Council of Ministers] if an All-Russian or All-Union convention or congress on the territory of the RSFSR is supposed to be convoked;
    b. the local Committee for Religious Matters, if a local convention is supposed to be convoked.
    The permission for convocation of republican conventions and conferences shall be granted by the Committee for Religious Matters of the appropriate republic.

21. Local, All-Russian and All-Union religious conventions and conferences may elect from among their members executive bodies in implementation of the decisions of the convention or conference. The list of members of the elected executive bodies shall be submitted simultaneously with the materials of the convention or conference to the authority which granted the permission for organizing the convention or conference in two copies in accordance with the

form determined by the Permanent Committee for Religious Matters at the [Council of Ministers].

22. Religious congresses [and conventions] and executive bodies elected by them do not possess the rights of a legal entity and, in addition, may not:
    a. form any kind of central fund for the collection of voluntary gifts from believers;
    b. make any kind of obligatory collection;
    c. own religious property, receive the same by contract, obtain the same by purchase, or hire premises for religious meetings;
    d. conclude any kind of contracts or legal transactions.

23. The executive bodies of religious societies or groups, as well as religious conferences [and conventions], may use exclusively in religious matters stamps, seals and stationery with the imprint of their names. Such stamps, seals and stationery may not include emblems or slogans established for Soviet agencies.

24. Religious conventions and conferences may be initiated and convoked by religious societies and groups of believers, their executive bodies and executive bodies of religious conferences [or conventions].

25. Objects necessary for the rites of the cult, whether handed over under contract to the believers forming the religious association, acquired by them, or donated to them for the purpose of the cult, are nationalized and shall be under the control of the Committee for Religious Matters at the city or district soviet.

26. Premises used for the dwelling of a watchman which are located near the prayer building shall be leased together with other religious property to believers by contract, free of charge.

27. Prayer buildings with objects shall be leased to believers forming religious associations for use by the Committee for Religious Matters at the city or district soviet.

28. Prayer buildings with objects in these buildings shall be received by contract from the representatives of the district or city soviet by no less than 20 members of a religious society for use by all believers.

29. In the contract concluded between believers and the city or district soviet [it] shall be required that the persons who receive a prayer building and religious objects for use (Art. 28) shall:
    a. keep and take care of it as state property entrusted to them;
    b. repair the prayer building, as well as pay expenses connected with the possession and use of the building, such as heating, insurance, guarding, taxes, [state and] local, etc.;
    c. use the property exclusively for the satisfaction of religious needs;
    d. compensate for any damage caused to the State by deterioration or defects of the property;
    e. keep an inventory of all religious objects, in which [inventory] shall be entered all newly obtained objects for the religious cult either by purchase, donation, transfer from other prayer buildings, etc., which are not owned by individual citizens. Objects which become unfit for use shall be excluded from the inventory with the consent of the authority which concluded the contract;
    f. admit, without any hindrance, the representatives of the city or district soviet to exercise control over the property with the exception of the time when religious ceremonies are performed.

30. Prayer buildings of historical or artistic value registered as such in the Ministry

of Education may be leased to believers on the same conditions, however, with the obligation to observe the regulations prescribed for registration and maintenance and the guarding of monuments of art and antiquity.

31. All local inhabitants of a corresponding faith have the right to sign the contract on the receipt of the buildings and religious objects for use and to obtain by this, after the leasing of property, similar rights of management over the property with persons who signed the original document.

32. Whoever has signed a contract may cancel his signature on the above-mentioned contract by filing the corresponding application to the agencies enumerated in article 4; this, however, does not free him from the responsibility for the good condition and safekeeping of the property during the period of the time prior to the filing of the above-mentioned application.

33. Prayer buildings shall be subject to compulsory fire insurance for the benefit of the appropriate local government at the expense of the persons who signed the contract. In case of fire, the insurance payment may be used for the reconstruction of the prayer building destroyed by fire, or upon decision of the appropriate local government for social and cultural needs of a given locality in full accordance with the Decree of August 24, 1925, on the Utilization of Insurance Payments Acquired for Prayer Buildings Destroyed by Fire.[12]

34. If there are no persons who wish to use a prayer building for the satisfaction of religious needs under the conditions provided for in Articles 27–33, the city or district soviet puts up a notice of this fact on the doors of the prayer building.

35. If, after the lapse of a week from the date of notice, no applications are submitted, the city or district soviet informs the higher authority. This information supplies data giving the date of the construction of the building and its condition, and the purpose for which the building is supposed to be used. The higher authority decides the further destination of the building in accordance with the provisions of Articles 40–42.

36. The transfer of a prayer building leased for the use of believers for other purposes (liquidation of the prayer building) may take place only according to a decision of the [Council of Ministers] of the autonomous republic or oblast which must be supported by reasons, in a case where the building is needed for government or public purposes. The believers who formed the religious society shall be informed regarding such decision.

37. If the believers who formed the religious society appeal to the [Council of Ministers] within two weeks from the date of the announcement of the decision, the case on the liquidation of the prayer building shall be conveyed to the Council. If the [Council] confirms the decision, the contract with the believers becomes null and void, and the property shall be taken away from them.

38. The lease of nationalized or private houses for the needs of religious associ-

---

12. This law, published in the collection of RSFSR laws (*Sobranie uzakoneny i rasporiazheny*, no. 58 [1925], text 470), provides that, as a rule, the insurance payments shall be used for the reconstruction of the prayer building destroyed by fire (Arts. 1 and 2). However, they may be used also for cultural needs, if the local government has made a decision on the liquidation of the prayer building in this district (Art. 3). Such decision may be appealed before higher authorities and carried out only if the higher authority has confirmed the decision of the local government. If confirmed, the money may be used for cultural needs of the district in the location of the prayer building destroyed by fire.

ations (Art. 10, par. 2) may be broken by a court decision in accordance with the general provisions of court procedure.

39. The liquidation of prayer buildings may be carried out in some instances by the Committee for Religious Matters by order of the city or district soviet in the presence of representatives of the local finance department and other interested departments as well as the representative of the religious association.

40. The religious property of the liquidated prayer building shall be distributed as follows:

    a. all objects of platinum, gold, silver and brocade as well as jewels shall be included in the account of the State fund and transmitted for disposal by local financial agencies or the Ministry of Education, if the objects were registered there;

    b. all objects of historical, artistic or museum value shall be transferred to the Ministry of Education;

    c. other objects, such as sacred images, priestly vestments, banners, veils and the like, which have special significance for the performance of religious rites shall be entrusted to believers for use in other prayer buildings or premises; they shall be included in the inventory of religious property in accordance with the general rules;

    d. such everyday objects as bells, furniture, carpets, chandeliers and the like shall be included in the account of the State fund and transmitted for disposal by local financial agencies or agencies of education if the objects were registered with these agencies;

    e. so-called expendable property, such as money, frankincense, candles, oil, wine, wax, wood and coal, shall not be taken away if the religious association will continue to exist after the liquidation of the prayer building.

41. Prayer buildings and wayside shrines subject to liquidation, which are registered in special local agencies for State funds, may be transferred for use free of charge to proper executive committees or city soviets under the condition that they will be continuously considered as nationalized property and their use for other purposes than stipulated may not take place without the consent of the Ministry of Finance.

42. Special local agencies for State funds shall register only such liquidated prayer buildings as are not included in the register of the Ministry of Education, such as monuments of art, or [those which] may not be used by local soviets as cultural or educational establishments (schools, clubs, reading halls, etc.) or dwelling houses.

43. When the religious association does not observe the terms of the contract or orders of the Committee for Religious Matters (on re-registration, repair, etc.) the contract may be annulled.

The contract may also be annulled upon the presentation of lower executive committees by the [Council of Ministers] of the autonomous republic, oblast, etc.

44. When the decision of the authorities mentioned in Article 43 is appealed to the [Council of Ministers] within two weeks, the prayer building and property may actually be taken from the believers only after the final decision of [the Council].

45. The construction of new prayer buildings may take place upon the request of religious societies under the observance of the general regulations pertaining to

construction and technical rules as well as the special conditions stipulated by the Permanent Committee for Religious Matters at the [Council of Ministers].

46. If the prayer building, because of dilapidation, threatens to fall apart completely or partly, the Committee for Religious Matters on the city or district soviet may request the executive body of the religious society or the representative of the group of believers to discontinue temporarily the holding of divine services and meetings of believers in such building until examined by the technical committee.

47. Simultaneously with the requirement on the closing of the prayer building, the officials exacting such requirement shall ask the appropriate agency of construction control to make a technical examination of the building. A copy of the letter shall be given to the agency which concluded the contract upon the leasing of the building and property to believers.

    If the building is registered by the Ministry of Education, a copy shall be given to the appropriate agency of the Ministry.

48. The [following persons] shall be invited with the right of deliberative vote to the examination procedure by the technical committee:
    a. the local representative of the Ministry of Education, if the building is registered by the Ministry;
    b. the representative of the Committee for Religious Matters at the appropriate city or district soviet;
    c. the representative of the religious association.

49. The decision of the technical committee stated in the examination document is binding and subject to execution.

50. If the technical committee decides that the building threatens to collapse, the committee must also indicate whether the building shall be demolished or made safe if appropriate repairs are made. In such case, the [examination] document shall describe in detail the necessary repairs for the prayer building and the date of completion. The religious association may not hold prayer or other meetings in the building until the repair work has been completed.

51. If the believers refuse to carry out the repairs as indicated in the [examination] document of the technical committee, the contract for the use of the building and religious property shall be annulled according to the decision of the [Council of Ministers] of the autonomous republic or oblast.

52. If, as required by the decision of the technical committee, the building shall be demolished, the contract for the use of the building and religious property shall be annulled according to the decision of the [Council of Ministers] of the autonomous republic or oblast.

53. [Any decision for the demolition of the prayer building] shall be carried out by the Committee for Religious Matters at the city or district soviet and the expenses defrayed from the sale of building material remaining after the demolition of the building. Any money left over shall be transferred to the Treasury.

54. The members of the groups of believers and religious societies may pool money in the prayer building or premises and outside it by voluntary collections and donations, but only among the members of the given religious association and only for the purpose of covering the expenses for the maintenance of prayer building or premises and religious property, and for the salary of the clergy and activities of the executive bodies.

    Any kind of compulsory collection of money for the benefit of religious associations is punishable under the provisions of the Criminal Code.

55. It is compulsory to enter in the inventory of religious property any kind of religious property, whether donated, or purchased with the money received through voluntary donations.

The donations made for the purpose of beautifying the prayer building or religious property shall be entered in the general inventory of the religious property which is in use by the religious association free of charge.

All other donations in kind made for indefinite purposes, as well as donations in money to cover the upkeep of prayer buildings (renovation, heating, etc.), or for the benefit of the clergy shall not be subject to entry in the inventory. The donations in money shall be entered by the cashier in the account book.

56. Expenditures of donated money may be carried out by the members of the executive body in connection with the purposes for which they are donated.

57. Prayer meetings of believers who formed a society or group may be held, without notification to or permission of the authorities, in prayer buildings or specially adapted premises which comply with the technical and sanitary regulations.

Divine services may be performed in the premises not specially adapted for these purposes, if notification [is made] to the Committee for Religious Matters.

58. Any kind of religious ceremonies or rites or display of objects of the cult in the buildings belonging to the State, public, cooperative or private institutions or enterprises is prohibited.

Such prohibition does not apply to the performance of religious rites in hospitals and prisons, in specially isolated rooms, if requested by dangerously ill or dying persons, or to the performance of religious ceremonies in cemeteries and in crematoria.

59. A special permission [granted] for each case separately by the Committee for Religious Matters is required for the performance of religious processions as well as the performance of religious rites in the open air. An application for such permission must be submitted at least two weeks prior to the ceremony.

Such permission is not required for religious processions connected with funerals.

60. Permission is not required for religious processions which are an inevitable part of the divine service and are made only around the prayer building, provided they do not disturb normal street traffic.

61. A permission of the agency which concluded the contract for the use of property is necessary for each religious procession as well as the performance of religious ceremonies outside the place where the religious association is situated. Such permission may be granted only with the agreement of the executive committee of the place where the procession or performance of ceremonies is supposed to take place.

62. A record of the religious societies and groups of believers shall be kept by agencies which register the religious association (Art. 6).

63. The registration agencies of religious associations (Art. 6) submit data to the Committee for Religious Matters at the city and district soviets in accordance with the forms and within the period established by the Permanent Committee for Religious Matters at the [Council of Ministers].

64. Surveillance over the activities of religious associations, as well as over the maintenance of prayer buildings and property leased to religious associations, shall be exercised by registration agencies, and in rural areas by village soviets.

C. Instructions of the People's Commissariat of the Interior of October 1, 1929 (as amended January 28, 1932)[13]

I. PURPOSE AND COMPOSITION

1. Citizens of the same cult, denomination, sect or doctrine who are 18 years of age or over may form religious societies or groups of believers for the joint satisfaction of their religious needs.
2. Believers who have formed a religious society or group may:
    - *a.* perform religious rites;
    - *b.* arrange prayer or general meetings of believers;
    - *c.* manage religious property;
    - *d.* conclude transactions of the civil law connected with the management of religious property and the performance of religious rites;
    - *e.* appoint clergymen for the performance of religious rites.
3. The religious associations may not:
    - *a.* create mutual credit societies, poorhouses, charity schools, hospices, dormitories for the poor, funeral funds, etc.;
    - *b.* establish cooperatives, producing unions, and, in general, use the property at their disposal for any other purpose other than the satisfaction of religious needs;
    - *c.* give material help to members of the association;
    - *d.* organize special prayer or other meetings for children, youth, and women;
    - *e.* organize scriptural, literary, sewing, labor or other meetings, groups, circles, sections, or such for teaching religion;
    - *f.* organize excursions and children's playgrounds;
    - *g.* organize libraries and reading rooms;
    - *h.* organize health resorts and medical care.

    Religious societies and groups do not enjoy the rights of a legal entity.
4. The membership of a religious society or group of believers may include only citizens who reside:
    - *a.* in the same city;
    - *b.* in the same city and vicinity;
    - *c.* in the same village; or
    - *d.* in several villages of the same district (raion).
5. A citizen may be a member of one religious association (society or group) of believers.

    Persons who belong to several religious associations may be prosecuted in accordance with [The Criminal Code].

    A citizen who desires to be a member of a religious association must submit

13. Originally published in N. Orleansky, *Zakon o religioznykh obedineniiakh RSFSR* [The law concerning the religious associations of the RSFSR] (Moscow, 1930). According to the Law on the Permanent Central Committee and Local Committees on Religious Matters of May 30, 1931, for matters relating to the administration of churches, special committees at the Council of Ministers and city and district soviets were organized which took over the activities formerly exercised by the People's Commissariat for the Interior. The Committee for Religious Matters at the Council of Ministers issued a new instruction on January 28, 1931, changing only the names of the authorities. This translation taken from the U.S. Senate, Committee on the Judiciary, *The Church and State Under Communism*, pp. 18–24.

a written or oral application to the executive body of the religious society or group of believers.

Members shall be accepted by the executive body or general assembly of the religious society or group of believers.

6. The activities of clergymen, preachers, preceptors, etc. are restricted to the area where the members of religious associations reside and to the place where the prayer premises are located.

The activities of clergymen, preachers, preceptors, etc., who permanently serve two or several religious associations, are restricted to the area where the believers who are members of these religious associations permanently reside.

A clergyman, preacher, preceptor, etc., may start his activities only after the date when the information respecting him has been submitted by the religious society or group of believers to the registration agency.

II. FORMATION AND EXPENDITURE OF MEANS

7. Members of a religious society or group of believers may collect in the prayer building voluntary donations (by collection boxes or plates) among all persons present.

Excepting the prayer building collection, only voluntary donations may take place among the members of a given religious society or group of believers.

8. Collections of voluntary donations among persons who are not members of a given religious association may be carried out only if permission is granted in accordance with the Law on the Collection of Voluntary Donations (*Sobranie Uzakoneny* . . . 1924, No. 8, Art. 81, and 1925, No. 52, Art. 388).

9. Religious associations may not establish compulsory membership fees, or introduce membership cards with monthly indications of donations.

Any kind of compulsory exaction of fees for the benefit of a religious association shall be subject to punishment under [the Criminal Code].

10. Religious associations may collect donations and spend them only for purposes connected with the maintenance of prayer buildings and religious property and for the performance of religious rites, as well as for remuneration to clergymen, watchmen and singers, the activities of executive bodies of religious societies or groups of believers, and executive bodies of religious conventions and conferences.

11. Pecuniary donations and donations in kind for the maintenance (renovation, heating, etc.) of prayer buildings or premises, or for the benefit of the clergy shall not be included in the inventory but may be spent by members of the executive body of a religious society or a representative of a group of believers.

Voluntary pecuniary donations shall be entered by the cashier in the account book.

Any kind of religious property, whether donated or purchased from voluntary donations, shall be entered in the inventory of the religious property.

Voluntary donations made in order to beautify the prayer building by adding a donated object, or in order to beautify the religious objects, shall be entered in the inventory of the religious property.

12. Executive bodies of religious conferences and conventions may receive voluntary donations, but they may not organize collections of voluntary donations or introduce any kind of compulsory fees or subscriptions.

Members of the executive bodies of religious conferences and conventions may spend donations received from believers and religious associations only for expenditures connected with the activities and needs of the executive body.

III. EXECUTIVE BODIES

13. For the execution of the functions connected with the management and use of religious property, as well as for outside representation, the religious association elects from among its members, at the general assembly of believers, by open ballot, an executive body:

    a. for a religious society—three members and two substitutes;
    b. for a group of believers—one representative and his substitute.

    Individual members of the executive body of a religious society or group of believers may be removed by the registration agency.

14. Individual citizens who are members of the executive body of a religious society or representatives of a group of believers may conclude transactions in their own names involving the management and use of the religious property, such as contracts respecting the employment of watchmen, the supply of firewood, renovation of the building and religious property, acquisition of products and property for the performance of religious rites and ceremonies, and they may engage in other activities closely and directly connected with the doctrine and rites of the given religious cult as well as conclude contracts respecting the rental of premises for prayer meetings.

15. A religious society or group of believers may elect, at the general assembly from among its members, an accounting committee of not more than three members and two substitutes for exercising control over religious property and money received through the collection of voluntary donations.

16. Local, republican, All-Russian and All-Union religious conferences and conventions may elect, from among their participants, executive bodies for the execution of decisions of the convention or conference.

    Decisions and decrees of the religious conferences and conventions and their executive bodies may be carried out only by voluntary action of the believers.

17. Executive bodies of religious conferences and conventions do not enjoy the rights of legal entities, and in addition to this, they may not:

    a. possess by contract or otherwise any religious property, acquire by purchase, or rent premises for prayer meetings;
    b. conclude any kind of contracts or transactions.

18. The area of activities of the executive bodies of religious conventions and conferences is restricted to the place where the religious societies or groups united by convention or conference are situated.

19. Executive bodies of religious societies or groups, as well as those of religious conventions and conferences, may use solely for religious matters stamps, seals, and stationery with their names [imprinted]. Such stamps, seals, and stationery may not include emblems or slogans established for Soviet government agencies.

20. All applications (statements, petitions, inquiries, etc.) of the religious associations to State authorities and responses to them are subject to the stamp duty with the exception of applications submitted to agencies of local soviets.

    Complaints regarding abuses and illegal activities of authorities are free from stamp duty no matter to which office they are submitted.

IV. MEETINGS AND CONVENTIONS

21. Prayer meetings, of the believers who have formed a religious society or group in prayer buildings or premises especially adapted for this purpose and considered satisfactory as to technical and sanitary conditions, may be arranged without notification to or permission of authorities.

Buildings and premises may be used after their inspection by the proper sanitary-technical committee whenever the representative of the Committee for Religious Matters and the fire brigade shall participate.

22. Prayer meetings, in premises which are not especially adapted for this purpose (e.g., dwelling houses), may be arranged only if permission for each separate case is granted by the proper authority.

Believers who have formed a religious society or group may notify the authorities concerning a series of prayer meetings held within a period of one year.

Believers who have not formed a society or group must notify authorities regarding each such prayer meeting separately.

23. Permission by the proper authorities is necessary for general assemblies of religious societies or groups.

24. The following shall be submitted in an application for the convocation of the assembly:
    a. the time and location of the assembly and the approximate number of participants;
    b. agenda of the assembly;
    c. the family name, name and patronymic of the responsible organizer (or organizers) of the assembly.

A receipt shall be given to the organizer by request upon the acceptance of the application if it fulfills the requirements mentioned above.

25. The application shall be submitted in writing:
    a. at least three days prior to the proposed prayer meeting;
    b. at least two weeks prior to the proposed assembly.

26. Information on the granting of permission or the denial of permission shall be transmitted to the organizer within seven days from the date of the submission of the application or, at any rate, no later than 24 hours prior to the proposed meeting or assembly.

27. Meetings of executive bodies and accounting committees of groups of believers or religious societies may be convoked without notice to or permission of the authorities.

28. The following may initiate and organize the convocation of a religious convention or conference: religious societies or groups of believers and their executive bodies as well as executive bodies of religious conventions and conferences.

The following data shall be submitted in the application for granting the permission for the convocation of the convention or conference:
    a. the time and location of the convention or conference;
    b. the number of delegates to the convention or conference;
    c. the territory covered by the convention or conference;
    d. list of items subject to discussion in the convention or conference;
    e. the family name, race, patronymic, profession and residence of the responsible organizer or organizers of the convention or conference.

A receipt to the organizer shall be given at his request upon the acceptance of the application if it fulfills the requirements.

29. Permissions for local, All-Russian and All-Union conventions or conferences may be granted:
    a. by the Permanent Committee for Religious Matters at the Council of Ministers in case an All-Russian or All-Union convention or conference is proposed to be convoked;

b. by the local Committee for Religious Matters if a local convention or conference is proposed to be convoked.

Permission for the convocation of a republican convention or conference shall be granted by the Committee for Religious Matters of the appropriate republic.

30. The application for permission of the convocation of a local or republican convention or conference shall be submitted at least one month prior to the proposed meeting, and of the All-Russian or All-Union conference or convention, at least two months prior to the proposed meeting.

    The responsible organizer shall be informed within two weeks of the decision on the granting or denial of permission for the convocation of a local or republican convention or conference, and of the convocation of an All-Russian or All-Union convention or conference within one month from the date of submission of the application.

31. Permission shall be denied if, according to its goal and the items on the agenda and the composition of the organizers or participants, the meeting, convention or conference is in conflict with the laws in effect in the territory of the RSFSR, threatens the social order and safety, or provokes discord and hostilities among the nations.

32. If a meeting, convention, or conference for which permission is required was arranged without permission, the persons organizing or convoking such a meeting, convention or conference shall be prosecuted in court.

V. PROCESSIONS AND CEREMONIES

33. Any kind of religious rites or ceremonies or display of objects of a cult in the premises of State, public, cooperative or private institutions and enterprises shall be prohibited.

    This prohibition shall not apply to:

    a. the performance of religious rites on the request of dying or dangerously ill persons in hospitals and prisons, if such rites or ceremonies are performed in specially isolated rooms, or to the performance of religious rites and ceremonies in cemeteries and crematoria;

    b. images of religious characters (statues and pictures) of artistic, historic or museum value which are exhibited in museums, galleries and other similar institutions.

34. Any kind of religious ceremonies, such as prayers, requiem masses, baptisms, the bringing of holy images (ikona), and the like, may be performed within the family or in apartments without the permission of or notification to authorities.

    The performance of religious rites may take place only if all persons living in rooms used in common are agreeable respecting the performance of such rites.

35. Permission of authorities is not required for religious processions which are an inevitable part of a divine service and are made only around the prayer building, providing they do not disturb street traffic.

36. Special permission, for each case separately, of the Committee for Religious Matters is required for the staging of religious processions as well as for the performance of religious rites outdoor.

    Permission is not required for religious services connected with a funeral.

37. The performance of religious rites as well as religious processions outside the place where the religious association is situated may be allowed by special permission, separately given for each case, issued by the agency which concluded the contract on the use of the religious property. Such permission may

be issued only if the executive committee of the district, in which the procession, rites or ceremonies are supposed to be performed, is agreeable to such performance.

38. The application requesting permission for religious processions or ceremonies shall be submitted by organizers in writing at least two weeks prior to the proposed procession or ceremonies.

    The application must contain the following data:
    a. the purpose of the procession or ceremony;
    b. date and hour of the beginning of the procession and its duration;
    c. detailed route of the procession;
    d. supposed number of participants;
    e. the family name, name, patronymic, profession and residence of the responsible organizer or organizers.

    A receipt shall be given to the organizer at his request upon the acceptance of the application.

    The decision on the granting or denial of permission for the performance of the procession or ceremony shall be transmitted to the responsible organizer within three days prior to the proposed procession or ceremony.

39. Permission shall be denied if the procession or ceremony is contrary to the laws in effect, provokes discord or hostilities among nations, threatens the social order or safety or may disturb street traffic.

40. For each procession or ceremony, there shall be a responsible master of ceremonies who is obliged to keep order during the procession or ceremony, observe that street traffic is not disturbed, and prevent any deviation from the purpose or route of the procession or ceremony as indicated in the permission.

41. If a procession or ceremony for which permission is required was organized without such permission and was not discontinued according to the demand of the administrative authorities, the persons organizing such procession or ceremony shall be prosecuted in court.

VI. THE REGISTRATION

42. The local religious associations of believers who are 18 years of age or over shall be registered as religious societies or groups of believers.

    No religious society may be organized with less than 20 citizens, however, a group of believers may be organized by citizens too few in number to organize a religious society.

43. A religious society or group of believers may start its activities only after registration by the Committee for Religious Matters at the proper city or district soviet.

44. The founders of a religious society or group of believers must submit two copies for registration of:
    a. the application according to established form;
    b. the list of founders of the group of believers, or of not less than 20 of a religious society, according to the established form.

    A receipt shall be given to the founders at their request upon the acceptance of the application, if it fulfils the requirements.

    Persons who submit false data in the application for registration shall be prosecuted according to the provisions [of the Criminal Code].

45. The registration agencies must register the religious society or group of belivers or advise the founders of the denial of the registration within one month from the date of the submission of the application.

46. The registration of a religious society or group of believers must be denied if its methods and forms of activities are contrary to the laws in effect, threaten the public order or safety, or provoke discord or hostilities among the nations.

VII. ACCOUNTING

47. A list of members of the executive bodies and accounting committees as well as a report on changes in this list shall be submitted within seven days by the religious society or group of believers to registration agencies.

    Such a list and report shall be submitted in two copies according to the established form.

    A receipt shall be given to the religious society or group of believers according to the established form upon acceptance of the list or report.

48. Data on the clergy, preachers, preceptors, etc. who serve the religious society or group of believers shall be submitted to the registration agency in two copies according to the established form.

    A receipt shall be given according to the established form upon acceptance of the date.

49. A religious association must submit to the registration agency a list of its members according to the established form.

    The first list shall include all members of the religious society or group of believers. By January 1 of each year, a report shall be submitted on changes in the list of members of the society or group.

50. If the provisions of the present instruction on the submission of data or reports are continuously violated by the religious society or group of believers, the registration agency may require the removal of the members of the executive body and the election of new members.

51. The materials of the religious convention or conference (records, decisions, reports) shall be submitted in two copies in accordance with the established form to the authority granting the permission for the convention or conference together with the list of members of the elected body.

    A receipt shall be given in accordance with the established form upon the acceptance of the materials and the list of members of the executive body.

52. Records on the religious societies and groups of believers shall be kept by the registration agencies.

53. The registration agencies shall submit, in accordance with the form established by the Committee for Religious Matters, the data on religious associations to higher authorities.

VIII. SURVEILLANCE

54. The activities of the religious societies and groups of believers are under the surveillance of the proper committee for religious matters.

55. In exercising surveillance, the proper committee for religious matters, as well as other authorities whose duty it is to safeguard the revolutionary order and safety, may send their representatives to each assembly or meeting of believers for the purpose of watching over order and safety.

    Persons sent to the assembly for supervision over order and safety may not participate in discussions or voting or engage in the leading of the assembly.

56. Persons sent to the assembly for supervision over order and safety are obliged to adjourn the assembly:

    a. in case of forcible activities of one part of the assembly toward another;

    b. in case of any deviation from the agenda submitted by the organizers of the assembly, violation of order, or inciting to the commission of crimes or infringements of the law, if such activities were not stopped by the presidium, or if the presidium, on the request of the person sent to the assembly, did not adjourn the assembly;

c. if the presidium of the assembly asks collaboration of the person sent to the assembly to adjourn the assembly which deviated from the provisions of the law.

The participants of the assembly declared adjourned must depart without delay. Persons failing to follow this demand shall be prosecuted.

57. Members of the militia, as well as the members of the local soviet, shall see to it that no forcible activities against persons are committed, no property demolished or abused, or other illegal activities performed during the processions and ceremonies.

58. Members of the militia, as well as local soviets and other authorities whose duty it is to safeguard the revolutionary order and safety, may send their representatives to any procession and ceremony for the maintenance of order and safety during the procession or ceremony.

Persons sent to the procession or ceremony for maintaining order and safety may break off the procession if the lawful orders of authorities are not observed and demand that the participants depart without delay.

59. Inspection of religious societies and groups of believers shall be performed, if necessary, by committees for religious matters at the city or district soviets.

The inspection of executive bodies of religious conventions and conferences shall be performed by the Committee for Religious Matters at the Council of Ministers.

Files and records, as well as money matters, shall be examined during the inspection.

IX. LIQUIDATION

60. A religious society or group of believers may be liquidated in accordance with the decision of the general assembly of the society or group.

The registration agency shall be informed within seven days regarding such decision.

61. In case of a disclosure in the activities of a religious association of deviations from the rules established for such association, the registration agency shall demand the correction of the defects by the date indicated by the agency.

If the religious society or group of believers refuses to correct the defects, as well as in the case of the disclosure of the violation of laws, the city or district committee for religious matters may ask the Committee for Religious Matters at the Council of Ministers to liquidate the society or group.

Such a decision shall be delivered to the executive body of the society or group.

62. The decision on the liquidation of the religious society or group of believers may be appealed before the Council of Ministers within two weeks from the date of the delivery of the decision.

In case of an appeal, the religious society or group of believers shall be liquidated only after the confirmation of the decision.

Liquidation of the religious society or group of believers shall be executed by the committee for religious matters at the city or district soviet.

63. The contract leasing the prayer building and religious property for the use of believers free of charge may be annulled according to the decision of the

Committee for Religious Matters at the Council of Ministers on the proposal of such Committee at the city or district soviet.

Believers who are members of the religious society or group shall be informed of such a decision.

64. The contract may be annulled if the religious association has not observed orders of authorities (on re-registration, renovation, etc.), as well as in the case when the prayer building is needed for State or public use.

65. If the believers who are members of the religious society or group, within two weeks from the date of announcement of the decision on the liquidation of the prayer building, take an appeal before the Council of Ministers, the contract shall be annulled, and the believers shall be deprived of the use of the building only after the confirmation of the decision.

The liquidation shall be carried out by the committee for religious matters at the city or district soviet in the presence of the representative of the finance department and other authorities interested in the case as well as of the representatives of the religious association.

D. Edict: On Administrative Liability for Violation of Legislation on Religious Cults of March 18, 1966[14]

The Presidium of the Supreme Soviet of the RSFSR decrees that the following activities are violations of the legislation on religious cults:

the refusal of leaders of religious associations to register such associations with the authorities;

the violation of established legislation on the organization and conduct of religious meetings, processions, and other cultic ceremonies;

the organization and conduct by ministers of the cult and members of religious associations of special meetings of children and youth, as well as of labor, literary, and other circles and groups, having no relation to the practice of the cult;

and carry with them a fine not exceeding fifty rubles, to be levied by administrative commissions or executive committees of the district or city Soviets of Workers' Deputies.

3. CRIMINAL LAW AND PROCEDURE OF THE RSFSR[15]

A. Criminal Code of the RSFSR

Article 28. Consequences of evasion of correctional tasks.

In the event that a person evades serving correctional tasks at the place of

14. Originally published in *Vedomosti verkhovnogo soveta RSFSR* [Bulletin of the Supreme Soviet of the RSFSR], no. 12 (1966), edict 219.

15. Articles 28, 70, 74, 122, 142 (par. 1), 143, 151, 186, 209, 227, 14, 5 originally published in *Ugolovnoe zakonodatelstvo soiuza SSSR i soiuznikh respublik* [Criminal legislation of the USSR and the union republics] (Moscow, 1963), and issues of *Vedomosti verkhovnogo soveta SSSR* and *Vedomosti verkhovnogo soveta RSFSR* from January 1, 1961, to July 15, 1965. Translation taken from Harold J. Berman, *Soviet Criminal Law and Procedure, the RSFSR Codes* (Cambridge, Mass.: Harvard University Press, 1966), pp. 157, 180, 196, 201, 204, 215, 224, 230, 257, 430. Articles 142 (par. 2, Ordinance on the Application of Article 142), 190–1, 190–3 translated by Harold J. Berman from *Vedomosti verkhovnogo soveta RSFSR*, no. 12 (1966), and no. 38 (1966).

work, the court may replace [the sentence] by correctional tasks at places determined by agencies in charge of application of such punishment. In the event of evasion of correctional tasks in the places determined by the designated agencies, the court may replace [the sentence] by deprivation of freedom, with every three days of the unserved term of correctional tasks to be replaced by one day of deprivation of freedom.

Article 70. Anti-Soviet agitation and propaganda.

Agitation or propaganda carried on for the purpose of subverting or weakening Soviet authority or of committing particular, especially dangerous crimes against the state, or circulating for the same purpose slanderous fabrications which defame the Soviet state and social system, or circulating or preparing or keeping, for the same purpose, literature of such content, shall be punished by deprivation of freedom for a term of six months to seven years, with or without additional exile for a term of two to five years, or by exile for a term of two to five years.

The same actions committed by a person previously convicted of especially dangerous crimes against the state or committed in wartime shall be punished by deprivation of freedom for a term of three to ten years, with or without additional exile for a term of two to five years.

Article 74. Violation of equality of rights of nationalities and races.

Propaganda or agitation for the purpose of arousing hostility or dissension of races or nationalities, or the direct or indirect restriction of rights or the establishment of direct or indirect privileges for citizens depending on the races or nationalities in which they belong, shall be punished by deprivation of freedom for a term of six months to three years, or by exile for a term of two to five years.

Article 122. Malicious evasion of payment for support or maintenance of children.

The malicious evasion by parents of payment, in accordance with a court decision, of the means for maintenance of minor children or of maintenance of adult children incapable of working who are dependent on them, shall be punished by deprivation of freedom for a term not exceeding three years, or by correctional tasks for a term not exceeding one year.

Article 142. Violation of laws on separation of church and state and of church and school.

The violation of laws on the separation of church and state and of school and church shall be punished by correctional tasks for a term not exceeding one year or by a fine not exceeding fifty rubles.

The same acts committed by a person who has previously been convicted for a violation of laws on separation of church and state and of church and school, and also organizational activity directed to the commission of these acts, shall be punished by deprivation of freedom for a term not exceeding three years.

Article 143. Obstructing performance of religious rites.

Obstructing the performance of religious rites, insofar as they do not violate public order and are not accompanied by infringement of the rights of citizens, shall be punished by correctional tasks for a term not exceeding six months or by social censure.

Article 151. Crimes against property of associations not constituting socialist organizations.

Crimes against the property of associations not constituting socialist organizations, committed with respect to property situated on the territory of the

RSFSR, shall be punished in accordance with the articles of the present chapter.

Article 186. Escape from place of exile.

Escape from a place of exile or en route to a place of exile shall be punished by deprivation of freedom for a term not exceeding one year.

Article 190–1. Circulation of knowingly false fabrications which defame the Soviet state and social system.

The systematic circulation in an oral form of knowingly false fabrications which defame the Soviet state and social system and, equally, preparation or circulation in written, printed, or any other form of works of such content, shall be punished by deprivation of freedom for a term not exceeding three years, or by corrective tasks for a term not exceeding one year, or by a fine not exceeding one hundred rubles.

Article 190–3. Organization of or active participation in group actions which violate public order.

Organization of and, equally, active participation in group actions which violate public order, or which are attended by clear disobedience of the legal demands of representatives of authority or which entail the violation of the work of transport or of state and social institutions or enterprises, shall be punished by deprivation of freedom for a term not exceeding three years, or by corrective tasks for a term not exceeding one year, or by a fine not exceeding one hundred rubles.

Article 209. Systematically engaging in vagrancy or in begging.

Systematically engaging in vagrancy or in begging, continued after warning given by administrative agencies, shall be punished by deprivation of freedom for a term not exceeding two years or by correctional tasks for a term of six months to one year.

Article 227. Infringement of person and rights of citizens under appearance of performing religious ceremonies.

Organizing or directing a group, the activity of which, carried on under the appearance of preaching religious beliefs and performing religious ceremonies, is connected with causing harm to citizens' health or with inducing citizens to refuse social activity or performance of civic duties, or with drawing minors into such group, shall be punished by a deprivation of freedom for a term not exceeding five years or by exile for a similar term with or without confiscation of property.

The active participation in the activity of a group specified in paragraph one of the present article, or systematic propaganda directed at the commission of acts specified therein, shall be punished by deprivation of freedom for a term not exceeding three years, or by exile for the same term, or by correctional tasks for a term not exceeding one year.

Note: If the acts of persons indicated in paragaraph two of the present article, and the persons themselves, do not represent a great social danger, measures of social pressure may be applied to them.

B. Ordinance: On the Application of Article 142 of the Criminal Code of the RSFSR.

In connection with questions arising from the practical application of Article 142 of the Criminal Code of the RSFSR, the Presidium of the Supreme Soviet of the RSFSR, on the basis of paragraph "C" of Article 33 of the Constitution of the RSFSR by way of clarification, explains that the following shall be understood as violations of the laws on separation of church and state and of

B. continued

school and church, involving criminal responsibility under Article 142 of the Criminal Code of the RSFSR:

the compulsory taking of collections and taxation for the benefit of religious organizations or ministers of the cult;

the preparation for mass dissemination, or the mass dissemination of written appeals, letters, leaflets, and other documents calling for the nonobservance of the legislation on religious cults;

the commission of fraudulent actions for the purpose of inciting religious superstition among the masses of the population;

the organization and conduct of religious meetings, processions, and other cultic ceremonies which violate the social order;

the organization and systematic conduct of religious instruction to minors in violation of established legislation;

the refusal to employ citizens or to admit them to educational institutions, their dismissal from work or expulsion from educational institutions, their deprivation of rights and privileges established by law, as well as other essential limitations of the rights of citizens on the grounds of their religion.

C. Code of Criminal Procedure
Article 14. Administration of justice on basis of equality of citizens before law and courts.

Justice in criminal cases shall be administered on the basis of equality of all citizens before the law and the courts, without regard to their social, property, or occupational status, nationality, race, or religion.

D. Law on Court Organization
Article 5. Equality of citizens before law and courts.

Justice in the RSFSR shall be administered on the basis of equality of citizens before the law and the courts, without regard to their social, property, or occupational status, nationality, race, or religion.

4. ANTIPARASITE LAWS

Edict of the Presidium of the Supreme Soviet of the RSFSR: On strengthening the struggle against persons who avoid socially useful work and lead an antisocial parasitic way of life.[16]

Our country, under the leadership of the Communist Party, has entered the period of expanded construction of communism. Soviet people are working with enthusiasm at enterprises, construction projects, collective and state farms and institutions, performing socially useful work in the family, observing the law, and respecting the rules of socialist community life.

However, in cities and in the countryside there are still individuals who are able to work but are stubbornly opposed to honest labor and lead an antisocial parasitic way of life. On collective farms such persons, enjoying the benefits established for collective farmers, avoid honest labor, undermine discipline, and thereby harm the artel's economy.

16. Originally published in *Vedomosti verkhovnovo soveta RSFSR*, no. 11 (May 18, 1961), edict 273, as amended in ibid., no. 38 (September 23, 1965), edict 932.

The parasitic existence of these persons as a rule is accompanied by drunkenness, moral degradation, and violation of the rules of socialist community life, which have an adverse influence on other unstable members of society.

It is necessary to wage a resolute struggle against antisocial, parasitic elements until this disgraceful phenomenon is completely eradicated from our society, creating around such persons an atmosphere of intolerance and general condemnation.

Taking into account the many expressions on the part of the working people that the struggle against antisocial elements be intensified, the Presidium of the Supreme Soviet of the RSFSR decrees:

1. To establish that adult able-bodied citizens who do not wish to perform a major Constitutional duty—to work honestly according to their abilities—and who avoid socially useful work, and carry on an antisocial parasitic way of life, shall be subject upon the order of an executive committee of a district (or city) Soviet of Workers' Deputies, to socially useful work at enterprises (construction sites), located in the region of their regular place of residence or in other localities within the boundaries of the given district, region or autonomous republics.

   Individuals who refuse socially useful work and carry on an antisocial, parasitic way of life, and who reside in the city of Moscow, the Moscow district, or the city of Leningrad, shall be subject, upon the order of a district (or city) people's court, to exile in specially designated localities for a period of from two to five years, and to enlistment in work at the place of exile.

   The decision of the executive committee of the district (or city) Soviet of Workers' Deputies on the enlistment of socially useful work or the order of the district (or city) people's court on exile shall be carried out only after an individual, who has refused socially useful work and has carried on an antisocial parasitic way of life, for the period of a month does not go to work in spite of warnings of the police authorities or social organizations.

2. The decision of an executive committee of the district (or city) Soviet of Workers' Deputies or the order of the district (or city) people's court on the application of coercive measures against a person who is avoiding socially useful work and who is leading an antisocial parasitic way of life shall be final and shall not be subject to appeal.

3. The exposure of persons avoiding socially useful work and leading an antisocial parasitic way of life, and the verification of all relevant circumstances shall be carried out at the initiative of state and social organizations and the declarations of citizens by organs of the police on the basis of materials in their possession. Upon completion of this verification, the organs of the police shall notify those persons involved of the necessity of going to work within a month. For the same purposes, organs of the police can send materials to social organizations for consideration.

   If after notification these persons do not follow the path of a life of honest labor, organs of the police shall send materials about them to the executive committee of the district (or city) Soviet of Workers' Deputies, and in cases provided for in part 2 of Article 1 of this Edict, with the agreement of the Procurator, to the district (or city) people's court.

4. If during the verification and examination of materials concerning a person who is leading a parasitic way of life signs of a criminal offence are established in his actions, his case shall be sent to agencies of the Procuracy.

5. The orders of the district (or city) people's courts on the exile of persons

avoiding socially useful work and leading a parasitic antisocial way of life shall be executed by organs of the police which also shall be entrusted with the responsibility for execution of decisions of the executive committees of the district (or city) Soviets of Workers' Deputies on sending such persons to work.

Administrative and social organizations of enterprises (construction sites) where these persons are sent to work are obliged to ensure that they are sent to work, and are to carry on educational work with them.

If a person sent to work by decision of the executive committee of the district (or city) Soviet of Workers' Deputies, or exiled by order of the district (or city) peoples' court in a specially designated locale, does not go to work, or having been put to work in fact does not work, then this person, upon representation of the organs of the police or of administrative and social organizations of enterprises (construction sites), is subject to corrective tasks imposed by the district (or city) people's court for a period of up to one year with retention of 10% of his earnings. In case of evasion of corrective tasks by such persons, upon representation of the organs for the preservation of social order the court may under the procedure provided in Article 28 of the Criminal Code of the RSFSR make substitution for their deprivation of freedom. The term of corrective tasks or deprivation of freedom shall not be considered a part of the term of exile.

Escape from the place of exile or en route to it shall be punished in accordance with Article 186 of the Criminal Code of the RSFSR.

6. If a person who has been exiled proves by his exemplary conduct and honest attitude toward work that he has reformed, he may, after expiration of not less than half of the term of exile, be released in advance upon the petition of social organizations to the district (or city) people's court at the place of exile.

7. To instruct the Council of Ministers of the RSFSR to adopt a decree on carrying out the necessary measures stemming from this Edict.

5. SECRET CIRCULAR OF THE STATE COUNCIL FOR THE AFFAIRS OF THE RUSSIAN ORTHODOX CHURCH[17]

I. Circular of the Council for Russian Orthodox Church Affairs.
Fundamental Points Concerning the Activity of the Cooperating Commission
of the Executive Committees and the Regional Soviets of Deputies of Workers
for Controlling the Observance of Legislation on Cults:

1. Public cooperating commissions for controlling the observance of the legislation on cults are to be established by the regional city executive committees.

2. The commissions are to be guided in their work by the laws, decrees, and orders of the highest legislative and executive organs of the Soviet state concerning religious cults, and also by the interpretations of the Council for Russian Orthodox Church Affairs of the Council of Ministers of the USSR on points concerning the application of legislation on cults.

3. The commission is to be made up of persons politically prepared, who because of their knowledge of this field are capable of controlling and supervising religious societies in the observance of Soviet legislation on cults.

17. Translated from *Vestnik russkogo studencheskogo khristianskogo dvizheniia* [Herald of the Russian Student Christian movement], 1967, no. 1, pp. 3–6.

Deputies of local soviets, workers of cultural-educational institutions and organs of public education, of finance institutions, propagandists, pensioners, workers in village soviets and local activists are to be drawn into the membership of the commission.

The size of the commission is to be determined by calculating the need for studying and controlling the activities of the religious societies (parishes) in the territory of the region, and also by the need of exposing and suppressing the illegal activities of unregistered religious groups.

The cooperating commissions are to be confirmed by the city executive committees and the regional executive committees. The vice-chairman or secretary of the city executive committee is to be made available to the commission.

4. The duties of the commissions include:

a. systematic study of religious conditions in populated areas (regardless of the presence or absence of officially active religious societies), to gather and analyze data on the frequency with which believers attend religious gatherings, to study the body of persons who attend church and fulfill religious rites (baptism, burial, marriage, confession), the degree to which religious societies and ministers of the cult influence and attract youth and children to religion and the rites, to verify the accuracy of the registering of religious rites, and through verification to stop instances of the baptisms of children without the consent of both parents;

b. to study continuously the ideological activity of the church (propagation and accommodation, the methods and means used by the ministers of the cult for expanding or limiting their influence on a certain part of the population, especially children and adolescents) and to ascertain which youth the ministers of the cult are attempting to prepare for and draw into religious work;

c. to consider and study the so-called "patronal" and other religious holidays held in populated areas, to analyze their adverse influence on production and work discipline, and to develop and introduce proposals aimed at liquidating these adverse occurrences;

d. to study the membership of religious societies (parish executive organs) and to expose their most active members;

e. to check closely the ministers of the cult and religious societies in their observance of Soviet legislation, to expose the attempts of the ministers of the cult to transgress Soviet laws, and to inform the executive committee of these violations at the proper time;

f. to help financial organs in exposing ministers of the cult who illegally perform religious rites in believers' homes and apartments and receive compensation without a receipt and do not declare this income on their income tax;

g. to expose persons not registered as ministers of a cult who illegally appear in populated areas and perform religious rites and to inform the executive committee of such persons.

One of the most important concerns of the cooperating commissions must be the seeking out of means and the introducing of concrete proposals aimed at limiting and weakening the activities of religious societies and ministers of the cult (within the framework of the law.).

The members of the commission are systematically to inform the chairman of the commission of their work and carefully to fulfill his instructions.

II. Explanatory Instructions of the Oblast Representative of the Council on Religious Affairs. Concluding a Contract with the "Group of Twenty," the Legal Organ of a Parish:

The text of the contract of your executive committee with the community of believers on the subject of transferring to them the free use of a church that is state property is now being sent.

The present contract is to be concluded with the entire community, i.e. the "Group of Twenty," and not with the community's executive organ, and is to be signed by the chairman of the soviet (in this instance, by the person who supervises religious cults) and by all the members of the "Group of Twenty."

It should be kept in mind that at present the "Groups of Twenty" in all the believing communities do not inspire special confidence. They are almost completely composed of elderly people, the uneducated, fanatics. We cannot entrust them with government property.

You should recommend that they create a new "Group of Twenty" composed of educated persons, persons capable of managing the community (no fanatics), who would honorably fulfill Soviet laws and your suggestions and recommendations.

When a satisfactory "Group of Twenty" is created, then sign the contract with them.

There should be no more than twenty persons in the "Group of Twenty." The "Group of Twenty" is composed of citizens who give the community of believers a declaration stating that they want to be members of the "Group of Twenty" and to shoulder the material responsibility for the property transferred to the community; they also report their age, education, place of work and their addresses.

In some churches there are contracts made on the opening of the church.

Contracts are signed in triplicate and a catalogue of the cult's property is attached to them, also in triplicate. Everything in the church, except those articles that are for sale, is to be included in the inventory.

Structures located on the church's property, dwellings, garages, barns and the like, except for the guardian's house and offices, and also houses with attached structures located beyond the limits of the church's property, are transferred to the community on a lease basis. A kolkhoz concludes the contract for transferring the buildings to the community by lease and collects the lease-money according to the proper article in the decree of the Soviet of People's Commissars of the RSFSR, March 26, 1926, point G (cf. housing laws of the 1957 edition, p. 542 for prayer buildings). This also applies to prayer houses.

The transfer of the prayer building and dwellings by a lease does not free the community from paying taxes (insurance, land rent, building tax). The leasing contract is concluded and signed by the kolkhoz's soviet.

After the contract has been signed and concluded, let the community of believers, i.e. the "Group of Twenty," choose its executive organ (chairman, vice-chairman, treasurer, and three members of the auditing commission).

It is desirable that you take part in the selection of members for the executive organ and select those persons who adhere to our line.

When everything is completed, the following items are to be sent to the representative of the Council on Religious Affairs in the oblast executive committee (oblispolkom) for registration: a copy of the contract with the catalogue of the cult's property, inventory, a copy of the lease contract, a list of the members of the "Group of Twenty" and a list of the members of the executive organ of the community and the auditing commission.

I suggest that you do not include employees of the church in the membership of the "Group of Twenty": priests, choir directors, guardians, janitors, stablemen, furnacemen, chauffeurs, makers of communion bread, bellringers.

Employees of the church can be selected by the community for the following posts in the "Group of Twenty": chairman, treasurer, vice-chairman, and for no others.

SELECTED BIBLIOGRAPHY
of English-Language Books
on
Religion in the Soviet Union

Compiled By
THOMAS E. BIRD AND ANDREW Q. BLANE

SELECTED BIBLIOGRAPHY

This bibliography is compiled for the general reader. It consists of a select list of books in English on religion in the Soviet Union, and is intended as a guide to the larger field within which the specialized essays of this volume find their place. The bibliography is selective rather than comprehensive. But the selection was made from a comprehensive list and after consultation with specialists on the separate religious communities in Russia. Although useful articles relevant to the topic abound, they are not included because of their number and because of the difficulties the general reader confronts in locating them. Brochures of substance are listed, as are books devoted mainly to religion in prerevolutionary Russia which also embrace the Soviet period,

The bibliography is arranged alphabetically by author and, where no author is given, by title. With few exceptions the list is made up of monographs. Two works (nos. 18 and 34) are bibliographies of special focus; two others (nos. 10 and 21) are chiefly document compilations. For the reader who seeks an introduction to and basic overview of religion in Soviet Russia the editors suggest Walter Kolarz, *Religion in the Soviet Union* (no. 52).

1. Alderson, Wroe, et al. *Meeting the Russians: American Quakers Visit the Soviet Union.* Philadelphia: American Friends Service Committee, 1956.
2. Ami, Ben, *Between the Hammer and Sickle.* Philadelphia: The Jewish Publication Society of America, 1967. Translation of Hebrew work published in 1965.
3. Anderson, Paul B. *People, Church, and State in Modern Russia.* New York: Macmillan, 1944.
4. ———. *Russia's Religious Future.* London: Lutterworth Press, 1935.
5. *The Atheist's Handbook.* Washington: U.S. Joint Publications Research Service, report no. 8,592, 1961. Translation of portions of a Russian work published in 1959.

6. Attwater, Donald. *The Christian Churches of the East.* Rev. ed., vol. 2. Milwaukee, Wisconsin: Bruce Publishing Co., 1962.

7. ———. *Leonid Feodorov and the Catholic Russians.* New York: Russian Center, 1954.

8. Bach, Marcus. *God and the Soviets.* New York: Crowell, 1958.

9. Bacon, E. *Central Asians Under Russian Rule: A Study in Cultural Change.* Ithaca: Cornell University Press, 1966.

10. Baron, J. B., and Waddams, H. M. *Communism and the Churches: A Documentation.* London: SCM Press, 1950.

11. Baron, Salo W. *The Russian Jew.* New York: Macmillan, 1964.

12. Bennigsen, Alexandre, and Lemercier-Quelquejay, C. *The Evolution of the Muslim Nationalities of the USSR and Their Linguistic Problems.* London: Central Asian Research Centre, 1961. Translation of French article published in 1960.

13. ———. *Islam in the Soviet Union.* New York: Praeger, 1967.

14. Bennigsen, George, ed. *Religion in Russia: A Collection of Essays Read at the Cambridge Summer School of Russian Studies, 1939.* London: Burns, Oates, and Washbourne, 1940.

15. Bilmanis, Alfreds. *The Church in Latvia.* New York: Drauga Vests, 1945.

16. Bourdeaux, Michael. *Opium of the People: The Christian Religion in the USSR.* London: Faber and Faber, 1965.

17. ———. *Religious Ferment in Russia.* New York: St. Martin's Press, 1968.

18. Braham, Randolph L., and Hauer, Mordecai M. *Jews in the Communist World: A Bibliography, 1945–1962.* New York: Pro-Arte Publishing Co., 1963.

19. Bourgeois, Charles. *A Priest in Russia and the Baltic.* Dublin-London: Burns, Oates, and Washbourne, 1953.

20. Casey, Robert Pierce. *Religion in Russia.* New York: Harper & Row, 1946.

21. *The Church and State Under Communism.* Vol. 1, pts. I (1964), II, III (1965): the USSR; vol. 4: Latvia, Lithuania, Estonia. Washington, D.C.: U.S. Senate Committee on the Judiciary.

22. *The Church Under Communism.* New York: Philosophical Library, 1953.

23. Cianfarra, Camille M. *The Vatican and the Kremlin.* New York: E. P. Dutton and Company, 1950.

24. *Conference In Defence of Peace of All Churches and Religious Associations in the USSR.* Moscow: Moscow Patriarchate, 1952. Translation of Russian work published in 1952.

25. Conquest, Robert. *Religion in the USSR.* New York: Prager, 1968.

26. Cooke, Richard J. *Religion in Russia Under the Soviets.* New York-Cincinnati: Abingdon Press, 1924.

27. Curtiss, John S. *The Russian Church and the Soviet State, 1917–1950*. New York: Columbia Press, 1940.
28. Decter, Moshe, ed. *Silence and Yearning: A Report and Analysis of the Status of Soviet Jewry*, New York: American Jewish Congress. (A special issue of *Congress Bi-Weekly*, 33, no. 18 [5 December 1966]).
29. Emhardt, William C. *Religion in Soviet Russia*. London: Mowbray, 1929.
30. Evans, Stanley G. *The Churches in the USSR*. London: Cobbett Publishing Co., 1943.
31. ———. *The Russian Church Today*. London: Zeno Publishers, 1955.
32. Fedotov, George P. *The Russian Church Since the Revolution*. New York: Macmillan, 1928.
33. *First Victims of Communism: White Book on the Religious Persecution in the Ukraine*. Rome: Analecta OSBM, 1953.
34. Fletcher, William C. *Christianity in the Soviet Union: An Annotated Bibliography and List of Articles of Works in English*. Los Angeles: University of Southern California, 1963.
35. ———. *A Study in Survival: The Church in Russia, 1927–1943*. New York: Macmillan, 1965.
36. Fletcher, William C., and Strover, Anthony J., eds. *Religion and the Search for New Ideals in the USSR*. New York: Praeger, 1967.
37. Frumkin, Jacob; Aronson, Gregor; and Goldenweiser, Alexis, eds. *Russian Jewry*. New York: Yoseloff, 1966.
38. Galter, Albert. *The Red Book of the Persecuted Church*. Westminster, Md: Newman Press, 1957.
39. Goldberg, Ben Z. *The Jewish Problem in the Soviet Union: Analysis and Solution*. New York: Crown, 1961.
40. Goldman, Guido G. *Zionism under Soviet Rule, 1917–1928*. New York: Herzel Press, 1960.
41. Greenberg, Louis. *The Jews in Russia*. Vol. 2. New Haven, Conn.: Yale University Press, 1951.
42. de Grunwald, Constantine. *The Churches and the Soviet Union*. New York: Macmillan, 1962. Translated by G. J. Robinson-Paskevsky from French work published in 1961.
43. Hecker, Julius F. *Religion and Communism*. New York: Wiley, 1934.
44. ———. *Religion under the Soviets*. New York: Wiley, 1934.
45. Iaroslavsky, Emelian. *Religion in the USSR*. New York: International Publishers, 1934. Translation of Russian work published in 1934.
46. *Islam and Russia: A Detailed Analysis of "An Outline of the History of Islamic Studies in the USSR" by N. A. Smirnov*. London: Central Asian Research Centre, 1956. Abridged translation of Russian work published in 1954.

47. Iwanov, B. I., ed. *Religion in the USSR*. Munich: Institute for the Study of the USSR, 1960. Translation of German work published in 1960.

48. Jackson, Joseph Harrison. *The Eternal Flame*. Philadelphia: Christian Education Press, 1956.

49. Johansen, Alf. *Theological Study in the Russian and Bulgarian Orthodox Churches Under Communist Rule*. London: Faith Press, 1963.

50. Kania, Wladyslaw. *Bolshevism and Religion*. New York: Polish Library, n.d. Translated by R. M. Dowdall from Polish work published c. 1945.

51. Kline, George L. *Religious and Anti-Religious Thought in Russia*. Chicago: University of Chicago Press, 1968.

52. Kolarz, Walter. *Religion in the Soviet Union*. New York: St. Martin's Press, 1962.

53. Kuegelgen, Carlo von, ed. *The Whited Sepulchre*. London: Lutterworth Press, 1935.

54. Ledit, Joseph. *Archbishop John Baptist Cieplak*. Montreal: Palm Publishers, 1963.

55. Lenin, V. I. *Lenin on Religion*. New York: International Publishers, 1932.

56. Lonsdale, Kathleen, ed. *Quakers Visit Russia*. London: East-West Relations Group of the Friends' Peace Committee, 1952.

57. Mailleux, Paul. *Exarch Leonid Feodorov: Bridgebuilder Between Rome and Moscow*. New York: P. J. Kenedy, 1964.

58. McCullaugh, Francis. *The Bolshevik Persecution of Christianity*. New York: Dutton, 1925.

59. Melish, William Howard. *Religion Today in the USSR*. New York: National Council of American-Soviet Friendship, 1945.

60. Meyendorff, John F. *The Orthodox Church*. New York: Pantheon, 1962. Translated by John Chapin from French work published in 1960.

61. Miliukov, P. N. *Religion and the Church*. Edited by M. Karpovich. New York: A. S. Barnes, 1960. Translated by Valentine Ughet and Eleanor Davis from Russian work published in 1930–37.

62. Mydlowsky, Lev. *Bolshevist Persecution of Religion and Church in the Ukraine: 1917–1957*. 2d rev. ed. London: Ukrainian Publishers, 1962.

63. Newton, Louie D. *An American Churchman in the Soviet Union*. Moscow: Union of Evangelical Baptists of the USSR, 1946.

64. Ormanian, Malachian. *The Armenian Church*. 2d rev. ed. London: A. R. Mowbray & Co., 1955.

65. Pennar, Jaan. *Islam and Communism*. New York: 1960.

66. Phillips, G. D. R. *Dawn in Siberia: The Mongols of Lake Baikal*. London: 1942.

67. Pollack, J. C. *The Faith of the Russian Evangelicals*. New York: McGraw-Hill, 1964.

68. Prokhanoff, I. S. *In the Cauldron of Russia*. New York: All-Russian Evangelical Christian Union, 1933.
69. *Religious Communities in the Soviet Union*. London: Press Department of the Soviet Embassy, 1941.
70. *The Russian Orthodox Church: Organization, Situation, Activity*. Moscow: Moscow Patriarchate, 1959. Translation of Russian work published in 1959.
71. *The Russian Orthodox Church in the Fight for Peace: Decisions, Epistles, Appeals, and Articles, 1948–1950*. Moscow: Moscow Patriarchate, 1950. Translation of Russian work published in 1950.
72. Savasis, J. *The War Against God in Lithuania*. New York: Maryland Books, 1966.
73. Schectman, Joseph B. *Star in Eclipse: Russian Jewry Revisited*. New York: Yoseloff, 1961.
74. Schwarz, Solomon M. *The Jews in the Soviet Union*. Syracuse: Syracuse University Press, 1951.
75. Scheinman, M. M. *Religion and Church in the USSR*. Moscow-Leningrad: Cooperative Publishing Society of Foreign Workers, 1933.
76. Spasov, G. *Freedom of Religion in the USSR*. London: Soviet News, 1951.
77. Spinka, Matthew. *The Church and the Russian Revolution*. New York: Macmillan, 1927.
78. ———. *The Church in Soviet Russia*. New York: Oxford University Press, 1956.
79. ———. *Christianity Confronts Communism*. New York-London: Harper, 1936.
80. *The Status of Soviet Jewry*. Washington, D.C.: B'nai B'rith, 1960.
81. Struve, Nikita. *Christians in Contemporary Russia*. New York: Charles Scribner's Sons, 1967. Translated by Lancelot Sheppard and A. Manson from French work published in 1962.
82. Swan, Jane. *A Biography of Patriarch Tikhon*. Jordanville, New York: Holy Trinity Russian Orthodox Monastery, 1964.
83. Szczesniak, Boleslaw, ed. *The Russian Revolution and Religion*. Notre Dame: University of Notre Dame Press, 1959.
84. Timasheff, N. S. *Religion in Russia 1917–1942*. New York: Sheed and Ward, 1942.
85. Torma, A., and Perlitz, H. *The Church in Estonia: The Fate of Religion and Church Under Soviet Rule in Estonia, 1940–1941*. New York: World Association of Estonians, 1944.
86. Trakiskis, A. *The Situation of the Church and Religious Practices in Occupied Lithuania*, pt. 1: "Under Soviet Occupation, 1940–1941." New York: Lithuanian Bulletin, 1944.

87. *The Truth About Religion in Russia.* Moscow: Moscow Patriarchate, 1944. Translation of Russian work published in 1944.
88. Valentinov, A. A. *The Assault of Heaven: A Collection of Facts and Documents Relating to the Persecution of Religion and Church in Russia Based Mainly Upon Official Sources.* London: Boswell Printing and Publishing Company, 1929. Translation of Russian work published in 1925.
89. Ware, Timothy. *The Orthodox Church.* Baltimore: Penguin Books, 1963.
90. Wheeler, Geoffrey. *Racial Problems in Soviet Muslim Asia.* London: Oxford University Press, 1962.
91. Wiesel, Elie. *The Jews of Silence.* New York: Holt, Rinehart, and Winston, 1966.
92. ———. *Will Soviet Jewry Survive?* New York: American Jewish Committee, 1967.
93. Yarmolinsky, Avrahm. *The Jews and Other Minor Nationalities Under the Soviets.* New York: Vanguard, 1926.
94. Zatko, James J. *Descent Into Darkness: The Destruction of the Roman Catholic Church in Russia, 1917–1923.* Notre Dame, Ind.: Notre Dame University Press, 1965.
95. Zenkovsky, Serge. *Pan-Turkism and Islam in Russia.* Cambridge: Harvard University Press, 1960.

CONTRIBUTORS

THOMAS E. BIRD is a member of the faculty of the City University of New York (Queens). He is the author of *Patriarch Maximos IV* (1964), founding editor of *Diakonia*, editor of *Russia and Orthodoxy* (1970), and a member of the United States Bishops' Commission for Dialogue with the Orthodox.

ANDREW Q. BLANE is a member of the faculty of the City University of New York (Lehman and Hunter). He is the editor of a forthcoming study of Russia and Orthodoxy.

BOHDAN R. BOCIURKIW is professor of political science and Director of Soviet and East European Studies at Carleton University, Ottawa. He has published articles in the *Canadian Journal of Economics and Political Science*, *International Journal*, *Canadian Slavonic Papers*, *Survey*, and other journals, as well as in numerous symposia. He is currently preparing a book on the Bolsheviks and religion.

ALEXANDER A. BOGOLEPOV has been, since 1951, professor of canon law at St. Vladimir's Orthodox Theological Seminary. He is the author of *The Church Under Communism* (1958), *Toward an American Orthodox Church* (1963), and *Church Reforms in Russia, 1905–1918* (1966).

JOAN DELANEY is a member of the Department of Slavic Languages and Literatures at the University of California, Berkeley. She is the author of the forthcoming *Edgar Allan Poe in Russia: A Study of Legend and Literary Influence*, and has contributed to several journals, including the *Slavic Review*, *Slavic and East European Journal*, and *Studia Slavica*.

FRANK H. EPP was editor of *The Canadian Mennonite* from 1953 to 1967. He is currently Director of Studies in International Conflict, attached to the Peace Section of the Mennonite Central Committee. In addition he is a part-time lecturer at the University of Ottawa. He is the author of *Mennonite Exodus: The Rescue and Resettlement of the Russian Mennonites Since the Communist Revolution* (1962), *An Analysis of Germanism and National Socialism in the Immigrant Press of a Canadian Minority Group, the Mennonites, in the 1930s* (1965), *Your Neighbor as Yourself: A Study on Responsibility in Immigration* (1968), and *Whose Land is Palestine? Current Claims in Historical Perspective* (1970).

R. H. EDWIN ESPY is the General Secretary of the National Council of the Churches of Christ in the USA.

WILLIAM C. FLETCHER was director of the Centre de Recherches et d'Etude in Geneva, Switzerland. He is the author of *Christianity in the Soviet Union: An Annotated Bibliography* (1963), *A Study in Survival: The Church in Russia, 1927–1943* (1965) and *Nikolai: Portrait of a Dilemma* (1968). He is the editor of *Religion and the Search for New Ideals in the USSR* (1967) and *Religion and the Soviet State: A Dilemma of Power* (1970). He has also contributed to several American and foreign journals.

J. J. GAPANOVICH was professor of history at the National Tsing Hua University in Peking from 1931 to 1953. From 1954 until his retirement in 1964 he was lecturer in Russian at the Australian National University in Canberra. Among his numerous publications are *The Koriaks of Kamchatka* (in Russian), *Russia in Northeast Asia* (vol. 1, *Colonization of the North;* vol. 2, *Wealth of the North*: in Russian), *Historiography Outside Russia*, and *Methods of Historical Synthesis*.

ZVI GITELMAN is professor of political science at the University of Michigan. He has contributed articles on Soviet Jewry to *Problems of Communism*, *Survey*, and *The Soviet System and Democratic Society: A Comparative Encyclopedia*. His article "Power and Authority in Eastern Europe" appears in *Change in Communist Systems* (1970).

GEORGE L. KLINE is a member of the faculty of Bryn Mawr College. He is the author of *Spinoza in Soviet Philosophy* (1952) and *Religious and Antireligious Thought in Russia* (1968). He was editor of and contributor to *Russian Philosophy* (1965), and translated V. V. Zenkovsky's *History of Russian Philosophy* (1953). He has contributed to numerous periodicals and symposia.

MESROB K. KRIKORIAN is the permanent representative of the Holy See of Etchmiadzin to the World Council of Churches in Geneva. He is the author of several books and studies, including a history of the Armenian Church (in Armenian, 1957, 1965), a biography of Catholicos Vazgen I (in Armenian) and *The Participation of the Armenian Community in Ottoman Public Life in Eastern Anatolia and Syria, 1860–1908* (1964).

Donald A. Lowrie is a past director of the YMCA Press. He has written numerous books, including *Rebellious Prophet: A Life of Nicolai Berdyaev* (1960) and *Christian Existentialism: A Berdyaev Anthology* (1967). He has published several monographs on the subject of religion in the Soviet Union and has contributed to many periodicals, American and foreign.

Paul Mailleux, S.J., is rector of the Pontifical Russian College in Rome. He is the author of *Exarch Leonid Feodorov: Bridge-builder Between Rome and Moscow* (1964).

Richard H. Marshall, Jr. is a member of the Department of Slavic Languages and Literatures of the University of Toronto. He is the author of *The Soviet Union: A Guidebook for Tourists* (1961) and a contributor to *Religion and the Soviet State: A Dilemma of Power* (1970). He has also contributed to such journals as the *Slavic Review, Slavic and East European Journal, Commonweal,* and *Diakonia*.

Elie Melia is a member of the faculty of St. Sergius Orthodox Theological Academy in Paris. He is also pastor of the Georgian Orthodox parish of St. Nina in Paris.

Joshua Rothenberg was for many years a senior research associate at the Institute of East European Jewish Affairs of the Philip W. Lown Graduate Center for Contemporary Jewish Studies. He is the author of *An Annotated Bibliography of Writings on Judaism Published in the Soviet Union, 1960–1965* (1969). His essay "Fifty Years of Jewish Religion in the Soviet Union" appeared in *Fifty Years of Soviet Jewry* (1969). He has also contributed to such periodicals as *Problems of Communism, Comparative Education Review, Jewish Social Studies,* and *Jewish Frontier*.

V. Stanley Vardys is professor of political science at the University of Oklahoma and Director of the University of Oklahoma Munich Center for Russian Language and Soviet Area Studies. He is the editor of and a contributor to *Lithuania Under the Soviets* (1965) and editor of *Karl Marx: Scientist? Revolutionary? Humanist?* (1970). His articles have appeared in the *Slavic Review*, *Russian Review*, *Foreign Affairs*, *Review of Politics*, *Problems of Communism*, and *Osteuropa*.

ALEXANDER VEINBERGS is President of the Federation of Latvian Lutheran Churches in America.

BERNHARD WILHELM is currently Director of Research at the Centre de Recherches et d'Etude in Geneva, Switzerland.

INDEX